8/10 ACMK
$5575

WORLD
The

A BRIEF HISTORY
Volume One: To 1500

FELIPE FERNÁNDEZ-ARMESTO

Tufts University

PEARSON
Prentice Hall

Upper Saddle River, NJ 07458

Maps by

Dorling Kindersley

D1089591

Library of Congress Cataloging-in-Publication Data

Fernández-Armesto, Felipe.
  The world: a brief history / Felipe Fernández-Armesto.
    p. cm.
  Condensed version of: The world : history. c2007.
  Includes bibliographical references and index.
  ISBN 0-13-600921-2
  1. Civilization--History. 2. World history. 3. Human ecology. I. Title.
  CB151.F48 2008
  909—dc22   2007029895

Executive Editor: Charles Cavaliere
Editorial Assistants: Maureen Diana, Lauren Aylward
Editor in Chief, Development: Rochelle Diogenes
Senior Development Editor: Gerald Lombardi
Senior Media Editor: Deborah O'Connell
Multimedia Specialist: Alison Lorber
Assistant Editor: Mayda C. Bosco
Director of Marketing: Brandy Dawson
Senior Marketing Manager: Kate Mitchell
Marketing Assistant: Jennifer Lang
Senior Managing Editor: Mary Carnis
Production Project Manager: Kathy Sleys
Operations Supervisor: Mary Ann Gloriande
Senior Art Director: Maria Lange
Cover Design: Maria Lange

Interior Design: Maria Lange/Kathy Mrozek
Design Support: Rob Aleman
Map Program Management: Gail Cocker-Bogusz, Scott Garrison
Cover Illustration: Corrin Skidds
Manager, Rights and Permissions: Zina Arabia
Manager, Visual Research: Beth Brenzel
AV Project Manager: Mirella Signoretto
Image Permission Coordinator: Craig A. Jones
Photo Researcher: Emma Brown
Composition/Full-Service Project Management: Frank Weihenig, Prepare, Inc.
Printer/Binder: Courier Companies, Inc.
Cover Printer: Phoenix Color Corporation

Maps designed and produced by DK Education, a division of Dorling Kindersley Limited, 80 Strand London WC2R 0RL. DK and the DK logo are registered trademarks of Dorling Kindersley Limited.

Credits and acknowledgments borrowed from other sources and reproduced, with permission, in this textbook appear on appropriate page within text or on page C-1.

Copyright © 2008 by Felipe Fernández-Armesto. All rights reserved. Printed in the United States of America. This publication is protected by Copyright and permission should be obtained from the publisher prior to any prohibited reproduction, storage in a retrieval system, or transmission in any form or by any means, electronic, mechanical, photocopying, recording, or likewise. For information regarding permission(s), write to: Rights and Permissions Department.

Pearson Prentice Hall™ is a trademark of Pearson Education, Inc.
Pearson® is a registered trademark of Pearson plc
Prentice Hall® is a registered trademark of Pearson Education, Inc.

Pearson Education Ltd.
Pearson Education Australia PTY, Ltd.
Pearson Education Singapore, Pte. Ltd.
Pearson Education North Asia Ltd.

Pearson Education, Canada, Ltd.
Pearson Educación de Mexico, S.A. de C.V.
Pearson Education–Japan
Pearson Education Malaysia, Pte. Ltd.

10 9 8 7 6 5 4 3 2 1
ISBN 13: 978-0-13-600887-3
ISBN 10: 0-13-600887-9

5 Rebuilding the World: Recoveries, New Initiatives, and Their Limits   96

PART 3   The Axial Age, from 500 B.C.E. to 100 C.E.   122

6 The Great Schools   124

9 The Rise of World Religions: Christianity, Islam, and Buddhism   210

17 The Ecological Revolution of the Sixteenth and Seventeenth Centuries 434

18 Mental Revolutions: Religion and Science in the Sixteenth and Seventeenth Centuries 462

19 States and Societies: Political and Social Change in the Sixteenth and Seventeenth Centuries   488

20 Driven by Growth: The Global Economy in the Eighteenth Century   516

21 The Age of Global Interaction: Expansion and Intersection of Eighteenth-Century Empires 538

22 The Exchange of Enlightenments: Eighteenth-Century Thought 562

CONTENTS

PART 9 The Frustrations of Progress to ca. 1900 586

25 Western Dominance in the Nineteenth Century: The Westward Shift of Power and the Rise of Global Empires 638

26 The Changing State: Political Developments in the Nineteenth Century 664

30   The Embattled Biosphere: The Twentieth-Century Environment   774

MAPS

MAPS

By the standards of astronauts, say, or science fiction writers, historians seem timid, unadventurous creatures who are only interested in one puny species—our species, the human species—on one tiny planet—our planet, Earth. But Earth is special. So far, we know of nowhere else in the cosmos where so much has happened and is happening today. By galactic standards, global history is a small story—but it's a good one.

Humans, moreover, compared with other animals, seem outward looking. Our concerns range over the universe and beyond it, to unseen worlds, vividly imagined or mysteriously revealed. Not just everything we do but also everything that occurs to our minds is part of our history and, therefore, part of this book, including science and art, fun and philosophy, speculations and dreams. We continually generate stories—new stories—at an amazing rate.

But the present passes instantly into the past. The present is always over, transformed into history. And the past is always with us, tugging at our memories, shaping our thoughts, launching and limiting our lives. So human history may seem narrowly self-interested, but it focuses on a riveting subject that is also our favorite subject—ourselves.

THE WAY OF HUMANKIND

Though the story of this book is a human story, it can never be merely human because, in isolation, humankind does not make perfect sense. Humans are animals, and to understand ourselves thoroughly and to know what, if anything, makes us unique, we have to compare ourselves with other animals. As with other animals, we are best studied in our habitats. We cannot begin to comprehend our own history except in context. Our story is inseparable from the climates where it takes place and the other life-forms that we depend on or compete with. All the elaborate culture we produce generates new, intimate relationships with the environment we refashion and the life-forms we exploit.

We are exceptionally ambitious compared to other animals, consciously remodeling environments to suit ourselves. We turn prairies into wheat lands, deserts into gardens, and gardens into deserts. We fell forests where we find them and plant them where none exist; we dam rivers, wall seas, cultivate plants, extinguish some species, and call others into being by selective breeding. Sometimes we smother terrain with environments we build for ourselves. Yet nothing we do liberates us from nature. As we shall see, one of the paradoxes of the human story is that the more we change the environment, the more vulnerable we become to ecological lurches and unpredictable disasters. Failure to establish a balance between exploitation and conservation has often left civilizations in ruins. History becomes a path picked across the wreckage. This does not mean that the environment determines our behavior or our lives, but it does set the framework in which we act.

We are an exceptionally successful species in terms of our ability to survive in a wide range of diverse climates and landscapes—more so than just about any other creatures, except for the microbes we carry around with us. But even we are still explorers of our planet, still trying to change it. Indeed, we have barely begun to change planet Earth, though, as we shall see, some human societies have devoted the last 10,000 years to trying to do it. We call ourselves masters, or, more modestly, caretakers of creation, but about 90 percent of the biosphere is too far underwater or too deep below the Earth for us to inhabit with the technology we have at present: These are environments that humans have only recently begun to invade and that we still do not dominate.

If we humans are peculiarly ambitious creatures, who are always intruding in the life of the planet, we are also odd compared to other animals in the way we generate change among ourselves. We are an unpredictable, unstable species. Lots of other animals live social lives and construct societies. But those societies are remarkably stable compared to ours. As far as we know, ants and elephants have the same lifeways and the same kinds of relationships that they have had since their species first appeared. That is not to say animals never change their cultures. One of the fascinating discoveries in primatology is that apes and monkeys develop cultural differences from one another, even between groups living in similar and sometimes adjacent environments. In West Africa, chimpanzees have developed a termite-catching technology. They "fish" with stripped branches that they plunge into termite nests but do not use tools to break open nuts. Chimps in a neighboring region ignore the termites but are experts in nut cracking, using rocks like hammers and anvils. In Sumatra in Indonesia, orangutans play a game—jumping from falling tress—that is unknown to their cousins in nearby Borneo. In East Africa, some male baboons control harems while others have one mate after another. In some chimpanzee societies, hunting and meat eating seem to have increased dramatically in recent times.

These are amazing facts, but the societies of nonhuman animals still change little compared with ours. So, alongside the theme of human interaction with the rest of nature is another great theme of our history: the ways our societies have changed, grown apart from one another, reestablished contact, and influenced one another in their turn.

THE WAY OF THIS BOOK

This book, then, interweaves two stories—of our interactions with nature and with each other. The environment-centered story is about humans distancing themselves from the rest of nature and searching for a balance between constructive and destructive exploitation. The culture-centered story is of how human cultures have influenced each other but also been different from each other. Both stories have been going on for thousands of years. We do not know whether they will end in triumph or disaster.

No one book can cover all of world history, and the fabric of this book is woven from carefully selected strands. Readers will see these at every turn, twisted together into yarn, stretched into stories. Human-focused historical ecology—the environmental theme—will drive readers back, again and again, to the same concepts: food, shelter, disease, energy, technology, art. (The last is a vital category for historians, not only because it is part of our interface with the rest of the world, but also because it forms a record of how we see reality and of how we see it change.) In the global story of human interactions—the cultural theme—we return constantly to the ways people make contact with each another: migration, trade, war, imperialism, pilgrimage, gift exchange, diplomacy, travel—and to their social frameworks: the economic and political arenas, the human groups and groupings, the states and civilizations, the sexes and generations, the classes and clusters of identity. In both stories, ideas and imagination play key roles, because most—perhaps all—of the changes we make happen first in our heads. We observe the world as it is, imagine it differently, and try to fend off our fears and realize our hopes.

The stories that stretch before us are full of human experience. "The stork feeds on snakes," said the ancient Greek sage Agathon, "the pig on acorns, and history on human lives." To build up our picture of human societies and ecosystems of the past we have to start with the evidence people have left. Then we reassemble it bit by bit, with the help of imagination disciplined by the sources. Anyone reading a history book needs to remember that interpreting evidence is a challenge—half burden and half opportunity. The subject matter of history is not the past directly because the past is never available to our senses. We have only the evidence about it. This makes history an art, not a science, a disciplined art like that of poetry disciplined by rhyme and meter, or a novel disciplined by character and plot, or a play disciplined by the limitations of stagecraft.

For a book like this, the sources set the limits of my imagination. Sometimes, these are concrete clues to what people really did—footprints of their wanderings, debris of their meals, fragments of their technologies, wreckage of their homes, traces of diseases in their bones. Usually, however, the sources reflect at best, not the way things were but the way people wished to represent them in their arts, crafts, and writings. Most sources—in short—are evidence of what happened only in the minds of those who made them. This means, in turn, that our picture of what went on in the world beyond human minds is always tentative and open to reinterpretation. The historian's job is not—cannot be—to say what the past was like, but rather, what it felt like to live in it, because that is what the evidence tends to reveal.

One of the most admirable historians of the twentieth century, R. G. Collingwood, who was also a professor of philosophy at Oxford, said that "all history is intellectual history." He was right. History—even the environmental and cultural history that is the subject of this book—is largely about what people perceived rather than what they really saw, what they thought or felt rather than what happened outwardly, what they represented rather than what was real. The nineteenth-century philosopher Arthur Schopenhauer, one of the most pessimistic thinkers ever, who drew on Hindu and Buddhist writings for his inspiration, said that history's only subject was "humankind's oppressive, muddlesome dream." He thought it made history pointless. I think it makes it intriguing.

Because the evidence is always incomplete, history is less a matter of describing or narrating or question-answering than it is of problem-posing. No one reading this book should expect to be instructed in straightforward facts or to acquire proven knowledge. The thrill of history is asking the right question, not getting the right answer. Most of the time, we can only hope to identify interesting problems that stimulate debate. And we have to accept that the debate is worthwhile for its own sake, even if we have insufficient knowledge to reach conclusions.

Historians do not even agree about which questions to ask. Some—including me—are interested in huge philosophical questions, such as how does history happen? What makes change? Is it random or subject to scientific laws? Do impersonal forces beyond human control—environmental factors or economics or some world force called fate, evolution, God, or progress—determine it? Or is change the externalization of ideas that people project onto the world? And if it's a mixture of all or some of these, what's the balance?

Some historians ask questions about how human societies function. How and why do societies grow and fragment and take different forms? How do people get power over others? How and why do revolutions happen and states and civilizations rise and fall?

Other historians like to pose problems about the present. How did we get into the mess we're in? Can we trace the causes of our problems back into the past and, if so, how far? Why do we have a globally connected world without global governance? Why is peace always precarious? Why does ecological overkill menace our environment? Having accounted—or failed to account—for the present, some historians like to focus on the future. They demand lessons from history about how to change our behavior or cope with recurrences of past difficulties. Others, again, search to make sense of the past, to find a way to characterize or narrate it that makes us feel we understand it.

Yet others—the majority, and again including me—like to study the past for its own sake and try to identify the questions that mattered to people at the time they first asked them. This does not mean that the sort of history found in this book is useless (although I do not necessarily think it would be a bad thing if it were). For to penetrate the minds of people of the past—especially the remote past of cultures other than your own—you have to make a supreme effort of understanding. The effort enhances life by sharpening responses to the streetscapes and landscapes, art and artifacts, laws and letters we have inherited from the past. And understanding is what we need most today in our multicultural societies and multi-civilizational world.

HOW THIS BOOK IS ARRANGED

After finding the time, accumulating the knowledge, posing the questions, stiffening the muscles, and summoning the blood, the big problem for the writer of a global history textbook is organizing the material. The big problem for the reader is navigating it. It is tempting to divide the world into regions or cultures or even—as I did in a previous book—into biomes and devote successive chapters to each. You could call that "world history," if you genuinely managed to cover the world. But "global history" is different: an attempt to see the planet whole, as if from an immense, astral height, and discern themes that truly transcend geographical and cultural boundaries. In this book, therefore, I try to look at every continent in just about every chapter (there are a couple of chapters that, for reasons described in their place, focus only on part of the world). Each chapter concentrates on themes from the two great global stories: how human societies diverge and converge, and how they interact with the rest of nature.

Because history is a story, in which the order of events matters, the chapters are arranged chronologically. There are 30 chapters—one for each week in a typical U.S. academic year (though of course, every reader or group of readers will go at their own pace)—and ten parts. I hope there is plenty to surprise readers without making the parts perversely defiant of the "periods" historians conventionally speak of. Part I runs roughly from 150,000 to 20,000 years ago, and, on the whole, the periods covered get shorter as sources accumulate, cultures diverge, data multiply, and readers' interests quicken. Of course, no one should be misled into thinking the parts are more than devices of convenience. Events that happened in, say, 1850, are in a different part of this book from those that happened in, say, 1750. But the story is continuous, and the parts could be recrafted to start and end at different moments.

At every stage, some parts of the world are more prominent than others, because they are more influential, more populous, more world-shaping. For much of the book, China occupies relatively more space, because China has, for much of the past, been immensely rich in globally influential initiatives. In the coverage of the last couple of centuries, Europe and the United States get a lot of attention: this is not "Eurocentrism" or "Westocentrism" (if there is such a word), but an honest reflection of how history happened. But I have tried not to neglect the peoples and parts of the world that historians usually undervalue: poor and peripheral communities, the margins and frontiers of the world, are often where world-changing events happen—the fault lines of civilizations, which radiate seismic effects.

HOW THIS BOOK HELPS STUDENTS

Pedagogy that Focuses and Enriches

The pedagogical features in *The World* help students engage with the narrative, provide reinforcement for learning, and enrich their study of world history.

Focus Questions open each chapter and encourage students to think critically while they read.

An Extensive and Integrated Map Program, created by Dorling Kindersley, one of the world's leading cartographic publishers, provides clear and innovative perspectives on both the larger themes and the particular events of world history.

Compelling Visual Sources, tightly coordinated with the text, include images never before published and captions that stimulate inquiry.

A Closer Look sections provide in-depth visual analysis of a specific cultural artifact. Detailed notes draw the viewer into close contact with the object.

Making Connections tables throughout the text offer visual summaries of important concepts. Instead of simply listing facts, these tools help students see connections that span across regions.

In-text Pronunciation Guides, embedded directly in the narrative, provide phonetic spellings for terms that may be unfamiliar to students.

Key Terms are defined in the Glossary and set in boldface type in the text

In Perspective sections end each chapter and ask students to consider the fundamental questions of a time period in world history.

HOW THIS BOOK SUPPORTS TEACHERS AND STUDENTS

An Extensive Teaching and Learning Package

The supplement package has been carefully crafted to enhance the instructor's classroom teaching experience and to provide students with resources that enrich the learning process.

Extensively revised and updated, the **Primary Source: Documents in Global History DVD** is both an immense collection of textual and visual documents in world history and an indispensable tool for working with sources. Extensively developed with the guidance of historians and teachers, the revised and updated DVD-ROM version includes over 800 sources in world history—from cave art to satellite images of the Earth from space. More sources from Africa, Latin America, and Southeast Asia have been added to this revised and updated DVD-ROM version. All sources are accompanied by headnotes and focus questions, and they are searchable by topic or region. The DVD comes with all new copies of *The World*. A stand-alone version can be purchased separately (0-13-178938-4).

myhistorylab www.myhistorylab.com With the best of Prentice Hall's multimedia solutions in one easy-to-use place, MyHistoryLab for *The World: A Brief History* offers students and instructors a state-of-the-art, interactive solution for world history. Organized by the main subtopics of *The World*, and delivered within a course-management platform (WebCT or Blackboard), or as a website, MyHistoryLab supplements and enriches the classroom experience and can form the basis for an online course.

www.prenhall.com/armesto The open-access companion website for *The World* includes study questions, flash cards, and interactive maps.

The **Instructor's Resource DVD** offers class presentation resources, including all of the maps and many of the illustrations from the text, PowerPoint presentations, and Classroom-Response System presentations.

The **Instructor's Guide to Teaching the World** provides everything instructors need to incorporate *The World: A Brief History* into their courses. An extensive Test-Item File, sample syllabi from users of *The World: A Brief History*, and teaching notes authored by David Ringrose, University of California, San Diego, enrich the utility of the Guide.

CourseSmart **CourseSmart Textbooks Online** is an exciting new *choice* for students looking to save money. As an alternative to purchasing the print textbook, students can *subscribe* to the same content online and save up to 50% off the suggested list price of the print text. With a CourseSmart eTextbook, students can search the text, make notes online, print out reading assignments that incorporate lecture notes, and bookmark important passages for later review. For more information, or to subscribe to the CourseSmart eTextbook, visit www.coursesmart.com.

vango notes Hear it. Get it. Study on the go with **VangoNotes**. VangoNotes is a digital audio study guide for *The World: A Brief History* that can be downloaded to an mp3 player. Students can study wherever they are or whatever they are doing by listening to the key concepts they need to know for each chapter of *The World.*

VangoNotes are **flexible**; students can download all the material directly to their mp3 players, or only the chapters they need. www.vangonotes.com

Study Guide, Volumes I and II, includes practice tests, essay questions, and map exercises.

 Titles from the renowned **Penguin Classics** series can be bundled with *The World: A Brief History* for a nominal charge. Please contact your Pearson Arts and Sciences sales representative for details.

DK **The Prentice Hall Atlas in World History, Second Edition** includes over 100 full-color maps in world history, drawn by Dorling Kindersley, one of the world's most respected cartographic publishers. Copies of the *Atlas* can be bundled with *The World* for a nominal charge. Contact your Pearson Arts and Sciences sales representative for details.

DEVELOPING *THE WORLD*

Developing a project like *The World* required the input and counsel of hundreds of individuals. We thank all those who shared their time and effort to make *The World* a better book.

Reviewers

Donald R. Abbott, San Diego Mesa College
Wayne Ackerson, Salisbury University
Roger Adelson, Arizona State University
Alfred J. Andrea, University of Vermont (Emeritus)
David G. Atwill, Pennsylvania State University
Mauricio Borrero, St. John's University
Leonard Blussé, Harvard University
John Brackett, University of Cincinnati
Gayle K. Brunelle, California State University—Fullerton
Fred Burkhard, Maryland University College
Antoinette Burton, University of Illinois
Jorge Cañizares-Esguerra, University of Texas—Austin
Elaine Carey, St. John's University
Tim Carmichael, College of Charleston
Douglas Chambers, University of Southern Mississippi
Nupur Chaudhuri, Texas Southern University
David Christian, San Diego State University
Duane Corpis, Georgia State University
Dale Crandall-Bear, Solano Community College
Touraj Daryaee, California State University—Fullerton
Jeffrey M. Diamond, College of Charleston
Brian Fagan, University of California—Santa Barbara
Nancy Fitch, California State University—Fullerton

Alison Fletcher, Kent State University
Patricia Gajda, The University of Texas at Tyler
Richard Golden, University of North Texas
Stephen S. Gosch, University of Wisconsin—Eau Claire
Jonathan Grant, Florida State University
Mary Halavais, Sonoma State University
Shah M. Hanifi, James Madison University
Russell A. Hart, Hawaii Pacific University
Phyllis G. Jestice, University of Southern Mississippi
Amy J. Johnson, Berry College
Deborah Smith Johnston, Lexington High School
Eric A. Jones, Northern Illinois University
Ravi Kalia, City College of New York
David M. Kalivas, Middlesex Community College
Frank Karpiel, College of Charleston
David Kenley, Marshall University
Andrew J. Kirkendall, Texas A&M University
Dennis Laumann, The University of Memphis
Donald Leech, University of Minnesota
Jennifer M. Lloyd, SUNY—Brockport
Aran MacKinnon, University of West Georgia
Moria Maguire, University of Arkansas—Little Rock
Susan Maneck, Jackson State University

Anthony Martin, Wellesley College

Dorothea Martin, Appalachian State University

Adam McKeown, Columbia University

Ian McNeely, University of Oregon

Margaret E. Menninger, Texas State University—San Marcos

Stephen Morillo, Wabash College

William Morison, Grand Valley State University

Laura Neitzel, Brookdale Community College

Kenneth J. Orosz, University of Maine—Farmington

Michael Pavkovic, Hawaii Pacific University

Kenneth Pomeranz, University of California—Irvine

Phyllis E. Pobst, Arkansas State University

Sara B. Pritchard, Montana State University

Norman Raiford, Greenville Technical College

Stephen Rapp, Georgia State University

Vera Blinn Reber, Shippensburg University

Matthew Redinger, Montana State University—Billings

Matthew Restall, Pennsylvania State University

Jonathan Reynolds, Arkansas State University

Richard Rice, University of Tennessee—Chattanooga

Peter Rietbergen, Catholic University (Nijmegen)

David Ringrose, University of California—San Diego

Patricia Romero, Towson University

Morris Rossabi, Queens College

David G. Rowley, University of Wisconsin—Platteville

Sharlene Sayegh, California State University—Long Beach

William Schell, Murray State University

Linda Bregstein Scherr, Mercer County Community College

Patricia Seed, University of California, Irvine

Lawrence Sondhaus, University of Indianapolis

Richard Steigmann-Gall, Kent State University

John Thornton, Boston University

Ann Tschetter, University of Nebraska—Lincoln

Deborah Vess, Georgia College & State University

Stephen Vinson, SUNY—New Paltz

Joanna Waley-Cohen, New York University

Anne M. Will, Skagit Valley College

John Wills, University of Southern California

Theodore Jun Yoo, University of Hawaii—Manoa

ACKNOWLEDGMENTS

Without being intrusive, I have tried not to suppress my presence—my voice, my views—in the text, because no book is objective, other than by pretense, and the reader is entitled to get to know the writer's foibles and failures. In overcoming mine, I have had a lot of help (though there are sure still to be errors and shortcomings through my fault alone). Textbooks are teamwork, and I have learned an immense amount from my friends and helpers at Pearson Prentice Hall, especially my editors, Charles Cavaliere and Gerald Lombardi, whose indefatigability and forbearance made the book better at every turn. I also thank the picture researcher Emma Brown and the members of the production and cartographic sections of the team who performed Herculean labors: Mary Carnis, managing editor; Kathleen Sleys, production project manager; Frank Weihenig, production editor; Marianne Gloriande, print buyer; Maria Lang, designer; Alison Lorber, media editor; and Maureen Diana, editorial assistant. Finally, Kate Mitchell has once again crafted a superb marketing campaign.

I could not have gotten through the work without the help and support of my wonderful colleagues at Queen Mary, University of London; the Institute of Historical Research, University of London; and the History Department of Tufts University. I owe special thanks to the many scholars who share and still share their knowledge of global history at the Pearson Prentice Hall Seminar Series in Global History, which now meets at Tufts University. David Ringrose of University of California, San Diego, was a constant guide, whose interest never flagged and whose wisdom never failed. Many colleagues and counterparts advised me on their fields of expertise or performed heroic self-sacrifice in putting all of the many pieces of the book together: Natia Chakvetadze, Shannon Corliss, Maria Guarascio,

Anita Castro, Conchita Ordonez, Sandra Garcia, Maria Garcia, Ernest Tucker (United States Naval Academy), David Way (British Library), Antony Eastmond (Courtland Institute), Morris Rossabi (Columbia University), David Atwill and Jade Atwill (Pennsylvania State University), Stephen Morillo (Wabash College), Peter Carey (Oxford University), Jim Mallory (Queens University, Belfast), Matthew Restall (Pennsylvania State University), Roderick Whitfield (School of Oriental and African Studies, University of London), Barry Powell (University of Wisconsin), Leonard Blussé (Harvard University), Guolong Lai (University of Florida), and Jai Kabaranda, my former graduate student at Queen Mary, as well as the many good people whose assistance I may have failed to acknowledge.

In making this abridged version of the original book, I have been able to make some small changes as well as many cuts. Readers inspired most of these, and I am especially grateful to the universities that gave me a chance to talk to teachers and students who have used or were going to use the book: Colorado State University; Jackson State University; Northern Kentucky University; Pennsylvania State University; Salem State University; the U.S. Air Force Academy; the US Naval Academy; the University at Buffalo (SUNY); the Ohio State University; the University of Arkansas, Little Rock; and the University of Memphis. I also learned a lot from the comments and feedback from subscribers to the H-World listserv. They are too numerous to name, but I owe special debts for self-sacrificingly generous help to Jack Betterly, Jerry Green, David Kalivas, and Peter Wozniak. I am also indebted to seminar-goers at the Boston Global History Consortium's Global History Seminar at Tufts University. But it has taken a long time to produce the book, and much of the good advice I've had, which came too late or required too much re-thinking for the time available, will only be reflected in future editions, if I am lucky enough to have any.

Felipe Fernández-Armesto
Tufts University
Fall 2007

About Felipe Fernández-Armesto

Felipe Fernández-Armesto holds the Prince of Asturias chair of Spanish Civilization at Tufts University where he also directs the Pearson Prentice Hall Seminar Series in Global History. Fernández-Armesto is a visiting professor of Global Environmental History at Queen Mary College, University of London, and is on the editorial board of the History of Cartography for the University of Chicago Press, the editorial committee of Studies in Overseas History (Leiden University), and the *Journal of Global History*. He has also served on the Council of the Hakluyt Society and was Chairman of Trustees of the PEN Literary Foundation. Recent awards include a Premio Nacional de Investigación (Sociedad Geográfica Española) in 2003, a fellowship at the Netherlands Institute of Advanced Study in the Humanities and Social Sciences, and a Union Pacific Visiting Professorship at the University of Minnesota (1999–2000). He won the Caird Medal of the National Maritime Museum in 1995 and the John Carter Brown Medal in 1999. In 2008, Fernández-Armesto will give the keynote address at the annual meeting of the World History Association.

The author, coauthor, or editor of over 25 books and numerous papers and scholarly articles, Fernández-Armesto's work has been translated into 24 languages. His books include *Before Columbus; The Times Illustrated History of Europe; Columbus; Millennium: A History of the Last Thousand Years* (the subject of a ten-part series on CNN); *Civilizations: Culture, Ambition, and the Transformation of Nature; Near a Thousand Tables; The Americas; Humankind: A Brief History; Ideas that Changed the World; The Times Atlas of World Exploration;* and *The Times Guide to the Peoples of Europe.* Two recent works are *Amerigo: The Man Who Gave His Name to America* and *Pathfinders: A Global History of Exploration* (which was awarded the World History Association Book Prize for 2006).

WORLD
The

A BRIEF HISTORY
Volume One: To 1500

FELIPE FERNÁNDEZ-ARMESTO
Tufts University

PART
One

Foragers and Farmers, to 5000 B.C.E.

Early art? Early science? Or both? In 2001, the discovery in ▶ South Africa of a stone carved 70,000 years ago showed that humans have used symbols for at least that long. These shapes, engraved in ochre, a soft reddish-brown stone that was a valuable, magical substance at the time, have been interpreted as a device to aid in counting or as a kind of calendar.

1.75 million to 1.25 million years ago
Homo erectus migrations out of East Africa

ENVIRONMENT

6 million years ago
Evolution of hominids/early humans

CULTURE

since 3 million years ago
Stone tools

150,000 to 20,000 years ago
Most recent Ice Age

since 20,000 years ago
Global warming

since ca. 10,000 years ago
Agriculture

since ca. 150,000 years ago
Homo sapiens

150,000 years ago
Fire, fire-hardened wood spears

since at least 100,000 years ago
Art, ritual, religion; first migrations out of Africa

since 20,000 years ago
Bow and arrow

Out of the Ice:
Peopling the Earth

The Spanish painter Francisco Goya painted these nightmare-visions in the mid-1820s on slivers of ivory, with novel techniques, burying the background in lamp-black, scratching the ivory to produce strange effects of light. He captured the fascinated unease with which human beings eye each other.

Francisco Goya y Lucientes, Spanish, 1746–1828. Boy Staring at an Apparition (1824–1825) Carbon Black and watercolor on ivory (Black wash heightened with vermilion and brown) 6.03 × 6.03 cm (2 3/8 × 2 3/8 in.) Museum of Fine Arts, Boston. Gift of Eleanor I. Arxiu Mas.

n exile in France in the 1820s, in the last years of his tortured, haunted life, Francisco Goya (1746–1828) etched nightmares—frightening faces stripped of every sane and civilized quality. The most abstract image captured the truth about how we understand human nature. A little boy, half bewildered, half fascinated, stares up at a baffling blur, recognizable as a human face because it inspires us with distinctive emotions: attraction, empathy, unease. But we perceive it unclearly. We think we know what it means to be human, but if anyone asks us to define humankind, we cannot do it. Or at least we cannot do it satisfactorily.

FRANCE

SO YOU THINK YOU'RE HUMAN

We can call humankind a species, but species are just categories for grouping to-gether closely related life forms, with boundaries that are fuzzy and subject to change. There is no standard of how closely related you have to be to a fellow crea-ture to be classed in the same species, or among species of the same sort, or, as bi-ologists say, "genus." DNA evidence reveals that all the people we now recognize as human had a common ancestor who lived in Africa, probably more than 150,000 years ago. If we go back 5 to 7 million years, we share ancestors with chimpanzees. Double the length of time, and the fossils reveal ancestors whom we share with other great apes. Further back, the flow of evolution erodes the differences between our ancestors and other creatures. If we accept the theory of **evolution**—and, in outline, it does present a true account of how life forms change—we cannot find any transforming moment in the past when humankind began. Species so like our-selves preceded us in the evolutionary record that, if we were to meet them today, we should probably embrace some of them as fellow humans, and puzzle over how to treat others.

Even today, there are nonhuman species—especially among the apes—whose humanlike qualities so impress people who work and live with them that they seem morally indistinguishable from humans and should, according to some biologists and philosophers, be included in the same genus and even the same moral commu-nity as ourselves, with similar rights. In terms of the sort of cultures they have, emo-tions they reveal, societies they form, and behaviors they adopt, chimpanzees share many characteristics with the fellow apes we call humans. To a lesser extent, gorillas

FOCUS questions

- WHERE IN the evolutionary record do humans begin?
- WHAT CAUSED the rapid population growth of *Homo sapiens*?
- WHY WAS the Ice Age a time of abundance?
- WHAT DOES its art tell us about Ice-Age society?
- WHEN DID *Homo sapiens* migrate to North and South America?
- HOW DID human life change when the Ice Age ended?

and orangutans are also like us. All of us apes use tools, learn from each other, practice altruism and deceit, like to play, detest boredom, and seem self-aware. Our bodies and our behaviors are so like those of chimpanzees that the physiologist and historian Jared Diamond has suggested we reclassify our species as a kind of chimp. Our relationship with other animals could come full circle. In the often-filmed story of *The Island of Dr. Moreau*, H. G. Wells (1866–1946) fantasized about a scientist who strove to produce perfect creatures by surgically combining human characteristics with those of other animals. Today, in theory, genetic engineering can produce such hybrids, prompting us to wonder at what point a hybrid would become human. The first big question for this chapter, then, is where in the evolutionary record does it make sense to talk about humans? When does the story of humankind begin?

Human Evolution

Paleoanthropologists—the specialists responsible for answering or, at least, asking the question about which species are human—give conflicting responses. The usual place to look is among creatures sufficiently like us to be classified, according to the present consensus, in the same genus as ourselves: the genus called "Homo" from the Latin word that means "human." A creature known as *Homo habilis* ("handy"), about 2.5 million years ago, chipped hand axes from stones. In calling this species the first humans, scholars defined humans as toolmakers—a now old-fashioned, indeed, discredited concept. *Habilis* also had a larger brain than earlier predecessors, but this is of doubtful significance. Ours is not the biggest-brained species in the evolutionary record. At one time, anthropologists backed a later species, *Homo erectus* ("standing upright"), of about 1.5 million years ago, as the first human, largely because they admired the flint tools and weapons that species carved. From finds over 800,000 years ago, a variant (or, perhaps, a different species) called *Homo ergaster* ("workman") appeared who later—at one site at least—stacked the bones of the dead. But reverence for the dead is not uniquely human, either. All these creatures, and others like them, have had champions who have claimed them as the first humans. Clearly, these instances of backing one set of ancestors over another reflect subjective criteria: supposed resemblance to ourselves. We are like the bereaved of some horrible disaster, scanning the remains of the dead for signs to prompt our recognition.

Species that occurred earlier than those we class under the heading "Homo," or who resembled us less, have tended to get labeled with names that sound less human. Anthropologists used to call them "pithecanthropoi"—literally, ape-men. Current terminology favors "**australopithecines**" ("southern ape-like creatures"), or "paranthropoi" ("next to humans"), as if they were identifiably nonhuman or prehuman. But in 1974, the archaeologist Dan Johansen made a discovery that blew away all notions of a clear dividing line. He spotted the bones of an australopithecine sticking out of the mud in Hadar in Ethiopia in East Africa. He dug her up and called her "Lucy" after the title of a Beatles song he happened to play that night in camp. Lucy had died over 3 million years ago. She was only about three feet tall, but she and her kind turned out to have characteristics that were thought to belong exclusively to later species of *Homo*. They walked on two legs and lived in family groups. Johansen discovered tools 2.5 million years old near the site the following year. In 1977, he found two-legged footprints, dating back 3.7 million years. Finds with similar characteristics may date as far back as 6 million years ago.

As evolution slowly grinds out species, who's human? Who's to say? It is tempting to reserve the term *human* for ourselves—members of the species we call **Homo sapiens.** Literally, the term *sapiens* means "wise," a grandiose name that betrays the foolishness of self-ascribed wisdom, for other species also have embarrassingly strong claims to "wisdom." One example is *Homo neanderthalensis,* who vanished only 30,000 years ago, and coexisted with our own ancestors for something like 100,000 years. Neanderthals had distinctive vocal tracts but could have interacted with *Homo sapiens* by nonverbal communication, just as we do today to talk with apes and even with humans whose spoken language we do not understand.

In most other respects, the two species of *Homo* were alike. **Neanderthals** were as big as *sapiens* and had a similar appearance; their brains were also similar but, on average, slightly larger. They followed the same hunting, foraging ways of life in overlapping habitats. They made the same kinds of tools our ancestors made, lived in the same types of society, ate the same foods, and had many of the same customs and rites. They cared for their old and sick and buried their dead with signs of honor that suggest a sense of religion. They also seem to have expected an afterlife, burying bears' jaws with their dead, as if to protect them and perhaps—though the evidence is uncertain—strewing flowers on some graves as if to help, honor, or adorn the deceased. Yet some paleoanthropologists seem determined to deny Neanderthals the name of humans—using arguments startlingly, frighteningly reminiscent of those that nineteenth-century scientific racism employed to deny full humanity to black people, claiming, for instance, that they were inferior and doomed to extinction. Evidence of Neanderthals' attainments is explained away. Assemblages of ritual objects found at their graves, detractors say, must be "tricks of evidence," deposited accidently by streams, winds, or animals.

Paleoanthropologists continue to dig up specimens that challenge believers in human uniqueness. In October 2004, excavators published news of a stunning find in southeast Asia on the island of Flores in Indonesia, which included the remains of a woman whose teeth, when they found her, were mashed to pulp, her bones rotted and soggy. She died 18,000 years ago. She was dwarfishly tiny. Her brain was barely as big as a chimpanzee's. But she had the power to subvert anthropological orthodoxy. *Homo floresiensis,* as her finders called her, proved that big brains do not make their possessors superior to other creatures. To judge from adjacent finds, these "hobbits," as the press dubbed them, had tools typical of early *Homo sapiens,* despite chimp-sized brains in imp-sized bodies. *Floresiensis* almost certainly made those tools. In known cases where nonhuman creatures lie alongside *sapiens*-made tools, *sapiens* ate them. But the remains of *floresiensis* showed no signs of butchering.

OUT OF AFRICA

Since no clear-cut line separates human from nonhuman species, we might rationally start our story with our last common ancestor. We all have a chemical component in our cells that a mother in East Africa passed on to her daughters over 150,000 years ago. We nickname her Eve after the first woman in Genesis. Of course, she was neither our first ancestor nor the only woman of her day. By the

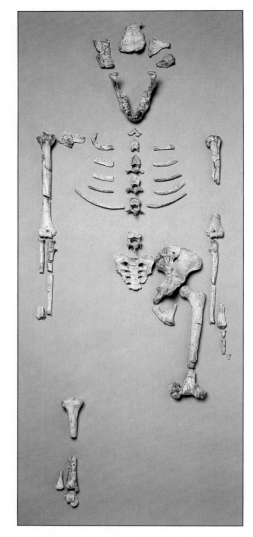

Lucy. The bones shown here aren't connected to each other, but modern imaginations have reconstructed the 3-million-year-old skeleton known as "Lucy," as human or nearly so. Lucy walked on two legs and was closer to humans, in evolutionary terms, than any non-human creature that exists today.

Stone tools. Paleoanthropologists have long used stone tool-making technologies to classify hominid cultures, because these artifacts have survived in relatively large numbers. The chopper on the left, of a pattern that dates from over 2 million years ago, was made by striking cobblestones against each other. Chimpanzees can be taught to make similar tools. The more elegant axe-blade in the center is of a kind that predominated over much of the world between about 1.5 million and 150,000 years ago. Though the size, shape, and presumably function of these tools varied, as the examples on the right show, the technology was surprisingly uniform around the world. No bone tools, for example, from the period survive.

best available estimates, there were perhaps 20,000 individuals of the species *Homo sapiens* at the time, all living in the same region. In 2003, archaeological evidence of Eve's world turned up in Herto, in Ethiopia. Three skulls about 160,000 years old had been stripped of flesh and polished, which suggests that the culture they belonged to practiced some death-linked ritual. The remains of a butchered hippopotamus lay nearby. We can begin to picture not only the appearance of the African Eve—we can do that by looking in a mirror—but also something of her way of life or, at least, life at a time close to her own.

Eve's home of mixed grassland and woodland was no Eden, but it suited our ancestors. Compared with competitor species, they had—as we still have—feeble bodies, weak senses of sight, smell, and hearing, poor digestions, and unthreatening teeth and claws. But they could make up for their deficiency as climbers by standing erect to look around them. Their profuse sweat kept them cool during long chases. With relatively accurate throwing-arms, they could ward off rival predators. With fire, they could manage grazing for the animals they hunted with fire-hardened spears and butchered with sharpened stones.

Peopling the Old World

From beginnings in East Africa, Eve's people spread over the world (see Map 1.1). But why? Why did they want to move? How did they adapt to new environments? Most species stay in the environments that suit them best. Even human migrants seek familiar surroundings or try to reproduce the feel of home by transporting their animals and transplanting their crops.

Yet *Homo sapiens* penetrated challengingly different environments: deep forests, where grassland habits were of limited use; cold climates, to which humans were physically ill suited; deserts and seas, which demanded technologies they had not yet developed. These new habitats bred unfamiliar diseases. Yet people kept on moving, through them and into them, with speed, range, and purpose unmatched in the dispersals of other creatures.

We can reconstruct routes, though the archaeological evidence is patchy, by measuring differences in blood type, genetic makeup, and

Early Human Migration

(All dates are approximate)	
150,000 years ago	Hypothetical African Eve (*H. sapiens*)
100,000 years ago	*H. sapiens* migrates out of Africa to Middle East
67,000 years ago	*H. sapiens* in China
60,000 years ago	*H. sapiens* reestablishes colony in Middle East
50,000 years ago	*H. sapiens* in Australia
40,000 years ago	*H. sapiens* in Europe
15,000 years ago	*H. sapiens* in the Americas

language among populations in different parts of the world. The greater the differences, the longer the ancestors of the people concerned are likely to have been out of touch with the rest of humankind. This is inexact science, because people are rarely isolated for long. There are, moreover, no agreed ways to measure the differences among languages. Still, for what it is worth, the best-informed research puts *Homo sapiens* in the Middle East by about 100,000 years ago. The colony failed, but new migrants reestablished it about 60,000 years ago. Settlement then proceeded along the coasts of Africa and Asia, probably by sea. The earliest agreed-upon archaeological evidence of *Homo sapiens* in China is about 67,000 years old (although some digs have yielded puzzlingly earlier dates for remains that seem like those of *Homo sapiens*).

The first colonizers of Australia arrived over 50,000 years ago in boats. At that time, water already separated what are now Australia and New Guinea from Asia. *Homo sapiens* reached Europe only a little later. Northern Asia and America—isolated by impenetrable screens of cold —were probably colonized much later. The most generally accepted archaeological evidence indicates the New World was settled no earlier than about 15,000 years ago.

If these dates are correct, the expansion of *Homo sapiens* implies remarkable population growth. Though we have no idea—beyond guesswork—of the actual numbers that migrated, we can estimate a figure in millions by the end of the process. A handful of Eve's children had multiplied to the point where they could colonize most of the habitable Old World in less than 100,000 years. But was the increase in population cause or effect of the migrations? And how did it relate to the other changes migration brought? Migrating groups were doubly dynamic: not just mobile, but also subject to huge social changes—divisive and violent, but also with constructive ways of organizing their lives. Migration, moreover, affected their understanding of the world and the way they interacted with the species they competed with, preyed on, and outlasted.

Migration, Population, and Social Change

As far as we know, everyone at the time lived by foraging and moved on foot. Because mothers cannot easily carry more than one or two infants, large numbers of children are unsuited to foraging life. Consequently, foragers limit opportunities to breed by strictly regulating who can mate with whom. Their main contraceptive method is a long period of lactation. Breast-feeding mothers are relatively infertile. The demographic growth that peopled the Earth is surprising, therefore, because it breaks the normal pattern of population stability in foraging communities. So how can we explain it?

Creatures like us, with short guts, weak jaws, blunt teeth, and only one stomach each, can chew and digest limited energy sources. So any increase in the range and amount of food available was a major evolutionary advantage. Cooking with fire probably helped, because it made food easier to digest. So did improved hunting technologies: drive lanes and corrals to herd animals for killing, and fire-hardened spears. The dating is debated, but all these developments were in place by the start of the migrations.

Whether or not new technologies empowered humans to migrate, perhaps new stresses drove them on, such as food shortages or ecological disasters. But no evidence supports this or fits with the evidence of rising population. In every other case we know of, in all species, population falls when food sources shrink. Another possible source of stress is warfare, for plague, famine, and natural disaster tend to

MAP 1.1

Early Human Migration 150,000–40,000 years ago

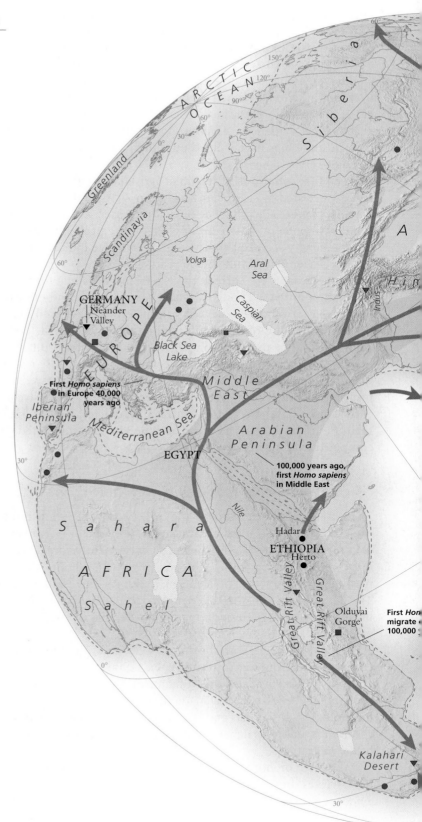

- *Homo erectus* migration, 1.75–1.25 million years ago
- *Homo sapiens* migration, 150,000–40,000 years ago
- possible coastal migrations
- ■ *Homo erectus* site
- ● *Homo sapiens* site
- ▼ Neanderthal site
- ▲ *Homo Floresiensis* site
- - - ancient coastline
- ancient lake

MAP EXPLORATION

www.prenhall.com/armesto_maps

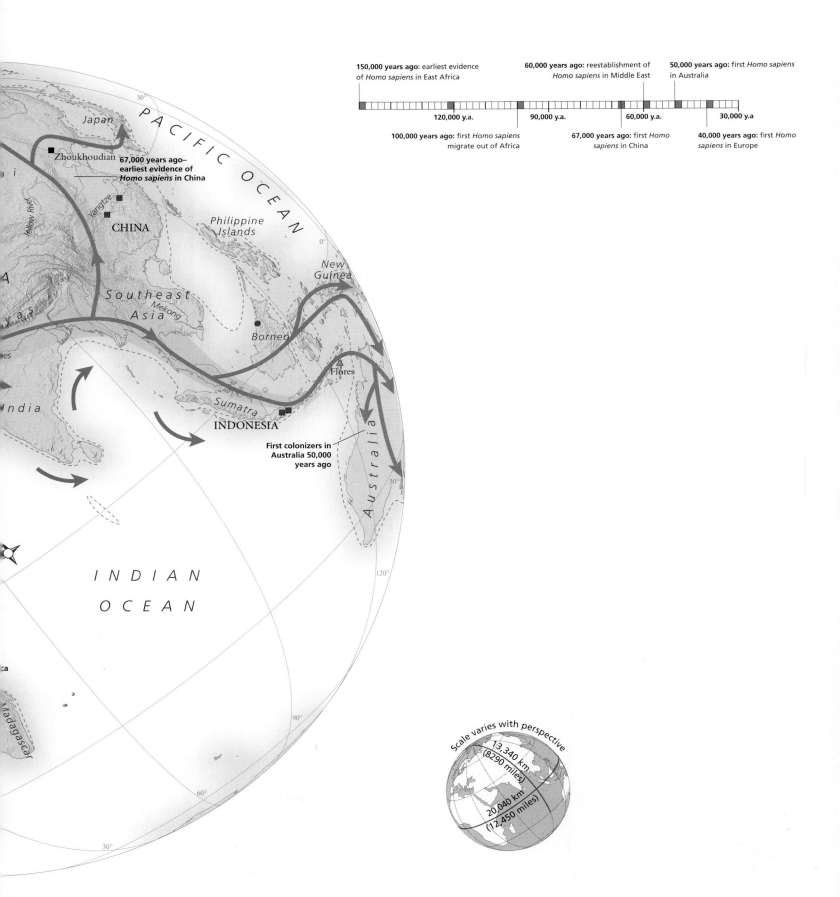

150,000 years ago: earliest evidence of *Homo sapiens* in East Africa

60,000 years ago: reestablishment of *Homo sapiens* in Middle East

50,000 years ago: first *Homo sapiens* in Australia

120,000 y.a.   90,000 y.a.   60,000 y.a.   30,000 y.a

100,000 years ago: first *Homo sapiens* migrate out of Africa

67,000 years ago: first *Homo sapiens* in China

40,000 years ago: first *Homo sapiens* in Europe

PACIFIC OCEAN

Japan

Zhoukhoudian

67,000 years ago–earliest evidence of *Homo sapiens* in China

Yellow River

Yangtze

CHINA

Philippine Islands

Southeast Asia

Mekong

Borneo

New Guinea

Flores

Sumatra

INDONESIA

First colonizers in Australia 50,000 years ago

India

Australia

30°

INDIAN OCEAN

120°

Madagascar

90°

60°

30°

Scale varies with perspective

13,340 km (8290 miles)

20,040 km (12,450 miles)

Margaret Mead, from "Warfare Is Only an Invention—Not a Biological Necessity"

Jane Goodall, from "The Challenge Lies in All of Us"

Chimp agression. Humans obviously share aggressive individual tendencies with other apes. The American naturalist Jane Goodall discovered that chimpanzees organize conflicts with other groups of chimpanzees: They practice warfare, in other words. This seems to support what some philosophers and psychologists long suspected: that war is a "natural" activity, or, if it is an effect of culture, that it arose early in the history of culture.

inhibit human action, whereas war spurs new responses. One of the most fascinating problems of history is how and when war started. According to one school of thought, war is natural. The commander of British forces in the Second World War, Bernard Montgomery (1887–1976), referred to a book on *The Life of the Ant* when people challenged him to justify war. Evolution, he meant, implanted aggressive and violent instincts in humans as it did in other animals. Romantics defend the opposite point of view. Human nature is essentially peaceful until competition corrupts it. War, according to Margaret Mead, the great liberal anthropologist of the 1920s and 1930s, was not a biological necessity but an invention that began or, at least, entered a new, more systematic phase, when settled communities started to fight one another to control land and resources. Indeed, the earliest archaeological proof we have of large-scale warfare—including the savage massacre of women and children—is a battle fought at Jebel Sahaba, near the modern border of Egypt and Sudan, about 11,000 years ago, when agriculture was in its infancy.

Yet organized warfare must really be much older. In the 1970s, the primatologist Jane Goodall observed warfare among chimpanzee communities in the forests of West Africa. When chimpanzee splinter groups secede from their societies, their former fellows try to kill them. Similar conflicts may have made early human splinter groups migrate to safety. It is an intriguing possibility, but, even if it were to prove correct, it poses other problems. What stresses could have caused people to divide and fight each other 100,000 years ago? Rising population again? Or are we driven back to more speculation about increasing competition for supposedly diminishing food stocks, or even to assertions about innate animal aggression?

In societies of increasing violence, men have enhanced roles. Among all primates, including humans, greater competitiveness in mating makes males, on average, bigger and stronger than females. In consequence, alpha males rule, or at least boss, most ape societies. Human males usually seem to bond more closely with each other, or form more or stronger alliances, than females. This, too, is useful in competitive circumstances, such as those of war and politics. Yet women are, in at least one respect, more valuable in most societies than men for a society can dispense with most of its men and still reproduce. That is why societies more commonly risk men in war than women. Women, moreover, are more easily mistaken as sacred because of the obvious correspondences between the cycles of their bodies and the rhythms of the heavens. Menstruation and the cycle of female fertility match the phases of the moon.

So how did male domination come to be normal in human societies? One theory ascribes it to a deliberate, collective power-seeking strategy by males, inspired by dislike of women or resentment or envy or a desire to get control of the most elementary of resources—the means of reproducing the species. By analogy with chimpanzees, a rival theory suggests that male dominance is a consequence of hunting, which, in the few chimpanzee groups known to practice it, is an almost exclusively male activity. Hunting increases male dominance in chimpanzee society because the hunters distribute the meat, in almost ritual fashion. Females line up and, in effect, beg for morsels. Female chimps often exchange sex for food, especially meat. By contrast, among bonobos, who are like chimps but are strictly plant eating, both sexes share foraging, and females tend to be socially equal or even dominant. Hunting, however, seems to be a recent development in chimpanzee society and to have followed and strengthened male dominance—not caused it.

MAKING CONNECTIONS

THE FIRST POPULATION BOOM: REASONS FOR POPULATION GROWTH

Fire-managed grazing of animals; driving lanes; corrals ⟶	*control over food supply*
Throwing-arms; fire-hardened spears ⟶ improved hunting ⟶	*improved diet*
Cooking with fire ⟶ improved taste and digestibility ⟶	*increase in range of available foods*
Sexual economic specialization ⟶ hunting and gathering ⟶	*women liberated for childbearing*

Without evidence to the contrary, it is unwise to assume that early in the migration period either sex monopolized political power. Still, migrating groups must have developed ways to liberate more women for childbirth or increase the fertile period of women's lives. Otherwise, population would have stagnated. Improved nutrition helped. Was there also some redistribution of economic activities, with men taking on more food-supplying roles?

As far as we know, in the earliest kind of sexual economic specialization, men did most of the hunting, while women did most of the gathering. Women's work seems to have been more productive in terms of calorific value per unit of energy expended. But we do not know when this specialization started or how rigid or widespread it was. In any case, the balance between hunted and gathered foods in the diets of the migrants varied with the environment. In known cases, hunters supplied about a third of the nutrition. The migrations, and the accompanying demographic changes, would have been impossible without both hunting and gathering.

The peopling of the Earth was such a long-lasting phenomenon that we can safely presume it had multiple causes operating in different combinations in different places and at different times. Then, too, some migrations were surely one-of-a-kind events. We can imagine, for instance, the first boat people who colonized Australia as the drop-outs of more than 50,000 years ago, opting out of a changing world to settle a new continent, where they could maintain a traditional way of life. In general, if people moved into new environments, they must have been drawn by an abundance of new resources elsewhere, not driven by a shortage of resources in their old homes. The era of opportunity coincided with, and was perhaps caused by, new trends in global climate.

THE LAST GREAT ICE AGE

Whatever caused it, the peopling of the world spanned the most convulsive period of climatic change that *Homo sapiens* experienced before our own times. The cooling and warming phases of the planet are regular occurrences, and one or the other is always going on. Every 100,000 years or so, a distortion in the Earth's orbit tugs the Northern Hemisphere away from the sun. On more frequent cycles, the Earth tilts and wobbles on its axis. When these phenomena coincide, temperatures change dramatically. Ice ages set in. A great cooling began about 150,000 years ago. The great migrations almost coincided with this, as if humans actively sought the cold (see Map 1.2).

PACIFIC
OCEAN

30° 0° Tropic of Cancer 30° 150° Beringia 60° 180°

Equator

90°

NORTH
AMERICA

Rocky Mountains

Vancouver

Cordilleran
Ice Sheet

Laurentide
Ice Sheet

Hudson
Bay

Mississippi Chicago

Ohio

Toronto

Boston

Greenland

Reykjavik Iceland

see inset

Great
Britain

Caribbean
Sea

Andes

ATLANTIC
OCEAN

M

North A

Andes

Amazon

S a h

SOUTH
AMERICA

60°

BRAZIL

Niger

0°

SWEDEN 60° 0° 30° 60° **RUSSIA**

Stockholm Volga Sungir

Star Carr Skateholm Moscow

YORKSHIRE Maininskaya

London **GERMANY** Oder **UKRAINE**

Dolní
Vogelherd Vestonice

FRANCE Willendorf **CZECH REP.**

DORDOGNE Laussel Carpathian
Mountains

Brassempouy Chauvet Black Sea
Lake

SPAIN

500 km

500 miles

0° 30°

PACIFIC
OCEAN

Kenniff Cave

Arnhem
Land

A
U
S
T
R
A
L
I
A

Yellow
Sea

Siberia

E
U
R
A
S
I
A

Yellow

South
China
Sea

Yangtze

Mekong

SOUTHEAST
ASIA

Himalayas

Ganges

Bay of
Bengal

Caspian Sea

U
R

Danube   Black Sea

Indus

Anatolia

Tigris

Euphrates

…ranean Sea

Arabian
Sea

INDIAN
OCEAN

1,000 km

1,000 miles

scale varies with perspective

N

a

Nile

F R I C A

Madagascar

NAMIBIA   Kalahari
Desert

Lion Cave

San

SOUTH AFRICA   LESOTHO

30°

180°   30°   0°   30°   150°

60°

Tropic of Cancer

Equator

Tropic of Capricorn

120°

90°

60°

Arctic Circle

MAP 1.2

The Ice Age

☐ extent of ice cover 20,000 years ago

☐ extent of ice cover 12,000 years ago

☐ tundra

☐ tundra and coniferous forests

☐ steppe

○ modern-city

◇ foraging settlement described on
page 22

◆ Ice-Age sites

San native people

--- ancient coastlines

〰 ancient lake

15

Ice-Age Hunters

The severity of the Ice Age is unimaginable, but it was not an entirely hostile world. For the hunters who inhabited the vast **tundra** that covered much of Eurasia, the edge of the ice was the best place to be. Over thousands of years of cold, many mammals had adapted by efficiently storing their own body fat—and that was the hunters' target. Dietary fat has a bad reputation today, but for most of history, most people have eagerly sought it. Relatively speaking, animal fat is the world's most energy-abundant source of food.

In some of the vast Ice-Age tundra, concentrations of small, easily trapped arctic hare could supply human populations. More commonly, however, hunters favored species they could kill in large numbers by driving them over cliffs or into bogs or lakes. The bones of 10,000 Ice-Age horses lie at the foot of a cliff in France, and remains of a hundred mammoths have turned up in pits in Central Europe. About 20,000 years ago, the invention of the bow and arrow revolutionized killing technology for smaller prey. While stocks lasted, there was a fat bonanza, achieved with relatively modest effort.

It is rash to suppose that Ice-Age communities were small, limited to 30 or 50 people, like modern hunter–gatherers. Today, hunter–gatherers survive only in regions of great scarcity, where the modern world has driven them. Back then, community size varied according to the available resources; we can rarely put a figure to a group because only partial traces of Ice-Age dwellings have survived.

For Ice-Age artists, fat was beautiful. One of the oldest artworks in the world is the Venus of Willendorf—a plump little carving of a fat female, 30,000 years old and named for the place in Germany where she was found. Critics have interpreted her as a goddess, ruler, or since she could be pregnant, a fertility symbol. Her slightly more recent look-alike, the Venus of Laussel, carved on a cave wall in France, evidently got fat the way most of us do: by enjoyment and indulgence. She raises a horn, which must contain food or drink.

Ice-Age people, on average, were better nourished than most later populations. Only modern industrialized societies surpass their intake of 3,000 calories a day. The nature of the plant foods they gathered—few starchy grains, relatively large amounts of wild vegetation—and the high ascorbic acid content of animal organ meats provided more vitamin C than an average American gets today. Abundant game guaranteed **Ice-Age affluence.** High levels of nutrition and long days of leisure, unequalled in most subsequent societies, meant people had time to observe nature and think about what they saw. The art of the era shows the sublime results. Like all good jokes, *The Flintstones*—the popular television cartoon series about a modern Stone-Age family—contains a kernel of truth. "Cave people" were like us, with the same kinds of minds and many of the same kinds of thoughts.

Ice-Age Art

In the depths of the Ice Age, a resourceful way of life took shape. We know most about Europe—especially southwest France and northern Spain, where extensive art has survived because it was made in deep caves evidently chosen because they were inaccessible. About 50 cave complexes contain thousands of paintings, mostly of animals.

 Marshall Sahlins, "The Original Affluent Society," from *Stone-Age Economics*

Venus of Laussel. An image of a woman carved in relief on a cave wall in central France more than 20,000 years ago reveals much about Ice-Age life: esteem for big hips and body fat, the love of revelry suggested by the uplifted drinking-horn, the involvement of women in presumably sacred activity, and the existence of accomplished, specialized artists.

Only now are the effects of tourism, too many respiratory systems, too many camera flashes, damaging these works in their once-secret caverns. Examples of sculptures, carvings, and other art objects are scattered across Europe, from the Atlantic to the Ural Mountains.

Footprints and handprints probably inspired the art, but what was it for? It surely told stories and had magical, ritual uses, as a way to reach a spirit-world inside or beyond the earth's depths or the cave walls. Some animal images are slashed or punctured many times over, as if in symbolic sacrifice. A good case has been made for seeing the cave paintings as aids to track prey. Hoof-prints, dung, seasonal habits, and favorite foods of the beasts are among the artists' standard stock of images.

Their technology was simple: a palette of red, brown, and yellow ochre (OH-ker), mixed with animal fat, and applied with wood, bone, and hair. Even the earliest works appeal instantly to modern sensibilities. The looks and litheness of the animal portraits spring from the rock walls, products of practiced hands and inherited learning. Carvings exhibit similar elegance—ivory sculptures of 30,000-year-old arched-necked horses from south Germany; female portraits from France and Moravia, over 20,000 years old; clay models of bears, dogs, and women fired 27,000 years ago in Russia.

Outside Europe, what little we know of the peoples of the time suggests that they created equally skillful work. Four painted rock slabs from Namibia in southwest Africa are about 26,000 years old, almost as old as any art in Europe, and bear similar animal images. The earliest paintings that decorate rocks in northernmost Australia show faint traces of long-extinct giant kangaroos and scary snakes. A clue to the very idea of representing life in art fades today from a rock face in Kenniff, Australia, where stencils of human hands and tools were made 20,000 years ago. But most of the evidence has been lost, weathered away on exposed rock faces, perished with the bodies or hides on which it was painted, or scattered by wind from the earth where it was scratched.

Ice-Age Culture and Society

The discovery of so much comparable art, of comparable age, in such widely separated parts of the world suggests an important and often overlooked fact. The Ice Age was the last great era of what we would now call a kind of **globalization.** That is, key elements of culture were the same all over the inhabited world. People practiced the same hunter–gatherer economy with similar kinds of technology, ate similar kinds of food, enjoyed similar levels of **material culture,** and—as far as we can tell—had similar religious practices.

The material culture—concrete objects people create—that many archeological digs yield offers clues to what goes on in the mind. A simple test establishes that fact. We can make informed inferences about people's religion, or politics, or their attitudes toward nature and society, or their values in general, by looking at what they eat, how they

The Ice Age

(All dates are approximate)	
150,000 years ago	Earth cools; last great Ice Age begins
18,000 years ago	Peak of Ice Age—farthest extent of ice cap
18,000 years ago	Warming of the Earth begins
16,000–8,000 years ago	Temperatures fluctuate; glaciers retreat; coastlines form
15,000–20,000 years ago	World emerges from Ice Age

 Cave art (Lascaux)

Cave art. Until they died out—victims of competition with and exploitation by settler communities—in the early twentieth century, the Southern Bushmen of South Africa made cave paintings similar to those their ancestors made more than 20,000 years ago. On rock surfaces and cave walls, shamans painted their visions of the creatures of the spirit-world, glimpsed in states of ecstasy on imaginary journeys beyond the ordinarily accessible world.

dress, and how they decorate their homes. For instance, the people who hunted mammoths to extinction 20,000 years ago on the Ice-Age steppes of what is now southern Russia built dome-shaped dwellings of mammoth bones on a circular plan 12 or 15 feet in diameter that seem sublime triumphs of the imagination. They are reconstructions of mammoth nature, humanly reimagined, perhaps to acquire the beast's strength or to conjure power over the species. Ordinary, every-day activities went on inside these extraordinary dwellings—sleeping, eating, and all the routines of family life—in communities, on average, of fewer than 100 people. But no dwelling is purely practical. Your house reflects your ideas about your place in the world.

Thanks to the clues material culture yields, we can make confident assertions about other aspects of Ice-Age people's lives: their symbolic systems, their magic, and the kind of social and political units they lived in. Although Ice-Age people had nothing we recognize as writing, they did have highly expressive symbols, which we can only struggle to translate. Realistic drawings made 20,000 to 30,000 years ago show recurring gestures and postures. Moreover, they often include what seem to be numbers, signified by dots and notches. Other marks, which we can no long interpret, are undeniably systematic. One widely occurring mark that looks like a P may be a symbol for female because it resembles the curves of a woman's body. What looks as if it might be a calendar was made 30,000 years ago in France. It is a flat bone inscribed with crescents and circles that may record phases of the moon.

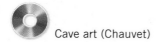
Cave art (Chauvet)

Clues to spiritual lives appear in traces of red ochre, the earliest substance that seems to have had a role in ritual. The oldest known ochre mine in the world, about 42,000 years old, is at Lion Cave in what is now Lesotho in southern Africa. The vivid, lurid color was applied in burials, perhaps as a precious offering, perhaps to imitate blood and reinvest the dead with life. The speculation that people might also have used ochre to paint their living bodies is hard to resist.

Those who controlled ritual wielded power. In paintings and carvings, we can glimpse the Ice-Age elite. Animal masks—antlered or lionlike—transform the wearer. From anthropological studies, we know such disguises are normally efforts to communicate with the dead or with the gods. Bringing messages from other worlds is the role of a **shaman** (SHAH-mehn), an intermediary between humans and spirits or gods. The shaman may seek a state of ecstasy induced by drugs or dancing or drumming, to see and hear visions normally inaccessible to the senses. He becomes the medium through which spirits talk to this world. Among the Chukchi hunters of northern Siberia, whose way of life and environment are similar to Ice-Age peoples', the shaman's experience is represented as a journey to consult the spirits in a realm that only the dead can normally enter. The shaman may adopt an animal disguise to acquire the animal's speed or strength or identify with an animal ancestor. Shamans' roles can be an awesome source of authority. They can challenge alpha males. Like other religions, shamanism involves spiritual insight, which people of both sexes, various levels of intellect, and all kinds of physique can acquire. It can replace the strong with the seer and the sage. By choosing elites who had the gift of communicating with spirits, Ice-Age societies could escape the oppression of the physically powerful or those privileged by birth.

Although we cannot be sure about the nature of the Ice-Age power class, we know it existed because of glaring inequalities in how Ice-Age people were buried. In a cemetery near Moscow, dated about 24,000 years ago, the highest-status person seems, at first glance, to have been an elderly man. His burial goods include a cap sewn with fox's teeth and about 20 ivory bracelets. Nearby, however, two boys

Shaman. In many societies, communication with the spirit-world remains the responsibility of the specialists whom anthropologists call shamans. Typically, they garb and paint or disguise themselves to resemble spirits or the animals deemed to have privileged access to realms beyond human sense. The shamans then "journey" to the spirits or ancestors in trances induced by dancing, drumming, or drugs. Shamans often acquire social influence and political authority as healers, prophets, and arbitrators.

of about eight or ten years old have even more spectacular ornaments. As well as ivory bracelets and necklaces and fox-tooth buttons, the boys have animal carvings and beautifully wrought weapons, including spears of mammoth ivory, each over six feet long. About 3,500 finely worked ivory beads had been drizzled over the head, torso, and limbs of each boy. Here was a society that marked leaders for greatness from boyhood and therefore, perhaps, from birth.

In our attempt to understand where power lay in Ice-Age societies, the final bits of evidence are crumbs from rich people's tables, fragments of feasts. Archaeologists have found ashes from large-scale cooking and the calcified debris of food at sites in northern Spain, perhaps from as long as 23,000 years ago. The tally sticks that survive from the same region in the same period may also have been records of expenditure on feasts. What were such feasts for? By analogy with modern hunting peoples, the most likely reason was alliance-making between communities. They were probably not male-bonding occasions, as some scholars think, because they are close to major dwelling sites where women and children would be present. Instead, from the moment of its emergence, the idea of the feast had practical consequences: to build and strengthen societies and enhance the power of those who organized the feasts and controlled the food.

Peopling the New World

The New World was the last part of the planet *Homo sapiens* peopled, but it is not easy to say exactly when or by whom. According to the formerly dominant theory, a gap opened between glaciers toward the end of the Ice Age. A race of hunters crossed the land link between North America and Asia, where the Bering Strait now flows, where no human hunter had ever trod before. The invaders found abundance so great and animals so unwary that they ate enormously and multiplied greatly. They spread rapidly over the hemisphere, hunting great game to extinction as they went. The story appealed to an unsophisticated form of U.S. patriotism. The Clovis people, as these hunters were dubbed after an early archaeological site in New Mexico, seemed to resemble modern American pioneers. They exhibited quick-fire locomotion, hustle and bustle, technical prowess, big appetites, irrepressible strength, enormous cultural reach, and a talent for reforging the environment.

By comparison, the truth about the peopling of the hemisphere is disappointingly undramatic. These first great American superheroes—like most of their successors—did not really exist. Although archeologists have excavated too few sites for a complete and reliable picture to emerge, a new theory dominates. We have evidence of early human settlement scattered from the Yukon to Uruguay and from near the Bering Strait to the edge of the Beagle Channel, over so long a period, in so many different geological layers, and with such a vast range of cultural diversity that one conclusion is inescapable. Colonists came at different times, bringing different cultures with them (see Map 1.3).

No generally accepted evidence dates any inhabited sites in the American hemisphere earlier than about 13,000 B.C.E. The first arrivals came when glaciers covered much of North America. They stuck close to the cold, where the game was fattest. They followed corridors between walls of ice or along narrow shores away from glaciers. Other arrivals came by sea and continued to come after the land bridge was submerged. Around 10,000 years ago, a catastrophic cluster of extinctions wiped out the mammoth, mastodon, horse, giant sloth, saber-toothed tiger, and at least 35 other large species in the Americas. New hunting techniques and

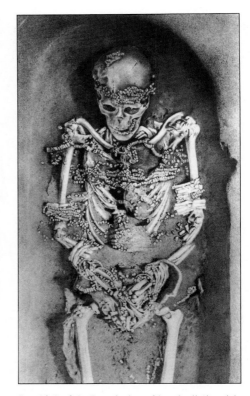

Sunghir burial. A profusion of beads distinguishes the graves of people of high status at Sunghir in Russia, from about 24,000 years ago. The distribution of signs of wealth in burials suggests that even in the Ice Age inequalities were rife and that status could be inherited.

 Clovis points

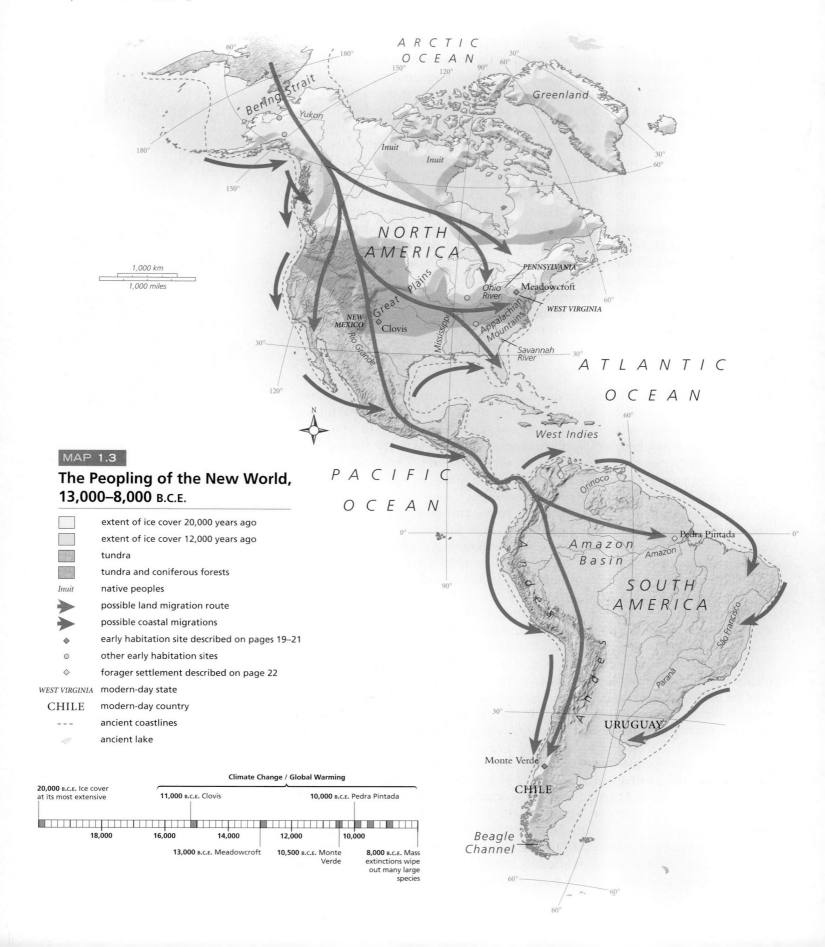

MAP 1.3

The Peopling of the New World, 13,000–8,000 B.C.E.

	extent of ice cover 20,000 years ago
	extent of ice cover 12,000 years ago
	tundra
	tundra and coniferous forests
Inuit	native peoples
➤	possible land migration route
➤➤	possible coastal migrations
◆	early habitation site described on pages 19–21
○	other early habitation sites
◇	forager settlement described on page 22
WEST VIRGINIA	modern-day state
CHILE	modern-day country
- - -	ancient coastlines
	ancient lake

Climate Change / Global Warming

20,000 B.C.E. Ice cover at its most extensive

11,000 B.C.E. Clovis

10,000 B.C.E. Pedra Pintada

18,000   16,000   14,000   12,000   10,000

13,000 B.C.E. Meadowcroft   10,500 B.C.E. Monte Verde   8,000 B.C.E. Mass extinctions wipe out many large species

perhaps new hunting peoples were probably partly responsible. But we can only explain the events in the context of vast climatic changes that affected habitats and the ecology on which these animals depended.

Many supposedly early sites of human habitation have proved to be delusions of overenthusiastic archaeologists—false, or, at best, unconvincing. A few sites, however, offer strong evidence of the antiquity and range of settlement. Most are in the eastern United States—a long way from Asia. It must have taken a long time for these people to get there from the vicinity of the modern Bering Strait. In the mid-1970s, 15,000-year-old basketwork and tools made with fine flints emerged from deep under the discarded beer cans that topped a dig at Meadowcroft, on the Ohio River, near the border of Pennsylvania and West Virginia. Archaeologists are investigating similar sites between the Ohio and Savannah Rivers. Later in the 1970s, excavations at Monte Verde in southern Chile revealed a 20-foot-long, wooden, hide-covered dwelling preserved in a peat bog for about 12,500 years. Nearby were a big mastodon-butchery and a space devoted to making tools. The inhabitants brought salt and seaweed from the coast, 40 miles away, and medicinal herbs from mountains equally far in the opposite direction. Half-chewed lumps of seaweed show the eaters' dental bites; a boy's footprints survive in the clay lining of a pit. If Meadowcroft is a long way from the colonizers' entry point near the Bering Strait, southern Chile is a world away again—almost as far as you can get in the Western Hemisphere. How long would it have taken the settlers of Monte Verde to cross the hemisphere, over vast distances and through many different environments, each demanding new forms of adaptation? Most specialists think it must have taken thousands of years. The question of the date of the first peopling of the New World therefore remains open.

SURVIVAL OF THE FORAGERS

As the ice cap retreated and the great herds shifted with it, many human communities opted to follow. Archeology has unearthed traces of their routes. Along the way, in what is now northern Germany, about 12,000 years ago, people sacrificed reindeer by weighting them with stones sewn into their stomachs and drowning them in a lake. About 1,000 years later, hunters as far north as Yorkshire in England found an environment as abundant as the cave artists' had been. Not only was it filled with tundra-loving species such as red deer, elk, and aurochs—huge, shaggy wild cattle—but also with wild boar in surroundings that were becoming patchily wooded.

At Skateholm in Sweden, about 8,000 years ago, hunters founded the largest known settlement of the era. It was a winter camp in an area where the 87 different edible animal species roamed. The people trapped river-fish, netted sea-birds, harpooned seals and dolphin, stuck pigs, and drove deer into pits or ponds. In summer, they moved farther north. They lie today in graves decorated with beads and ochre and filled with the spoils of their careers, including antlers and boar's tusks. Their burly dogs are buried nearby, sometimes with more signs of honor than humans were given, for hunting prowess and skill in war determined status. Many of the human dead bear wounds from man-made weapons. Women have only a third as many wounds as the men: evidence of sexual specialization.

The most persistently faithful followers of the ice were the North American Inuit. About 4,000 years ago, they invented the blubber-filled soapstone lamp. Now they could follow big game beyond the tundra and into the darkness of an arctic

Bushmen. Though now obliged to adopt a mixed economy, supported in part by farming and donations of food, the San or Bushmen of southern Africa have been among the most conservative of the world's peoples. They maintained their foraging way of life, essentially unchanged, for millennia—despite neighbors' attempts to exterminate them. This record of survival contrasts with the rapid turnover of more ambitious civilizations that radically modify their environments, usually with disastrous results.

winter. They could track the musk ox to the shore of the ocean and the caribou on its winter migrations, when its fur is thickest and its fat most plentiful. This way of life persisted until the late twentieth century, although the people who first practiced it have disappeared. Migrants from the Arctic Ocean replaced them 1,000 years ago.

Climate change trapped other foraging peoples in environments where they had to develop new ways of life. Some of these environments offered new kinds of abundance. Here were life-filled rivers, lakes, and broad-leaved forests, rich in acorns (nutritious food for humans with enough time to fine-grind them). New World prairies held apparently inexhaustible stocks of bison. Between unstable periods of climate change around 12,000 years ago, foragers even colonized dense, tropical forests in southeast Asia and in the New World at Pedra Pintada in Brazil where the Amazon River now flows. This is a region where foragers today have to struggle to find foods they can digest, but it seems to have been more environmentally diverse toward the end of the Ice Age.

Some societies perpetuated their foraging life in hot, arid deserts, as different from the best hunting grounds of the Ice Age as it is possible to imagine. This required two forms of adaptation. First, thinly dispersed populations had to create collaborative networks. Such interdependence explains why peoples who live in ecologically shaky homelands often require people to marry outside the group and why they regard hospitality to strangers as a sacred obligation. Second, poor environments demanded that inhabitants develop what we might call orally transmitted science. For only with accurate and extensive knowledge of their habitat can people survive in harsh environments.

The San or Bushmen of southern Africa's Kalahari Desert illustrate the difficulties and solutions. Their domain has shrunk in the last few centuries, as Bantu farmers, Khoi herdsmen, and white invaders have overrun much of their former territory. But their heartland was already dry at the time of the San's first occupancy, about 14,000 years ago. The increased rainfall that usually followed the retreat of the ice hardly fell here. There are underground rivers but few permanent water holes. The people watch for rare signs of rain and hurry to gather the vegetation that accompanies it. The scrubland plant foods, including water-bearing tubers and a kind of cactus, supply 30 percent of their sustenance. The rest comes from game, which grazes on tough desert shrubs that humans cannot digest. To kill large game is almost impossible with a Bushman's bow. He wounds the beast with a poisoned barb and follows it at a run for many miles until it drops from exhaustion and the effects of the drug, before butchering the heavy animal and dragging it home. Bushmen who persist with this demanding way of life to this day are pursuing a commitment that has grown out of generations of invested emotion. As difficult as it may be for us to understand, the San would find it heart-wrenching to change their way of life for the mere sake of efficiency, convenience, or material gain.

In one sense, the world's food supply still depends on foraging. The amount of food from hunting actually increased in the twentieth century, which may go down in history not only as the last age of hunting but also as the greatest. World over today, we practice a highly specialized, mechanized, and unusual form of hunting—deep-sea trawling. Fish farming is likely to replace it in the future, but in any case, deep-sea fishing is a historical throwback.

IN PERSPECTIVE: After the Ice

In the post–Ice-Age world, little by little, over thousands of years, most societies abandoned foraging and adopted farming or herding to get their food. Among peoples who still live close to the ice cap, the Inuit remain faithful to their hunting tradition in North America. Most of their Old World counterparts, however, have long abandoned it. In Eurasia, though some hunting cultures still cling to the old ways at the eastern end of Siberia, the peoples on the western Arctic rim—the Sami (or Lapplanders) of Scandinavia and their neighbors, the Samoyeds and Nenets—adopted reindeer herding over 1,000 years ago. The Ice-Age way of life, if not over, is drawing to a close. Hunting is now thought of as a primitive way to get food, long abandoned except as an aristocratic or supposedly manly sport.

The disappearance of foraging seems a remarkable turnaround for a predator-species such as *Homo sapiens*. There was a time before hunting, when our ancestors were scavengers, but for hundreds of thousands, perhaps millions, of years, foraging was reliable and rewarding. It fed people through every change of climate. Its practitioners spread over the world and adapted successfully to every kind of habitat. Humans dominated every ecosystem they entered. They achieved startling increases in their numbers, which we struggle to explain. They founded more varied societies than any other species (though the differences among these societies were slight compared to later periods). They had art-rich cultures with traditions of learning and symbolic systems to record information. They had their own social elites, political customs, ambitious magic, and practical methods to exploit their environment.

Our next task is to ask why, after the achievements recounted in this chapter, did people abandon the foraging life? Renouncing the hunt and pursuing new ways of life after the Ice Age are among the most far-reaching and mysterious transformations of the human past. If the puzzle of why *Homo sapiens* spread over the Earth is the first great question in our history, the problem of why foragers became farmers is the second.

CHRONOLOGY

(All dates are approximate)

Over 3 million years ago	Lucy
2–1 million years ago	*Homo erectus* migrates from East Africa to Africa and Eurasia
100,000 years ago	*Homo sapiens* migrates out of Africa
67,000 years ago	*Homo sapiens* in Asia
50,000 years ago	*Homo sapiens* colonizes Australia and New Guinea
	Homo sapiens reaches Europe
30,000 years ago	Last Neanderthals vanish
20,000–15,000 B.C.E.	World emerges from the Ice Age
20,000 B.C.E.	Invention of the bow and arrow
13,000 B.C.E.	*Homo sapiens* in the Americas

PROBLEMS AND PARALLELS

1. When does the story of humankind begin? Is it possible to define what it means to be human?

2. How do Neanderthals and *Homo floresiensis* challenge definitions of *Homo sapiens*?

3. Why did *Homo sapiens* migrate out of Africa? How did migration change people's relationships with each other and with their environment?

4. Why did the population of *Homo sapiens* increase so rapidly?

5. Which stresses could have caused early peoples to divide and fight each other? Which theories have been put forward for how war started?

6. How did male domination come to be normal in human societies? What impact did sexual economic specialization have on early societies?

7. Why was the Ice Age a time of affluence? What role did shamans play in Ice-Age society?

8. Why has the foraging life persisted today?

DOCUMENTS IN GLOBAL HISTORY

- Margaret Mead, from "Warfare Is Only an Invention—Not a Biological Necessity"
- Jane Goodall, from "The Challenge Lies in All of Us"
- Marshall Sahlins, "The Original Affluent Society," from *Stone-Age Economics*

- Cave art (Lascaux)
- Cave art (Chauvet)
- Clovis points

Please see the Primary Source DVD for additional sources related to this chapter.

READ ON

F. Fernández-Armesto, *Humankind: A Brief History* (2004) traces debates over the boundaries of the concept of humankind. Jared Diamond's book on the human overlap with apes is *The Third Chimpanzee* (1992). The works of F. de Waal, especially *The Ape and the Sushi Master* (2001), and those of J. Goodall, especially *The Chimpanzees of Gombe* (1986), are fundamental for understanding the issues. B. Sykes, *The Seven Daughters of Eve* (2001), is the best introduction to the use of DNA in paleoanthropology. C. Stringer and C. Gamble, *In Search of the Neanderthals* (1995), is an interesting review of human engagement with Neanderthal remains. The classic novel by W. Golding, *The Inheritors* (1963), is an imaginative attempt to envisage Neanderthal life.

Good general introductions to human evolution include R. G. Klein, *The Human Career* (1999), and I. Tattersall, *The Fossil Trail* (1997). C. Gamble, *Timewalkers: The Prehistory of Global Colonization* (1994), is an excellent account of the migrations. On fire, J. Goudsblom, *Fire and Civilization* (1993),

is a classic, which the author has kept up-to-date in recent editions. R. Wrangham's views appeared in "The Raw and the Stolen," *Current Anthropology*, vol. xl (1999), 567–594. On war, K. Lorenz, *On Aggression* (1966), and R. Ardrey, *The Territorial Imperative* (1997), are controversial classics. J. Haas, ed., *The Anthropology of War* (1990) and L. H. Keeley, *War Before Civilization* (1997), survey the evidence.

On sex roles, G. Lerner, *The Creation of Patriarchy* (1987), and E. Martin, *The Woman in the Body: A Cultural Analysis of Reproduction* (1992), set the terms of debate. J. Peterson, *Sexual Revolutions* (2002), is an invaluable short survey.

On the conditions of Ice-Age life, M. D. Sahlins, *Stone Age Economics* (1972), is a stimulating classic. T. D. Price and J. A. Brown, eds., *Prehistoric Hunter-Gatherers* (1985) is an important collection of studies. On the art, the most illuminating works include S. J. Mithen, *Thoughtful Foragers* (1990), and J. D. Lewis-Williams, *Discovering Southern African Rock Art* (1990).

On the peopling of the New World, the challenging and readable work of J. Adovasio, *Before America* (2004), makes a stimulating starting point. S. Mithen, *After the Ice* (2004) is an engaging and imaginative introduction to the post–Ice-Age world.

The material on the San, L. van der Post's much maligned classic, *The Lost World of the Kalahari* (1977) is a thrilling read. For up-to-date studies, see L. Marshall, *The !Kung of Nyae Nyae* (1976), and E. Wilmsen, *Land Filled with Flies* (1989).

CHAPTER 2

Out of the Mud: Farming and Herding After the Ice Age

In environments that have no plants that humans can digest, herding is a life-giving option: Animals and humans live in mutual dependence. Humans protect the flocks from predators; their livestock convert grasses and shrubs into meat and milk. But, as with the Somali herdsmen pictured here, herders' lives are often precarious in marginal environments, because domesticated animals host disease-bearing organisms that can infect humans. Typically, herding cultures cope with restricted diets by developing a tolerance to digest dairy foods after infancy.

I n August 1770, Captain James Cook, charting the Pacific Ocean for Britain's Royal Navy, paused at an island off the north coast of Australia. He named it Possession Island, for to Cook's mind, it was waiting to be grabbed. The natives had left no marks of possession on its soil. Plants they could have domesticated—"fruits proper for the support of man"—grew wild. The people, Cook wrote, "know nothing of cultivation. ... It seems strange."

AUSTRALIA

He was puzzling over one of the most perplexing problems of history—the difference between foragers and farmers, food procurers and food producers. To most people, in most societies, for most of the time, food is and always has been the most important thing in the world. Changes in how we eat are among history's big changes. The biggest of all came after the Ice Age, as the world warmed: **husbandry**—breeding animals and cultivating crops—began to replace hunting and gathering.

Together, farming and herding revolutionized humans' place in their ecosystems. Instead of merely depending on other life forms to sustain us, we forged a new relationship of interdependence with species we eat. We rely on them for food; they rely on us for their reproduction. Husbandry was the first human challenge to evolution. Instead of evolving species through **natural selection**, farming and herding proceed by what might be called unnatural selection—sorting and selecting by human hands, for human needs, according to human agendas.

Herding and tilling also changed human societies. By feeding people on a vastly greater scale, agriculture allowed societies to get hugely bigger than ever before. We can only guess at the absolute figures, but in areas where farming has replaced foraging in modern times, population has increased fifty- or even a hundredfold. Larger populations demanded new forms of control of labor and food distribution, which, in turn, nurtured strong states and powerful elites.

Society became more volatile and, apparently, less stable. In almost every case, for reasons we still do not understand, when people begin to practice agriculture, the pace of change quickens immeasurably and cumulatively. States and civilizations do not seem to last for long. Societies that we think of as being most evolved turn out to be least fitted for survival. Compared with the relative stability of forager communities, societies that depend on agriculture are prone to lurch and collapse. History becomes a path picked among their ruins.

FOCUS questions

- WHY ARE settled foragers better off than farmers?
- WHAT KINDS of environments are suited to herding?
- WHAT KINDS of environments were suited to early agriculture?
- WHERE DID farming start, and what were the first crops?
- GIVEN THE disadvantages, why did people farm?

James Cook, from *Captain Cook's Journal During His First Voyage Round the World*

The rice fields of Bali in Indonesia are among the most productive in the world, using varieties of rice and techniques for farming it that are about 1,000 years old. Irrigation channels, maintained and administered by farmers' cooperatives, distribute water evenly among the terraces. Though originally a lowland crop, favoring swampy conditions, rice adapts perfectly to upland environments and to terrace farming.

Still, for Captain Cook, and for most people who have thought about it, it was strange that people who had the opportunity to practice agriculture should not take advantage of it. The advantages of agriculture seem so obvious. The farmer can select the best specimens of edible crops and creatures, collect them in the most convenient places and pastures, crossbreed livestock, and hybridize plants to improve size, yield, or flavor. By these methods, farming societies build up large populations. Usually they go on to create cities and develop ever more complex technologies. To Cook and his contemporaries in Europe, who believed that progress was inevitable and that the same kind of changes are bound to happen everywhere, peoples who clung to foraging seemed baffling.

THE PROBLEM OF AGRICULTURE

Cook and others at the time saw only two explanations for why foragers might reject agriculture: They were either stupid or subhuman. Early European painters in Australia depicted indigenous people as apelike creatures, grimacing oddly and crawling in trees. Colonists ignored the natives, or, when they got in the way, often hunted them down—as they would beasts. But native Australians rejected more than agriculture. In some areas, they shunned every technical convenience. On the island of Tasmania, in the extreme south of Australia, where the natives became extinct soon after European settlement began, they seemed to have forgotten every art of their ancestors: bows, boats, even how to kindle fire. In Arnhem Land, in the extreme north, they used boomerangs to make music but no longer as weapons for the hunt. Progress, which the European discoverers of Australia believed in fervently, seemed to have gone into reverse. Australia was not only on the exact opposite side of the world from England, but also it was a topsy-turvy place where everything was upside down.

We can, however, be certain that if natives rejected agriculture or other practices Europeans considered progressive, it must have been for good reasons. Native Australians did not lack the knowledge necessary to switch from foraging to farming had they so wished. When they gathered wild yams or the root known as nardoo, they ensured that enough of the plant remained in the ground to grow back. In many regions, too, they used fire to control the grazing grounds of kangaroos and concentrate them for hunting, a common technique among herders to manage pasture and among tillers to renew the soil. Along the Murray and Darling Rivers, aborigines even watered and weeded wild crops and policed their boundaries against human and animal predators. They could have planted and irrigated crops, farmed the grubs they liked to eat, penned kangaroos, and even tried to domesticate them. In the far north of Australia, aboriginal communities traded with the farming cultures of New Guinea. So they could have learned agriculture from outsiders.

If the aborigines did not farm, it must have been because they were doing well without it. Similar cases all over the world support this conclusion. Where wild foods are abundant, there is no incentive to domesticate them. Of course, people often adopt practices that do them no good. We can concede this general principle, but, case by case, we still want to know why.

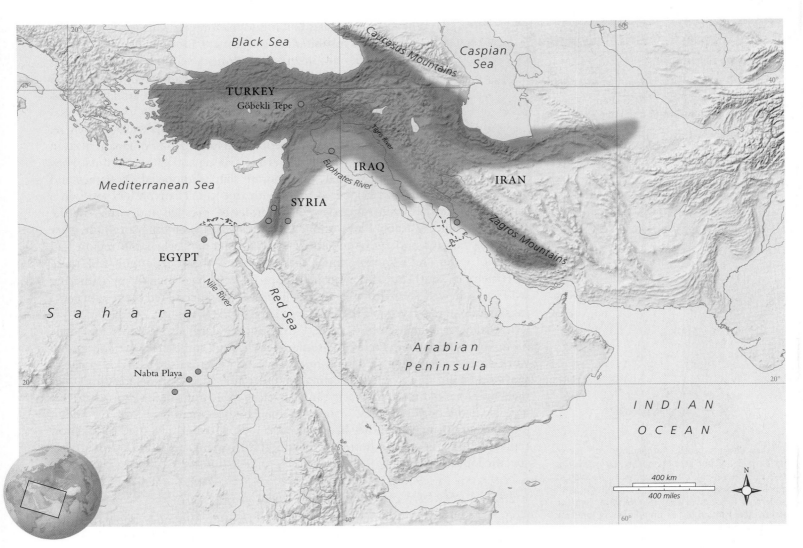

Preagricultural Settlements

Under some conditions, people can settle in one place without the trouble of farming. Archaeological evidence from the Middle East shows this. After the Ice Age, a frontier zone between forest and grassland stretched across the eastern shore of the Mediterranean and what are now Iran, eastern Turkey, and Iraq (see Map 2.1). Forests were full of nuts, which gatherers ground into flour. Grasslands bred vast quantities of wild grass with edible seeds. These foods could all be warehoused between harvests and had the additional advantage of maturing at different times. Dense herds of gazelle provided more nutrition for hunters to bring home. Food was so plentiful that foragers did not have to move around much to find it.

By about 14,000 to 15,000 years ago, permanent settlements arose throughout the region: clusters of dwellings made of wood on stone foundations, or cut from soft stone and roofed with reeds. Villages had distinctive habits, which almost amounted to badges of identity. Some favored gazelle toe bones for jewelry; some preferred fox teeth and partridge legs. Villagers married within their own communities, as inherited physical characteristics show: People were relatively short in some villages or had distinctive palates in others. They cut plans of their fields on limestone slabs, which suggests that they had a sense of possession that Captain Cook would have recognized.

MAP 2.1

Preagricultural Settlements in the Middle East

forest
grassland
TURKEY   modern-day country
●   preagricultural settlement
----   ancient coastlines

Early Forager Settlements

(All dates are approximate)	
15,000 years ago	World emerges from the Ice Age
14,000–15,000 years ago	Permanent settlements appear in Middle East
13,000 years ago	Honshu Island, Japan
10,000 years ago	Nabta Playa, Egypt; Göbekli Tepe, Turkey

Overuse deforms bones. Archaeology can reconstruct how ancient people behaved by measuring the deformities in their skeletons. The woman whose toe this was lived in a community of early sedentary foragers in what is now Syria. She evidently spent much of her time kneeling, presumably to grind the acorns and kernels of wild wheat on which her people relied for food.

When archaeologists first found the foragers' villages in the 1930s, they assumed the inhabitants were farmers. But their remains, on the whole, show better health and nourishment than the farming peoples who followed. A diet rich in seeds and nuts had ground down their teeth, but—unlike the farmers—they had none of the streaked tooth-enamel common among the under-nourished.

Similar evidence of preagricultural settlements exists elsewhere. The Jomon (JOHM-mehn) people of Honshu Island, Japan, lived in permanent villages 13,000 years ago, fishing and gathering nuts. They made pots for display, in elaborate shapes, modeled on flames and serpents and lacquered them with tree sap. Their potters were, in a sense, magicians, transforming clay into objects of prestige and ritual. In the Egyptian Sahara, at Nabta Playa, about 40 plant species, including sorghum, grew alongside hearths and pit ovens about 10,000 years ago, when the region had plenty of water and a cooler climate than now. At Göbekli Tepe (goh-BEHK-lee TEH-peh) in southeast Turkey, contemporaries who lived mainly by gathering wild wheat hewed seven-ton pillars from limestone and decorated them with carvings of animals and symbols that look suspiciously like writing.

Small, permanent houses suggest that nuclear families—parents and children—predominated in these early settlements, though some sites have communal work areas for grinding seeds and nuts. The way skeletons are muscled suggests that women did slightly more kneeling (and therefore slightly more grinding) than men, and men did more throwing (and therefore more hunting) than women. But both sexes did both activities. Male and female bodies began to reconverge after a long period during which they had evolved to look differently. As food production replaced hunting and gathering, war and child rearing became the main sex-specific jobs in society.

The Disadvantages of Farming

In the early stages of moving from foraging to farming, the food supply becomes less reliable because people depend on a relatively small range of farmed foods or even on a single species. Communities become vulnerable to ecological disasters. Famine is more likely as diet narrows. When people have to plant and grow food as well as gather it, they use more energy to get the same amount of nourishment (although domesticated foods, once harvested, tend to be easier to process for eating). The need to organize labor encourages inequalities and exploitation. Concentrations of domesticated animals spread disease, such as smallpox, measles, rubella, chicken pox, influenza, and tuberculosis.

So the problem is really the opposite of what Cook supposed. Farmers' behavior, not foragers', is strange. Husbandry in some ways makes life worse. No one has put the problem better than the historian of agronomy, Jack L. Harlan: "The question must be raised: Why farm? … Why work harder for food less nutritious and a supply more capricious? Why invite famine, plague, pestilence and crowded living conditions?"[1]

HUSBANDRY IN DIFFERENT ENVIRONMENTS

The most obvious contrast in environments is between **herders** and **tillers**. Herding developed where plants were too sparse or indigestible to sustain human life, but animals could convert these plants into meat—an energy source that people can access by eating the animals. In some places, roamed by crea-

○ MAKING CONNECTIONS ○

FORAGERS AND FARMERS COMPARED

FORAGERS	FARMERS
Food procurers	**Food producers**
hunt and gather	husbandry (breed animals, cultivate crops)
Fit into nature	**Change nature**
little environmental impact	herders: some environmental impact tillers: massive environmental impact
Manage the landscape	**Nature remade and reimagined**
Dependence on wild animals and plants	**Interdependence between humans, plants, and animals** animals and plants exploited and domesticated
Stable food supply	**Unstable food supply**
nomadic foragers move in response to environmental change	small range of farmed foods increases vulnerability to ecological disasters, change of climate
Stable population	**Expanding population**
• relatively little labor needed • population control available, mainly by managed lactation	• breeding livestock and cultivating plants lead to increased food supply • increased population • concentrations of domesticated animals spread disease
Stable society	**Radically changed, unstable society**
• kinship and age fix individual's place in society • sexes usually share labor by specializing in different economic tasks	• need to control labor and food distribution leads to social inequalities • work shared between the sexes, increased reliance on female labor • strong states develop with powerful elites, complex technologies

tures with herd instinct, people could manage herds instead of hunting them. Breeding enhanced qualities that evolution did not necessarily favor, such as docility; size; and yield of meat, milk, eggs, and fat. But herds, on the whole, kept to traditional patterns of migration, and people continued to accompany them—driving the beasts, now, rather than following them. Domesticated animals remained recognizably the heirs of their wild ancestors, and the landscapes through which they traveled did not change much, except that the herds' feeding and manure probably encouraged the grasses they ate to flourish at the expense of other plant species.

In other environments, tilling develops where the soil is suitable or enough ecological diversity exists to sustain plant husbandry or mixed farming of plants and animals. In the long run, tillage of the soil changed the world more than any previous innovation by Homo sapiens. From postglacial mud, people coaxed what we now call "**civilization**"—a way of life based on radically modifying the environment. Instead of merely trying to manage the landscape nature provided, farmers recarved it with fields and boundaries, ditches and irrigation canals. They stamped the land with a new look, a geometrical order. Agriculture enabled humans to see the world in a new way—to imagine that magic and science had the power to change nature. Such power, in turn, changed people's sense of where they fit into the panorama of life on Earth. Now they could become lords or, in more modest moments or cultures, stewards of creation.

 Jack Harlan, from *Crops and Man*

Masai. Humans need vitamin C, but the meat and dairy products from herds do not supply much of it. So people in herding cultures eat half-digested plants from animals' stomachs and organ meats, such as the liver, in which vitamin C tends to get concentrated. Fresh blood—drawn here from the veins of a calf by Masai women in Kenya—is also a useful source of the vitamin. Drinking blood confers an added advantage: Nomads can draw it from their animals "on the hoof," without slaughtering them or halting the migrations of their flocks.

Herders' Environments

In tundra and evergreen forests, where cold shortens the growing season, too little humanly digestible plant food thrives to keep large communities alive. People can remain foragers—and primarily hunters, seeking the fat-rich species typical of such zones—like the Inuit in the North American Arctic, who hunt seal and walrus, or they can become herders, like the Sami and Samoyeds of northern Europe and northwest Asia, who live off reindeer.

Similarly, the soils of the world's vast grasslands—known as prairie in North America, pampa in South America, steppe in Eurasia, and the **Sahel** (sah-HEHL) in Africa—have, for most of history, been unfavorable for tillage. Though there are favorable patches, the sod is mostly too difficult to turn without a steel plow. The peoples of the Eurasian and African grasslands were probably herding by about 5000 B.C.E. Native American grassland dwellers of the New World, on the other hand, retained a foraging way of life because available species—bison, various types of antelope—were more abundant for the hunt and less suitable for herding.

For those who choose it, herding has three special consequences.

First, it imposes a mobile life. The proportion of the population who follow the herds—and, in some cases, it is the entire population—cannot settle in permanent villages. Herder peoples can build on a large scale. The Scythians, for instance, people of the western Asian **steppe** who first domesticated the horse and invented the wheel and axle about 6,000 to 7,000 years ago, built impressive stone structures. But these were underground tombs, dwellings for the dead, while the living inhabited temporary camps. Some herding societies in Asia and Africa have become rich enough to found cities for elites or for specialist craftsmen or miners. In the thirteenth century C.E., a city of this type, Karakorum in Mongolia, was one of the most admired in the world. On the whole, however, herding does not favor cities or the kind of culture that cities nourish, such as monumental buildings, large-scale institutions for education and the arts, and industrial technology.

Second, since herders breed from animals that naturally share their grassland habitats, their herds consist of such creatures as cattle, sheep, horses, goats—milk-yielding stock. To get the full benefit from their animals, herding peoples have to eat dairy products. To modern, milk-fed Americans, this may sound normal. But it required a modification of human evolution. Most people, in most parts of the world, do not naturally produce lactase, the substance that enables them to digest milk, after infancy. They respond to dairy products with distaste or even intolerance.

Third, the herders' diet, relying heavily on meat, milk, and blood, lacks variety compared to diets in more ecologically diverse environments. If you eat organ meats, drink animal blood, and prepare dairy products to harness beneficial bacteria, you can get everything the human body needs, including adequate vitamin C, but herding peoples, although they often express contempt for farmers, prize cultivated plants and import them at great cost or take them as tribute or booty. They also value products of tree-rich environments, such as timber, silk, linen, and cotton.

So conflict arose not from herders' hatred of farmers' culture but from a desire to share its benefits. On the other hand, farmers have not normally had to depend on herding cultures for meat or dairy products. Typically, they can farm their own animals, feeding them on the waste or surplus of their crops or by grazing them between their areas of tillage or at higher altitudes above their fields. Therefore, in herder–settler warfare, the herders have typically been aggressive and the settlers defensive, until about 300 years ago or so, when the war technology of sedentary societies left herding societies unable to compete.

Tillers' Environments

The first prerequisite for farming was soil loose enough for a dibble—a pointed stick for poking holes in the ground—to work. At first, this was the only technology available. Where the sod had to be cut or turned—where, for instance, the soil was heavy, or dense, or sticky—agriculture had to wait for the more advanced technology of the spade and the plow.

Equally necessary for agriculture were water to grow the crop, sun to ripen it, and nourishment for the soil. Farming can exhaust even the richest soils. Flooding and layering with silt or dredging and dressing new topsoil is needed to replace nutrients. Alternatively, farmers can add fertilizer, such as ash from burned wood, leaf mold from forest clearings, or dung, from bird colonies or domesticated animals.

Three broad types of environment suited early agriculture: swampy wetlands, uplands, and alluvial plains, where flooding rivers or lakes renew the topsoil. (Cleared woodlands and irrigated drylands are also suitable for agriculture, but as far as we know, farming never originated in these environments. Rather, outsiders brought it to these areas from someplace else.) Each of the three types developed with peculiar characteristics and specialized crops.

SWAMPLAND Swamp is no longer much in demand for farming. Nowadays, in the Western world, if we want to turn bog into farmland we drain it. But it had advantages early on. Swamp soil is rich, moist, and easy to work with simple technology. At least one staple grows well in waterlogged land—rice. We still do not know where or when rice was first cultivated, or even whether any of these wetland varieties preceded the dryland rice that has gradually become more popular around the world. Most evidence, however, suggests that people were producing rice on the lower Ganges River in India and in parts of southeast Asia some 8,000 years ago, and in paddies in the Yangtze River valley in China not long afterward.

Where rice is unavailable, swampland cultivators can adapt the land for other crops by dredging earth, making mounds for planting and ditches for water-dwelling creatures and plants. In the western highlands of New Guinea, the first agriculture we know of started fully 9,000 years ago in boggy valley bottoms. Drains, ditches, and mounds still exist in the Kuk swamp there. More extensive earthworks were in place by 6000 B.C.E. The crops have vanished—biodegraded into nothingness—but the first farmers probably planted **taro**, the most easily cultivated, indigenous native root. Modern varieties of taro exhibit signs of long domestication. A diverse group of plants—sago, nuts, and native bananas, yams, and other tubers—was probably added early. At some much disputed point, pigs arrived.

Variety of crops made New Guinea's agriculture sustainable. Variety may also help explain why farming remained a small-scale enterprise there. New Guinea never generated the big states and cities that grew up where the range of crops was narrower and agriculture more fragile. It may sound paradoxical that the most advantageous crop range produces the most modest results, but it makes sense. One of the pressures that drives farming peoples to expand their territory is fear that a crop will fail. The more territory you control, the more surplus you

○ MAKING CONNECTIONS

HERDERS AND TILLERS COMPARED

HERDERS	TILLERS
Environment	**Environment**
tundra, evergreen forests of northern Eurasia, grasslands, uplands	swampy wetlands, alluvial plains, temporal forests, irrigated deserts, some uplands
Way of life	**Way of life**
mobile	settled
Diet	**Diet**
reliance on meat, milk, and blood, sometimes supplemented by cultivated plants from tillers	reliance on cultivated plants, supplemented by meat and dairy from their own animals
Culture	**Culture**
does not favor development of cities, large-scale institutions, industry	tends to become urban, with large-scale institutions, industry

desire for goods from farming cultures, need for extensive grazing land

possessive attitude to land

mutual incomprehension and demonization

violence between herders and tillers

can warehouse, the more manpower you command, and the more productive your fields. Moreover, if you farm an environment with a narrow range of food sources, you can diversify only by conquering other people's habitats. The history of New Guinea has been as violent as that of other parts of the world, but its wars have always been local and the resulting territorial adjustments small. Empire-building was unknown on the island until European colonizers got there in the late nineteenth century.

We know of no other swamps that people adapted so early, but many later civilizations arose from similar sorts of ooze. We do not know much about the origins of agriculture among **Bantu** speaking peoples in West Africa, but it is more likely to have begun in the swamp than in the forest. Swampland is suited to the native yams on which Bantu farming first relied. Waterlogged land is also the favorite habitat of the other mainstay of Bantu tradition, the *oil palm*. The earliest archaeological evidence of farming based on yams and oil palms dates from about 5,000 years ago in swampy valley bottoms of Cameroon, above the forest level.

Swampland also contributed to agriculture along the Amazon River in South America 4,000 or 5,000 years ago. At first, the crops were probably richly diverse, supplemented by farming turtles and mollusks. Later, however, from about

500 C.E., farmers increasingly focused on bitter manioc, also known as cassava or yucca, which has the great advantage of being poisonous to predators. Human consumers can process the poison out. Olmec civilization, which, as we shall see in Chapter 3, was enormously influential in the history of **Mesoamerica**, was founded in swamps thick with mangrove trees about 3,000 years ago.

UPLANDS Like swamplands, regions of high altitude are not places that people today consider good for farming. There are three reasons for this: First, as altitude increases, cold and the scorching effects of solar radiation in the thin atmosphere diminish the variety of viable plants. Second, slopes erode (although relatively rich soils then collect in valleys). Finally, slopes in general are hard to work with plows. Still, this does not stop people who do not use plows from farming them, and in highlands suitable for plant foods, plant husbandry or mixed farming did develop.

The Andes Highlands usually contain many different microclimates at various altitudes and in valleys where sun and rain can vary tremendously within a short space. Some of the world's earliest farming, therefore, happened at surprisingly high altitudes. Evidence of mixed farming survives from between about 12,000 and 7,000 years ago near Lake Titicaca, 13,000 feet up in the Andes Mountains of South America. Here, in the cave of Pachamachay, bones of domesticated llamas cover those of hunted species. The domesticated animals fed on quinoa (kee-NOH-ah), a hardy grain that grows at high altitudes thanks to a bitter, soapy coating that cuts out solar radiation. The llamas ingested the leafy part and deposited the seeds in their manure. Their corrals therefore became nurseries for a food fit for humans to grow and eat.

The earliest known experiments in domesticating the potato probably occurred at about the same time in the same area—between 12,000 and 7,000 years ago. Potatoes were ideal for mountain agriculture. Some naturally occurring varieties grow at altitudes of up to 14,000 feet. Eaten in sufficient quantities, moreover, potatoes provide everything the human body needs to survive. High-altitude varieties have a hidden advantage. Whereas wild lowland potatoes are poisonous and need careful processing to become edible, the concentration of poison in potatoes diminishes the higher you climb. There is an obvious evolutionary reason for this. The poison is there to deter predators, which are most numerous at low altitudes.

The potato gave Andean mountain dwellers the same capacity to support large populations as peoples of the valleys and plains, where a parallel story began in the central coastal region of what is now Peru. There, around 10,000 years ago, farmers grew sweet potato tubers, perhaps the New World's earliest farmed crop. Andean history became a story of highland–lowland warfare, punctuated by the rise and fall of mountain-based empires.

Mesoamerica The Mesoamerican highlands, which are less high and less steep than those of the Andes, produced their own kind of highland-adapted food: a trinity of *maize*, *beans*, and *squash*. This combination grows well together and when eaten together provides almost complete nutrition. The earliest surviving specimens of cultivated maize are 6,000 years old, developed from a wild grass known as teosinte (TEE-eh-SIN-tee), which is still found in central Mexico, along with the wild ancestors of domesticated beans. Botanists estimate that people domesticated beans about 9,000 years ago (see Figure 2.1). The earliest domesticated squashes date from about the same period. The fact that their wild ancestors have disappeared suggests that farming here might have started with squashes when gatherers of wild beans and grains needed to provide food for times of drought. Squash grows well during arid spells severe enough to wither teosinte and blight beans.

FIGURE 2.1 TEOSINTE AND MAIZE. The form of teosinte from which early farmers in Mesoamerica developed maize no longer exists. But the diagram illustrates the stages through which Mesoamericans may have bred teosinte into maize, until they developed the characteristic thick, densely packed cobs familiar today. Unlike teosinte, maize cannot germinate without human help.
Permission of The University of Michigan Museum of Anthropology.

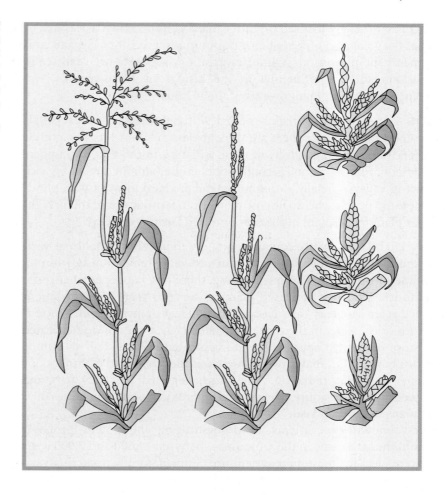

Teff—the staple grain of early Ethiopian civilization—remains unique to the region, where it is still harvested regularly. But, as the picture shows, it more closely resembles wild grasses than modern high-yielding food grains. The starchy ears are tiny and require much labor to mill. So, like many traditional staples, teff faces the threat of extinction today from the competition of commercial hybrids or genetically modified varieties, promoted by powerful corporations.

The Old World The Old World had no potatoes, quinoa, or maize for highland farmers to work with. The hardiest staples available in most of Eurasia and Africa were *rye* and *barley*. Surprisingly, however, people in lowlands first domesticated both of them in what are now Jordan and Syria, probably about 10,000 years ago. Rye germinates at just a couple degrees above freezing, but its drawbacks made it more popular as a winter crop in wheat-growing lowlands than as a mountain staple. Its yield is lower, and it is less nutritious than other grains. Rye is also extremely vulnerable to fungus infection. Barley did not fulfill its potential to be an Old World equivalent of quinoa or potatoes until the sixth century C.E., when it became the staple food in Tibet.

The only other Old World grain with similar potential was Ethiopia's indigenous grass called *teff*. Though its tiny grains make teff laborious to cultivate and process, it was suited to the region's fertile soil and temperate climate above 7,200 feet. Although farmers in Ethiopia cultivated teff at least 5,000 years ago, they never had to rely on it absolutely. Some varieties of *millet*—the name of a huge range of grasses whose seeds humans can digest—had superior yields. Over time, millet displaced teff, which never became a major staple outside Ethiopia.

ALLUVIAL PLAINS Although swamps and rain-fed highlands have produced spectacularly successful agriculture, farmers get the best help from nature in alluvial plains, where river-borne or lake-borne mud renews the topsoil. If people can channel the floods to keep crops from being swept away on these plains, sediment restores nutrients and compensates for lack of rain. Alluvial soils in arid climates sustained, as we shall see in the next chapter, some of the world's most productive economies until late in the second millennium B.C.E. *Wheat* and barley grew in the black earth that lines Egypt's Nile River, the floodplains of the lower Tigris and Euphrates Rivers in what is now Iraq, and the Indus River in what is now Pakistan. People first farmed millet on alluvial soils in a cooler, moister climate in China, in the crook of the Yellow River and the Guanzhong (gwang-joe) basin around 7,000 years ago. And in the warm, moist climate of Indochina in what is now Cambodia, three crops of rice a year grew on soil that the annual counterflow of the Mekong River created. The Mekong becomes so torrential that the delta—where the river enters the sea—cannot funnel its flow, and water is forced back upriver.

Smaller patches of alluvium, deposited by floods, nourished the world's earliest known fully farming economies. Among the first was Jericho on the Jordan River in modern Israel. Today, the Jordan valley is crusted with salt and sodium. Ten thousand years ago, however, Jericho overlooked an alluvial fan that trickling streams washed down from the hills, filling the river as it crept south from the Sea of Galilee. The river Jordan was thick with silt. The banks it deposited formed the biblical "jungle of Jericho," from where lions raided the sheepfolds. Here, rich wheat fields created the landscape the Bible called "the garden of the Lord." Desert people, such as the Israelites were tempted to conquer it.

In much the same period, between about 9,000 and 11,000 years ago, farming towns also appeared in Anatolia in Turkey. Çatalhüyük (chah-tahl-hoo-YOOK), the most spectacular of them, stood on an alluvial plain that the river Çarsamba flooded. Nourished by wheat and beans, the people filled an urban area of 32 acres. Walkways across flat roofs, not streets as we define them, linked a honeycomb of dwellings. You can still see where the occupants swept their rubbish—chips of bone and shiny, black flakes of volcanic glass called obsidian—into their hearths.

By exchanging craft products—weapons, metalwork, and pots—for primary materials such as cowrie shells from the Red Sea, timber from the Taurus Mountains in Anatolia, and copper from beyond the Tigris, the inhabitants of Çatalhüyük became rich by the standards of the time. Archeologists have unearthed fine blades, obsidian mirrors, and products of the copper-smelting technology that these people developed.

Yet the inhabitants of Çatalhüyük never got safely beyond the mercy of nature. They worshipped images of its strength: bulls with monstrous horns and protruding tongues, crouching leopards who guard goddesses leaning on grain bins, fuming volcanoes, giant boar with laughing jaws and bristling backs. This is surely farmer's art, animated by fear. Most people died in their late twenties or early thirties. Their corpses were ritually fed to vultures and jackals—as surviving paintings show—before their bones were buried in communal graves. Çatalhüyük became

Jericho skull. No one knows why people in Jericho, in the eighth millennium B.C.E., kept skulls, painted them with plaster, and inserted cowrie shells into the eye sockets. But these decorated skulls have, in a sense, helped the dead to survive. Some of the skulls even show traces of painted hair and mustaches.
Ashmolean Museum, Oxford, England, U.K.

doomed as the waters that supplied it dried up. But it lasted for nearly 2,000 years, remarkable longevity by the standards of later cities. Along with Jericho and other settlements of the era, it showed how farming, despite its short-term disadvantages and the sacrifices it demanded, could sustain life through hard times.

THE SPREAD OF AGRICULTURE

The development of food production was not a unique occurrence—a one-of-a-kind accident or a stroke of genius. Rather, farming was an ordinary and fairly frequent process that could therefore be open to a variety of explanations. Scholars used to suppose that it was so extraordinary it must have begun in some particular spot and that **diffusion** spread it from there—carried by migrants or conquerors, or transmitted by trade, or imitated. The last 40 years of research have shown, on the contrary, that the transition to food production happened over and over again, in a range of regions and a variety of environments, with different foodstuffs and different techniques (see Map 2.2). Nevertheless, connections between neighboring regions were unquestionably important in spreading husbandry. Some crops were undoubtedly transferred from the places they originated to other regions.

Europe

It seems likely (though disputed) that migrants from Asia colonized Europe. They brought their farming materials and knowledge with them, as well as their **Indo-European languages**, from which most of Europe's present languages descend. Colonization was a gradual process, beginning about 6,000 years ago. Early farmers may have cleared some land, but probably did not undertake large-scale deforestation. Well-documented cases from other forest environments suggest that early agriculturists in Europe found trees useful and even revered them. So large-scale deforestation more likely occurred naturally, perhaps through tree diseases.

Asia

Similar migrations probably spread farming to parts of Central Asia south of the steppeland. The farming that developed in alluvial environments in Anatolia and the Jordan valley colonized or converted every viable part of the region by 8,000 or 9,000 years ago, crossing the Zagros Mountains (in what is now Iran) and, by about 6,000 years ago, spreading comprehensive irrigation systems between oases in southern Turkmenistan, which had a moister climate than it has now. In southern Pakistan remnants of domestic barley and wheat in mud bricks and the bones of domestic goats confirm the presence of agriculture about 9,000 years ago. This is also the site of the world's earliest surviving cotton thread, strung through a copper bead about 7,500 years ago. In the Indian subcontinent, the sudden emergence of well-built villages in the same period was probably the result of outside influence.

The Americas

In much of North America, maize spread northward from its birthplace in central Mexico. The process took thousands of years and demanded the development of new varieties as the crop crossed climate zones. The best estimate puts maize farming in the southwestern United States about 3,000 years ago. Meanwhile, some North American peoples began to farm sunflowers and sumpweed for their edible seeds and roots. In South America, the idea of agriculture spread from, or across, the high Andes, through the upper Amazon basin.

Her seated position and uptilted head seem to suggest authority, as do the predatory felines that guard the throne, as if in obedience to someone able to command nature.

Her bulbous breasts and exaggerated sex organs suggest the importance of fertility to the society in which this image was crafted.

THE FERTILITY GODDESS OF ÇATALHÜYÜK

In recent times, the so-called "fertility goddess" or "Earth Mother" of Çatalhüyük has become a cult-object for feminists, who make pilgrimages to the site. But what her image was for, and what it represents, are unknown.

The folds of fat around her joints suggest a degree of obesity amounting to clinical pathology or physical deformity. Most human societies, for most of history, have admired body fat on both men and women.

What can we infer from this image about the status of women in early agricultural societies?

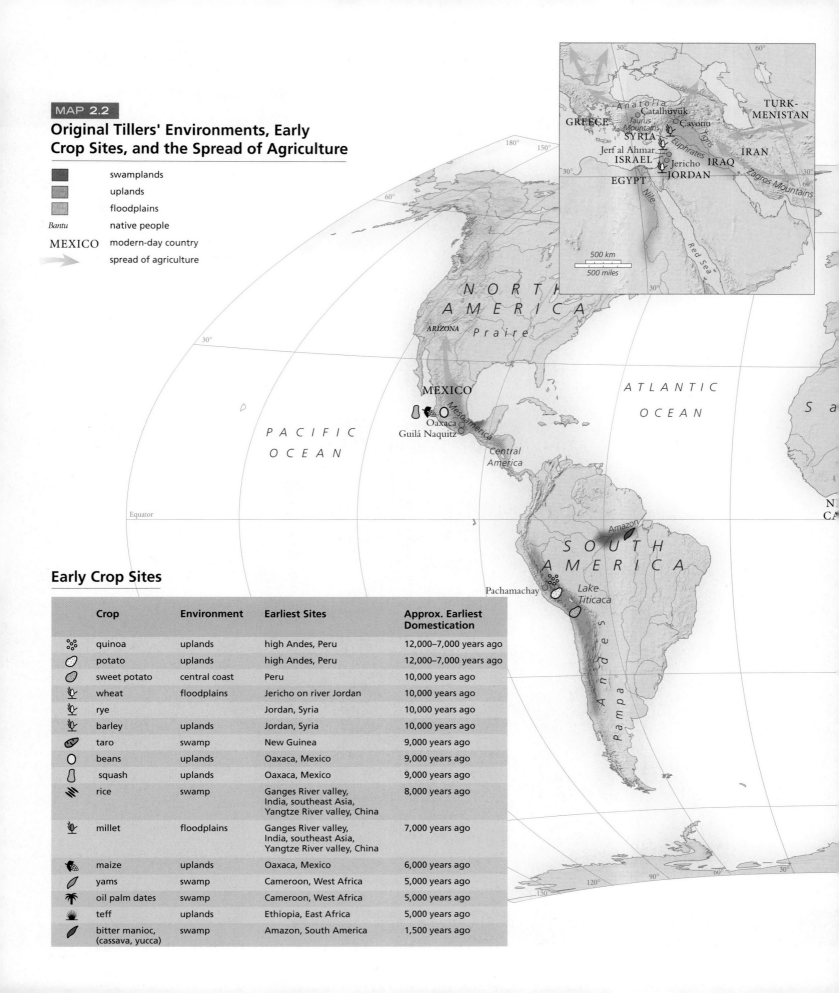

MAP 2.2

Original Tillers' Environments, Early Crop Sites, and the Spread of Agriculture

- ◼ swamplands
- ◼ uplands
- ◻ floodplains
- *Bantu* native people
- MEXICO modern-day country
- → spread of agriculture

Early Crop Sites

	Crop	Environment	Earliest Sites	Approx. Earliest Domestication
	quinoa	uplands	high Andes, Peru	12,000–7,000 years ago
	potato	uplands	high Andes, Peru	12,000–7,000 years ago
	sweet potato	central coast	Peru	10,000 years ago
	wheat	floodplains	Jericho on river Jordan	10,000 years ago
	rye		Jordan, Syria	10,000 years ago
	barley	uplands	Jordan, Syria	10,000 years ago
	taro	swamp	New Guinea	9,000 years ago
	beans	uplands	Oaxaca, Mexico	9,000 years ago
	squash	uplands	Oaxaca, Mexico	9,000 years ago
	rice	swamp	Ganges River valley, India, southeast Asia, Yangtze River valley, China	8,000 years ago
	millet	floodplains	Ganges River valley, India, southeast Asia, Yangtze River valley, China	7,000 years ago
	maize	uplands	Oaxaca, Mexico	6,000 years ago
	yams	swamp	Cameroon, West Africa	5,000 years ago
	oil palm dates	swamp	Cameroon, West Africa	5,000 years ago
	teff	uplands	Ethiopia, East Africa	5,000 years ago
	bitter manioc, (cassava, yucca)	swamp	Amazon, South America	1,500 years ago

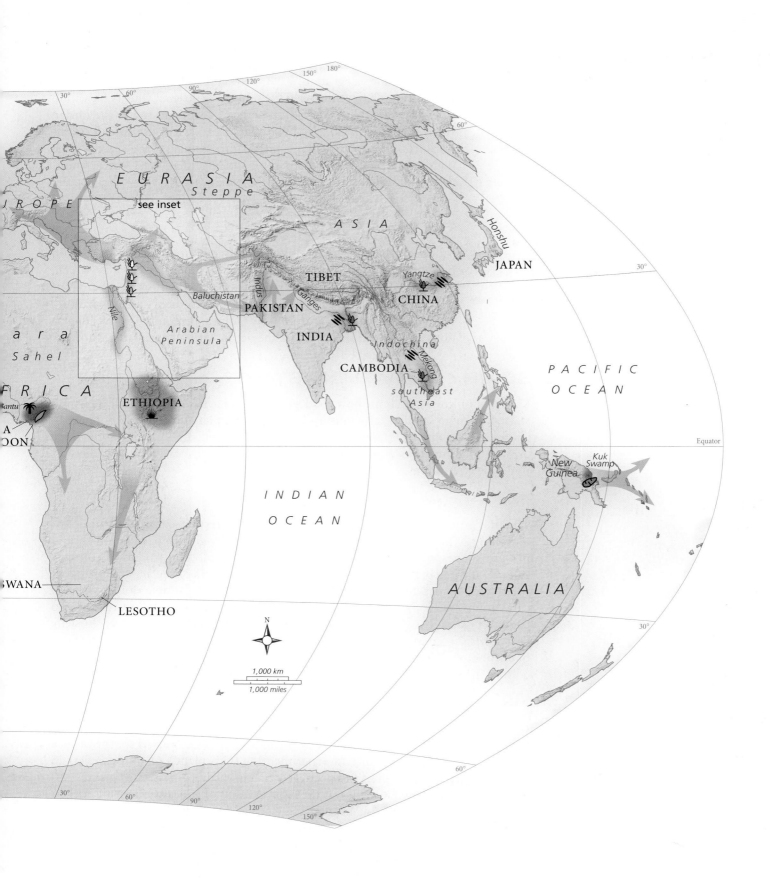

EURASIA

Steppe

EUROPE

see inset

A S I A

ASIA

Honshu

JAPAN

CHINA

Yangtze

TIBET

Baluchistan

Indus

Ganges

PAKISTAN

INDIA

*Arabian
Peninsula*

Nile

Indochina

Mekong

CAMBODIA

*southeast
Asia*

PACIFIC

OCEAN

Equator

a r a

Sahel

FRICA

Bantu

ETHIOPIA

A

OON

New
Guinea

*Kuk
Swamp*

INDIAN

OCEAN

SWANA

LESOTHO

AUSTRALIA

N

1,000 km
1,000 miles

30°

The Spread of Agriculture

(All dates are approximate)	
9,000 years ago	Evidence of agriculture in Indian subcontinent; farming spreads by diffusion in the Egyptian Sahara and Nile valley
8,000–9,000 years ago	Farming spreads from Jordan valley and Anatolia to central Asia, south of the steppe
6,000 years ago	Migrants from Asia bring farming materials and knowledge with them to Europe
4,500–5,000 years ago	Bantu expansion spreads farming from West Africa southward
3,000 years ago	Maize moves northward from Mexico to southwestern United States

Africa

How agriculture spread in Africa is less clear than in other regions. People began to cultivate similar plant foods in the Egyptian Sahara and in the Nile valley about 9,000 years ago. It therefore looks as if one region might have influenced the other. A little later, wheat cultivation along the Nile followed developments of a similar kind in the Jordan valley. Between 4,500 and 5,000 years ago, agriculture spread southward from West Africa along with Bantu languages. We can trace the path from what are now Cameroon and Nigeria in West Africa, southward and then eastward across the Sahara to the Nile valley, before turning south again.

The Pacific Islands

Scholars debate when agriculture originated in the Pacific Islands. In particular, we do not know how or when the sweet potato—which, together with the pig, is the basis of food production in most of the region—got there. The most widely respected theory sees agriculture as the result of diffusion from New Guinea. It required many adaptations as it spread slowly across the ocean with seaborne migrants.

SO WHY DID FARMING START?

Knowing or guessing about how food production started does not tell us why it started. Though scholars ferociously advocate rival explanations, we do not have to choose among them. Different explanations, or different combinations of the same explanations, may have applied in different places. We can group the theories under seven headings.

Population Pressure

The first group of theories explains agriculture as a response to stress from population growth and overexploitation of wild foods. Logically, population should not grow if resources are getting scarce. But anthropological studies of contemporary cultures making the transition to agriculture in southern Africa support the theory. Apparently, once farming starts, people cannot abandon it without catastrophe. A ratchet effect makes it impossible, while population rises, to go back to less intensive ways of getting food. As an explanation, however, for why agriculture arose in the first place, population pressure does not match the facts of chronology. In most places, growth was more probably a consequence of agriculture than a cause.

The Outcome of Abundance

In direct opposition to stress theory, a group of theories claims that husbandry was a result of abundance, a by-product of the leisure of fishermen in southeast Asia who devoted their spare time to experimenting with plants. Or hill dwellers in northern Iraq, whose habitat was peculiarly rich in easily domesticated grasses and grazing herds, invented it. Or it was the natural result of concentrations of pockets of abundance in Central Asia in the post–Ice-Age era of global warming. As temperatures rose, oases opened up where different species congregated peacefully. Humans discovered they could domesticate animals that would otherwise be rivals, enemies, or prey. Abundance theory may explain why agriculture developed in some key areas, but not why, in good times, people would want to change how they got their food and take on extra work.

The Power of Politics

Stress theory and abundance theory may apply to why agriculture arose in different areas, but they cannot be true simultaneously. Therefore, beyond the food supply, it is worth considering possible political or social or religious influences on food strategies. After all, food not only sustains the body. It also confers power and prestige. It can symbolize identity and generate rituals. In hierarchically organized societies, elites nearly always demand more food than they can eat, not just to ensure their security but also to show off their wealth by squandering their waste.

In a society where leaders buy allegiance with food, competitive feasting can generate huge increases in demand, even if population is static and supplies are secure. Societies bound by feasting will always favor intensive agriculture and massive storage. Even in societies with looser forms of leadership or with collective decision making, feasting can be a powerful incentive to boost food production and storage, by force if necessary. Feasting can celebrate collective identity or cement relations with other communities. Then, too, people could process most of the early domesticated plants into intoxicating drinks. If farming began as a way to generate surpluses for feasts, alcohol must have had a special role.

Cult Agriculture

Religion may well have been the inspiration for farming. Planting may have originated as a fertility rite, or irrigation as libation, or enclosure as an act of reverence for a sacred plant. To plow or dibble and sow and irrigate can carry profound meaning. They can be rites of birth and nurture of the god on whom you are going to feed. In exchange for labor—a kind of sacrifice—the god provides nourishment. Most cultures represent the power to make food grow as a divine gift or curse or a secret that a hero stole from the gods. People have domesticated animals for use in sacrifice and prophecy as well as for food. Many societies cultivate plants that play a part at the altar rather than at the table. Examples include incense, ecstatic or hallucinatory drugs, the sacrificial corn of some high Andean communities, and wheat, which, in orthodox Christian traditions, is the only permitted grain for the Eucharist. And if religion inspired agriculture, alcohol as a drink that can induce ecstasy might have had a special appeal. In short, where crops are gods, farming is worship.

Climatic Instability

Global warming, as we saw in Chapter 1, presented some foragers with thousands of years of abundance. But warming is unpredictable. Sometimes it intensifies, causing drought; sometimes it goes into temporary reverse, causing little ice ages. Its effects are uneven. In the agrarian heartland of the Middle East, for example, warming squeezed the environment of nut-bearing trees but favored some grasses. The forest receded dramatically as the climate got drier and hotter between about 13,000 and 11,000 years ago. The new conditions encouraged people to rely more and more on grains for food and perhaps try to increase the amount of edible wheat. Gatherers who knew the habits of their plants tended them more carefully. It was, perhaps, a conservative, even a conservationist strategy: a way to keep old food stocks and lifestyles going under the impact of climate change.

Cult agriculture. Chimú goldsmiths (Chapter 14) produced this ceremonial dish, which depicts the succession of the seasons, presided over by the central figure of the maize god, and offerings of the characteristic starches of the Peruvian lowlands—maize, cassava, sweet potatoes. By the time this object was made, however, around 1200 C.E., maize varieties had been adapted for varied environments, including uplands and temperate climates.

Agriculture by Accident

In the nineteenth century, the most popular theory of how farming started attributed it to accident. One can hardly open a nineteenth-century book on the subject without encountering the myth of the primitive forager, usually a woman, discovering agriculture by observing how seeds, dropped by accident, germinated on fertilized soil. The father of the theory of evolution Charles Darwin (1809–1882; see Chapter 25), himself, thought something similar:

> The savage inhabitants of each land, having found out by many and hard trials what plants were useful ... would after a time take the first step in cultivation by planting them near their usual abodes. ... The next step in cultivation, and this would require but little forethought, would be to sow the seeds of useful plants; and as the soil near the hovels of the natives would often be in some degree manured, improved varieties would sooner or later arise.[2]

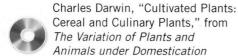

Charles Darwin, "Cultivated Plants: Cereal and Culinary Plants," from *The Variation of Plants and Animals under Domestication*

Darwin makes accident interact with human action. But historians are never satisfied to fall back on what would or might have happened (though this may be necessary to help understand remote or poorly documented periods). We want to know—and it is the historian's job to try to tell us—what really did happen. Assuming that anything a "savage" does requires "little forethought" does not fit with what we now know of human nature. Cleverness occurs at every period of history and in every type of society—in New Guinea as well as in New York, in antiquity as well as in modernity.

Production as an Outgrowth of Procurement

Still, the accident theory may be right in one respect. Early practitioners may not have consciously thought of food production as a different strategy from foraging. It makes sense, for instance, to see herding as a natural development of some hunting techniques, such as improving a species by culling weak or old animals, managing grazing by setting fires, driving herds down lanes to a place of slaughter, or corralling them for the kill. Similarly, farming and gathering might have been parts of a single continuous attempt to manage food sources. It is hard to tell where one leaves off and the other begins. The Papago Native Americans of Arizona drift in and out of an agrarian way of life as the weather permits, using patches of surface water to grow fast-maturing beans.

The archaeological evidence has begun to yield clues to how gatherer communities of southwestern Asia transformed themselves into farming communities after the Ice Age. Grasses on the whole are naturally too indigestible to be human food. But the region produced wild barley and two kinds of wheat—einkorn (EYEN-korn) and emmer (EH-mehr). Archaeologists have found ground fragments of these grains from 14,000 to 15,000 years ago. The kernels are hard to free from their tough, inedible covering, so people who ate large amounts of them may have had an incentive to try to breed varieties that were easier to process. At first, the gatherers beat sheaves of wheat with sticks where they grew and collected edible seeds in baskets as they fell. As time went on, they cut stalks with flint sickles, which meant that fewer seeds fell when the wheat was harvested. This new method suggests that people were selecting preferred seeds for replanting. Modern experiments show that this process could produce a self-propagating species within 20 years. Alternatively, the new method itself might have encouraged changes in the species because heavier, larger seeds would be more likely to fall to the ground at the point of harvesting. Eventually, new varieties would emerge, but the process would be slower.

Einkorn is one of the few wild grasses that yield kernels that human stomachs can digest. It was a principal food source for the early sedentary foraging cultures of the Middle East, and one of the first species farmers adopted. But its grains are hard to separate from their tough husks, which helps explain why farmers strove to produce new varieties of grain by selection and hybridization.

Even earlier, humans used a similar process with snails and other mollusks, which are an efficient food, self-packaged in a shell for carrying and cooking. People can isolate aquatic varieties, such as mussels and clams, in a pool, or enclose a snail-rich spot with a ditch. Moreover, snails are grazers and do not need to be fed with foods that humans would otherwise eat themselves. They can be herded without the use of fire, any special equipment, personal danger, or the need to train leashed animals or dogs to help. By culling small or undesirable types by hand, the early snail farmers could soon enjoy the benefits of selective breeding. Shell mounds from the late Ice Age or soon thereafter contain varieties of snails that are bigger on average than today's, so it looks as if the snail eaters were already selecting for size. Sometimes large-scale consumption of mollusks preceded that of foods that the more elaborate technologies of the hunt obtained. In southern Greece, a huge dump of snail shells nearly 13,000 years old was topped first by red deer bones with some snail shells, and then, nearly 4,000 years later, by tuna bones.

IN PERSPECTIVE: Seeking Stability

Gathering, hunting, herding, and tillage, which our conventional chronologies usually place one after the other, were complementary techniques to obtain food. They developed together, over thousands of years, in a period of relatively intense climatic change. The warming, drying effects of the post–Ice-Age world multiplied opportunities and incentives for people to experiment with food strategies in changing environments. The naturalist David Rindos described early farming as a case of human–plant symbiosis, in which species developed together in mutual dependence, and—in part at least—evolved together: an unconscious relationship, until some foodstuffs needed human help to survive and reproduce. For instance, maize seeds would not fall to the ground unless a human removed the husks.

Some food procurers and early food producers were surprisingly alike: Their settlements, art, religious cults, even foods (although obtained by different means) were often of the same order. The similarities suggest that the transition to agriculture was an attempt to stabilize a world convulsed by climatic instability—a way to cope with environmental change that was happening too fast and to preserve ancient traditions. In other words, the peoples who switched to herding or farming and those who clung to hunting and gathering shared a common, conservative mentality. Both wanted to keep what they had.

Perhaps, then, we should stop thinking of the beginnings of food production as a revolution, the overthrow of an existing state of affairs and its replacement by an entirely different one. Rather, we should think of it as a **climacteric** (kleye-MAK-tehr-ihk)—a long period of critical change in a world poised

CHRONOLOGY

(All dates are approximate)

15,000 B.C.E.	End of Ice Age
14,000–13,000 B.C.E.	First permanent settlements in Middle East
11,000 B.C.E.	Appearance of Jomon culture, Japan
10,000–5000 B.C.E.	Mixed farming and potato cultivation develop (South America)
9000–7000 B.C.E.	Farming towns appear in Anatolia and Egypt
8000 B.C.E.	Rye and barley cultivation in Jordan and Syria; farming spreads from Jordan and Anatolia to Central Asia
7000 B.C.E.	"Trinity" of maize, beans, and squash develops in Mesoamerica; farming spreads in Egyptian Sahara and Nile valley; evidence of agriculture in Indian subcontinent; earliest evidence of agriculture in New Guinea
6000 B.C.E.	Rice cultivation in India, southeast Asia, and China
4000 B.C.E.	Scythians domesticate the horse and invent wheel and axle; Indo-European languages spread as migrants from Asia colonize Europe; millet farmed in Yellow River valley, China
5000–2000 B.C.E.	River valley civilizations flourish
3000 B.C.E.	Teff cultivated in Ethiopia; Bantu languages and agriculture begin to spread southward from West Africa; earliest specimens of cultivated maize (Mexico)
1000 B.C.E.	Maize cultivation moves northward from Mexico to southwestern United States

 David Rindos, from "Symbiosis, Instability, and the Origins and Spread of Agriculture: A New Model"

between different possible outcomes. Indeed, the concept of climacteric can be a useful way to understand change throughout the rest of this book as we confront other so-called revolutions that were really uncertain, slow, and sometimes unconscious transitions.

If early farmers' motivations were conservative, in most cases they failed. On the contrary, they inaugurated the spectacular changes and challenges that are the subject of the next chapter.

PROBLEMS AND PARALLELS

1. How was husbandry, with its emphasis on "unnatural selection," the first human challenge to evolution?

2. What are the disadvantages of farming compared to foraging?

3. How did agriculture affect the pace of change in human society? Why were agricultural settlements less stable than foraging communities?

4. What are the relative benefits of farming and herding? Why was violence between farmers and herders common until recently?

5. What were the prerequisites for early agriculture? Why were alluvial plains the most hospitable environment for early agricultural communities?

6. Why did farming start at different places and at different times around the world? What are some of the rival theories advocated by scholars?

7. Why is the beginning of food production more of a climacteric than a revolution?

DOCUMENTS IN GLOBAL HISTORY

- James Cook, from *Captain Cook's Journal During His First Voyage Round the World*
- Jack Harlan, from *Crops and Man*
- Charles Darwin, "Cultivated Plants: Cereal and Culinary Plants," from *The Variation of Plants and Animals under Domestication*

- David Rindos, from "Symbiosis, Instability, and the Origins and Spread of Agriculture: A New Model"

Please see the Primary Source DVD for additional sources related to this chapter.

READ ON

The lines of the argument are laid down in F. Fernández-Armesto, *Near a Thousand Tables* (2002). The method of classifying events in environmental categories comes from F. Fernández-Armesto, *Civilizations* (2001). Indispensable for the study of the origins of the agriculture are J. R. Harlan, *Crops and Man* (1992); B. D. Smith, *The Emergence of Agriculture* (1998); D. Rindos, *The Origins of Agriculture* (1987); and D. R. Harris, ed., *The Origins and Spread of Agriculture and Pastoralism in Eurasia* (1996). K. F. Kiple and K. C. Ornelas, eds., *The Cambridge World History of Food* (2000) is an enormous compendium.

I. G. Simmons, *Changing the Face of the Earth: Culture, Environment, History* (1989) is a superb introduction to global environmental history, as is B. De Vries and J. Goudsblom, eds., *Mappae Mundi: Humans and Their Habitats in a Long-Term Socio-Ecological Perspective* (2004).

The quotation from Darwin comes from his work of 1868, *The Variation of Animals and Plants under Domestication.*

On feasts, M. Dietler and B. Hayden, *Feasts: Archaeological and Ethnographic Perspective on Food, Politics, and Power* (2001) is an important collection of essays. M. Jones, *Feasts* (2007) is now the best study, with invaluable insights on early agriculture.

O. Bar-Yosef and A. Gopher, eds., *The Natufian Culture in the Levant* (1991) is outstanding. On Çatalhüyük, up-to-date information is in M. Özdogan and N. Basgelen, eds., *The Neolithic in Turkey: The Cradle of Civilization* (1999), and I. Hodder, *Towards a Reflexive Method in Archaeology* (2000), but the classic J. Mellaart, *Çatal Huyuk* (1967) is more accessible. On Jericho, the classic work is by Kenyon, *Digging up Jericho; The Results of Jericho Excavations* (1957).

PART TWO

Farmers and Builders, 5000 to 500 B.C.E.

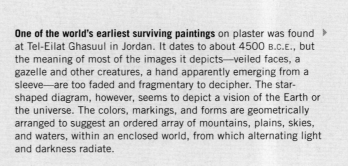

One of the world's earliest surviving paintings on plaster was found ▶ at Tel-Eilat Ghasuul in Jordan. It dates to about 4500 B.C.E., but the meaning of most of the images it depicts—veiled faces, a gazelle and other creatures, a hand apparently emerging from a sleeve—are too faded and fragmentary to decipher. The star-shaped diagram, however, seems to depict a vision of the Earth or the universe. The colors, markings, and forms are geometrically arranged to suggest an ordered array of mountains, plains, skies, and waters, within an enclosed world, from which alternating light and darkness radiate.

ENVIRONMENT

ca. 4500 B.C.E.
Irrigation

ca. 3500 B.C.E.
Horses domesticated

since 5000 B.C.E.
Intensive agriculture, bronze metallurgy: Tigris-Euphrates, Nile, Indus, Yellow Rivers

CULTURE

since ca. 3500 B.C.E.
Complex, hierarchical societies and states

ca. 3000–1000 B.C.E.
Continued warming

ca. 1200–800 B.C.E.
Widespread environmental crises

ca. 1800 B.C.E.
Spread of iron technology

ca. 3200 B.C.E.
Writing

ca. 2000 B.C.E.
Epic of Gilgamesh

ca. 1000 B.C.E.
Mediterranean maritime
colonialism begins

CHAPTER 3

The Great River Valleys: Accelerating Change and Developing States

Nebamun's tomb from about 1500 B.C.E. shows the Egyptian vizier hunting in the lush Nile delta, abundant in fish below his reed-built boat, prolific in the bird- and insect-life flushed from the blue thickets at his approach. He grabs birds by the handful and wields a snake like a whip.
© Copyright The British Museum

Witnesses in court swear to tell "the whole truth." This would be a risky oath for a historian to take because we see the past only in glimpses and patches. Sometimes-contrasting, sometimes-contradictory sources confuse or distract us. To get close to the whole picture, we have to shift perspective, dodging and slipping between rival viewpoints. With every shift, we get a bit more of the picture—like glimpsing the depths of a forest, between the leaves and the trees.

GREAT RIVER VALLEYS

The boldest possible perspective shift is imaginary, to envision history from a viewpoint outside it—perhaps from an enormous distance of time and space, and ask how it might look to a visitors from a remote future in another world. They would have an enviable advantage: objectivity, which we, who are entangled in our history, can never attain. Today, globalization is spreading uniform ways of life across the world, but galactic observers could see that, since agriculture started, the main theme of our past has been increasingly rapid cultural divergence. Compared with foragers, herders and tillers generated more change of all kinds. More spectacular, however, were the differences that separated farming cultures from each other.

Some of them came to occupy vast zones, feed huge populations, and sustain spectacular material achievements—including cities, monumental arts, and world-changing technologies. Other farmers' societies remained relatively small and static. This does not mean they were backward or primitive. Their modest scale and relative isolation kept them stable. These were peoples who succeeded in adapting to climate change without subjecting their societies to social and political convulsions, which were often part of the price other peoples paid for material achievements that seem impressive to us. The big problem we need to look at in this chapter, then, is what made the difference?

It is also worth asking whether within these diverse societies we can detect any common patterns. This is a long-standing quest for historians and, especially, for sociologists, who look for models that they can use to describe and predict how societies change. At a simple level, intensified agriculture clearly unlocks a potential pattern. More food makes it possible to sustain larger populations, to concentrate them in bigger settlements, and to divert more manpower into nonagricultural activities. But intensification also requires organization, and, broadly speaking, the more intensive the farming, the more organized it has to be. It calls for someone—or some group—with power to divide land, marshal labor, and regulate the distribution of water and—if necessary—fertilizer. Surplus production needs to be guarded in case crops fail or natural disasters strike. A legal elite is necessary to resolve the frequent disputes that arise in thickly settled communities, where people have to compete for resources. So, intensively farmed areas all tend to develop similar political institutions and personnel, including bureaucrats and enforcers.

FOCUS questions

- WHY DID intensified agriculture lead to cultural differences?
- WHERE DID the first great river valley civilizations develop?
- HOW CAN we account for the similarities and differences in political institutions, social structure, and ways of life in the four great river valleys?
- HOW DID the river valley states expand?
- IS WRITING a defining characteristic of civilization?
- WHY IS cultural divergence one of the main themes of human history since the beginning of agriculture?

These effects are the themes of this chapter, which focuses on the most conspicuous examples, in regions with common environmental features. The next chapter follows the crises, catastrophes, and transformations large-scale farming societies faced up to the end of the second millennium B.C.E. Chapter 5 covers the recovery or renewal of ambitious states and cultural experiments after the crises had passed.

• • • • •

GROWING COMMUNITIES, DIVERGENT CULTURES

Most of the communities that early agriculture fed resembled the forager settlements that preceded them. They were small and did not change much over time. Lack of evidence means that we mostly have to infer what we think we know about them. So with no reason to think otherwise, we assume that early farming societies in New Guinea, North America, along the Amazon River in South America, and among the Bantu people in West Africa were like those in most of the rest of the world. They were extended family businesses where everyone in the community felt tied to everyone else by kinship. Elsewhere, owing to greater resources or to the enlivening effects of cross-cultural contacts through migration or trade, different patterns prevailed. Communities became territorially defined. Economic obligations, not kinship, shaped allegiance. Chiefs or economic elites monopolized or controlled the distribution of food.

Scholars have tried to divide subsequent change in societies of this type into sequences or stages of growth—chiefdoms become states, towns become cities. But these are relative terms, and no hard-and-fast lines divide them. At most, differences are a matter of degree. For instance, we think of chiefdoms as having fewer institutions of government than states. In chiefdoms, the chief and a few counselors handle all the business of government. In a state, those functions get split among groups of specialists in, say, administering justice, handling revenue, or conducting war. In practice, however, we know of no community that does not delegate at least some power, and no state where the responsibilities of different government departments do not merge or overlap.

Similarly, the difference between a small city and a big town or a small town and a big village is a matter of judgment. Some of the characteristics we traditionally associate with particular lifeways turn out, in the light of present knowledge, to provide little or no help for defining the societies in which they occur. Metallurgy, pottery, and weaving, for example, exist among herding and foraging peoples, as well as in settled communities.

However, where many people settle together, predictable changes usually follow. As markets grow, settlements acquire more craftsmen, who engage in more specialized trades and who organize into more and larger units. As they get bigger, settlements and politically linked or united groups of settlements also expand the number of government functions. Where once there was just a chief and his counselors, now there are aides, advisers, officials, and administrators.

Densely settled communities also tend to divide their populations into more categories. This usually happens in two ways. On the one hand, as society gets bigger, people seek groups within it of manageable size, with whom to identify and to whom to appeal for help in times of need. On the other hand, rulers organize subjects into categories according to the needs of the state, which include collective labor, taxation, and war. The categories get more numerous and varied as opportunities for economic specialization multiply and as more districts or quarters appear in growing settlements. In some cases, these categories resemble what, in our society, we call classes, that is, groups arrayed horizontally, one above or below another according to power, privilege, or prosperity. For most of history, however, it is misleading to speak of classes. Societies were more usually organized vertically into groups of people of widely varying rank and wealth, linked by some form of common allegiance. They might feel bound by a place of origin, or a locality or neighborhood, or a common ancestor, or a god, or a rite, or a family, or a sense of identity arising from shared belief in some myth (see Figure 3.1).

So, if we want to try to trace the early history of cultural divergence, we should look for certain sorts of changes, namely, intensified settlement, population concentrated in relatively large settlements, multiplying social categories and functions of government, emergence of chiefs and fledgling states, and increasingly diversified and specialized economic activity. Between 5000 and 3000 B.C.E., we can detect these changes in widely separated places around the world. We can take a few examples in a selective tour through cultures launched into divergent futures.

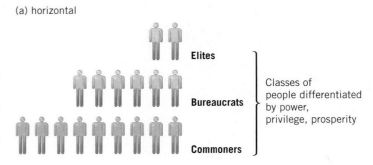

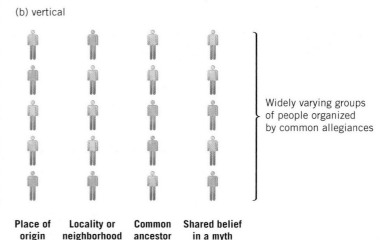

FIGURE 3.1 HORIZONTAL AND VERTICAL ORGANIZATIONS OF SOCIETY

Intensified Settlement and Its Effects

In the New World, Mesoamerica and Central America remained a region of small villages. We can document monumental cities and large states there only from about 2000 B.C.E. In North America, agriculture barely appeared. By contrast, at the base of the high Andes in South America, archaeology has unearthed early evidence of many different social rankings, economic specializations, and grossly unequal concentrations of wealth and power.

In about 3500 B.C.E., large farming settlements began to appear on alluvial plains in coastal Peru, north of present-day Lima, and especially in the Supe Valley, which has over 30 archaeological sites. The most impressive was Aspero, where by the mid–third millennium B.C.E. 17 mounds supported half a dozen platforms and various terraces, with large, complex dwellings and storehouses. The platforms were built up with loads of rubble in uniform containers, which suggests that a system existed to measure the labor of different groups of workers. An infant's grave gives us a glimpse into the society and perhaps the politics of the time. Under a grinding stone he lies painted with red ochre, wrapped in textiles, and scattered with hundreds of beads. This is evidence of heritable wealth and, perhaps, power in an economy dependent on grain where a flour-making tool literally marked the difference between life and death.

Covering over 32 acres, Aspero must have had a big population—uniquely big by the standards of the Americas at the time. There were, however, many settlements of between two and three thousand people. They were trading centers where people exchanged the products of different ecosystems—marine shells, mountain

Trade enriches. Gold-laden graves in a 6,000-year-old cemetery at Varna, Bulgaria, lie by an inlet beside a wood-built village that is quite different from mud-walled settlements in the interior, where the graves are under the houses. The Varna culture vanished—overwhelmed perhaps by horse-tamers from the nearby steppes.

Stonehenge

foods, and featherwork made from the brightly colored birds that lived in the forests east of the Andes.

Comparable developments occurred across Eurasia (see Map 3.1). In Eastern Europe, for instance, innovations in technology and government emerged, without, as far as we know, any influence from outside the region. Europe's oldest copper mine at Rudna Glava in modern Serbia made the region a center of early metallurgy. In Tisza in what is now Hungary, over 7,000 years ago, smelters worked copper into beads and small tools—magic that made smiths powerful figures of myth. To the people who left offerings, the mines were the dwellings of gods.

In Bulgaria of the same period, trenches and palisades surrounded settlements, with gateways exactly aligned at the points of the compass, as in later Roman army camps. Here prospectors traded gold for the products of agriculture. No place in prehistoric Europe gleams more astonishingly than Varna on the Black Sea, where a chief was buried clutching a gold-handled axe, with his penis sheathed in gold, and nearly 1,000 gold ornaments, including hundreds of discs that must have spangled a dazzling coat. This single grave contained more than three pounds of fine gold. Other graves were symbolic, containing earthenware masks without human remains. At Tartaria in Romania, markings on clay tablets look uncannily like writing.

A little to the east, also around 5000 B.C.E., in what is now Ukraine, the earliest known domesticators of horses filled their garbage dumps with horse bones. In graves of about 3500 B.C.E., as if for use in an afterlife, lie covered wagons, arched with hoops and designed to be pulled by oxen, rumbling on vast wheels of solid wood: evidence that rich and powerful chiefdoms could carry out ambitious building projects despite a herding way of life that required constant mobility. Few other societies in the world were rich enough to bury objects of such size and value. Central Eurasia became a birthplace for early transportation technology. For instance, the earliest recognizable chariot dates from early 2000 B.C.E., in the southern Ural Mountains that divide Europe from Asia.

Meanwhile, monumental building projects, on a scale only agriculture could sustain and only a state could organize, were under way in the Mediterranean. The remains of the first large stone dwellings known anywhere in the world are on the island of Malta, which lies between Sicily and North Africa. Here, at least half a dozen temple complexes arose in the fourth and third millennia B.C.E. They were built of limestone around spacious courts shaped like clover leaves. The biggest temple is almost 70 feet wide under a 30-foot wall. Inside one building was a colossal, big-hipped goddess attended by sleeping beauties—small female models scattered around her. There were altars and wall carvings—some in spirals, some with deer and bulls—and thousands of bodies piled in communal graves. We wonder how Malta's soil, so poor and dry, could sustain a population large and leisured enough to build so lavishly.

Even on Europe's Atlantic edge, in the fourth millennium B.C.E., luxury objects could find a market and monumental buildings arose. Some of the earliest signs of the slow-grinding social changes lie among the bones of aristocrats in individual graves with the possessions that defined their status and suggest their way of life—weapons of war and drinking cups that once held liquor or poured offerings to the gods. Then come the graves of chiefs, buried under enormous standing stones, near stone circles probably designed to resemble glades that preceded them as places of worship. In the Orkney Islands, for instance, off the north coast of Scotland, settled about 5,500 years ago, an elaborate tomb at Maes Howe lies close to a temple building, filled with light on midsummer's day. Nearby stone circles hint on

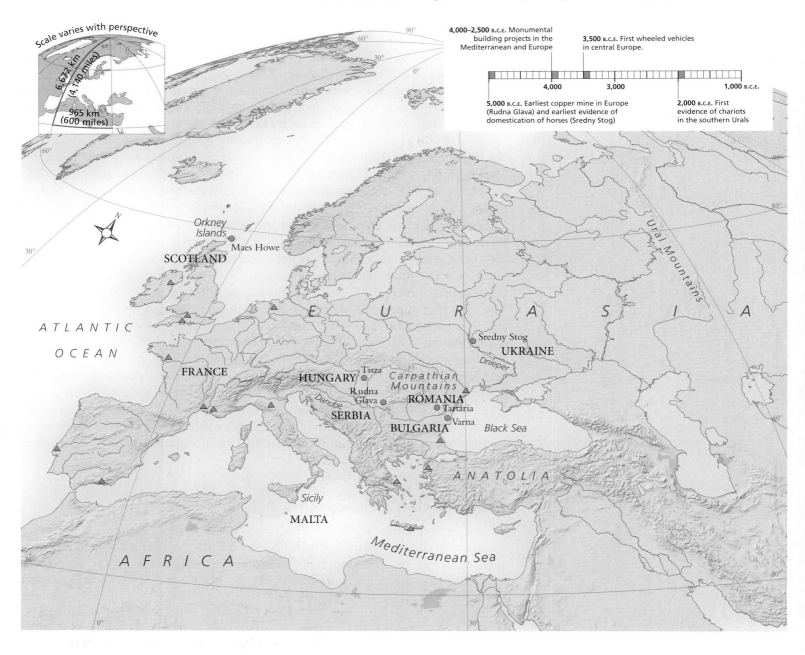

Scale varies with perspective

6,672 km (4,140 miles)

965 km (600 miles)

4,000–2,500 B.C.E. Monumental building projects in the Mediterranean and Europe

3,500 B.C.E. First wheeled vehicles in central Europe.

4,000   3,000   1,000 B.C.E.

5,000 B.C.E. Earliest copper mine in Europe (Rudna Glava) and earliest evidence of domestication of horses (Sredny Stog)

2,000 B.C.E. First evidence of chariots in the southern Urals

Orkney Islands
Maes Howe
SCOTLAND

ATLANTIC OCEAN

FRANCE

HUNGARY
Tisza
Rudna Glava
SERBIA
Danube
ROMANIA
Tartaria
Varna
BULGARIA

Sredny Stog
UKRAINE
Dnieper

Carpathian Mountains

Black Sea

ANATOLIA

Sicily

MALTA

Mediterranean Sea

AFRICA

E U R A S I A

Ural Mountains

a smaller scale at attempts to monitor the Sun and, perhaps, control nature by magic. A stone-built village to the west has hearths and fitted furniture still in place. It is tempting to imagine this as a far-flung colonial station, preserving the styles and habits of a distant home in southwest Britain and northwest France, where the big tombs and stone circles are found.

THE ECOLOGY OF CIVILIZATION

In this world of increasing diversification, four river valleys stand out in terms of scale: the middle and lower Nile in Egypt; the Indus and the now dried-up Saraswati (sah-rah-SWAH-tee) (mainly in what is now Pakistan); the Tigris and Euphrates in what is now Iraq; and the Yellow River in China. Between 5000 and 2000 B.C.E., people in these regions exploited more land and changed at a faster

MAP **3.1**

Intensified Settlements in Western Eurasia, 5,000–2,000 B.C.E.

●   Places described in text

▲   other important archaeological sites

MALTA   modern day country

pace than those in other regions. Change was measured in terms of intensified agriculture, technological innovation, development of state power, and construction of cities.

In recent times, these valleys have occupied disproportionate space in our history books and a privileged place in our store of images and memories. Their ruins and relics still inspire movie makers, advertisers, artists, toy makers, and writers of computer games. They shape our ideas of what civilizations ought to be. When we hear the word *civilization*, we picture Egyptian pyramids, sphinxes, and mummies; Chinese bronzes, jades, and clays; Mesopotamian ziggurats—tall, tapering, steplike temples—and writing tablets smothered with ancient wedge-shaped letter forms. Or we conjure the windblown wrecks of almost-vanished cities in landscapes turning to desert. We even call these seminal—or nursery—civilizations, as if they were seed plots from which civilized achievements spread around the world. Or we call them great civilizations, and begin our conventional histories of civilization by describing them.

Civilization is now a discredited word. People have abused it as a name for societies they approve of, which usually means societies that resemble their own. Or they have misapplied it as the name of a supposedly universal stage of social development, even though we have no evidence that societies follow any universal course of development. We can, however, understand a civilization as a society that, for good or ill, engages ambitiously with its environment, seeking to remodel the rest of nature to suit human purposes. In this sense of the word, the four river valleys housed societies more civilized than earlier cases we know of. They modified the landscape with fields and irrigation works or smothered it with monumental buildings on a scale that no people before attained or, perhaps, even conceived.

THE GREAT FLOODPLAINS

The four river valleys shared certain environmental features: a gradually warming and drying climate; relatively dry soils; and a reliance on seasonally flooding rivers and, therefore, on irrigation. If we consider them, together, however, we can see how relentless divergence opened cultural chasms inside this common ecological framework.

The Ecology of Egypt

In the north, where the Nile empties into the Mediterranean, distinctive food sources and useful plants complemented what farmers could grow in the irrigated lands to the south. In the delta's teeming marshlands, birds, animals, fish, and plants clustered for the gatherer and hunter. A painter showed Nebamun—a scribe and counter of grain who lived probably about 3,500 years ago—hunting in a land "full of everything good—its ponds with fish and its lakes with birds. Its meadows are verdant; its banks bear dates; its melons are abundant." Fish fed on lotus-flowers. Thickets of rushes and papyrus provided rope and writing paper.

Most of Egypt, however, lay above the delta. The Nile flows from south to north, from the highlands of Ethiopia in Central Africa to the Mediterranean, and where the ground breaks from higher altitudes or where the riverbed narrows, dangerous rapids hinder navigation. Soil samples reveal the history of climate change. By about 4,000 years ago, the valley was already a land of "black" earth between "red" earths. Floods fed the fertile, alluvial black strip along the Nile; slowly drying red desert lay

Making bread. Some of the activities portrayed in ancient Egyptian tomb-offerings seem humdrum. Beer-making or—as in this example, nearly 3,000 years old—bread-making, are among the most common scenes. But these were magical activities that turned barely edible grains into mind-expanding drinks and a life-sustaining staple food.

on either side. Hunting scenes painted at Memphis, Egypt's first capital, in the Nile delta, showed game lands turning to scrub, sand, and bare rock. Rain became rare, a divine gift, according to a pious king's prayer to the Sun, dropped from "a Nile in heaven." Thirst was called "the taste of death." Other lands had rain, as an Egyptian priest told a Greek traveler, "Whereas in our country water never falls on fields from above, it all wells up from below."

The Nile turns green with algae in early summer, then red with tropical earth in August. In September and October, if all goes well, the river floods and spreads the dark, rich silt thinly over the earth. Between floods, the nitrogen content of the soil decreases by two-thirds in the top six inches. But the annually renewed topsoil grew some of the densest concentrations of wheat in the ancient world. If the flood is too high, the land drowns. If the level of the river falls below about 18 feet, drought follows. In one of the oldest surviving documents of Egyptian history, probably of about 2500 B.C.E., a king reveals a dream. The river failed to flood because the people neglected the gods who ruled beyond the rapids, where the waters came from. Still, compared to the other river valleys of the period, the Nile flood waters were—and still are—exceptionally regular and, therefore, easy to exploit.

The economy guaranteed basic nutrition for a large population, not individual abundance. Most people lived on bread and grainy, nutritious beer in amounts only modestly above subsistence level. A surplus generated trade, which made up for the country's lack of timber and aromatic plants for perfumes and incense. The wall carvings of a memorial to Queen Hatshepsut, who reigned around 3,500 years ago, reveal vast stores of grain and live cattle unloaded in the land of Punt, at the far end of the

Food aid. Egypt exported surplus food across the Red Sea in exchange for the luxury aromatics, especially incense, of the land of Punt, whose queen, depicted in a painting perhaps 3,500 years old, appears comically—or realistically?—obese. Like modern Westerners, but unlike most people in most cultures, the Egyptians esteemed thin body shapes.

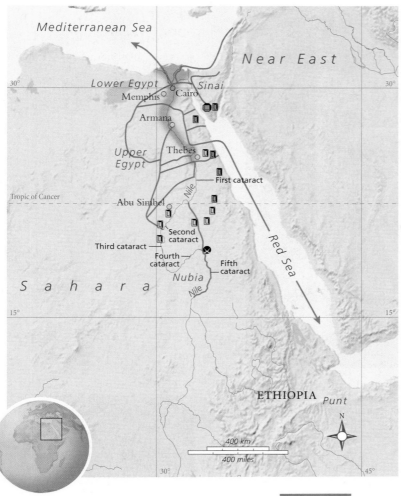

MAP **3.2**

Ancient Egypt

●   modern city

→   trade route

Trade Goods

▪   gold

▪   copper

●   turquoise

⊗   ivory

Red Sea in East Africa, in exchange for scented trees to grace a temple garden and exotic animals for the Egyptian royal zoo. Most of the courtly luxuries that today's Western museum goers see in exhibits on ancient Egypt came from trade, raids, and conquest. Gold and ivory, for example, came from Nubia, an African kingdom beyond the cataracts, and copper and turquoise came from Sinai, a region of desert uplands that link Egypt to the Near East (see Map 3.2).

Shifting Rivers of the Indus Valley

In the Indus valley, the sparse remains of the society called Harappan, after one of its earliest excavated cities, lie beyond historians' reach. The rising water table has drowned evidence of the earliest phases, and scholars have not been able to decipher the writing system. Here the Indus and Saraswati Rivers were more powerful and capricious than the Nile, changing course and cutting new channels that might deprive settlements of water supplies. Ultimately, perhaps, they were fatally unpredictable, for Egypt lasted thousands of years longer. When the Indus altered course and the Saraswati dried up, Harappan cities dwindled to faint traces in the dust.

But three to five thousand years ago, the Indus floodplain was broader than the Nile's. The Indus and Saraswati flooded twice a year—first with the spring snowmelt when the rivers rose, and then in summer when warm air, rising in Central Asia, sucks moisture in from the sea. As a result, farmers here could grow two crops annually. The basic patterns were the same as in Egypt. Wheat and barley grew on rainless, irrigated soil, and cattle grazed on marginal grassland. No region was as rich as the Nile delta, but Harappa had a coastal outpost at the seaport of Lothal, on the Indian Ocean, in a land of rice and millet (see Map 3.3).

The Harappan heartland had few valuables of its own. As in Egypt, the basis of its wealth was the surplus of its agriculture. Around 2000 B.C.E., the

Harappan seals. In the last couple of centuries, scholarly code-crackers have worked out how to read most of the world's ancient scripts. But the writing on Harappan seals remains elusive. The seals seem to depict visions and monsters—but the messages they conveyed were probably of routine merchants, data-stock-taking, and prices. In most cases that we know of, writing was first devised to record information too uninteresting for people to confide to memory.

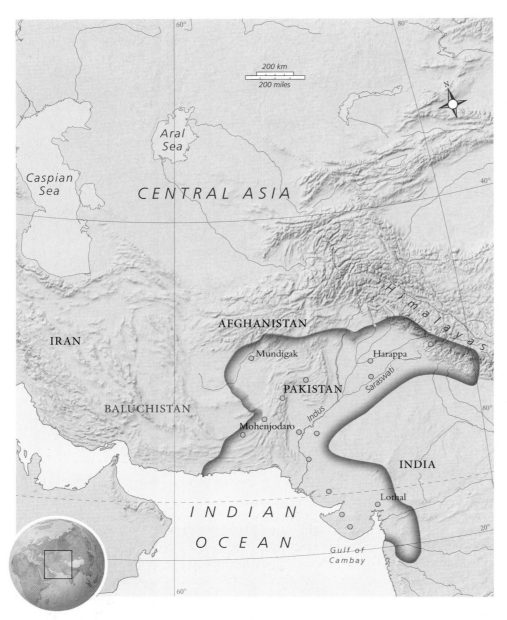

MAP 3.3

Harappan Civilization

extent of Harappan culture

Harappan site

INDIA   modern-day country

Harappan-culture area was the biggest in the world, stretching over half a million square miles. This was, perhaps, evidence of weakness rather than strength. Territorial expansion was the Harrapan solution to feeding its increasingly dense population in the heartland, and no society can keep expanding forever.

Most surviving Harappan art is engraved on seals used to mark trading goods. These little masterpieces capture how people of the time saw their world. Some show naturalistic representations of animals, feasting tigers, and elegant bulls. Violations of realism, however, are more characteristic and include jokey elephants and rhinoceroses. Perplexing scenes, probably from Harappan mythology, include magical transformations of human into tiger, starfish into unicorn, horned serpent into tree.

Fierce Nature in Early Mesopotamia

The Nile and the Indus spill and recede according to a reasonably predictable rhythm, but the Tigris and Euphrates flood at any time, washing away dikes, overflowing

MAP **3.4**

Early Mesopotamia

▨   fertile crescent

●   place described on pages 60–66

IRAN   modern-day country

- - -   ancient coastlines

—   ancient irrigation and water works

→   trade route

▲   ziggurat

MAP EXPLORATION

www.prenhall.com/armesto_maps

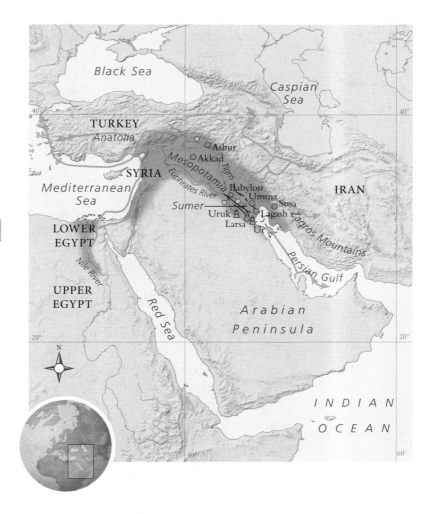

ditches. At other times, desert sandstorms choke the farmers and bury their crops. In the wind, according to the poets, earth shattered "like a pot." "Will new seed grow?" asked a proverb. "We do not know. Will old seed grow? We do not know."

In lower Mesopotamia, where the first big cities sprang up around 3000 B.C.E., the rivers fell through a parched landscape from a distant land of rain, like trickles across a windowpane. Even with irrigation, the summers were too harsh and dry to produce food for the early cities, which had to rely on winter crops of wheat and barley, onions, chickpeas, and sesame. Rain fell then more often than it does today, but it was largely confined to winter when ferocious storms made the sky flare with sheet lightning. "Ordered by the storm-god in hate," according to a poet, "it wears away the country." The floods that created the life-giving alluvial soils were also life-threateningly capricious. Unleashed in early summer by mountain rains, rivers could swell and sweep away crops (see Map 3.4).

Meanwhile, earth and water, the benign forces that combined to create the alluvial soil, were also celebrated in verse. The goddess Nintu personified Earth—zealous, jealous mother, yielding nourishment, suckling infants, guarding embryos. Water, to awaken the land's fertility, was a male god, Enki, empowered "to clear the pure mouths of the Tigris and Euphrates, to make greenery plentiful, to make dense the clouds, to grant water in abundance to all ploughlands, to make corn lift its head in furrows and to make pasture abound in the desert." But Nintu and Enki were subordinate deities, at the beck and call of storm and flood.

The ferocity of the climate demanded hardy plants, so Mesopotamia produced much more barley than wheat. Exhausting digging raised dwellings above the flood and diverted and conserved water. The people who lived along the lower stretches of the river depicted themselves in their art as dome-headed, potbellied lovers of music, feasts, and war. But they were necessarily resourceful people who made ships in a country with no timber, worked masterpieces in bronze in a part of the world where no metal could be found, built fabulous cities without stone by baking mud into bricks, and dammed rivers as the Marsh Arabs of southern Iraq do to this day—with brushwood, reeds, and earth.

The Good Earth of Early China

Mesopotamia and Harappa traded with each other. Mesopotamia and Egypt were close to each other and in constant touch. The map shows, however, that long distances and physical barriers surrounded China's Yellow River valley (see Map 3.5). Nevertheless, perhaps in part because the environment was similar, developments here unfolded in familiar ways.

The Yellow River collects rain in the mountains of Shaanxi province, where rapid thaws bring torrents of water. Where it disgorges, the stream broadens suddenly and periodically overflows. Here the climate has been getting steadily drier for thousands of years. The region today is torrid in summer, icy in winter, stung

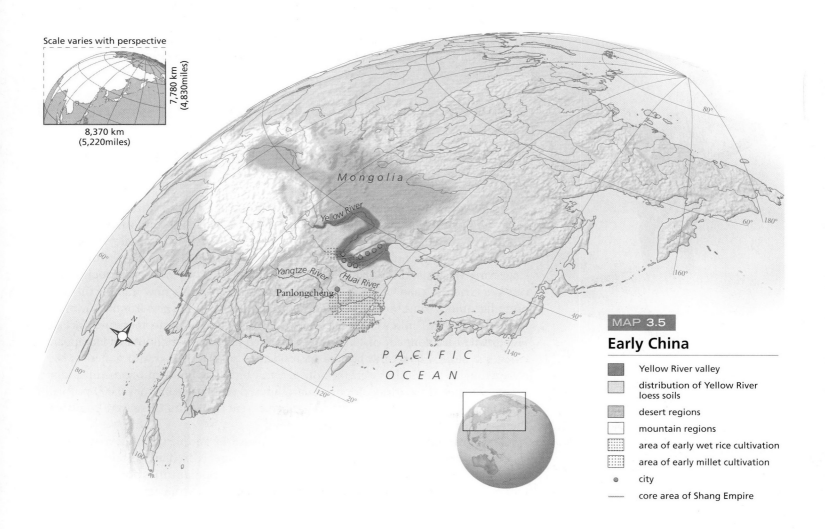

Scale varies with perspective

7,780 km (4,830 miles)

8,370 km (5,220 miles)

Mongolia

Yellow River

Yangtze River

Huai River

Panlongcheng

PACIFIC OCEAN

N

MAP 3.5

Early China

- Yellow River valley
- distribution of Yellow River loess soils
- desert regions
- mountain regions
- area of early wet rice cultivation
- area of early millet cultivation
- city
- core area of Shang Empire

by chill, gritty winds, and rasped by rivers full of ice. The winds blow dust from the Mongolian desert over the land, creating the crumbly, yellow earth that gives the river its name. This soil is almost sterile if it is not watered, but the fierce, unpredictable flood coaxes it into amazing fertility. The river needs careful management, with dikes to stem the flood, ditches to channel it, and artificial basins to conserve water against drought.

When farmers first began to till them, these lands were a sort of savanna, where grasslands mixed with woodland. Three or four thousand years ago, water buffalo were still plentiful, together with other creatures of marsh and forest. In the *Shi Jing*, a collection of ancient songs, poets rhapsodize about the toil of clearing weeds, brush, and roots. "Why in days of old did they do this task? So that we might plant our grain, our millet, so that our millet might be abundant." During the Shang dynasty, between about 3000 and 1000 B.C.E., millet sustained what were perhaps already the densest populations in the world and kept armies of tens of thousands of warriors in the field. The earliest known cultivators cleared the ground with fire before dibbling and sowing. They harvested each cluster of ears by hand and threshed seeds by rubbing between hands and feet. Crop rotation secured the best yields. Eventually soya beans provided the alternating crop, but it is not clear when soya cultivation began.

Even at its wettest, the Yellow River valley could not sustain a rice-eating civilization. Rice could become a staple only when people colonized new areas. Later poets recalled expansion from the Yellow River southward as a process of conquest, grasping at the Yangtze River. But conquest makes more interesting myths than colonization does. Colonists and conquerors probably combined with other communities, where similar changes were already in progress, in a slow process of expansion on many levels, beginning more than 3,500 years ago.

CONFIGURATIONS OF SOCIETY

All four valleys faced the same problems—population was growing denser and society becoming more complex. Yet they adopted contrasting solutions.

Patterns of Settlement and Labor

We do not know how many people lived in the great river-valley civilizations, but they surely numbered millions. In Egypt, the people were spread fairly uniformly throughout the narrow floodplain of the Nile. Cities strewed the other three valleys. In lower Mesopotamia for instance, Ur, Abraham's home in the bible story, had royal tombs of staggering wealth and towering ziggurats, built over 4,000 years ago—inspired, as recent archaeology shows—by even earlier structures in what is now Iran. By the second millennium B.C.E. towns also marked the growth of China: new frontier towns—modest places like Panlongcheng, or Curled Dragon Town, in the northern province of Hubei, where a colonnade of 43 pillars surrounded the governor's house. In Harappan cities, the streetscapes—the layouts of residential and administrative zones—were always roughly identical, as were the houses. Every brick was uniform—sometimes kiln baked, sometimes pan dried. Mohenjodaro housed perhaps 50,000 or 60,000 people, and Harappa over 30,000. No other settlements were as big, but there were plenty of them—at least 1,500 are known to archaeology.

Population density made specialization possible. People could devote themselves to particular crafts and trades. Each sex specialized in certain occupations. Outside the home, urban life created new opportunities for specialized female labor. Women and children, for instance, were the textile workers in

Excerpt from the *Shi Jing*

Dancing girl. One of a collection of bronze figures known as "dancing girls" unearthed at Mohenjodaro. Their sinuous shapes, sensual appeal, and provocative poses suggest to some scholars that they may portray temple prostitutes. They are modeled with a freedom that contrasts with the formality and rigidity of the handful of representations of male figures that survive from the same civilization (see page 68).
Dancing girl. Bronze statuette from Mohenjo Daro. Indus Valley Civilization. National Museum, New Delhi, India. Borromeo/Art Resource, NY

◉ MAKING CONNECTIONS ◉

THE ECOLOGY OF CIVILIZATIONS

REGION →	ENVIRONMENTAL DIVERSITY →	PRIMARY MODIFICATION →	ECONOMIC CONSEQUENCES →
Egypt (Nile River)	Delta: marshlands, ponds, lakes; upriver: "black earth," alluvial plain created from regular floods from central African headwaters; bordered by Sahara Desert, with scattered oasis	Exploitation of lush delta flooded alluvial plain with irrigation	Everyday abundance of basic commodities (wheat, barley, cattle) leads to population increase, regional trade
Indus (Indus, Saraswati Rivers)	Wide alluvial floodplain, frequent changing river courses, varied climate—coastal outposts, hot interior, upriver Himalayan headwaters; flooding twice a year from spring snowmelt and monsoon rains	Widespread irrigation of rainless upriver regions; grazing on grasslands, marsh areas	Agricultural surplus with two harvests a year; rapid population growth, urbanization
Mesopotamia (Tigris, Euphrates Rivers)	Delta: marshlands, ponds, lakes, waterways; upriver alluvial plains flooded irregularly; harsh summer sandstorms, intense heat; winter floods, rainstorms; lack of forests, stone	Irrigation; dependence on winter crops: barley, wheat, onions, chickpeas; intensive plowing; digging of dikes and ditches to divert and store water	Widespread cultivation of grains leads to regional trade; use of mud brick for housing, temples
China (Yellow River)	Unpredictable river floods surrounding areas creating loess soil—basis of agriculture; probably more rainfall than the other three regions	Dikes, irrigation canals control flooding; creation of basins to conserve water; early exploitation of savanna grasslands, buffalo, and other animals; farming based on millet, later supplanted by soya	Gradual expansion/colonization southward toward rice-growing region of Yangtze River

Ashur, a large city in northern Mesopotamia, and probably wove cotton in Harappan cities. Moreover, women were not necessarily excluded from power. These societies employed them as rulers, prophetesses, and priestesses and included them as subjects of art. Yet art also depicted women in servile roles. For instance, pouting, languid bronze dancing girls—or are they temple prostitutes?—figure among the few artworks excavated from Harappan cities of the second millennium B.C.E. Mesopotamian law codes and Chinese texts show people increasingly inheriting status from their fathers rather than their mothers, and depict women's talents increasingly focused on the family home and child rearing. This is understandable because population increase created more domestic work, while increasingly ambitious agriculture and construction were more efficiently entrusted to males. Concentrating on domestic life, however, gave women opportunities to exercise informal power. Surviving texts show some of the consequences. Women could initiate divorce, recover their property, and, sometimes, win additional compensation on divorce. A wife, says the Egyptian *Book of Instructions*, "is a profitable field. Do not contend with her at law and keep her from gaining control."

 Ptahhotep, from the Egyptian *Book of Instructions*

Politics

All four river valley societies shared, in one respect, a type of environment suited to tyranny, or, at least, to strong states exercising minute control over subjects' lives. Even without agriculture, people could have no security of life without collective action to manage the floods. Even foragers would need ditches and dikes to protect wild foodstuffs and defend dwellings. The importance of collectively managing the floods helps account for the obvious resemblances between the political systems of all these regions. All practiced divine or sacred kingship; all had rigid social hierarchies; all placed the lives and labor of the inhabitants at the disposal of the state. The mace head of an Egyptian king of the fourth millennium B.C.E. shows him digging a canal. Proverbially, a just judge was "a dam for the sufferer, guarding lest he drown." A corrupt one was "a flowing lake."

We can see how one irrigation system worked, in Larsa in Mesopotamia, from the archive of a contractor named Lu-igisa, which has survived from around 2000 B.C.E. His job was to survey land for canal building, organize the laborers and their pay and provisions, and supervise the digging and the dredging of accumulated silt. Procuring labor was the key task—5,400 workers to dig a canal and 1,800 on one occasion for emergency repairs. In return, he had the potentially profitable job of controlling the opening and closing of the locks that released or shut off the water supplies. Failure was fatal. "What is my sin," he complained when he was fired, "that the king took my canal from me?"

The Egyptian State

In Egypt, defying nature meant more than refashioning the landscape. Above all, it meant stockpiling against disaster, to safeguard humans from the invisible forces that let loose the floods. A temple at Abu Simbel had storehouses big enough to feed 20,000 people for a year. The taxation yields proudly painted on the walls of a high official's tomb are an illustrated menu for feeding an empire: sacks of barley, piles of cakes and nuts, hundreds of head of livestock. The state as stockpiler existed, it seems, not to redistribute goods but for famine relief.

Methods of collecting and storing grain were as vital as the systems of flood control, precisely because the extent of the flood could vary from one year to the next. The biblical story of Joseph, an Israelite who became a pharaoh's chief official and saved Egypt from starvation, recalls "seven lean years" at one stretch. Such bad times were part of folk memories, as were spells when "every man ate his children." A tomb scene from the city of Amarna shows a storehouse with only six rows of stacked victuals, including grain sacks and heaps of dried fish, laid on shelves supported on brick pillars. A strong state was an inseparable part of this kind of farsightedness. Grain had to be taxed under compulsion, transported under guard, and kept under watch.

 Excerpts from *The Amarna Letters*

If pharaohs were highly glorified storekeepers, what did the Egyptians mean when they said their king was a god? Furthermore, how could pharaohs bear the names and exercise the functions of many gods, each with a separate identity? A possible aid to understanding is the Egyptian habit of making images. The image "was" the god only when the god inhabited the image. The pharaoh's person could provide a similar opportunity for a god to take up residence. In a letter from around 1350 B.C.E., pharaoh is "my Sun-god" and the ruler of a city in Palestine "thy servant and the dirt whereon thou dost tread." Some 400 years earlier, a father, Sehetep-ib-Re, wrote advice to his children—"a counsel of eternity and a manner

Weighing the soul. About 4,500 years ago, Egyptian sensibilities changed. Instead of showing the afterlife as a prolongation of life in this world, tomb-painters began to concentrate on morally symbolic scenes, in which gods interrogate the dead and weigh their good against their evil deeds.
© The Trustees of The British Museum

of living aright." The king is the Sun-god, but he is more. "He illumines Egypt more than the sun, he makes the land greener than does the Nile."

In Egypt the law remained in the mouth of the divine pharaoh, and the need to put it in writing was never strong. Instead, religion defined a moral code that the state could not easily modify or subvert. The evidence comes from Egyptian tombs. Early grave goods include the cherished possessions and everyday belongings of this world, suggesting that the next world would reproduce the inequalities and lifestyles of this one. At an uncertain date, however, a new idea of the afterlife emerged. This world was called into existence to correct the imbalances of the one we know. It is particularly well documented in ancient Egyptian sources that most of the elite seem to have changed their attitude to the afterlife around 2000 B.C.E. Earlier tombs are antechambers to a life for which the world was practical training. Tombs built later are places of interrogation after a moral preparation for the next life.

Wall paintings from the later tombs show the gods weighing the souls of the dead. Typically, the deceased's heart lies in one scale, and a feather symbolizing truth lies in the other. The jackal-headed god of the underworld, Anubis, supervises the scales. The examined soul renounces a long list of sins that concentrate on three areas: sacrilege, sexual perversion, and the abuse of power against the weak. Then the good deeds appear: obedience to human laws and divine will, acts of mercy, offerings to the gods and the spirits of ancestors, bread to the hungry, clothing to the naked, "and a ferry for him who was marooned." The reward of the good is a new life in the company of Osiris, the sometime ruler of the universe. For those who fail the test, the punishment is extinction.

Statecraft in Mesopotamia

Unlike Egypt, a single state under a single ruler, Mesopotamia was divided into numerous small rival kingdoms, each based on a single city. In Mesopotamia, kings were not gods, which is probably why the earliest known law codes come from there. The codes of Ur from the third millennium B.C.E. are fragmentary—essentially, lists of fines. But the code of King Lipit-Ishtar of Sumer and Akkad, around 2000 B.C.E., is clearly an attempt to regulate the entire society. It explains that the laws were divinely inspired. Their purpose was to make "children support the father and the father children, ... abolish enmity and rebellion, cast out weeping and lamentation ... bring righteousness and truth and give well-being."

 *The Code of Lipit-Ishtar*

Gilgamesh, king of Uruk, hero of the world's earliest known work of imaginative literature, shown in a relief more than 3,000 years old, kills the Bull of Heaven. The bull was a personification of drought. It was part of a king's job to mastermind irrigation.
Royal Museums of Art and History, Brussels, Belgium. Copyright IRPA-KIK, Brussels, Belgium

excerpts from the *Epic of Gilgamesh*

Hammurabi, ruler of Babylon in the first half of the 1700s B.C.E., gets undue credit because his code happens to survive intact, having been carried off as a war trophy to Persia. It is engraved in stone and shows the king receiving the text from the hands of a god. It was clearly intended to substitute for the physical presence and utterance of the ruler. "Let any oppressed man who has a cause come into the presence of the statue of me, the king of justice, and then read carefully my inscribed stone, and give heed to my precious words. May my stone make his case clear to him." These were not laws as we know them, handed down by tradition or enacted to restrain the ruler's power. Rather, they were means to perpetuate royal commands. Obedience was severely enforced in Mesopotamia—to the vizier in the fields, the father in the household, the king in everything. "The king's word is right," says a representative text, "his word, like a god's, cannot be changed."

Even if we had no written evidence to confirm it, royal power would gleam from the luxurious artifacts that filled rulers' tombs, evidence of the realm's wealth: a gilded harp carved in the form of a ram; dice and gaming boards of inlaid shell and polished stone; lively animals sculpted in gold and silver; tapering vessels of gold, and golden cups modeled on ostrich eggs. The stunning collections of jewelry seem to have religious themes, as if each had a distinct ritual function.

In Mesopotamian carvings, the king is commonly the biggest figure in any scene that includes him. He drinks. He receives supplicants who petition his help and citizens and ambassadors who pay him tribute. He presides over armies and processions of chariots drawn by wild asses. He carries bricks to build cities and temples, purifying them with fire and consecrating them with oil. To form the first brick from the mud was the king's exclusive right, and bricks from the state kilns were stamped with royal names. Royal seals make plain why this was. They show gods building the world up out of mud. They mix it, carry it up ladders, and fling mud bricks up to the men who set them layer by layer. The transformation of mud into city was royal magic.

Oracles—means of supposed access to knowing the future—told kings what to do. Augurers were the hereditary interpreters of oracles. They read the will of the gods in the livers of sacrificed sheep, the drift of incense, and, above all, in the movements of heavenly bodies. Their predictions of royal victory, danger, anger, and recovery from sickness fill surviving records. Religion, however, did not necessarily limit royal power. Kings firmly controlled the oracles and sometimes slept in temples to induce prophetic dreams, especially during a crisis, such as the failure of the floods. Of course, the predictions they reported may have merely legitimated the policies they had already decided to follow.

Yet these rulers were there to serve the people: to mediate with the gods on behalf of the whole society, to organize the collective effort of tillage and irrigation, to warehouse food against hard times, and to redistribute it for the common good.

The most famous relic of ancient Mesopotamian literature, the *Epic of Gilgamesh*, sheds further light on the nature of leadership. There was a real Gilgamesh, or at least a king of that name who ruled the city of Uruk, probably around 2700 B.C.E. The poem quotes a proverbial saying about him: "Who has ever ruled with power like his?" In the surviving versions, written down, perhaps about 1800 B.C.E., the same natural forces that molded the Mesopotamian environment shaped the story. When Gilgamesh, the hero of the poem, confronts a monster who breathes fire and plague, the gods blind the attacker with a scorching wind. When Gilgamesh explores the Ocean of Death to find the secret of immortality, he encounters the only family to have survived a primeval flood. The disaster, wrought by divine whim, had destroyed the rest of the human race and even left the gods themselves "cowering like dogs crouched against a wall."

The First Documented Chinese State

The earliest recorded kingship traditions of China resemble those of Egypt and Mesopotamia, with the same connection between royal status and the management of food and water. The legendary engineer-emperor Yu the Great was praised for having "mastered the waters and caused them to flow in great channels." Early folk poetry describes a period of city building after his time, so fast "that the drums could not keep pace." The legendary ruler Tan-fu supervised builders of houses and temples, as they "lashed the boards and erected the frames."

The earliest China we know of was a unitary state. The dynasty known as Shang dominated the Yellow River valley for most of the second millennium B.C.E. Diviners, whose job was to detect the gods' messages, heated animal bones and turtle shells to breaking point and read the gods' answers to questions along the lines of the cracks. Scribes transcribed the answers onto the fragments, so the bones tell of the lives and duties of kings. The king was most often engaged in war and sometimes in diplomacy and marriage, which later emperors called "extending my favor." To soldiers, "our prince's own concerns" rolled them "from misery to misery" and gave them homes "like tigers and buffaloes . . . in desolate wilds." The court treasury held millet, turtle shells, and oracle bones in tribute.

Above all, the king was a mediator with the gods, performing sacrifices, preparing for and conducting oracle readings, breaking the soil, praying for rain, founding towns. He spent half his time hunting—presumably as a way to entertain counselors and ambassadors, train horsemen, and supplement the table. Scholars claim to detect an increasingly businesslike tone in the oracles. References to dreams and sickness diminish as time goes on; the style becomes more terse and the tone more optimistic. Sometimes the bones reveal revolutions in the conduct of rites from reign to reign, evidence that kings fought tradition and tried to give the world a stamp of their own. Tsu Jia, for instance, a king of the late second millennium B.C.E., discontinued sacrifices to mythical ancestors, mountains, and rivers and increased those to historical figures. Beyond reasonable doubt, he was modifying the practices of the longest-lived and most renowned of his dynasty, Wu Ding (woo-ding).

The chronology is uncertain, but Wu Ding must have ruled about 1400 B.C.E. He was remembered 1,000 years later as a conqueror and glorious hunter. One of his 64 consorts was buried in the richest known tomb of the period, with her human servants, dogs, horses, hundreds of bronzes and jades, and thousands of cowrie shells, which were used as money. Although there is room for confusion because of the habit of calling different people by the same name, court records probably identify her correctly. Wu Ding repeatedly consulted the oracles about her childbeds and sickbeds. She was one of his three principal wives and an active participant in politics. She had a domain of her own and could mobilize 3,000 warriors.

As mediator with the gods, the king was a substitute for the shaman, the middleman between humans and gods, eliciting the "sharp-eared, keen-eyed" wisdom of ghosts and spirits and restoring contact with heaven after disordered times. By taking over the divination of bones and turtle shells, the king transferred to the state the most important political functions of magic and religion—foretelling the future and

 Tan-fu the Duke, from the *Shi Jing*

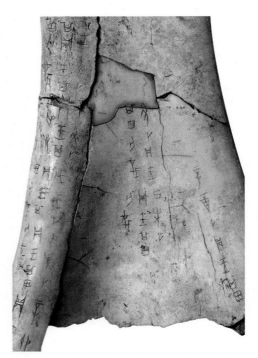

Oracle bones in China in the second millennium B.C.E. were heated until they cracked. Specialist diviners—shamans at first, later royal appointees—read the future along the lines of the cracks, scratching their interpretations into the bone. Most predictions were formal and even banal. This example says characteristically, "If the king hunts, there will be no disaster."

The Great River Valleys

(All dates are approximate)

5000 B.C.E.	Beginning of intense agriculture in great river valleys; use of plows widespread in Mesopotamia
3000 B.C.E.	Menes unites Upper and Lower Egypt; large cities appear in lower Mesopotamia (Sumer)
2500 B.C.E.	Sargon of Akkad conquers Sumer; cities of Harappa and Mohenjodaro flourish
2000–1000 B.C.E.	Shang dynasty (China)
2250–2000 B.C.E.	Ziggurat of Ur
2000 B.C.E.	Law code of Lipit-Ishtar (Mesopotamia); concept of afterlife becomes more moralistic in Egypt
1800 B.C.E.	*Epic of Gilgamesh* written down
1700 B.C.E.	Law code of Hammurabi
1500 B.C.E.	Reading of oracle bones becomes secularized in China; beginning of gradual expansion of Yellow River valley southward toward Yangtze

interpreting the will of the spirits. The king became the guardian of a secular bureaucracy—a slowly developing corps of court historians, who could acquire experience on which predictions could be based more reliably than on the shamans' supposed insights.

At this stage, the Chinese viewed kingship in practical terms—how well the ruler looked after his subjects' well-being. Shang rulers claimed to have come to power as executors of divine justice against an earlier—doubtless mythical—dynasty, the Xia (SHEE-ah), whose last representative had forfeited his right to rule by "neglecting husbandry": failing, that is, in his duty to look after the realm as a farmer cares for his fields. The earliest scholars' texts that describe the emergence of China probably reflect traditional propaganda fairly accurately. They depict kind, generous rulers who fostered the arts of peace. The Yellow Emperor, a mythical figure, was credited with inventing the carriage, the boat, the bronze mirror, the cooking pot, the crossbow, "and a kind of football." Poems and popular legends, however, reveal more of the bloody business of kingship, which inherited ancient clan leaders' rights of life and death. An axe engraved with the emblems of the executioner—hungry smiles and devouring teeth—signified the original term for rulership. "Bring your tongues under the rule of law," says a late Shang ruler in an approving poet's lines, "lest punishment come upon you when repentance will be of no avail."

Wealth and warfare were inseparable essentials of kingship. Tombs of Shang rulers around 1500 B.C.E. display the nature of their power: thousands of strings of cowrie shells, bronze axes and chariots, lacquerware, and hundreds of intricately carved treasures of jade and bone. The greatest treasures were bronzes of unparalleled quality, cast in ceramic molds. Bronze making was the supreme art of Shang China, and its products were a privilege of rank. Thousands of human sacrifices, buried with kings to serve them in the next world or to sanctify their tombs were—to those who buried them—among the cheapest sacrifices.

Ruling the Harappan World

In the Harappan world, the extraordinary consistency in urban layout and building design did not necessarily arise from political unity. Hierarchically ordered dwelling spaces hint at a class or even a more rigid caste structure. In a class system, individuals can rise or fall through the ranks of society. In a caste system they are stuck with the status with which they are born. In Harappan cities, the extensive communal quarters must have had something to do with the organization of manpower—soldiers, perhaps, or slaves, or scholars. Huge warehouses suggest a system to distribute food. The waste-disposal system looks like a masterpiece of urban planning, with clay pipes laid under the streets. The uniform bricks must have come from state kilns and pans. The imposing citadels or fortresses enclosed spaces that might have had an elite function, like the spacious bathing tank at Mohenjodaro. Harappan sites, however, have no rich graves, and the absence of kingly quarters or regal furnishings tempts us to imagine Harappan societies as republics or theocracies.

Normally, for a society like Harappa's, whose writings we cannot read, archaeological evidence tells us what little we know. We would hope to learn something from works of art, but no pictorial art has survived, and Harappan artists seem to have produced little sculpture, except on a small scale in clay and bronze. One extraordinary figure from Mohenjodaro, of great seriousness, with almond eyes and rigidly fluted beard, wears a headband with what looks like the setting for a gem. He has a rich garment slung over one shoulder and extends what is left of his arm in what must have been a symbolic or ritual gesture. He has been called a priest-king or a philosopher-king, but these romantic terms are valueless. With no context for interpreting him, we can only describe him.

The Politics of Expansion

Although just about everything in Harappan politics remains mysterious, the reach of the culture seems so vast it is hard to imagine how it can have spread so far, into a range of different environments, except by force of arms. A sense of what the Harappan frontier was like—expanding and violent—grips you when you see the garrisons that reached toward the interior of Asia, in unirrigatable deserts and siltless hills. In what is now northern Afghanistan, lapis lazuli and copper were traded at oasis settlements that reached westward toward the Caspian Sea. Mundigak, a fortified trading center, was equipped to house entire caravans. Today, behind formidable walls with square bastions, the wreck of a great citadel lunges over the landscape, baring rows of deep, round columns at its flank, like the ribs of a huge, squat beast crouched to guard the routes of commerce.

In Egypt, Mesopotamia, and China, the sources are ample enough to reveal how states grew by conquest. In Egypt, the Nile was the spine that supported a unitary state. More than the source of life-giving mud, the river was a highway through a long, thin land. Culture and trade could flow freely from the coast to the cataracts. Models and paintings of river craft are among the most common decorations of tombs. At Thebes, you can still see painted scenes of grain-laden barges, and others with oil jars and bundles of fodder, docking by the marketplace.

The river was politically unifying, too. Pharoahs took the river route for inspection tours of the kingdom, mooring at royal docks with brick shrines and exercise yards for chariots. Egypt was an empire shaped like the fans Egyptians used to rake and beat their wheat—the long staff of the Nile linked to the spread of the delta where the river meets the Mediterranean. Mythology preserved the

⊙ MAKING CONNECTIONS ⊙

POLITICS AND STATE POWER IN GREAT RIVER VALLEY SOCIETIES

STATE →	LEADER & SYMBOLIC ROLE →	METHOD OF UNIFICATION →	RULER'S MEANS OF CONTROL →
Egypt	Pharaoh (herdsman) sometimes functions as god	Organizing labor to manage floods; distributing food; use of Nile River as highway to unify, control	Pharaoh's commands, policies function as law, regarded as divine
Mesopotamia city-states	Kings/royals meditate, lead worship, receive oracles	Organizing labor; distributing food; competition with other city-states	Earliest law codes; rituals performed by oracles guide decision making
China	Emperor/engineer, builder, hunter, takes on shamans' role in receiving prophecies	Organizing dike building, irrigation; use of Yellow River as highway to unify and control	Ritual divination using oracle bones—foretelling future, interpreting will of spirits
Harappa	Uncertain if singular ruler or priests dominated ruling class	Harnessing river, irrigation; distributing food; engineering and construction of complex urban systems	Unknown; widespread standardization of measurements and trade point to coordination/leadership

memory of a prehistoric Egypt divided into an upriver South Kingdom, or Upper Egypt, and Lower Egypt, occupying the delta region. Pharaohs wore a double crown to recall this past. Egypt's traditional lists of dynasties began with Menes, who supposedly conquered the delta from his own kingdom in the south around 3000 B.C.E. He united the kingdoms and founded Memphis, his capital, at the point on the Nile where Upper and Lower Egypt joined, a little to the south of modern Cairo.

Conveyance by river was one of the features this world had in common with heaven. To accompany the immortals as they were ferried across the sky, the pharaoh Cheops was provided with transport. In one pit adjoining his pyramid lies the barge that carried his body to the burial place. Egyptologists are currently excavating an adjoining pit, where his celestial boat is buried. In this sailing vessel, he would navigate the darkness, joining the fleet that bore the Sun back to life every night.

In retrospect, the unity of Egypt seems "natural"—river shaped. Mesopotamia was not so easy to unify. Competition was probably the driving force behind Mesopotamian city-states. Inscriptions addressed to their cities' patron gods are full of victories against rivals, each one's propaganda contradicting the others. Around 2000 B.C.E., the most boastful author of inscriptions, Lugal Zagesi, king of the city of Umma in Sumer, claimed more. The supreme god, Enlil, "put all the lands at his feet and from east to west made them subject to him" from the Persian Gulf to the Mediterranean.

This was almost certainly just a boast. Left to themselves, the warring Sumerian city-states could never have united for long. Around 2500 B.C.E., however, invaders from northern Mesopotamia forced political change. The conquering king, Sargon of Akkad, was one of the great empire builders of antiquity. His armies poured downriver and made him King of Sumer and Akkad. "Mighty mountains with axes of bronze I conquered," he declared and dared kings who came after him to do the same. His armies were said to have reached Syria and Iran.

Such a vast empire could not last. After a century or two, native Sumerian forces expelled Sargon's successors. Nevertheless, his achievement set a new pattern—an imperial direction—for the political history of the region. City-states sought to expand by conquering each other. For a time, Lagash, a northern neighbor of Ur, dominated Sumer. One of its kings was the subject of 27 surviving images. We have no better index of any ruler's power. But around 2100 B.C.E., Ur displaced Lagash. The new capital began to acquire the look for which it is renowned, with showy ziggurats and daunting walls. Within a few years more, tribute, recorded on clay tablets, was reaching Ur from as far away as the Iranian highlands and the Lebanese coast. A 4,000-year-old box—the soundbox of a harp, perhaps—gorgeously depicts the cycle of royal life in imperial Ur—victory, tribute-gathering, and celebration. Thereafter, leadership in the region shifted among rival centers, but it always remained in the south.

In China, itineraries for royal travel dating around 1500 B.C.E. reveal a different political geography. Kings constantly rattled up and down the great vertical artery of the realm, the eastern arm of the Yellow River, and frenziedly did the round of towns and estates to the south, as far as the river Huai. Occasionally, they touched the northernmost reach of the Yangtze River. This was a telltale sign. Shang civilization was expanding south from its heartlands on the middle Yellow River, growing into a regionally dominant superstate. Gradually, the worlds of Chinese culture and politics absorbed the Yangtze valley. The result was a unique state containing complementary environments: the millet-growing lands of the Yellow River, the rice fields of the Yangtze. The new ecology of China helped protect it against ecological disaster in either zone. It also formed the basis of the astonishingly resilient and productive state seen in subsequent Chinese history. The consequences will be apparent throughout the remainder of this book. For most of the rest of our story, China wields disproportionate power and influence.

Moreover, the broadening of China's frontiers stimulated rulers' ambitions. They became boundless. Religion and philosophy conspired. The sky was a compelling deity: vast and pregnant with gifts—of light and warmth and rain—and bristling with threats of storm and fire and flood. A state that touched its limits would fulfill a kind of "manifest destiny"—a reflection of divine order. Comparing the state to the cosmos prompted rulers to seek a dominion as boundless as the sky's. The Chinese came to see imperial rule over the world as divinely ordained. Emperors treated the whole world as rightfully or potentially subject to them. By the time of the Zhou, the dynasty that succeeded the Shang, the phrase **mandate of heaven** came into use to express these doctrines.

The concept of the mandate of heaven spread to neighboring peoples. On the Eurasian steppes, the immense flatlands and vast skies encouraged similar thinking. We have no documentation for the ambitions of the steppe dynasties until much later. But, as we shall see, steppelanders with conquest in mind repeatedly challenged empires around the edges of Eurasia in the first millennium B.C.E. It is probably fair to say that for hundreds, perhaps thousands, of years the concept of a right to rule the world drove imperialism in Eurasia.

Literate Culture

It used to be thought—some people still think—that one reason the early Egyptians, Mesopotamians, Chinese, and Harappans qualified as "civilized" was because they were the first to use symbolic methods to record information and pass it on to future generations.

Mesopotamians devised the wedge shapes of the writing known as **cuneiform** to be easily incised, or cut, in the clay tablets used to keep records. The hieroglyphs of the earliest Egyptian texts and the symbols carved on Chinese oracle bones were **logograms**, stylized pictures that provoked mental associations with ideas they were intended to represent or with the sounds of their spoken names. The surviving Harappan texts marked the cord or sacks of merchants' goods. Archaeologists have retrieved many of them from heaps of discarded produce.

So, these civilizations all developed useful and expressive writing systems. For three reasons, however, we can no longer claim that writing was a special and defining feature that made these the first civilizations. First, writing systems originated independently in widely separated parts of the world and were far more varied than traditional scholarship has supposed. Notched sticks and knotted strings can be forms of writing as much as letters on a page or in an inscription. Some writing systems were much older than the civilizations of the river valleys.

Second, it is not clear why we should consider writing special compared to information-retrieval systems based on memory. The earliest writing systems were usually employed for trivia—merchants' price lists, tax collectors' memoranda, potters' marks, and similar jottings. Real art—the great creative poems and myths, like the *Epic of Gilgamesh*—were too sacred for writing to taint and too memorable for such a crude method of transmission. Instead, for centuries, people memorized them and transmitted them orally from one generation to the next.

Finally, how much information does a system have to be able to convey before we can call it writing? Will knotted strings or notched sticks do? Surviving Shang oracle bones of the second millennium B.C.E. bear the ancestral language of modern Chinese. Yet a symbolic system of recording information appears on pottery more than 2,000 years older from Banpo in the Yellow River region. The symbols might be numerals and potters' marks. They do not seem to be connected sentences because the symbols are simple and used one at a time. So is this writing or something else unworthy of the name? Turtle shells recently discovered at Wuyang (woo-yahng) in China, which are thousands of years older, bear marks that we can only explain as part of a system of symbolic representation.

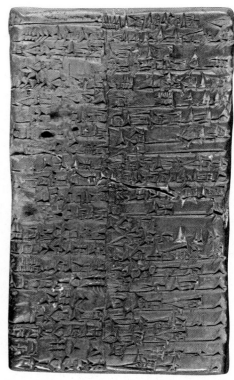

Early writing. In almost all known cases, writing was devised to record neither wisdom nor art, but only tedious data, such as prices and tax returns. This clay tablet from a collection at the Library of Congress is written in Sumerian and concerns the wages paid to named supervisors of day laborers. It dates to 2039 B.C.E.

Instead of restricting our definition of writing, we ought to feel awe at the adventure of combining isolated symbols to tell stories and make arguments. But familiarity disperses awe. Some cultures may have taken thousands of years to make this leap, even while they used writing systems for other purposes, such as labels, oracles, bureaucracy, and magic charms.

IN PERSPECTIVE: What Made the Great River Valleys Different?

Still, the fact remains that, thanks in part to writing, the civilizations of the four great river valleys—or, at least, the three whose writings we can decipher—are, to us, the best known of their time. For that reason, not because of their supposed influence on other peoples, they fairly occupy so much space in books like this one. Studying their written works helps us identify at least two reasons for the cultural divergence of the era, of which they are extreme examples. First, in part, divergence was environmentally conditioned. That is, the greater or more diverse the resource base, the bigger and more durable the society it feeds. The great river valleys were large, continuous areas of fertile, easily worked soil, and for farming societies, exploitable land is the most basic resource of all. Environmental diversity gave the river valley peoples extra resources, compared with civilizations in less privileged regions. Egypt had the Nile delta at hand. In the Yellow River and Yangtze valleys, China had two complementary ecological systems. Mesopotamia had a hinterland of pastures, and Mesopotamia and Harappa had access to each other by sea.

Second, interactions matter. Societies learn from each other, compete with each other, and exchange culture with each other. The more societies are in touch with other societies, the more these activities occur. By contrast, isolation retards. Egypt was in touch with Mesopotamia and Mesopotamia with Harappa. China's relative isolation perhaps helps explain its late start in some of the common processes of change that these societies all experienced. All these societies enclosed, within their own bounds, relatively large zones of exchange. But all were remarkably self-contained. As we shall see in the next chapter, however, travel and trade were increasingly important. These were the means of communicating the cultures from the great river valleys to other regions, some of which were less environmentally fortunate. Invasions and migrations, too, were—and still are—effective forms of interaction because they shift many people around, and people carry their culture with them.

The grandeur of the great river valley civilizations raises questions about their sustainability. Their wealth and productivity excited envy from outsiders and invited attack. Continued population growth demanded ever more intensive exploitation of the environment. At the same time, climates and ecosystems continued to change. The vast collective efforts required for irrigation, storage, and monumental building left huge classes of people oppressed and resentful of elites. As a result of these and other stresses, beginning around 1500 B.C.E., transformation or collapse threatened all these societies. Meanwhile, peoples in less easily exploitable environments found the will and means to reproduce, challenge, or exceed the achievements of these four civilizations. The question of how well they succeeded is the focus of the next chapter.

CHRONOLOGY

(All dates are approximate)

5000–2000 B.C.E.	Four great river valley civilizations develop: Middle and Lower Nile, Egypt; Indus and Saraswati Rivers; Tigris and Euphrates Rivers, Mesopotamia; Yellow River, China
3000 B.C.E.	Menes unites Upper and Lower Egypt
2500 B.C.E.	Cities of Harappa and Mohenjodaro flourish; Sargon of Akkad conquers Sumer
2250–2000 B.C.E.	Ziggurat of Ur built
2000–1000 B.C.E.	Shang dynasty, China
1800 B.C.E.	*Epic of Gilgamesh* written down
1700 B.C.E.	Law code of Hammurabi

Because they all made use of bronze, nineteenth-century archaeology—classifying societies according to their characteristic technology—called the era of the great river valley civilizations the Bronze Age. In the late second millennium B.C.E., the crises that afflicted them seemed to herald transition to an "Iron Age." Such labels no longer seem appropriate. Though there were bronze-using and iron-making societies, there was never an "age" of either. Some societies in Africa never used bronze. Many societies never took up iron. Few employed iron to make tools and weapons until well into the first millennium B.C.E. Although bronze making came to have an important place in the economies and art of many Eurasian peoples during the second millennium B.C.E., other societies achieved similar standards of material culture and developed comparable states without it. In any case, there are aspects of civilization—ways of thinking and feeling and behaving—more deeply influential than technology, "more lasting"—as a Roman poet said of his poems—"than bronze," and therefore more worthy of attention.

PROBLEMS AND PARALLELS

1. How did the distinctive ecological differences of the four great river valleys affect their economic activity?

2. How did environmental transformations caused by humans (such as irrigation) affect the great river valley civilizations, both positively and negatively?

3. What was the connection between religion and political leadership in Egypt, Mesopotamia, and China? What is the evidence for these relationships?

4. What methods did rulers use to expand their states in China, Mesopotamia, the Indus valley, and Egypt? How did each area's environment affect this expansion?

5. What do the writing systems of China, Mesopotamia, Indus valley, and Egypt tell us about each society's politics, religion, and economy?

6. Why are the ways a civilization thought, felt, and behaved not adequately conveyed by labels such as "Bronze Age"?

DOCUMENTS IN GLOBAL HISTORY

- Stonehenge
- Excerpts from the *Shi Jing*
- Ptahhotep, from the Egyptian *Book of Instructions*
- Excerpts from *The Amarna Letters*

- *The Code of Lipit-Ishtar*
- excerpts from the *Epic of Gilgamesh*
- Tan-fu the Duke, from the *Shi Jing*

Please see the Primary Source DVD for additional sources related to this chapter.

READ ON

R. L. Burger, *Chavín and the Origins of Andean Civilization* (1993) is an excellent introduction to the Peruvian material. H. Silverman, ed., *Andean Archaeology* (2004) contains some important recent research.

L. Nikolova, *The Balkans in Later Prehistory* (1999) is authoritative on the southeastern European sites. C. Renfrew, ed., *Problems in European Prehistory* (1979) includes some vital contributions. D. V. Clarke, *Skara Brae* (1983) is a useful pamphlet on those of the Orkneys. For the vexed question of the "rise" of "civilization," K. Wittfogel, *Oriental Despotism* (1967) is the now almost universally repudiated classic on the subject. K. W. Butzer, *Early Hydraulic Civilization in Egypt*

(1976) is a pioneering classic on the ecological dimensions. B. J. Kemp, *Ancient Egypt* (1989) is an excellent introduction.

G. Algaze, *The Uruk World System* (1993) is an important study of the origins of Mesopotamian civilization.

K. C. Chang, *Art, Myth and Ritual* (1983) and *Shang Civilization* (1980) are indispensable on China. E. L. Shaughnessy, *Sources of Western Zhou History* (1992) is immeasurably illuminating.

B. and R. Allchin, *The Rise of Civilization in India and Pakistan* (1982) is particularly useful for Harappa, on which the studies collected by G. Possehl, ed., *Harappan Civilization* (1993) are an important supplement.

A Succession of Civilizations: Ambition and Instability

One measure of the influence of the Hittites is the durability of their art. This relief, from Carchemish in Phoenicia, dates from at least two centuries after the Hittite empire collapsed but continues to reflect Hittite conventions and values. The winged sun was a symbol other regional empires adopted.

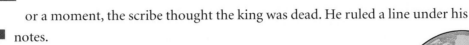

HATTI

For a moment, the scribe thought the king was dead. He ruled a line under his notes.

They formed a grim, faltering record of an old man's regrets: his hatred of his treacherous sister—"a serpent" who "bellows like an ox"; the faithlessness of his adopted heir—"an abomination ... without compassion"; the disloyalty of relatives—"heedless of the word of the king." The dying monarch railed against his daughter, too. "She incited the whole land to rebellion." Rebels taunted him, "There is no son for your father's throne. A servant will sit on it."

With his last bit of strength, Hattusili, the great king of the Hittites, ruler of the land of Hatti, south of the Black Sea, and of an empire that touched upper Mesopotamia and the Mediterranean, sought to keep a grasp on power beyond the grave. With no suitable adult to succeed him, he decided that his infant grandson must be the next king. The administrators of the kingdom must protect the child and prepare him for manhood, reading to him every month his grandfather's testament, with its warnings against disloyalty and its exhortations to mercy, piety, and forgiveness.

Around the deathbed in the city of Kussara, in a room gleaming with lapis lazuli and gold, the assembled warriors and officials contemplated an insecure future. But the king was not yet dead. He stirred, striving to speak. The scribe, straining to catch the royal words, scratched hurried characters onto his clay tablet. A woman's name fell from the king's lips: Hastayar. Who was she? Wife or concubine, sorceress or daughter? No one now knows. But she was at the bedside, consulting with the old women who were the court's prophetesses, even as the king's life ebbed. With Hattusili's last breath came these final words: "Is she even now interrogating the soothsayers? ... Do not forsake me. Interrogate me! I will give you words as a sign. Wash me well. Hold me to your breast. Keep me from the earth."

● ● ● ● ●

FOCUS questions

- WHY WERE the Hittite, Cretan, and Mycenean states more fragile than the great river valley civilizations?
- WHAT FUNDAMENTAL problems to their survival did all large ancient civilizations face?
- WHY DID Harappan civilization disappear?
- WHAT WERE the continuities between the Shang and the Zhou in China?
- WHERE DID the first states arise in the New World?
- WHY WAS Egypt able to survive when other ancient civilizations collapsed around 1000 B.C.E.?

Hattusili dictated this deathbed testament in about 1600 B.C.E. It is the most intimate and lively document to survive from its time, our only glimpse of a king with his guard down, disclosing his own personality. It also reveals the nature and problems of a state at this time: the all-importance of the person of a king, the sacred nature of his word, the ill-defined rules of succession, the power and jealousies of military and administrative elites, an intelligence system that relied on soothsayers, and an atmosphere of danger and insecurity. In short, it was a political environment made to be volatile.

In the Hittite kingdom, we see the great themes of the second millennium B.C.E. First, features that characterized the great river valley civilizations of the previous chapter began to emerge in other environments. These features included intensive agriculture, densely distributed populations, stratified societies (with higher and lower classes), large cities, and states often seeking to build empires. Second, the number of complex states—those with large-scale systems to organize production, control distribution, and regulate life—rapidly increased. These new states also developed a great variety of political institutions and ways to structure society and organize economic activity. Finally, accelerating change claimed victims. By about 1000 B.C.E., war, natural disaster, environmental overexploitation, and social and political disintegration had strained or shattered most of the big states and civilizations that had emerged from the transition to agriculture.

Students of history often dislike this period, with its bewildering succession of empires and civilizations that rise and fall, sometimes with baffling speed. Textbook pages resemble a bad TV soap opera—crowded with action, empty of explanation, with too many characters and too few insights into their behavior. To make sense of the millennium between 2000 and 1000 B.C.E., we need to understand the problems associated with accelerating change. This was a period of climacteric: an era of critical change that extinguished some civilizations, changed others, and might have wiped all of them out. The question for this chapter, then, is, why were some ambitions in the world of around 3,000 years ago realized and others were not? What made the difference between success and failure for states and civilizations?

THE CASE OF THE HITTITE KINGDOM

Anatolia (an-a-TOH-lee-ah), where Hattusili's kingdom took shape, seems an unlikely place to found a large state. Most of it suffered alternating seasonal extremes that scorched and froze crops. Rainfall was, and still is, less than 20 inches a year. (Western Europe and North America receive two or three times more.) Desert stretched between cultivatable patches.

Yet from the central part of this region, between about 1800 and 1500 B.C.E., the people who called themselves children of Hatti—Hittites—drew thousands of such patches and millions of people into a single network of production and distribution, under a common allegiance and built a state we can call an empire. It had palace complexes, storehouses, towns, and armies. And all were comparable in scale with those of the river-valley peoples of the last chapter. Egyptian pharaohs treated Hittite kings as equals. When one pharaoh died without heirs, his widow sent to the king of Hatti for "one of your sons to be my husband, for I will never take a servant of mine and make him my husband." We can picture the Hittites with the help of images they have left us of themselves: hook-nosed, short-headed, and arrayed for war. But how did their state and empire happen in such a hostile environment?

The Importance of Trade

Hatti became a regional power through enrichment by trade. In the second millennium B.C.E., new potential trading partners arose as the economic center of gravity in Mesopotamia gradually shifted upriver. Changes in the course of the Tigris and Euphrates Rivers stranded formerly important cities. Accumulations of silt kept merchants offshore. Wars at the far end of the Persian Gulf and the disappearance of some of the great cities of the Indus valley probably disrupted commerce in the Arabian Sea and Persian Gulf. New opportunities, meanwhile, arose in the north as economic development created new markets, or expanded old ones, in Syria, the Iranian highlands, and Anatolia (see Map 4.1).

For instance, the archives of Ebla, an independent city-state in Syria, reveal exchanges with Mesopotamia. Ebla's commerce was a state monopoly. Its merchants were ambassadors. A dozen foreign cities delivered gold, silver, copper, and textiles to its markets and treasury. Its royal granary stored enough food for 18 million meals. The most complete surviving record of a tour of inspection of the state warehouses names 12 kinds of wheat, abundant wine and cooking oil, and more than 80,000 sheep. The city's ceramic seals, ivory figurines, and metalwork reached the courts of chiefs in central Anatolia.

With the shift of economic activity from Lower to Upper Mesopotamia and beyond, networks of traders spread, east and north, from growing upriver cities such as Ashur on the Tigris and Mari on the Euphrates. Thousands of documents—16,000 in Ebla, 17,000 in Mari—describe wealthy private merchants underwritten by the state and stateless middlemen who served as deal makers. Trade forges social obligations, establishes new relationships of power, and legitimates old ones. Merchant-diplomats carried gifts between palaces. The king of the city of Ugarit (OOH-gahr-riht) rewarded an official called Tamkaru for this kind of work with a grant of land in the mid-1200s B.C.E. Leaders who accumulated imported luxuries or who were tough enough to tax passing trade could reinvest in more goods or buy the allegiance of other chiefs. They might build palace centers like those of Mesopotamia and Egypt to redistribute goods.

Business had its human side. The royal family of Ashur had a farm at a frontier trading post on the routes to Anatolia and the Mediterranean. Over 1,000 people lived there—migrants from Ashur, exiled foreigners, prisoners of war. The steward, permanently frustrated by impractical orders, frustrated the king in turn, who wrote: "What is this, that whatever I tell you, you fail to do as I say?" The supply of beer and tableware to entertain passing embassies provoked many quarrels. So did the problems of enforcing tolls on luxuries.

Anitta, king of Kanes, early in the second millennium had "a throne of iron and a sceptre of iron." Iron was new, originating in this region but still rare and soft, smelted at a temperature only slightly higher than that required for copper. The technique of

Ebla's palace walls in the mid–third millennium B.C.E. were 40 or 50 feet high. The ceremonial court in the foreground was 165 feet long. The holes show where pillars supported the roof. Akkadian invaders destroyed the palace around 2300 B.C.E. but left intact the precious archives that recorded the range of trade with Mesopotamia, Anatolia, and Egypt.

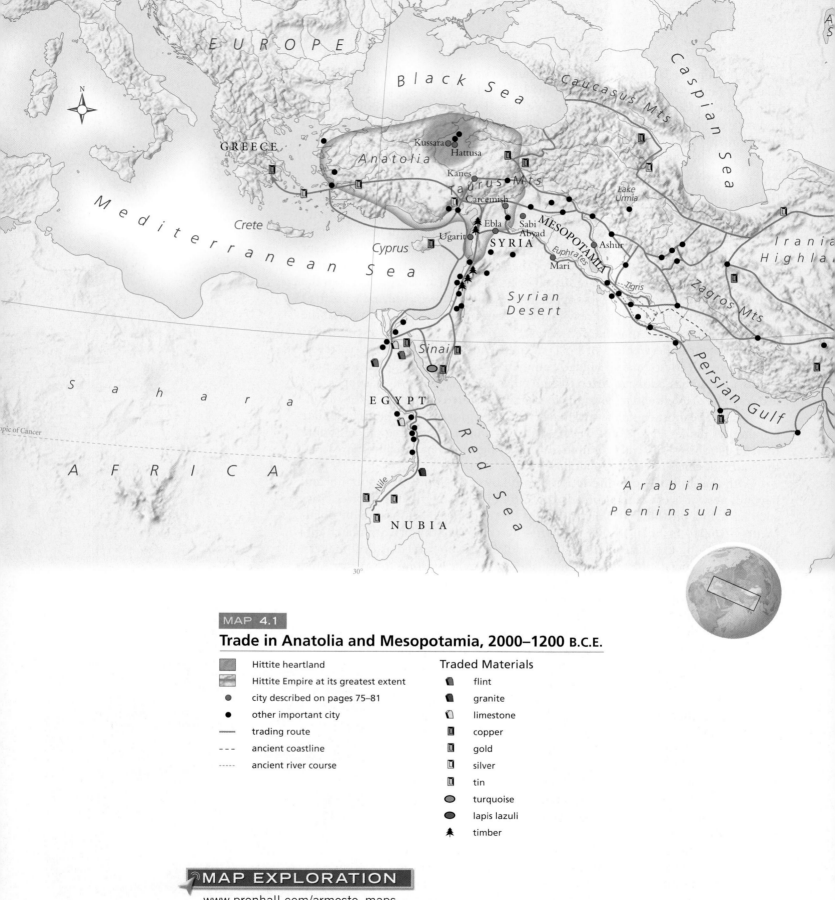

MAP 4.1

Trade in Anatolia and Mesopotamia, 2000–1200 B.C.E.

	Hittite heartland
	Hittite Empire at its greatest extent
●	city described on pages 75–81
●	other important city
—	trading route
- - -	ancient coastline
·····	ancient river course

Traded Materials

	flint
	granite
	limestone
	copper
	gold
	silver
	tin
	turquoise
	lapis lazuli
🌲	timber

MAP EXPLORATION

www.prenhall.com/armesto_maps

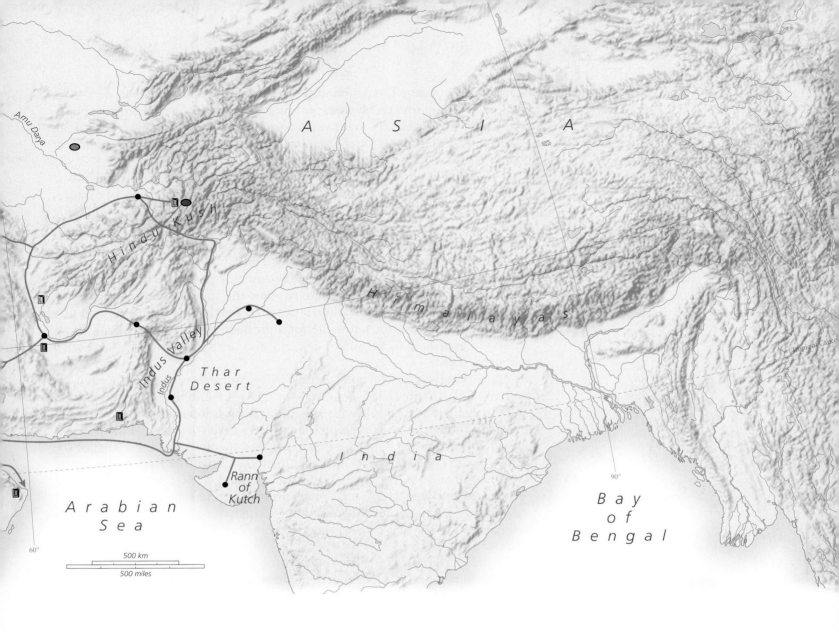

combining it with carbon to make it hard was unreliable. Bronze remained the metal of choice for weapons and agricultural tools. One of the towns Anitta saw as a rival was Kussara, the hometown of the dynasty that later founded the kingdom of Hatti. According to one of his inscriptions, he demolished the place and cursed it, so that it might never arise again. The curse failed. His example, however, inspired the Hittites and showed them how trade and conquest could build a state.

Hittite Society and Politics

The Hittite kingdom brought farmers and herders into a single state and economic system. This was how to make the most of the rugged Anatolian environment, with its small concentrations of cultivatable soil surrounded by marginal grazing land. Herders' wool combined with small farmers' food production. Such mixed farming by independent peasants—not bonded or enslaved workers or wage earners—was of the highest importance. Livestock produce fertilizer to help feed growing populations. Milk-rich diets can improve human fertility. The consequences are more opportunity for economic specialization, urbanization, and the mobilization of manpower for war.

The surviving inventory of the estate of a typical Hittite peasant lists one house for his family of five, three dozen head of livestock, one acre of pasture, and three and a half acres of vineyard, with 42 pomegranate and 40 apple trees. The pasture must have been for his eight oxen. His goats, hardier animals, presumably foraged where they could. Farmers like these were the manpower that, for a time, made Hatti invincible. Children worked the farms during military campaigns, which usually coincided with sowing and harvest. Peasants were willing, presumably, to support the state that in turn protected them, for Hittite law laid down harsh penalties for theft or trespassing on private property. We do not know the total productivity of the economy, but a single silo excavated in the major city, Hattusa, held enough grain for 32,000 people for a year.

Hittite Land Deed

Hatti's king was the sun god's earthly deputy. Subjects called him "My sun," as modern monarchs are called "Your Majesty." His responsibilities were war, justice, and relations with the gods. Hardly any case at law was too trivial to be referred to the king, although, in practice, professional clerks dealt with most of them. A vast household surrounded him: "the Palace servants, the Bodyguard, the Men of the Golden Spear, the Cupbearers, the Table-men, the Cooks, the Heralds, the Stable boys, the Captains of the Thousand." It was a bureaucratic court, where writing perpetuated the king's commands and conveyed them to subordinates. The court was vast, too, because it had to house a huge harem. Royal concubines were rivets of the kingdom. The king's many daughters contributed to the harems of allies and tributaries.

To judge from surviving law codes, Hittites observed many apparently arbitrary sexual taboos. Intercourse with pigs or sheep was punishable by death, but not cases involving horses or mules. Hittites evidently measured the civilization of other societies by the severity of their incest laws. Their own code forbade intercourse between siblings or cousins. Any sexual act, however, was polluting in some degree and had to be cleansed by bathing before prayer. If we knew more about Hittite religion, we might understand their morality better. Strong sexual taboos are usually found in "dualist" religions, alongside belief in the eternal struggle of forces of good and evil or spirit and matter. Hittite attitudes toward sex contrasted with those in Mesopotamia, where—in what seems to have been a more typical pattern—sex was in some sense sacred, and temples employed prostitutes.

In some ways, Hatti was a man's world, with the masculine attitudes and values typical of a war state. The oath army officers took indicates this:

Hittite Soldiers' Oath

> Do you see here a woman's garments? We have them for the oath. Whoever breaks these oaths and does the king harm, let the oaths change him from a man to a woman! Let them change his soldiers into women, and let them dress in the fashion of women and cover their heads with a length of cloth! Let them break the bows, arrows and clubs in their hands and let them take up instead the distaff and the looking-glass!

Women, however, exercised power. Old women acted as diviners at court. Others, lower down the social scale, were curers, waving sacrificial piglets over the victims of curses, with the cry, "Just as this pig shall not see the sky ..., so let the curse not see the sacrificers!"

Fragility and Fall: The End of Hatti

The Hittite state was formidable in war. It had to be. Its domestic economy was fragile and its homeland poor in key resources. It needed to grow. Conquests were the only way to guarantee food for an increasing population and tin to make bronze weapons. But even successful conflicts can weaken a state by overextending its power and disrupting its trade. Growth butts against immovable limits. In Hatti's case, those limits were the frontiers of Egypt and Mesopotamia.

The Hittite kingdom suffered from other weaknesses. As with all communities that made the transition to agriculture, it was vulnerable to famine and disease. Around 1300 B.C.E., King Mursili II reproached the gods for a plague: "Now no one reaps or sows your fields, for all are dead! The mill-women who used to make the bread of the gods are dead!" A couple of generations later, there was reputedly "no grain in Hatti," when Puduhepa—a formidable royal spouse—wrote to Egypt demanding some as part of the dowry of her daughter. For one of the last Hittite kings, Tudhaliya IV, an order not to detain a grain ship bound for his country was "a matter of life and death." Nomadic prowlers from the hinterlands were another common hazard. People the Hittites called Kaska invaded repeatedly to grab booty or extort protection. On at least one of their raids, they robbed the royal court.

In the last few decades of the 1300s B.C.E., the Hittite state was in decline. Hatti lost southern provinces to an expanding kingdom in Upper Mesopotamia. The oaths the king demanded from his subordinates have an air of desperation: "if nobody is left to yoke the horses . . ., you must show even more support . . . . If . . . the chariot-driver jumps down from the chariot, and the valet flees the chamber, and not even a dog is left, . . . your support for your king must be all the greater." Among the last documents the court issued are complaints that subject kings were neglecting tribute or diplomatic courtesies. After 1210 B.C.E., the Hittite kingdom disappeared from the record.

The Hittites	
(All dates are approximate)	
1800–1500 B.C.E.	Hatti develops into an empire
1300 B.C.E.	Plague strikes Hatti
1210 B.C.E.	Last recorded mention of Hatti

INSTABILITY AND COLLAPSE IN THE AEGEAN

The Hittite story is a case study of the problems of global history in the second millennium B.C.E. It demonstrates how agrarian communities became consolidated into states, elevated into empires, and how most of them failed to survive past 1000 B.C.E. Echoes, parallels, and connected cases occurred in many regions near the experiments in civilization building that we discussed in the last chapter.

The civilization scholars call Minoan or Cretan, for instance, took shape in the second millennium on the large Mediterranean island of Crete, which lies between what are now Greece and Turkey. Nearby in the southern Peloponnese, the peninsula that forms the southern part of Greece, the civilization we call Mycenean emerged. Both have inspired Western imaginations. Europeans and Americans view Crete and Mycenae as part of their history, assuming that they can trace the civilization of classical Greece—and therefore of the Western world—to these glamorous, spendthrift cultures of 3,500 years ago. That now seems doubtful. Crete and Mycenae were almost as mysterious to the Greeks as they are to us, and almost as remote. Still, they are worth studying for their own sake and the light they cast on their times.

Crystal vase. Under the elite apartments, Cretan palaces contained workshops where craftsmen made luxuries for elite consumption and for export, such as this crystal vase, about 3,500 years old, from the palace of Zakros, and the unguents and perfumes that vessels like this contained.

Cretan Civilization

Crete is big enough to be self-sustaining, but mountains cover two-thirds of it leaving little land to cultivate amid devastating droughts and earthquakes. But wall paintings from around 2000 B.C.E., when the first palace-storehouses arose there, show fields of grain, vines, and orchards of olives, almonds, and quince. Forests of honey and venison surround gardens of flowers. The seas seem full of dolphin and octopus, under skies where partridge and brightly colored birds fly.

This lavish world was carved from a tough environment, harsh soil, and dangerous seas. And it depended on two despotic methods to control an unpredictable food supply: organized agriculture, embracing, as in Hatti, both farming and herding, and state-regulated trade. The function of the palace as storehouse was a vital part of the system. The greatest palace complex on the island, Knossos, covers more than 40,000 square feet. When it lay in ruins, visitors from Greece who saw its galleries and corridors imagined an enormous maze, built to house a monster who fed on human sacrifices. In fact, the labyrinth was an immense storage area for clay jars, 12 feet high, filled with wool, wine, cooking oil, and grain, some still in place.

Stone chests, lined with lead to protect the foodstuffs they contained, were like strongboxes in a central bank waiting to be distributed or traded. Cretan ships brought ivory and ostrich eggs from Africa and baboons from Egypt. Craft workshops inside the palaces added value to imports by spinning and weaving fine garments, delicately painting stone jars, and hammering gold and bronze into jewels and chariots. Palace records suggest a staff of 4,300 people.

Yet Knossos and buildings like it were also dwellings of an elite who lived in luxury. Squat columns with tops like fat pumpkins supported majestic staircases. Pillars were lacquered red, and the wall paintings glowed with a wonderful sky blue—scenes of feasting, gossiping, playing, and bull leaping. At Zakros, a site that was never plundered, you can see marble-veined chalices, stone storage jars, and a box of cosmetic ointment with an elegant little handle in the form of a reclining greyhound.

Lesser dwellings, grouped in towns, were tiny imitations of the palace. Many had columns, balconies, and upper-storey galleries. In the houses of more prosperous inhabitants, colorful, delicate pottery, stone vases ground into seductively sinuous shapes, and elaborately painted baths survive in large numbers. Yet at lower levels of society, there was little surplus for luxury or time for leisure. Few people lived beyond their early forties. If the purpose of the state was to recycle food, its efficiency was limited. Skeletons show that the common people lived near the margin of malnutrition.

The cities' environment was destructive. On the nearby island of Thera, which a volcanic eruption blew apart around 1500 B.C.E., ash and rock buried the lavish city of Akrotiri. Knossos and similar palaces along the coasts of Crete were all rebuilt once or twice on an increasingly generous scale, after unknown causes, possibly earthquakes, destroyed them.

Fortifications—evidence of internal warfare—began to appear. At the time of the last rebuilding of Knossos, generally dated around 1400 B.C.E., a major change in culture occurred. The archives began to be written in an early form of Greek. By this time, the fate of Crete seems to have become closely entangled with another Aegean civilization—the Mycenean.

Mycenean Civilization

The fortified cities and gold-rich royal tombs of the Mycenean civilization began to appear early in the 1500s B.C.E. States in the region already had kings who made war, hunted lions, and inhabited palace-storehouses similar to those of Crete. At Pylos, one of the largest Mycenean palaces, clay tablets list the vital and tiresome routines of numerous palace officials: levying taxes, checking that the landowner class observed its social obligations, mobilizing resources for public works, and gathering raw materials for manufacture and trade. Workshops turned out bronze-ware and perfumed oils for export to Egypt and the Hittite empire. Trade reached north as far as Scandinavia (see Map 4.2), for eastern Mediterranean elites craved Baltic amber for glowing jewels.

The essential duty of the palace bureaucrats was to equip their rulers for almost constant warfare. Palaces were heavily fortified. As well as fighting each other, the kingdoms felt the threat of the barbarian hinterland, which may, in the end, have overwhelmed them. Paintings on the walls of Pylos show warriors, in the boar's-head helmets also worn on Crete and Thera, in battle with skin-clad savages.

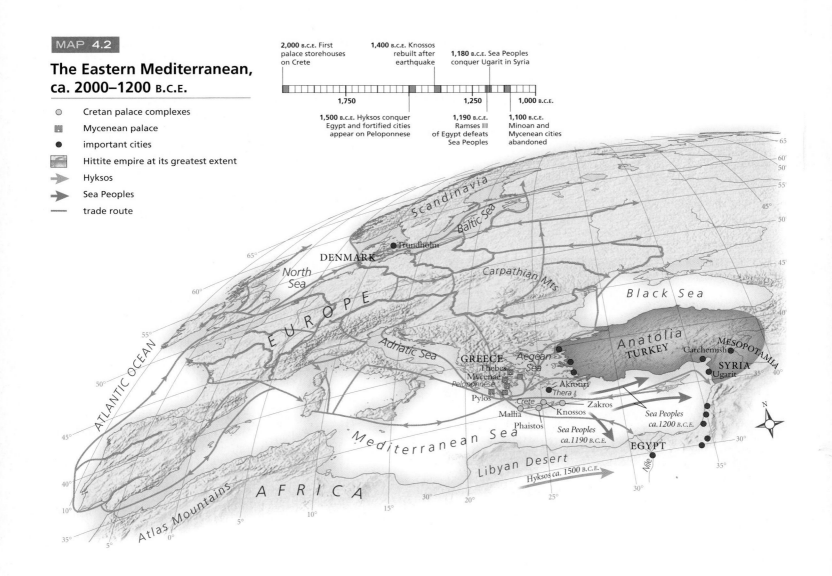

MAP 4.2

The Eastern Mediterranean, ca. 2000–1200 B.C.E.

○ Cretan palace complexes

▥ Mycenean palace

● important cities

▦ Hittite empire at its greatest extent

➤ Hyksos

➤ Sea Peoples

— trade route

2,000 B.C.E. First palace storehouses on Crete

1,500 B.C.E. Hyksos conquer Egypt and fortified cities appear on Peloponnese

1,750

1,400 B.C.E. Knossos rebuilt after earthquake

1,250

1,190 B.C.E. Ramses III of Egypt defeats Sea Peoples

1,180 B.C.E. Sea Peoples conquer Ugarit in Syria

1,000 B.C.E.

1,100 B.C.E. Minoan and Mycenean cities abandoned

Stunned by earthquakes, strained by wars, Mycenean cities followed those of Crete into abandonment by 1100 B.C.E. What is surprising is not, perhaps, that they should ultimately have perished, but that their fragile economies, sustained by elaborate and expensive methods of collecting, storing, and redistributing food, should have managed to feed the cities and support the elite culture for so long.

A GENERAL CRISIS IN THE EASTERN MEDITERRANEAN WORLD?

Although we could explain the extinction of Crete, Mycenae, and Hatti in terms of local political failures or ecological disasters, it is tempting to try to relate them to a general crisis in the eastern Mediterranean. For not only was the grandeur of the Aegean civilizations blotted out and the Hittite empire of Anatolia overwhelmed, but nearby states also reported fatal or near-fatal convulsions. The Egyptians almost succumbed to unidentified **Sea Peoples**, who exterminated numerous states and cities in the region. Meanwhile, in Upper Mesopotamia, an anguished king of Ashur prayed to Assur (AHS-soor), the city's god, "Darkness without sunshine awaits the evil-doers who stretch out threatening hands to scatter the armies of Assur. Wickedly, they conspire against their benefactor."

Crete and Mycenae

(All dates are approximate)	
2000 B.C.E.	First palace-storehouses on Crete
1400 B.C.E.	Knossos (Crete) rebuilt after earthquake; early Greek language used at Knossos
1100 B.C.E.	Cretan (Minoan) and Mycenean cities abandoned

The Egyptian Experience

Egypt had survived invasion before the Sea Peoples. Perhaps toward 1500 B.C.E., the Hyksos (HIUK-sohs) arrived, sweating from the Libyan desert, to overwhelm the land. Like so many nomadic conquerors of sedentary cultures around the world, the Hyksos became Egyptianized before they were expelled. For their part, Egyptians considered all foreigners barbarians and viewed them with contempt.

But the narrowness of the fertile Nile valley was a cause of unease, and Egyptians alternated between arrogance and insecurity. On the one hand, desert and sea constituted protection against barbarian attack. Egypt was flanked by almost uninhabitable spaces, difficult to cross, whereas civilizations, like those of Mesopotamia and Harappa, with more attractive environments at their frontiers, were under constant threat from marauders and invaders. On the other hand, sea and desert were the realm of Seth, the god of chaos who threatened to overwhelm the cosmic order of life along the Nile.

Exposure to invasion continued. The descent of the Sea Peoples—about 1190 B.C.E.—is well documented because the pharaoh who defeated them, Ramses III, devoted a long inscription to his achievement. It is glaring propaganda, a celebration of the pharaoh's power and preparation: "Barbarians," it says vaguely, "conspired in their islands . . . . No land could withstand their arms." A list of victims follows, including Hatti and cities along the eastern Mediterranean. "They were heading for Egypt, while we prepared flame before them . . . . They laid their hands on the land as far as the edges of the Earth, their hearts confident and trusting, 'We will succeed!'" The Nile delta, however, "made

Sea Peoples. "Now the northern peoples in their isles were quivering in their bodies," says the inscription that accompanies a ship-borne battle-scene of the reign of Ramses III. "They penetrated the channels of the mouths of the Nile.... They are capsized and overwhelmed where they stand.... Their weapons are scattered on the sea." Pharaohs' propaganda tended to lie or exaggerate, but the "Sea Peoples" really existed, and Egypt really escaped conquest or colonization by them.

like a strong wall with warships ... I was the valiant war-god, standing fast at their head. Those who came forward together on the sea, the full flame was in front of them at the river mouths, while a stockade of lances surrounded them on the shore. They were dragged in, enclosed, and prostrated on the beach, killed and made into heaps."

The Roots of Instability

The pharaoh's boasts reflect real events. Other documents confirm the existence of the Sea Peoples. For example, when the city of Ugarit in Syria fell, probably early in the twelfth century B.C.E., never to be reoccupied, messages begging for seaborne reinforcements were left unfinished. The reply from the governor of an inland trading center on the way to Hatti and Mesopotamia was typical—too little, too late: "You must remain firm. . . . Surround your towns with ramparts ..., and await the enemy with great resolution."

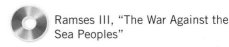 Ramses III, "The War Against the Sea Peoples"

The image of a general crisis brought about by barbarian invasions has appealed to Western historians influenced by a familiar episode of their own past: the decline and fall of the Roman Empire. A general crisis also fits with a popular conception of the past as a battlefield of barbarism versus civilization. However, such an idea is, at best, an oversimplification because both barbarism and civilization are relative, subjective terms.

We can best understand the intruders as a symptom of a broader phenomenon of the period: the widespread instability of populations driven by hunger and land shortages. Egyptian carvings show desperate migrants, with oxcarts full of women and children. From Mesopotamia and Anatolia comes evidence of marauders in the late thirteenth century B.C.E. But migrants probably did not cause the decline of the states they ravaged. Rather, they were among its consequences. Environmental and economic historians have scoured the evidence unsuccessfully for some sign of a deeper trauma, such as earthquakes or droughts or commercial failures, that might explain grain shortages and disrupted trade.

The causes of the crisis lay in common structural problems of the states that faltered or failed, namely, their ecological fragility and unstable, competitive politics. In this respect, the crisis was even more general, not just confined to the civilizations around the eastern Mediterranean where the Sea Peoples roamed. If we turn to trace the fate of communities elsewhere in Asia, and even to some examples in the New World, we can detect similar strains and comparable effects.

Instability in the Eastern Mediterranean

(All dates are approximate)	
1500 B.C.E.	Hyksos conquer Egypt
1200 B.C.E.	Sea Peoples attack Mesopotamia and Anatolia
1190 B.C.E.	Ramses III defeats Sea Peoples

THE EXTINCTION OF HARAPPAN CIVILIZATION

In the Indus valley, city life and intensive agriculture were in danger of collapse even when they were at their most productive. Many sites were occupied only for a few centuries. Some sites were abandoned by about 1800 B.C.E., and by 1000 B.C.E., all had dwindled to ruins. Meanwhile, in Turkmenia, on the northern flank of the Iranian plateau, relatively young but flourishing fortified settlements on the Oxus River (Amu Darya) shrank to the dimensions of villages. Some scholars believe a sudden and violent invasion was responsible, while others think of a gradual ecological disaster.

Selections from the *Rig Veda*

The Evidence of the *Rig Veda*

A collection of hymns and poems called the ***Rig Veda*** (rihg VEH-dah) inspired the invasion theory. The people who created this literature of destruction were sedentary speakers of an Indo-European language, living in what is now the Punjab, the area north of the Indus valley where northern India and Pakistan meet from about 1500 B.C.E. They were not newcomers or nomads, though strong in horses and chariots. When poets wrote down the *Rig Veda*, around 800 B.C.E., after centuries of oral transmission, it still had the power to carry hearers and readers back to a lost age of heroes.

The hymns tell of a people who wanted a world of fat and opulence, basted with butter, flowing with milk, dripping with honey. They valued boasting and drinking. Their rites of fire included burning down their enemies' dwellings. Their favorite god, Indra, was a "breaker of cities," but this was part of his generally destructive role, which included mountain smashing and serpent crushing.

Some of the cities seem already to have been in ruins when the *Rig Veda* poets beheld them. Excavators who claimed that they could read traumatic events at Mohenjodaro, in the bones of massacre victims and scorch marks on the walls, seem to have been wrong. Few of the supposed massacre victims have any wounds. Instead of a single violent event, the more likely explanation speaks of a gradual decline—a climacteric, a point at which Harappan civilization collapsed, and its cities were abandoned.

The Environment of Stress

The climate was getting drier in the Indus valley. The Saraswati River disappeared into the advancing Thar Desert. Yet not even the loss of a river adequately explains the abandonment of the cities. The Indus River is still disgorging its wonderful silt, year by year, over vast, shining fields, which would have been sufficient to maintain the urban populations. Presumably, something happened to the food supply that was connected with the drying climate or human mismanagement of environmental resources—the cattle and hinterland products that supplemented the wheat and barley of the fields.

In addition—or instead—the inhabitants apparently fled from some plague more deadly than the malaria that anthropologists have detected in buried bones. In an environment where irrigation demands standing water, mosquitos can breed. Malaria is inevitable. The people left, "expelled by the fire-god," as the *Rig Veda* says, and "migrated to a new land." This is probably an exaggeration. People stayed on or squatted in the decaying cities, inhabiting the ruins for generations. But the fall of Harappan civilization remains the most dramatic case of large-scale failure in the second millennium B.C.E. In broad terms, Harappa suffered essentially the same fate as the Hittite and eastern Mediterranean civilizations: The food distribution system outran the resource base. And when networks of power began to break down, invaders broke in.

The Collapse of Harappan Civilization

(All dates are approximate)	
1800 B.C.E.	Some Harappan cities abandoned
1000 B.C.E.	All Harappan cities in ruins
800 B.C.E.	*Rig Veda* written down

CONFLICT ON THE YELLOW RIVER

China's problems toward the end of the second millennium B.C.E. were part of what looks increasingly like a global pattern, yet different in some ways from those of Egypt or Harappa. China suffered no large-scale population loss, no wholesale abandonment of regions, no wreck of cities.

The basis of the Shang (shawng) state had always been shaky. War, rituals, and oracles are all gamblers' means of power, vulnerable to the lurches of luck. Manipulating the weather, the rains, the harvests, for instance, was part of the king's job, but in reality, of course, it was not one he could accomplish. Failure was built into his job description. It was a common problem for monarchs of the time, exposing pharaohs to blame for natural disasters, driving Hittite kings to depend on soothsayers.

The late Shang state was shrinking. Beginning about 1100 B.C.E., the names of subject, tribute-paying, and allied states gradually vanished from the oracle bones. The king's hunting grounds grew smaller. The king became the sole diviner and commander, as the numbers at his disposal fell. Former allies became enemies.

Meanwhile, just as Mesopotamian culture had been exported to Anatolia and Cretan ways of life to Mycenae, so Shang was exported beyond the Shang state. New chiefdoms were developing in less favorable environments under the influence of trade. As far away as northern Vietnam and Thailand, bronze-making techniques similar to those of China appeared at the courts of chiefs. More ominously and closer to home, right on the Shang border, a state arose in imitation and, increasingly, in rivalry: Zhou (jaow).

Bronze drum. This intricate geometric design on the face of a Vietnamese drum shows a sunburst at the center. Rulers often displayed these impressive bronze drums as emblems of their royal status.

The Rise of Zhou

The earliest Zhou sites—of the 1100s B.C.E.—are burials in the mountains of western China. This was probably not the Zhou heartland but the area they had migrated to from grazing country farther to the north. Their own legends recalled time spent "living among the barbarians." The Zhou were highland herders, an upland, upriver menace to the Shang, just as Akkad was to Sumer in Mesopotamia.

According to chronicle evidence, Shang-style turtleshell oracles had inspired the Zhou to conquest, and later Zhou rulers upheld that tradition. Chronicles composed in the third century B.C.E. tell the same story as texts hundreds of years older. If they can be believed, the Zhou "captured"—as they put it—the Shang state in a single battle in 1045 B.C.E. at Muye. They annexed it as a kind of colony and established garrisons all along the lower Yellow River to the coast. Archaeological evidence shows that they shifted the center of the empire north, to the hilly region west of where the Yellow River turns toward the sea.

The Zhou Political System

Inscriptions on bronze loving cups are the only contemporary written sources to survive from the period of Zhou supremacy, which lasted from about 1000 through the 700s B.C.E. Those who could afford them—and, of course, few could—recorded their inheritances, their legacies to their families, and, above all, the key moments in their family's relationships with the imperial house. Documenting the family's achievements was related to a belief in inherited virtue. Indeed, as an adviser to an early Zhou king put it: "there is nothing—neither wisdom nor power—that is not present at a son's birth."

The inscriptions tend to combine self-praise and self-justification. Shortly before 1000 B.C.E., for instance, a king's nephew recorded how he had been made ruler of the colony of Xing (shing). He tells us first of the royal decision to make the appointment. Then we get the circumstances: The nominee performs a rite of gratitude. He accompanies the king on a lake hunt in a ship with a red banner. The

Zhou China

1100 B.C.E.	Shang state in decline
1045 B.C.E.	Zhou overthrow Shang at Battle of Muye
1045–700 B.C.E.	Zhou supremacy

king bags a goose and gives the nominee a black axe. "In the evening, the lord was awarded many axe-men as vassals, two hundred families, and was offered the use of a chariot-team in which the king rode; bronze harness-trappings, an overcoat, a robe, cloth and slippers." The gifts apparently mattered a great deal because all such inscriptions mention them. The special clothes conferred status. The newly ennobled lord then commissioned a commemorative cup, which bore the inscription "With sons and grandsons, may he use it for ever to confer virtue, invoke blessings, and recall the order to colonize Xing."

The Zhou did not continue all Shang traditions. Despite pious declarations, they gradually abandoned divination by bone oracles. Though they extended China's cultural frontiers before their own state dissolved in its turn in the eighth century B.C.E., their leaders were not universal emperors in the mold of the Shang, ruling all the world that mattered to them. Rival states multiplied around them, and their own power tended to erode and fragment. But they originated the ideology of the **mandate of heaven**, which "raised up our little land of Zhou." All subsequent Chinese states inherited the same notion that the emperor was divinely chosen. Furthermore, all subsequent changes in rule appealed to the same claim that heaven transferred power from a decayed dynasty to one of greater virtue. The Zhou created an effective myth of the unity and continuity that dominated how the Chinese came to think of themselves. This myth is now the part of the standard Western view of China, too, as a monolithic state—massive, uniform, durable, and hungry for world dominance.

STATE-BUILDING IN THE AMERICAS

On a relatively smaller scale and over a longer time span, communities in parts of the New World experimented with some of the same processes of state-building and civilization that we have seen in the Old World. Some peoples of the Andean region and in Mesoamerica were particularly ambitious in modifying their environments.

Cerro Sechín. As urban life and monumental building spread upland from the river valleys of coastal central Peru in the second millennium B.C.E., warfare and rites of human sacrifice spread with them. Walls at Cerro Sechín are carved with scenes of warriors overseeing the severed heads and cleft bodies of their victims.

Andean Examples

About 3,500 years ago, experiments in civilization spread from alluvial areas on the Peruvian coast to less obviously favorable environments (see Map 4.3). In Cerro Sechín (SER-roh se-CHIN), only about 300 feet higher than the Supe (SOO-peh) valley in north-central Peru (see Chapter 2), an astounding settlement existed in about 1500 B.C.E. on a site of about 12 acres. On a stone platform 170 feet square, hundreds of carved warrior images slash their victims in two, exposing their entrails, or slicing off their heads in a rite of victory. By about 1200 B.C.E., nearby Sechín Alto (se-CHIN al-toh) was one of the world's great ceremonial complexes, with gigantic mounds erected to perform rituals, and monumental buildings arrayed along two boulevard-like spaces, each more than a mile long, at its heart. The biggest mound covers 30 square miles and is almost 140 feet tall.

These places, and others like them, suggest new experiments to manage the environment and coordinate food production in numerous small, hilly areas, each irrigated by a gravity canal and organized from a central seat of power. The violent carvings of Cerro Sechín show the price paid in blood to defend or enlarge them.

In the same period—in the last three centuries or so of the second millennium B.C.E.—farther up the coast, new settlements took shape around the Cupisnique (KOO-pees-nee-keh) gorge. Though the environment was similar, the physical remains suggest a different culture and different politics. Huaca de los Reyes (WA-kah deh las RAY-ess), for instance, had dozens of stucco-fronted buildings and colonnades of fat pillars, each up to 6.5 feet thick, guarded by huge, saber-toothed heads in clay. At Pampa de Caña Cruz (PAM-pah deh KAN-yah krooss), a gigantic mosaic, 170 feet long, represented a similar head, embedded in the earth, so that a viewer could only appreciate its shape from a height humans could not reach—but their gods, perhaps, could. These regions traded with nearby highlands, where building on a monumental scale followed soon afterward at sites that exhibit extraordinary cultural diversity.

Most Andean experiments in civilization were short-lived. With modest technologies, they struggled to survive in unstable environments. At irregular intervals, usually once or twice a decade, **El Niño** (el NEEN-yo)—the periodic reversal of the normal flow of Pacific currents—drenched the region in torrential rain and killed or diverted the ocean fish. Population levels outgrew food supplies, or overexploitation impoverished the soil, or envious neighbors unleashed wars.

The city of Chavín de Huantar (cha-VEEN deh wan-tar) began to emerge about 1000 B.C.E., over 3,300 feet up in the Andes. Chavín demonstrates how people could achieve prosperity and magnificence at middling altitudes. Essential prerequisites were command of trade routes and the availability of diverse foodstuffs in the microclimates of mountain environments. Gold-working technology, already at least 1,000 years old in the highlands, provided objects for luxury trade. Forest products from east of the mountains were also in demand in the lowland cities. Chavín was in the middle of these trades.

Even in the impressive world of early Andean civilizations, the sheer workmanship of Chavín stood out and attracted imitators in architecture, water management, engineering, metalwork, and ceramics. Today the ceremonial spaces, storehouses, and barrack-like dwellings inspire speculation about how this society was organized and ruled. The best clues are probably in the sculptures of humans half-transformed into jaguars, often with traces of drug-induced ecstasy. Nausea and bulging eyes contort their faces; their nostrils stream with mucus. Here is the evidence of a society ruled by shamans.

Developments in Mesoamerica

States developed in the Andes the same way they developed in the Old World—as responses to the stimulation of trade. Both followed the model described in Chapter 3: beginning with intensified agriculture, leading to population density, economic specialization, growing markets, and trade. In the Andes, the model emerged from the soil of Aspero in the Supe valley and climaxed in Chavín. In Mesoamerica, however, stunning experiments in civilization began, as far as we know, without the benefit of trade.

The culture we call Olmec (OL-mek) arose in southern Mexico in the second millennium B.C.E. (see Map 4.3). We can picture the Olmecs with help from portraits they left: heads, carved from stones and columns of basalt, each of up to 40 tons, toted or dragged over distances of up to 100 miles. Some have jaguarlike masks or almond eyes, parted lips, and sneers of cold command. Perhaps they, too, are shaman-rulers with the power of divine self-transformation, though they are never as thoroughly transformed as the coca-crazed shamans of Chavín.

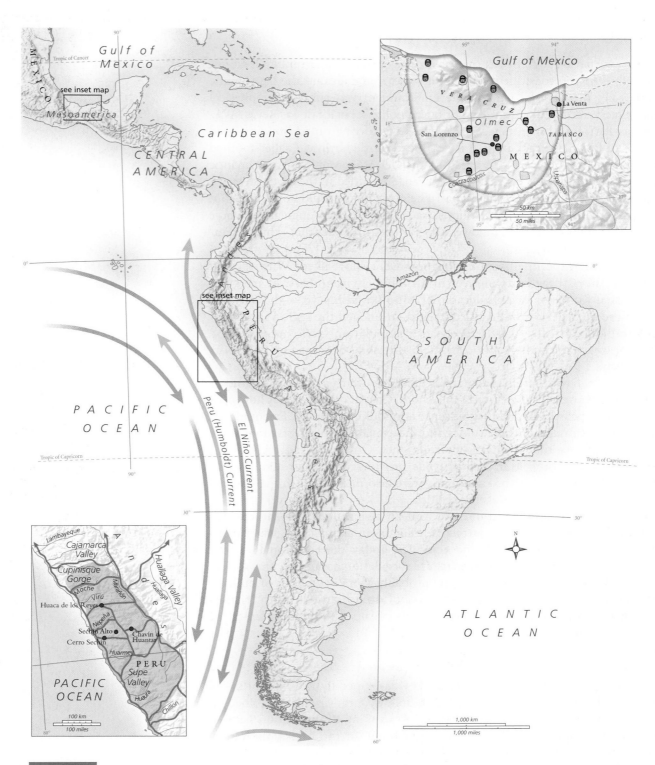

MAP 4.3

State-Building in the Americas, ca. 1500–1000 B.C.E

	Olmec cultural area		Olmec sculptural site
	Chavín cultural area	PERU	modern-day country
→	normal flow of Pacific Ocean current	*TABASCO*	state province
→	El Niño current		
PERU	modern-day country		
TABASCO	state province		

The swamps of southern Mexico had supported agriculture for at least 1,000 years before the first monumental art and ceremonial centers in the Olmec tradition appeared. The Olmec chose settlement sites where they could exploit a variety of environments. Marshy lakes, full of aquatic prey, were alluring to settlers. They dredged mounds for farming from the swamp and, between the mounds, coaxed canals into a grid for raising fish, turtles, and perhaps caymans.

The agricultural mounds became the model for ceremonial platforms. The earliest known ceremonial center was built around 1200 B.C.E. Two large centers soon followed, at La Venta, deep among the mangrove swamps, and at nearby San Lorenzo. By about 1000 B.C.E., San Lorenzo had substantial reservoirs and drainage systems, integrated into a plan of causeways, plazas, platforms, and mounds. At La Venta, there are early examples of the ritual spaces that fitted into these gridworks. The center was built with stones toted and rolled from more than 60 miles away. The focus of La Venta is a mound over 100 feet tall—evidently a setting for the most important rituals. One of the ceremonial courts has a mosaic pavement that resembles a jaguar mask that its creators appear to have deliberately buried. Similar buried offerings were placed under other buildings, perhaps the way some Christians bury relics from saints in the foundations and altars of churches. Although the stone buildings—those that survive—were designed for ritual life, these were cities: dense settlements clustered around the ceremonial centers.

Two unsolved problems exist in connection with the Olmecs: How and why did intensive food production begin? And how and why did ambitious attempts to modify the environment begin? Monumental building requires ample food to support manpower and generate energy. Many scholars still believe that the Olmecs could have produced sufficient food by slashing forest clearings, setting fire to the stumps, and planting seeds directly in the ash. But as far as we know, no society using such methods ever prospered the way the Olmecs did. It is more likely that the transition to city-building began when the Olmecs started farming high–yielding varieties of maize. With beans and squash, maize provided complete nourishment. The three plants together were so important to Olmec life that they depicted them on gods' and chieftains' headgear.

It looks as if a determined, visionary leadership energized by shamanism drove Olmec civilization forward. An exquisite scene of what seems to be a ceremony in progress suggests the seemingly pivotal role of shamanism. Archaeologists found it buried in sand, perhaps as an offering. Carved figures with misshapen heads, suggesting that the skull was deliberately deformed, stand in a rough circle of upright stone slabs. They wear nothing but loincloths and ear ornaments. Their mouths are open, their postures relaxed. Similar figures include a were-jaguar—half jaguar, half human. Others carry torches on phallic staffs. Or else they kneel or sit in a restless posture, as if ready to be transformed from shaman into jaguar, as other works depict. For the rites these figures suggest, the Olmecs built stepped platforms—forerunners, perhaps, or maybe just early examples of the angular mounds and pyramids typical of later New World civilizations.

Rulers were buried in the sort of disguises they wore for ritual performances. They became fantastic creatures with a cayman's body and nose, a jaguar's eyes and mouth, and feathered eyebrows that evoke raised hands. They lay in pillared chambers with bloodletting tools of jade or stingray spine beside them. We can still see their images carved on thrones of basalt, where they sat to shed blood—their own and their captives'.

Shaman. Masks, music, and dance often play roles in bringing about shamanic ecstasy. This ceramic flute-player from Chavín de Huántar in the Peruvian Andes, of the mid–first millennium B.C.E., wears a jaguar mask, with the bulging eyes and dilated nostrils typical of a visionary trance.

State-Building in the Americas

(All dates are approximate)	
1500 B.C.E.	Cerro Sechín (Peru)
1200 B.C.E.	Sechín Alto (Peru)
1000 B.C.E.	Chavín civilization emerges
1000 B.C.E.	Olmec cities of San Lorenzo and La Venta flourishing
500 B.C.E.	End of Chavín civilization
300 B.C.E.	Olmec civilization in decline

Believers in the diffusionist theory of civilization have often hailed the Olmecs as the mother civilization of the Americas. Diffusionism states, in brief, that civilization is such an extraordinary achievement that only a few gifted peoples created it. It then diffused—or spread by example and instruction—to less inventive peoples. This theory is almost certainly false. Rather, several civilizations probably emerged independently in widely separated places.

Nevertheless, Olmec influence seems to have spread widely in Mesoamerica and perhaps beyond. Numerous aspects of Olmec life became characteristic of later New World civilizations: mound building; a tendency to seek balance and symmetry in art and architecture; ambitious urban planning around angular temples and plazas; specialized elites, including chieftains commemorated in monumental art; rites of rulership involving bloodletting and human sacrifice; a religion rooted in shamanism with bloody rites of sacrifice and ecstatic performances by kings and priests; agriculture based on maize, beans, and squash.

ASSESSING THE DAMAGE

By 1000 B.C.E., failed states littered the landscape. Some of the world's spectacular empires broke up. Mysterious catastrophes cut short the histories of complex cultures. Food distribution centers controlled from palace labyrinths shut down. Trade was disrupted. Settlements and monuments were abandoned. Harappan civilization vanished, as did Crete's and Mycenae's. Hatti was obliterated.

In Mesopotamia, Akkadian armies spread their language the length of the Tigris and Euphrates. Sumerian speech dwindled from everyday use to become—like Latin in the Western world today—a purely ceremonial language. Sumer's cities crumbled. Their memory was preserved chiefly in the titles that invaders from uplands and deserts used to dignify the rule of their own kings. Ur declined to a cult center and tourist resort.

Something similar occurred in China, which succumbed to conquerors from neighboring uplands. The civilization survived, but its center of gravity was shunted upriver. As we shall see in Chapter 5, when numerous competing kingdoms in turn succeeded Zhou in the 700s B.C.E., continuity was not broken. Society and everyday life remained essentially intact. This was a pattern often repeated in Chinese history. In the New World, meanwhile, Mesoamerica and the Andean region undertook environmentally ambitious initiatives, but none showed much staying power.

The Survival of Egypt

Though there were more losers than winners after the climacteric of the second millennium B.C.E., the outstanding case of endurance was Egypt. Invasions in the late second millennium failed, and the basic productivity of the agrarian system remained intact. But even Egypt was reined in.

Nubia (NOO-bee-ah)—the region upriver of the cataracts, in what is now Sudan—disappeared from Egyptian records by 1000 B.C.E. This was a major reversal because Egypt had constantly tried to extend its empire along the Nile. The abundant ivory, the mercenaries that Nubia supplied, and the river trade that made gold in Egypt "as plentiful as the sand of the sea" had long drawn Egypt southward. Egypt originally became interested in Central Africa when the explorer Harkhuf made three expeditions around 2500 B.C.E. He brought back "incense, ebony, scented oil, tusks, arms, and all fine produce." Harkhuf's captive pygmy, "who dances divine dances from the land of the spirits..." fascinated the boy pharaoh Pepi. Writing to the explorer, the pharaoh commanded the utmost care in guarding him: "inspect him ten times a night. For my Majesty wishes to see this pygmy more than all the products of Sinai and Punt."

Contact and commerce led to the formation of a Nubian state in imitation of Egypt, beyond the second cataract. From about 2000 B.C.E. on, Egypt tried to influence or control this state, sometimes by erecting fortifications, sometimes by invasion, sometimes by pushing its own frontier southward. Pharoahs' inscriptions piled curses on the Nubians as the latter became more difficult to handle. Eventually, around 1500 B.C.E., Pharoah Tut-mose I conquered the kingdom of Kush and made Nubia a colonial territory. Egypt studded Nubia with forts and temples. The last temple, to Ramses II, at Abu Simbel, was the most crushingly monumental that Egyptians had built for 2,000 years. It has remained a symbol of power ever since. But during the reigns of his immediate successors, disastrously little flooding of the Nile, on which the success of Egyptian agriculture depended, was recorded. This was the era, toward the end of the thirteenth century B.C.E., when Egypt came closer to collapse than at any time since the invasion of the Hyksos. To abandon Nubia in the late second millennium B.C.E., after investing so much effort and emotion, shows how severe Egypt's need for retrenchment must have been.

◯ MAKING CONNECTIONS ◯

INSTABILITY: CONDITIONS LEADING TO DOWNFALL OF KINGDOMS 2000–1000 B.C.E.

KINGDOM AND REGION →	PRIMARY PROBLEMS →	CONSEQUENCES
Egypt	Exposure to invasion; limited areas of soil fertility; occasional grain shortages	Famines, land shortages, and sizable migrations; invasion by Sea Peoples exploits instability
Hatti—Northern Anatolia	Growth overlaps with frontiers of Egypt, Mesopotamia; overextension of power; disruption of trade through warfare; vulnerability to famine and disease in early stages of agriculture	Nomadic prowlers attack during weak periods, conquered subjects revolt
Crete—Aegean Sea	Uneven organization of labor; distribution of food; competition with other city-states; destruction of environment; little fertile soil; dangerous seas	Social inequality, internal warfare combine with nearby volcanic activity and earthquakes to force abandonment of cities, palaces
Mycenean Civilization	Barbarian raiders from north attracted by wealth of palaces; earthquakes; social inequality; internal warfare	Social inequality, internal warfare combine with nearby volcanic activity and earthquakes to force abandonment of cities, palaces
Harappa and Mohenjodaro: Indus River	Gradually drying climate; evidence of earthquakes, shifting riverbeds, disease; overuse of environmental resources	Gradual collapse of food distribution system; political control; cities and towns abandoned
Shang and Zhou Dynasties—China	Overdependence of Shang leaders on rituals, oracles, war, conquest to manipulate harvest, weather	Collapse of Shang rule; rise of Zhou state; shifting center of empire; lessened dependence on divination by bone oracles

CHRONOLOGY

(All dates are approximate)

2500 B.C.E.	Egypt expands southward
2000–1000 B.C.E.	Climacteric: critical and accelerating change; state-building in Hatti, Crete, Egypt; Shang China, the Andes, and Mesoamerica
2000 B.C.E.	Nubian state formed, emulating Egypt, Cretan civilization emerges
1800–1500 B.C.E.	Hittite kingdom flourishes
1500 B.C.E.	Mycenean civilization appears; Cerro Sechín flourishes in Andes (Peru)
1210 B.C.E.	Last record of Hatti
1190 B.C.E.	Ramses III defeats Sea Peoples
1100 B.C.E.	Cretan and Mycenean cities abandoned; Shang state in decline; Harappan cities in ruin; Chavín civilization emerges; Nubia disappears from Egyptian records
300 B.C.E.	Olmec civilization declines (Mesoamerica)

IN PERSPECTIVE: The Fatal Flaws

Paradox racked the most ambitious states of the era. They were committed to population growth, which imposed unsustainable goals of expansion on overextended frontiers. They were founded on intensified methods of production, which drove them to overexploit the environment. They concentrated large populations, making them more vulnerable to famine and disease. Enemies surrounded them, jealous of their wealth and resentful of their power. They created more enemies by inspiring rivals and imitators in their hinterlands. When their food distribution programs failed, disruptive migrations resulted. Their rulers condemned themselves to failure and rebellion because they lived a lie, manipulating unreliable oracles, negotiating with heedless gods, bargaining with hostile nature. If Harappan society was unsustainable in the silt-rich Indus valley, how realistic were the Hittite or Olmec or Cretan or Andean ambitions in much less favorable environments?

In some cases, the traditions that failed or faltered during the great climacteric reemerged elsewhere. In others, dark ages of varying duration—periods of diminished achievement, about which we have little evidence—followed the climacteric. Chavín survived for about 500 years, until about 500 B.C.E., but during the following several centuries, people in the Andes attempted nothing on a comparable scale. After the Olmec stopped building on a large scale, probably in the 300s B.C.E., they had no successors for many centuries. Squatters occupied the cities of Harappa and Mycenae. The literacy of these civilizations was lost, their writing systems forgotten. When writing resumed in these regions centuries later, the inhabitants had to invent new alphabets.

Our next problem is to penetrate that darkness and trace the displaced traditions from failed states. We want to examine the context that would produce a different world after the climacteric, post-1000 B.C.E. In the last millennium B.C.E.—thanks to an extraordinary blossoming of intellectual and spiritual life—the world was literally rethought.

PROBLEMS AND PARALLELS

1. How did the features that characterized the great river valley civilizations begin to emerge in other environments in the second millennium B.C.E.?

2. Why did the number of complex states rapidly increase during this period?

3. Why did the Hittite kingdom fall? Why did Cretan and Mycenean civilization collapse and disappear in this period, while Egypt survived?

4. What factors might account for the long-term survival of Chinese civilization and the collapse and disappearance of Harrapan/Indus valley civilization?

5. Why is the period between 2000 and 1000 B.C.E. a climacteric in global history?

DOCUMENTS IN GLOBAL HISTORY

- Hittite Land Deed
- Hittite Soldiers' Oath

- Ramses III, "The War Against the Sea Peoples"
- Selections from the *Rig Veda*

Please see the Primary Source DVD for additional sources related to this chapter.

READ ON

T. Bryce, *Life and Society in the Hittite World* (2002) is incomparable in its field. To understand the nature and importance of trade, the books of M. W. Helms, *Ulysses' Sail* (1988) and *Craft and the Kingly Ideal* (1993) are of great help. M. Heltzer, *Goods, Prices and the Organisation of Trade in Ugarit* (1978), and E. H. Cline, *Sailing the Wine-Dark Sea* (1994) are valuable studies of particular trade routes.

The best book on Crete is now O. Dickinson, *The Aegean Bronze Age* (1994). E. D. Oren, ed., *The Sea Peoples and Their World* (2000) is an important collection.

Leading works on the so-called Indo-Europeans are J. P. Mallory, *In Search of the Indo-Europeans* (1989), and C. Renfrew, *Archaeology and Language* (1987). The books listed for Chapter 3 by Shaghnessy, Posspehl, and Bulger remain important for this chapter.

Especially useful on the Olmecs are M. D. Coe, ed., *The Olmec World: Ritual and Rulership* (1996), and E. Benson and B. de la Fuente, eds., *Olmec Art of Ancient Mexico* (1996). D. O'Connor, *Ancient Nubia* (1994) is a good introductory work.

CHAPTER 5

Rebuilding the World: Recoveries, New Initiatives, and Their Limits

The elephant wall of Anuradhapura, the city in northern Sri Lanka that became a courtly center in the second half of the first millennium B.C.E., when kings endowed it with great irrigation cisterns, monumental trees, and sites of sacrifice, pilgrimage, and monastic life. The elephants guard a stupa—a dome-like spiritual dwelling place for the Buddha—built in the second century B.C.E. (See pp. 111–112.)

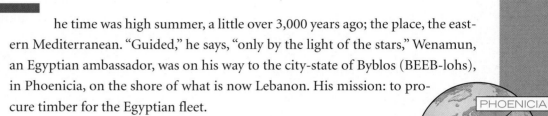

PHOENICIA

The time was high summer, a little over 3,000 years ago; the place, the eastern Mediterranean. "Guided," he says, "only by the light of the stars," Wenamun, an Egyptian ambassador, was on his way to the city-state of Byblos (BEEB-lohs), in Phoenicia, on the shore of what is now Lebanon. His mission: to procure timber for the Egyptian fleet.

On arrival he set up an altar to Egypt's chief god, Amun. King Zeker Baal kept Wenamun waiting for weeks. Then the king suddenly summoned the ambassador in the dead of night. Presumably, the summons was a negotiating ploy. Wenamun, however, reported it as a change of heart. The ambassador recorded the dialogue that followed—doctored, no doubt, but still revealing.

"I have come," Wenamun began, "for timber for the great and august ship of Amun, king of gods." He recalled that Zeker Baal's father and grandfather had sent wood to Egypt, but the king resented the implication that it was tribute.

"They did so by way of trade," he replied. "When you pay me I shall do it... I call loudly to the Lebanon which makes the heavens open, and the wood is delivered to the sea."

"Wrong!" retorted Wenamun. "There is no ship which does not belong to Amun. His also is the sea. And his is the Lebanon of which you say, 'It is mine.' Do his bidding and you will have life and health."

In the end, the Egyptians had to pay Zeker Baal's price: four jars of gold and five of silver, unspecified amounts of linen, 500 ox hides, 500 ropes, 20 sacks of lentils, 20 baskets of fish. "And they felled the timber," Wenamun wrote, "and they spent the winter at it and hauled it to the sea."

● ● ● ● ●

The Egyptian ambassador's story opens a window into a world recovering from the crises and climacteric of the late second millennium B.C.E. The confidence of a small city-state like Byblos in the face of demands from a giant like Egypt seems astounding. But increasing trade and cultural exchange inspired it.

The question for this chapter, then, is what happened between 1000 and 500 B.C.E. that led some places to recover from the failures of the second millennium? The investigation will equip us to approach a far bigger problem in the next part of this book: How do we explain the vitality and influence—the intellectual and spiritual achievements—of some groups and centers in Eurasia in the period that followed?

FOCUS questions

● WHY WAS the Phoenician alphabet so significant in world history?

● WHAT WERE the political and economic foundations of the Assyrian Empire?

● WHAT ROLES did colonization and trade play in Greek and Phoenician cultures?

● WHY DID the Zhou state decline in China?

● HOW WAS civilization built anew in India and Sri Lanka?

● HOW DID geography influence the transmission of culture in the Americas and Africa?

Equally important is the problem of why new initiatives were so rare, late, and slow beyond Eurasia. In particular, why did promising states in the Americas and sub-Saharan Africa wither instead of thrive in this period? Why, for example, was Greece's dark age after the fall of Mycenae so much shorter than the dark ages of the Andes after Chavín or Mesoamerica after the Olmecs? Why did big states and monumental cities appear later in sub-Saharan Africa than in China, India, or the Mediterranean? And why did so much historical initiative—the power of some human groups to influence others—become so concentrated in a few regions?

The best way to approach these questions is to look first at recovery in the Middle East, the Mediterranean, China, and India, before turning to see how isolation frustrated Africa and the Americas.

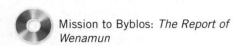

Mission to Byblos: *The Report of Wenamun*

TRADE AND RECOVERY IN THE MIDDLE EAST

Byblos was one of the largest city-states of Phoenicia, a maritime culture along the eastern coast of the Mediterranean (see Map 5.1), from where, beginning early in the first millennium B.C.E., traders and colonists spread. Meanwhile, however, new, land-based empires arose that grew rich as much by conquest as by trade, threatening and eventually engulfing Phoenicia.

The Phoenician Experience

In front of them, Phoenicians had waters accessible through excellent harbors. Behind them, they had forests for shipbuilding and timber exports. What they did not have was much land to farm. They turned, therefore, to industry and trade.

Their wealth was the stuff of other peoples' stories. Phoenician cities stood, as the biblical prophet Ezekiel said of Tyre, "at the entry of the sea . . . a trader for the people of many isles. Their ports ring with precious metals, exude aromas of spice, and swirl with dye-steeped textiles. But the basis of everything is shipbuilding: the timbers from Lebanon, the oak for the oars, benches of ivory, sails of Egyptian linen, and mariners and builders from the Phoenician coast."

This was a period when the only way to trade with a region that did not have its own merchant class was to colonize it. According to legend, the Phoenicians' earliest colonies were at Carthage in what is now Tunisia and at Cadiz in Spain by around 800 B.C.E., followed by Malta and Sardinia. From these bases, Phoenician navigators broke into the Atlantic and established a trading post as far away as Mogador on the northwest coast of Africa.

Where they built cities, the Phoenicians were agents of cultural exchange, borrowing from all over the eastern Mediterranean, while exporting some of their religious cults. In Carthage, newborn babies rolled from the arms of statues of their gods, Baal and Tanit, as sacrifices into sacred flames.

The colonies remained, even when the cities of Phoenicia fell to foreign raiders or rulers. In 868 B.C.E. the king of Assur (see Chapter 4) "washed his weapons in the Great Syrian Sea," and his successors continued to grab tribute from Phoenicia for over a century. Egypt-

Phoenicia

(All dates are approximate)	
1000 B.C.E.	Phoenicia trades and colonizes in the Mediterranean
800 B.C.E.	Carthage founded as a Phoenician colony
700 B.C.E.	Malta and Sardinia colonized
500 B.C.E.	Carthage seeks control of Mediterranean trade
146 B.C.E.	Carthage destroyed by the Romans

ian, Babylonian, and Persian rulers preyed on the region. By 500 B.C.E., Carthage aspired to be an imperial capital of its own, fighting to control Mediterranean trade—first with Greek cities, then with Rome. It had a fine harbor in the center of the Mediterranean and a fertile hinterland of flocks, wheat fields, vineyards, and irrigated gardens.

A Roman poet later recalled Phoenicians as "a clever people who prospered in war and peace. They excelled in writing and literature and the other arts, as well as in seamanship, naval warfare, and ruling over an empire." Their records might illuminate for us the dark age of lack of sources after the fall of Mycenae, but the Romans, who defeated Carthage in three wars and destroyed the city in 146 B.C.E., were too thorough in victory. The Phoenician language and almost the whole of Phoenician literature disappeared. Only fragments of stone inscriptions survive, along with the Phoenicians' unique gift to the world, the alphabet.

All writing systems, as far as we know, except those indebted to the Phoenician, are based on syllables, logograms, or some combination of both. In the former, each sign represents a syllable. In the second type, a sign stands for an entire word. Both methods require the user to know a large number of signs—dozens in the syllabic system and hundreds or even thousands in a logographic one. Systems in the Phoenician tradition, on the other hand, suit societies with wide literacy and cheap writing materials. The Greeks seem to have gotten the idea of an alphabet and some of the symbols from the Phoenicians. From there, the idea spread to the Romans and other European peoples who, in turn, transmitted it around the world.

The Assyrian Empire

By 1000 B.C.E., Hatti's extinction was Assur's opportunity (see Chapter 4). Kings of Assur, who were already wide-scale raiders, forged a state along the Upper Tigris. By about 750 B.C.E., Assyrian rulers were contending for more than regional power, calling themselves "Kings of the World" (see Map 5.1).

In northern Mesopotamia, the Assyrian kings replaced local rulers with governors, who ran provinces too small to mount successful rebellions. Beyond this core, Assyrian supremacy was looser, adjusted to local feeling and custom. In Babylon, for instance, the king of Assyria performed the rite of allegiance to the city god; in Gaza, near the border between modern Israel and Egypt, he was enrolled among local divinities. Elsewhere, he destroyed temples and statues of gods to demonstrate his power and then restored them to show his generosity.

An ideology of domination is obvious in the remnants of Assyria that archaeologists have dug up: in the crushing weight of palace gates, the gigantic scale of the royal beasts that guard them, and the monumental sculptures, with their endless portrayals of battles and tribute bearers. The king was not divine but heroic and intimate with gods. In portraits he kills bulls and lions and consults heaven, while winged spirits attend him. He literally entertained gods in his bedchamber. Attendants brought the statues of gods in and offered them food and libations.

Inscriptions from the reign of King Ashurbanipal (ah-shoor-BAH-nee-pahl) in the mid–seventh century B.C.E. capture the character of the Assyrian state. He was probably the most self-celebrated monarch in Mesopotamian history. While never dethroning war as the Assyrians' priority, he made a cult of literacy, looting the learning of Babylon for his library at Nineveh (NIH-neh-veh). He was proud of the canals dug and the wine pressed in his reign, the 120 layers of bricks in the foundations of his palace, the offerings he made of first fruits to "the temples of my land." A portrait survives of him picnicking with his wife under a vine and the dangling head of a slain enemy.

Winged bull. "May the guardian bull, the guardian genius, who protects the strength of my throne, always preserve my name in joy and honor until his feet move themselves from this place." An inscription left by King Esarhaddon, son of Sennacherib, explains the function of the winged bulls—usually carved with the portrait heads of kings—that guarded Assyrian gates and throne rooms. *Human-headed winged bull and winged lion (lamassu). Alabaster (gypsum); Gateway support from the Palace of Ashurnasirpal II (ruled 883–859 B.C.E.). Limestone. H: 10' 3/1/2". L: 9' 1". W: 2" 1/2". The Metropolitan Museum of Art, Gift of John D. Rockefeller, Jr., 1932. (32.143.2) Photography © 1981 The Metropolitan Museum of Art.*

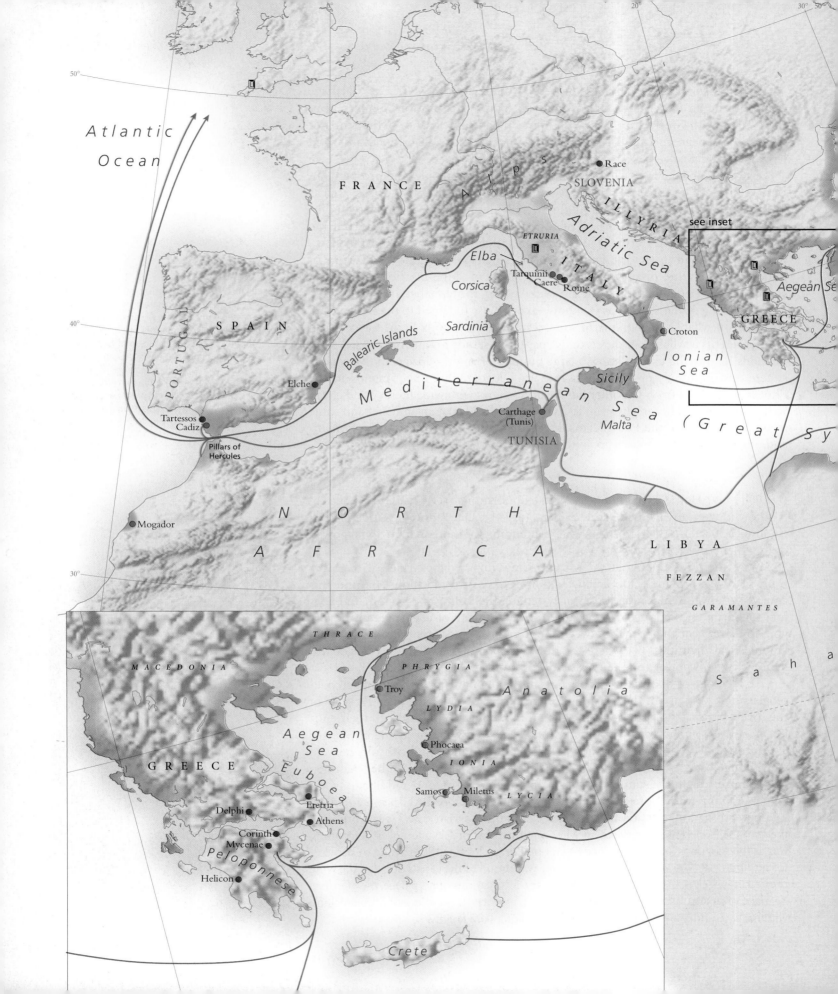

Atlantic
Ocean

FRANCE

SLOVENIA
Race

ILLYRIA

Adriatic Sea

ETRURIA
Elba
ITALY
Tarquinii
Caere
Rome

Corsica

GREECE

see inset

Aegean Se

SPAIN

Sardinia

Croton

PORTUGAL

Balearic Islands

Elche

Ionian
Sea

Mediterranean

Sea (Great Sy

Sicily

Tartessos
Cadiz

Carthage
(Tunis)

Malta

Pillars of
Hercules

TUNISIA

Mogador

NORTH

LIBYA

AFRICA

FEZZAN

GARAMANTES

THRACE

Sahara

MACEDONIA

PHRYGIA

Troy

Anatolia

LYDIA

Aegean
Sea

Phocaea

GREECE

Euboea

IONIA

LYCIA

Samos
Miletus

Delphi
Eretria

Athens

Corinth
Mycenae

Peloponnese

Helicon

Crete

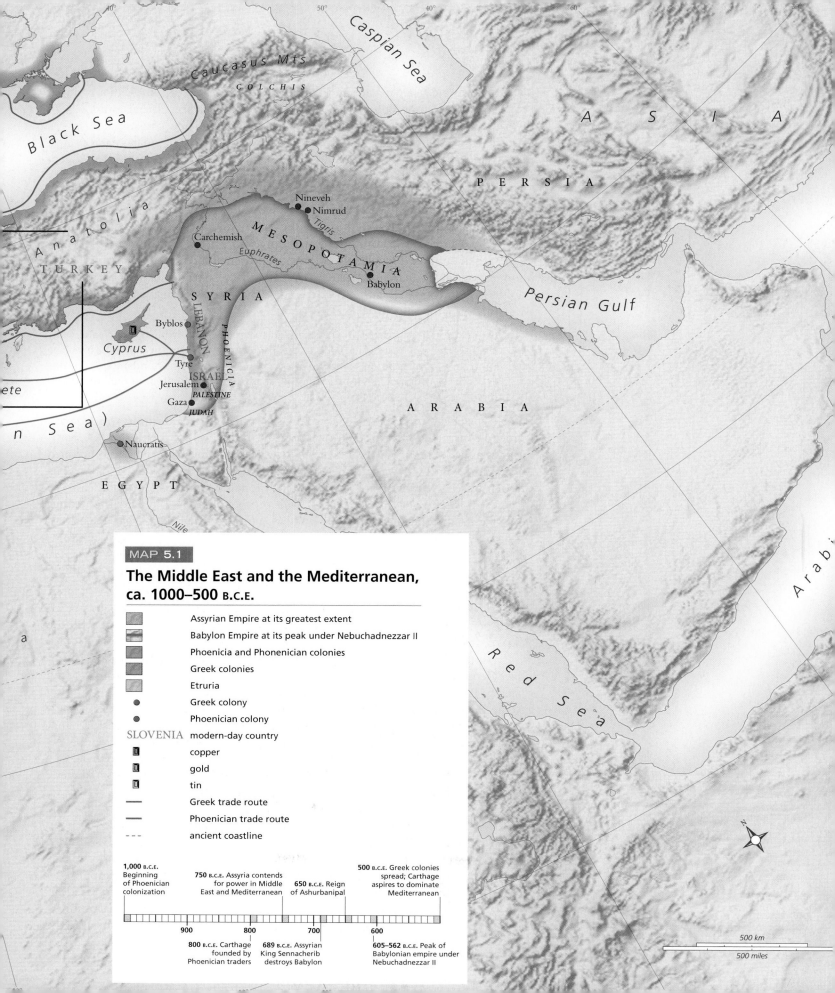

Black Sea

Caspian Sea

Caucasus Mts
COLCHIS

A S I A

Anatolia

P E R S I A

TURKEY

Nineveh
Nimrud

M E S O P O T A M I A

Carchemish

Tigris

Euphrates

S Y R I A

Babylon

LEBANON

Byblos

Cyprus

PHOENICIA

Persian Gulf

Tyre

ISRAEL

Jerusalem

A R A B I A

PALESTINE

Gaza

JUDAH

ete

n Sea)

Naucratis

E G Y P T

Nile

Red Sea

Arab

MAP 5.1

The Middle East and the Mediterranean, ca. 1000–500 B.C.E.

Assyrian Empire at its greatest extent
Babylon Empire at its peak under Nebuchadnezzar II
Phoenicia and Phonenician colonies
Greek colonies
Etruria
● Greek colony
● Phoenician colony
SLOVENIA modern-day country
copper
gold
tin
Greek trade route
Phoenician trade route
--- ancient coastline

1,000 B.C.E. Beginning of Phoenician colonization

750 B.C.E. Assyria contends for power in Middle East and Mediterranean

650 B.C.E. Reign of Ashurbanipal

500 B.C.E. Greek colonies spread; Carthage aspires to dominate Mediterranean

900   800   700   600

800 B.C.E. Carthage founded by Phoenician traders

689 B.C.E. Assyrian King Sennacherib destroys Babylon

605–562 B.C.E. Peak of Babylonian empire under Nebuchadnezzar II

500 km
500 miles

To celebrate a new palace and flaunt his wealth, Ashurbanipal held a banquet for 16,000 citizens, 5,000 visiting dignitaries, 1,500 palace officials, and 47,074 workmen "summoned from all over the kingdom." They consumed history's biggest meal: 10,000 jugs of beer; 10,000 skins of wine; 30,000 quarts each of figs, dates, and shelled pistachios; 1,000 each of lambs and fat oxen; 14,000 sheep; 20,000 pigeons; 10,000 eggs; 10,000 desert rats; and hundreds of deer. "For ten days I gave them food, I gave them drink, I had them bathed, I had them anointed. I honored them and sent them back to their lands in peace and joy."

Like Egyptian and Chinese rulers, the Assyrian kings sought to enhance their power by claiming to communicate with forces in Nature—a doomed enterprise. When their supposed magic failed, they lost power, and competing factions arose. Some Assyrian monarchs asserted their legitimacy so vigorously as to make us doubt it. Ashurbanipal's father tried to secure the succession against rebellion with 150 lines of oaths and curses:

> Just as the noise of doves is persistent, so may you, your women, your sons, your daughters have no rest or sleep. Just as the inside of a hole is empty, may your inside be empty. Just as gall is bitter, so may you, your women, your sons, your daughters, be bitter . ... May your waterskin break in a place of thirst and famine, so that you die of thirst.

In the background of internal conflicts was a harem of ambitious women with time to conspire in favor of their own sons. In the early eighth century B.C.E., Sammuramat was one such woman who effectively ruled the empire and accompanied her son to war. Naqia was another. She was virtual coruler with her husband, Sennacherib (seh-NAH-keh-rihb), the Assyrian monarch famed for descending on the Hebrew holy city of Jerusalem "like a wolf on the fold." She did everything kings did, from dedicating inscriptions to building a palace and receiving war dispatches.

The Babylonian Revival

As the cities of southern Mesopotamia declined, trade shifted upriver to Babylon. To Assyrians, Babylon was always the great prize, and it became part of their empire. But Babylonians frequently rebelled. In 689 B.C.E., Sennacherib massacred or dispersed the population and dug channels across the site of the city, with the aim of turning it into a swamp.

Ashurbanipal resumed the policy of vengeance. In 649 B.C.E., he was said to have deported 500,000 people from their homes to prevent anyone from stealing back to Babylon, "and those still living," he announced, "I sacrificed as an offering to the spirit of my grandfather, Sennacherib." Yet the name of Babylon was a rallying point for native resistance to Assyria. A reversal of fortunes was at hand. Overextended Assyria succumbed to enemies in the 620s. In the late seventh century B.C.E., Nabopolassar masterminded a Babylonian revival. His boast was that he "defeated Assyria, which, from olden days had made people of the land bear its heavy yoke."

Babylon now became an imperial metropolis again, exploiting the vacuum Assyria's collapse left. Its fame peaked during the long reign (605–562 B.C.E.) of Nebuchadnezzar (neh-boo-kahd-NEH-zahr) II. Ancient Greek guidebooks attributed two of the seven wonders of the world to him: the terraced "hanging" gardens of Babylon, supposedly built to please a concubine, and city walls broad enough to race four chariots abreast. Nebuchadnezzar was a master of theatrical gestures, a genius at attracting esteem. He cultivated an image of himself as the

Assyria and Babylon

(All dates are approximate)

750 B.C.E.	Assyria becomes an empire
689 B.C.E.	Sennacherib destroys city of Babylon
620s B.C.E.	Assyrian empire falls; Ashurbanipal is last king
605–562 B.C.E.	Peak of Babylonian empire under Nebuchadnezzar II

● MAKING CONNECTIONS

CONDITIONS LEADING TO RECOVERY IN MIDDLE EAST AND MEDITERRANEAN

STATE →	TYPE OF LEADERSHIP AND INITIATIVES →	EFFECTS
Phoenician city-states	Merchant elites; economy based on trade and proximity to forest, mineral, metal resources; colonization of Mediterranean	Spread of Phoenician technical knowledge, culture, and alphabet throughout Mediterranean
Assyrian Empire	Powerful king with provincial governors; cult of personality combined with ideology of domination; palace-building, other monumental architecture	Imperial state based on upper Tigris River spreads to lower Mesopotamia, Mediterranean coast
Babylonian Empire	Strong city-state asserts independence, becomes imperial center after decline of Assyrians; large-scale building projects; monumental architecture	Large metropolis becomes regional political/trade/cultural center; Babylon and Egypt battle for control of regional resources

restorer of ancient glories by rebuilding ziggurats and city walls all over Mesopotamia. On what survives of his showy works, bulls, lions, and dragons strut in glazed brick.

Whether because Nebuchadnezzar overreached himself or because his dynasty could produce no more dynamic leaders, his was Babylon's last era of greatness. In effect, Babylon and Egypt fought each other to exhaustion in their efforts to replace Assyria. Five centuries later, the Greek geographer Strabo reflected that Babylon had been "turned to waste" by the blows of invaders and the indifference of rulers. "The great city has become a great desert."

GREECE AND BEYOND

In the late second millennium B.C.E., when the Sea Peoples and other displaced communities disrupted the eastern Mediterranean and threatened Egypt (see Chapter 4), a similar upheaval took place on land. Migrants from the north swept into southern Greece, eradicating literate culture. Refugees streamed across the Aegean and Ionian Seas to Italy, Anatolia, and islands in the eastern and central Mediterranean.

The Greek Environment

By early in the first millennium B.C.E., the Mycenean palace centers were in ruins. The only stone or rubble buildings from this period that we know of in Greece were on the island of Euboea. Few iron tools were available for farming. Barley was the staple crop, laboriously cultivated. Most Greeks lived by goat farming and in thatched huts.

Industry and trade were ways to escape. In the tenth century B.C.E. Athens, Corinth, and a few other centers exported finely decorated pots and pressed olives—the only surplus farm product—for their oil. Neighboring peoples considered the Greeks' barley unfit to eat. But olive oil was exportable and came from a crop whose care was seasonal and left time for seafaring. Olives would grow in ground that grains disdained at altitudes over 2,000 feet. It had many uses. Olive oil added fat to poor diets and could be used as lamp-fuel or for cleansing the body. Olive processors invested profits in promoting trade. Commercial enterprise lined the Aegean and Ionian Seas with cities and, from the mid–eighth century B.C.E.

onward, spread over the Mediterranean and the Black Sea. The Greeks lived, they said, "around a sea, like frogs around a pond."

The Greek poet Hesiod recorded a conversation that evokes the way Greece took to the sea. Perses, his younger brother, was lolling around their humble farm while Hesiod sweated at the plow. "Greece and poverty are sisters," Perses began. "How can I make money easily?" Hesiod recommended working on the land. But Perses was the type of person who asks for advice only because he wants to confirm his own opinion. He revealed what he really wanted: "to buy and sell in distant markets." "Please don't be a fool," rejoined Hesiod. "Money may be all you want in life, but it is not worth the risk of drowning. . . . Be moderate, my brother. Moderation is best in everything."

All over Greece, however, men like Perses won the arguments. Greek writers included merchants and explorers among their heroes, something unthinkable, for example, in China of the time, which valued only farmers, warriors, and scholars. In the 500s B.C.E., trade was growing so rapidly that some Greek states introduced their own coinage and designed and built new, larger types of ships.

Greek Colonialism

By Hesiod's time, iron tools improved agriculture and increased food production, which in turn led to an increase in population. But more people meant more demands on food and land. Now, not only were the Greeks a trading people, but they also became colonizers (see Map 5.1). Greek experience echoed that of Phoenicia: city-communities at home, outreach by sea, colonies abroad.

The Greeks founded colonies on the advice of gods who spoke through oracles. At Delphi, where smoke rose from deep crevices in the earth, a priestess uttered divine pronouncements from a three-legged throne cast in the form of writhing serpents. One supplicant went to the shrine to find a remedy for childlessness, with no thought of starting a colony, and received orders to found Croton in southern Italy. Others were told to colonize to escape famine. Founding colonies became so much a part of Greek life that a comic playwright speculated on the chances of founding one in the sky. "Not that we hate our city," the would-be colonists protest, "for it is a prosperous mighty city, free for all to spend their wealth in, paying fines and fees."

Most colonists were outcasts, exiles, and criminals—frontiersmen forging a new society. But wherever they went, they reproduced Greek ways of life. At Naucratis in the Nile delta, for example, colonists dedicated shrines to cults from their home towns—the goddess Hera of Samos and the Sun-god Apollo of Miletus. In the sixth and fifth centuries B.C.E., offerings to Aphrodite, goddess of love, show a steady stream of Greek sex-tourists to the lively local brothels. Such sober travelers as Solon, the great lawgiver of Athens, also visited Naucratis. They came to Egypt on business or on a grand tour in search of enlightenment from a great civilization.

Meanwhile, growing contacts inspired Greek artists and thinkers. The sea washed new cultural influences back toward Greece. Unlike so many of the earlier systems that were developed to catalog merchandise or record trade transactions, the Greek alphabet was rapidly used to record creative literature and preserve epic poems that bards once recited at warriors' drinking parties. Poems attributed to the bard Homer, for instance, were written down in their surviving versions probably toward the end of the second century B.C.E. They have been revered—and imitated—ever since in the West for the brilliance with which they evoke war and seafaring. The *Iliad* tells a story of the interplay of gods and mortals during a mili-

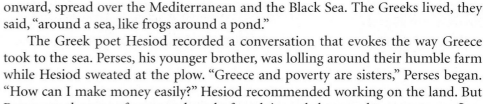

Hesiod, excerpt from *Works and Days*

Olive harvest. The export of olive oil was vital to Greece's recovery from the so-called "dark ages" that followed the fall of Mycenean cities. Greece's poor soils and hot climate could not produce much else that was salable abroad. Solon, the legendary lawgiver, supposedly compelled the Athenians to grow olives. Scenes of laborious techniques to harvest olives from their trees decorate this vase by the most prolific Athenian artist of the late sixth century B.C.E., known as the Antimenes Painter.

tary expedition from Mycenae to the city of Troy in what is now Turkey. The *Odyssey* recounts the wanderings of one of the heroes of the same war on his way home. The *Iliad* bristles with ships' masts. The *Odyssey* is loud with waves. Greek literature rarely strayed far from the sea.

Early Greek Society

Greeks had a remarkably uniform set of ideas about themselves—"our community of blood and language and religion and ways of life." Some of their notions were mythical, and Western tradition has multiplied the myths. We have idealized the Greeks as originators of our civilization and embodiments of all our values. However, scholars have been revising almost everything that has traditionally been said about them. The Greek gods appear no longer as personifications of virtues and vices but as unpredictable and often demonic manipulators. Their world—and the imagination of most Greeks who shared it—was run not by reason but by weird and bloody rites, goat dances, orgiastic worship, sacrifices, signs, and omens.

Greeks lived in relatively small communities of citizens who saw themselves living together out of choice. Political institutions took many different forms, including hereditary and elected monarchies and states with ruling elites, defined by blood or wealth. *Demokrateia* meant a state where supreme power belonged to an assembly of all citizens. But most Greeks disapproved of such an arrangement. Only privileged males were citizens. Women were excluded. So were slaves, who made up 40 percent of the population in the fifth century B.C.E. Athens. In some Greek states, citizens used bits of broken pottery as ballots on which to scrawl their votes to exile unpopular leaders. When we look at them now, we see fragments of an oppressive system that made slaves of captives, victims of women, battle fodder of men, and scapegoats of failures.

Families—groups based on monogamous couples and their descendants—were the basis of society in Greek communities. When Aristotle, the greatest of Greek scholars, speculated in the fourth century B.C.E. about the origins of the state, he assumed that it arose from the voluntary alliance of families. In Athens, some of the earliest group burials known to archaeologists are in family plots. Typically, girls married at age 14 or 15 to men twice their age. So men dominated. "The Greeks," said a writer of the fourth century B.C.E., "expect their daughters to keep quiet and do woolwork."

Myth eliminated women from Athenian origins—the founders of the community supposedly sprang from the soil. Wives and daughters did not normally inherit property. They rarely appeared in public, except as emotional mourners or as priestesses in religious cults. In art of the first half of the millennium, men are shown more and more in the company only of other men, women only with other women. Women's function was to serve the community by bearing and raising children and thereby increasing manpower for production and war. In the city-state of Sparta—which Greeks always regarded as "utterly different" from other Greek states—all women had to train for motherhood, and women who died in childbirth were commemorated in the same way as heroic warriors killed in battle.

 Aristotle, "The Creation of the Democracy in Athens"

 Plutarch on education and family in Sparta

Greek women. Women collecting water from a fountain was a common subject for Greek painters of water pots. This example from the Greek colony of Vulci in Italy, where the native population esteemed women more highly than the Greeks did, follows a standard Greek pattern. It shows the women in profile, forming a line at a fountain with a lion's-head spout under a roof supported by slender columns.

Scholars used to infer Greek values and morality from philosophical writings, but now we also look to popular plays and satires and find that the average Greek's social attitudes were different from the philosophers'. Athenian elites, for instance, tended to idealize homosexual relationships between older men and boys, but the playwrights' audiences despised them. At times, Plato (see Chapter 6) called for women to be men's equal partners, but popular literature almost always presented women as despicable. Even women who were intellectually superior to men were portrayed as dangerous or vulgar.

One of the discredited notions is of Greek "purity"—the idea that the Greeks were a self-made civilization, owing almost nothing to other cultures. To some extent, this was one of their myths of themselves: a way of differentiating themselves from foreigners. Indeed, the Greeks went beyond mere imitation when they received influences, whether from abroad or from an antiquity that they saw as their own. But they were heavily indebted to what they called Asia, which to them included Egypt, and, especially, to parts of Anatolia and the Ionian islands. Here—as we shall see in the next chapter—the learning we call Greek first appeared. Greece was open to the eastern Mediterranean, and influences from around the sea's rim fashioned Greek culture.

The Spread of State-Building and City-Building

Phoenician and Greek colonization and trade made the Mediterranean a highway of cultural exchange. Around and across its peninsulas lay a thick crust of peoples who could build up surplus resources, strong states, monumental cities, literate culture, and vibrant art (see Map 5.1). Most of them tend to get left out of books on global history, because they are ill known or underrated. But they help us see the Phoenicians and Greeks in context. They also help us understand what made the Mediterranean a potential forge of empires and fount of influence for the future. A tour is in order.

The lands of the Thracians lay along the Aegean Sea, north and east of Greece. Their written works have perished, and surviving inscriptions are indecipherable. But archaeology gives us inklings of their culture.

Because Thrace was close to trading centers of the eastern Mediterranean, its chiefs made an early start accumulating wealth and state-building. They practiced rites of fire, commemorated in spiraling incisons that swirled on their hearths. A fine example imitates a shimmering Sun. A horseback hero dominated their art. In surviving examples he wrestles a three-headed monster, leads a bear in triumph, and does battle among severed heads.

Around 500 B.C.E., energetic rulers unified the Thracian city-states into a kingdom and sought to expand their domain. These were flesh-and-blood figures whom we know from Greek sources, not mythic heroes. In 429 B.C.E., the Thracian King Sitalkes invaded Macedonia in northern Greece. There he built a palace-city of 12.5 acres, mostly of mud bricks and painted stucco. His failure to build a permanent empire marks a new period, when Thracian states squirmed to survive alongside mightier neighbors.

To the Thracians' west, along the coast of the Adriatic Sea around 500 B.C.E., lay Illyria, whose rulers and elites were buried with hoards of gold and silver and sacrifices of oxen and boar. An urn found in present-day Slovenia depicts the luxurious life of an Illyrian court. Warriors parade. Hawkers and deer hunters stalk. Dignitaries display their authority with double-headed scepters or play on pipes. Voluptuous, long-haired women feed them.

THRACIAN HORSEBACK HERO

Pre-Christian fragments of Thracian art sometimes survive because Christians recycled them as building material for churches. This heroic figure on a horse was a favorite subject for Thracian artists. Goldsmiths had depicted a similar figure, known to historians as "The Master of the Animals," for centuries.

Dominating a rearing horse and calmly feeding a lion, the hero has powers of control over sometimes unconquerable and savage forces of nature. The posture of the horse has signified command in Western art and imagery ever since.

The hero's servant contributes to mastery of the horse by pulling its tail. Perhaps in an attempt to represent Alexander the Great (r. 336–323 B.C.E.) as divine, later artists copied this feature in their depictions of him.

Two women are often onlookers in pre-Christian sacred scenes from Thrace.

How does this image shed light on state-building and cultural exchange in the Mediterranean world around 500 B.C.E.?

Greece and the Mediterranean

(All dates are approximate)	
1000–900 B.C.E.	End of Greek dark ages
750 B.C.E.	Trade expands and Greek cities line the Mediterranean
500s B.C.E.	Greek colonies spread
500 B.C.E.	Thracian city-states united
500 B.C.E.	Illyrian, Garamantine, Etruscan, and Spanish civilizations thrive
100 B.C.E.	The *Iliad* and the *Odyssey* probably written down

Across the Mediterranean, in the ferociously hot and dry region of Libya called the Fezzan (feh-ZAN), lived the Garamantes. They dug nearly 1,000 miles of irrigation tunnels under the Sahara, carving out the limestone that lies between the water table and the sand. On all sides, desert surrounded their cities. The Garamantes grew wheat where they could and barley elsewhere. No records of their own survive, but early Greek descriptions call them a slave-trading elite, driving four-horse chariots. Romans depicted their tattooed and ritually scarred faces under ostrich-plume helmets.

On the north shore of the Mediterranean, stretching like a garter across central Italy, was Etruria, the land of the Etruscans. Their "loamy, fat and stoneless" soil had to be plowed nine times to make a furrow, so they needed iron mines and powerful smelting technology. Much of the region, however, lay under malarial marshes that the Etruscans drained. Their language, which their neighbors could not understand, became a soothsayers' tongue in Roman times and was then forgotten. So we cannot decipher their inscriptions.

We can, however, glimpse Etruscan culture through their arts. Theater was their specialty, but soothsaying was the skill they esteemed most, reading omens from sheep's livers and the flight of birds. These were borrowed techniques. Like the Phoenicians (and perhaps thanks to trade with them), Etruscan culture drew from all over the Mediterranean.

Etruscan cities were the earliest in Italy. The biggest, at Caere, could have accommodated 20,000 inhabitants. The layout of their tombs imitated their houses, as if to prepare for an afterlife. At Caere, a warrior lies alongside two chariots, with shields and arrows nailed to the walls. But the tomb was not made for him. Its best chamber houses a heavily bejeweled woman. Strewn around her, gold, silver, and ivory objects are marked with her name: Larthia.

Among the Etruscans, women had freedom Greeks and Romans of the time mistook for immodesty. They could go out of their homes, attend games, dine with men. In Greek art, the only women who did such things were prostitutes, but Etruscan wives routinely dined with their husbands. In one tomb, a married couple was buried under a portrait showing them reclining as companions, side by side on a couch, in the way Mediterranean elites of the time typically ate dinner. With easy affection, he draws her close, as she offers him flowers. Since mirrors and combs often display inscriptions, we can assume upper-class Etruscan women were literate.

In Greek and Roman eyes, Etruscans spent too much time on grooming and dress, like characters in TV ads, and wantonly displayed their bodies, like beach cultists in modern California. Accusations that Etruscans performed sexual acts in public may be only slight exaggerations. On the wall of one tomb, a half-naked couple shares a bed. Banquet

A ceramic sarcophagus from a richly painted Etruscan burial chamber of the sixth century B.C.E. at Cerveteri in central Italy. The couple is shown together, hospitably sitting up as if to entertain visitors. They appear in death as they might have in life—reclining together at a dinner party, exchanging affection with vivid realism. The scene would be unimaginable in Greece at the time, where women were confined to subordinate roles.
Sarcophagus of a married couple on a funeral bed. Etruscan, from Cerveteri, 6th century BCE. Terracotta. Lewandowski/Ojeda. Musée Louvre, Paris, France. RMN Réunion des Musées Nationaux/Art Resource, NY

scenes show nude serving boys, as in Greece—but this may have been normal attire, or lack of it, for the young.

Beyond Etrona lay Spain, where Greeks said, "the god of riches dwells." From western Spain comes a belt decorated with a hero in combat with a lion and a huge funeral monument depicting a banquet of monsters—one with two heads, one with a forked tongue—feeding on wild boar. In another scene, a hero challenges a fire-breathing monster. The region evidently had an elite with the resources to build on a large scale and the power to inspire heroic and terrible images of authority.

From eastern Spain comes an imposing female sculpture—startling in its realism—called the Lady of Elche. Originally, she was probably enthroned in a tomb. A hollow space in her back may have held an offering to the gods or the ashes or bones of a human fellow occupant. Her luxurious dress, elaborate hairstyle, grand headdress, and enormous jewels leave no doubt of her social status or the wealth of the society that produced her.

From deep inside the steamship age, it is hard to imagine how inhibiting was the strength of the eight-knot current—the "rapacious wave," a Greek poet called it—that stoppered the entrance from the Mediterranean to the Atlantic "sea of darkness." But Greek and Phoenician traders forced their way through to Tartessos, in southern Spain, where the banks of the Rio Tinto are blotched with the flow of copper-bearing ores, and miners dug deep underground galleries.

Greek tales help us reconstruct Tartessos's history. In the mid–first millennium B.C.E., King Arganthonios was said to have subsidized the city walls that protected the marketplace of Phocaea at the other end of the Mediterranean. For a transition of this kind, from pastoralism to plutocracy, trading partners were essential. But Tartessos belongs to a long tradition of civilization-building in Spain, dimly detectable in even earlier treasure hordes. Native cultures, given the resources, were capable of spontaneous economic growth.

Lady of Elche. The limestone sculpture known as the Lady of Elche evokes the splendor of Iberian civilization in the first millennium B.C.E. Carved with startling realism, she was originally enthroned and housed in a tomb, with offerings concealed in a hollow in her back. Her luxurious dress, elaborate hair, and bulging jewels were glamorously painted.

EMPIRES AND RECOVERY IN CHINA AND SOUTH ASIA

Summaries nearly always distort. But the story of this chapter so far is of formerly marginal regions becoming—at least for a while—rich and powerful, like Phoenicia and Greece, Assyria and Babylon, and parts of the western and central Mediterranean, as if to replace the old centers of power and wealth in Lower Mesopotamia, Hatti, and Crete. This suggests problems to bear in mind when confronting what happened in China and South Asia in the same period: Were the traditions of the Shang and Zhou, in China, and of Harappa in India passed on to successors in new places? Or was the continuity of history ruptured and a new beginning made in new locations?

The Zhou Decline

The Zhou claimed that they were divinely chosen to rule the world (see Chapter 4). But as their supremacy spread, the realm became increasingly decentralized, and rituals to appease the gods became ever more elaborate: The vessels got bigger, the ceremonies larger scale, the hymns of praise to ancestors more extravagant. "Heaven's mandate is unending," intoned the court poets and congregations, with evident unease. A poet in the provinces disagreed: "Drought has become so severe, . . . glowing, burning. . . . The great mandate is about to end."

King Li (lee) ascended the throne in 857 B.C.E. Chroniclers portrayed him as self-indulgent and heedless of advice. A bronze inscription preserves Li's own version: "Although I am but a young boy, I have no leisure day or night," sacrificing to ancestors, elevating "eminent warriors" and well-recommended sages. But there was more urgent business than these ceremonial acts. In 842 B.C.E., rebels drove him from his capital, eventually installing the young heir, Xuan (shoo-ehn). For a reign of 46 years, Xuan held off the main external threat, the Western barbarians, while trying to confront natural disasters with magic.

When he died in 782 B.C.E.—reputedly murdered by the ghost of a subordinate he had unjustly executed—an earthquake hit. Following tradition, the poet blamed the disaster on the government's shortcomings. But the problems went deeper. As wealth trickled outward from trade, outlying states grew more insubordinate. In 771 B.C.E., people whom the Zhou called "Dog barbarians" drove them from their ancestral lands forever.

The Zhou moved east, to a region glorious under the Shang, but now divided among 148 Zhou relatives or nominees. Consolidation and reconfiguration reduced the number, and by the sixth century B.C.E., the former empire had been transformed into jostling states (see Map 5.2). Leadership among them was usually determined by war—and, within states, by assassination and massacre. Instability can inhibit cultural and economic development and unleash violence. Yet the consequences were, in some respects, the opposite. As we shall see in Chapter 6, politically fragmented environments fostered intellectual endeavor. Indeed, well before the turn of the mid-millennium, this fact was also evident in South Asia.

MAP 5.2

China and South Asia, ca. 750 B.C.E.

- China during Warring States Period
- barbarian incursions
- Ganges River Valley
- Sinhalese cultural area

South Asia: Relocated Centers of Culture

After the erosion and disappearance of the Harappan cities, Indian history differed in an important respect from other regions of large-scale state-building and city-building. Recovery in Europe, Mesopotamia, Phoenicia, and China depended on the survival or revival of previous traditions or on stimulation by outside influences. But India provides proof that such conditions were not necessary.

Historical orthodoxy has long insisted that something of the Harappan past—migrants, culture—must have survived. Indian civilization seems to deserve a pedigree as old as the Indus cities, and those cities, in turn, deserve to have left lasting traditions. But written and archaeological sources are few, and we have no evidence of continuities or unmistakable transmissions of culture across the dark, undocumented centuries of Indian history. When civilization did reemerge in South Asia in the first millennium B.C.E., it was in the Ganges valley and the island of Sri Lanka, which was once known as Ceylon.

The Ganges Valley

After a lapse of centuries, iron axes cleared the way for farming in the Ganges valley, a different environment from the hot, dry floodplains of the Indus valley. It was a region of abundant rain and rich forests. We have no knowledge that the Ganges received colonists from Harappa at the time. The only artifacts from the region during this period are fine copperware, which no one has found in the art of the Indus people, although some decorative designs may be similar.

Later Indian cultural history does not exhibit strong evidence that Harappan culture was transplanted to the Ganges either. Only pottery fragments exist with glazes similar to Harappan wares. Moreover, the first urban sites and fortifications in the Ganges valley have none of the telltale signs of Harappan order: no seals, no weights and measures, no uniform bricks. This makes it hard to believe that the Ganges civilization could be the Harappan civilization transplanted. On the contrary, the lack of material evidence makes early Indian civilization seem even more distant from the Harappan than Greek civilization was from the Cretan and Mycenean. In only one respect does the world of the Ganges clearly resemble that of Harappa—we know all but nothing about its political and social life.

The literature of its sages, however, survives in abundance. It is impossible to find evidence for traditional claims that the earliest texts originate from orally transmitted traditions from deep in the previous millennium. But surviving versions could have begun to be written down early in the first millennium B.C.E. The theoretical sections of these texts, the **Upanishads** (oo-PAH-nee-shadz), show the recollection of a time when teaching passed from one generation to another by word of mouth. *Upanishad* means something like "the seat close to the master."

 Excerpt from the Upanishads

One of the earliest Upanishads tells how the powers of nature rebelled against nature itself—how the lesser gods challenged the supreme god **Brahman** and failed. "But the fire could not burn straw without Brahman. The wind could not blow the straw away without Brahman." On its own, the story might suggest no more than a doctrine of divine omnipotence, similar to the doctrines Jews, Christians, and Muslims hold. But in the context of the other Upanishads, it seems part of a more general, mystical belief in the oneness of the universe,

India and Sri Lanka

(All dates are approximate)

1000 B.C.E.	Civilization emerging in Ganges valley
800 B.C.E.	Upanishads probably written down
? B.C.E.	*Sinhalese* colonize Sri Lanka
500 C.E.	*Mahavamsa* probably written down

infinite and eternal. Such a "theory of everything" does not appear in the thought of earlier civilizations.

Sages of the time proclaimed two more new ideas. The first was that matter is an illusion. The world is Brahman's dream; the creation of the world was like a falling asleep. Sense organs can tell us nothing that is true. Speech is illusory since it relies on lips and tongues. Thought is illusory, since it happens in—or at least passes through—the body. Most feelings are illusory because our nerves and guts register them. We can glimpse truth only in purely spiritual visions or certain kinds of feeling, like selfless love and unspecific sadness, which do not arise from particular physical stimuli. Second, the Upanishads describe a cycle of reincarnation or rebirth. Through a series of lives virtuously lived, the soul can advance toward perfection, at which time its identity is submerged in the divine "soul of the world" known as Brahman.

These ideas are so startling and innovative that we want to know how they occurred. And who were the patrons and pupils of the sages who uttered them? Why did society value such sublimely unworldly speculations? We have no evidence on which to base answers to these questions. But ideas from about the sixth century B.C.E. to about the first century C.E. are antiquity's most influential legacy to us and the subject of our next chapter. They still inform the questions that confront our religions and philosophies and mold how we think about them.

Building Anew in Sri Lanka

South Asia's other nursery of large-scale cities and states was in Sri Lanka, off the southern tip of India, in the Indian Ocean (see Map 5.2). Here, the *Mahavamsa* (ma-ha-VAHM-sah), chronicles of the long-lived "Lion Kingdom," are deceptive documents. In surviving versions, they were written down in what Westerners think of as the sixth century C.E. to justify the ruling *Sinhalese* (sihn-hah-LEHZ) people. The chronicles begin the history of the kingdom with a credible event: colonization by seafarers from the Gulf of Cambay, on the edge of the Harappan culture area. But the Sinhalese had no known connection with the Harappans. They became large-scale builders and irrigators but produced nothing to rival the logic, creative literature, mathematics, and speculative science written down along the Ganges about 2,500 years ago.

The heartland of the early kingdom was in the relatively dry northern plateau, where annual rainfall is heavy, but long dry spells are common. Nowadays in the dry zone, rice cultivation relies on village reservoir tanks dug out of seasonal streams, dammed with earth. There is not always enough water for annual crops of rice. Even if we allow for changes in the climate, the Sinhalese colonists could not have built great cities without hydraulic ingenuity. Even before the adoption of Buddhism, which tradition dates to the third century B.C.E., Anuradhapura (an-uh-rad-POO-ra) was a large and splendid capital, with the largest artificial reservoir in the world.

So civilizations can arise without the help of either recovered traditions or stimulation from outside influences. Yet the question remains, if people in the Ganges valley and Sri Lanka could build states and cities without traditions from the past or influences from outside, why were the Americas and most of Africa relatively dormant for so long, despite the promising starts described in earlier chapters?

THE FRUSTRATIONS OF ISOLATION

In discussing developments in the Americas and Africa, we have to allow for a trick of the evidence. The cultures of Eurasia churned out documents and literature, much of which we can read today. This alone accounts for their dominant place in historical tradition, compared with cultures that employed other, less accessible ways to record events and ideas. In the West, prejudice also favors Eurasian cultures over others. We pay more attention to history that seems to anticipate the way we live now. Sometimes we read into that history the origins of our own societies. Conversely, we overlook or fail to recognize history that appears too different from our own.

Compared to Eurasia, the geography of the Americas and sub-Saharan Africa discourages communication and cultural exchange (see Map 5.3). Much of Africa and Central and South America lies in the tropics, where dense rain forests make it difficult and unhealthy for any outsider attempting to cross them. Africa has relatively few rivers, and for the most part, they do not allow long-range navigation. In Eurasia, cultural exchange was rapid. It happened across zones of similar climate, with no need for either the people or the food plants and livestock they brought with them to adapt. Cultural transmission in Africa and the Americas, on the other hand, had to cross vast chasms of climate from north to south and south to north, calling for different survival strategies along the way.

Monsoonal wind systems in Asia and relatively stable weather in the Mediterranean favor navigation, whereas exposed shores and hostile winds enclose much of sub-Saharan Africa. Except in the Caribbean, the Americas have none of the narrow seas that encourage communication in parts of Europe and Asia. Even the civilizations of the Ganges and Sri Lanka, though they originated independently, could take advantage of the communications systems of maritime Asia and trans-Eurasian trade routes to link up with China and southwest Asia by land and sea.

Developments in North America

Still, there were developments beyond Eurasia. In the American far north, the Dorset culture transformed life. People there began to build semisubterranean longhouses and stone alleys for driving caribou into lakes. Their art realistically depicted all the species that shared their environment.

The critical new technology was the blubber-fueled soapstone lamp, which enabled the Dorset people to go far from home in the Arctic darkness, tracking the musk ox and caribou. No longer limited to the forest, the users of oil lamps could also hunt on the ice, where abundant fat game waited without competitors and where the climate preserved carcasses. People of the Dorset culture speared seals and harpooned walruses from kayaks on the open sea. Now that their prey was too fat to be felled by arrows, they abandoned the bow for the barbed harpoon. Ingenious notched blades stayed in the victim's flesh until it was so tired that it could be hauled in, butchered, and sped home on hand-drawn sleds with runners of walrus ivory.

Equally dramatic new ways of life developed in the same period—between the late second and mid–first millennia B.C.E.—on the lower Mississippi River and the coast of the Gulf of Mexico. The culture—called Poverty Point after the location of its biggest site in Louisiana—worked in copper and manufactured tools and jewelry. Trade goods arrived along the Mississippi, Red, and Tennessee Rivers. More

North America

Civilizations developing between 1000 and 500 B.C.E.

Dorset culture—Northwest Canada to the Arctic

Poverty Point—Gulf of Mississippi

Foraging communities—Ohio River valley

San Juan and Tucson basins—Southwest United States

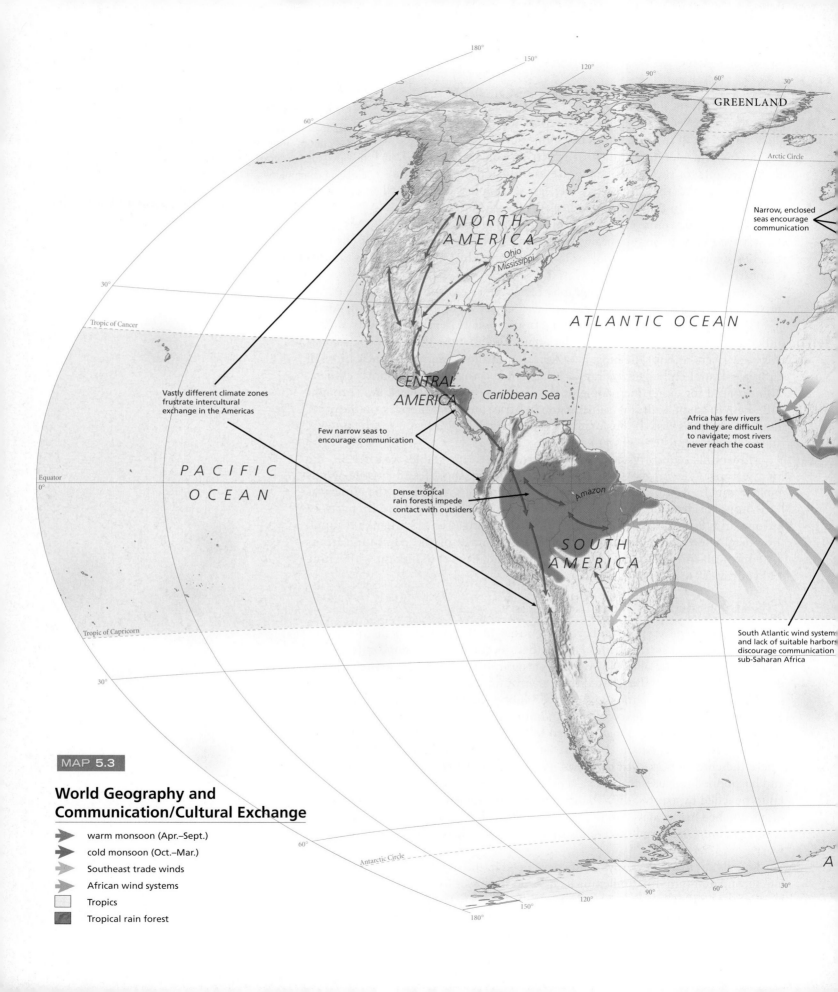

GREENLAND

Arctic Circle

NORTH
AMERICA

Ohio
Mississippi

ATLANTIC OCEAN

Narrow, enclosed
seas encourage
communication

CENTRAL
AMERICA

Caribbean Sea

Vastly different climate zones
frustrate intercultural
exchange in the Americas

Few narrow seas to
encourage communication

Africa has few rivers
and they are difficult
to navigate; most rivers
never reach the coast

PACIFIC
OCEAN

Equator
0°

Dense tropical
rain forests impede
contact with outsiders

Amazon

SOUTH
AMERICA

Tropic of Cancer

Tropic of Capricorn

South Atlantic wind system
and lack of suitable harbors
discourage communication
sub-Saharan Africa

Antarctic Circle

MAP 5.3

World Geography and
Communication/Cultural Exchange

- warm monsoon (Apr.–Sept.)
- cold monsoon (Oct.–Mar.)
- Southeast trade winds
- African wind systems
- Tropics
- Tropical rain forest

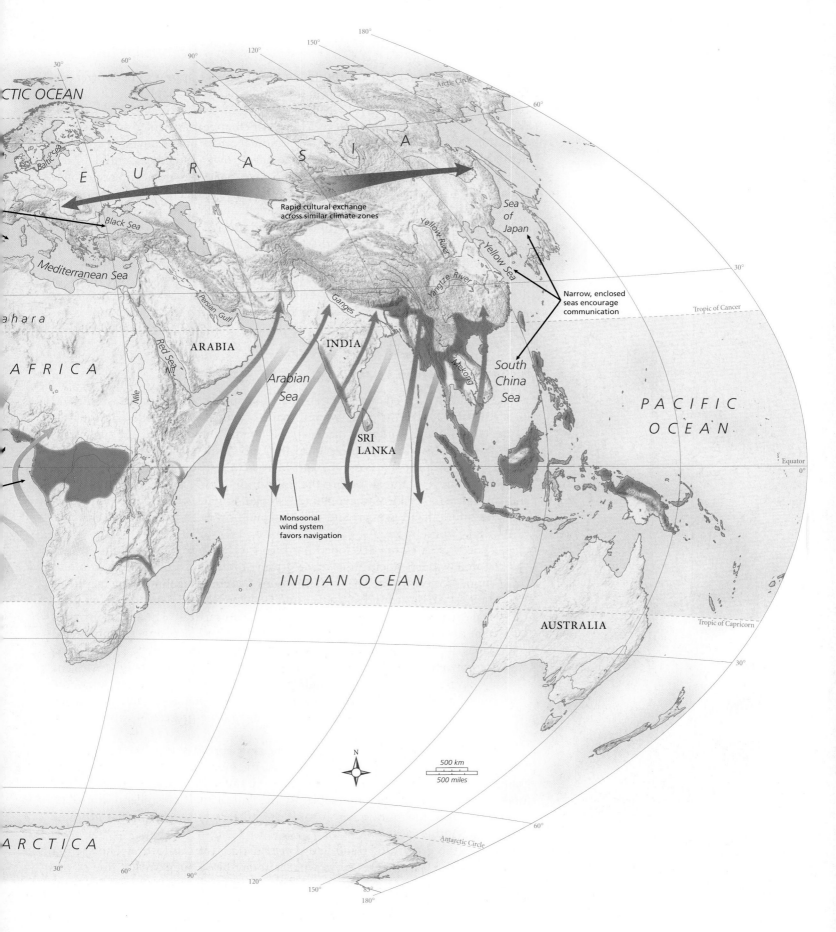

Rapid cultural exchange
across similar climate zones

Narrow, enclosed
seas encourage
communication

Monsoonal
wind system
favors navigation

ARCTIC OCEAN

EURASIA

Baltic Sea

Black Sea

Mediterranean Sea

Sahara

AFRICA

ARABIA

Red Sea

Nile

Persian Gulf

INDIA

Ganges

Arabian
Sea

SRI
LANKA

Yellow River

Yellow Sea

Sea
of
Japan

Yangtze River

Mekong

South
China
Sea

INDIAN OCEAN

PACIFIC
OCEAN

AUSTRALIA

ANTARCTICA

Arctic Circle

Tropic of Cancer

Equator

Tropic of Capricorn

Antarctic Circle

N

500 km
500 miles

than a hundred sites, grouped around ten major centers, appear to be forager settlements comparable to settlements in the Middle East (see Chapter 2). The biggest covers a square mile and is divided by a series of semicircular earthen ridges. Alongside is a mound almost 70 feet high, which appears oriented to the spring and autumn equinox. The mound is a ceremonial center unlike anything seen earlier in Mesoamerica and, therefore, likely to have grown up independently.

Meanwhile, burial mounds in the Ohio River valley provide evidence of new social patterns and perhaps chiefdoms. Here, settled foragers planted grains and sunflowers to supplement the food they gathered and hunted, painted their dead, and buried them with ornaments of copper and shell.

In the same period, contact with Mesoamerica brought about changes in parts of the Southwest. In the San Juan and Tucson basins in Arizona, people developed a variety of maize that matured in 120 days. They could now cultivate maize in drier areas where squash also grew. From around 500 B.C.E., the number of sites with traces of beans increased. Farmers here were working toward the same complete system of nutrition—maize, squash, beans—that the Olmecs had developed in Mexico (see Chapter 4).

New Initiatives in Africa

As in North America, change between 1000 and 500 B.C.E. in Africa was slow and localized compared to the most dynamic parts of Eurasia. Nonetheless, four developments are worth mentioning (see Map 5.4). First, around 750 B.C.E., Egypt weakened, and a Nubian state reemerged on the Upper Nile (see Chapter 4), with its chief cities at Napata (na-PAY-tuh) and Meroe (MEHR-oh-ee). Egyptian culture had long influenced Nubia. Late in the millennium, however, the language of the Nubian court changed from Egyptian to a Nubian tongue, which shows that Nubia was becoming less Egyptian and more Sudanic or, as some scholars say, more African.

Heads sculpted from coarse-grained clay, in what is now central Nigeria, in the second half of the first millennium B.C.E., are not just fine works of art—as this example of the first century B.C.E. shows. They are also evidence of the technical accomplishments of the craftsmen who made clay tubing for the forges in which iron tools were made.

Second, Africans developed hard-iron technology. This was almost certainly an independent discovery. African smiths had smelted soft iron and copper for centuries. The first iron foundries emerged along the Niger River in West Africa around 500 B.C.E., and again, perhaps independently, in Central Africa's Great Lakes region soon after. Natural drafts fanned the furnaces that melted the iron ore through long clay tubes. The people who made the tubes also left clay heads—wide-eyed, open-mouthed, partly shaved, with decoratively scarred foreheads. The use of fired clay suggests how Africans may have made the breakthrough in iron forging. These people knew the seemingly magical uses of fire—how fire turns hard what is soft and helps make art out of mud. Forging iron was a further stage in the process of exploring the potential of fire.

Third, Bantu languages continued their slow spread south (see Chapter 1), reaching Central Africa by about 1000 B.C.E. In this region, farmers could grow grains as well as yams, a major improvement in nutrition. Surplus production of food made trade with Nubia possible. By the end of the first millennium B.C.E., thanks, perhaps, to improved iron tools, Bantu farmers reached what are now Kenya and South Africa.

Finally, the growth of trade had consequences for the future. The slaving activities of the Garamantes from what is today Libya suggest that one of the major routes to tropical Africa was already developing across the Sahara from the Mediterranean. The other great potential link was across the Indian Ocean from Asia to the Horn of Africa in what is today Somalia and Ethiopia. This

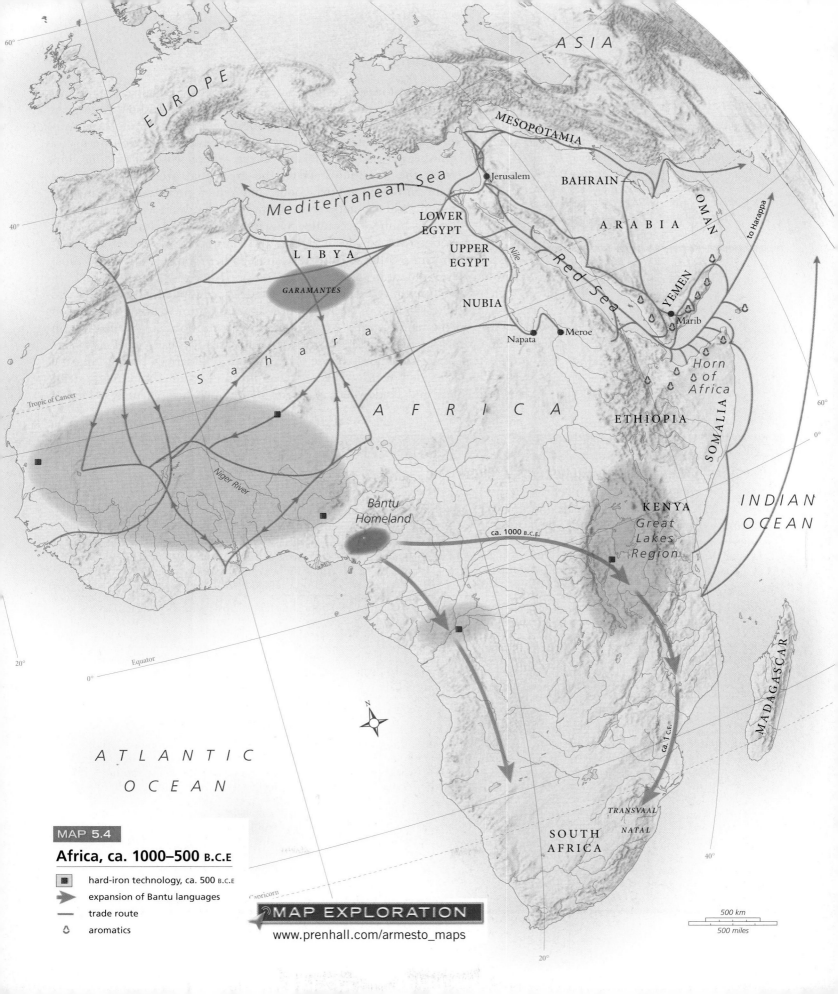

ASIA

EUROPE

MESOPOTAMIA

Mediterranean Sea

BAHRAIN

OMAN

to Harappa

Jerusalem

LOWER
EGYPT

ARABIA

LIBYA

UPPER
EGYPT

Nile

Red Sea

YEMEN

Marib

GARAMANTES

NUBIA

Napata   Meroe

Horn
of
Africa

Sahara

SOMALIA

Tropic of Cancer

AFRICA

ETHIOPIA

Niger River

KENYA
Great
Lakes
Region

INDIAN
OCEAN

Bantu
Homeland

ca. 1000 B.C.E.

Equator

N

MADAGASCAR

ATLANTIC
OCEAN

ca. 1 C.E.

TRANSVAAL

NATAL

Capricorn

SOUTH
AFRICA

40°

MAP 5.4

Africa, ca. 1000–500 B.C.E

▪ hard-iron technology, ca. 500 B.C.E

➤ expansion of Bantu languages

— trade route

⚱ aromatics

MAP EXPLORATION
www.prenhall.com/armesto_maps

500 km

500 miles

Africa/Southwest Arabia

(All dates are approximate)

1000s B.C.E.	Bantu languages expanding southward
900s B.C.E.	Sabaean empire grows
750 B.C.E.	Nubian kingdom reemerges
500 B.C.E.	First iron foundries along Niger River
100s B.C.E.	Bantu languages reach South Africa

link was at least as important for the history of civilization in East Africa as the link to the Mediterranean was to Europe. We do not know when this route opened, but developments in southern Arabia provide clues about how it may have begun. Southern and southeast Arabia has fertile valleys, where seasonal streams flow from the mountains. Here, the areas that are now Oman and Bahrain forged copper goods, and Yemen produced frankincense and myrrh, aromatic resins from trees that were used in perfumes and, as biblical accounts show, for religious rituals. Some of these goods reached Mesopotamia and Harappa. But when those civilizations collapsed in the second millennium B.C.E., so did most economic development in this region.

Only Saba in southwest Arabia, closest to Africa, continued to grow. This was where the biblical Queen of Sheba supposedly came from to King Solomon in Jerusalem in the tenth century B.C.E. Numerous inscriptions survive from soon after that time. A temple outside Marib (MA-rihb), the Sabaeans' chief city, bears bronze plaques commemorating victories—scenes of warriors brandishing the severed hands of their victims. This same temple houses bronze sculptures—tribute from kings and landowners, some, evidently, personal likenesses. Piecing

○ MAKING CONNECTIONS ○

AMERICAS, AFRICA, AND EURASIAN CIVILIZATIONS: 1000–500 B.C.E.

REGION →	MEANS OF CULTURAL, ECONOMIC, POLITICAL DEVELOPMENT →	DISTINCTIVE ACHIEVEMENTS
Greece	Seaborne trade; colonization of Mediterranean basin; extensive cultural exchange	New forms of government (*demokrateia*) and communities (*poleis, ethne*); colonial autonomy; highly developed written literature
Zhou Dynasty/Warring States Period (China)	Centralized rule; elaborate court rituals; ancestor worship; trade and taxation; constant threat from barbarians	Political instability fosters intellectual endeavors
Ganges Valley	Highly developed spiritual literature (Vedas, Upanishads); agriculture with iron tools; little understanding of political, economic policies	First philosophies focused on doctrine of reincarnation, *maya* (matter as illusion), large-scale urban settlements, fortifications
Sri Lanka	Sophisticated water-management systems combined with urbanization	Large-scale cities, early adoption of Buddhism from neighboring India
North America	In the far north: decentralized communities, simple technologies, group hunting techniques; South/Midwest: widespread trade networks connecting to Mesoamerica, settlements	Northern regions: long-term adaptation to hostile environments, gradual depletion of wildlife; South/Midwest: forager settlements, mound building, mixed agriculture/hunting–gathering culture
Sub-Saharan Africa/southwest Arabia	Widespread trade, cultural exchange with hard-iron technology accelerating tool and weapon making, spread of Bantu language	Growth of Nubian state south of Egypt; sophisticated art, industry in Niger region; building and farming techniques spread with Bantu speakers; trade and state-building in southwest Arabia (Saba)

together the inscriptions, we see how the Sabaean state expanded at its neighbors' expense. Understanding what happened in Saba is the best way to study one of the most intriguing problems in the next part of this book—the growth of great states and great ambitions in East Africa.

IN PERSPECTIVE: The Framework of Recovery

The climacteric of the late second millennium B.C.E. damaged and changed the frameworks of civilization but in most cases did not break them. Recovery was possible because traditions survived—or could be revived—or because there were stimulating outside influences. In Greece and India, people forgot the art of writing and had to reinvent it from scratch centuries later. Recovery sometimes happened in new places and among new peoples. After the extinction of the Harappan world, civilization gradually emerged in India, far from the Indus. In Sri Lanka, monumental irrigation works and buildings arose. In Mesopotamia and China, the centers of activity and initiative were relocated, but, again, the continuities of tradition, which are the foundations of progress, were never entirely lost. Traditions spread through neighboring regions. Greek civilization crystallized on the edges of the Greek world, in islands and small colonies around the Ionian and Aegean Seas. Fertilized by Phoenicia and Greece, a ring of ambitious cities and states formed around the Mediterranean and Black Seas.

People continued to make ambitious attempts to modify the environment, transforming new areas. In parts of Eurasia, the pace of state-building and economic expansion quickened. The imperial experiments between 1000 and 500 B.C.E. failed to take hold, but efforts to expand borders and dominate other states became a feature of regions where change was accelerating. Political instability among competing states stimulated technological change: hotter furnaces, more iron. It also, perhaps, multiplied the opportunities of patronage for artists and intellectuals. An "age of sages" was detectable in India and would soon be apparent in other parts of Eurasia.

In the Mediterranean and what we think of as the Middle East, between 1000 and 500 B.C.E., state-building and growing trade led to imperial ambitions that eventually failed. Elsewhere, imperial projects ran out of steam or into trouble—as in China—or simply did not happen. Was this because the contenders were too well matched? Or was it because the economic environment was too undeveloped or the ecological environment too fragile? Or was it because no conqueror had found an enduring formula or a means to solidify states that were prone to failure? Whatever the problems that frustrated imperial ambitions in the first half of the millennium, states soon found ways to overcome them. The second half of the millennium was remarkabl enot only as an age of sages in Eurasia but also as an age of robust empires. A zone of connected, communicating cultures began to take shape across Eurasia and the Mediterranean, from the Pacific to the Atlantic. They nourished each other. Faint links were beginning to put parts of this central zone in touch with northern Europe and Africa. In the rest of the world, isolated cultures,

CHRONOLOGY

(All dates are approximate)

1000–500 B.C.E.	Traditions and states of the late second millennium recover; Dorset culture in American far north thrives; peoples of lower Mississippi and Gulf of Mexico develop new ways of life
1000 B.C.E.	Civilization reemerges in Ganges valley; Bantu languages continue slow spread southward
800 B.C.E.	Phoenicians colonize the Mediterranean
771 B.C.E.	Zhou driven eastward from their ancestral lands
750–500 B.C.E.	Rapid expansion of Greek trading and colonization
750 B.C.E.	Egypt declines and Nubian state reemerges
605–562 B.C.E.	Peak of Babylonian Empire
500 B.C.E.	Carthage seeks control of Mediterranean trade until destroyed by Romans in 146 B.C.E.; West Africans develop and spread hard-iron technology southward
100s B.C.E.	Bantu languages reach present-day South Africa

still organized in kinship groups, chiefdoms, or small states, were able, at best, to develop small regional networks.

As a result, the focus of the next part of this book is on Eurasia and, in particular, the regions where sages founded well-rooted intellectual traditions that still shape the way we think: in China, India, southwest Asia, and Greece. These were homelands of huge ambitions to understand the world, change it, or conquer it. Their stories occupy the next chapters.

PROBLEMS AND PARALLELS

1. Why was the ruler of the city-state of Byblos able to stand up to a giant nation-state like Egypt?

2. Why did the Phoenician writing system play such an important role in the "recovery" of the Mediterranean world?

3. How did rulers such as Ashurbanipal and Nebuchadnezzar II enhance and extend their imperial states?

4. Why was Greek cultural influence so important for the Mediterranean world?

5. What evidence for the continuity of Harrapan/Indus valley culture exists in the civilizations of South Asia in the first millennium B.C.E.?

6. How did the interplay of cultures in the Mediterranean and Indian Ocean basins in the first millennium B.C.E. affect the development of civilizations in those areas? How did the isolation characteristic of cultures in the Americas affect the development of civilizations there?

DOCUMENTS IN GLOBAL HISTORY

- Mission to Byblos: *The Report of Wenamun*
- Hesiod, excerpt from *Works and Days*

- Aristotle, "The Creation of Democracy in Athens"
- Plutarch on Education and Family in Sparta

Please see the Primary Source DVD for additional sources related to this chapter.

READ ON

H. Goedicke, ed., *The Report of Wenamun* (1975) is a first-rate edition of the text. S. Moscati, ed., *The Phoenicians* (1968), and M. A. Aubet, *Phoenicians and the West* (1993) introduce the Phoenicians and their colonies. The standard works by H. W. F. Saggs, *The Might That Was Assyria* (1984), and *The Greatness That Was Babylon* (1962) are still valuable introductions, as is J. Oates, *Babylon* (1979). J. and D. Oates, *Nimrud* (2001) describes the palace.

S. Hornblower, *Greek World* (1983), and O. Taplin, *Greek Fire* (1989) make exciting introductions to the Greeks. J. Boardman, *The Greeks Overseas* (1964) covers Greek colonization admirably. C. Morgan, *Athletes and Oracles* (1990) is a splendid study. S. B. Pomeroy, *Goddesses, Whores, Wives, and Slaves: Women in Classical Antiquity* (1995); C. B. Patterson, *The Family in Greek History* (1998); and L. Foxhall and J. Salman, eds., *When Men Were Men* (1998), deal with women. The quotation from Hesiod on page 104 is from I. Morris and B. Powell, *The Greeks* (2006).

R. F. Hoddinott, *The Thracians* (1981); J. Wilks, *The Illyrians* (1992); C. M. Daniels, *The Garamantes of Southern Libya* (1970), and R. Harrison, *Spain at the Dawn of History* (1988) are outstanding on their respective subjects.

For the Zhou see page 110 above. On the Upanishads, J. Mascaro, *The Upanishads* (1965) is the best edition in translation; N. S. Subrahmanian, *Encyclopedia of the Upanishads* (1985) is a valuable companion.

On North America, B. Trigger and W. E. Washburn, *The Cambridge History of the Peoples of North America* (1996–2000) is an invaluable guide. B. Fagan, *Ancient North America: The Archaeology of a Continent* (1991) is a helpful introduction.

For Bantu languages in particular and the African background in general, J. Ki-Zerbo, ed., *The UNESCO General History of Africa*, i (1993) is of great value.

PART Three

The Axial Age, from 500 B.C.E. to 100 C.E.

Babylonian world map The world as seen from ▶ Babylon in the mid–first millennium B.C.E. The circle represents the ocean. The towers of Babylon can be seen just inside the ring. Other cities are indicated by circles and the Tigris and Euphrates Rivers by lines.
British Museum, London, UK/Bridgeman Art Library

ENVIRONMENT

since 800 B.C.E.
Trans-Mediterranean trade

since 3000 B.C.E.
Steppe pastoralism

CULTURE

650–550 B.C.E.
Zoroaster

ca. 623–543 B.C.E.
Buddha

551–479 B.C.E.
Confucius

since 300 B.C.E.
Silk Roads;
Monsoon driven Indian
Ocean trade

since 100 B.C.E.
Mediterranean–Atlantic trade

ca. 550–334 B.C.E.
Persian Empire

427–347 B.C.E.
Plato

334–323 B.C.E.
Alexander's
Empire

ca. 300–223 B.C.E.
Mauryan Empire

240 B.C.E.–400s C.E.
Roman Empire

221 B.C.E.–
220s C.E.
Han Empire

ca. 3–33 C.E.
Jesus

CHAPTER 6 The Great Schools

The Buddha's first sermon, depicted here in a Kushanese relief of the late second or early third century C.E. The Buddha squats under a lotus tree, on a pedestal decorated with a prayer wheel. The attentive figures who stand by his pedestal among the onlookers who surround him are probably the patrons who commissioned this sculpture. Kushanese art—from the mountainous northwest of the Indian subcontinent and Afghanistan—combines influences from India, Persia, Greece, and China, demonstrating the vitality of cultural exchange across Eurasia.

Scenes from the Life of Buddha, late 2nd–early 3rd century, Kushan dynasty, Stone. Courtesy of the Freer Gallery of Art, Smithsonian Institution, Washington, D.C.

J ust over halfway through the first millennium B.C.E., a frustrated adminis-
trator in the police service set out from the small Chinese state of Lu, south
of the Yellow River, on a journey in search of a worthy master. Conflicting
traditions claim him as the descendant of kings and the child of a
humble home. By what is said to be his own account, he was a studious
child, who worked his way through his education, learning menial jobs,
including grain counting and bookkeeping. He could never get ahead in the
bureaucracy of Lu, perhaps because he was openly disgusted with the
immorality of its politics. A book later published under his name recounts the
history of his times in deadpan fashion, listing the violence and injustice of the
kings and aristocrats, without any apparent moralizing. The effect heightens the reader's
revulsion.

The exile never found the ideal ruler he sought. Instead, he lived by attracting pupils and
left a body of thought that still influences ideas on the conduct of politics and the duties and
opportunities of daily life. For him—and for most other thinkers in an era disfigured by the
disintegration of China—loyalty was the key virtue: loyalty to God, to the state, to one's family, and to the true meanings of the words one uses. Most of the world knows him today by a
name that is a corruption of his honorific title: "Master Kong"—Kong Fuzi (koong foo-tzeh)
in Chinese, "Confucius" in the West.

● ● ● ● ●

The importance of Confucius is a reminder of how much the world of our own day owes to
the world of his—how thinkers of the time influenced the way we think now. Heroic teachers gathered disciples and handed down traditions. Typically, followers treated the founders
with awestruck reverence, recast them as supermen or even gods, and clouded our knowledge of them with legends and lore. We can unpick enough evidence, however, to get tentative pictures of outstanding examples of some of them—some we even know by name—and
some impression of what they taught.

These sages came up with ideas so influential as to justify a term that has become popular with scholars: the **axial age**. Different writers assign different meanings to this term. In
this chapter and the next, it designates the 500 years or so, roughly up to the beginning of the
Christian era. The image of an axis suits the period for three reasons. First, the areas in which
the thought of the sages and their schools unfolded stretched, axis-like, across Eurasia, in
regions that bordered on and influenced each other (see Map 6.1). Second, the thought of

FOCUS questions

- WHAT DO historians mean by the term *axial age*?
- WHAT WERE the main areas of axial-age thinking in Eurasia?
- WHAT WERE the most important religious ideas that developed during the axial age?
- WHAT SIMILARITIES developed among Chinese, Greek, and Indian science and medicine during the axial age?
- HOW DID political pessimists differ from optimists in their ideas about human nature and the role of government?
- WHY WAS the axial age confined to such a limited area of the world?

the period has remained central to, and supporting of, so much later thought, as its influence spread with developments described throughout the rest of this book. The religious leaders of the time founded traditions of such power that they have huge followings. The secular thinkers ran out, as if with their fingernails, grooves of logic and science in which people still think. They raised problems of human nature—and of how to devise appropriate social and political solutions—that still preoccupy us. And, third, because disciples wrote down much of their teaching, a body of texts has survived to become reference points for later study.

No one should try to study this material expecting it to be easy. We could dodge the difficulties by talking about the personalities instead of the problems of the axial age. But this chapter is designed to concentrate on what the axial-age sages thought and why they thought it—not on their lives and characters. So, after briefly outlining who the sages were and where they operated, we shall turn to the religious, political, and scientific ideas that characterized the age and made it "axial"—the shared features, which for students of global history are the most interesting.

Finally, the big problem arises: Why was there an axial age at all? Why did so much enduring thinking happen in such a relatively concentrated period? I try to explore this question, toward the end of the chapter, by investigating the networks to which the sages and their disciples belonged. The next chapter describes the political and economic contexts that surrounded, nourished, and transmitted axial-age ideas.

China, India, Greece, and southwest Asia were the linked locations in which axial thinking happened. So we also have to keep in mind the problem of why other parts of the world seem to have experienced nothing similar. If Africa, or the Americas, or the Pacific world, or western or northern Europe, or northern or Central Asia had comparable sages and schools, they left no record, and we know nothing of them. But, of course, they did produce traditions of thought that had local or regional influence, inviting us to try to understand why they have not survived and to make comparisons between the Eurasian arena of the axial age and other parts of the world.

THE THINKERS OF THE AXIAL AGE

As we saw in the last chapter, the work of thinkers of great depth and complexity was recorded earlier in India. Gradually, however, as disciples began to confide sages' secrets to writing, evidence emerged that issues similar to those already familiar in Indian sources (see Chapter 5) were attracting attention in other parts of Asia.

In what we now call Iran, the sage usually known as Zoroaster (zoh-roh-AHS-tehr) is dated to around the late seventh and early sixth centuries B.C.E. Texts ascribed to him are so partial, corrupt, and obscure that we cannot reconstruct them with confidence. As practiced by his followers, however, Zoroastrianism assumed that conflicting forces of good and evil shaped the world. The single good deity, Ahura Mazda (ah-HOO-rah MAHZ-dah), was present in fire and light;

the rites of his worshippers were connected with dawn and fire-kindling, while night and darkness were the province of Ahriman, the god of evil. Similar ideas, which dominated mainstream thinking in Iran for 1,000 years, have appeared in other Eurasian religions. Zoroastrian communities are still scattered around the world. For reasons we shall come to, however, Zoroaster had no comparable successor in his homeland.

In India, meanwhile, around the middle of the millennium, texts of the Veda multiplied. In particular, teachings about Brahman, handed down in the early Upanishads and described in Chapter 5, were studied and written down. Alongside this defining of Brahmanism in written texts, new thinking explored the moral implications of religious life, in a world of competing states comparable to that of China. Vardhamana Jnatrputra, for instance, whose life is traditionally assigned to the sixth or early fifth century B.C.E., is universally known as "Mahavira" (ma-ha-VEE-rah)—"the great hero." He founded **Jainism** (JAH-een-izm), a way of life designed to free the soul from evil by ascetic practices: chastity, detachment, truth, and charity. But Jainism is so demanding that it could only be practiced with full rigor in monasteries and religious communities. It never drew a following outside India.

Gautama Siddharta (GAW-teh-mah sihd-ARTH-ah), however, who probably lived between the mid–sixth and early fourth centuries B.C.E., founded in India a religion of potentially universal appeal. Or perhaps the tradition he launched is better described as a code of life than as a religion, since Gautama himself seems never to have made any assertions about God. Rather, he prescribed practices that would liberate devotees from the troubles of this world. Gautama, whose followers called him "the Buddha" or "Enlightened One," taught that a combination of meditation, prayer, and unselfish behavior could achieve happiness. The object was escape from desire—the cause of unhappiness. For the most privileged practitioners of what came to be called Buddhism, the aim was the ultimate extinction of all sense of self in a mystical state, called **nirvana** or "extinction of the flame." Devotees gathered in monasteries to help guide each other toward this end—but individuals in worldly settings could also achieve it. Many early Buddhist stories of the attainment of enlightenment concern people in everyday occupations, including merchants and rulers. This helped create powerful constituencies for the religion. To liberate the soul from the world, either by individual self-refinement or by losing oneself in selflessness, was likely to be a long job. In the meantime, the soul could expect to be recycled by reincarnation. The distinctive element in the Buddhist view of this process was that it was ethical. A principle of justice—or at least of retribution—would govern the fate of the soul, which would be assigned a "higher" or "lower" body in each successive life according to how virtuous it had been in its previous incarnation.

Critics sometimes claim that these new religions were really forms of old magic: that the desire to "escape the world" or "extinguish the self" or achieve "union with Brahman" was, in effect, a bid for immortality, and that mystical practice was a kind of alternative medicine designed to prolong or enhance life. Or else such practices as prayer and self-denial could be seen as a bid for the charismatic power of self-transformation of the shaman (see Chapter 1), obtained without using mind-bending drugs. These analyses may have some validity. The Buddha called himself healer as well as teacher. Many legends of the era associate miracles of therapy with founders of religions. The identification of detachment from the world with the pursuit of immortality is

Zoroastrians. Though persecuted almost to extinction in Iran, the land of its birth, Zoroastrianism survives among exiled communities, especially in India, the United States, and Western Europe. Here Zoroastrian priests in London mark the New Year by kindling sacred light.

Siddhartha Gautama: *Identity and Nonidentity*

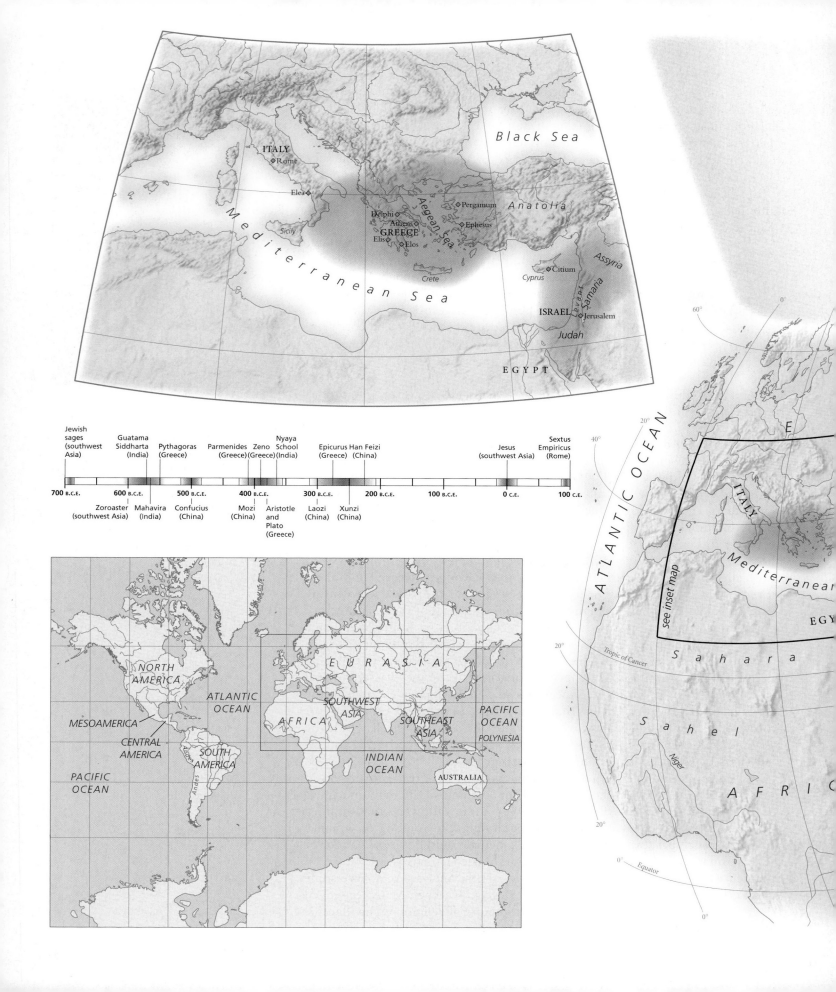

Black Sea

ITALY
◇Rome

Elea◇

Aegean Sea

Delphi◇
Athens◇
GREECE
Elis◇
◇Elos

Pergamum◇

Ephesus◇

Anatolia

Sicily

Crete

Mediterranean Sea

Cyprus

◇Citium

Assyria

Levant

Samaria

ISRAEL

◇Jerusalem

Judah

EGYPT

Jewish sages (southwest Asia)

Guatama Siddharta (India)

Pythagoras (Greece)

Parmenides (Greece)

Zeno (Greece)

Nyaya School (India)

Epicurus (Greece)

Han Feizi (China)

Jesus (southwest Asia)

Sextus Empiricus (Rome)

700 B.C.E. — 600 B.C.E. — 500 B.C.E. — 400 B.C.E. — 300 B.C.E. — 200 B.C.E. — 100 B.C.E. — 0 C.E. — 100 C.E.

Zoroaster (southwest Asia)

Mahavira (India)

Confucius (China)

Mozi (China)

Aristotle and Plato (Greece)

Laozi (China)

Xunzi (China)

NORTH AMERICA

EURASIA

ATLANTIC OCEAN

MESOAMERICA

CENTRAL AMERICA

AFRICA

SOUTHWEST ASIA

SOUTHEAST ASIA

PACIFIC OCEAN

POLYNESIA

SOUTH AMERICA

Andes

INDIAN OCEAN

AUSTRALIA

PACIFIC OCEAN

ATLANTIC OCEAN

60°

40°

E

20°

ITALY

Mediterranean

EGY

see inset map

Sahara

Tropic of Cancer

Sahel

Niger

AFRIC

20°

20°

0°

Equator

0°

60°

0°

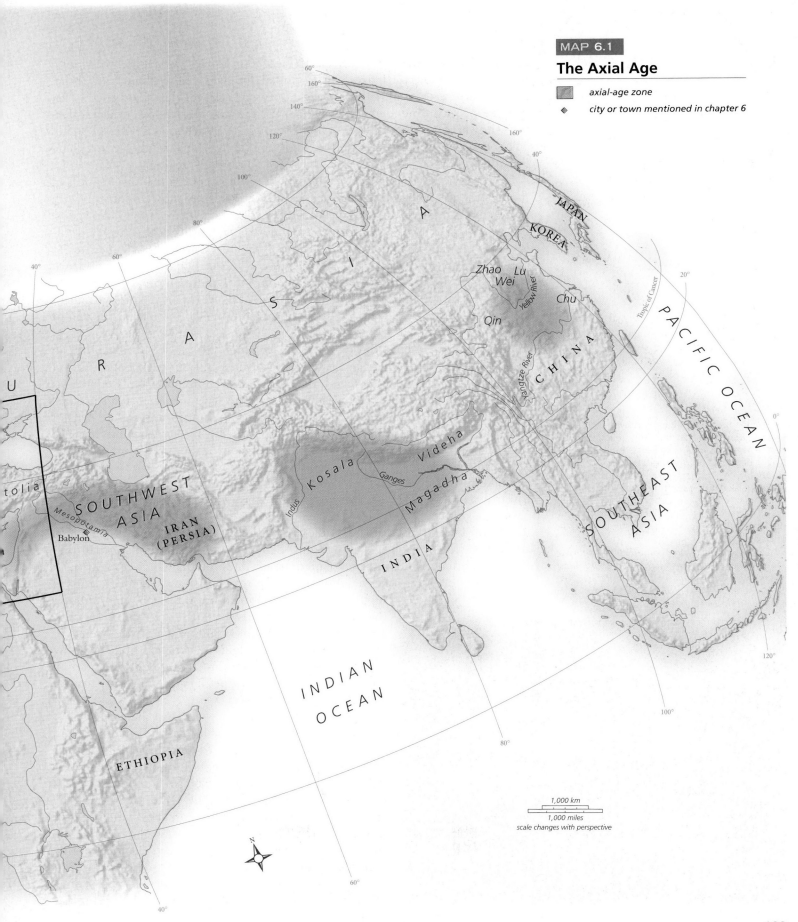

MAP 6.1

The Axial Age

axial-age zone

city or town mentioned in chapter 6

60°
160°
140°
120°
100°
80°
60°
40°

JAPAN
KOREA
Zhao
Lu
Wei
Chu
Qin
Yellow River
Yangtze River
CHINA
A
S
I
A
E
U
R
A
S
I
A

Tropic of Cancer

PACIFIC OCEAN

40°
20°
0°

U
tolia

SOUTHWEST
ASIA
Mesopotamia
Babylon
IRAN
(PERSIA)

Indus
Kosala
Ganges
Videha
Magadha
INDIA

SOUTHEAST
ASIA

ETHIOPIA

INDIAN
OCEAN

120°
100°
80°
60°
40°

N

1,000 km
1,000 miles
scale changes with perspective

explicit, for instance, in writings attributed to Laozi (low-tzeh), probably a fourth-century B.C.E. figure, who founded **Daoism** (daow-ihzm) in China. Amid the insecurities of life among the warring states described in the last chapter, he recommended disengagement to give the Daoist power over suffering—power like that of water, which erodes even when it seems to yield: "There is nothing more soft and weak; for attacking the hard and strong there is nothing better."

Yet, the new religions were genuinely new. They upheld the effectiveness of moral practice, alongside rituals, as ways to adjust humans' relationship with nature or with the divine: not just sacrificing offerings fittingly to God or gods, but also modifying how people behaved toward each other. They attracted followers with programs of individual moral progress, rather than with rites to appease nature. In other words, they were emerging as religions of salvation, not just of survival. They promised the perfection of the human capacity for goodness, or "deliverance from evil"—attainable in this world or, if not, by transfer to another world after death, or by a transformation of this world at the end of time.

Traditions developed during the axial age among Jews also showed a drift in this direction. This relatively small and politically insignificant people of southwest Asia's Mediterranean coastal region demands attention because of the enormous long-term influence of some Jewish thinking. The Jews inhabited the war zone described in the last chapter. Traditionally, in the attempt to retrieve the facts of early Jewish history, scholars have relied on supposedly historical narratives in the Bible, the sacred writings of the Jews. But archaeological investigation has made this history increasingly difficult to confirm. So any account has to be tentative.

Like most people, the Jews seem to have started with a religion tailored toward worldly ends, worshipping a tribal deity who promised material success and victory. Their sacred writings, however, tell a story of disillusionment: of defeats and dispossessions by their enemies. From the eighth century B.C.E., Egyptian, Assyrian, and Babylonian inscriptions confirm that Jews inhabited two kingdoms called Israel and Judah, which fought each other and fell victim to neighboring empires. Large-scale deportations— including a massive forced migration to Babylon after the fall of the Jews' holy city of Jerusalem in the 580s B.C.E.—incited a "diaspora mentality": exiles' sense of loss, resignation, nostalgia, defeat, and hope. "By the waters of Babylon," as psalmists put it, "we lay down and wept. . . . If I ever forget Jerusalem, let my tongue cleave to my mouth."

Instead of turning the Jews against their deity, their disasters inspired them to see him as the only true God, beside whom all other gods were false. Sufferings were trials of faith and punishments for sin—especially for failures to acknowledge God's uniqueness. God promised deliverance, if not in this life, then in the afterlife, or at the end of history, or, at best, in a remote future, as a reward for fidelity to prescribed rituals and rules of life, known as "the Law." Jews differed among themselves about what deliverance would mean. For some, it would be individual immortality; for some, relief from a sense of sinfulness; for some, the elimina-

Laozi, from the *Tao Te Ching*

Exile of the Jews. "The king of Assyria carried the Israelites away to Assyria." This relief from the palace of the invading king seems to illustrate the scene described in the biblical Book of Kings (II.18:11), as soldiers take prisoners from the fortress of Lachish, which the Assyrians captured in 701 B.C.E. The Bible says that the Hebrew king then "stripped the gold from the doors of the Temple of the Lord" in an attempt to buy off the invaders.

Judean exiles carrying provisions. Detail of the Assyrian conquest of the Jewish fortified town of Lachish (battle 701 B.C.). Part of a relief from the palace of Sennacherib at Nineveh, Mesopotamia (Iraq). Erich Lessing/Art Resource, N.Y.

tion of evil from the world; for some, national independence; for some, an empire over their enemies.

The last great teacher of the age—the greatest, in terms of the scale of his influence—was the Jew we usually call Jesus, who died in or about 33 C.E. To the secular historian, Jesus is best understood as an independent-minded Jewish rabbi, with a radical message. Indeed, some of his followers saw him as the culmination of Jewish tradition, embodying, renewing, and even replacing it. The name *Christ*, which his followers gave him, is a corruption of a Greek attempt to translate the Hebrew term *ha-mashiad*, or **Messiah**, meaning "the anointed," which Jews used to designate the king they hoped for at the end of history to bring heaven to earth. Jesus' message was uncompromising. The Jewish priesthood should be purged of corruption, the temple at Jerusalem "cleansed" of money-making practices. More controversially, some of his followers understood him to claim that humans could not gain divine favor by appealing to a kind of bargain with God—the "covenant" of Jewish tradition. God freely gave or withheld his favor, or grace. According to Jewish doctrine, God responded to obedience to laws and rules. But Jesus' followers preferred to think that, however righteously we behave, we remain dependent on God's grace. No subsequent figure was so influential until Muhammad, the founder of Islam, who died six centuries later, and none thereafter for at least 1,000 years.

The religious teachings of the sages were highlights in a world teeming with other new religions, most of which have not survived. In a period when no one recognized a hard-and-fast distinction between religion and secular life, spiritual ferment stimulated intellectual innovation. It is still hard to say, for instance, whether Confucius founded a religion. After all, he ordered rites of veneration of gods and ancestors but disclaimed interest in worlds other than our own. The many other schools of the axial age in China shared similar priorities but mixed what we would now think of as secular and religious thinking. Confucius's opponent, Mozi (moh-tzeh), is a case in point. He taught a philosophy of **universal love**, on secular grounds, 400 years before Jesus' religious version.

Other innovators formulated ideas that belong in what we would now classify as secular thought. Greek sages, for instance, whose work overlapped with that of the founders of new religions in Asia, taught techniques for telling good from evil and truth from falsehood that we still use. The towering figures were two teachers of the fourth century B.C.E.: Aristotle, a physician's son from northern Greece, who was, perhaps, the most purely secular thinker of the age, and his teacher, the Athenian aristocrat, Plato. Aristotle left work on science, logic, politics, and literature unequalled in the West for centuries, while Western philosophy is often jokingly dismissed as "footnotes to Plato." Logicians, scientific observers, and experimenters in China paralleled these achievements, as did thinkers in India of the school known as Nyaya, who shared confidence in reason and the urge to analyze it, resolving arguments step by step.

THE THOUGHTS OF THE AXIAL AGE

There is no easy way to analyze the thinking of the axial age. Textbook writers usually divide the subject by regions, because scholars tend to specialize in regions. This method, however, conceals the fact that an almost continuous zone across Eurasia stretching from China, through India, southwest Asia, and the Mediterranean Levant, to Greece linked these regions together (see Map 6.1).

A thematic approach, of the kind attempted over the next few pages, helps reveal connections and contrasts. We start with religious ideas, bearing in mind the now-familiar warning that religion and secular life were overlapping categories for most thinkers at the time.

Religious Thinking

Of new thoughts of God formulated or developed in the axial age, three proved especially influential in global history: the idea of a divine creator, responsible for everything else in the universe; the idea of a single God, uniquely divine, or divine in a unique way; and the idea of an involved God, engaged in the life of the world.

CREATION Gods and spirits are hard to imagine. It is even harder to imagine nothing. But the idea of nothing enabled thinkers to understand nature in a new way. For once you have got your head around the concept of nothing, you can imagine creation from nothing.

Before the axial age, creation narratives, as far as we know, were not really about creation, but were explanations of how the universe came to be the way it is. Ancient Egyptian creation myths tell of a creator transforming chaos into a world endowed with time: but the chaos was there for him to mold. The eternal being whom early Indian writings call Brahman created the world out of himself, "as a spider spins its web." "How could it be so," sneered one text of the Upanishads, "that being was produced from non-being?" Most Greek philosophers agreed. Plato's creator-god did not start from nothing but rearranged what was there. Buddhists saw no beginning to the universe and no need for a creator.

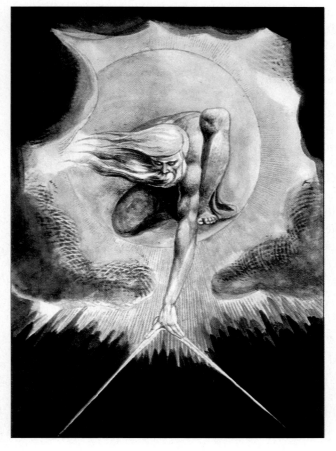

The Creator. The British poet and artist William Blake (1757–1827) was explicit; he painted visions. His version of the Creation—probably now the most famous in the world—is certainly visionary but has obvious sources. It calls the Bible to mind, as God measures "a world without form, and void." The use of rushing wind to suggest the Holy Spirit, and of sun rays to signify Jesus, are among the oldest conventions of Christian art. God's stooped posture and his dividers, flashing like lightning, recall medieval paintings of God as the architect of the cosmos (see Chapter 13).

Some ancient Greek poetry, however, described a world-beginning without prior matter. Emotion or thought was the prime mover of the universe. As the Gospel according to John put it in the late first century C.E., "In the beginning was the logos"—literally, the thought, which English translations usually render as "the word." Of all the early Christian accounts of Jesus' life, John's was the gospel Greek thought influenced most heavily. Most other Christian accounts relied heavily on traditions peculiar to Jesus' own people, the Jews, who brought an unusual philosophical twist to divine thinking: the idea of a creator who always existed but who made everything else out of nothing.

Conclusions followed. The creator was unique, for nothing else could precede creation; he was purely spiritual, since there was no matter until he made it; he was eternal—he existed, that is, outside time—since he was not himself a product of creation; he was therefore unchanging; nothing greater than he could be conceived: His power had no limits.

MONOTHEISM The idea of a unique God, who monopolizes power over nature, is now so familiar, at least in the West, that we can no longer sense how strange it is. Yet, until the first millennium B.C.E., as far as we know, most people who imagined an invisible world—beyond nature and controlling it—supposed that it was crowded with gods, the way creatures crammed nature. To systematize the world of the gods in the axial age, Greeks arrayed gods in order. Persians reduced them to two—one good, one evil. In Indian *henotheism*, a multiplicity of gods collectively represented divine unity.

For Jews, Yahweh (YAH-weh), their tribal deity, was, or became, their only God. The chronology is insecure, and we do not know whether the Jewish creation theory was cause or consequence of this development. Their writings called him "jealous"—unwilling to allow divine status to any rival. Fierce enforcement of his sole right to worship was part of the covenant in which Yahweh's favor was exchanged for obedience and veneration. "I am Yahweh your God. . . . You shall have no other gods to rival me."

Jews were not obliged to impose the Yahweh cult on others. On the contrary, for most of history, they treated it as a treasure too precious to share with non-Jews. Elsewhere, monotheism seemed unappealing. Buddhism dispensed with the need for a creator by upholding that the universe was itself infinite and everlasting. When asked about the existence of God, Buddha, in the recollection of his disciples, always answered evasively. In India, China, and Greece, the idea of a unique creator left options for polytheism: If one being inhabited eternity, why—in strict logic—might not others? Other uniqueness can be divided: You can shatter a rock, parse a statement, refract light. So maybe the uniqueness of God is of this kind. Alternatively, it could be a kind of comprehensiveness, like that of "Nature," "the Earth," or the sum of everything. God is one—any good Brahmanist would acknowledge—in the sense that everything is one. In any case, if God's power is without limits, surely he can create other gods.

Despite these arguments, three developments have conspired, in the long run, to make the God of the Jews the favorite God of much of the world. First, the Jews' own "sacred" history of sacrifices and sufferings gave a compelling example of faith. Second, a Jewish splinter group, which recognized Jesus as—so to speak—the human face of God, opened its ranks to non-Jews. Christianity built up a vigorous and sometimes aggressive tradition of trying to convert non-Christians everywhere. Thanks in part to a message adaptable to all sorts of cultural environments, it became, over nearly 2,000 years, the world's most widely diffused religion. Finally, early in the seventh century C.E., the prophet Muhammad studied Judaism and Christianity, and incorporated the Jewish understanding of God in Islam, the rival religion he founded. In its turn Islam attracted almost as many followers. Today, well over a third of the world's population subscribes to the tradition of Jewish, Christian, and Muslim monotheism (see Figure 6.1).

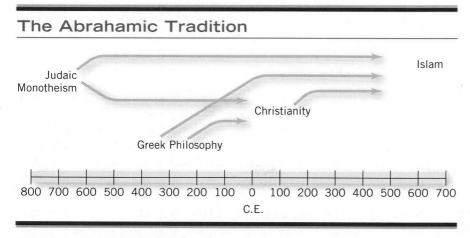

The Abrahamic Tradition

Islam

Judaic Monotheism

Christianity

Greek Philosophy

800 700 600 500 400 300 200 100 0 100 200 300 400 500 600 700

C.E.

FIGURE 6.1 THE ABRAHAMIC TRADITION

Divine love. "I am the good shepherd," said Jesus, according to the Gospel of John (10:14), "and I lay down my life for my sheep." During the persecutions that punctuated the first 300 years of the history of the Church, Christian artists interpreted the New Testament's many texts about "straying" and "lost" sheep as metaphors for the souls of martyrs, whom Jesus gathered into his fold. This third-century example shows how Christians continued the heroic and aesthetic conventions of classical sculpture.

"The Good Shepherd," marble, height: as restored 99 cm, as preserved 55 cm, head 15.5 cm. Late 3rd century A.D. Vatican Museums, Pio-Christian Museum, Inv. 28590. Courtesy of the Vatican Museums.

DIVINE LOVE Having created, did God remain interested in creation? Most Greek thinkers of the era ignored or repudiated the suggestion. Aristotle's description of God is of a perfect being, who needs nothing else, who has no uncompleted purposes, and who feels neither sensibility nor suffering. "The benevolence of heaven" was a phrase much used in China around the midpoint of the millennium, but this seems a long way short of love. Mozi, as even his philosophical adversaries admitted, "would wear out his whole being for the benefit of humankind." But his vision of humankind bound by love was not theologically inspired. Rather, he had a romantic vision of a golden age of "Great Togetherness" in the primitive past.

The claim that God's interest is specially focused on humans seems suspiciously self-centered. Gradually, however, axial-age thinking made it believable by insisting that humankind was higher than other animals. There were dissenting traditions. Philosophers in southern Italy in the late sixth century B.C.E. taught that "All things that are born with life in them should be treated as kindred." Religious Jains' reverence for animals' souls was—and still is—so intense that they swept the ground to avoid walking on insects. But the biblical God makes "man in His own image" as the last word in creation and gives humans dominion over all other animals.

In the second half of the millennium, thinkers in other traditions formulated similar ideas. In the mid–fourth century B.C.E., Aristotle developed a hierarchy of living souls, in which the human soul was superior to those of plants and animals, because it had rational as well as "vegetative" and "sensitive" faculties. The Chinese formula was similar, as, for example, Xunzi (shoon-tzeh) put it early in the next century: "Man has spirits, life, and perception, and in addition the sense of justice; therefore he is the noblest of earthly beings." Humans could exploit stronger creatures because they were able to form societies and act collaboratively. Buddhism ranked humans as higher creatures than others for purposes of reincarnation. For Jews humans were lords or stewards of creation, uniquely empowered to communicate directly with God.

Late in the axial age, some Jews began to use the image of **divine love** to express this relationship—perhaps to cope with the frustrations of their history, in which they had never recovered political independence. Jesus and his followers seized on the identification of God with love. Love is a universal emotion. By making God's love embrace all humans—rather than favoring a chosen race or a righteous minority—Christianity acquired universal appeal. Creation became an act of love consistent with God's nature. This solved a lot of problems, though it raised another—why does a loving God permit evil and suffering?

New Political Thinking

The evidence was glaringly ambiguous: Were misdeeds the result of corrupted goodness or inherent evil? Were human beings by their very nature good or bad? "The nature of man is evil—his goodness is only acquired by training," said Xunzi, for instance, in the mid–third century B.C.E. He believed that the original state of humankind was a grim swamp of violence, from which progress painfully raised people. Confucius, on the other hand, thought, "Man is born for uprightness. If he lose it and yet live, it is merely luck." Since the axial age, political solutions to the problem of human nature have always been of two contrasting kinds: those that emphasize freedom, to release human goodness, and those that emphasize discipline, to restrain human wickedness.

The biblical book of Genesis contained the most widely favored compromise. God made humans good and free. The abuse of freedom made people bad. Logically, this was unpersuasive. If Adam was good, how could he use freedom for evil? To escape this trap, Genesis added a diabolical device. The serpent (or other devilish agents in other traditions) corrupted goodness from outside. This has left politics with a difficult balancing act, which no system has ever adequately accomplished, between freedom and force.

POLITICAL PESSIMISM For pessimists, the way to overcome human deficiencies was to strengthen the state. Plato was a member of an Athenian gang of intellectuals and aristocrats, who felt qualified for power and therefore resented democracy. His recommendations included censorship, repression, militarism, regimentation, rigid class structure, extreme collectivism, selective breeding of superior human beings, and deliberate deception of the people by the state. Political power should be concentrated in a self-electing class of philosopher-rulers called **Guardians.**

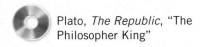
Plato, *The Republic*, "The Philosopher King"

Their qualification for office would be intellectual superiority, guaranteed by a mixture of heredity and education, which would make them selfless in their private lives and godlike in their ability to see what was good for the citizens. They would achieve Plato's declared objective: "the greatest happiness of the whole, and not that of any one class." He wrote so persuasively that this reasoning has continued to appeal to state builders ever since. "There will be no end to the troubles of states, or indeed, of humanity," he claimed, "until philosophers become kings in this world, or till those we now call kings and rulers really and truly become philosophers." His Guardians, however, became the inspiration and the intellectual ancestors of elites, aristocracies, party hacks, and self-appointed supermen whose justification for tyrannizing others has always been that they know best.

Chinese counterparts exceeded the severity even of Plato's thinking. For most of the time, they were in the minority: The consensus among the sages was that the ruler should be bound by law (a point in which Aristotle, at the other end of Eurasia, agreed). Confucius even said that ethics should override obedience to the law. In the fourth century B.C.E., however, a school of thought in China known as the **Legalists** denounced ethics as a "gnawing worm" that would destroy the state. Society required only obedience. Law and order were worth tyranny and injustice.

This was a new twist in the history of thinking about law. The explanation lies in the terror of the times. Legalist doctrine was born in a time of civil disaster and has tended to resurface in bad times ever since. Legalists laughed off earlier sages' belief in the innate goodness of people. The best penalties were the most severe: cutting off heads, slicing or ripping people in half, roasting them alive. As well as in the worship of order, ancient Chinese Legalism anticipated modern fascism, for instance, in advocating and glorifying war, recommending economic self-sufficiency for the state, denouncing capitalism, praising agriculture, and insisting on the need to suppress individualism in the interests of state unity.

Legalism: selections from the writings of Han Fei

POLITICAL OPTIMISM But most sages of the axial age were optimists. They thought human nature was essentially good. Hence, the political doctrines of Confucianism, which demanded that the state should liberate subjects to fulfill their potential. Hence, too, the democracy Greek sages advocated, which entrusted citizens (though not, of course, women or slaves) with a voice in political affairs.

Chinese thinkers applied similarly individualistic doctrines, but they did not question monarchy. The state was meant to reflect the universe. Its unity could not be compromised. All that could be expected was that the ruler should consult the

The Great Wall of China. Legend assigns the Great Wall of China to the Warring States period in the third century B.C.E. In fact, it took centuries to build and was often rebuilt thereafter. Little of the surviving workmanship, which stretches for some 4,000 miles, is more than 500 years old. Chinese culture now extends way beyond it, but the wall has an important place in the formation of Chinese identity—defining the supposed boundary of the non-Chinese world, displaying the ambition and achievement of Chinese civilization.

people's interests and views and should face the subjects' right to rebel against tyranny. "Heaven sees according as the people see," said Mencius, Confucianism's outstanding spokesman. "Heaven hears according as the people hear." This was a reminder to the ruler, not a recipe for republicanism. Nor does Indian literature of the time mention popular institutions. But some Indian states did have elites hundreds or thousands strong that ruled as a group, electing leaders for fixed terms among themselves.

Meanwhile, in Greece, a variety of political experiments unfolded, including republican, aristocratic, and even democratic systems. Aristotle made a masterly survey of them in the fourth century B.C.E. He thought monarchy was the best system in theory, but not in practice, because it was impossible to ensure that the best man would always be the ruler. More practical was aristocratic government, in which a manageable number of superior men administered the state. But it tended to generate into the self-interested rule of the wealthy or permanent power for an hereditary clique. Democracy could lead to demagogues and mob rule. The best system was a carefully crafted mixture in which aristocracy predominated, under the rule of law. Broadly speaking, this was embodied in the Roman state of the second half of the millennium (see Chapter 8), which became, in turn, the model for most republican survivals and revivals in Western history. Even when, toward the end of the axial age, Rome abandoned republican government and restored what was in effect a monarchical system, Romans still spoke of their state as a republic and the emperor as merely the chief magistrate.

In politics, Jesus preached a subtle sort of subversion. A new commandment to "love one another," he claimed, could replace virtually all laws. The Kingdom of Heaven was more important than the empire of Rome. In one of history's great ironic jokes, Jesus advised fellow Jews, in effect, to despise or even ignore the state: "Render unto Caesar that which is Caesar's and unto God that which is God's." All Jews at the time would have understood what this meant, for everything, to them, was God's.

For society at large, Jesus was equally dangerous, welcoming social outcasts—prostitutes, tax collectors, "sinners," and heretics. He favored the weak against the strong: children, women, the lame, the blind, and beggars—the "meek," who, he promised, "shall inherit the earth." In view of the radical nature of this bias, it is unsurprising that Jewish and Roman authorities combined to put him to death. His followers then turned from political activism to spiritual preparation for personal salvation.

Challenging Illusion

New thinking about reason and reality, and the relationship between them, flourished alongside or within the work of the religious leaders. Perhaps the most startling feature that united the thought of the axial age across Eurasia was the sages' struggle against illusion—their effort to see beyond appearances to underlying realities. "People dwelling in a cavern," said Plato, "see only the shadows … that the fire throws onto the wall of their cave." Senses deceive. We are mental cave dwellers. How can we see out of our cave?

Mathematics

The question inspired innovations in mathematics. Indian sages discovered in numbers a limitless universe. Jain speculators about the age of the cosmos invoked mind-bogglingly big numbers, partly to demonstrate how impossible it was to attain the infinite. Workers in arithmetic discovered unreachable numbers: ratios that could never be exactly determined, but that seemed to underpin the universe—π, for instance (22 divided by 7), which determined the size of a circle, or the complex ratio that Greek mathematicians called the "Golden Number" (roughly 1.618) and seemed to represent perfection of proportion. The invention of geometry showed how the mind can reach realities that the senses obscure or warp: a perfect circle, a line without magnitude. Reality can be invisible, untouchable, and yet accessible to reason.

A figure of enormous importance in unfolding these mysteries (for that is what they were to people at the time) was Pythagoras. His life spanned the Greek world. He was born on an island in the Aegean, around the mid–sixth century B.C.E., but spent most of his teaching life in southern Italy. He attracted stories—he communed with the gods; he had a golden thighbone; he was not a mere man but a unique being, between human and divine.

He was the first thinker, as far as we know, to formulate the idea that numbers are real. They are obviously ways we have of classifying objects—two flowers, five flies. But Pythagoras thought that two and five really exist, quite apart from the objects they enumerate. They would still exist, even if there were nothing to count. He went further. Numbers are the basis on which the cosmos is constructed. "All things are numbers," was his way of putting it. Numbers determine shapes and structures—we still speak of "squares" and "cubes"—and numerical proportions underlie all relationships. Geometry, Pythagoras thought, is the architecture of the universe.

Not everyone was equally enthusiastic about the cult of numbers. "I sought the truth in measures and numbers," said Confucius in a text, which, though he probably did not really write it, reflects the prejudices of the third-century B.C.E. Daoist who compiled it, "but after five years I still hadn't found it." Still, the exploration of numbers was widespread among axial-age sages. **Rationalism**—the doctrine that unaided reason can elicit truth and solve the world's problems—was among the results.

Reason

The first pure rationalist we know by name was Parmenides, who was from a Greek colony of southern Italy in the early fifth century B.C.E. He started with geometry. If you believe geometrical figures are real, you believe in the truth of a supersensible world—for a perfect triangle, for instance, is like God: No one has ever seen one, though crude man-made approximations are commonplace. The only triangles we know about are those in our thoughts. Parmenides therefore suggested that the same might be true of everything else.

In some ways, the consequences are impressive. If, say, a pink rose is real by virtue of being a thought rather than a sensible object, then a black rose is equally real. The nonexistence of anything is an incoherent concept. Few of Parmenides's followers were willing to go that far, but reason did seem able to open secret caverns in the mind, where truths lay. "Fire is not hot. Eyes do not see": These were the numbing, blinding paradoxes of the fourth-century B.C.E. Chinese philosopher Hui Shih (hway-sheh)—who wrote five cartloads of books. They show that data act directly on the mind, which processes them before they become sensations. Thought does not have to arise from experience. For a true rationalist, the best laboratory is the mind, and the best experiments are thoughts.

In partial consequence, rationalism became an escapist's alternative to reality. Parmenides, for instance, thought he could prove that change was illusory and differences deceptive, and that only the unchanging and eternal were real. One of his successors, Zeno of Elea, invented famous paradoxes to demonstrate this: An arrow in flight always occupies a space equal to its size; therefore, it is always at rest. You can never complete a journey because you always have to cross half the remaining distance first. Matter is indivisible because "if a rod is shortened every day by half its length, it will still have something left after ten thousand generations."

Early in the second half of the millennium, teachers in India, Greece, and China proposed rules for the correct use of reason. Practical issues probably underpinned these movements. For pleading in courts, arguing between embassies, persuading enemies, and praising rulers, it was important to make arguments watertight. Logic was a fascinating by-product of these practical needs.

The Nyaya school

The most rigorous and systematic exposition was Aristotle's, strapping common sense into intelligible rules. He was the best-ever analyst of how reason works, in as much as it works at all. According to Aristotle, we can break valid arguments down into phases, called **syllogisms**, in which we can infer a necessary conclusion from two premises that prior demonstration or agreement have established to be true. If the premises are "All men are mortal" and "Socrates is a man," it follows that "Socrates is mortal."

At roughly the same time in India, the Nyaya school of commentators on ancient texts analyzed logical processes in five-stage breakdowns. Their conception, however, was in one fundamental way different from Aristotle's. They claimed reason was a kind of extraordinary perception that God conferred. Nor were they strictly rationalists, for they believed meaning did not arise in the mind. God, tradition, or consensus conferred it on the object of thought.

Science

Meanwhile, another route through the thought of the axial age led to science. As with the exploration of reason, the starting point was distrust of the senses. As a Daoist text of the third century B.C.E. points out, some metals seem soft but can combine to form harder ones; lacquer feels liquid but can be made dry by the application of another liquid. First appearances are deceptive. The science of the axial age sought to penetrate the veil and expose underlying truths. "Truth," said Democritus around the turn of the fifth and fourth centuries B.C.E., "lies in the depths." Although no strictly scientific texts from India survive from this period, the Upanishads contain similar warnings about the unreliability of appearances (see Chapter 5).

The idea of a distinction between what is natural and what is supernatural was, as far as we can tell, new. Previously, science seemed sacred, medicine magical. The earliest clear evidence of a shift in thinking is Chinese. In 679 B.C.E. the sage Shen Xu (shahn shoo) taught that ghosts were the products of the fears and guilt of those who see them. Confucius deterred followers from thinking "about the dead until you know the living." Confucians professed interest in human affairs—politics and practical morality—and indifference to the rest of nature. But as far as they did delve into nature studies, it was to dig out what they regarded as superstition: claims that inanimate substances had feelings and wills, that spirits inhabit all matter, or that the natural world is responsive to human sin or goodness. "The fact," says a Confucian text of about 239 B.C., "that water leaves the mountains is not due to any dislike on the part of the water but is the effect of height. The wheat has no desire to grow or be gathered into granaries." "Natural" causes displaced magic.

In Greece, the origins of science were inseparable from magic, nature worship, and shamanistic attempts to penetrate the mysteries of unseen worlds. For science to thrive in a world that most people believed gods and sprites and demons still

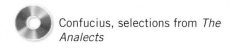

Confucius, selections from *The Analects*

Delphi. Around Mount Parnassus, north of Athens, Greeks found or founded many shrines consecrated to Earth and Nature, as well as the most famous oracular site, at Delphi, where priestesses uttered obscure prophecies, supposedly under the influence of hallucinogenic fumes that rose from a fissure in the ground. Nearby, the circular sanctum known as the Tholos was built in the fourth century B.C.E., at or near the place where the Greeks' predecessors had located the navel of the Mother-Goddess or, as we might now say, the center of the Earth.

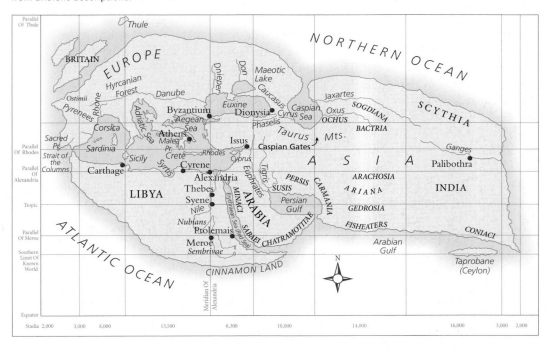

MAP 6.2

The World According to Eratosthenes

Eratosthenes (ca. 275–195 B.C.E.) directed the Library of Alexandria and made a remarkably accurate estimate of the size of the globe. His world map has not survived but a version can be reconstructed from ancient descriptions.

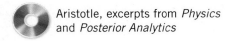

Aristotle, excerpts from *Physics* and *Posterior Analytics*

ruled, a method was needed to observe nature systematically, order the information, and test the resulting hypotheses. Aristotle was the best representative of Greek science in its maturity. "We must have facts," he said and proceeded to gather them in enormous quantities. Like the perfect example of a "nutty professor," he prowled around his lecture room, dissected flies, and noted every stage in the incubation of birds' eggs. Other highlights of Greek science of the period included Archimedes's discovery of the mechanics of leverage in the mid–third century B.C.E., and, slightly later, the work of Eratosthenes, who produced an almost exactly accurate calculation of the size of the planet (see Map 6.2).

Chinese practical science—systematic investigation of nature through observation and experiment—probably arose, in parallel with that of Greece, from Daoist doctrines of nature. Habits of observation and experiment developed from magical and omen-seeking practices of early Daoism. The Daoist word for a "temple" means *watchtower*—a platform from which to observe the natural world and launch naturalistic explanations of its phenomena. Daoism has, in Confucian eyes, a reputation for magical mumbo-jumbo because its priests practice strange ceremonies, many of which seem indebted to the magical fallacy that nature responds to human ritual. But Daoism also teaches that Nature—to the one who would control it—is like any other beast to be tamed or foe to be dominated—it must be known first.

So Daoism encouraged scientific practice: observation, description, classification, and experiment. In second-century B.C.E. China, for instance, Daoist legend told of Yi (yee) the archer, who on sage advice sought the medicine of immortality away in the west, when the weed that would confer it was growing outside his door.

Daoist texts often have amusing dialogues between craftsmen who know their work and rationalists who persuade them to do it in a different way, with ruinous results. Grand theory is discouraged as an intrusion of reason into the workings of wisdom, which can be attained only by gaining knowledge. Chinese science has always been weak on theory, strong on technology.

Medicine

Controversy followed between magic and medicine—or was it just between rival forms of magic? Illness, like any abnormal state, including madness, could be the result of possession or infestation by a spirit, a "demon"—to recycle a commonly used word for it. Or some diseases could have material causes, others spiritual. Or all could be a mixture of the two. Or sickness could be a divine affliction earned by sin.

In Greece in the late fifth century B.C.E., a secular school known as the Hippocratics tried to monopolize the medical profession, at the expense of rival healers who were attached to temples. The Hippocratics thought that health was essentially a state of balance among four substances in human bodies: blood, phlegm, and black and yellow bile. Adjust the balance, and you alter the patient's state of health. This condemned patients in the West for centuries to treatment mainly by diet, vomiting, laxatives, and bloodletting. The theory was wrong—but it was genuinely scientific, based on observation of substances the body expels in pain or sickness.

A treatise sometimes attributed to Hippocrates himself—supposed founder of the school—advocates a naturalistic explanation for epilepsy, which many people at the time assumed to be a form of divine possession. The test is: Find a goat exhibiting the same symptoms that a human epileptic does. "If you cut open the head, you will find that the brain is ... full of fluid and smells foul, convincing proof that the disease and not the deity is harming the body." The method sounds bizarre, but the conclusion is impressive. "Personally," the Hippocratic writer went on, "I believe that human bodies cannot be polluted by a god." A similar shift of business into the hands of secular medical specialists occurred in China. Xunzi, who died in 235 B.C.E., scorned a man who "having got rheumatism from dampness beats a drum and boils a suckling pig as an offering to the spirits." Result: "a worn-out drum and a lost pig, but he will not have the happiness of recovering from sickness." Religious explanations of disease remained. But the Hippocratics and their Chinese counterparts started a presumption that has gained ground ever since: Nothing needs to be explained in divine terms. The physical world is all there is.

These changes had close parallels in India. In the earliest known Indian work of medicine, the Arthaveda (ahr-thah-VEH-dah), which dates from the early first millennium B.C.E., diseases and demons are more or less identical and are treated with charms or drugs. From the sixth century B.C.E. onward, however, we see evidence of professional medical training and literature. Work largely complete by the second century C.E. summarizes these medical teachings. Writings attributed to Susutra, who probably lived in the sixth century B.C.E., concern surgery; writings attributed to Charaka (which may be the name of a school rather than a person) concentrate exclusively on diet and drugs. A saying attributed to Charaka is strikingly similar to the morals of the Greek

Ayurvedic medicine. This medical textbook, first published in 1593, and based on *The Canon of Medicine* written by the great Muslim scholar Avicenna early in the eleventh century, is still used by students at the Unani Medical College in Hyderabad, India. Ayurvedic treatments are usually herbal, although diet and exercise are also important remedies. The illustration and text shown here concern the muscles of the human body.

Axial-Age Science and Medicine

Sixth century B.C.E.	Susutra (India)
Late fifth century B.C.E.	Hippocrates (Greece)
ca. 250 B.C.E.	Archimedes (Greece)
d. 235 B.C.E.	Xunzi (China)
ca. 200 B.C.E.	Eratosthenes (Greece)

Hippocrates: "If you want your treatment to succeed, to earn wealth, to gain fame, and to win heaven hereafter ... seek the good of all living creatures, strive with your whole heart to cure the sick." The similarities among Indian, Greek, and Chinese axial-age medicine are so remarkable that historians often assume that they influenced each other. There is, however, no direct evidence for this influence.

Skepticism

A consequence of the rise of a scientific point of view was the suspicion that the world is purposeless. In particular, this line of thinking challenged another axial-age orthodoxy: If the world was purposeless, it was not made for humans, who were reduced to insignificance. What Aristotle called the "Final Cause"—the purpose of a thing, which explains its nature—becomes incoherent. The world is a random event.

In around 200 B.C.E., this was such a dangerous idea that a skeptical Chinese treatise, the *Liezi* (lee-ay-tzeh), avoided direct advocacy of it by putting it into the mouth of a small boy, who challenged a pious host for praising the divine bounty that provided good things for his table. "Mosquitoes suck human blood, wolves devour human flesh but we do not therefore assert that Heaven created man for their benefit." The greatest-ever exponent of a purposeless cosmos was the Chinese philosopher of the first century C.E., Wangchong (wahng-chohng). Humans, he said, live "like lice in the folds of a garment. When fleas buzz in your ear, you do not hear them: How could God even hear men, let alone concede their wishes?" Some materialist thinkers still assert that the whole notion of purpose is superstitious and that asking why the world exists or why it is as it is is pointless.

In a world without purpose, there is no need for God. The name of the Greek philosopher Epicurus, who died in 270 B.C.E., has become unfairly associated with the pursuit of physical pleasure—which he certainly recommended, albeit with restraint. A far more important element of his thought was his interpretation of the atomic theory. In a world of atoms and voids, there is no room for "spirits." Since atoms are subject to "random swerves," there can be no fate. Since atoms are perishable, and everything is composed of them, there can be no immortal soul. Gods, if they exist at all, inhabit an imaginary world from which "we have nothing to hope and nothing to fear." Epicurus's arguments were formidable, and materialists and atheists kept returning to them. At about the end of the first century C.E., the Roman writer Sextus Empiricus suggested, like a modern Marxist, that "some shrewd man invented fear of the gods" as a means of social control. The doctrines of an all-powerful and all-knowing god were devised to suppress freedom of conscience. "If they say that God controls everything, they make him the author of evil," he concluded. "We express no belief and avoid the evil of the dogmatisers."

In revulsion from the big, unanswerable questions about the nature of reality, skeptical thinkers and their schools refocused philosophy on practical issues. One of the great anecdote-inspiring characters of ancient Greece was Pyrrho of Elis, who accompanied Alexander the Great's invasion of India in 327–324 B.C.E. (see Chapter 7) and imitated the indifference of the naked sages he met there. On board ship on the way home, he admired and shared the calm response of a pig to a storm. Since, he argued, you can find equally good reasons on both sides of any argument, the only wise course is to stop thinking and judge by appearances. More effective was the argument that all reasoning starts from assumptions; so none of it is secure. Mozi had developed a similar insight in China around the beginning of the fourth century B.C.E. Most problems were matters of doubt. "As for what we now know, is it not mostly derived from past experience?"

Later Greek philosophy focused on the best practical choices for personal happiness or for the good of society. **Stoicism**, for instance, is the outstanding example, both for the coherence of Stoic ideas and for the scale of their influence. Stoicism appealed to the Roman elite and through them had an enormous effect on Christianity. First taught in the school that Zeno of Citium founded in Athens in the late fourth century B.C.E., Stoicism started from the insight that nature is morally neutral—only human acts are good or evil. The wise man therefore achieves happiness by accepting misfortune. Further Stoic prescriptions—fatalism and indifference as remedies for pain—were similar to teachings preached at about the same period at the far end of Eurasia, especially by Buddha and his followers, or Laozi and his. People have sought the "happiness priority" in so many contrasting ways that it is hard to generalize about its overall effect on the history of the world. Stoicism, however, was certainly its most effective manifestation in the West. It has supplied, in effect, the source of the guiding principles of the ethics of most Western elites ever since it emerged.

Skeptics and Stoics

Fourth century B.C.E.	Pyrrho of Elis (Greece)
Late fourth century B.C.E.	Zeno of Citium (Greece)
d. 270 B.C.E.	Epicurus (Greece)
First century C.E.	Wangchong (China)
First century C.E.	Sextus Empiricus (Rome)

AXIAL AGE–AXIAL AREA: THE STRUCTURES OF THE AXIAL AGE

Monotheism, republicanism, Legalism, rationalism, logic, science (including scientific medicine), skepticism, the most enduring religions and ethical systems—the tally of new thinking in the axial age looks impressive by any standards, but especially because of its legacy to us. Why was this period so productive? Why was it confined to so few societies around the globe?

The structures that underpinned the work of the axial-age thinkers were important for making it happen. The schools and sages formed four obvious and sometimes overlapping categories. First, there were professional intellectuals, who sold their services as teachers, usually to candidates for professional or public office, but perhaps also to those who sought happiness or immortality or, at least, health. A second class sought the patronage of rulers or positions as political advisers. Many sages belonged to both these groups. Aristotle, for instance, taught in Athens but also served as a royal tutor to the prince who later became Alexander the Great (see Chapter 7). Confucius eked out life as a teacher, but not for want of a calling to serve states. A third category was made up of prophets or holy men, who emerged from ascetic lives with inspired messages for society. A fourth was composed of charismatic leaders with visions to share with and, if possible, impose on their peoples.

Most sages fitted into networks. Though lonely, hermitlike existence was an ideal that many of them recommended, affected, and even sought, few, if any, of these sages were genuinely isolated thinkers. They usually depended on contacts. Networks stimulated innovation, nourished competition, fertilized ideas, and gave emotional support. Plato wrote all his works as dialogues and conversations—which make the function of the network visible. The Confucian Mencius, the Daoist Zhuangzi (jwahng-tzeh), and Hui Shi, the analyst of language, competed and debated. Plato's teacher, Socrates, was in contact and conflict with all the Greek schools of his day, attacking those known as Sophists for allegedly putting the elegance of an argument as more important than its truth. Epicurus

The Academy of Athens. Romans continued to admire the philosophy of classical Greece. The Acropolis of Athens is recognizable in the background of this mosaic, preserved in the ruins of Pompeii. The columns and gardens recall what the setting of Plato's Academy at Athens was really like.

and Zeno of Citium established schools in Athens within a few years of each other toward the end of the fourth century B.C.E.

Formal institutions of education played their part in defining networks and stimulating competition. We know little of how they functioned, but the Academy of Athens, founded in 380 B.C.E., had a garden and lodgings for students, which Plato purchased. Members took meals in common and contributed to costs according to their means. Master–pupil relationships created traditional or what we might call cross-generational networks. Socrates taught Plato, who taught Aristotle. Traditions of this sort can get rigid, but clever pupils often innovate by reacting against their masters' teaching (something all textbook writers should bear in mind) and set up chains of revisionism from one generation to the next. Confucius was a critic of the establishment of his day. Mohists, similarly, opposed Confucians. A succession of masters as well as a series of conflicts linked Mozi to Confucius. Han Feizi (hawn fay-tzeh), a Confucian pupil, founded the Legalist school in reaction to his teacher, Xunzi (see Figure 6.2).

Disciples confided masters' works to writing. The Upanishads were probably transmitted orally before they were finally written down. Socrates wrote nothing. Jesus wrote nothing himself that has survived—only, as far as we know, a few words scratched in the dust. Buddha's teachings were too sacred—his first disciples thought—to confide to writing and had eventually to be retrieved from memories when it was finally decided to write them down. Does this mean that the axial age is a trick of the evidence? That the ideas of its sages became so influential only because they were eventually written down? Not entirely, but it does mean that its thoughts have come down to us in a way that other regions and other periods did not have or did not use.

Some thinkers of the axial age were rich men. Plato could endow his own school with his own money. Buddha and Mahavira, the founder of Jainism, were princes.

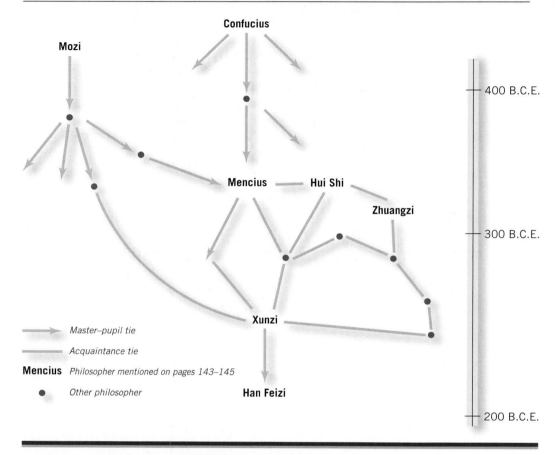

Network of Chinese Philosophers, 400–200 B.C.E.

FIGURE 6.2 NETWORK OF CHINESE PHILOSOPHERS, 400–200 B.C.E.
Adapted from R. Collins, *The Sociology of Philosophies* (Cambridge, MA: Belknap Press, 1998) p. 55.

Usually, however, intellectuals need patrons or employers to survive. The politically fragmented worlds of axial-age Greece, China, and India had plenty of potential patrons. A wandering scholar like Confucius might not retain a patron for long—but he could turn to others. This made for independence of thought and liberated political philosophy to criticize rulers. Every subsequent age has successfully adapted Confucius's message, but he addressed it to his own time. Hence his emphasis on the renewal of tradition, the resumption of sacred rites, the restoration of land and property to their rightful owners. Of course, royal patrons are rarely disinterested. In mid–fourth century B.C.E. China, Mencius found his patron, the King of Wei, interested only in schemes to improve military efficiency. Also at the court of Wei, Hui Shi turned his talent for argument to negotiations with other states.

To patronize sages became a source of princely prestige. In China the prince of Zhao allegedly had 1,000 scholars at his court toward the mid–third century B.C.E. The state of Chu supported the followers of Mozi against the Confucians. Qin, supposedly a "barbarian" kingdom on the edge of the Chinese culture area, was home to thousands of scholars. When its ruler burned books in the 220s B.C.E., it was less perhaps an act against learning than a gesture of partisanship on behalf of thinkers he favored.

○ MAKING CONNECTIONS ○

THINKERS AND THOUGHTS OF THE AXIAL AGE

REGION →	SAGE / THINKER AND TIME PERIOD →	PHILOSPHY/ RELIGION →	DISTINCTIVE IDEAS
Southwest Asia	Jewish sages, ca. 700–500 B.C.E.	Judaism	Monotheism; trials of faith; punishments for sin; covenant with God
Southwest Asia	Zoroaster, ca. 600 B.C.E.	Zoroastrianism	Eternal conflict between good and evil (dualism)
India	Gautama Siddharta, ca. 560 B.C.E.	Buddhism	Meditation; karma; Four Noble Truths; escaping desire
India	Mahavira, ca. 559 B.C.E.	Jainism	Sanctity of life; nonviolence (*ahimsa*)
Greece	Pythagoras, ca. 550 B.C.E.	Mathematics	Geometrical and mathematical ideas; ratios; ideas that numbers are real
China	Confucius, ca. 500 B.C.E.	Secular philosophy	Loyalty to God, state, and family; importance of ethics and right conduct
Greece	Parmenides, ca. 425 B.C.E.	Rationalism	Objects of thought are more real than sense perception
China	Mozi, ca. 400 B.C.E.	Secular philosophy	Universal love
Greece	Zeno, ca. 390 B.C.E.	Stoicism	Nature is morally neutral; happiness achieved by accepting misfortune
Greece	Aristotle and Plato, ca. 380 B.C.E.	Secular philosophy	Logic; science; political thought
India	Nyaya school, 350 B.C.E.	Rationalism	Logic; reason as an extraordinary perception conferred by God
China	Laozi, ca. 300 B.C.E.	Daoism	Detachment from world; quest for immortality
Greece	Epicurus, ca. 280 B.C.E.	Skepticism	Centrality of matter; soul is not immortal; if God exists he is indifferent to human affairs
China	Xunzi, ca. 250 B.C.E.	Secular philosophy	Human goodness can be attained through progress and freedom
China	Han Feizi, ca. 225 B.C.E.	Legalism	Only good is the good of the state; law and order more important than tyranny and injustice
Southwest Asia	Jesus, ca. 30 C.E.	Christianity	Importance of faith, divine love

In India, too, among the states that shared the Ganges valley, similar rivalries and opportunities existed. The Veda contains fragments of sages' dialogues with kings, in which the kings sometimes out-argued the sages. Buddhism relied on rulers' patronage in the kingdoms of Kosala and Magadha. Mahavira was related to the rulers of Videha, where his doctrines enjoyed official favor. His followers debated with Buddhists for supremacy in Magadha. As we shall see in the next chapter, political unification and large-scale imperialism did not promote intellectual productivity. One reason why Zoroaster had no comparably influential successors in Persia is probably because Persia rapidly became an imperial power. In China, India, and Greece the axial age waned as empires grew at the expense of small states, even though the empires themselves spread axial-age ideas.

In some places, popular support also nourished the intellectuals. Sages and holy men are useful to the public in times of political dissolution. Their wisdom and objectivity make them sought after to arbitrate between neighbors or to take the place of absent justice. Public interest is apparent in the multiplicity of schools and the willingness of pupils to seek the benefit of masters' expertise. Learned writings attracted readers. Democritus, an exponent of atomic theory in the early fourth century B.C.E., was credited with 60 books. Heraclitus, one of the first generation of Greek sages, refused to take on pupils. But he nonetheless deposited his writings in the famous temple of the goddess Artemis at Ephesus on the western coast of Anatolia— in effect, his local public library.

CHRONOLOGY
(All dates are approximate)

600 B.C.E.–100 C.E.	Teachers and their disciples influence thinking all across Eurasia
	Spread of Zoroastrianism for next 1,000 years primarily in present-day Iran
	Teachings about Brahman begin to be written down; Buddhism develops in India
	Confucianism, Daoism, and Legalism spread in China
	Legacy of Plato and Aristotle to Western philosophy
	Proponents of secular medicine (Susutra in India, Hippocrates in Greece, and Xunzi in China)
580 B.C.E.	Forced migration of Jews from Jerusalem to Babylon creates a "diaspora mentality," influential up to present times
33 C.E.	Jesus and spread of Christianity over the next two millennia

IN PERSPECTIVE: The Reach of the Sages

Although the new thinking of the axial age was confined to parts of Asia and Europe, it was a worldwide story because of how axial-age thinking later spread and shaped thoughts and feelings in every clime and continent. Empires that are the subject of the next chapter helped to spread it. Trade and colonization, which can be traced at intervals throughout the rest of this book, spread axial thought across the planet. The Roman Empire carried Greek science and philosophy into Western Europe. Buddhism became a state ideology in the first empire to cover almost all of India. The Chinese Empire became a growing arena in which Buddhism, as well as native Chinese thought, spread within and across China's widening borders. Japan's and Korea's intellectual traditions developed from Chinese-inspired starting points. Migration and trade bore Indian thinking into southeast Asia. Christianity fused Jewish and Greek intellectual traditions and spread them—ultimately—all over the world. Islam shared much of the same heritage and spread it almost as far. Buddhism is the third, in terms of numbers of followers, of the three World Religions of today. Alongside Christianity and Islam, both of which developed after the axial age, it has spread over many different countries and cultures, whereas most religions tend to remain specific to their cultures of origin. We do not fully understand the reasons for Buddhist success in this respect, but we shall trace its history in this book. But the scale of demands Buddhism makes on its followers is well suited to a variety of walks of life.

As a result of the spread of the work of the sages and their schools, the thought of the modern world has a familiar ring to a student of the axial age. It seems astonishing that today, after all the technical and material progress of the last 2,000 years, we should remain so dependent on the thought of such a distant era and have added so little to it. We debate the same issues about the nature of reality, using the same tools of logic and science. We struggle with the same problems about the relationship of this world to others, and most of us still follow religious traditions founded by axial-age sages. We search for a balance between the same kinds of optimistic and pessimistic assessments of human nature that people of the axial age identified, and we seek resolutions of similar conflicts of political ideas that arise as a result. To a remarkable extent, we express ourselves in terms the ancient sages taught.

Although the sages and schools of the axial age were confined to Eurasia, comparisons with other parts of the world help us understand how cultural contacts shape and spread what people think and believe. Over and over again, readers of this book will see and will have seen, for example, how ways of thought and life and worship radiated outward from kernel regions: from Mesoamerica, for example, into North and Central America; or from parts of the Andes along the coasts and mountain chains of South America and across the Amazon valley; or from the Ethiopian highlands into surrounding areas; or from centers on the Niger River in West Africa into the Sahel and the forest; or from western Polynesia deep into the Pacific. But the relatively isolating geography of the Americas, sub-Saharan Africa, and the Pacific worked against the kinds of comparatively intense exchange that were possible across Eurasia.

It is impossible to trace to their outer limits the networks that bound the axial-age sages. But the similarities between their thoughts across Eurasia suggest that long-range cultural exchanges must have been going on among them. This was perhaps the critical difference that made Eurasian societies relatively prolific in a period when we know of no comparable achievements in intellectual life anywhere else in the world. Our next task is therefore to look not only at the changing political frameworks of the axial age, but also at the evidence of the spread and strength of long-range cultural contacts in the world of the time.

PROBLEMS AND PARALLELS

1. What were the similarities among the ideas of the great sages of the axial age? How do they influence the way we think now?

2. How did the idea of divine love alter humankind's relationship with God and the world?

3. How did religious ideas affect political thought in the axial age? Why were most axial-age sages optimists rather than pessimists?

4. How did axial-age science investigate nature? How did axial-age medicine distinguish itself from magic?

5. What roles did networks, schools, and patrons play in spreading axial-age thinking?

6. What comparisons can be made between the axial age and the way culture radiates outward from kernel regions in other parts of the world?

DOCUMENTS IN GLOBAL HISTORY

- Siddhartha Gautama: *Identity and Nonidentity*
- Laozi, from the *Tao Te Ching*
- Plato, *The Republic*, "The Philosopher King"
- Legalism, selections from the writings of Han Fei

- The Nyaya school
- Confucius, selections from *The Analects*
- *Aristotle*, excerpts from *Physics* and *Posterior Analytics*

Please see the Primary Source DVD for additional sources related to this chapter.

READ ON

The Analects of Confucius is the best work with which to begin study of the sage. Many editions are available: R. Dawson, *Confucius* (1982) is perhaps the best general introductory account of the subject. E. L. Shaughnessy, *Before Confucius* (1997) gives the background to the thought of the period of the Hundred Schools. T. De Bary, ed., *Sources of Chinese Tradition* (2000) is an excellent introductory anthology of extracts from key texts. J. Needham, *Science and Civilisation in China* (1961), i and ii, with vol. vii by C. Habsmeier, set Chinese thought—not only on science—in global context, stressing the priority of Chinese achievement in antiquity and the Middle Ages. N. Sivin, *Medicine, Philosophy and Religion in Ancient China* (1996) collects essays on the links between Dao and science. For Chinese political thought, see S. DeGrazia, *Masters of Chinese Political Thought* (1973) for a selection of texts and B. I. Schwartz, *The World of Thought in Ancient China* (1985), for a critical guide.

R. Zaehner, *The Dawn and Twilight of Zoroastrianism* (2003) is an unsurpassed classic. R. Gotshalk, *The Beginnings of Philosophy in India* (1998) can be recommended on the Upanishads; for texts, E. Deutsch, *A Source Book of Vedanta* (1971) has a good selection. A. T. Embree, ed., *Sources of Indian Tradition* (1988) collects some useful texts. R. Gombrich, ed., *The World of Buddhism* (1991) is a superb introduction to its subject, especially good on Buddhist monasticism. K. H. Potter, ed., *Encyclopedia of Indian Philosophies* (1994), 6 vols., is a comprehensive guide to Indian thought.

On the Jewish and Jesusian concept of God, K. Armstrong, *A History of God* (1993), and J. Miles, *God: A Biography* (1995) are suggestive and instructive; the revisionist M. S. Smith, *Origins of Biblical Monotheism* (2001) can also be recommended. C. S. Lewis, *The Four Loves* is a classic work contrasting the Jesusian notion of divine love with other traditions. The version in *The New Jerusalem Bible* is the most reliable modern translation of the gospels and has manageable and instructive notes. On Jesus, G. Vermes, *Jesus the Jew* (1973) is provocative, enlightening, and gripping. C. P. Thiede and M. D'ancona, *The Jesus Papyrus* (1997) too, offers an invigorating challenge to conventional thinking. M. Staniforth, trans., *Early Jesusian Writings* (1968) collects some of the texts that did not make it into the Bible.

W. K. C. Guthrie, *A History of Greek Philosophy* (1962) is a model of scholarship; the sixth and last volume, *Aristotle: An Encounter* is also an intensely personal and fascinating study of the single most important thinker in the history of Western thought. A. A. Long, *Hellenistic Philosophy* (1974) takes up the story where Guthrie leaves off. The classic work by E. R. Dodds, *The Greeks and the Irrational* (1957) remains a valuable corrective to conventional thinking. O. Taplin, *Greek Fire* (1990) is an accessible and up-to-date study of ancient Greek thought. M. L. West, *The East Face of Helicon* (1997) settles the controversy about where Greek ideas "originally" came from. R. Collins, *The Sociology of Philosophies* (1998) makes an important contribution to tracing the connections that made schools of thinkers and forged the contacts between them.

The Great Empires

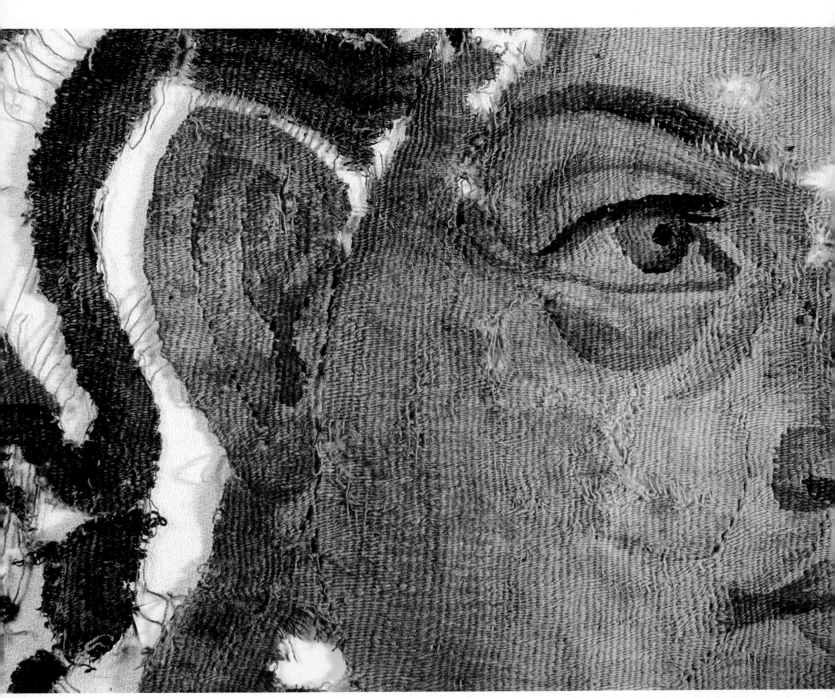

China and Rome on the Silk Roads. A face with Caucasian features on a woolen weaving from the first or second century C.E. is evidence that the Chinese and the Romans were linked by trade. The cloth was discovered in a grave on the Silk Roads in Xinjiang. The face was stitched into a pair of pants and woven in a style not used by the Chinese.

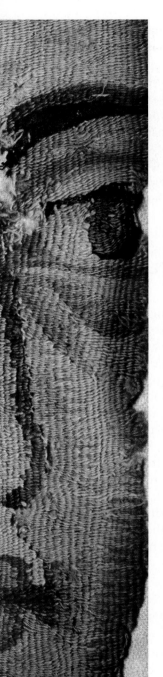

I n about 33 B.C.E., Maecenas, one of the Roman Empire's leading ministers, gave a small farm to a penniless poet. The farm was just what Horace wanted. For the rest of his days, he devoted much of his best poetry to celebrating the simple, rural life and praising his patrons. In one poem, he imagined Maecenas worrying over what the Chinese might be plotting. In others, Horace pictured Augustus, the Roman emperor, fathering a future conqueror of China. This was outrageous flattery, since there was no likelihood of the Roman and Chinese empires having much contact of any kind, let alone going to war. In 97 C.E., China did send an envoy to Rome, but he turned back at the Black Sea.

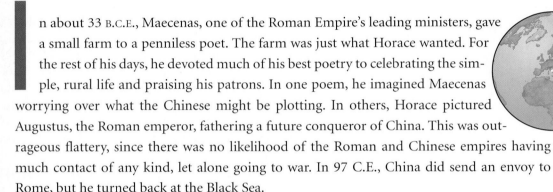

That was as close as the Roman and Chinese empires ever came to direct mutual dealings. But that Horace was aware of China, and realized that events at the far end of Eurasia could affect Roman interests, shows how the world was, as we say now, getting smaller, as land trade routes opened communications across Eurasia; traffic grew along the existing maritime routes of the Indian Ocean, and, finally, sea travel began to connect the Mediterranean with northern Europe's Atlantic shores. The trade routes of the Phoenician and Greek trailblazers described in Chapter 5 led north from the Strait of Gibraltar to the tin-producing British Isles. Their colonies were staging posts in the making of a new economy—helping goods, people, and ideas cross or get around the watershed that divides Mediterranean from Atlantic Europe.

• • • • •

Not only did travelers and trade expand communications, but also the need for big armies and the growth of commerce created a demand for stronger, bigger states—empires that included many political communities in common allegiance. The new empires of the period took shape first in southwest Asia, then around the Mediterranean, and finally in China and India. They established common frontiers or frontier zones of conflict and culture exchange. Around them, chiefs, enriched by trade, turned into kings.

FOCUS questions

- WHY WERE trade routes so important to axial-age empires?
- HOW DID the Persian Empire benefit its inhabitants?
- HOW WAS Rome able to conquer and rule a vast empire?
- HOW DID Asoka seek to unify his empire?
- WHAT WAS the significance of the Han dynasty for China?
- WHERE DID the first potentially imperial states arise in the Americas?

The empires spilled people, technology, and means of life into frontier areas that had been little populated. Cultivated crops and domesticated livestock transformed previously undisturbed ecosystems. At an increasing rate, neighbors who had lived by hunting and foraging for wild plants adopted agriculture, following the empires' example. Those who continued to resist change were cast as enemies and savages. In the great grasslands, the steppes of central Eurasia, where tilling the soil was impossible, empires formed with a different sort of economy, based on herding livestock. A pattern began that lasted for some 2,000 years of violence between these nomad empires that lived by herding and the sedentary farmers who lived near them.

Meanwhile, beyond the routes that connected Eurasian empires, foragers and small-scale farmers survived. They could minimize risk by minimizing change. Most of them took this option. In parts of the New World, however, experiments in embracing change and attempting to control it continued. Large-scale interventions in the environment and imaginative adaptations of human society took forms that were familiar from Eurasia. Agriculture led to urbanization, long-range commerce, and eventually imperialism. Seen from today's perspective, the Americas seemed to be reliving the history of the Old World.

ROUTES THAT DREW THE OLD WORLD TOGETHER

As a general rule in history, bigger states mean more exchange over longer distances. In part, this is simply because they facilitate trade and travel within their own expanding borders; in part, because they generate increasing contacts with each other through commerce, diplomacy, and war. To understand the cultural exchanges of the period—how and why they happened and to what extent—we therefore have to understand the political framework: where and how new states formed; how their horizons broadened; what were the new institutions—the mechanisms for conveying commands and exacting obedience—that enabled them to function over unprecedented distances.

State-building and the development of communications are mutually dependent processes. Routes of commerce are the lifelines of empires: pumping them with resources, equipping them with new ideas and technologies, laying down tracks for their armies to follow. We must begin, therefore, by drawing in the long-range causeways of the period: the sea lanes and land routes that crossed Eurasia, making possible the cultural exchanges of the axial age and the new political developments in the empires the routes linked (see Map 7.1).

The Sea Routes of the Indian Ocean

The world maps Indian geographers of the axial age drew look like the product of stay-at-home minds. Four—then, from the second century B.C.E. onward, seven—continents radiate from a mountainous core. Around concentric rings of rock flow seven seas, made up respectively, of salt, sugarcane juice, wine, butter, curds, milk, and water.

Real observations, however, underlay the metaphors of the maps. The world was grouped around the great Himalaya Mountains and the triangular, petal-like form of India, with the island of Sri Lanka falling from it like a dewdrop. The ocean was divided into separate seas, some imaginary or little known, but others representing real routes to frequented destinations and commercial centers. The Sea of Milk, for instance, corresponds roughly to what we now call the Arabian Sea, and led to Arabia and Persia. The Sea of Butter led to Ethiopia.

Stories of Indian seafaring from late in the first millennium B.C.E. appear in the *Jatakas*, collected tales of Buddhahood—guides to how to become enlightened. Here, piloting a ship "by knowledge of the stars" is a godlike gift. The Buddha saves sailors from cannibalistic goblin-seductresses in Sri Lanka. He puts together an unsinkable vessel for a pious explorer. A merchant advised by an enlightened sage buys a ship on credit and sells the cargo at a profit of 200,000 gold pieces. A guardian-deity saves shipwreck victims who have combined commerce with pilgrimage "or are endowed with virtue or worship their parents." Similar legends appear in Persian sources, like the story of Jamshid, a hero who is both king and shipbuilder and who crosses oceans "from region to region with great speed."

Accounts of real voyages back these stories. Toward the end of the sixth century B.C.E., Darius I—an emperor enthusiastic for exploration—ruled Persia. He ordered a reconnaissance of the Indian Ocean from the northern tip of the Red Sea, around Arabia, to the mouth of the Indus River in northern India. A canal built from Suez on the Red Sea to the Nile indicates there must have been traffic for it to serve, traffic that the canal increased.

What Indian mapmakers called the Seas of Milk and Butter were, to Greek merchants, "the Erythraean Sea," from which traders brought back aromatics—especially frankincense and myrrh—and an Arabian cinnamon substitute called cassia. Important ports for long-range trade lined Arabia's shores. At Gerrha, for instance, merchants unloaded Indian manufactures. Nearby, Thaj also served as a good place to warehouse imports. Egyptian merchants endowed temples in south Arabia with incense in the third century B.C.E.

from *The Periplus of the Erythraean Sea*

The reason for the long seafaring, sea-daring tradition of the Indian Ocean lies in the regularity of the monsoonal wind system. Above the equator, northeasterlies prevail in winter, but when winter ends, the winds reverse direction. For most of the rest of the year, they blow steadily from the south and west, sucked toward the Asian landmass as air warms and rises over the continent. By timing voyages to take advantage of these predictable changes, navigators could be confident of a fair wind out and a fair wind home.

◯ MAKING CONNECTIONS

THE DYNAMICS OF EMPIRE

ENVIRONMENT →	SOCIETY →	ECONOMY →	COMMERCE →	POLITICS
Cultivated crops and livestock transform ecosystems across Eurasia	Foragers adopt agriculture	Urbanization leads to increased trade over longer distances	Increased contact between regions leads to conflict, war, diplomacy, and cultural exchanges	Increased commerce, conflicts, numerous routes of communication provide opportunities for stronger, bigger states that can manage many political communities more efficiently

MAP 7.1

Eurasian Trade, ca. 500 B.C.E.–100 C.E.

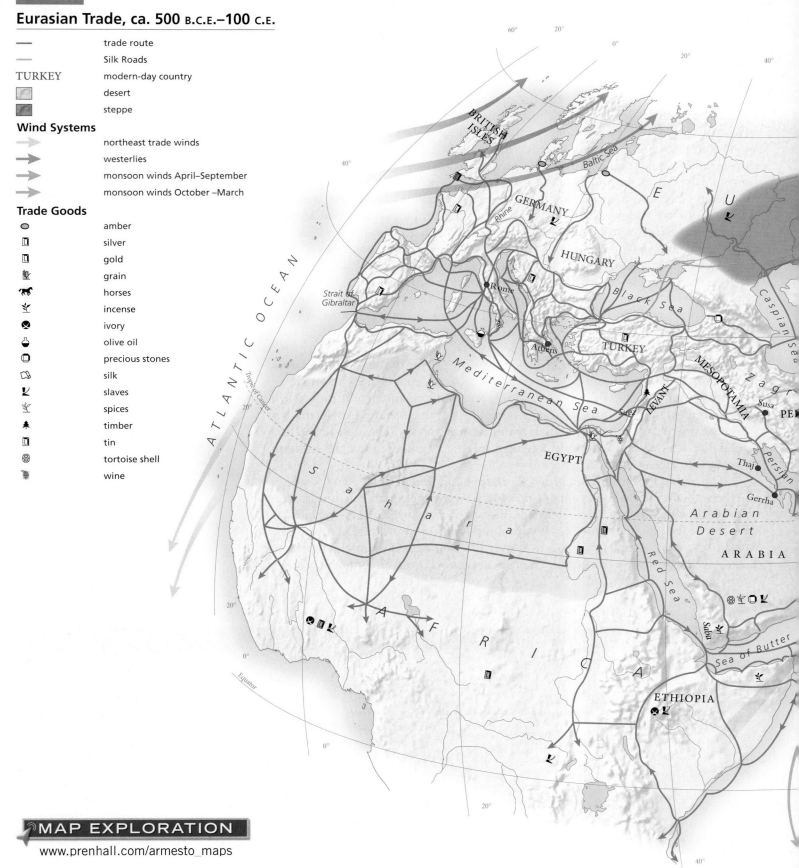

———	trade route
———	Silk Roads
TURKEY	modern-day country
▨	desert
▨	steppe

Wind Systems

⟶	northeast trade winds
⟶	westerlies
⟶	monsoon winds April–September
⟶	monsoon winds October –March

Trade Goods

⬭	amber
▯	silver
▯	gold
⚘	grain
🐎	horses
⚘	incense
⬤	ivory
⬦	olive oil
⬯	precious stones
⬚	silk
⚑	slaves
⚘	spices
♠	timber
▯	tin
⊕	tortoise shell
⬤	wine

BRITISH ISLES
Baltic Sea
GERMANY
Rhine
HUNGARY
Black Sea
Rome
Athens
TURKEY
Mediterranean Sea
Suez
LEVANT
MESOPOTAMIA
Susa
PE
Zagr
Caspian Sea
Thaj
Persian
Gerrha
Arabian Desert
ARABIA
EGYPT
Red Sea
Saba
Sea of Butter
Strait of Gibraltar
ATLANTIC OCEAN
Tropic of Cancer
S a h a r a
A F R I C A
ETHIOPIA
Equator

60° 20° 0° 20° 40°
40°
40°
20°
0°
20°
40°
20°
20°
0°

MAP EXPLORATION
www.prenhall.com/armesto_maps

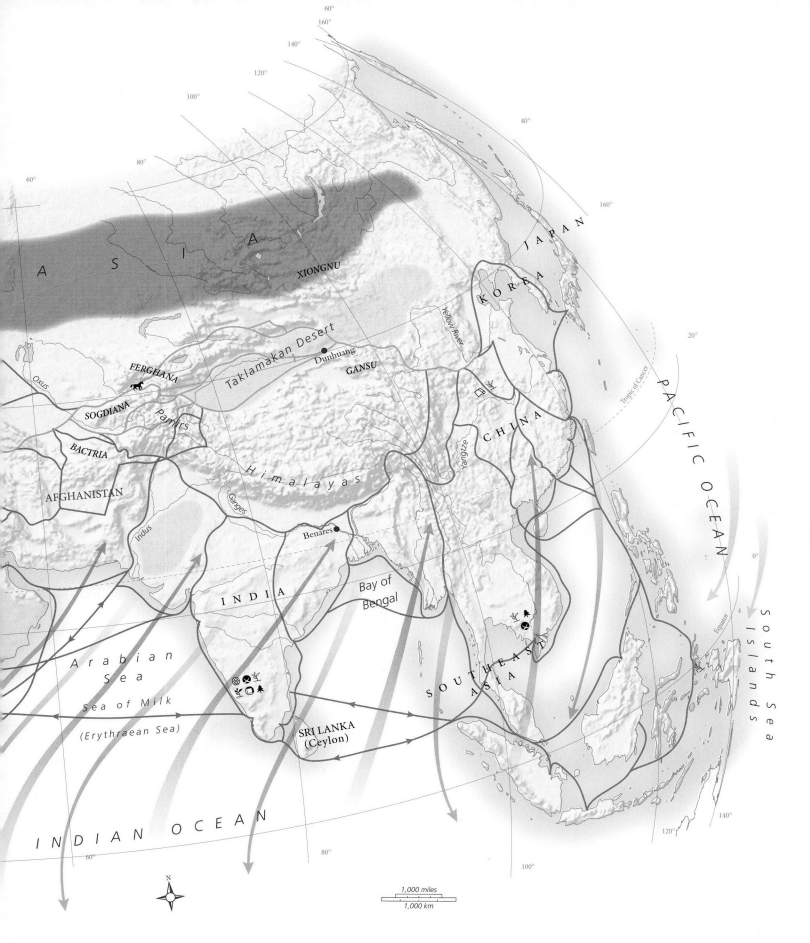

ASIA

XIONGNU

Oxus

FERGHANA

SOGDIANA

Pamirs

BACTRIA

AFGHANISTAN

Indus

Ganges

Taklamakan Desert

Dunhuang

GANSU

Himalayas

Benares

INDIA

Arabian
Sea

Sea of Milk

(Erythraean Sea)

SRI LANKA
(Ceylon)

Bay of
Bengal

INDIAN OCEAN

Yellow River

KOREA

JAPAN

CHINA

Yangtze

SOUTHEAST
ASIA

PACIFIC OCEAN

Tropic of Cancer

Equator

South Sea
Islands

N

1,000 miles

1,000 km

Agatharchides of Knidos describes Saba

It is a fact not often appreciated that, overwhelmingly, maritime exploration has been made into the wind, presumably because it was at least as important to get home as to get to anywhere new. This was how the Phoenicians and Greeks opened the Mediterranean to long-range commerce and colonization (see Chapter 5). The same strategy enabled South Sea Island navigators of this period to explore and colonize the Pacific (see Chapter 10). The monsoonal wind system in the Indian Ocean freed navigators from such constraints. One must try to imagine what it would be like, feeling the wind, year after year, alternately in one's face and at one's back. Gradually, would-be seafarers realized how the wind would change regularly, and so could risk an outward voyage without fearing that they might be unable to return home.

The Indian Ocean has many hazards. Storms wrack it, especially in the Arabian Sea, the Bay of Bengal, and the deadly belt of bad weather below about ten degrees south of the equator. But the predictability of a homeward wind made this the world's most benign environment for long-range voyaging. The fixed-wind systems of the Atlantic and Pacific were almost impossible to cross with ancient technology. We know of no round trips across them. Even compared with other navigable seas, the reliability of the monsoon season offered other advantages. No reliable sources record the length of voyages in this period, but, to judge from later statistics, a trans-Mediterranean journey from east to west, against the wind, would take 50 to 70 days. With the monsoon, a ship could cross the entire Erythraean Sea, between India and a port on the Persian Gulf or near the Red Sea, in three or four weeks in either direction.

Land Routes: The Silk Roads

In the long run, sea routes were more important for global history than land routes. They carried a greater variety of goods faster, more economically, and in greater amounts. Nevertheless, in the early stages, most Eurasian long-range trade was small scale—in goods of high value and limited bulk. Goods moved through a series of markets and middlemen. In the axial age, the land routes that linked Eurasia were as important as the sea routes in establishing cultural contacts: bringing people from different cultures together, facilitating the flow of the ideas of the axial-age sages, transmitting the works of art that changed taste and the goods that influenced lifestyles.

From around the middle of the first millennium B.C.E., Chinese silks appeared here and there across Europe. By the end of the millennium, we can trace the flow of Chinese manufactured goods from the southern Caspian to the northern Black Sea, and into what were then gold-rich kingdoms in the southwest Eurasian steppe. Meanwhile, roads that kings built and maintained crossed what are now Turkey and Iran, penetrated Egypt and Mesopotamia, reached the Persian Gulf, and, at their easternmost ends, touched the Pamir Mountains in Afghanistan and crossed the Indus River.

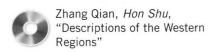
Zhang Qian, *Hon Shu*, "Descriptions of the Western Regions"

Merchants could also use these routes. The first written evidence of presumed commerce across Eurasia appears in a report from Zhang Qian, a Chinese ambassador who set out for one of the Greek-ruled kingdoms established in Central Asia in the wake of Alexander the Great in ca. 139 B.C.E. From the time of his mission, "specimens of strange things began to arrive" in China "from every direction."

In 111 B.C.E., a Chinese garrison founded the outpost of Dunhuang (deen-hwang)—the name means "blazing beacon"—beyond China's western borders, amid desert and mountains. Here, according to a poem inscribed in one of the caves where travelers sheltered, was "the throat of Asia," where "the roads to the western ocean" converged like veins in the neck. We now call them the **Silk Roads.** They led to the markets of Central Asia and linked up with routes that branched into Tibet, or doubled back toward India, or continued westward across the Iranian plateau.

From Dunhuang, the Silk Roads skirted the Taklamakan (tahk-lah-mah-KAHN) Desert, clinging to the edges, where water drains from the surrounding mountains, haunted, in Chinese accounts, by screaming demon drummers—personifications of the ferocious winds. The desert deterred even bandits, and the mountains offered protection from the predatory nomads who lived beyond them.

A few years after the founding of Dunhuang, a Chinese army, reputedly of 60,000 men, traveled to secure the mountain passes at the western end and to force the horse breeders of Central Asia to trade. A painted cave shows the general, Wudi (woo-dee), kneeling before the "golden men"—idols taken, or perhaps mistaken, for Buddhas—that Chinese forces seized. In ca. 102 B.C.E., the Chinese invaded Ferghana and obtained 30,000 horses in tribute. Meanwhile, caravans from China reached Persia, and Chinese trade goods became common along the eastern Mediterranean.

Trade across Eurasia exposed great disparities in wealth between East and West. These differences helped to shape the history of that region over the next 2,000 years. Already in the first century C.E., the Roman geographer, Pliny, worried about it. The Roman world produced little that its trading partners wanted, whereas the silks of China and the spices and incense of Arabia and the Indian Ocean were much in demand in Rome. The only way people in Europe could pay for them was in cash—gold or, more commonly, silver. Nowadays, we would call this an adverse **balance of trade**—the value of Europe's imports from Asia far surpassed the value of its exports. The problems of financing it, by finding enough silver and ultimately of overcoming and reversing it by finding and supplying goods Asians wanted to buy, became a major theme of the history of the West and, in the long run, as we shall see, of the world.

THE FIRST EURASIAN EMPIRE: PERSIA

Iran commanded a central position in the developing trade across Eurasia, linking Central Asian markets to those of southwest Asia and the Mediterranean. So—in view of the way trade and empire are mutually nourishing—it is not surprising that the first of the great empires of the axial age originated here.

In earlier periods, Akkadians and Assyrians had carried the traditions of lowland Mesopotamia north into their hills, like booty. Now conquerors from the adjoining and even higher tableland used the same traditions to create a new state. This state became the biggest the world had yet known: the Persian Empire.

The Persian Heartland

Its heartland consisted of scatterings of good soil and precious water in a vast, arid plateau. Ragae, with its brackish streams and sweet wells, overlooked the Zagros (ZAH-grohs) Mountains. Hamadan lay in a valley watered with springs, known for good fruit and inferior wheat. Fars was the richest area in ancient times. Water from the Zayinda Rud enriched the plain of Isfahan (IHS-fah-hahn). Rivers—including the Tigris and Euphrates—laced the southwest. Here, at the old trading city of Susa, on the border of the Mesopotamian world, the

China and the Silk Roads	
ca. 500 B.C.E.	Chinese silks appear in Europe
ca. 139 B.C.E.	Zhang Qian sets out for Bactria
111 B.C.E.	Chinese found Dunhuang
102 B.C.E.	Chinese invade Ferghana

Heavenly horse. Chinese artists have favored horses as subjects in almost every period but never more than during the Han dynasty (206 B.C.E.–220 C.E.), when an intense effort to import fine horses from Central Asia enriched China's equine bloodstock. More than for their utility, horses inspired artists—as in this example from Wuwei (Gansu province) of the second century C.E.—as symbols of the fleeting, ever-changing nature of human life.

The Art Archive/Picture Desk, Inc./Kobal Collection

○ MAKING CONNECTIONS

TRADE ROUTES AND THEIR CONNECTIONS

LONG-RANGE ROUTES →	ADVANTAGES →	GEOGRAPHICAL SCOPE →	COMMERCE AND EXCHANGE →	POLITICAL SYSTEMS
Sea Route: Indian Ocean	Changeable, predictable monsoon winds lead to reliable schedules; great variety and amount of goods can be carried via ship (emporium trading); seaborne trade usually faster than land routes	East Africa, Arabia, India, southeast Asia; canal between Red Sea and Nile River eventually connects to Mediterranean	Aromatics (incense), spices, gold, and "thousands of other things" (including wild animals)	African kingdoms, Indian empires and kingdoms, Arabian tribal chiefdoms, Mediterranean empires
Land Route: Silk Roads across Eurasia	Less investment needed to embark on small-scale trading expeditions; more cultural contacts between vastly different peoples; widespread trade of high-value items	China, Bactria, Sogdiana, Persia, Mesopotamia, Anatolia, Caspian/Black Sea, Mediterranean	Spices, silk, gold, silver, cloth, horses, aromatics	Imperial China, Central Asian kingdoms, Egypt, nomadic tribes of Middle East, Persian Empire, Roman Empire, Mediterranean city-states
Sea Route: Mediterranean	Relatively high population densities along the coastal Mediterranean provides more opportunities for trade, numerous ports; shorter distances, calmer waters than vast Indian Ocean routes	Europe, North Africa, southwest Asia, Black Sea, with Red Sea–Nile canal connections to Arabia, Indian Ocean route	Grain, wine, olive oil, timber, metals	Greek city-states/colonies, Egypt, North African city-states, Roman Empire

Persians established the capital of their state. Generally, between mountains and deserts, lay narrow strips of good pasture and land, watered by seasonal streams that could be irrigated for farming. Like the old Hittite Empire (see Chapter 4), Persia was another alliance of farmers and flocks. Hymns that are among the earliest sources for Iranian history praise herders and husbandmen as followers of truth and pronounce their nomadic enemies "adherents of lies, who uproot crops and waste livestock," which would be better employed fertilizing farmland. Farming communities' depictions of bull sacrifice show spurting blood transformed into sprouting wheat.

The founding of the Persian Empire is traditionally credited to Cyrus the Great, a general from Fars. Toward the mid–sixth century B.C.E., he launched a coup to take over one of the biggest successor-states of Assyria, the kingdom of the Medes. His subsequent campaigns stretched from Palestine to Afghanistan. His power reached almost the farthest limits the Persian Empire would ever attain. His inscriptions call him simply, "I, Cyrus, the Achaemenid" (ah-KEE-meh-nihd)—the name of the family to which he belonged. But he headed a conquest state, poor in resources, with a need to keep growing. The Persian Empire gradually adopted the

Persepolis. Reliefs that line the approach to the audience chamber of the ruler of Persia at Persepolis show exactly what went on there: reception of tribute, submission of ambassadors. The figures look uniform at first, but their various styles of beards, headgear, and robes indicate the diversity of the lands from which they came and, therefore, the range of the Great King's power.

Old World–conquering ambitions of Sargon of Akkad (see Chapter 3) and the Assyrians but with a difference: The Persians put these ambitions into practice.

The empire joined two regions—Mesopotamian and Persian—that mountains had formerly divided. At its greatest extent, it reached the Aegean coast, Egypt, and India beyond the Indus River. It relied on long-range trade and needed to invest in communications. By early in the fifth century B.C.E., nearly 1,700 miles of road from Susa to Sardis crossed the empire. Royal armies tramped them at a rate of 19 miles a day, and "Nothing mortal," it was said, "travels as fast as the royal messengers." The road was also a channel for tribute. Carvings at the imperial city of Persepolis, founded around the end of the sixth century B.C.E., show ivory, gold, and exotic animals arriving at the court of the ruler of Persia.

Persian Government

Persia was more than a robber empire. The empire provided a canal linking the Nile to the Red Sea and irrigation works on the Oxus and the Karun Rivers. Forts beyond the Caucasus Mountains kept steppe nomads at bay. At Jerusalem, Cyrus the Great undertook to rebuild the temple that symbolized the city's sanctity for the Jews. The gesture was typical of the way Persian rulers conciliated the subjects they acquired. In gratitude, the biblical prophet Isaiah hailed Cyrus as God's anointed.

Greeks accused Persians of treating their kings like gods, in the Egyptian manner, but this charge was unjust. Persian kings were not gods, but their right to rule was god given. The other practices that Greeks found peculiar were the Persian love of luxury—a criticism excused, perhaps, by envy—and their respect for women. Surviving Achaemenid ration lists—the records of wages and payments in kind that court personnel received—assign professions by sex. These show that royal attendants could be of either sex and that women could supervise mixed groups of men and women and earn higher wages than men. It was not, however, a society of sexual equality. Scribes had to be male, while servers of rations—the lowest category by pay—had to be female. Mothers got extra rations for the birth of boys. Nevertheless, women could

Religious freedom in ancient Persia: the "Cyrus Cylinder"

Rise and Fall of the Persian Empire

Sixth century B.C.E.	Cyrus the Great founds Achaemenid dynasty
Early fifth century B.C.E.	Completion of royal road from Susa to Sardis
490 and 480 B.C.E.	Unsuccessful efforts to conquer Greece
334 B.C.E.	Alexander conquers Persian Empire

hold property in their own right. This gave them a political role as what, in modern American politics, would be called "campaign funders"— backers and patrons of men who sought power. Greek sources, exaggerating the amount of power women enjoyed as a result, blamed every lurch of palace politics on female willfulness. For Greeks, who barred women from political life in their own communities, saw them as dangerous agents of chaos in other cultures' states.

The Persian–Greek Wars

Greeks who lived on and beyond the western edge of the Persian Empire were in a giant's shadow. They needed to find ways to cope with insecurity and defeat fear. In about 500 B.C.E., the ruler of Miletus, a Greek colony on the shore of western Anatolia, had a map of the world that showed two roughly equal areas—an exaggeratedly large Europe at the top, like a protruding lip over Asia and Africa crammed into the lower half. The agenda was clear. Asia was reduced to a manageable conquest.

The map looked brash but concealed unease. Rumors claimed that the Persians wanted to conquer Europe because "its trees were too fine for anyone but the Great King to possess." More likely, the empire was committed to expanding because it needed tribute from subject-lands to support it. In any event, the Greeks saw the Persians as a threat but did not feel threatened enough to stop feuding with each other even when the Persians prepared to invade Greece. The oracle of Delphi (Chapter 5) even advised submitting to Persian rule, with its reputation for efficiency, generosity, and respect for trade. In the wars that followed, Greek unity occurred only in dire moments of Persian invasion. Persia, after testing the difficulties of conquering Greece in unsuccessful invasions in 490 and 480 B.C.E., was generally content to keep these enemies divided, while prioritizing Persian rule over rich, soft Egypt.

The sea became the effective frontier between the Greek and Persian worlds. A Persian decree of 387 B.C.E. sums it up: The king "deems it right that the cities in Asia be his . . . The other Greek cities, both small and great, shall be independent," while most of the Greek colonies on the islands of the Aegean were divided between Persia and Athens. This was an indication that Athens—best resourced of the Greek cities because it controlled silver mines—had imperial ambitions of its own, which many Greek states found more menacing than those of Persia.

The Empire of Alexander the Great

Not even Athens could assert long-term hegemony in Greece. Macedon, however, could. Macedon is an example of a now familiar fact: On the edges of civilizations, chiefdoms developed into states. This northern kingdom had what to southern Greeks was a barbarian background, but Greece profoundly influenced its culture. Increasingly, in the fourth century B.C.E., Macedonians saw themselves as Greeks. Aristotle (see Chapter 6) served as a tutor to the royal court.

In 338 B.C.E., King Philip of Macedon imposed unity by force on the Greeks and revived the idea of conquering Persia. When he was assassinated—allegedly by a Persian-backed conspiracy—two years later, his 19-year-old son, Alexander, inherited his father's ambitions. For Philip, attacking Persia was probably intended to focus his uneasily united realm on an external enemy. Alexander's motivation, however, has baffled historians. Was he seeking to vindicate his dead father? Or to reenact legendary romances of Greek campaigns in Asia, which filled his head from his boyhood reading? Or was he full of insatiable ambition to leave "no world unconquered" as some early biographers claimed? Did he have humdrum economic aims? He certainly showed interest in opening up Indian Ocean trade or seizing control of its routes. He ordered reconnaissance by sea of the routes between India, Persia, and Arabia and began, just before his death, to plan the conquest of Arabia.

Probably, his ambitions grew with his success. Alexander destroyed the Persian Empire at lightning speed in three years' campaigns from 334 B.C.E. (see Map 7.2). When the last Persian emperor died at his own officers' hands, perhaps because he had decided to abandon resistance, Alexander proclaimed himself "Great King." His success seems inexplicable except in terms of the interconnected skill and luck of the battlefield. The Persian Empire was essentially strong, well run, and easily governed. Alexander took it over intact, maintained its methods of control, and divided it among his subordinates.

Success and flattering omens convinced him that he enjoyed divine favor— perhaps, even, that he was divine. His methods became increasingly arbitrary, his character increasingly unpredictable. He dealt with disloyalty first by judicial murder, then assassination, then slaughter by his own hand, then arbitrary executions. In the last years of his life, his control slipped. He failed to impose Persian rituals of homage on his Greek and Macedonian followers who felt that it was demeaning to prostrate themselves before a mere mortal, even if he was a king. He sought conquests beyond Persia's frontiers, but his troops became insubordinate, and he had to halt his invasion of India, shortly after crossing the Indus. Characteristically,

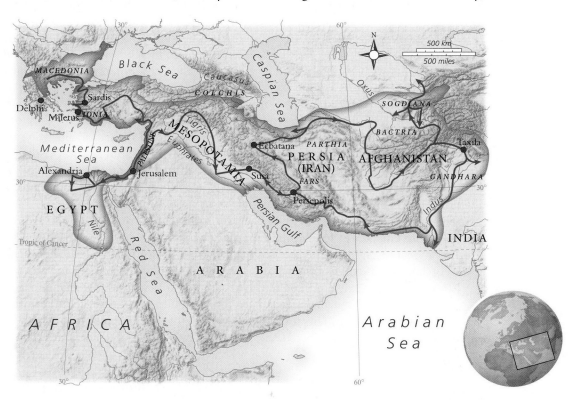

 MAP 7.2

The Empire of Alexander the Great

Empire of Alexander at its greatest extent

→ route of Alexander the Great

Alexander saved face by pretending he had submitted not to the demands of his men, but to warnings from the gods. He had just set the conquest of Arabia as his next objective when he fell dead at age 32, from unknown causes, after a drinking bout—the favorite Macedonian form of excess.

It was what modern publicists might call "a great career move." He became the world's most written-about hero. Epic romancers embroidered his life with wonder stories of his uncontainable prowess. They credited him with exploring the depths of the ocean and ascending to heaven in a chariot drawn by ravens. An epic poem celebrated him in Malay. Kings in India, Ethiopia, and Scotland named themselves after him.

His empire did not outlast him. But long-term, long-range cultural exchanges throve in the states among which it fragmented. On the frontiers of India, the kingdom of Gandhara combined Buddhist religion and Greek-style art. In Alexandria, the city Alexander founded at the Nile Delta, Greek and Egyptian traditions fused. Through the kingdoms of Bactria and Sogdiana, the trade of the Silk Roads funneled. A Persian rump state, Parthia, arose in the Iranian heartland. A power vacuum arose in the eastern Mediterranean that none of Alexander's many imitators could fill. The eventual beneficiary was Rome.

THE RISE OF ROME

One of the great unsolved puzzles of history is how a small city-state of obscure origins and limited manpower conquered the Mediterranean, extended its frontiers to the Atlantic and North Sea, and transformed almost every culture it touched. The Romans started as a community of peasants, huddling for defense in an unstrategic spot. The site of Rome had poor soil, no metals, and no outlet to the sea. Its inhabitants became warlike by necessity. They had no way to gain wealth except at their neighbors' expense.

Horace, "Dulce et Decorum est Pro Patria Mori"

The Romans organized for war and made victory their supreme value. Roman citizens owed the state at least 16 years of military service. They learned—to quote Horace again—that "to die for the fatherland is sweet and fitting." Their generals celebrated victories in triumphal public parades, showing off booty and prisoners. Roman education emphasized the virtues of patience and endurance. As a result, Rome was well equipped to tough out defeats. Like those other great imperialists, the nineteenth-century British, they could "lose battles but win wars."

This was particularly evident in the Punic Wars the Romans fought against Carthage (see Chapter 5) for domination of the western Mediterranean. The background is clear enough. In the late third century B.C.E., Roman armies reached the limits of landward expansion in Italy. They turned their aggression toward the wealth of Sardinia, Sicily, and Spain. Carthage, the most formidable naval empire of the western Mediterranean, already had colonies, allies, and subject-communities there. Reluctantly, the Romans took to the sea to fight the Carthaginians. This was remarkable, as the Romans hated the sea. "Whoever first dared to float a ship," wrote Horace in about 30 B.C.E., "must have had a heart of oak covered with a triple layer of bronze." Carthage recovered from every defeat, until in 146 B.C.E. Rome finally destroyed it and turned the western Mediterranean into a zone free of rivals. Historians generally regard these wars as the crucial episode in the ascent of Rome.

Meanwhile, Rome also engaged the major powers of the eastern Mediterranean. Macedon was annexed to Rome in 148 B.C.E., after 50 years of intermittent wars. The rich kingdom of Pergamum in Anatolia was next. When its last king died, he willed his kingdom to the Roman people in 133 B.C.E. Then came Syria and Palestine. When Rome annexed Egypt in 30 B.C.E., it controlled virtually all the shores of the Mediterranean (see Map 7.3).

MAP 7.3

The Roman World

	extent of Roman Empire ca. 120 C.E.
	Parthian Empire ca. 120 C.E.
Celts	peoples
●Fayyum	place described on pages 160–166
—	maritime trade routes
	wine
	olive oil
	garum (fish sauce)
	honey
	slaves
	horses
	wool
	flax/linen
	murex (purple dye)
	marble
	timber
	gold
	tin
	copper

290 B.C.E.: Rome reaches limits of landward expansion in Italy

148 B.C.E.: Rome annexes Macedon

30 B.C.E.: Augustus becomes first emperor of Rome

43 C.E.: Rome invades Britain

400 B.C.E.   300 B.C.E.   200 B.C.E.   100 B.C.E.   1 C.E.   100 C.E.   200 C.E.

264 B.C.E.: Outbreak of first war between Rome and Carthage

146 B.C.E.: Rome destroys Carthage in final war

51 B.C.E.: Conquest of Gaul completed by Julius Caesar

27 B.C.E.: Rome annexes Egypt

106 C.E.: Conquest of Dacia completed

Tombstone of a Roman Soldier. The Roman Empire shifted people across vast distances. This tombstone in Cologne, Germany, records a veteran soldier, Marcus Valerius Celerinus, who married and settled locally after his legion was transferred to Germany from his home in southern Spain, late in the first century C.E. His wife, Marcia Procula, sits in a subordinate position, ready to serve him from a basket of fruit. The inscription proclaims the image "from life" of Marcus, naming his tribe, his citizenship of his birthplace in Spain, and his status as a veteran of the Tenth Legion. Marcus reclines to dine, the way a Roman gentleman would. At his elbow is his slave. A table with wine cups and a wine jar stand beside him.

The Roman Frontiers

The Roman Empire was an empire of coasts, with the sea as it central axis. It therefore exposed long, vulnerable frontiers to landward. On the African and Levantine shores, Roman territory seemed protected by deserts. The European flank, however, despite 100 years of further conquests, never seemed secure. There was no reliable barrier against attack. An endless quest for security led beyond the Mediterranean to the Rhine and the Danube Rivers. In the first and early second centuries C.E., Rome subdued Dacia, where deadly womenfolk were said to torture prisoners. The result was an even longer and more irrational frontier.

Roman expeditions also invaded Germany as far as the Elbe River, but the Germans seemed too barbaric to absorb. They were "wild creatures" incapable of laws or civilized arts, according to Velleius, a Roman cavalry officer who fought them around 4 B.C.E. Julius Caesar (d. 44 B.C.E.), whose methodical generalship extended the empire to the Rhine, regarded that river as the limit of civilization. So Rome abandoned the Germans to their own devices. This was probably a mistake. Almost all speakers of Germanic languages beyond Switzerland and the Rhineland were left outside the empire, seething with resentment and vengefulness at their exclusion from the wealth they associated with Rome. If Rome had absorbed them and the other sedentary peoples beyond its frontiers, as China did at the other end of Eurasia, the Roman Empire might have proved as durable as China's. The sedentary peoples China absorbed on its frontiers guarded the Chinese Empire against nomadic outsiders.

Imperial Culture and Commerce

Retired soldiers—Latin-speaking and schooled in allegiance to Rome—helped spread a common culture across the empire, settling in lands where they had been stationed, marrying local women. On his tombstone in Cologne, in the Rhineland, the image of a retired veteran from southern Spain reclines; his wife and son serve food and wine from an elegant, claw-footed table. A tombstone in northern Britain commemorates a 16-year-old boy from Roman Syria.

Roman culture was so well known in Britain that mints in the third century C.E. could stamp coins with references to the poetry of Virgil—the epic poet who, in the reign of Augustus (r. 27 B.C.E.–14 C.E.), celebrated Rome's foundation myth. Everywhere, the empire promoted the same classical style for buildings and urban planning: symmetrical, harmonious, based on Greek architecture. The artistic traditions of subject-peoples became provincial styles. For instance, the last monuments of the funerary art of the pharaohs are the Fayyum portraits, which stare from the surfaces of burial caskets in Roman Egypt. They are recognizably in an ancient Egyptian tradition, yet faces as realistic and sensitive as these might be found in portraits anywhere in the Roman Empire.

Engineering was the Romans' ultimate art. They discovered how to make cement, which made unprecedented feats of building possible. Everywhere the empire reached, Romans invested in infrastructure, building roads, sewers, and aqueducts. Amphitheatres, temples, city walls, public baths, and monumental gates were erected at public expense, alongside the temples that civic-minded patrons usually endowed. The buildings serviced new cities, built in Rome's image, where there were none before, or enlarged and embellished cities that already existed. The biggest courthouse in the empire was in London, the widest street in Italica, a Roman city in southwest Spain. Colonists in Conimbriga, on the coast of Portugal, rebuilt their town center in the first century C.E. to resemble Rome's. Trade as well as war shipped elements of common culture around the empire. Rome exported Mediterranean amenities—villas, cities, mosaics—to the provinces, or forced Mediterranean crops like wine grapes and olive trees to grow in unlikely climates.

As industries became geographically specialized, trade and new commercial relationships crisscrossed the empire. In the first century C.E., merchants from the Duero valley in Spain were buried in Hungary. Greek potters made huge jars to transport wine from Spain to southern France. In southwest Spain, huge evaporators survive from the factories where garum—the empire's favorite fish sauce—was made from tuna and mackerel. The lives of cloth merchants from northeast France are engraved on a tomb at Igel, on the frontier of Germany. They conveyed bales of cloth by road and river and sold it in elegant shops, lavishing their profits on banquets to lord it over their farming neighbors.

Of course, as the empire grew, political institutions changed. When Rome was a small city-republic, two annually elected chief executives, called consuls, shared power between themselves, subject to checks by the assembly of nobles and notables known as the senate, and by the tribunes, representatives of the common citizens. Increasingly, as the state expanded, in the emergencies of war, power was confided to individuals called dictators, who were expected to relinquish control when the emergency was over. In the second half of the first century B.C.E., this system finally broke down in struggles between rival contenders for sole power. In 27 B.C.E., all parties accepted Augustus, who had emerged as victor from the civil wars, as head of state for life, with the right to name his successor.

Effectively, henceforth, Rome was a monarchy, though Romans, schooled in republicanism, hated to use the word. Part of the consequence of Roman distaste for kings was that the rules of succession to supreme power were never perfectly defined. Augustus called himself *princeps*—a word roughly equivalent to "chief" in English. Gradually, however, "emperor" took over as the name people normally used to designate the ruler. The Latin term—*imperator*—originally meant an army commander, and the army, or parts of the army, often in rivalry with each other, increasingly dethroned and elected emperors.

Unified command and sustained leadership helped to make the growing empire manageable, but the problem remained of melding such diverse and widespread peoples into a single state. A common sense of belonging spread, as Rome granted Roman citizenship to subject-communities. Envoys from allies on the Atlantic and Black Sea came to Rome to hang offerings in the temple of Jupiter, "greatest and best" of Rome's guardian gods. Yet this was by no means a uniform empire. It was so big that it could only work by permitting the provinces to retain their local customs and religious practices. At one level it was a federation of cities, at another a federation of peoples. Everywhere, Rome ruled with the collaboration—sometimes enforced—of established elites. Spanish notables with barbarous names followed Roman law in legal decisions that they ordered to be carved in bronze. Hebrew princes and Germanic chiefs ruled as imperial delegates. Celts were Rome's partners in the west, Greeks in the east, where Greek rather than Latin was the most widespread common tongue and served at most levels as the language of government.

Fayyum portrait. When Egypt became a Roman province in 30 B.C.E., burial practices remained the same: Mummies were encased in painted caskets. But the style of painting that depicted the deceased gradually took on Roman conventions of portraiture, as in this lovely example of a young woman from the mid–second century C.E.

 Pliny the Elder, from *The Natural History*

Roman Expansion

ca. 290 B.C.E.	Rome reaches limit of expansion in Italy
148 B.C.E.	Rome annexes Macedon
146 B.C.E.	Rome destroys Carthage
133 B.C.E.	Pergamum added to Roman Empire
30 B.C.E.	Rome annexes Egypt
106 C.E	Conquest of Dacia completed

Celtic conspicuous consumption. This wine vessel, buried with the queen or princess to whom it belonged in the mid–first millennium B.C.E., was as tall as she was. Too big and heavy to handle, it was just for show. Like the wine it contained, it was imported from the Mediterranean. Greek soldiers and chariots decorate the rim. Serpent-haired Gorgons form handles, inside which lions climb—all symbolizing the owner's power.

The Celts

Celts dominated Western Europe by the mid–first millennium B.C.E. They occupied present-day France, Britain, Ireland, and most of Spain. Their settlements were widespread in Central Europe and even reached Anatolia. Everywhere they lived in numerous chiefdoms and small states. What united them was language. They all spoke mutually intelligible versions of a single tongue.

Stories about the Celts made Roman gooseflesh ripple. They hunted human heads and hung them on their saddles. They stitched sacrifice victims for burning inside wicker images of gods. They had a reputation for drunkenness. A 35-year-old Celtic hostess in central France was buried with a Greek wine vessel so large that it had to be imported in sections and assembled on arrival. The Celts' courage was also renowned. Roman sculpture shows them dead or dying but never giving up.

Despite their fierce and undisciplined reputation, the Celts had a way of life that Romans recognized as civilized. They were supposedly suspicious of writing wisdom down, but many inscriptions survive, including laws, administrative records, and a calendar to foretell the future. There were modest Celtic towns in France and Spain. The town of Numancia, which was rich in iron, was a minor metropolis by Celtic standards. Covering almost 1,800 square feet, it was arranged in neat streets up to 21 feet wide. The dwellings of Numancia were of mud and thatch on a rubble base, but the inhabitants enjoyed fresh water and sanitary drainage.

By the time Rome seriously began to wage war on them—early in the last quarter of the second century B.C.E.—the Celts of what is now France had a society Romans acknowledged as like their own: no longer organized along tribal lines but according to wealth, prowess, and ancestry. Nobility was measured in livestock, not land. Peasants paid their rents in calves, pigs, and grain. After ferocious initial resistance to Roman conquest, Celts usually accepted Romanization and became enthusiastic collaborators in the Roman Empire. Generally, they welcomed the enriching economic consequences of the peace the Romans enforced.

THE BEGINNINGS OF IMPERIALISM IN INDIA

Meanwhile, beyond the eastern frontiers of Persia, in India, Alexander's threat seems to have had an immediately galvanizing effect. When one of his generals recrossed the Indus in 305 B.C.E., he found the states of the Ganges valley confederated under a leader from the delta region, Candragupta (chahn-drah-GOOP-tah). The sources are hazy, however, until the next reign, that of Asoka (ah-SHOH-kah), which began in the 260s B.C.E. The *Arthasastra* (ahr-SHAS-trah) describes the political world of Asoka. More importantly, his thoughts and deeds come to life in the decrees and self-reflective ruminations he had inscribed on pillars and rock faces. If it were not such an awful pun, one would say that the rock inscriptions are hard evidence.

Excerpts from the *Arthasastra*, "The Duties of Government Superintendents"

The sources show, first, the extraordinarily long reach of Asoka's power (see Map 7.4). Second, the evidence reveals an expanding realm, constantly reforging environments. "The king shall populate the countryside," says the *Arthasastra*, "by creating villages on virgin land or by reviving abandoned village sites. . . . Like a barren cow, a kingdom without people yields nothing."

The same source describes two main types of environment—one rainy and the other requiring irrigation—and specifies suitable crops for both: rice, millet, wheat, barley, six sorts of beans, four types of oil seeds, various vegetables, herbs,

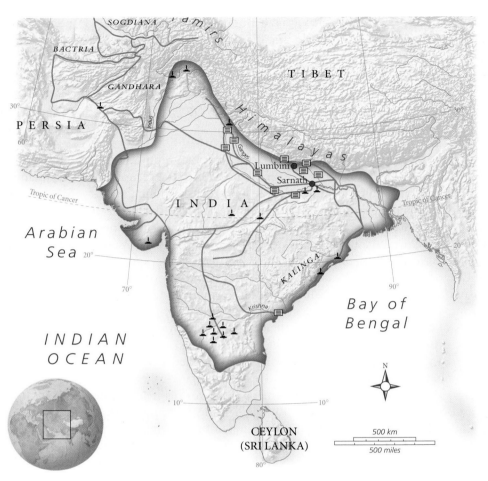

MAP 7.4

The Reign of Asoka, ca. 268–223 B.C.E.

- maximum extent of Asoka's empire
- ⊥ pillar edict of Asoka
- ▤ rock inscription of Asoka
- —— trade route

and spices. The king is responsible for irrigation and should encourage others to irrigate by exempting them from the water tax. Pasture, mines, and forests (for obtaining war elephants) are all worthy objects of conquest. Roads are emphasized, with signposts and wells at nine-mile intervals. Regulating trade—including coinage, weights, and measures—and processing the raw materials of royal lands are also part of the ruler's job.

Government

Methods and means of government reflected central control. Peasants paid a quarter of their produce in tax, apparently directly to the king. Army leaders received pay in cash, rather than being given a share of royal power, as was customary in later Indian states. Asoka's inscriptions portray a hands-on ruler. He "received reports at all times"—in his harem or gardens, his carriage, or his barns, where he inspected his livestock. "And whatever I order by word of mouth, whether it concerns a donation or proclamation or whatever urgent matter is entrusted by my officers, if there is any dispute or deliberation about it at the Council, it is to be reported to me immediately."

The *Arthasastra* expresses an ideology of universal rule and uniform justice. It is hard to know, however, what this meant in practice. India was already becoming a **caste** society, where social rank was inherited, unchangeable, and made sacred by religious sanctions. Brahmanical literature (see Chapter 5) treated women as if

The stupa of Sanchi. The Emperor Asoka (r. ca. 272–223 B.C.E.) built the first shrine at Sanchi, near Bhopal in India, to honor a place made holy by the footprints of the Buddha. Enriched by the donations of pilgrims, it was adorned by dozens of elaborate structures over thousands of years. The northern gateway, shown here, is elaborately carved with scenes of legends of the Buddha's life and with tales of exemplary charity.

they were imperfectly human, though Buddhism admitted them to one form of high status as nuns. Few other occupations were open to them. There were state-run weaving shops for unmarriageable women, including retired prostitutes, the elderly, and the deformed. The king had female bodyguards, but this was because women's social exclusion made them trustworthy: They had nothing to gain by rebelling.

Asoka and His Mental World

The rock inscriptions are, in a sense, Asoka's autobiography, disclosing an extraordinary personal story of spiritual development. The first secure date in his reign is the conquest of Kalinga, a kingdom in eastern India around 260 B.C.E. In his commemorative inscription, he expresses regret for the suffering he caused: 150,000 deportees, 100,000 killed, "and many times that number who perished." He goes on: "The Beloved of the gods [meaning Asoka himself] felt remorse, for . . . the slaughter, death and deportation of the people is extremely grievous to the Beloved of the gods, and weighs heavily on his mind." The inscription then gets to what one suspects is the real point: "The Beloved of the gods believes that one who does wrong should be forgiven. . . . And the Beloved of the gods conciliates the forest tribes of his empire, but he warns them that he has power even in his remorse, and he asks them to repent, lest they be killed."

So, in part at least, Asoka's remorse was intended as a warning, and he could hardly have won such a large empire except by war. Still, within a few years, the repudiation of conquest became a major theme of his inscriptions. "Any sons or grandsons I may have should not think of gaining new conquests. . . . The Beloved of the gods considers victory by the teaching of the Buddha to be the foremost victory." Asoka put the policy of conquest-by-conversion into practice, sending missionaries to the kingdoms that replaced the old Persian Empire and to Sri Lanka (see Chapter 5). His descendants, he hoped, would adhere to this policy "until the end of the world."

How are we to explain Asoka's extraordinary behavior? His realm was expanding into areas where city life was only starting or, in northwest India, only reviving after the disappearance of the Harappan civilization. In the absence of existing bureaucracies, Asoka had to resort to the one disciplined, literate group available: the Buddhist clergy. This was the period when Buddhist scriptures were being recorded. Asoka recruited the scribes to his service, decreeing that monks, nuns, and his lay subjects should hear the scriptures frequently and meditate upon them.

These words are the telltale trace of Asoka's bargain with the clergy, probably made in the tenth year of his reign, 258 B.C.E. About this time, too, he made a much-publicized pilgrimage to the scene of the Buddha's enlightenment. In a further inscription, he claimed he had made society holy—where "gods mingle with men"—for the first time in India.

As the Buddhist clergy became more powerful, however, the monks' rivalry for the gifts of the pious and their theological disputes threatened the peace of the realm. So Asoka forbade them to speak ill of one another. "Concord is to be recommended, that men may hear one another's principles and obey them." Asoka's alliance with religion was the shape of things to come. As we shall see, it became a practice of kings all over the world, bringing common problems and advantages.

The language of Buddhism also infused Asoka's declarations of policy: "All men are my children. . . . There is no better work than promoting the welfare of the whole world." The disadvantaged were specifically included—slaves and servants, women and prisoners. Officials toured the empire to instruct people in

Asoka's version of Buddhist ethics: family loyalty, piety for holy men, mercy toward living creatures, and personal austerity. He made such tours himself, taking more pleasure in distributing alms and consulting holy men, he said, than in all other pleasures. These activities replaced hunting, formerly a royal obligation, now banned.

Toward the end of Asoka's reign, it appeared that his enlightenment was beginning to damage the empire. He tightened laws on the treatment of animals, forbidding the slaughter of young livestock and animals that were nursing their young. Fishless days were imposed. "Chaff, which contains living things must not be set on fire. Forests must not be burned to kill living things, or without good reason. An animal must not be fed with another animal." Gelding and branding were restricted. These decrees must have caused outrage and threatened livelihoods. The emperor's pride in the 25 amnesties he granted to imprisoned criminals can hardly have endeared him to their victims. His condemnation of all rituals as trivial and useless compared with a life in accordance with Buddhist doctrine alienated ordinary people. Perhaps worst of all, his policy against conquests meant the empire could not expand and turned the violence of the military classes inward.

Only 25 years after Asoka's death in 232 B.C.E., his empire (which historians call the Mauryan Empire) broke up into separate states. But state-forming, environment-modifying habits had spread throughout India. The economic infrastructure—the routes of commerce, the enhanced range of resources—was not invulnerable. But the Mauryan infrastructure was unforgettable and it could usually be repaired or reconstructed, if necessary, after future wars and environmental disasters.

CHINESE UNITY AND IMPERIALISM

Even after 500 years of division among warring states, the ideal of imperial unity remained in China. Real unity, however, required force. Of all the warring states, Qin was the most marginal, occupying relatively infertile uplands, far from the rice-growing regions. The intelligentsia of most other states considered its people imperfectly civilized.

Toward the mid-third century B.C.E., Qin began what, in retrospect, looks like a systematic strategy of rejecting the very idea of empire. In 256 B.C.E., its ruler discontinued all imperial rites, in effect dissolving the empire. Ten years later, a new king of Qin, Shi Huangdi (shee hwang-dee), declared that having been dismantled, the empire could be replaced. Over the next 25 years, he systematically isolated and conquered rival kingdoms and declared himself "First Emperor" of a new monarchy. "If," he declared, "the whole empire has suffered, . . . it is because there were nobles and kings." In other words, with himself as sole ruler, a unified China would enjoy peace and prosperity.

Our picture of his reign comes from histories compiled one or two generations later. They are distorted partly by the awe Shi Huangdi inspired and partly by revulsion from his oppressive rule. They were based not on what he actually did, but on the sometimes unrealistic ambitions his decrees reveal. To judge by these sources, he aimed to break the aristocracy, abolish slavery, outlaw inheritance practices that concentrated wealth in noble hands, and replace the power of kings and lords with a uniform system of civil and military districts under his own appointees. He ordered the burning of hundreds of people he considered disloyal and, reputedly, of thousands of books. Only useful technical manuals and the writings of the Legalist

The Reign of Asoka	
ca. 268–232 B.C.E.	Reign of Asoka
260 B.C.E.	Conquest of Kalinga
258 B.C.E.	Conversion to Buddhism
ca. 200 B.C.E.	Breakup of Asoka's empire

Excerpts from *The Edicts of Asoka*

Terracotta warriors. Though his life and reign were short, everything else about Shi Huangdi (r. 221–210 B.C.E.), the Qin ruler who conquered China, was on a monumental scale. The size and magnificence of his tomb, guarded by an army of terracotta warriors, echoes the grandeur of his engineering works and the scope of his ambitions and uncompromising reforms.

school (see Chapter 6) were allowed. Uniformity was the keynote of the new state. Laws, coinage, measurements, script, even axle lengths of carts had to be the same all over the kingdom. Unauthorized weapons were melted down.

Shi Huangdi's demonic energy is obvious in everything he attempted. He mobilized 700,000 laborers to build a network of roads and canals. He knocked the Great Wall of China together out of older fortifications, as protection against nomad attacks. When he died in 210 B.C.E., he was buried with thousands of life-size clay models of soldiers and servants—each with different facial and body features—to accompany him into the next life. He was a showman of power on a huge scale—which is usually a sign of insecurity. His empire was too fragile to last, but sweeping away the warring states made it easier for his successors to rebuild an enduring Chinese Empire.

Unity Endangered and Saved

The first instinct of the rebels who overthrew his feeble son in 207 B.C.E. was to restore the system of the Warring States period. The result was chaotic warfare, with one of the rebel leaders, Liu Bang (lee-oh bahng), emerging victorious over all the others. He put in place a carefully tempered version of Shi Huangdi's system. Restored kings had small territories within military districts. Peasants owed the state two years' military service plus one month's labor a year, which must have seemed lenient compared to Shi Huangdi's demands.

Legalism remained the dominant political philosophy. Liu Bang put most of his former allies to death and showed contempt for Confucianism. In the long run, however, only Confucian scholars and officials could supply the literate administrators that a growing state needed. Gradually, especially in the 50-year reign of Han Wudi (hawn woo-dee), beginning in 141 B.C.E., Confucianism became the state ideology again.

Liu Bang called his dynasty "Han" after the portion of the country he received in the carving up of Shi Huangdi's realm. In the period of expansion that began in the late second century B.C.E., Han China became the essential China that we see on maps of later eras. Chinese began to call themselves Han.

The return of peaceful conditions under the Han dynasty stimulated a population explosion. The population of 20 million in Shi Huangdi's day probably tripled by the end of the millennium. In part, the huge increase was also probably a consequence of the increased size and environmental diversity of the state. Rice-growing and millet-growing regions could again exchange supplies in each other's bad times. The government coped with disasters, such as drought, famine, or earthquakes, by massive frontier colonization programs and redistributing population on a large scale. Forced migrations peopled newly conquered provinces in the southeast at the same time that settlers were encouraged to migrate south toward the Huai valley. These movements shifted the distribution of population, making the Yangtze River the main axis of China. Meanwhile, in the north in 120 B.C.E., 700,000 families were moved into a new conquest beyond the province of Shaanxi, which famine had devastated.

The Han dynasty lasted from 206 B.C.E. to 220 C.E., despite a succession system that bred palace conspiracies. Succession was determined by designating a principal wife to be the mother of each emperor's heir. This gave empresses' families a unique opportunity to profit from the emperor's favor. But the advantage rarely lasted more than two generations—less, if the empress failed to produce a future emperor. Consequently, every empress's family was tempted to seize power for itself—and most tried. In these circumstances, a dynasty that survived a long time was a triumph against the odds.

The Menace from the Steppes

The other main problem China faced in this period emerged from the steppelands, north of the Great Wall and the Silk Roads. The region had a bad reputation. Its climate was inhospitable, its soil unworkable, its native herdsmen savage. In some ways, however, it was a good place to start building an empire. It bred plenty of horses and men accustomed to the saddle. Its people were voracious because they were poor. It was a vast, flat tract of land, with few geographical obstacles to the creation of a large state. Because the steppeland fringed the Silk Roads, leaders of steppelander bands could conduct raids, amass treasure, and use their wealth to build up large followings.

Chinese booty, ransom, and protection money enriched war chiefs who became wealthy enough to extend their followings beyond their own kin. According to Chinese evidence, compiled much later—which is all we have—the first great stepplander state emerged late in the third century B.C.E., among people the Chinese called Xiongnu (shee-ohng-noo). The leader styled himself "Son of Heaven," which was a Chinese imperial title and therefore suggests Chinese influence. His warriors hunted heads—exhibiting scalps from their bridles, making enemies' skulls into cups. The basis of their success in war was their skill in mounted archery. Sheep, horses, cattle, and camels were the mainstay of their economy—guaranteeing the advantages of mixed pastoralism, with milk yields of different species of animals peaking at different times. In about 176 B.C.E., they conquered Gansu (gohn-soo), at the western end of the Great Wall, and became a serious, constant nuisance to China.

Confucian doctrine advocated what we would now call appeasement: "Your Majesty has but to manifest your virtue towards them and extend your favors to cover them, and the northern Barbarians

The Qin and the Han

ca. 256 B.C.E.	Ruler of Qin discontinues imperial rites
ca. 247 B.C.E.	Shi Huangdi becomes ruler of Qin state; beginning of Qin expansion
214 B.C.E.	Construction of Great Wall begins
210 B.C.E.	Death of Shi Huangdi
206 B.C.E.	Beginning of Han dynasty
141 B.C.E.	Han Wudi becomes Han emperor
ca. 139 B.C.E.	Embassy of Zhang Qian to Central Asia
220 C.E.	Collapse of Han Dynasty

The Han and the Xiongnu

Third century B.C.E.	First Xiongnu state emerges
ca. 176 B.C.E.	Xiongnu conquers Gansu
127–120 B.C.E.	Chinese mount successful operations against the Xiongnu

will undoubtedly come of their own accord to pay you tribute at the wall." This policy was not as feeble as it sounds. Many neighboring peoples genuinely felt the "peaceful attraction" of Chinese rule, and Chinese culture absorbed huge numbers of subject-peoples. The Xiongnu, however, were unresponsive to such methods.

In the late second century B.C.E., Han efforts to recruit allies against them failed. But in the 120s B.C.E., the Chinese mounted a series of successful operations. The fortification of the Silk Roads followed. For a while around the turn of the millennium, the Xiongnu even abandoned hostilities. Thereafter, weakened by civil wars, they succumbed to celebrated campaigns in the late first century C.E., while pressure accumulated from neighbors to the north and east, who, in their turn, were beginning to move toward statehood.

BEYOND THE EMPIRES

The edges of empires bred states. The Xiongnu were not the only example of economic and political development in China's shadow. Large-scale state formation also occurred in the same period in Japan and Korea, under Chinese influence, and at the other end of Eurasia, among the Scythians and Sarmatians, pastoral peoples whose lands bordered the Roman and Persian Empires.

Japan and Korea

In the fourth century B.C.E., a rice-growing, bronze-using culture known to archaeologists as Yayoi emerged in Japan. It gradually developed into a state system, under the stimulus of contacts with China. According to Chinese records, in about 200 C.E., one of the Japanese states, Yamatai, conquered the others, under the rule of a female shaman. When she died, 1,000 attendants were burned at her burial. This is the first inkling we have of a unified Japanese state.

Korean states developed faster. The Chinese were in touch with three Korean states—Silla, Paekche, and Koguryo. The Chinese sources are so vague, and the archaeological evidence so scanty, that historians can say nothing reliable about the political history of these realms. But their rulers were buried in impressive tombs, and grave goods reveal something of the nature of power and trade: iron weapons, gold diadems and chains, bronze ornaments that imitate Chinese work.

The Western Eurasian Steppe

Meanwhile, at the other end of the Eurasian steppe, in Ukraine and southern Russia, states formed among the pastoral peoples known as Scythians and Sarmatians. Scythian states formed in and around Crimea (creye-MEE-ah), a peninsula that juts into the Black Sea, where Greek trader-colonies lived. Here was the Scythian center of Neapolis, a ruler's court covering 40 acres and surrounded by a stone wall. Sarmatian royal courts throve beyond the rivers Dneiper and Don.

On one level, Greek writers sensed this pastoral, nomadic world was alien, wild, and menacing. The fifth-century B.C.E. Greek historian, Herodotus, told of a legendary traveler who undertook a mysterious, dreamlike journey to their land, beyond the river Don in modern Ukraine. On another level, the nomads were familiar trading partners. Greek craftsmen depicted them in everyday scenes, milking ewes or stitching their sheepskin cloaks. Greek and Celtic trade goods filled princely graves in the last half of the first millennium B.C.E.

Much of this art was produced under the patronage of Scythian and Sarmatian princes and is echoed in their own goldsmiths' work. A gold cup, for instance, from

At the Edge of Empires	
Seventh century B.C.E.	First written evidence of the Scythians
ca. 500 B.C.E.	Silla, Paekche, and Koguryo states dominate Korea
Fourth century B.C.E.	Yayoi culture emerges in Japan
ca. 200 B.C.E.	Sarmatians displace Scythians

A gold cup of the mid–first millennium B.C.E. shows why Scythian art was admired in the classical world. Despite the Scythians' fierce reputation, their goldwork usually shows peaceful images of camp life, vividly depicted, such as this scene in which one warrior binds another's leg.

a royal tomb near the Black Sea shows bearded warriors in tunics and leggings at peace or, at least, between wars. They tend one another's wounds, fix their teeth, mend their bowstrings, and tell campfire tales. A Sarmatian queen of the first century C.E. stares, in Greek clothes and hairstyle, from the center of a gold crown. When we look at their art, we can never be sure whether these people were happy in their own traditions or envious of the sedentary empires—probably a bit of both.

Mesoamerica

Far more remarkable than these cases of state-building by peoples on the edges of existing empires are independent but comparable developments that began in this period in Mesoamerica (see Map 7.5). Chiefdom-formation and state-building had a long history in the Americas, but every innovation had been blocked or

Monte Albán and Teotihuacán

➡	Monte Albán
➡	Teotihuacán
○	settlement
●	place mentioned on page 174
OAXACA	modern province

frustrated. The geography and vast climate zones of the Americas discouraged communication and cultural change (see Chapter 5).

Now, at least two centers sprang into what might fairly be called a potentially imperial role. Monte Albán (MON-tay al-BAHN) in Oaxaca was the first. In a period of social differentiation early in the millennium, the region had deer-fed elite, buried in stone-lined graves with jade-bead lip studs and earrings. Population growth accompanied their supremacy, with increasing exploitation of irrigation and the spread of settlement into areas of sparse rainfall. Around the mid-millennium, ever-larger settlements appeared, with ritual mounds and the first engraved picture-writing, or glyphs. We do not know how to read this writing, and the inscriptions are all short—perhaps only names and dates. From about the same time and place, we have the first evidence of what the ritual platforms were for: a carving of a human sacrifice, with blood streaming from a chest sliced open to pluck out the heart.

Not long after this, Monte Albán began to draw in population from surrounding settlements. It was a natural fortress, enhanced by defensive walls. From a modest village, Monte Albán became a city of perhaps 20,000 people by about 200 B.C.E., when the population stabilized. Faded carvings proclaim its warlike values in parades of sacrifice victims. A palace and a reservoir that could have held 20,000 gallons of water suggest a familiar story: collective effort under strong rule. The main plaza contains 40 huge carved stones—probably of the second century B.C.E. These are "conquest slabs," listing the names of subject-cities and the tribute these cities had to pay.

Monte Albán casts light on the later and more spectacular case of Mesoamerican empire-building. Teotihuacán (tay-oh-wah-tee-KAHN), in the valley of Mexico, about 450 miles north of Albán, was destined to be a far greater metropolis. At 6,000 feet above sea level, a little higher than Monte Albán, its agriculture was based on what were by then the region's standard products: maize, beans, and squash. Around the end of the millennium, perhaps as the result of a war, a migration as sudden as Albán's shifted almost the entire population of the valley of Mexico to Teotihuacán. The building of the towering Sun Pyramid began. By about 150 C.E., 20 monumental pyramids were in place. The other buildings included some apparently for housing people from distant lowland sites: ambassadors, tribute bearers, hostages.

The art of Teotihuacán suggests an ecologically fragile way of life, dependent on rainfall and unreliable gods to deliver fertile soil and crops. The artists imagined the sky as a serpent whose sweat fell as rain and fed the plant life of Earth, where sacrificers in serpent masks scattered blood from hands lacerated with cactus spikes or impaled human hearts on bones. Yet the city and the reach of its trade and power grew for over 350 years. At its peak, Teotihuacán was big enough to house well over 100,000 people. Carvings over 625 miles away depicted its warriors, and its trade goods and tribute came from a similarly wide area.

IN PERSPECTIVE: The Aftermath of the Axial Age

The axial age left three legacies: a remarkably durable heritage of ideas, less secure though lengthening routes for trade and cultural exchange in Eurasia, and a fragile group of empires. In some ways, these legacies seemed interdependent. The empires added little to the intellectual achievements that preceded them, but they did safeguard, enshrine, and nurture them. The Romans, for example, adopted and fostered Greek learning. Persian emperors adopted Zoroastrian rites. Asoka

Monte Albán. The builders of Monte Albán (Oaxaca, Mexico) reshaped the 1,500-foot-high mound on which it stands to fit their idea of how a city should be: 50 acres of terraces supporting temples, palaces, and garrisons. This was truly an imperial metropolis, decorated with gaudy, gory slabs depicting dismembered captives.

became the patron of Buddhism in India. The Han rehabilitated Confucianism. The empires developed sea and land communications in Eurasia. The road-building programs, the Chinese effort to scout and fortify the Silk Roads, and the interest Alexander and his Persian predecessors took in Indian Ocean navigation all demonstrate that.

The collapse of the Persian Empire and the rapid unraveling of Asoka's empire showed that the world was not yet safe for large-scale imperialism. But the pattern of state-building seems to have been irresistible. New states on the edges of the existing Eurasian empires—and, as we shall see in the next chapter, in parts of Africa where contacts with Eurasia were multiplying—suggest this pattern. The New World resembled a "parallel universe" where, despite the environmental differences, histories similar to those of parts of Eurasia and Africa were beginning to unfold.

CHRONOLOGY

Seventh century B.C.E.	First written evidence of the Scythians
Sixth century B.C.E.	Cyrus the Great founds Persian Empire
Fifth century B.C.E.	1,700 miles of road cross Persian Empire
	Chinese silks appear in Europe
	Silla, Paekche, and Koguryo states dominate Korea
Fourth century B.C.E.	Yayoi culture emerges in Japan
334 B.C.E.	Alexander conquers Persian Empire
Third century B.C.E.	Roman Empire expands beyond Italy
	First Xiongnu state emerges north of China
ca. 268–232 B.C.E.	Reign of Asoka (India)
206 B.C.E.	Beginning of Han dynasty in China
200 B.C.E.	Population of Monte Albán reaches 20,000 (Mesoamerica)
127–120 B.C.E.	Chinese mount successful operations against the Xiongnu
27 B.C.E.	Augustus becomes first emperor of Rome
ca. 150 C.E.	Teotihuacán at peak of its influence (Mesoamerica)
220 C.E.	Collapse of the Han dynasty

PROBLEMS AND PARALLELS

1. How do travel and trade create a demand for stronger, bigger states? How do cross-cultural contacts, larger road networks, and increased communication benefit or disadvantage states?

2. What were the advantages and disadvantages of sea routes versus land routes for commerce and communication in the ancient world?

3. What common factors contributed to the fall of the empires discussed in this chapter?

4. How did each empire try to meld together diverse peoples into a single state? Did they succeed or fail?

DOCUMENTS IN GLOBAL HISTORY

- from the *Periplus of the Erythraean Sea*
- Agatharchides of Knidos describes Saba
- Zhang Qian, *Hon Shu*, "Descriptions of the Western Regions"
- Religious freedom in ancient Persia: the "Cyrus Cylinder"
- Horace, "Dulce et Decorum est Pro Patria Mori"

- Pliny the Elder, from *The Natural History*
- Excerpts from the *Arthasastra*, "The Duties of Government Superintendents"
- Excerpts from *The Edicts of Asoka*

Please see the Primary Source DVD for additional sources related to this chapter.

READ ON

For Indian maps, J. B. Harley and D. Woodward, eds., *History of Cartography* (1987), vol. ii is fundamental. L. Feer, *A Study of the Jatakas* (1963) is a good introduction to those texts. The texts I cite on the Erythraean Sea are easy to consult in L. Casson, ed., *The Periplus of the Erythraean Sea* (1989), and S. Burstein, ed., *Agatharchides of Cnidos: On the Erythraean Sea* (1989). P. Horden and N. Purcell, *The Corrupting Sea* (2000), and D. Abulafia, ed., *The Mediterranean in History* (2003) are the best histories of the Mediterranean; for the link to the Atlantic, see B. Cunliffe, *Facing the Ocean* (2001). On the Indian Ocean, M. Pearson, *The Indian Ocean* (2003) is a masterly survey; the demanding work of K. Chaudhuri, *Asia before Europe* (1991) repays the effort it requires.

On the Silk Roads, the outstanding book is now the British Library exhibition catalog edited by S. Whitfield, *The Silk Roads* (2004). On Dunhuang, see R. Whitfield et al., eds., *Cave Temples of Dunhuang* (2000). J. Mirsky, *The Great Chinese Travelers* (1976), collects extracts from key texts, including the journey of Zhang Qian.

On the Persian Empire, *The Cambridge History of Iran* (1993) is unbeatable. On women, I follow M. Brosius, *Women in Ancient Persia* (1998). On the Persian Wars, P. Green, *The Greco-Persian Wars* (1996) is authoritative. S. Hornblower, *The Athenian Empire* (2000) is a superb study. The same author's *The Greek World* (1983) provides the

backdrop down to the time of Alexander, on whom R. Lane Fox, *Alexander the Great* (1973) is both scholarly and irresistibly readable. My remarks on Alexander's legacy are indebted to G. Cary, *The Medieval Alexander* (1967), which is a wonderful book.

On the Romans, T. Cornell, *The Beginnings of Rome* (1995) takes the story down to the Punic Wars. A. Goldsworthy, *The Fall of Carthage* (2004) is a history of those wars. R. Syme, *The Roman Revolution* (1939) is a classic of abiding interest and importance, centered on the rise of Augustus and a monarchical system of government. The best study of Virgil is probably R. Jenkyns, *Virgil's Experience* (1999).

For Celtic history, N. K. Chadwick, *The Celts* (1971), remains standard. H. D. Rankin, *Celts and the Classical World* (1987) is particularly interesting on Greek and Roman images. M. J. Green, *Celtic Art* (1997) is a good introduction.

On India in this period, F. R. Allchin, ed., *The Archaeology of Early Historic South Asia* (1995) is fundamental. R. Thapar, *Asoka and the Decline of the Mauryas* (1961) is insightful and close to the sources. R. McKeon and N. A. Nikam, *The Edicts of Asoka* (1959) analyzes these important sources.

For the Qin-Han revolution D. Twitchett and M. Loewe, eds., *The Cambridge History of China* (1986) is invaluable. Li Xueqin, *Eastern Zhou and Qin Civilizations* (1985) is excellent on the background. For the Xiongnu, as for all steppeland history, the classic work of R. Grousset, *The Empire of the Steppes* (1970) remains fundamental.

For Japan and Korea, *The Cambridge History of Japan* (1993) is inescapably useful. W. Hong, *Paekche of Korea and the Origins of Yamato Japan* (1994) is helpful on the links between the two regions. K. Mizoguchi, *An Archaeological History of Japan* (2002) surveys the archaeological evidence.

The Scythians and Sarmatians have inspired much good work. Useful introductions are supplied in T. Talbot Rice, *The Scythians* (1957); E. Phillips, *The Royal Hordes* (1965); and T. Sulimirski, *The Sarmatians* (1970). On Mesoamerica, J. A. Hendon and R. A. Joyce, *Mesoamerican Archaeology* (2004) has the most up-to-date account.

For Monte Albán, R. E. Blanton, *Monte Albán* (1978) is the standard work. For Teotihuacán, important works include J. C. Berlo, ed., *Art, Ideology and the City of Teotihuacán* (1993), and R. Storey, *Life and Death in the Ancient City of Teotihuacán* (1992).

Fitful Transitions, from the Third Century to the Tenth Century

The world map of Beatus of Liebana. The eighth-century Spanish monk, Beatus of Liebana, illustrated his Commentary on the last book of the Bible with a world map. Almost all those who later made copies of his work produced versions of their own maps. In this one, from 1109, the picture of Adam, Eve, and the serpent indicates the presumed location of the Garden of Eden, at the extreme limit of the East. Europe is the disproportionately large, nearly square shape at the lower left.

ENVIRONMENT

200–400
Spread of maize cultivation into North America

CULTURE

220
Breakup of Han Empire

200s on
Spread of Buddhism to east Asia

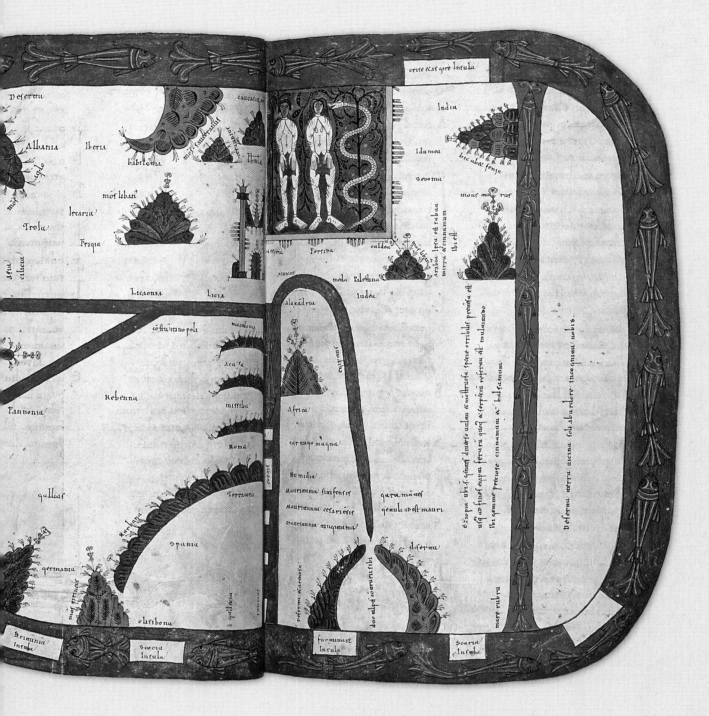

mid–500s
Plague in Arabia
and eastern Mediterranean

600–800
Growing trans-Saharan trade;
Polynesian diaspora

800–1000
"Internal colonization" in
China, Japan, western Europe

300s on
Spread of Christianity
in Roman world

400s
Breakup of Roman Empire

630 on
Rise and spread of Islam

8 Postimperial Worlds: Problems of Empires in Eurasia and Africa, ca. 200 to ca. 700 C.E.

Detail from a Mayan vase, early sixth century c.e. The color scheme of red on a gold background is characteristic of ceramics from Tikal, while the bird-like symbols with forked, blood-sucking tongues on the bottom row have similarities with glyphs from Teohituacán.

They arrived in January 378, soon after the beginning of the rains, in the tropical lowlands of what is now eastern Guatemala. They came from Teotihuacán, 7,500 feet high in the mountain-ringed valley of central Mexico, across hundreds of miles of mountains and forests, to the land of the Maya, whose environment, culture, and language were different from their own. The Maya called the leader of the group Siyaj K'ak (SEE-ah kah-AK), meaning "fire born," and added a nickname, "The Great Man from the West." But why had he come?

MESOAMERICA

His destination was Tikal (tee-KAHL), where limestone temples and gaudily painted rooftop reliefs rose above dense forest. Tikal was one of the oldest and largest of the many city-states among which the Maya world was divided. Its population at the time was perhaps over 30,000. But while Tikal was a giant by Maya standards, Teotihuacán was probably more than three times its size: no mere city-state, moreover, but the nerve center of an empire that covered the valley of Mexico and spilled into neighboring regions. Teotihuacáno influence and tribute gathering probed further still.

Relations between Tikal and Teotihuacán were important for both cities, because of the complementary ecologies of their regions (see Map 8.1). The Maya supplied Mexico with products unavailable in the highlands, including the plumage of forest birds for ornament, rubber for the ball games the elites of the region favored, cacao, jade, and incense. But visitors like Siyaj K'ak were rare, or even, perhaps, unprecedented. As they approached, day by day, along the river now called San Pedro Mártir, the communities they passed through handed on the news to neighbors down the line. What were the newcomers' intentions? Were they invaders or invitees? Envoys or adventurers? Were they mercenaries, perhaps, or a marriage party? Had they come to arbitrate disputes or to exploit them for their own purposes?

FOCUS questions

- WHY DID Teotihuacán rise and decline as an imperial state?
- WHY DID the Roman Empire collapse in the west but survive in the east?
- WHY WAS China better adapted for long-term survival than Rome and India?
- WHAT WERE the bases for Ethiopia's prosperity?
- WHY WERE the Arabs able to conquer such a vast empire so quickly?
- HOW DID the Muslims treat conquered peoples?
- HOW DID states in Korea, Tibet, and Japan develop?

The inscriptions that record the events are too fragmentary to answer these questions. But they tell a suggestive story. When Siyaj K'ak reached Tikal on January 31, his arrival precipitated a revolution. On that very day, if the inscriptions can be taken literally, the life of the city's ruler, Chak Tok Ich'aak (chak tek eech-AH-AK) (or "Great Jaguar Paw," as historians used to call him), came to an end. He "entered the water," as the Maya said, after a reign of 18 years, ending the supremacy of a royal line that had supplied 13 kings. The monuments of his dynasty were shattered into fragments or defaced and buried: slabs of stone on which images of kings were carved, with commemorations of the wars they fought, captives they took, astronomical observations they recorded, and sacrifices they offered to the gods—sometimes of their own blood, sometimes of the lives of their captives.

Siyaj K'ak installed new rulers not only in Tikal but also in other, smaller cities in the region over the next few years. The supremacy of Teotihuacán, or at least of Teotihuacános, was part of the new order. A rash of new cities was founded from Tikal, though they seem quickly, in most cases, to have asserted or exercised independence. It would exceed the evidence to speak of the birth of a new regional state or the foundation of a new province of the empire of Teotihuacán. But we can confidently assert that contacts across Mesoamerica were growing, that state formation was quickening and spreading, and that a complex political pattern was emerging: jealous Maya cities, competing and combining, with elites often drawn or sponsored from central Mexico.

• • • • •

Tikal

The influence and power of Teotihuacán were close to their maximum. Teotihuacános founded colonies wherever the city needed supplies. Chingú (cheen-GOO), near the later site of Tula (TOO-lah), was one, where lime was exported for Teotihuacán's gigantic building projects. San Ignacio in Morelos was another, supplying avocados, cacao, and cotton, which would not grow in the highlands but was vital for everyday clothing and the quilted armor warriors favored.

In part, pressure of population drove this expansion. Teotihuacán probably produced or attracted more people than it could contain. In any case, to sustain a growing city, Teotihuacán needed a growing empire. The basic foodstuffs the city consumed—maize and beans—were part of the ecosystem of its own region. But the concentration of population that had to be fed was enormous by the standards of preindustrial cities anywhere in the world and probably required extra supplies from farther away. The cotton and the luxuries and ritual objects on which elite life depended had to come from other climes. Teotihuacán had its own mines of obsidian—the black volcanic glass of which the cutting blades of tools and weapons were made. But it had no other resources to export. It had to be a military state.

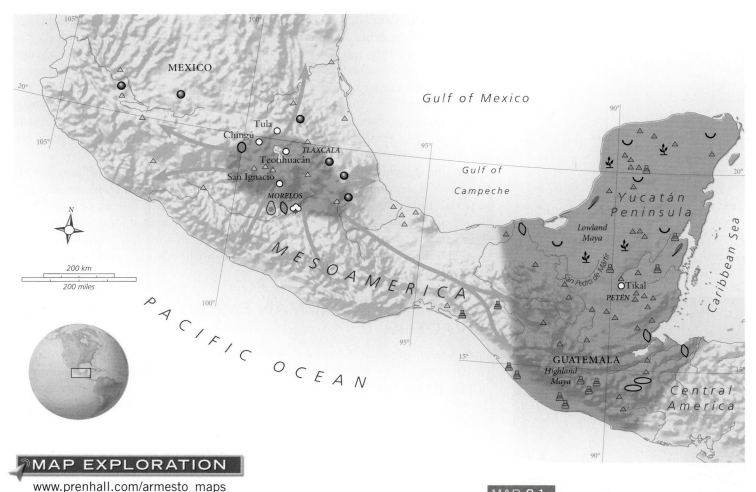

MAP EXPLORATION

www.prenhall.com/armesto_maps

MAP 8.1

The Maya and Teotihuacán

▨	Maya
▨	Teotihuacán and directions of influence
⚎	Mayan temple
△	important Mayan site
△	important Teotihuacán site
●	obsidian mine
MEXICO	modern-day country
PETÉN	modern-day province or region
○	city described or mentioned on pages 181–184

Products Supplied from Maya to Teotihuacán

◖	cacao
⚘	incense
◯	jade
⬎	plumage
∪	rubber

Products Supplied to Teotihuacán from Neighboring Colonies

◖	avocado
◗	cacao
⬡	cotton
◗	lime

We do not know how the state was organized. Unlike the Maya, the Teotihuacános produced no art depicting kings and, as far as we know, no chronicles of royal activities. Some curious features, however, show up in the archaeological record. During the fourth century, many families were shifted from small dwellings into large compounds, as if the city were being divided among rival, or potentially rival, focuses of allegiance. From the mid–fifth century, there are signs of internal instability. One of the most lavish temples was demolished. Thick, high internal walls divided different quarters of the city from each other. New building gradually ceased. Meanwhile, Teotihuacáno influence over distant areas withered. At an uncertain date, probably around the mid–eighth century, a traumatic event ended Teotihuacán's greatness. Fire wrecked the center of the city, and much of the population fled. Teotihuacán remained a city of perhaps 30,000 people, but it never again displayed imperial trappings or ambition. It is hard to resist the impression that the empire had overreached itself. No single city or empire of comparable dimensions replaced Teotihuacán. But people in Mesoamerica remembered it, conserved its influence, and tried to imitate it, as they entered a period of kaleidoscopic change, in which small, well-matched states fought among themselves without ever settling into an enduring pattern.

Teotihuacán was one of the world's most out-of-the-way empires—isolated from most of the others that arose in or after the axial age. Yet it was typical of its time. Other new imperial initiatives of the era—in the formative Islamic world and in Ethiopia—succumbed to remarkably similar challenges. Even the old empires struggled with similar problems. In Rome, India, China, and Persia, imperial traditions inherited from the axial age were extinguished or suffered periods of fragmentation or submersion by invaders whom the natives regarded as barbaric. And on the edges of empires in transformation, as well as within them, new states felt the effects.

In this chapter and the next two, we have to face the questions of how, if at all, these stories are connected, and why their outcomes differed. How, for instance, imperial unity revived in China but not in the other affected areas, or why Christianity and Islam, but not Buddhism, became almost monopolistic ideologies in their areas of dominance. Less pressing, perhaps, but no less interesting, is the problem of how the history of the rest of the world echoes or connects with the fates of Eurasia's empires.

THE WESTERN ROMAN EMPIRE AND ITS INVADERS

On Rome's Capitoline Hill stands a bronze statue of the Emeperor Marcus Aurelius (r. 161–180), triumphantly horsed, holding a globe, wielding Roman power at its height. Yet the empire had abiding problems: sprawling size; a long, vulnerable land frontier; the unruly behavior of politicized soldiery, with Roman armies fighting each other to make and unmake emperors; the uneasy, usually hostile relationship with Persia. Two new dangers were increasingly apparent. First, for most of the elite, Christianity seemed subversive. To the pious, Rome's greatness was at the disposal of the gods. To the practical, Roman unity depended on politically charged cults of the divine emperor and patron-gods of Rome. Second, Germanic peoples beyond the empire's borders in Europe coveted Roman wealth. The prosperity gap was like that between "North and South," on a global level, today—inspiring fear in the prosperous and envy in the poor.

Marcus Aurelius anticipated ways in which the empire would cope with these problems for the next three centuries. He sensed the need to divide government, making his adoptive brother coemperor and delegating to him responsibility for the eastern frontier. This sort of division was to be a recurrent formula for saving the state from crisis. He repudiated fancy theories in favor of practical ethics (see Chapter 6). His was a dark world, glinting with campfire light, as he fought to keep the Danube frontier secure. He snatched moments on campaign to write his *Meditations* in Greek, which was the common language of the eastern half of the empire and the prestige language favored for philosophy. "Renew yourself," he wrote in a memo to himself, "but keep it brief and basic."

In combination with threats from Persia and the convulsions of Roman politics, Germanic invasions in the third century almost dissolved the empire. In the late fourth century, the struggle to keep out the immigrants became hopeless. They came usually in relatively small, mobile war parties, numbering hundreds or at most a few thousand, composed of men detached from their traditional kinship structures by loyalty to a "ring giver"—a warlord who could buy allegiance with booty, protection money, ransom, extortion, or mercenary service. Trinkets of warband service survive in burial sites: armbands set with jewels or onyx or inscribed with reminders of loyalty, rings bulging with garnets.

The philosopher at war. *The Meditations* of the Emperor Marcus Aurelius (r. 161–180) were written in military camps while he was campaigning against the barbarians on the empire's northern frontiers. His statue atop the Capitol at Rome has always symbolized dynamism and power, not only because of the commanding gesture of the emperor, but also because of the power his horse displays with its flared nostrils and stamping hoof.

Marcus Aurelius, from *The Meditations*

The biggest bands of migrants, numbering tens of thousands at a time, and traveling with women and children, were driven by stresses that arose in the Eurasian steppelands. Here, the mid and late fourth century was a traumatic time, when war, hunger, plague, exceptional cold, or some combination of such events induced unprecedented mobility, conflict, and confusion. The Roman historian and retired soldier, Ammianus Marcellinus, reported a conversation with some Huns, reputedly the most ferocious of the steppeland peoples of the time. "Ask," he said, "who they are and whence they came—and they cannot tell you." Fear of the Huns glistens between the lines of every account: fear of their monstrous appearance, which Roman writers suspected must be produced by self-deformation; fear of their mounted archery; fear of their merciless treatment of enemies. Late in the fourth century, the Huns broke out of their heartlands in the depths of Asia—perhaps on the northeast borders of China, where many scholars identify them with the people the Chinese called Xiongnu (see Chapter 7). A kind of ricochet effect set in, as peoples collided and cannoned off each other, like balls on a pool table. Or perhaps all the turbulence of peoples, Germans and steppelanders alike, was the result of common problems: cold weather, shrinking pastures; or new sources of wealth, such as trade and booty, enriching new classes and disrupting the traditional stability of the societies concerned. Whatever the reasons, in the late fourth and early fifth centuries, displaced communities lined up for admission into the enticing empires of Rome, Persia, China, and India.

Ammianus Marcellinus on the Huns

The hardest part of the story to appreciate is what it felt like for those who took part. Inklings emerge from the earliest surviving poem in what is recognizably German: the *Hildebrandslied*, the story of a family split in the conflicts of the fifth century. Hildebrand's wife was left "in misery"; his baby grew into his battlefield adversary. The boy, raised in ignorance of his father's identity, unwittingly rejected his present of gold and jewels, "which the King of the Huns had given him." Only the first few lines survive of the terrible climax, in which father and son fight to the death. The story shows the chaotic, divisive effects of the migrations, the interdependence of the worlds of Germans and Huns.

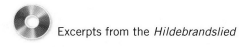
Excerpts from the *Hildebrandslied*

Germans were not nomadic by custom but, according to their own earliest historian, Jordanes, who wrote in the sixth century, were "driven to wander in a prolonged search for lands to cultivate." In 376, for instance, a reputed 200,000 Visigothic refugees were admitted into the Roman Empire. But the Romans then left them to starve, provoking a terrible revenge at the battle of Adrianople in 378 when a Roman emperor died along with most of his army. From 395 to 418, the Visigoths undertook a destructive march across the empire. In 410, they sacked Rome, inspiring speculations about the end of the world among shocked subjects of the empire, before settling as paid "guests" and, in effect, the masters of the local population in southern France and northern Spain. Other Germanic peoples found the Visigoths' example irresistible. Rome's frontier with the Germans was becoming indefensible (see Map 8.2).

Jordanes, *Deeds of the Goths*, Book Twenty-Six

Changes Within the Roman Empire

Meanwhile, the center of power in the dwindling empire shifted eastward into the mostly Greek-speaking zone, where barbarian incursions were more limited. In 323, the Emperor Constantine elevated a dauntingly defensible small garrison town into Constantinople, an imperial capital.

From here, in the fourth and fifth centuries, the emperors were able to keep invaders out of most of the eastern provinces or limit immigration to manageable

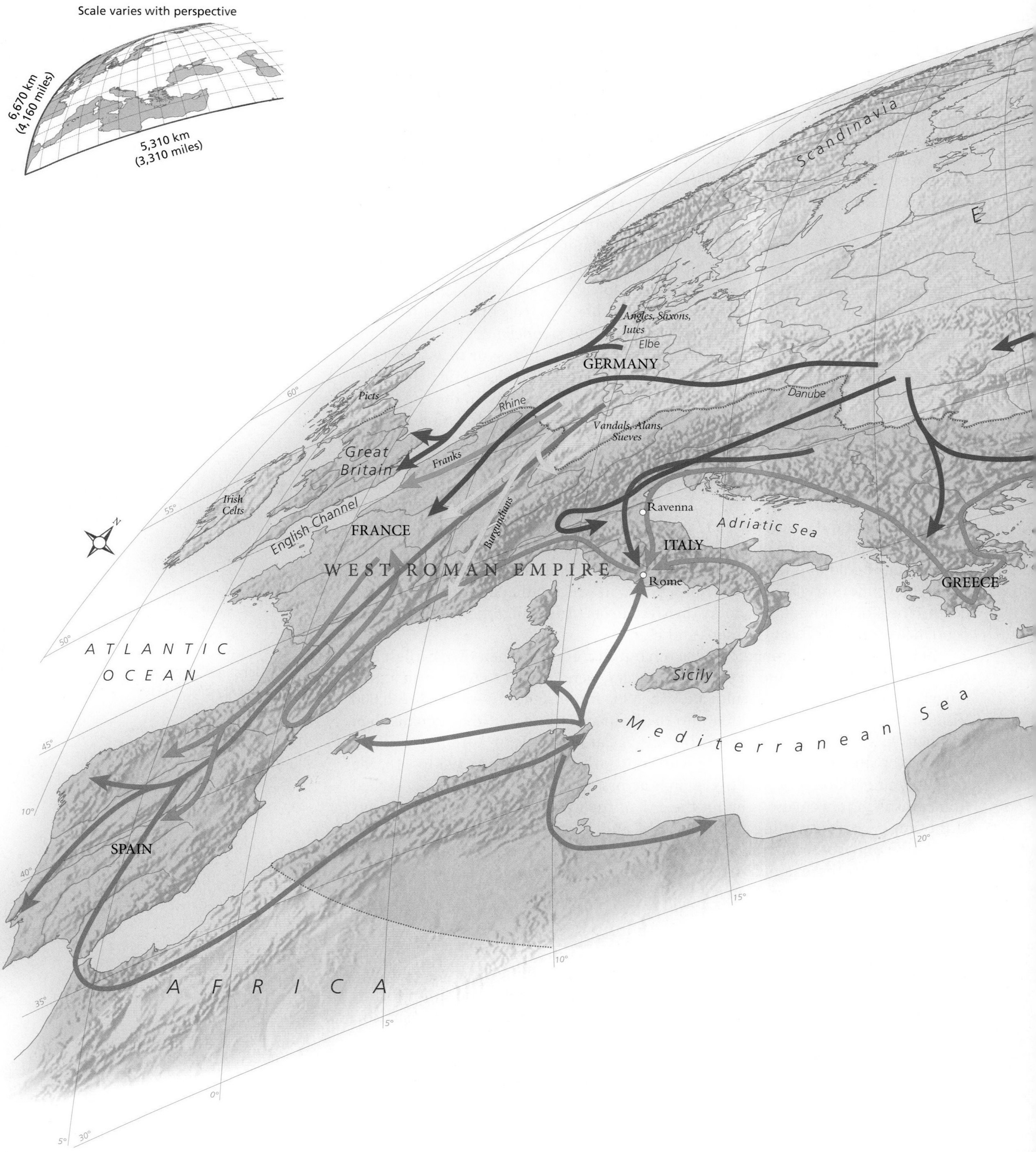
Scale varies with perspective
6,670 km
(4,160 miles)
5,310 km
(3,310 miles)
Scandinavia
E
Angles, Saxons,
Jutes
Elbe
GERMANY
Picts
Rhine
Danube
Vandals, Alans,
Sueves
Great
Britain
Franks
Irish
Celts
English Channel
FRANCE
Burgundians
Ravenna
Adriatic Sea
ITALY
WEST ROMAN EMPIRE
Rome
GREECE
ATLANTIC
OCEAN
Sicily
Mediterranean Sea
SPAIN
AFRICA
60°
55°
50°
45°
40°
35°
30°
10°
5°
0°
5°
10°
15°
20°

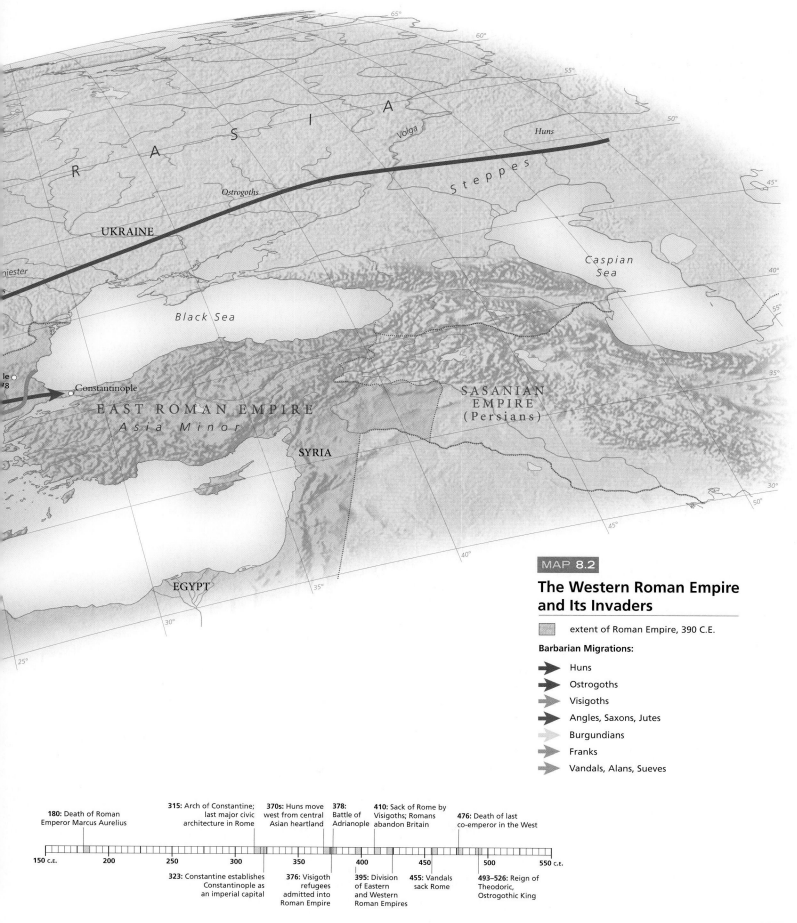

EURASIA

Volga

Huns

Ostrogoths

Steppes

UKRAINE

Dniester

Caspian Sea

Black Sea

Constantinople

EAST ROMAN EMPIRE
Asia Minor

SYRIA

SASANIAN EMPIRE
(Persians)

EGYPT

MAP 8.2

The Western Roman Empire and Its Invaders

◻ extent of Roman Empire, 390 C.E.

Barbarian Migrations:

➤ Huns

➤ Ostrogoths

➤ Visigoths

➤ Angles, Saxons, Jutes

➤ Burgundians

➤ Franks

➤ Vandals, Alans, Sueves

180: Death of Roman Emperor Marcus Aurelius

315: Arch of Constantine; last major civic architecture in Rome

370s: Huns move west from central Asian heartland

378: Battle of Adrianople

410: Sack of Rome by Visigoths; Romans abandon Britain

476: Death of last co-emperor in the West

150 C.E. 200 250 300 350 400 450 500 550 C.E.

323: Constantine establishes Constantinople as an imperial capital

376: Visigoth refugees admitted into Roman Empire

395: Division of Eastern and Western Roman Empires

455: Vandals sack Rome

493–526: Reign of Theodoric, Ostrogothic King

Stilicho. The late Roman Empire increasingly relied on immigrant mercenaries for its defense. The Vandal Stilicho (right) was one of the best, defending—as a Roman poet of the time said—"all within the sun's fiery orbit" in trust for the emperors of Rome. "All virtues meet in thee." He married an emperor's niece and maneuvered to make his son, Eucherius, also shown here, emperor. His daughter married an emperor. But, falsely accused of treachery, he loyally gave himself up for execution in 408 C.E. These ivory panels are examples of an art form traditionally used to commemorate Roman consuls.

proportions or to numbers needed for imperial defense. In the west, however, the empire could not control the incursions. Supplies and reinforcements from Constantinople could easily reach the provinces from Italy's Adriatic coast eastward, whereas the western Mediterranean lay beyond the terrible navigational bottlenecks between Italy, Sicily, and North Africa. The Rhine was easily crossed—especially in the cold winters of the early fifth century, when the river often froze. From there, invaders usually swung through northern France toward Spain, or turned south to reach Italy.

Impeded by war, long-range exchanges of personnel and commerce became increasingly impractical in the west. Communications decayed. Aristocrats withdrew from traditional civic responsibilities—retiring to their estates, struggling to keep them going amid invasions. Bishops replaced bureaucrats. In localities from which imperial authority vanished, holy men took on the jobs of judges. Almost everywhere, barbarian experts in warfare took military commands. Garrisons withdrew from outposts of empire beyond the Rhine, the Danube, and the English Channel. After 476, there was no longer a coemperor in the west. Regional and local priorities replaced empirewide perspectives. The most extreme form of the dissolution of authority inside the empire was the establishment of kingdoms led by foreigners, as Germans—settled as uneasy allies, entrusted with imperial defense, and quartered at the expense of their host communities—gradually usurped or accepted authority over non-Germanic populations. Where such kingdoms delivered peace and administered laws, they replaced the empire as the primary focus of people's allegiance.

The "Barbarian" West

At the time, writers of history and prophesy, peering through the twilight of the empire, could not believe Roman history was over. Rome was the last of the world monarchies the Bible foretold. Its end would mean the end of time. Everyone, including barbarian kings, pretended that the empire had survived. Germanic settlers were all, in varying degrees, susceptible to Romanization, and their kings usually showed deference to imperial institutions. A Visigothic leader, Athawulf, vowed "to extirpate the Roman name," but ended by marrying into the imperial family and collaborating with Rome. Burgundian kings in what is now eastern France continued a flattering correspondence with the emperors in Constantinople for as long as their state survived. The Franks, who occupied most of France in the late fifth and early sixth centuries, adorned their monarchs with emblems of Roman governors and consuls. No barbarians were proof against the appeal of Roman culture. Vandals, whose name has become a byword for destruction, had themselves portrayed in Roman-style mosaics. Even the Germanic settlers of Britain, most of whom had had virtually no contact with the Roman Empire, recalled the rule of Roman "giants" in their poetry.

Yet the limits of barbarian identification with Rome were of enormous importance. The notion of Roman citizenship gradually dissolved. Although the barbarians envied Roman civilization, most of them hankered after their own identities and—not surprisingly amid the dislocation of the times—clung to their roots. Many groups tried to differentiate themselves by upholding, at least for a time, unorthodox versions of Christianity. Some of their scholars and kings took almost as much interest in preserving their own traditional literature as in retaining or rescuing the works of classical and Christian writers. Law codes of barbarian kingdoms prescribed different rules for Germans and Romans.

The realm of the Ostrogothic king, Theodoric, was typically hybrid. He ruled Italy from 493 to 526. A church wall in his courtly center at Ravenna displays his palace, with throne room of gold, curtained like a sanctuary. His tomb is the burial mound of a Germanic king but is also in the style the Roman aristocracy of his era favored. Boethius, his chief minister, who was a Roman senator, not a Goth, worked hard to Romanize him, clinging to the old order, banking on the domestication of barbarian invaders. Imprisoned by Theodoric for his Roman partialities, he wrote *The Consolation of Philosophy*, fusing the Stoical value system of happiness with the Christian tradition of deference to God. Happiness and God, Boethius argued, were identical.

The Collapse of Empire in the West

162–180	Reign of Emperor Marcus Aurelius, high point of Roman Empire
Third and fourth centuries	Germanic migrants enter empire in increasing numbers
323	Founding of Constantinople
378	Battle of Adrianople, Roman emperor killed
Late fourth century	Huns break out of Central Asia
410	Visigoths sack Rome
476	End of empire in the west

 Pliny the Elder, from the *Natural History*

STEPPELANDERS AND THEIR VICTIMS

Because Germanic peoples lined the zone between Rome's frontier and the Eurasian plains, steppeland peoples like the Huns made relatively few and brief forays into the Roman Empire. Empires centered in China, Persia, and India, by contrast, had to cope with the steppelanders directly (see Map 8.3). In some ways, invading herdsmen were easier to deal with than the Germans who were used to settled agriculture. Their techniques of warfare were less flexible, ill equipped for mountain terrain on the frontiers of Persia or India, or amid rice paddies in China. When successful as conquerors, the steppelanders were usually easier to wean from their cultural traditions than the Germans, assimilating to Chinese or, in some cases, to Indian ways within a few generations.

China

China's empire, moreover, was better adapted for survival than Rome's. Thanks to China's roughly round shape, centrally retained armies could get quickly to any point on its frontiers. No invaders threatened the long sea coast. Subject-peoples tended to embrace Chinese identity with surprising enthusiasm. Above all, size, productivity, and technical inventiveness made China self-sufficient, if necessary. No adverse balance of trade, such as Rome endured, drained wealth out of the empire. China's internal market was huge—more internal trade meant more wealth.

But, like Rome, China under the Han dynasty never solved the most basic problem of imperial government: how to secure the succession of emperors. Factionalism and rebelliousness bred in imperial households. To offset the danger, emperors relied ever more heavily on **eunuchs**, whom Roman emperors, too, regarded as perfect servants, and whose inability to father families of their own

"A Parthian shot" now means a cutting parting remark—so-called from the tactics Parthian mounted archers used in defending their homeland in what is now Iran and Iraq against the Romans. Retreating, or pretending to retreat, they turned in their saddles to shoot at their pursuers. Steppelander armies copied or developed this technique on their own. This 2,000-year-old Chinese design shows a Turkic warrior wielding a double-curve bow, constructed to be compact but with high tensile strength for use on horseback.

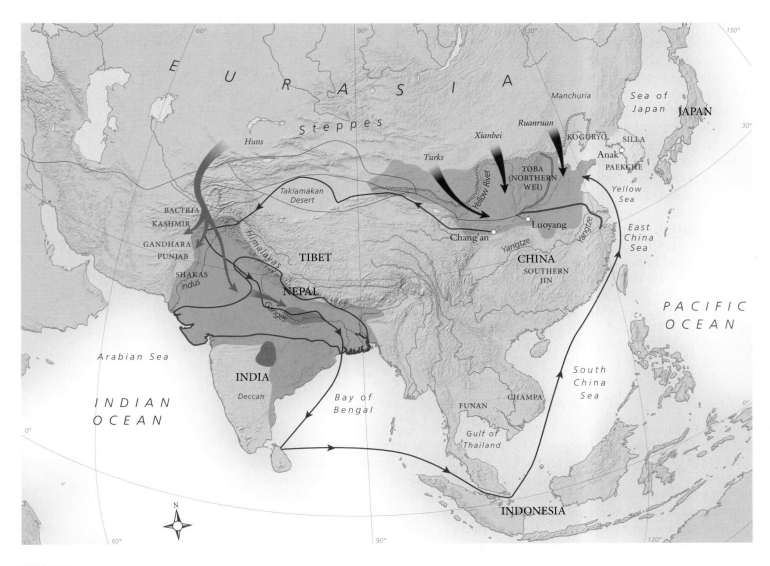

MAP 8.3

Steppelanders and Asian Kingdoms, ca. 300–700 C.E.

- ▢ farthest extent of Toba Wei, ca. 500 C.E.
- ▢ kingdom of Candra Gupta I
- ▢ farthest extent of Gupta dynasty, ca. 500 C.E.
- ▢ Vakataka dynasty
- — Harsha's empire, ca. 650 C.E.
- ➡ Hun invasions
- ➡ Steppeland migrants into China
- ➡ Journey of Faxian, 405–411 C.E.

- 〜〜〜 Great Wall
- — Grand Canal
- — Silk Roads
- *Xianbei* people

Scale varies with perspective

made them proof against dynastic ambitions. The long-term result was to create another faction and a new focus of resentment, as eunuchs usurped control over the succession. As in Rome, armies in China contended for the power to make and unmake emperors. Rivalry between armies and eunuchs precipitated civil war in 184, when Chang Chueh (chahng joo-ay), a wandering medic, whose plague rem-

MAKING CONNECTIONS

CHINA AND ROME COMPARED

	CHINA	ROME
Geography	Round shape ensures that centrally located armies can get quickly to any point on frontier. Numerous rivers and canals facilitate communication	Long land frontier and narrow sea lanes impede movement of troops and information
Culture	Subject peoples embrace Chinese identity; barbarian immigrants adopt Chinese customs and language	Germanic peoples beyond empire's borders covet Roman wealth. "North–South" prosperity gap leads to envy and hostility. Limited identification by barbarians with Rome.
Economy	Size, productivity, and technical inventiveness lead to self-sufficiency	Adverse balance of trade drains wealth out of the empire

edy made him a popular hero, proclaimed rebellion against eunuch rule. The army emerged ascendant from nearly 40 years of war that followed.

In 220, the last Han emperor was forced to abdicate in favor of a new, army-backed dynasty, known as Jin. But the former patterns of politics resumed. Civil war became chronic, made worse by emperors' efforts to divide their responsibilities along lines similar to those Rome adopted, giving members of the imperial family regions to run. Steppeland migrants and marauders played increasingly important roles in the wars. Contenders for disputed succession called in rival barbarian armies. In 304, the leader of one of these armies proclaimed himself emperor, and his son drove the Jin south, into the Yangtze valley. The old capital, Chang'an (chahng-ahn), filled with "weeds and thorns." Northern China became a kaleidoscope of kingdoms and self-styled empires, continually reshaken by warlords, adventurers, and Turkic and Mongol migrants. Toward the end of the fifth century, the ruler of the ascendant barbarians, the Xianbei (shee-on-bay), introduced Chinese rites, including the state cult of Confucius. But the state he founded fragmented in its turn. The old aristocracy resisted Chinese values, while the court practiced Chinese-style cycles of factionalism, family rifts, and civil wars.

India

Although the invasion routes into India from the steppes look formidable on the map, they were poorly guarded (see Map 8.3). In the fourth century, a ruler of Maghada who called himself Candra Gupta (CHAN-drah GOOP-tah), after a hero of the time of Alexander the Great, attempted to restore the unity of the Indian subcontinent. His dynasty, the Guptas, never established as wide a dominion as that of Asoka (see Chapter 7), but they did weaken the states of India's northwest frontier. The Huns who began to infiltrate India around 415 were, presumably, part of the fallout of the same catastrophes that spilled steppelanders into the Roman and Chinese Empires.

The morale of the population favored the invaders. Writers generally agreed that they were living in the *Kaliyuga*, the age of decline. A play written by Kalidasa—who probably lived in the fourth century—depicted alienated classes in a morally corrupt state, where officials practised torture and extortion on accused innocents. It was

The End of Dynasties in China and India

220	Last Han emperor forced to abdicate
304	Contenders for Chinese throne call in barbarian armies
415	Huns begin to infiltrate India
ca. 467	Demise of Gupta Empire

Faxian, *Record of Buddhist Countries*, Chapter Sixteen

Korean crown. Before Buddhism became rooted there in the sixth century C.E., Korean rulers were buried with fabulous treasures. This crown, with antler-like ornaments, is from one of the many royal burial mounds of the kingdom of Silla. It shows the influence of Chinese and Central Asian goldsmiths' work.

hard for the empire's poorest subjects to identify with a system that perpetuated their poverty by making social rank inherited. According to Faxian (faw-shee-ahn), a Chinese Buddhist pilgrim in India in 405–411, the "untouchables" of the lowest caste had to sound a clapper in the street to warn against their polluting presence.

The loose-knit Gupta political system, which covered most of India as far south as the Deccan, showed little resilience. The decline of the empire is conventionally dated from 467—less than a decade before the last emperor in Rome was forced to abdicate. Subsequent Gupta emperors are barely known, except by name, from contemporary sources. Yet within another 50 years or so, the Hunnic realm seems to have become one Indian state among many. Indian unity—such as it was—dissolved among a multitude of principalities in the north and a few relatively large, unstable kingdoms in the south.

NEW FRONTIERS IN ASIA

For the Chinese and Gupta Empires, the barbarian invasions inaugurated times of troubles, but it was a time of opportunity for developing states on their frontiers, where imperial power might otherwise have inhibited or repressed development. An early Gupta inscription mentions developing states around the frontiers: the Shaka dynasty in western India and the Vakatakas, whose daughters the Guptas took in marriage in the Deccan. The conditions favored similar effects in other parts of Asia.

Korea

Refugees from China, for instance, fled from the nomad invaders in search of tamer barbarians, to whom to offer their services as technicians or sages. Dong Shou—to take a case in point—was a scholar who escaped from the Xianbei in 337, and took refuge in neighboring Koguryo (koh-goo-ryuh), an emerging state in what is now southeastern Manchuria and northern Korea. After a prosperous career, he was buried at Anak, amid wall paintings that document the history of Koguryo at the time. Buddhist and Daoist emblems mingle with scenes of the life of the kingdom: proudly displayed images of prosperity and strength, including irrigation works, rice production, people and horses eating, and a procession of well-armored soldiers. While China dissolved, Koguryo expanded. A memorial of King Kwanggaet'o, erected at the time of his death in 413, credits him with the conquest of 64 walled towns and 1,400 villages. Continuing prosperity—the result of the introduction of ox-drawn plows and irrigation for rice fields—can be measured in the results of the census the Chinese took when they eventually conquered Koguryo in 667–668. The country had 176 walled cities and 697,000 families. Unlike other communities whom the Chinese considered barbarians, however, Korean states had, by then, too much self-pride and too long a history of achievement to adopt Chinese identity.

Meanwhile, similar histories unfolded in the southern Korean kingdoms of Silla (shil-lah) and Paekche (pak-jay). Although the iron trade contributed to the enrichment of these states, they were agrarian kingdoms whose wealth was in manpower. They fought one another to gain population. Paekche paid a ransom of 1,000 households, for instance, when raiders from Koguryo occupied its capital. Silla resolutely followed Chinese models of state-building. In 520, King Pophung began to give positions of power and social prestige to Confucian scholars. The kingdom, however, also had a caste system of its own. Many positions were open only to those ranked as possessing "sacred bone"—the rank of the royal family— and "true bone," the birthright of the courtly elite. (This distinction disappeared after 653, when a true bone became king.) Silla unified the Korean peninsula in over 100 years of warfare from the mid–sixth century.

Funan

Meanwhile, the turbulence of central Eurasia, which periodically disrupted the Silk Roads, favored states along the maritime route across Eurasia, beside monsoonal seas. Chinese travelers' accounts give us glimpses into their world. Funan occupied a stretch of territory wrapped around the coast of the Gulf of Thailand. Chinese officials singled it out as a possible tributary or trading partner in the third century. Its culture was almost certainly borrowed from India. By Chinese reports, it was a repository of learning, rich enough to levy taxes in "gold, silver, pearls and perfumes." Its success depended on its role as a middleman in Chinese trade with Indonesia and the Bay of Bengal.

THE RISE OF ETHIOPIA

The most remarkable state favored by growing commerce across monsoonal seas was Ethiopia, a country at the limit of the Indian Ocean network. The right balance between accessibility and isolation was the key to Ethiopia's success. High altitude made the emergent state defensible and guaranteed it a temperate climate in tropical latitudes. Axum (AHK-soom), the capital, was around 7,200 feet up.

Outsiders saw Axum as a trading state, where all the exotic goods of Africa awaited: rhino horn, hippo hides, ivory and obsidian, tortoise shell, monkeys, slaves. Objects manufactured in China and Greece found their way to Axumite tombs. The frequent use of Greek in inscriptions, alongside the native language, indicates a cosmopolitan community. Ethiopian products could reach the outside world through the Mediterranean via Roman and later Byzantine Egypt and with the Indian Ocean via the Red Sea. The highlands could dominate the long Rift valley land route to the south, to lands rich in gold, aromatics, slaves, and ivory.

But the corridor from the Ethiopian highlands to the sea is long and leads to dangerous waters. For the people of Axum, intent on their farming, trade was a sideline. They stamped ears of wheat on their coins. The highlands were fertile enough to produce two or three crops a year. Food mentioned in inscriptions includes wheat, beer, wine, honey, meat, butter, vegetable oils, and the world's first recorded coffee.

The material remains of the culture include finely worked ivory, metalwork, and huge, cubical tombs lined with brick arches. Three enormous stone pillars, each of a single slab of locally quarried granite, towered over the city. The largest was 160 feet tall and weighed nearly 500 tons—bigger than any other monolith ever made. Depictions of many-storied buildings or figures of hawks and crocodiles adorned the pillars. According to a Greek visitor's description, the central plaza of the city had a four-towered palace and thrones of pure marble, smothered with inscriptions, and statues of gold, silver, and bronze.

Inscriptions from early in the fourth century recorded what people at the time regarded as the key events of politics: numbers of captives; plunder in livestock; oaths of submission; doles of bread, meat, and wine granted to captives; their punitive relocation in distant parts of the empire; thank offerings for gods who bestowed victory—native gods at first, then, from the 340s, the Christian God. The ambitions of the kings seemed to tug across the strait to Arabia (see Chapter 5). Early in the sixth century, King Kaleb launched an expedition to conquer southern Arabia, much of which the Ethiopians occupied for most of the rest of the century.

Stela of Axum. Until the rulers of Ethiopia adopted Christianity in the mid–fourth century, they invested huge amounts of capital and labor to create gigantic stelae—still the biggest structures made of single blocks of stone anywhere in the world. The largest examples—which reach well over 100 feet high—stood on ground long used for burials and probably marked important tombs. They have the skyscraper-like form of towering buildings. This art form climaxed in the early fourth century, just before Ethiopian priorities switched to church building, and the last stelae were left to topple or perhaps were never even hoisted into position.

The Rise of Ethiopia

340s	Spread of Christianity in Ethiopia
Early sixth century	King Kaleb begins conquest of southern Arabia
530s	Environmental crisis undermines control of south Arabia

THE CRISES OF THE SIXTH AND SEVENTH CENTURIES

Ethiopian control of south Arabia probably faltered because of an environmental crisis in the 530s. Plague played a part in the collapse of the irrigation states of southern Arabia and drove migrants northward, some seeking refuge in Roman-controlled Syria, others swelling the cities of Mecca and Medina. Twice during the Ethiopian occupation, the great dam at Marib broke. The losses of irrigation water were so traumatic that they became a major theme for poets' laments.

These disasters roughly coincided with other, more widespread catastrophes. In 535, the skies of the Northern Hemisphere darkened. A massive volcanic eruption in Indonesia split Java from Sumatra and spewed ash into the atmosphere. Thanks to the diminished sunlight, temperatures fell. The new conditions suited some disease-bearing microorganisms. A plague-bearing bacillus ravaged Constantinople. A disease that resembled smallpox devastated Japan. Even in central Mexico graves contain evidence of a severe decline in health toward the mid–sixth century. In the same period, the Eurasian steppes overspilled anew, impelling horseborne warbands into Europe: refugees, perhaps, from plague. Historians still debate how far these events are connected and whether a single volcanic explosion can account for them. Still, the sixth century marked a low point from which reformers could launch revivals of endangered traditions and rally weakened states.

In India, for instance, early in the seventh century, Harsha, king of Thanesar, tried to fill in the political fissures and reconstruct an empire (see Map 8.3). He devoted his reign of 41 years to the reunification of most of the Ganges basin. Rulers in Punjab, Kashmir, and Nepal paid him tribute. He made tireless tours of his realm, collecting tribute, giving alms, dispensing judgments. But even in the biography Harsha himself commissioned, practical compromises with kingly ideals are evident. The book describes the poor, gathering fragments of grain left after the king's camp has moved on. The king's elephants trample the hovels of peasants who can defend themselves only by hurling clods of earth. Harsha's dominion was an improvised conquest, and his achievement did not survive him. He had, however, more successful counterparts in China and Rome.

JUSTINIAN AND THE EASTERN ROMAN EMPIRE

Though the eastern Roman Empire remained a single state, it, too, was transformed. In the perceptions of its leaders, it remained "Roman," even after 476, when the emperors no longer had any power in Rome itself. Nowadays, however, historians prefer the term *Byzantine Empire* from "Byzantium" (bih-ZAN-tee-uhm), the former name of Constantinople. From the sixth or seventh centuries onward, use of Latin—always restricted in the eastern provinces to fairly high levels of administration—dwindled. Most invaders were defeated, turned away, bought off, or deflected by diplomacy, but migrants seeped through the frontiers.

Justinian (r. 527–565) was the last emperor to adopt a grand strategy of imperial reunification, giving equal importance to recovery in the west and defense and expansion in the east. He aimed to be a restorer but was more suited to be a revolutionary—"a born meddler and disturber," a chronicler who knew him called him. As the heir of a peasant-turned-soldier whom the army had elected to rule, he enjoyed thumbing his nose at established elites. He infuriated bishops with his

Theodora. According to court gossip, Theodora (ca. 500–548), wife of the Roman Emperor Justinian (r. 527–565), was a former prostitute of insatiable sexual appetite. But the propagandist who portrayed her in mosaic, in the church of San Vitale at Ravenna, depicted her as a sacred figure, towering over priests and nobles and equal in stature to her husband. She approaches the altar arrayed in jewels—a convention used in the art of the time to personify the Church—bearing a gift of communion wine to be converted miraculously into the blood of Christ.

attempts to reconcile conflicting theological opinions. His tax policies made the rich howl with anguish. He was a great lawgiver who had himself depicted as the biblical Moses and yet broke all the rules himself. Typically, Justinian outraged straitlaced courtiers by choosing a notoriously dissolute actress named Theodora to be his empress. He relied on her strength and intellect. She was the counselor of every policy and the troubleshooter of every crisis. In the famous mosaic portrait of her in the church of San Vitale at Ravenna in Italy, she wears jewels of triumph and a cloak embroidered with images of kingship and wisdom.

Justinian had the ill-disciplined energy of all insomniacs as he paced the palace corridors at night "like a ghost," as hostile courtiers said. He thought big. His projects included importing silk from China and allying with Arabs and Ethiopians against Persia. He built Constantinople's cathedral to be the biggest church in the world and, when it fell down, built it again. His reconquests from barbarian kingdoms reunited most of the Mediterranean world. Buildings he erected stretched from Morocco to the Persian frontier. He left his partially restored empire impoverished but enlarged. The robust performance of the eastern empire under Justinian seems impressive compared with the more radical transformation of the empire in the west. In particular, the eastern empire survived the new wave of barbarian invasions that was about to overwhelm Rome's old enemy, Persia.

 Prologue of the *Corpus Juris Civilis*

THE NEW BARBARIANS

The barbarian invasions were not yet over. The Lombards invaded Italy in 568 from the north, just in time to gather the spoils of Justinian's wars, in which Romans and Goths had exhausted each other. On a plaque made to adorn the helmet of their King Agilulf, winged figures brandish drinking horns of a traditional

Germanic court along with placards marked "Victory" of a kind carried in Roman triumphs. Agilulf's sumptuous cross—all Christian barbarian kings had something similar—is a wand of victory: a sign to conquer by. In the late seventh century, the Bulgars, another invader-people from the steppes, crossed the Danube and set up as the elite of a state that stretched from the northern Balkans almost to Constantinople. In his shrine at Arkona, on the Baltic, the four-headed deity of the Slavs was perhaps already developing the thirst for wine for which he later became notorious. During the seventh and eighth centuries, in an expansion almost undocumented and never explained, Slavs spread over most of eastern Europe from the Baltic to southern Greece. Meanwhile, in North Africa, the Berbers, upland pastoralists, mobilized camel-borne war bands to terrorize the southern Mediterranean shore. In Scandinavia, in the eighth century, warriors who fought on sleds, with prows carved with the heads of monsters, took to the sea.

THE ARABS

These all proved formidable enemies of what was left of the Roman world. But most formidable of all the loiterers on the threshold were the Arabs or, more precisely, nomadic, Arabic-speaking peoples of central Arabia. They lived astride the trade routes of the peninsula, between Romanized communities and city-states in the north, and the maritime-oriented kingdoms of the seaboard. In the seventh century, they were transformed from a regional nuisance into a dynamic force. The preceding period in Arabia has a bad press—represented as chaotic and morally clueless, until the prophet Muhammad brought peace and justice in the 620s and early 630s. But the contrast between the periods before and after the Prophet's arrival may be too sharply drawn.

The few glimpses the sources give us suggest that Arab society was already demographically robust, militarily effective, and—at least in its poetry—artistically creative. "Poetry, horses, and numbers of people" were the standards by which different communities measured their rival merits. It is true, however, that Arabia was politically divided and riven by internal wars among tribes.

The tribes had also come to depend on war: raiding the Byzantine, Persian, and Arab cities that were scattered around the edges of the region and milking their trade. In one respect the transformation of these Arabs resembled that of other nomadic peoples mobilized for war by social change. As trade and banditry concentrated wealth, new styles of leadership dislocated the traditional, kinship-based structures of society and created an opportunity for a single, charismatic leader to unite an overwhelming force. In the Arabs' case, however, Muhammad's distinctive character marked him out from all other such leaders. His impact changed every aspect of life it touched. The Prophet taught a religion that was as rigorously monotheistic as Judaism, as humane and potentially as universal as Christianity, as traditional as paganism, and—for its time—more practical than any of them. More than a religion, Islam—literally "submission" to God—was also a way of life and a blueprint for society, complete with a demanding but unusually practical moral code, a set of rules of personal discipline, and the outline of a code of civil law.

Islam

A belief dear to Islamic scholars represents Muhammad as God's mouthpiece and therefore, in human terms, utterly original. His teachings crackle and snap with the noise of a break with the past. He picked up Jewish concepts: monotheism, providence, history ruled by God. The inspiration of Islam combined elements bor-

Pre-Islamic Arabic poetry: "The Poem of Antar"

rowed from Judaism and Christianity with a measure of respect for some of the traditional rites and teachings of pagan traditions in Arabia.

Muhammad claimed to have received his teaching from God, through the Archangel Gabriel, who revealed divine words into his ear. The resulting **Quran** (kuh-RAHN) was so persuasive that hundreds of millions of people believe him to this day. By the time of his death, Muhammad had equipped his followers with a dynamic social organization, a sense of unique access to God, and a conviction that war against nonbelievers was just and sanctified. Warriors were promised an afterlife in a paradise where sensual pleasures were like those of this world—lush gardens, young women. Muhammad's legacy gave Muslims (those who "submit" to God's message) administrative and ideological advantages against potential enemies. Yet the opportunity for the Arabs to become an imperial people arose as much, perhaps, from the weakness of the Byzantine and, especially, the Persian Empires as from the dynamics of their own society.

Sasanian victory. Huge rock carvings were traditional media of propaganda for Persian kings. None celebrates a more spectacular victory than that of Shapur I (r. 241–272) at the battle of Edessa in 260 C.E., when he took the Roman Emperor Valerian captive. The sculptor captured Valerian in another sense by showing him bending the knee in submission, while his cloak billows in the wind. The realism of the art enhances its symbolic significance, suggested by Shapur's huge crown, bulging physique, imperious gestures, and the stamp of his horse's hoof.

The Arabs Against Persia and Rome

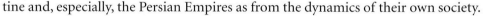

Of the old Eurasian empires, Persia's was the most successful in fending off steppeland turbulence. The Sasanians, Persia's ruling dynasty from 226, however, concentrated their power in the most defensible part of the empire, in the highlands of Fars and in and beyond the Zagros Mountains. A commanding position in the world, along trade routes that linked the Mediterranean to the Indian Ocean and the Silk Roads, gave them the resources to maintain their traditional hostility to Rome—symbolized in a rock carving of 260, where the Roman emperor, Valerian, grovels at the feet of Persian captors. Yet mutual respect tempered Persia's wars against Rome. Each empire recognized the other as civilized, while condemning all other neighbors as barbarians. In the 380s, Rome and Persia responded to the barbarian menace by making peace.

The peace lasted throughout the steppeland turbulence of the fifth century, but at the beginning of the sixth century, as other dangers seemed to recede, war between Romans and Persians resumed with lethal intent—like a sparring partnership that turns deadly. By the time of the Arab conquests, the two giant empires had worn each other out. Mountains had protected Persia from northern steppeland invaders—but the Arab frontier to the southwest was flat. The Muslim Arabs absorbed the Persian Empire in its entirety in a series of campaigns from the late 630s to the early 650s. Syria, Palestine, Egypt, and North Africa—Rome's wealthiest and most populous provinces—fell to Arab or Arab-led armies by the early eighth century.

THE MUSLIM WORLD

The Muslims' conquests functioned like a single empire, gradually spreading Islam, the Arabic language, and a common Muslim identity and introducing more or less uniform principles of law and government. (See Map 8.4.) Flexibility brought

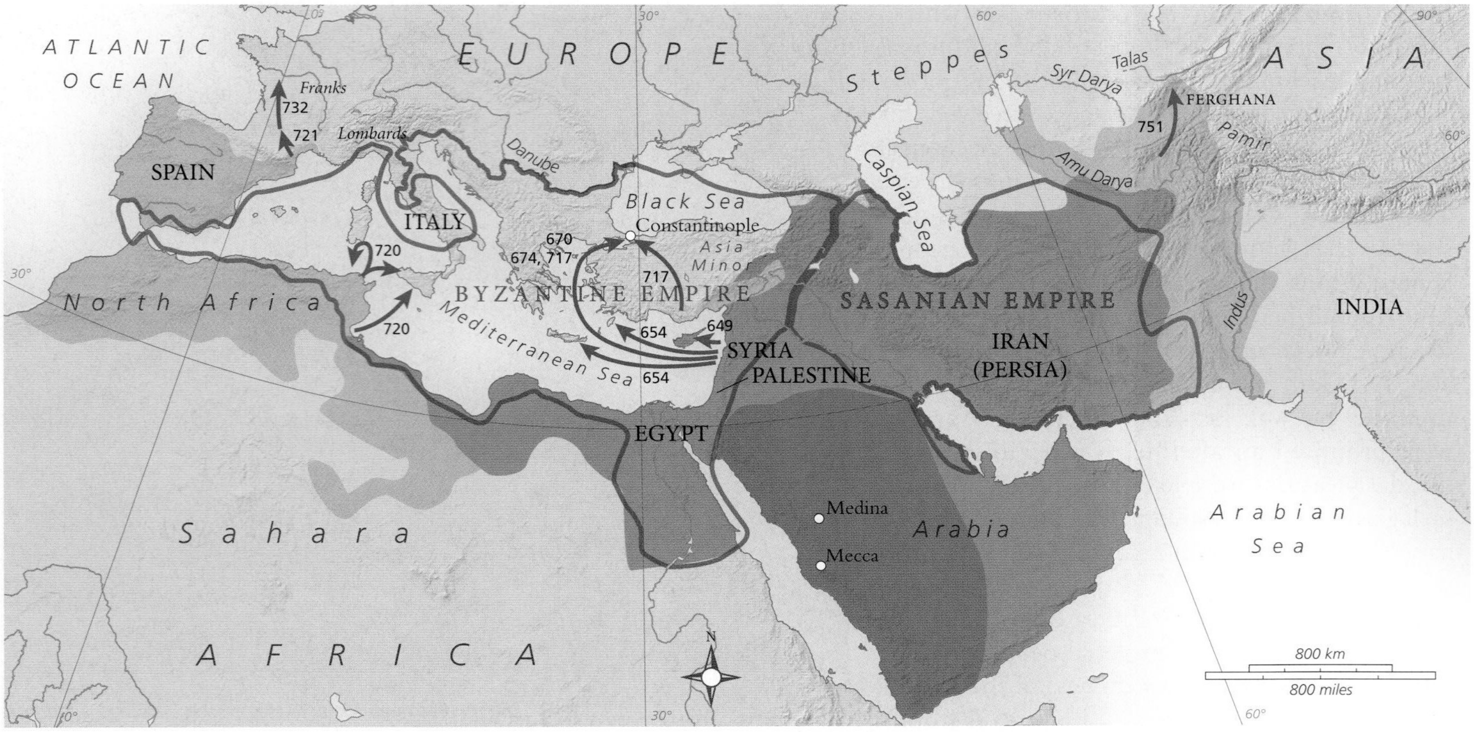

MAP 8.4

The Muslim World, ca. 756

▓ Muslim-ruled lands by 634

▒ Muslim-ruled lands by 656

░ Muslim-ruled lands by 756

→ Muslim invasions, with dates

— Byzantine Empire ca. 610

— Sasanian Empire ca. 610

⟳ MAP EXPLORATION

www.prenhall.com/armesto_maps

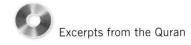

Excerpts from the Quran

success. Although Arabs and descendants of the Prophet's own tribe enjoyed social privileges, every male Muslim could share a sense of belonging to an imperial elite. Although women were repressed, they at least had important rights: to initiate divorce (albeit under stricter conditions than those that applied to men); to own property and retain it after divorce; to conduct business in their own right. Christians and Jews, though vulnerable to periodic persecution and compelled to pay extra taxes, were normally allowed to worship in their own way. So, at first, were the Zoroastrians of Persia, who, though despised as pagans, were too numerous to alienate. Although other forms of paganism were forbidden, many traditional shrines and pilgrimages were resanctified as suitable for Muslim devotion.

But the Islamic world was too big to remain a single empire. And the precepts Muhammad left his followers at his death were not intended for a large state. For his followers, he was both prophet and ruler. Whereas Jesus invited individuals to respond to God's grace, Muhammad, more straightforwardly, called them to obey God's laws. Whereas Moses legislated for a chosen people, the Jews, and Jesus preached a "kingdom not of this world," Muhammad aimed at a code of behavior covering every department of life. He failed, however, to leave a code that was anything like comprehensive. So schools of jurisprudence set out to fill in the gaps by inferring Muhammad's principles from such laws as he did make in his lifetime, applying them more generally and, in some cases, adding insights from reason, common sense, or custom. The **Sharia**—literally, the desert-dweller's "way to water"—was both a religious discipline and a law code for the state. The principles of law were unchangeable: revealed to the masters of the eighth and ninth centuries, whose interpretations of Muhammad's tradition were regarded as divinely guided. The reconciliation of the various schools' opinions, however, has always allowed some opportunities for development.

● MAKING CONNECTIONS ●

EMPIRES IN TRANSFORMATION

EMPIRE/ REGION →	EXTERNAL ENEMIES →	INTERNAL WEAKNESSES →	STRENGTHS →	SURVIVAL STRATEGIES →	SUCCESSOR STATE
Teotihuacán/ Mesoamerica	Resentful tributary city-states	Overpopulation; reliance on imports; limited resources to export	Widely emulated culture; extensive trade network	Continual expansion to sustain population growth; installing friendly rulers in neighboring regions	—
Roman/ Mediterranean	Germanic border peoples; Huns from Eurasian steppes; Persians	Sprawling, vulnerable land frontiers; politicized military; Christian threat to paganism; internal disorder; mass migrations; uncertain succession of leadership; adverse balance of trade	Occasional strong leaders; strong military tradition; eastern provinces easily defended and supplied	Division of leadership responsibility under Marcus Aurelius (162); division of empire after Constantine (d. 337); transfer of capital to Constantinople	Byzantine Empire in east; Germanic and barbarian kingdoms in west
Han/China	Steppeland raiders and migrants	Uncertain succession of leadership; feuding imperial factions; warlords	Circular shape facilitates movement of troops and information; Chinese culture imitated by barbarians; strong internal economy	Use of eunuchs for administration; promotion of Chinese customs and language among barbarians	Jin dynasty followed by civil war and political fragmentation
Gupta/India	Huns	Cultural pessimism (age of Kaliyuga); poor defenses; inequality fostered by caste system; corrupt bureaucracy	Several strong leaders (Candra Gupta)	Differing layers of local authority linked together	Hunnic states and other principalities; kingdom of Harsha
Sasanian/ Persia	Romans; nomadic Arabs	Exhaustion after continuous wars with Rome	Commanding geographic position; strong defenses; effective diplomacy	Concentrating power in most defensible areas; diplomacy with Rome	Islamic caliphate

One consequence of the way Islam developed was that where Jesus had proclaimed a sharp distinction between the secular and the spiritual, Muslims acknowledged no difference. The supreme Islamic authority, the **caliph** (KAY-lihf)—literally, the "successor" of the Prophet—was, Christians said, both pope and emperor. The problem of identifying who was caliph split Islam between rival

Islamic Expansion

570–632	Life of Muhammad
630–early 650s	Muslim conquest of Iraq, Syria, Palestine, Egypt, Persian Empire
ca. 700	Muslim conquest of North Africa
ca. 715	Muslim conquest of Spain
751	Battle of Talas; Arabs defeat Chinese

claimants and incompatible methods of choosing a caliph within a generation of Muhammad's death. The major division that eventually developed was between **Shia** (SHEE-ah) (meaning "party"), which regarded the caliphate as the prerogative of Muhammad's nephew, Ali, and his heirs, and **Sunni** (SOO-nee) (meaning "tradition"), which maintained that the Muslim community could designate any member of Muhammad's tribe to hold the office. The rift has never healed, and although Sunnism became the dominant tradition in the Islamic world, schisms multiplied and, with them, internal conflicts, rival caliphates, and secessionist states.

For as long as unity prevailed, the limits of Arab expansion show both its explosive nature and its reliance on mobilizing the resources and manpower of conquered or converted communities to make further conquests. When Arab expansion began to run out of impetus, in the second decade of the eighth century, armies owing allegiance to the successors of Muhammad, under Arab generalship, were operating in northern Spain. More or less at the same time, they were destroying Zoroastrian temples in Central Asia and a Buddhist shrine in northern India. At its northeast extremity, the Arab effort even touched the outermost frontier of Chinese imperialism, west of the Pamir Mountains, where, in the first half of the eighth century, local rulers played off the Chinese against the Arabs to maximize their own power. In 751, Chinese and Arab armies met in direct conflict for the first and last time, on the banks of the Talas River. The result was victory for the Arabs and their Turkic allies. After this, China withdrew permanently behind the Pamirs, and most of Central Asia became securely part of the world of Islam.

RECOVERY AND ITS LIMITS IN CHINA

At home, China faced familiar problems, with only internal conflicts to weaken it and only the well-known threat from the steppelands to hold at bay. China's recovery from the crisis of the sixth century started later than Rome's under Justinian but lasted longer. A professional soldier, Yang Jian (yahng ihee-en; r. 581–605) proclaimed himself emperor, put to death 59 princes of the dynasty he had formerly served, and launched a strategy to re-create the empire (see Map 8.5). It proved remarkably easy. As a Chinese who had proved that he could master barbarians on the battlefield, Yang Jian was an attractive candidate for the throne.

Conscious of his lack of traditional credentials except success, the new emperor looked to Buddhism to legitimize his rule and to Legalism (see Chapter 6) for practical guidance in government. Law, he said, should "suit the times." In other words, there were no sacred, everlasting, or universal principles. He vowed "to replace mercy with justice"—and demonstrated his commitment by endorsing the condemnation of his own son to death for embezzlement. He affected contempt for Confucian bookworms and controlled the court by violent displays of temper. His workaholic and frugal ways—he rationed the palace women's cosmetics—were the characteristics that most impressed observers.

Yang Jian's brutal, strong-arm methods were appropriate to a time of reunification by force. In 605 his successor Yangdi reverted to tradition, announcing the revival of clemency, Confucian learning, and "ancient standards." The great triumph of his reign was the reintegration of the Yellow River and Yantgze valleys by an improved and extensive canal system, the Grand Canal. This was the kind of project that ought to have identified the dynasty with the "ancient

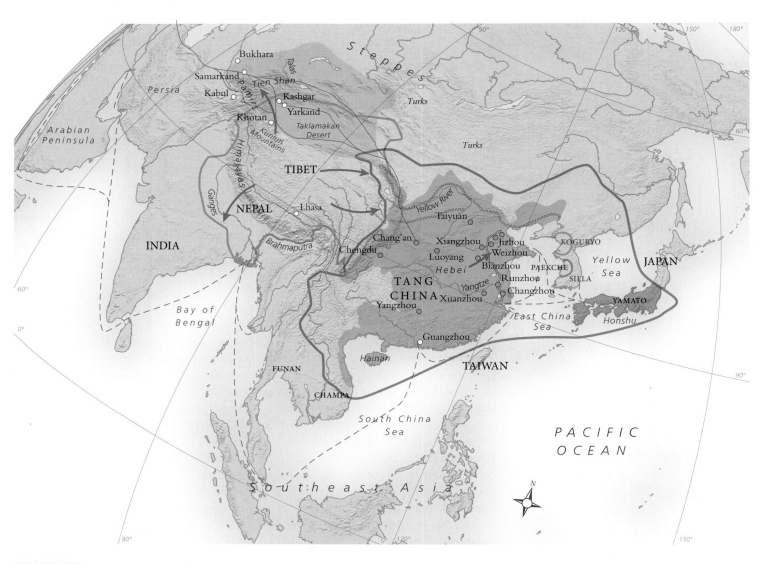

Scale varies with perspective

MAP 8.5

Tang China, Tibet, and Japan, ca. 750 C.E.

- Tang Empire at its greatest extent
- areas of temporary Tang control
- Yamato state
- approximate extent of Chinese cultural influence
- Tibetan Empire ca. 750 C.E.
- ➤ Tibetan invasions
- Silk Roads
- 〰〰 Great Wall
- ═ Grand Canal
- – – maritime trade routes
- ● city with over 300,000 inhabitants
- ○ other major city

3,333 km (2,071 miles)

8,392 km (5,214 miles)

virtue" Confucians prized. It was in the tradition of the great engineering emperors of legend, back to Yu the Great (see Chapter 3). The regime, however, forfeited this potential goodwill by the forced labor and taxes the canal-building demanded. An attempt to conquer Korea was ruinous and unsuccessful—the usual prelude to a political revolution.

Rise of the Tang

In 617, as the throne toppled, the most respected family in the kingdom, the Li, led a rebellion. Li Yuan (lee yoo-ehn), head of the family, was well connected in the army and secured neutrality or support from nomad princes. The reconquest of the country from rival rebels was not complete until about 624, but the exhaustion and disenchantment of the country favored a period of peace. The new dynasty, which called itself Tang (tahng), relied at first on this comfortable mood. The second emperor of the dynasty, Taizong (teye-tzong), took an interventionist, reformist line. He favored the skeptical, scientific tradition, derided omens and magic potions, and held ceremonies when he pleased, not when seers told him to. He rationalized the administration, cutting down the numbers of posts and administrative divisions and subdivisions, creating a new, handpicked bureaucracy for the provinces that he selected by examination, and simplified the law codes.

Empress Wu

Taizong's reforms did much to stabilize the empire. Dynastic crises no longer threatened to dissolve the state. A grueling test occurred in 690, when a woman seized the throne. On the face of it, this was unlikely to happen. Two collections of anecdotes—the *Nüjie* (noo-jay) and *Nüchunyu*—(noo-chuan-yoo) dominated perceptions of women as idle and promiscuous: a virtuous woman got up early and applied herself to household chores. Women were largely excluded from education—a limitation against which the *Nüjie* protested—and barred from the examinations for the state service. The only route to power was through the dangerous, overpopulated imperial harem. Wu Zhao's (woo jow) combination of beauty and brains impressed Taizong. Her recommendation of torture, brutality, and slaughter as methods of government supposedly amused him. She sought power by seducing the emperor's heir. As the former emperor's concubine, she was ineligible to be the next empress, but she maneuvered her way around that obstacle with ease. In 655, she married the heir to the throne, replacing his official wife, whom she tortured to death. Similar methods ensured her ascendancy during her husband's lifetime and as effective regent during the next two reigns. To secure her own elevation to the rank of emperor, she mustered every disaffected faction. The Buddhist clergy were her agents, proclaiming her as an incarnation of God, circulating propaganda on her behalf around the empire. Urged by 60,000 petitioners, she became emperor—literally, because she did not rule as an empress but used the masculine title emperor.

Tang Decline

These extraordinary and—to most people at the time—unnatural events hardly disturbed the continuity of the Tang and provoked no serious attempts at provincial succession of the kind that had been routine under previous dynasties. Resentment accumulated, however, under the less resolute rule of Wu's successors. In the

Lady-in-waiting. Though the politics of Tang China could be turbulent, they never disturbed the serenity of the arts of the imperial court. Women were frequently depicted. Many images of women as servants or, as in this example, as imperial ladies-in-waiting have survived because they were often placed as offerings in tombs. But portraits of female artisans—especially silk-makers—poets, students, equestrians, and matriarchs are also common, showing that, in an era that produced a female emperor, many occupations and roles were open to women.
Dagli Orti/Picture Desk, Inc./Kobal Collection

mid–eighth century, the defenses of the empire were beginning to look shaky as defeats by nomads became increasingly frequent. A frontier general, An Lushan (ahn loo-shawn), was selected as scapegoat. He had therefore little recourse except to rebel. The ensuing civil war confirmed the militarization of society, which, owing to the demands of frontier wars, was already happening anyway: 750,000 men were under arms in the 750s. Governors became virtually autonomous rulers of their provinces. About a quarter to a third of the empire was effectively outside imperial control. Peasants lived, it was said, "without a penny to their name."

To "bring the provinces under the rule of law" was now the watchword. "Only then can proper order be restored to the realm." Tax reforms in 782 decreed a single, uniform system throughout the empire. In practice, local authorities were left to fulfill quotas. Emperors took the initiative against the autonomous provinces and even began to restore control of provincial armed forces to the central government. But they failed to control the most wayward province, Hebei (huh-bay), which was effectively independent by 822. Meanwhile the provinces that remained supposedly subject to direct imperial control gained power at the expense of a central government that the efforts at recovery had impoverished. Governors enjoyed long tenures, levied unauthorized taxes, appointed local nominees to administrative positions, and acquired ever-larger revenues and retinues. Central government recovered some taxpayers. There were 2.5 million registered households in 807, 5 million in 839. This was still little more than half the figure attained before An Lushan's revolt. Imperial power became confined to the Yangtze valley.

IN THE SHADOW OF TANG: TIBET AND JAPAN

In the shadow of Tang China, some promising states emerged. Tibet and Japan provide contrasting examples (see Map 8.5).

Tibet

At the time of the presumed beginnings of the first Tibetan state in the sixth century, the Chinese spoke of Tibetans in the conventional language used for barbarians, as pastoralists who "sleep in unclean places and never wash or comb their hair." In the river valleys of Tibet, however, sedentary agriculture was possible. An agricultural transformation in the fifth century brought barley to these areas as a staple crop. Once a cereal food was available in large amounts, the advantages of a cold climate for storage helped to create food surpluses. A land from which small numbers of nomads eked a precarious living now became a breeding ground of armies that could march on far campaigns with "ten thousand" sheep and horses in their supply trains.

Before the seventh century, divine monarchs ruled Tibet, "descended," according to early poems, "from mid-sky, seven stories high," and aspiring to rule "all under heaven." Like other divine kings, they were liable to be sacrificed when their usefulness expired. At an unknown date in the sixth century, kings who ruled until they died a natural death replaced this system. Long reigns, with stability and continuity, were now possible. The first king known from more than fragmentary mentions was Songtsen Gampo. His reign, from about 627 to 650, marked an unprecedented leap in Tibetan power. China bought him off with a Chinese bride in 640. Preserved among a cache of documents in a

Recovery and Its Limits in China

581	Yang Jian proclaims himself emperor (Sui dynasty)
605	Yangdi becomes emperor
609	Grand Canal completed
617	Yangdi deposed; rebellion ensues
618	Li Yuan begins reconquest of China from rival rebels; beginning of Tang dynasty
626	Beginning of reign of Taizong, second Tang emperor
690	Wu Zhao (Empress Wu) seizes throne
755–763	Rebellion of An Lushan
822	Province of Hebei effectively independent

 Dezong, on the art of government

 Chinese descriptions of Tibetans

The Rise and Decline of Tibet

Fifth century	Barley introduced as a staple crop
627–650	Reign of Songtsen Gampo
Early ninth century	Beginning of Tibetan decline

The Potala Palace, towering above the valley of Lhasa, stands on the supposed site of the palace of the kings of Tibet in the seventh and eighth centuries. The present construction, however, began to rise in the mid–seventeenth century. The building is designed to suggest mystical power—cloud-shrouded, hard of ascent, overwhelming.

Treaty between Tibet and China, 821 C.E.

cave on the Silk Road is the oath of allegiance he exacted: "Never will we disobey any command the king may give." In practice, however, in most of the communities he conquered, he simply levied tribute, rather than practicing direct rule or close supervision.

Tibetan aggression continued for most of the next 250 years. Tibetan armies conquered Nepal and invaded Central Asia. A pillar at Lhasa, the Tibetan capital, erected before 750, records campaigns deep inside China. In 821 a Chinese ambassador described the Tibetan war camp, where shamans in tiger skins banged drums before a tent "hung with gold ornaments in the form of dragons, tigers and leopards." Inside, in a turban "the color of morning clouds," the king watched as chiefs signed the treaty with China in blood.

The kings' tastes were increasingly cosmopolitan. Ten of them, including Songtsen Gampo, lie under small mounds at Phyongrgyas, where "dead companions" attended them—now no longer sacrificed but appointed to guard and tend the graves without direct contact with the outside world. Pillars in Indian, Central Asian, and Chinese styles and a guardian lion modeled on a Persian original attest to the role of Tibet as a cultural crossroads. Their metal smiths' ingenuity was famous. Mechanical toys of gold dispatched as gifts to the Chinese court included a horse with moving limbs and a tiger with roaring jaws. Tibetan chain mail had an almost magical reputation for deflecting missiles. Yet even this could not protect the Tibetans from the effects of the instability of the era of Tang decline, which must have disrupted trade, while the power of the steppelanders limited Tibetan opportunities to raid or expand. In the early ninth century, Tibet suffered defeats on all fronts. Rebellions ensued. Tibet signed its last treaty as an equal with China in 823. Its last known king was assassinated in 842.

Japan

Better prospects of enduring experiments in statecraft existed on the remoter edges of Chinese cultural influence, in Japan, where the steppeland menace could not reach. Chinese culture began to arrive in Japan from Korea when a Buddhist monk became tutor at a Japanese court in about 400. The Korean kingdom of Paekche sent scholars and Buddhist scriptures. The leading state in Japan, Yamato, was a maritime kingdom, attracted by Korean and Chinese civilization, and at least as interested in expanding onto the mainland of Asia as in growing within the Japanese islands. Around 475, the king of Yamato applied to China for the rank of general and minister. He claimed his ancestors had conquered "55 kingdoms of hairy men to the east and 65 barbarian kingdoms to the west." Crossing the sea to the north, he added, they had subjugated 95 kingdoms. "The way to govern is to maintain harmony and peace, thereby establishing order." The ruler, one of the Korean advisers suggested, should "try to make farmers prosperous. . . . After he has followed this policy for three years, food and soldiers will become plentiful." From the mid–sixth century, Japan was following this sort of program, organizing royal estates, taking censuses.

Early in the seventh century, direct contact with China opened. The first Japanese embassy to China presented greetings "from the Son of Heaven in the land where the sun rises to the Son of Heaven in the land where the sun sets." The Chinese dismissed this as impertinence. Their accounts make the queen who ruled Japan at the time say, "As barbarians living in an isolated place beyond the sea, we do not know propriety and justice." It is not clear that the Japanese really saw themselves like that. They staked a claim to equality with China—and imperial rank—that subsequent Japanese regimes never abandoned.

In the 640s, the dynasty narrowly beat off a bid for the throne from a Chinese immigrant family. Reform of the administration then began in earnest. The drive to centralize by breaking up and replacing traditional power structures is reflected in a decree of 645 that blamed clan chieftains for dividing up the land, engaging in conflict, unjustly exploiting labor, and impoverishing peasants "who lack enough land to insert a needle." Landlords were forbidden "to increase, by one iota, the miseries of the weak." Indirectly, China's invasion of Korea in the 660s boosted imperial rule in Japan. Korean refugees were appointed to court rank. After victory in a civil war of 672, the ruling dynasty of Japan was unchallenged. Japan solved the problem that bedeviled the politics of other empires—devising a secure way to ensure the succession—by two means. First, women's aptitude to rule was accepted. This increased the dynasty's stock of suitable candidates for the throne. Indeed, until the 770s, when a disastrous empress inspired lasting revulsion against women rulers, most rulers were women. Second, from 749, it became normal for rulers to abdicate and watch over the transmission of power to their heirs. The system worked well until the mid–ninth century, when a single courtly family, the Fujiwara, established an effective monopoly over supply of the chief wives for successive emperors. Thereafter, in the Japanese system of government, the emperor presided over the realm, but a dynasty of court favorites or chief ministers usually did the ruler's job. The last big political development—the

⊙ MAKING CONNECTIONS ⊙

DEVELOPING FRONTIER STATES

STATE/REGION/PERIOD →	IMPERIAL NEIGHBOR →	RESOURCES/ORGANIZATION →	ACHIEVEMENTS
Koguryo, Silla, Paekche/Korea ca. 300–500	China	Chinese religious influence—Buddhism and Daoism; Chinese migrants and technical knowledge	Complex irrigation system for rice cultivation; hundreds of walled towns; strong military
Funan/Indochina ca. 100–400	India, China	Indian cultural influences; commercial traders strategically located between India and China	Sophisticated culture; wealthy mercantile class; expansion around Gulf of Thailand
Ethiopia/Africa ca. 300–500	Rome, Byzantine Egypt	Accessible to Indian Ocean trade routes, isolated enough to be defensible; temperate climate; trade center connecting Africa to India and Arabia	Productive agriculture system—up to three crops a year; developed industry (metalwork, ivory) and large-scale urbanization
Tibet/Central Asia ca. 500–800	China, India	Development of barley as primary cereal crop for vast high-altitude plateau; food surpluses and strong military	Long-term alliance/tributary, relationship with China; stable leadership; conquest of neighboring kingdoms
Japan/East Asia ca. 400–600	China, Korea	Chinese/Korean cultural influences; strategic position for maritime trade; isolated and defensible; organization of royal estates; censuses	Long-term tributary relationship with China; gradually centralized power structure to maximize productivity; stable power structure with some women emperors

CHRONOLOGY

All dates are c.e.

220	End of Han dynasty in China
323	Founding of Constantinople
340	Spread of Christianity in Ethiopia
Third and fourth centuries	Germanic invasions of Roman Empire; Huns break out of Central Asia
ca. 375	Teotihuacán (Mesoamerica) at peak of its influence and power
Fifth century	Introduction of barley as a staple crop in Tibet
400	Beginning of Chinese influence in Japan
410	Visigoths sack Rome
415	Huns begin to infiltrate India
467	Death of last-known Gupta emperor (India)
476	End of western Roman Empire
493–526	Reign of Theodoric, Ostrogothic king
527–565	Reign of Justinian, Byzantine emperor
ca. 535	Massive volcanic eruption in Indonesia
570–632	Life of Muhammad
Seventh century	Beginning of Slav expansion in eastern Europe
609	Grand Canal completed in China
627–650	Reign of Songtsen Gampo in Tibet
630–720	Rapid Arab expansion
667–668	Chinese conquest of Koguryo (Korea)
690	Beginning of reign of Empress Wu (China)
751	Arabs defeat Chinese at battle of Talas

search for a means to harness Buddhism for state service while preserving Japan's native religion—belongs in the next chapter.

IN PERSPECTIVE: The Triumph of Barbarism?

Had Siyaj K'ak been able to continue his journey from Teotihuacán and cross the ocean to Eurasia he might have been gratified by the contrast between the stability and growth of the empire he represented and the perils that beset the empires of the Old World. In the year of his arrival, the Visigoths challenged Roman might at Adrianople. The crises that accompanied the traumas of the Eurasian steppelands and the migrations of Germanic and steppelander peoples into neighboring empires were already beginning. One measure of the instability that ensued is particularly striking. In much of Europe and India, the fifth and sixth centuries were so chaotic that record keeping collapsed, and we can no longer reconstruct a complete outline even of the most basic facts of political history—the names and chronology of kings and dynasties. By contrast, in the same period, for the Maya world Siyaj K'ak visited, we know far more about the rulers of many city-states, whose records are inscribed in stone in meticulous detail.

Yet, despite the waves of migrants and invaders that washed over Old World empires in the half millennium or so from about 200 onward and the crises they provoked, the most remarkable feature of the period is perhaps the durability of old orders. Cultural conflicts usually follow battlefield victories. And even where the so-called barbarians defeated the empires, they tended to get conquered in their turn by the cultures of their victims. The German invaders of the Roman world were partly Romanized, while the eastern Roman empire survived, centered on Constantinople. Steppeland conquerors played havoc with the political unity of India—but the cultural transformations of India happened from within. "Barbarians" disrupted China politically but did not disturb the continuity of Chinese civilization. On the contrary, when barbarians settled within China, they adjusted to Chinese ways. Indeed, Chinese civilization overspilled China into Korea, Japan, southeast Asia, and Tibet. The instability of the steppes damaged the land-bound trade of Eurasia, but the commerce of the Indian Ocean continued to grow, and the development of Ethiopia was among the consequences.

Still, despite continuities that survived the barbarians, the world was transformed. Rather than the world of empires that had dominated the densely populated belt of the axial age, it might be proper to speak of a world of civilizations. Western civilization was a hybrid—partly Germanic, partly Christian, partly Roman in heritage. The Islamic world was far more innovative, but it had, in some respects, a similar profile: with a biblical heritage, reinterpreted by Muhammad, and the learned legacies of Rome, Greece, and Persia, under an Arab elite from outside the empires, established by conquest but susceptible to the cultural influence of its victims. In both Islam and Christendom, notions of universal empire survived: the caliphate, Byzantium. But neither could maintain unity in practice, and the respective regions became arenas of states contending for the imperial legacy or ignoring it. In India, political fragmentation under the impact of barbarian invasion was more thoroughgoing, in China less so. In both, however, the invaders and immigrants were like chameleons, taking on the cultural hues of their new environments. In both, moreover, the traditional culture spread into new areas and new states, such as those of south India, and China's neighbors. So nowhere, by the eighth century, except in Ethiopia, was there any longer a civilization that was confined to a single state.

Even at the end of a chapter crowded with politics, we still have not reached the deepest transformative influences on the period. One of the traditional limitations of history textbooks is that politics, which generates most of the sources, tends to dominate the foreground. But politics is full of short-term changes, while ideas and environmental influences generate the sea changes. The next two chapters explore the religious transformations that made this world of civilizations distinct, in particular, from the empires that preceded them, and the discovery and development of resources that not only renewed the Old World, but also opened up new frontiers in other parts of the globe.

PROBLEMS AND PARALLELS

1. How were imperial traditions inherited from the axial age extinguished or fragmented by the year 500?

2. How does the history of Teotihuacán echo Eurasian developments in this period?

3. What were the differences between the ways that China and Rome dealt with steppeland migrants and invaders? Why was China more successful?

4. How did the Byzantine Empire and the barbarian kingdoms in Western Europe continue the traditions of Rome?

5. To what extent was Ethiopia able to achieve a balance between accessibility and isolation?

6. How did states develop on the edges of empires during this period?

7. Why were the Arabs able to conquer a vast empire in so short a time?

8. How was the world that recovered from the crises of the third through seventh centuries a world of civilizations?

DOCUMENTS IN GLOBAL HISTORY

- Tikal
- Marcus Aurelius, from *The Meditations*
- Ammianus Marcellinus on the Huns
- Excerpts from the *Hildebrandslied*
- Jordanes, *Deeds of the Goths*, Book Twenty-Six
- Pliny the Elder, from the *Natural History*
- Faxian, *Record of Buddhist Countries*, Chapter Sixteen

- Prologue of the *Corpus Juris Civilis*
- Pre-Islamic Arabic poetry: "The Poem of Antar"
- Excerpts from the Quran
- Dezong, on the art of government
- Chinese descriptions of Tibetans
- Treaty between Tibet and China, 821 C.E

Please see the Primary Source DVD for additional sources related to this chapter.

READ ON

Helpful information on relations between Teotihuacán and the Maya is in D. Drew, *The Lost Chronicles of the Maya Kings* (1999); R. Hassig, *War and Society in Ancient Mesoamerica* (1992); and S. Martin and N. Grube, *Chronicle of the Maya Kings and Queens* (2000), which is also a lavish compendium of facts and images. G. Braswell, *The Maya and Teotihuacán* (2003) is an important revisionist study that challenges the account of Siyaj K'ak' above.

On the transformation of the Roman world, Peter Brown, *The World of Late Antiquity* (1989) is the ideal introduction—sprightly and subtle. A. H. M. Jones, *The Later Roman Empire* (1964) is a classic study of undiminished interest. J. Herrin, *The Formation of Christendom* (1987) is assured, fluent, and in touch with the sources. A. Cameron et al., eds., *The Cambridge Ancient History*, xiv (2000) is forbiddingly comprehensive and magisterial. R. Collins, *Early Medieval Europe* (1991) is a vigorous, thoughtful textbook. The classic works by F. Lot, *The End of the Ancient World and the Beginning of the Middle Ages* (2000), and by H. Pirenne, cited below, can still be recommended in combination with more recent scholarship.

There are many editions of the *Meditations of Marcus Aurelius*. On Constantine, R. Macmullen, *Constantine* (1987) is standard. Sources on his conversion are collected in M. Edwards, trans., *Constantine and Christendom* (2003). D. Bowder, *The Age of Constantine and Julian* (1978) is valuable in setting the context. M. Grant, *The Emperor Constantine* (1993) is lively and readable. R. Macmullen, *Christianity and Paganism in the Fourth to Eighth Centuries* (1997) is a valuable introduction. A. Momigliano, *The Conflict of Paganism and Christianity in the Fourth Century* (1964) is a collection of classic studies. R. Lane Fox, *Pagans and Christians* (1987), and K. Hopkins, *A World Full of Gods* (1999) are also helpful. On the transformation of the city of Rome, B. R. Ward-Perkins, *From Classical Antiquity to the Middle Ages* (1985) sets the context of urban change in Italy, while P. Llewellyn, *Rome in the Dark Ages* (1993) is a graphic account of the reemergence of Rome as the pope's capital.

W. Goffart, *Barbarians and Romans* (1980) is an introductory overview. E. A. Thompson, *A History of Attila and the Huns* (1972) is a classic study, still vital. There are many editions of the *Hildebrandslied*, but I know of no substantial critical studies in English except F. Norman, *Three Essays on the Hildebrandslied* (1973). The most useful study of the Christianity of Germanic invaders of the Roman Empire is

E. A. Thompson, *The Visigoths in the Time of Ulfila* (1966). J. M. Wallace-Hadrill, *The Barbarian West* (1952) is the best possible introduction to the Germanic kingdoms; his *The Long-Haired Kings* (1962) is an absorbing collection of essays on the same subject, which should be read in conjunction with I. N. Wood, *The Merovingian Kingdoms* (1994). *The Consolation of Philosophy* is widely available in many editions. For Boethius's life and thought, J. Marenbon, *Boethius* (2003) is excellent, and H. Chadwick, *Boethius* (1981) is both authoritative and concise. S. Williams and G. Friell, *The Rome That Did Not Fall* (1999) is a helpful essay on the survival of the empire in the east. See now the revisionist, archaeologically informed survey of B. R. Ward-Perkins, *The Fall of Rome and the End of Civilization* (2005).

The steppes are covered in R. Grousset, *The Empire of the Steppes* (1970). Volume iii of *The Cambridge History of China* (1978) covers this period admirably. S. A. M. Adshead, *Tang China* (2004) provides an introduction to that dynasty. C. P. Fitzgerald, *The Empress Wu* (1955) is a captivating classic biography. R. K. Dwivdki and D. L. Vaish, *A History of the Guptas* (1985), and S. Goyal, *History and Historiography of the Age of Harsha* (1992) provide a political and cultural outline of India. W. E. Henthorn, *A History of Korea* (1971) is particularly good on this period.

On Axum, see the works of Munro-Hay and Phillipson mentioned in Chapter 9.

On Justinian, *The Secret History of Procopius* (1927) is an irresistibly engaging, albeit cruelly prejudiced, source. Balanced modern studies include J. A. S. Evans, *The Age of Justinian* (1996), and R. Browning, *Justinian and Theodora* (1971). G. Greatrex, *Rome and Persia at War* (1998) admirably covers the Persian wars of this period.

For an understanding of Byzantium in this period, A. Cameron, *Changing Cultures in Early Byzantium* (1996) is an authoritative, clear, and insightful collection. M. Grant, *From Rome to Byzantium* (1998) is a readable narrative. M. Whittow, *The Making of Orthodox Byzantium* (1996) is invaluable on the development of a distinctive religious culture. A. Cameron and J. Herrin, *Constantinople in the Early Eighth Century* (1984) is helpful. M. Angold, *Byzantium* (2001) is a good overview. W. E. Kaegi, *Byzantine Military Unrest* (1981) takes an interesting approach. On eunuchs, see K. Ringrose, *The Perfect Servant: Eunuchs and the Social Construction of Gender in Byzantium* (2003). On the Bulgars, O. Minaeva, *From Paganism to Christianity* (1996) wields fascinating artistic evidence. On Lombard Italy and its context, C. Wickham, *The Long Eighth Century* (2000) and *Early Medieval Italy* (1990) are excellent.

A. Hourani, *History of the Arab People* (2003) is probably the best overall survey of Arab history. M. A. Cook, *Muhammad* (1983) is a brief and brilliant introduction. Some of the same author's important essays are collected in *Studies in the Origins of Early Islamic Culture and Tradi-tion* (2004). M. Cook and P. Crone, *Hagarism: The Making of the Islamic World* (1977) is a groundbreaking study. M. Hodgson, *The Venture of Islam*, 3 vols. (1974) is a marvelous classic. G. R. Hawting, *The First Dynasty of Islam* (2000) is an efficient narrative of the early caliphate. On the impact of the Arab conquests, all students should read—critically, of course—the classic—by H. Pirenne, *Mohammed and Charlemagne* (1939).

CHAPTER 9 The Rise of World Religions: Christianity, Islam, and Buddhism

Priests, officials, and bystanders (shown prostrating themselves, on the right) greet the pilgrim Xuanzang on his return to China from India, where he had traveled to find Buddhist scriptures. Pack horses bear the 75 sacred texts he had acquired to a temple on the left. Monks at the rear carry holy relics.

n 872, Ibn Wahab, a Muslim traveler from Iraq, arrived in China. The emperor called for illustrated scrolls to be put before the visitor.

Ibn Wahab recognized the portraits of biblical prophets and patriarchs. I said, his account continues, Here is Noah with his ark, which saved hm when the world was drowned ...

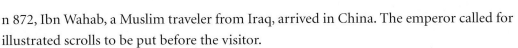

At these words, the emperor laughed and said, You have identified Noah, but, as for the ark, we do not believe it. It did not reach China or India.

That is Moses with his staff, I said.

Yes, said the emperor, but he was unimportant and his people were few.

There, I said, is Jesus, surrounded by his apostles.

Yes, said the emperor. ... His mission lasted only thirty months.

Then I saw the Prophet on a camel ... and I was moved to tears. Why do you weep? asked the emperor.... He and his people founded a glorious empire. He did not live to see it completed, but his successors have. ... I saw also other pictures, which I did not recognize. The interpreter told me that they were the prophets of China and India.

• • • • •

The anecdote illustrates three themes of the time: the effectiveness of communications across Eurasia; the superiority of Chinese knowledge; and the subject of this chapter—the beginnings of the ascent of Christianity, Islam, and Buddhism to be *world religions,* with followings in all sorts of physical and cultural environments. Most religions do not spread beyond their cultures of origin. Christianity, Islam, and Buddhism were unusual. They aspired to be universal, and became global.

FOCUS questions

- WHY DID Buddhism, Christianity, and Islam become world religions?
- HOW DID commerce spread religion in parts of Eurasia and Africa?
- WHY DID missionaries seek to convert rulers and elites?
- HOW DID Christian and Muslim rulers deal with religious minorities?
- WHY WAS monasticism more important for Christianity and Buddhism than for Islam?
- WHAT ROLE did women play in the spread of world religions?
- HOW DID world religions accommodate themselves to local cultures?

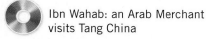

Ibn Wahab: an Arab Merchant visits Tang China

Historians often claim to be interested in the past for its own sake. If we also want to understand our own world and trace the emergence of its key features, we have to confront the problem of why Christianity, Islam, and Buddhism began to acquire the global acceptance they have today. So in this chapter, we have to stay in Eurasia and Africa—in the parts where these three religions had penetrated by Ibn Wahab's time—and catch up in the next chapter with changes occurring in the meantime in other parts of the world.

There has never really been an "age of faith." Of course, there are plenty of sincere individual conversions, spiritually inspired or intellectually induced. Most people, however, in most periods, experience religion only superficially. If they do undergo real conversion or spiritual rebirth, it happens sporadically and rarely lasts long. Nor should we judge the spread of religion by the extent of people's intellectual grasp of it. If you ask most Christians or Muslims or Buddhists about the doctrines of their faiths, they will usually give you, at best, a shallow account. Their religion may not affect their ethical behavior much. Instead of understanding religion as belief, or spiritual experience, or doctrine, or ethics, we should treat it here as cultural practice, and say that a religion has "spread" where and when many people take part in its rites and identify with their fellow worshippers as members of a community. Four processes enabled Islam, Buddhism, and Christianity to take off and spread: war, trade, missionary activity, and elite—especially royal—sponsorship (see Map 9.1)

COMMERCE AND CONFLICT: CARRIERS OF CREEDS

Forcible conversion is—strictly speaking—no conversion at all. "There is no compulsion in religion," says the Quran. The Catholic Church forbids using force to spread faith. Buddhism, too, has no place for coercion. But force sometimes works.

In the Islamic World

The Arabic word **jihad** (jee-HAHD) literally means *striving*. Muhammad used the word in two contexts: first, to mean the inner struggle against evil that Muslims must wage for themselves; second, to denote real war against the enemies of Islam. These have to be genuine enemies, who "fight against you to the death." But in Muhammad's day the community he led was almost constantly at war, and Chapter Nine of the Quran seems to legitimate war against all "polytheists" and "idolaters." After the Prophet's death, his successors turned the doctrine of jihad against the "apostates" who abandoned Islam because they considered that their obligations to Muhammad had ended when he died. It was then used to proclaim successful wars of aggression.

Holy war seems an appropriate translation for "jihad": an enterprise sanctified by obedience to what are thought to be the Prophet's commands and rewarded by the promise of martyrdom. According to a saying traditionally ascribed to Muhammad, martyrs go straight to the highest rank of paradise, for "they fight," as the Quran says, "in the cause of Allah and they slay the enemy or are slain." This is

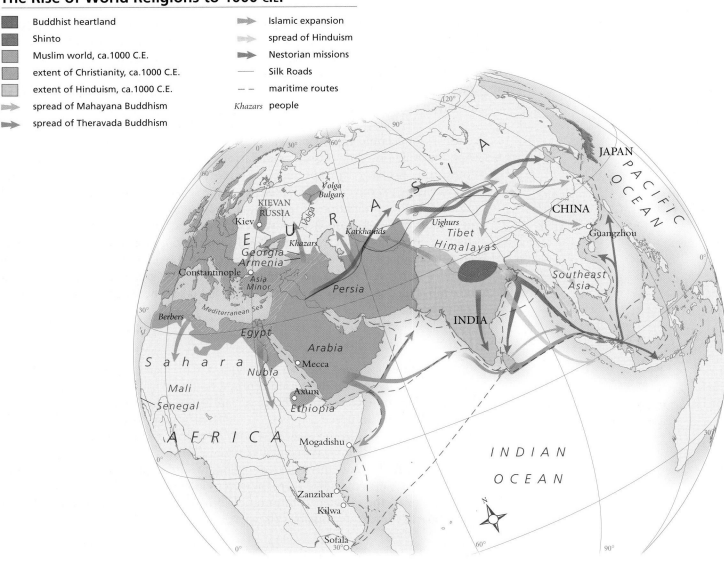

MAP 9.1

The Rise of World Religions to 1000 C.E.

	Buddhist heartland		Islamic expansion
	Shinto		spread of Hinduism
	Muslim world, ca.1000 C.E.		Nestorian missions
	extent of Christianity, ca.1000 C.E.		Silk Roads
	extent of Hinduism, ca.1000 C.E.		maritime routes
	spread of Mahayana Buddhism	*Khazars*	people
	spread of Theravada Buddhism		

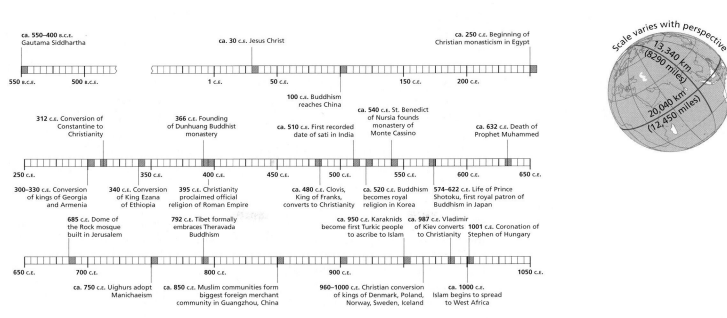

213

no more bloodthirsty than many passages in the Bible and needs no more to be taken literally than Paul's injunction to Christians to "fight the good fight." But it can justify war and implies a link between war and the spread of Islam. A tenth-century Muslim jurist summed up the tradition as it had evolved by that time. Enemies could either submit to Islam or pay a poll tax for the privilege of persisting in their own religion. "Failing that, we will make war against them."

That was theory. Practice was not always so clear-cut. But in the first couple of centuries of Islamic expansion, victorious Muslim armies did normally aim to wipe out religions they classed as idolatrous and to tax Christians, Jews, and, at times, other privileged groups, such as Zoroastrians in Persia. The result would not necessarily be to convert people to Islam, in the sense of changing their hearts and minds. But the elimination of traditional priesthoods and the destruction of former places of worship opened up spaces in which Islam, the religion of the conquerors, could take root. Moreover, God seemed to endorse Islam. If traditional religion became a badge of resistance to conquest, it withered when that resistance failed. In northwest Africa, for instance, when the last great Berber revolt against the Arabs failed in 703, the woman who had led it sent her sons to receive instruction in Islam.

In Christendom

So, slowly, faith followed the flag of conquest. Christian conquerors also abused religion to justify war. In the eighth century, the Frankish king Charlemagne gave the pagan Saxons in Germany a choice of baptism or death. In the ninth, Alfred the Great of England imposed baptism on defeated pagans as a condition of peace. Olaf, king of Norway in the early eleventh century, massacred or mutilated pagans who refused Christianity. It seemed consistent with the nature of the Lord of Hosts, as the Bible frequently referred to God, to spread Christianity by war. Yet in all these cases, and others like them, however violent and arbitrary the beginnings of Christianity, the affected communities joined Christian civilization and built springboards for further missions elsewhere.

In the Buddhist World

Less well known is that much of the early spread of Buddhism relied on similar strategies by royal strongmen. As in Christendom, Buddhist rulers practiced remarkable intellectual contortions to justify the imposition by violence of a doctrine of peace and love. Asoka (see Chapter 7) was not alone in priding himself on conquests allegedly achieved "by **dharma**"—the teachings of Buddha. Asoka's near contemporary, Kaniska, King of Peshawar in what is today Pakistan, enforced Buddhism on his own subjects, as did King Vattagamani, in Sri Lanka, early in the first century B.C.E. In the mid–eleventh century C.E., when King Anuruddha (ah-non-ROOD-dah) introduced Buddhism to Burma, he showed his piety by waging war on the neighboring Mon kingdom to gain possession of holy scriptures.

Trade

War can spread religions, but after the time of Asoka, Buddhism never became the ideology of a widely successful conqueror until the sixteenth century; nor did Christianity, until European empires began to spread it around the world. Meanwhile, both religions had to spread with individual journeys beyond political frontiers. Even Islam overspilled the boundaries of Muslim conquests.

Trade was probably at least as important as war. The temples of Dunhuang are full of images of the role of the Silk Roads in spreading Buddhism. Merchants who rested at the monastery there endowed thousands of paintings that still line chambers carved from the rock. According to tradition, a Chinese monk began to hollow the caves out of the cliff face in 366. Many of the paintings portray individual merchants in acts of worship, often with their families and sometimes in the company of their ancestors. In one image, brigands, converted by a Buddhist merchant they have captured, join him in prayer. In others, merchants ransom themselves from bandits by acts of piety. In others, famous Buddhas and sages travel roads familiar to the merchants to visit Buddhist shrines in India and acquire sacred texts.

Manichaeanism and the Uighurs

Buddhism met rival religions along the Silk Roads. The Uighurs (OOEE-goors) were a pastoral, Turkic-speaking people who dominated the steppeland north of the roads for 100 years from the 740s. On service as mercenaries during the Chinese civil wars of the mid–eighth century, they picked up **Manichaeanism** (mah-nih-KEE-ahn-ih-sihm), a religion of obscure origin, probably rooted in a heretical form of Zoroastrianism (see Chapter 6). Mani (MAH-nee), its supposed founder in Persia in the third century, divided the universe into realms of spirit, which was good, and matter, which was evil. This kind of dualism was an ancient and influential idea. But although Mani relentlessly sought to spread his religion, it had never previously captured the allegiance of a state. On the contrary, Zoroastrians, Christians, Muslims, and even (in China, in 732) Buddhists persecuted it. Now, however, the Uighur ruler proclaimed himself the "emanation of Mani," and Manichaean zealots became his counselors, rather as Buddhist and Christian rulers chose clergy as advisers and bureaucrats. Indeed, a Uighur bureaucracy developed, using its own language and script. According to a ninth-century inscription, Manichaeanism transformed "a barbarous country, full of the fumes of blood into a land where the people live on vegetables, from a land of killing to a land where good deeds are fostered." Uighur monarchs endowed temples in China and sponsored the collecting of Manichaean scriptures. However, Buddhism and, to a lesser extent, Christianity ultimately replaced Manichaeanism among the Uighurs, and the creed of Mani never caught on to the same extent anywhere else.

Christianity on the Silk Roads

Christianity was only moderately successful along the Silk Roads. Relatively few Christians, especially from Western Europe, engaged in long-range trade. Among Christian peoples who did have strong vocations for commerce, the Armenians avoided trying to convert others so as not to invite persecution by non-Christian rulers. **Nestorians**—Christians named after Nestorius, Bishop of Constantinople in the fifth century, who regarded the human Jesus as merely human, quite distinct from the divine Jesus—had a network of monasteries and communities that reached China. But the Nestorians remained a thin and patchy presence across a vast area.

Dunhuang. The Silk Roads spread Buddhism as well as trade. Here—in a tenth-century example of the thousands of devotional paintings merchants endowed at the monastery of Dunhuang in Central Asia—a convert and his family pray at the feet of a Bodhisattva. Many Chinese converts to Buddhism retained the family values characteristic of Confucianism.

Camel caravan is still the most practical way to cross the Sahara, and camels still carry part of the traditional salt trade there. Like other long-range trade routes, those across the Sahara in the Middle Ages were avenues for the transfer of culture, spreading Islam, for example, from North Africa to the kingdoms of the West African Sahel and the Niger valley.

Islam on Trade Routes

If Buddhism dominated much of the Silk Roads, Islam spread almost equally effectively by trade along the sea routes of Asia and across the Sahara. Muslim merchant communities founded mosques, elected or imported preachers, and sometimes attracted local people to join them. Muhammad's commands for peaceful conversion were at least as strong as those for jihad. "Call unto the way of thy Lord with wisdom and fair exhortation," the Quran commands. According to a contemporary estimate, thousands of Muslims constituted the biggest of the foreign merchant communities that perished in Guangzhou in a rebel massacre in 879. In the same period, as East African ports became integrated into the trade routes of the Indian Ocean, they developed Muslim communities.

In West Africa, way beyond the African frontiers of the caliphates, immigration and acculturation along the Saharan trade routes prepared the way for Islamization. Arab visitors to Soninke chiefdoms and kingdoms from the ninth century noted that some people followed "the king's religion," while others were Muslims. On this frontier, Islam lacked professional missionaries. Occasionally, however, a Muslim merchant might interest a trading partner or even a pagan ruler in Islam. A late eleventh-century Arab writer tells such a story, from Malal south of the Senegal. At a time of terrible drought, a Muslim guest advised the king that if he accepted Islam, "You would bring Allah's mercy on the people of your country, and your enemies would envy you." Rain duly fell after prayers and Quranic recitations. "The king, together with his descendants and the nobility, became sincerely attached to Islam, but the common people remained pagans."

War, Trade, and Religion

366	Founding of Dunhuang
Fifth century	Nestorius, bishop of Constantinople
Seventh and eighth centuries	Rapid Islamic expansion
Mid–eighth century	Uighurs adopt Manichaeanism
Ninth century	Seaborne pilgrims begin to arrive in Mecca; Muslim merchant communities thrive in major Chinese ports
Mid–eleventh century	King Anuruddha introduces Buddhism to Burma; Islam begins to penetrate East and West Africa

MONARCHS AND MISSIONARIES

Although not much practiced by Muslims in this period, conversion of kings was one of the main strategies Buddhist and Christian missionaries employed to spread their faiths. They learned to start at the top of society because religion, like other forms of culture, tends to trickle downward, encouraged by the example the power of leaders imposes.

For Christians, in particular, the strategy of targeting elites marked a profound innovation in the history of the Church. Christianity in antiquity was branded—not altogether justly—as a "religion of slaves and women." It appealed to a low level of society and, at first, to those with a low-level education. In its earliest days, it was actually unwelcoming to persons of high status, like the rich young man in the

Gospels whom Jesus sent away grieving, or the well-to-do for whom admission to the Kingdom of God was as if through the eye of a needle. In apostolic times, converts of respectable status were few and modest: a Roman army officer; a tax collector; an Ethiopian envoy mentioned in the Acts of the Apostles; the "most excellent Theophilus," who was probably a Roman official, addressed by a gospel-writer. Over the next two to three centuries, the Church embraced people of all classes in the towns of the empire—thanks especially to Christian women, who became the evangelizers of their own husbands and children. But Christianity remained a minority religion, unable to capture the allegiance of rulers or the institutions of states. In the first half of the fourth century, however, three spectacular conversions inaugurated an era in which efforts at conversion targeted the top. The rulers of three great states adopted Christianity: the Roman Emperor Constantine, King Ezana of Ethiopia, and King Trdat (tuhr-DAHT) of Armenia.

Constantine

Like so many future invaders and tourists from the north, Constantine, commander of the Roman army in Britain from 306, was seduced by the feel and flavor of Mediterranean culture. The standard tale of the beginning of his conversion to Christianity is not credible. In 312, he was heading south, intent on capturing the Roman throne for himself. Approaching the decisive battle at Milvian Bridge, not far from Rome, he saw a vision that he later described as "a cross of light, superimposed on the sun"—perhaps like the cross-like clouds mountaineers have reported in the Alps, or perhaps an unusual grouping of planets, or perhaps just a dream. As Constantine already worshiped the Sun, the image appealed. The priorities reflected in the accompanying message, "In this sign, conquer!" reflected Constantine's. He was looking for a Lord of Hosts rather than a God of Love. An alternative account of the conversion may be Constantine's own. It is a stock story of revelation by grace. "I did not think that a power above could see any thoughts which I harbored in the secret places of my heart … but Almighty God, sitting on high, has granted what I did not deserve."

Everywhere politics was so deeply implicated in royal religion that it is hard to resist skepticism about the spirituality of royal converts and the sincerity of their conversions, just as today we prudently disbelieve politicians who claim to be "born again." Bet hedging was the usual strategy. The emperor was the chief priest of the official pagan cults and was worshiped as divine. His role could not suddenly lose its traditional character. Official religion continued. Court poets and orators classified Constantine's victims in battle as divine sacrifices and his birth as a gift of the gods. One of them constructed a framework of paganism over which the emperor's Christianity could fit: "you have secret communion with the Divine Mind, which, delegating our care to lesser gods, deigns to reveal itself to you alone." Constantine continued to personify the Unconquered Sun in official portraits. The sacredness of the emperor's person, however, could now be redefined in Christian terms by calling him God's deputy on Earth and, in deserving cases, making him a saint after his death. In coins his sons issued, the hand of God guides Constantine into heaven on a chariot, like the prophet Elijah's in the Bible.

Imperial patronage profoundly affected Christianity. Constantine himself became, according to his own propaganda, "like an apostle"—settling disputes between theologians, influencing the election of bishops. During the fourth century, Christianity gradually began to displace the old cults as the official religion of the empire. Pulpits spread imperial propaganda. Millions of subjects of the empire

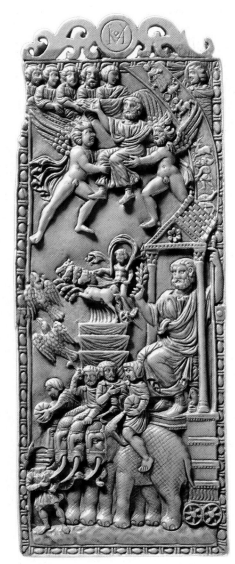

Christian and pagan cultures were so similar and so mixed in the fourth-century Roman Empire that it is sometimes hard to tell them apart. Here an emperor, having ridden in life in triumph on an elephant, is hoisted skyward by the chariot of the sun, which pagans worshiped as a god and Christian artists used as an image for Christ. Winged spirits ascend with the emperor's soul, through the spheres of heaven, marked by the signs of the zodiac, top right, to the heavenly home of his ancestors. This is one of the last works of art that portrays a Roman emperor in a predominantly pagan setting.

began to go to church—without necessarily embracing, or even understanding, Christian doctrines. More than ever, learned and aristocratic classes, who had previously despised Christianity, blended its teachings with the philosophy of classical antiquity. Christian virtues blended with those of Stoicism (see Chapter 6). Christian pacifism withered as Christians supported the empire's wars.

Ezana

The adoption of Christianity at the court of Ethiopia at Axum in the 340s illustrates a similar dilemma for a war leader seeking to appropriate a religion of peace. The inscriptions of King Ezana were bloodthirsty documents, full of conquests and captives. As his reign unfolded, they remained bloody but became increasingly high-minded, full of the concept of the good of the people and service to the state. The king still waged wars but grew moralistic about justifying them. One adversary "attacked and annihilated one of our caravans, after which we took to the field." The king of neighboring Nubia (see Chapter 4) was guilty of boastfulness, raiding, violation of embassies, and refusal to negotiate. "He did not listen to me," Ezana complains, "and uttered curses." The new tone reflects the growing influence of Christian clergy.

Before the 340s, Ezana described himself as "son of Mahreb," a war god. Suddenly, he dropped the claim and waged war in the name of the "Lord of heaven and Earth" or "the Father, Son and Holy Spirit." His last monument proclaims, "I cannot speak fully of his favors, for my mouth and my spirit cannot fully express all the mercies he has done to me… He has made me the guide of my kingdom through my faith in Christ." He toppled the great stone pillars of Axum or ceased to erect them and began to build churches.

Trdat

To become Christian was to join the growing common culture—vertex of a triangle of Christian states, Ethiopia, Rome, Armenia. For Armenia, the evidence is too indistinct to yield a clear picture of what happened. A supposed letter King Trdat wrote in the late third century to an anti-Christian Roman emperor declares "loathing for Christians" and a promise to persecute them. His eventual submission to baptism supposedly arose in revulsion from the fate of 33 nuns whom he had put to death. Gregory the Illuminator—Trdat's former friend, whom he imprisoned in a pit of snakes—stirred his remorse. This looks like a theologically crafted tale of a change of heart induced by divine grace. The whole story seems loosely modeled on that of the Apostle Paul in the Bible—the persecutor turned converter. Trdat's conversion occurred sometime between 301 and 314. The latter date seems likely, as by then Constantine had begun to favor Christianity, and Trdat favored alignment with Rome against Persia.

Early Conversions to Christianity

312	Emperor Constantine of Rome
ca. 301–314	King Trdat of Armenia
340s	King Ezana of Ethiopia

From *The Life of St. Nino*

Diplomatic Conversions

In the Caucasus Mountains near Armenia, at about the same time, tradition credits an unnamed slave woman (whom later tradition called Nino) with converting the people we now know as the Georgians. Her prayers cured a queen's illness. When the king proposed to shower the slave with rewards, "She despises gold," said the queen. "The only way we can repay her is to worship divine Christ who cured me thanks to her prayers." The story sounds made up. The verifiable fact, however, is that the priests who launched the Georgian state church came from Constantine's empire. Christianity was a political option for small states striving to preserve their independence and playing Persia against Rome.

The Georgian kingdoms of Iberia and Lazica pried themselves free of Persian dominance, partly by opting for Roman support. By the early sixth century, a Roman ambassador to Lazica could hardly restrain his enthusiasm for a people who were "in no way barbarians, long association with the Romans having led them to adopt a civilized and law-abiding way of life." From 522, the kings of Lazica ceased to accept election by the emperors of Persia and chose to be invested by those of Rome.

Religious allegiances changed with political alliances. Poised between Christian and Muslim powers, the rulers of the Khazars (HAH-zahrs)—Turkic pastoralists between the Black Sea and the Caspian, who built up a state that endured for 400 years from the early seventh century—adopted, at different times, Christianity, Islam, and Judaism in their efforts to preserve their independence.

Buddhist Politics

Buddhist missionaries also displayed partiality for royal and imperial disciples. The Chinese emperor Ming was supposed to have introduced Buddhism as the result of a vision in the late first century. This was untrue, but it is evidence of the importance the Buddhist clergy who invented the tale attached to imperial patronage. As we saw in the last chapter, Buddhism became the favorite spiritual resource of usurpers of the Chinese throne who wanted to legitimize their rule and of monarchs who needed a propaganda machine. But no Buddhist emperor ever suspended the traditional rites and sacrifices that Chinese emperors were required to perform. Only Yang Jian in the sixth century (see Chapter 8)—a skeptic contemptuous of all religion—had the nerve to do that.

Buddhism had, moreover, to contend with Chinese belittlement of anything foreign. Indeed, the measure of Buddhism's success is that, until "Westernization" began in the late nineteenth century, it was the only movement of foreign origin ever really to catch on in China. Sporadic bursts of imperial favor enabled Buddhists to establish an enormous network of monasteries that became magnets of piety for millions of people. The scale of Buddhism's ascent appeared during one of the spasms of persecution of Buddhism in which emperors occasionally indulged. In the 820s through the 840s, thousands of monasteries were dissolved, and 250,000 monks and nuns forced back into lay life.

Korea

In the neighboring Korean kingdom of Koguryo, the rise of Buddhism began in the late fourth century, when barbarian invasions of China enriched Koguryo with refugees. Fugitive Chinese monks reconciled Buddhism with royal responsibilities under the old, indigenous religion. King Kwanggaet'o dedicated a temple with the inscription, "Believing in Buddhism, we seek prosperity." King Changsu (r. 413–491) is depicted at the tomb of his predecessor performing Buddhist as well as native rites. The rest of Korea resisted Buddhist intrusions at first, perhaps because of the importance of local religious rites as part of the ceremonial of kingship. The kings of Silla, for instance, derived prestige from their claim to have

The monastery church at Jvari ("the Cross") in Georgia occupies a hilltop where St. Nino, a female evangelist traditionally credited with helping to spread Christianity in Georgia in the fourth century, is said to have paused to pray. A church on the site is documented from the seventh century, but the existing building resembles Western churches of the ninth and tenth centuries.

arisen from a dynasty of holy men. State formation in Korea was essentially a process of extending uniform religious rites to one community after another.

The launch of Buddhism as a royal religion in southern Korea is traditionally ascribed to the personal conversion of King Song in Paekche and King Pophung of Silla, despite noble opposition, in the 520s or 530s. Monks, like the chief minister Hyeyong in the mid–550s, became useful state servants. Won'gwang, who returned from China in 602 to head the bureaucracy, adapted dharma for political purposes. Serve your lord with loyalty and "face battle without retreating" became precepts of the faith. Having adapted to one political system in the sixth century, Korean Buddhism did so again, under new political conditions, in the tenth century, when the reform of the Korean administration along Chinese lines filled the bureaucracy with men trained in Confucianism. The scholar-administrator Ch'oe Sungno expressed the ensuing compromise well in 982: "Carrying out the teachings of Buddha is the basis for the cultivation of the self. Carrying out the teachings of Confucius is the source for regulating the state."

Japan

Japan was the scene of the most remarkable working compromise between a new, universal religion and kingly commitment to traditional paganism. The first image of the Buddha in Japan was said to have arrived as a diplomatic gift from Korea in 538. The pious efforts of the Soga clan—immigrants from China—supposedly spread the new religion around the end of the sixth century. Underlying the tale is a political saga. The traditional "way of the gods"—**Shinto** in Japanese—was the reigning dynasty's special responsibility. The Soga aimed to replace them and saw Buddhism as the path to power.

A traditional anecdote captures the true lines of the debate that raged in the mid–sixth century. "All neighboring states to the west already honor Buddha," the Soga pointed out. "Is it right that Japan alone should turn her back on this religion?" But native ministers replied, "The rulers of this country have always conducted seasonal rites in honor of the many heavenly and earthly spirits of land and grain."

The search was on for a synthesis that would harness Buddhism for the state without disturbing the traditional Shinto ideology and magic of the monarchy. Prince Shotoku (574–622), the first great royal patron of Buddhism in Japan, realized the value of the Buddhist clergy as potential servants of the state. He wrote learned commentaries on Buddhist doctrine and founded monasteries. His injunctions include, "The emperor is heaven and his ministers are Earth. . . . So edicts handed down by the emperor must be scrupulously obeyed." Endorsed from the court, Buddhism flourished. The Japanese census of 624 counted 816 monks. By 690, 3,363 monks received gifts of cloth from the throne.

A reaction set in. The traditional elite feared Buddhism as a foreign menace to the imperial rites. Early eighth-century law codes banned wandering monks from "speaking falsely about misfortunes or blessings based on mysterious natural phenomena," "deluding the people," and begging without permit.

Prince Shotoku. As regent for the first reigning Japanese empress in the early seventh century, Prince Shotoku, shown here with two of his sons in a Korean painting of nearly two centuries later, used his influence to promote contacts with China, remodel the Japanese government on Chinese lines, and spread Buddhism in Japan.

Various measures attempted to prevent monasteries from abusing their tax-exempt status.

The advances of Buddhism, however, were irresistible. A Buddhist scripture warned kings that "if they do not walk in the law, the holy men go away and violent calamities arise." In the 730s, the monk Gembo returned from China with 5,000 volumes of Buddhist scriptures and endeared himself by curing an empress's depression. In 747, 6,563 monks were ordained at a palace ceremony. Buddhist rituals originally intended in India to treat snakebites, poison, and disease were used in Japan to protect the state. The outcome was a characteristically Japanese compromise. No one in Japan, it is often said, was purely Buddhist. The traditional Shinto shrines played a part in the devotions even of monks, as they still do. Even Empress Shotoku in the 760s, whose Buddhist devotion was unsurpassed, never tried to tamper with the traditional rites.

The Introduction of Buddhism in Korea and Japan

Late fourth century	Chinese refugees introduce Buddhism in Koguryo
ca. 520–530	Kings of Paekche and Silla convert to Buddhism
538	First image of Buddha arrives in Japan
574–622	Life of Prince Shotoku, first great royal patron of Buddhism
Seventh century	Rapid expansion of Buddhism in Japan under royal patronage

Tibet

According to a legend crafted in Tibet about 500 years after the supposed event, a Chinese or Nepalese wife of King Songtsen Gampo brought Buddhism there in the sixth century. The true story was of long, slow monastic colonization. Though Songtsen Gampo probably patronized Buddhist monks and scholars, who frequented his court in the households of the Nepalese and Chinese princesses of his harem, he continued to represent himself as divine.

Even King Trisong Detsen in the second half of the eighth century, whom Buddhists hailed as a model of piety and their opponents denounced as a traitor to the traditional royal religion, depicted himself as both the divine defender of the old faith and the enlightened enthusiast of the new. In 792, he presided over a great debate between Indian and Chinese champions on the question of whose traditions better represented the Buddha's doctrine. The issue was decided in favor of the Indian traditional moral disciplines (**Theravada Buddhism,** as it is usually called), by which the soul might advance to Buddhahood by tiny incremental stages of learning and goodness, lifetime after lifetime, rather than the **Mahayana Buddhism,** argued by Chinese spokesmen, who claimed that the soul could achieve Buddhahood in one lifetime. Mahayana Buddhism, which also took root in Japan, is known as the "greater vehicle" because its proponents believe that it can carry more people to salvation than Theravada Buddhism, the "lesser vehicle."

But this debate was premature. Tibet was hardly yet a Buddhist country, nor could one tradition of Buddhism be imposed in the contexts in which Buddhism spread: missionary work and monastery founding; the spread of culture along the routes of merchant caravans; and the ebb and flow of armies, that transmitted ideas as the tide shifts pebbles.

By the time of Tibet's treaty with China in 821, Buddhism had made real progress. The treaty invoked Buddhist as well as pagan gods, and after traditional sacrifices and blood-smearing rites, the Buddhists among the treaty's

Samye monastery. The first Buddhist monastery in Tibet was reputedly founded at Samye in the valley of Lhasa. It illustrates the importance of royal patronage in bringing Buddhism to Tibet. According to legend, King Trisong Detsen in the 770s invited an Indian sage into the kingdom, who consecrated the site of the monastery after a battle with the demons who infested it.

negotiators withdrew for a celebration of their own. King Ralpachen was so devout that he let monks sit on his prodigiously long hair. But a reaction set in at his death in 836, and Buddhism survived in Tibet only precariously awaiting renewal by a new wave of monastic colonization. Its main rival was not the old religion but **Bon.** Of the origins of this faith, we know nothing reliable, but it was similar and heavily indebted to Buddhism. The sayings of the great Bon-po sage, Gyerspungs, closely resembled those of Buddhist masters: Existence is like a dream. "Validity is vacuity." Truth must "transcend sounds and terms and words." The main difference lay in the sages' attitude to India. Buddhists acknowledged that their teaching came from there, whereas Bon-pos traced it to a legendary land in the west, and regarded their mythical founder, Shen-rab, as the original Buddha.

India

Ironically, the effort to combine Buddhism with traditional kingship failed most conspicuously in India itself, the Buddha's homeland. In the sixth century, kingdoms multiplied in India, and kings granted revenue and property to holy men to found religious establishments, in an effort to gain their support. Kings made relatively few grants, however, to Buddhists. The circumstances of the period—the conflicts with the Huns (see Chapter 8) and the crumbling of political unity—seem to have driven popular piety back to the worship of local gods, as if the troubles of the time were proof that Buddhism had failed.

Xuanzang's descriptions of the caste system

Rites and practices associated with the traditions we now call **Hinduism** were taking hold. Indeed, some holy men set out to systematize them as an alternative to Buddhism. The development of the caste system—in which everyone has an unchangeable ritual rank, defined at birth, that determines one's place in society—indicates how Hinduism was spreading. The caste system was not yet fully defined, but according to the description of India in 630 through 645 by Xuanzang (shoo-en-tzang), the greatest Chinese Buddhist manuscript collector, butchers, fishermen, actors, executioners, and scavengers were ritually unclean and had to live outside city limits. Almost everyone acknowledged the superiority of the highest caste, the priestly Brahmans. The spread of blood sacrifice also shows that Buddhism was in retreat. Kings sacrificed horses, in defiance of Buddhist teaching, but protected cows, which Hinduism regards as sacred. The first **sati**—the burning of a widow on her husband's funeral pyre—was recorded in 510. The Palas dynasty of Bengal in the eighth to the eleventh centuries was the last nominally Buddhist reigning family in India. Most Indian kings preferred to stake their power on devotion to traditional gods rather than on Buddhism.

The Margins of Christendom

In Christendom, the *Constantinian model*, according to which conversion begins with the ruler, prevailed for most of what we think of as the Middle Ages. Almost every conversion of a nation or a people, as related in medieval sources, began with the conversion of a king. There were exceptions. Clovis, for instance, the Frankish chief who took over most of Gaul (modern France) in the 480s, gave up his claim to descent from a sea god for allegiance to the Church, which promised victories and supplied literate administrators. But conversions among the Frankish people preceded or accompanied Clovis's. In Iceland, where supposedly "democratic" decision making is generally supposed to have prevailed, the collective adoption of Christianity was resolved in the assembly of the people in 1000, but the law speaker who presided over the assembly, Thorgeirr Thorkelsson, withdrew to meditate or commune with the gods for a day and a night before lending his decisive influence to the debate. Of course, Christianity was also spread in undocumented or barely documented ways: movements of population, journeys of merchants and envoys. But missionary strategy focused on leaders as means of mobilizing peoples.

In northern and eastern Europe, a great sequence of royal conversions in the late tenth and early eleventh centuries more or less established the frontier of Christendom, beginning with Harold Bluetooth in the 960s in Denmark and Mieszko of Poland in 966. In Norway, a year or two after the king's confirmation as a Christian in 995, a popular assembly endorsed the new religion. In Sweden King Olof Skötkunung began minting coins with Christian symbols on them before 1000. He established an uninterrupted sequence of Christian rulers. The coronation of Stephen of Hungary in 1001 settled the Christian destiny of that country.

Vladimir and the Rus

No case was more significant for the future than that of Vladimir, ruler of Kiev in what is today Ukraine, in 987–988, for his adherence ensured that Christianity would be privileged among the eastern Slavs—including the Russians, who became Europe's most numerous people. Vladimir was the descendant of Scandinavians as well as Slavs, pagans on both sides (see Chapter 10). Like many great saints, he sinned with gusto. His harem was said to contain over 800 girls. Russians trace proverbs in praise of drunkenness to his invention. He left a reputation, in the words of a German chronicler, as "a cruel man and a fornicator on a huge scale."

Among his people, paganism was entrenched by terror. The horror of a human sacrifice among the Rus profoundly impressed a Muslim ambassador who witnessed it in 922. The slave girl chosen to die with her master sang songs of farewell over her last cups of liquor before ritually copulating with her executioners. An old woman called the Angel of Death then wound a cord around her neck and handed the slack to men standing on either side. Warriors beat their shields to drown the victim's screams. While the cord was tightened, the Angel of Death plunged a dagger repeatedly in and out of the girl's breast. The funeral pyre, built on a ship, was then lighted, and the fire fed until it burned to ashes.

 Ibn Fadlan's journey to Russia

To replace this religion, and break the power of its priests, Vladimir needed something equally powerful. The traditional story of his emissaries' quest led first to the Bulgars, who "bow down and sit, look hither and thither like men possessed, but there is no joy in them, only sorrow and a dreadful stench. Their religion is not good. Then we went to the Germans, and we saw them celebrating many services in their churches, but we saw no beauty there. Then we went to the Greeks, and they led us to the place where they worship their God [the church of Hagia Sophia that Justinian had built in Constantinople]; and we knew not whether we were in heaven or on Earth; for on Earth there is no such vision or beauty and we do not know how to describe it. We only know that there God dwells among men."

Vladimir's decision in favor of Orthodox Christianity owed more to politics than aesthetics. Conversion was the price he paid for the hand of a Byzantine princess whom he demanded with threats. Imperial Byzantine princesses were not normally permitted to marry foreign suitors, for, according to the tenth-century emperor, Constantine VII, "just as each animal mates with its own species, so it is right that each nation should also marry and cohabit not with those of other race and tongue but of the same tribe and speech." Marriages between imperial princesses and foreign

The Spread of Christianity

ca. 500	Clovis, king of the Franks, converts to Christianity
960	Harold Bluetooth of Denmark converts
966	Conversion of King Mieszko of Poland
ca. 988	Vladmir of Kiev adopts Orthodox Christianity
ca. 997	Norway and Sweden convert to Christianity
1000	Iceland converts to Christianity
1001	Coronation of Stephen of Hungary as a Christian monarch

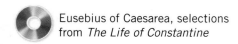

Eusebius of Caesarea, selections from *The Life of Constantine*

rulers diminished the divinely sanctioned dignity of the Byzantine monarchy and opened the way for foreign rulers to claim the Byzantine throne. Vladimir solemnly evicted his idols. The thunder god, Perun, was dragged through the dust before being flung in a river. Vladimir imposed Christianity by violence, while making it more acceptable by ordering that Christian liturgy be conducted in the Slavonic language the Rus spoke, rather than in Greek.

Islam and the Turks

The magnetism Christianity exerted on the frontiers of Christendom was paralleled in the Islamic world. Around the mid–tenth century, the Karakhanids (kah-rah-HAHN-ihds) became the first Turkic people to subscribe to Islam—apparently as a result of the favorable impression they derived from raiding Islamic territory. This was an event pregnant with consequences for the future, because the Turks would bring to the Islamic world a vital infusion of manpower and expertise in war—"the army of God, whom I have installed in the East," according to a legendary saying of the Prophet.

Islam's attraction for them is easier to express than explain. Their values were warlike. Boys were not named until they had "lopped off heads in battle." Even women were war trained and "made the enemy vomit blood." Yet some of their leaders saw attractions in Islam. In 962, Altigin (AHL-tee-geen), a Turk who had adopted Islam while serving as a slave in Persia, founded at Ghazni (GAHZ-nee) in Afghanistan a Muslim state that was to exert great influence in the future. In about 985, a Turkic chief, Seljuk (SEHL-jook), who dreamed of "ejaculating fire in all directions" and conquering the world, ruled a small state in Central Asia. His descendants supplied some of the Islamic world's most effective frontiersmen.

TRICKLE DOWN: CHRISTIANIZATION AND ISLAMIZATION

From converted rulers and conquered elites, religions trickled down to the rest of society. For Christians, for example, Constantine's patronage was an extraordinary windfall. At the time, despite the gradual accumulation of converts among the socially respectable and intellectual, Christianity had remained one among many popular eastern cults. It still bore the marks of its origins as a Jewish heresy, founded by a rabbi whose birth and death were, in the world's eyes, equally disreputable. Its scriptures were, by the sophisticated standards of the Greek schools of rhetoric and philosophy, so badly written as to embarrass all educated Christians.

Now, after the conversion of Constantine, according to the fourth-century Christian historian Eusebius, "It felt as if we were imagining a picture of the kingdom of Christ and that what was happening was no reality but a dream." There were subsidies for the Church, exemptions from fiscal and military obligations for the clergy, jobs in the state service for Christians, and the assurance, from the emperor's own hand, that the worship of Christians benefited the empire.

The rise of the Church from persecution to predominance was completed in 395, when the emperor Theodosius proclaimed Christianity the official religion of the Roman Empire and reduced pagan traditions to the underprivileged status formerly imposed on Christians. From the late fourth century onward, nobility and sanctity converged. So many young aristocrats became monks that monasteries came to resemble "noblemen's clubs." Christianity guaranteed the best opportunities for promotion in the army and bureaucracy and for personal enrichment.

○ MAKING CONNECTIONS ○

FACTORS AIDING THE SPREAD OF UNIVERSAL RELIGIONS

RELIGION →	WAR →	TRADE →	MISSIONARIES →	ELITES
Buddhism	Early rulers Asoka, Kaniska, Anuruddha invoke "dharma" (teachings of Buddha) in violent conquests	Silk Roads fundamental to spreading Buddhism via traveling monks and monasteries housing merchants, pilgrims	Missionaries/pilgrims important—Xuanzang (China); conversion of kings a primary means of accelerating social acceptance	Emperor Ming (China); King Song (Korea); Prince Shotoko (Japan); Trisong Detsen (Tibet)
Christianity	Charlemagne, other rulers (Alfred the Great of England, Olaf of Norway) justify war, conquest by forcible conversion	Few long-distance Christian traders along Eurasian trade routes; Nestorians a thin and patchy presence along Silk Roads	Converting kings and elite groups a fundamental strategy	Constantine (Roman Empire); Ezana (Ethiopia);. Trdat (Armenia); Vladimir (Kiev, Russia)
Islam	Jihad justifies both interior struggle and warfare against polytheists, idolaters, apostates; continual warfare against non-Islamic neighboring states	Effectively spread via land and sea routes across Africa. Dispersal of Muslim–merchant communities throughout south and southeast Asia	Traveling merchants; conversion encouraged by specific social/political policies favoring Muslims (beneficial tax system, legal codes)	Especially important in Turkic areas (Central Asia): tenth-century leaders Altigin, Seljuk

Those who accepted it subscribed to a cultural package associated with success. Ethiopian sources are too meager for certainty, but in Armenia, too, the continuing progress of Christianity depended, at least until the Arab conquest in the eighth century, on royal and aristocratic initiatives.

To some extent, parallel considerations applied within the Islamic world. Because the Muslim conquests were vast, and the conquerors relatively few in number, Muslim rulers could not exclude non-Muslims from positions of authority. The caliph Umar (OO-mahr) I expelled non-Muslims from Arabia in 635, but without the services of Christians and Jews in the rest of the Middle East, or of Zoroastrians in Persia, the administrations of the eighth- and ninth-century caliphates would have been understaffed. Still, by favoring Muslims, discriminating against non-Muslims, and insisting on the exclusive use of Arabic as the language of administration, rulers created a climate of prejudice in favor of Islam among elites. Even mild persecution could exert considerable pressure. The caliph Umar II (r. 717–720) tried to exclude Christians and Jews from public offices. He also forbade them to build places of worship or lift their voices in prayer. They had to wear distinctive clothing and were forbidden saddles for their horses. If a Muslim killed a Christian, his penalty was only a fine. Christians could not give valid testimony against Muslims in legal cases. Later caliphs sporadically renewed persecution. In 807, Caliph Harun al-Rashid (hah-ROON ahr-rah-SHEED) ordered all churches on the frontiers of his empire demolished and reinforced the clothing laws against Christians. In the 850s, the caliph al-Mutawakkil (ahl-moo-tah-WAH-keel) ordered that Christian and Jewish graves should be level with the ground. Converts

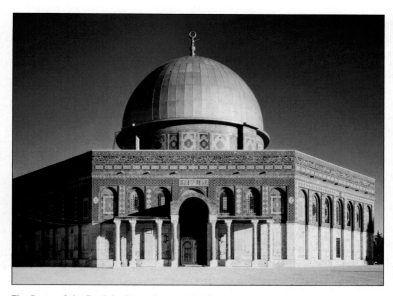

The Dome of the Rock in Jerusalem marks the spot where, according to Muslim tradition, the Prophet Muhammad ascended to paradise. The Caliph Abd al-Malik had it built in the late seventh century, marking as sacred to Islam a city that Christians and Jews already revered. The splendor and scale of the building out-dazzled and dwarfed the nearby Church of the Holy Sepulcher and the remains of the last Jewish Temple.

to Islam, on the other hand, could rapidly ascend through the ranks of society.

For most Christian and Jewish subjects of Islamic states, the tax system—which exempted Muslims from most charges—was the focus of discrimination. Indeed, many people proclaimed themselves Muslims simply to take advantage of reduced tax rates, until Al-Hajjaj (ahl-hah-JAHL), the brutal governor of Iraq in the 690s and early 700s, reimposed the old tax levels on supposedly phoney converts.

Partly because Islam tolerated some other religions, the conquered societies were slow to become Islamized. Indeed, substantial Christian minorities have survived in Egypt, Iraq, Syria, and, especially, Lebanon to this day. Some historians have tried to measure the rate of acceptance of Islam by calculating the numbers of people who gave their children Muslim-sounding names. This method suggested to Richard W. Bulliet, its greatest exponent, that only 2.5 percent of the population of Iran were converted to Islam in the seventh century. Not until the early ninth century was the majority of the population Muslim. The remainder were Islamized during the ninth and tenth centuries. The significance of name giving is broadly cultural, in most places, rather than specifically religious. But the names people were given or adopted do help to demonstrate roughly the rate at which Islam became the dominant influence on the culture of Iran.

RELIGIOUS LIVES: THE WORLD OF MONKS AND NUNS

In Buddhism and Christianity, monasticism grew as these religions spread and, in turn, became a major cause of their success.

Christian Monasticism

As a result of the triumph of Christianity as an elite religion, the Church became the great upholder of Roman standards of learning, art, and government. This is not surprising among aristocratic bishops, whose family traditions were of power. Pope Gregory the Great (r. 590–604) organized the defenses of Rome (see Chapter 8), launched missions of spiritual reconquest to pagan parts of Western Europe, and reimposed on the western empire a kind of unity by the sheer range of his correspondence. In Visigothic Spain, Isidore of Seville (ca. 560–636) passed the learning of classical Greece and Rome on to future generations in the form of an encyclopedia.

It was harder to domesticate the church's own barbarians—the antisocial ascetics and hermits, whose response to the problems of the world was to withdraw from them or rail at them from their caves. The monastic movement made their lives "regular," in houses of work, study, and prayer to benefit society as a whole. There is no scholarly consensus on the origins of monasticism. Christians perhaps got it from Buddhists, or maybe it arose independently as hermits and holy men clubbed together for mutual support. The earliest recorded Christian monastic communities emerged in Egypt in the second century, among ascetics seeking to imitate Jesus' period of self-exile in the desert. Of the many rules of life for monks written in the following centuries, the most influential rule in the western church was that of Benedict of Nursia.

Isidore of Seville's T-O map of the world

The only certain date in his life is 542, when a king visited him at his monastery of Monte Cassino in southern Italy. Benedict started as a typical, obsessive ascetic, in a cave, where food was lowered to him while he disciplined the lusts of the flesh in a convenient thorn bush. In one of the earliest surviving illustrations of his life, the cave mouth is jagged and bloody. When he established his own community, he rededicated the pagan shrine of the Roman god Jupiter on the spot to St. Martin, the patron of poverty, who gave half his cloak to a beggar. The nearby pagan shrine of Apollo became the chapel of John Baptist, the biblical voice crying in the wilderness. These rededications disclose Benedict's program: the practice of charity in refuge from the world.

His book of rules for monks borrowed freely from others. But its superiority and universality were recognized almost at once, and there has hardly been a monastic movement or revival in the West since then that has not been based on or deeply influenced by it. The animating principles are the quest for salvation in common and the subordination of individual willfulness. Benedict banned extremes of mortification in favor of steady spiritual progress, manual labor, study, and prayer in private and in common. He devised a means to make civilization survive, for monastic study also embraced the learning of ancient Greece and Rome. Monasteries became centers for colonizing wasteland and wilderness. Monks sought "desert" frontiers to build new monasteries, and lay people followed them.

 The Rule of St. Benedict

 from the *Confession of St. Patrick*

Buddhist Monks

Monasticism was even more important in Buddhism than in Christianity, since most Buddhist clergy were subject to monastic discipline. In practice, Buddhist monasteries performed particular functions, especially in transmitting learning, similar to those of monasteries in Christendom. The 50,000 ancient manuscripts preserved in the library cave of Dunhuang—a precious time capsule, sealed for 800 years in the tenth century—are a measure of the importance of scholarship in Buddhist monasteries. The business of retrieving, translating, editing, and purifying the best written evidence of the Buddha's teachings turned monks into giants and heroes of learning. The first Chinese to be ordained as a Buddhist priest, for instance, in about 250, was Zhu Shixing (joo-sha-shang). He was nearly 80 years

⊙ MAKING CONNECTIONS   ⊙

THE RELIGIOUS LIFE

RELIGION →	EXAMPLES OF RELIGIOUS COMMUNITIES →	MONASTERY FUNCTIONS/ACTIVITIES
Christianity	Egyptian monasteries, second century; Benedictine monasteries, Italy and Europe, sixth century onward	Scholarly (preservation, translation of ancient manuscripts); cultural (lay people followed monks in reclaiming desert regions); religious (Benedict's widely followed program focused on steady spiritual progress, manual labor, study, and prayer)
Buddhism	Silk Road monasteries (ca. 200–800)	Scholarly (transmission of learning; translation and preservation of texts); secular and religious education, centers of lay life (reading groups, pilgrimage sites, inns for travelers, and granaries for food storage)
Islam	Sufi monasteries, Turkey/Mideast (ninth century and after)	Mystical orders focusing on intense spiritual practices (dancing, prayer, study) organized into brotherhoods, sisterhoods

old when he made a pilgrimage to India to procure a manuscript of the Buddha. Exhausted by the journey, he handed it to his disciples to carry to China before he died. Kumarajiva, translator into Chinese of the most famous of Buddhist scriptures, the **Lotus Sutra,** in the early fifth century, was said to be able to memorize 30,000 words a day. As in Christendom, Buddhist monastic libraries diversified into secular learning, imaginative literature, and administrative and historical records of life way beyond the monastery walls. They were centers of lay life, too, hosting reading clubs for believers, including groups of women, who would pay fines—such as a jug of wine or bowl of cereal—for failure to attend meetings. And monasteries functioned as objects of pilgrimage, inns for travelers, and granaries to store food against hard times.

Sufism

Strictly speaking, there should never have been anything like monasticism in Islam. The Quran condemns it. But Christian influence was not easy to filter out of early Islam. In the early eighth century, Hasan al-Basri quoted Jesus to support his view that asceticism is God's "training ground that his servants might learn to run to him." He advocated fasting and meditation to induce a mystical sense of identity with God. When, toward the end of the same century, the female mystic, Rabia al-Adawiyya (rah-BEE-yah ahl-dahWEE-yah), experienced a vision of Muhammad, he asked her if she loved him. "My love of God has so possessed me," she replied, "that no space is left for loving or hating any but him." Groups of devotees founded houses of common life, or, at least, schools in which they trained in mystical techniques and cultivated the tradition these thinkers established. Though fellow Mus-

The Lotus Sutra. Composed between the first century B.C.E. and the second century C.E., the *Lotus Sutra* is the most important text of Mahayana Buddhism. This printed version, from around 1000 C.E., shows the Western Paradise of the Amitabha Buddha and his court of Bodhisattvas.

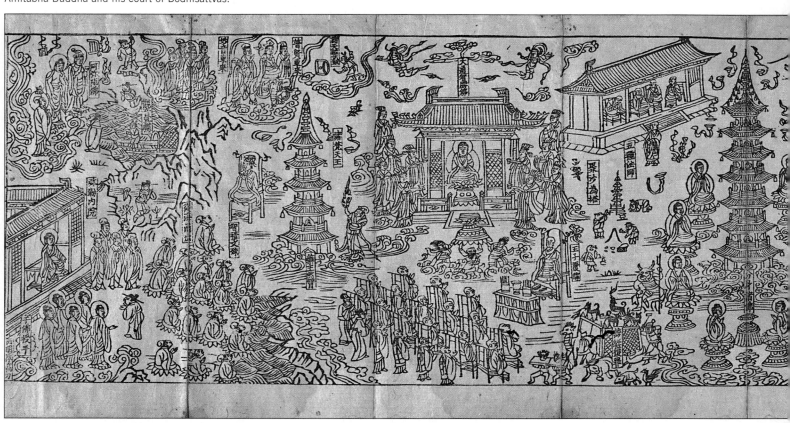

lims often suspected these **Sufis** (SOO-fees) of being heretical, Sufism supplied Islam with some of its supplest thinkers and most dedicated and successful missionaries.

Religious Women

In Christianity, Buddhism, and the Islamic world, women acquired new roles, inside the home as guardians of religious tradition for their children, and outside the home as members of religious orders. Nuns played the same role as monks in prayer and scholarship. In some places, both sexes shared the same houses of religion, often under female leadership. At Whitby in seventh-century England, the formidable Abbess Hilda ruled one of the largest and most learned religious establishments of the day. Nunneries played an important part in Buddhist life in China and Japan as schools for women. The empresses Shotoku of Japan (see Chapter 10) and Wu of China (see Chapter 8) were nuns before their ascent to power. In the Buddhist world, the nun's vocation was often a stage before returning to secular life in households where husbands had several wives and concubines. In Islam, which allowed men to have up to four wives, there was relatively little spare woman power. So female monasticism never developed, and female Sufis—though often individually influential—were rare. Only exceptionally strong-minded women like Rabia al-Adawiyya could pursue their vocations in a life of renunciation of marriage.

Early Monasticism

ca. 250	Zhu Shixing is the first Chinese to be ordained Buddhist priest
Second century	Earliest Christian monastic communities (Egypt)
Sixth century	Life of Saint Benedict
Seventh century	Abbess Hilda rules important religious establishments
Late eighth century	Rabia al-Adawiyya, Islamic Sufi mystic

 Rabia al-Adawiyya, "Brothers, My Peace Is in My Aloneness"

IN PERSPECTIVE: The Triumphs of the Potential World Religions

The story of this chapter has been of cultural change rather than religious conversion. Some of the conditions—violence, mass migration, enforced refugeeism, pestilence, famine, natural disaster, "culture shock," and demographic collapse—constitute, on a large scale, influences comparable to the traumas that often precede individual conversion. Yet, when we monitor the public progress of Christianity, Islam, and Buddhism, we glimpse, at best, shadows of individual religious experience. Instead, we see shrines multiplying; congregations growing; influence deepening on laws, rites, customs, and the arts.

By around 1000, all three religions had demonstrated their adaptability to different cultures and climates (see Map 9.2). Buddhism had big followings in China, Japan, Tibet, and southeast Asia and had spread into Central Asia along the Silk Roads. Christianity had a near monopoly in Western Europe and spilled east and north into Scandinavia and the Slav lands, while retaining the allegiance of communities scattered through Asia. Islam, dominant in southwest Asia and North Africa, spread by conquest, conversion, and migration among Turkic peoples and around the trade

Scale varies with perspective

4,444 km
(2,762 miles)

3,867 km
(6,228 miles)

ICELAND

SCANDINAVIA

NORWAY

SWEDEN

SCOTLAND

IRELAND

Whitby

DENMARK

Baltic Sea

Elbe

ENGLAND

Saxons

POLAND

GERMANY

Rhine

Slavs

RUS

60

Kiev

ATLANTIC OCEAN

FRANKISH KINGDOM

Alps
Po

ITALY

Nursia

Rome

Monte Cassino

Braga

Seville

HUNGARY

UKRAINE

Dnieper

Volga

Khazars

Balkans

Danube

Black Sea

Caucasus

GEORGIA

Constantinople

ARMENIA

GREECE

Sicily

30°

North Africa

Mediterranean Sea

Cyprus

SYRIA

to Central Asia

Baghdad

IRAQ

Jerusalem

Muslim ruled
by 750 C.E.

Alexandria

EGYPT

Red Sea

Nile

Arabian Peninsula

N

Mecca

MAP 9.2a

The Christian World, ca.1000 C.E.

	Catholic Christianity	→	missions
	Orthodox Christianity	†	important church or monastery
	Christian churches believing Jesus to be wholly divine (Monophysite)	*Saxons*	people
	Nestorian Christianity		
	area with significant Christian minorities today		

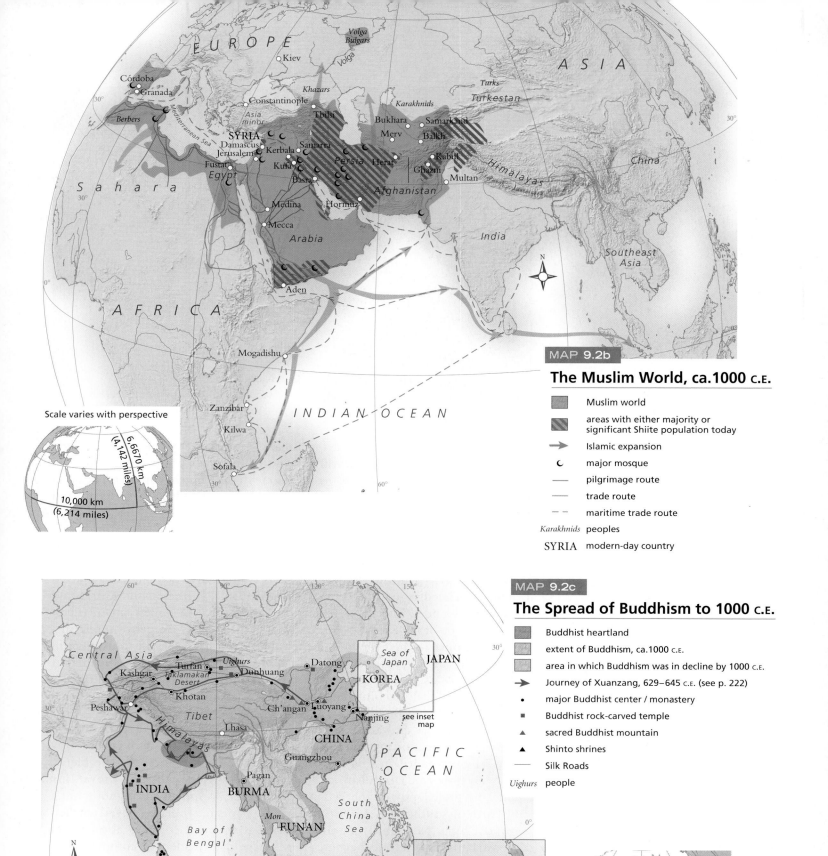

MAP 9.2b

The Muslim World, ca.1000 C.E.

- Muslim world
- areas with either majority or significant Shiite population today
- → Islamic expansion
- ☾ major mosque
- — pilgrimage route
- — trade route
- – – maritime trade route
- *Karakhnids* peoples
- SYRIA modern-day country

MAP 9.2c

The Spread of Buddhism to 1000 C.E.

- Buddhist heartland
- extent of Buddhism, ca.1000 C.E.
- area in which Buddhism was in decline by 1000 C.E.
- → Journey of Xuanzang, 629–645 C.E. (see p. 222)
- • major Buddhist center / monastery
- ■ Buddhist rock-carved temple
- ▲ sacred Buddhist mountain
- ▲ Shinto shrines
- — Silk Roads
- *Uighurs* people

The Kaaba. Promoters of new religions often had to reconsecrate pagan sites—it was easier to do that than to persuade worshippers to abandon them. Muhammad, for instance, made pilgrimage to the black rock housed in a building known as the Kaaba in Mecca compulsory for Muslims. As the picture shows, tens of thousands of pilgrims circle the site each year at the beginning of a series of annual rituals called the hajj. But the rock had already been a place of pagan pilgrimage in Arabia and a shrine of many gods for generations, perhaps centuries, before Muhammad's time.

routes of the Indian Ocean and the Sahara. Among them, the three religions seemed to have carved up the world known to Ibn Wahab, whom we encountered at the start of this chapter discussing religion with the Chinese emperor. The bases from which all three religions would expand further, especially in the sixteenth and seventeenth centuries (see Chapter 18), had been laid.

Their competitive advantages with religions they displaced were already evident. Pagan groves and temples became churches. Local deities reemerged as saints. Excavations at the shrine of the Irish saint, Gobnet, for instance, have yielded 130 anvils dedicated to the smith god, Goibhnin. In Scotland, the goddess Brigid, associated with childbirth, became St. Bride. In the Islamic world, old sacred sites blended into the new religious landscape. The holiest site of Islam, the black stone of the **Kaaba** in Mecca, where Muslims have to perform pilgrimage at least once in their lifetimes if they able, was a pagan shrine. Muslims still perform the same rites—kissing the stone, running the course of the stream that flows nearby—as their pagan predecessors did. Buddhists had no difficulty incorporating local gods into the vast Buddhist pantheon or sanctifying local shrines with relics of Buddhas.

This flexibility and adaptability made Christianity, Islam, and Buddhism suitable for projection around the world. This does not explain, of course, why other religions failed in this respect or never made the attempt. The blend, which we now call Hinduism, of local Indian religions with the universally applicable philosophy of the Vedas (see Chapter 3) spread throughout India and parts of southeast Asia, but no farther. Daoism, similarly, never reached beyond China. Nor, until migrants carried it to small colonies abroad, did Zoroastrianism penetrate beyond Iran, where it struggled to compete with Islam. Traditional paganism, Manichaeanism, and the many cults that came and went, leaving little trace in the record, withered in the face of Christian, Muslim, or Buddhist competition. Some religions, such as Bon in Tibet, Shinto in Japan, and, as far as we know, the religions of sub-Saharan Africa, had no universal aspirations and were designed only for their traditional followers. To judge from later artistic evidence, there was a good deal of exchange between the local and regional religions of Mesoamerica from the twelfth century to the sixteenth. We cannot say how much farther they might have spread had Christianity, arriving in the 1500s, not transformed the religious profile of the region. In the Americas, in sub-Saharan Africa, and in regions of which we know even less, such as Australia and the Pacific, the same reasons that inhibited the spread of other forms of culture also tended to limit the communicability of religions. There were no great, long-range avenues of communication, such as the Silk Roads and the monsoonal ocean. The kind of competition that Islam, Christianity, and Buddhism generated never took effect.

CHRONOLOGY

(All dates are C.E.)

Second century	Earliest Christian monastic communities (Egypt)
ca. 250	Zhu Shixing becomes first Chinese to be ordained as Buddhist priest
ca. 314	King Trdat of Armenia converts to Christianity
ca. 340	King Ezana of Ethiopia converts to Christianity
366	Founding of Dunhuang monastery, western China
395	Proclamation of Christianity as official religion of Roman Empire
ca. 520	Conversion of kings of Paekche and Silla to Buddhism
538	First image of Buddha arrives in Japan
Sixth century	Life of Benedict of Nursia
Seventh and eighth centuries	Rapid expansion of Islam; spread of Buddhism in Tibet
Ninth century	Seaborne Muslim pilgrims begin to arrive in Mecca
ca. 988	Vladimir of Kiev converts to Orthodox Christianity

Even as they changed the societies in which they triumphed, the new religions changed in their turn, compromising with vested interests, modifying their messages to suit mighty patrons, serving the needs of warriors and kings, even becoming organs of the state, instruments of government, means of training bureaucrats, and communicating with subjects. A further consequence of expansion was that different traditions within each of the religions lost patience or touch with each other. Christians in different parts of the world adopted different theologies. In Ethiopia, for instance, the church believed that Jesus was wholly divine, with no distinctly human person. The Nestorian Christians of the Silk Roads preached the opposite doctrine: that the human Jesus was wholly human, leaving his divine nature in heaven. Theological differences gradually drove Christians in Europe apart. After 792, most congregations in Western Europe modified the creed, the basic statement of Christian belief, to make the Holy Spirit "proceed" from "the Father and the Son" rather than "the Father" alone. Most churches in eastern Europe denounced the new wording as heresy. Different Islamic states subscribed variously to Shiism and Sunnism (see Chapter 8) and to different interpretations of Islamic law. In Buddhism divisions between followers of the Theravada and Mahayana traditions were sometimes just as bitter.

Although all these religions had started by appealing to people of modest or marginal social position, they "took off" by converting rulers and elites, who favored new religions—spiritual merits apart—because they saw advantages in doing so. The support of the church, for instance, was expensive for rulers and aristocrats. But it was worth it because it meant that God and his angels and saints became one's allies and friends. We can measure the value a typical royal convert got from the deal in the weight of gold and jewels in the votive crown that the seventh-century Spanish Visigothic king Reccesvinth hung in the sanctuary of his royal church. In return for such rich gifts, matched by comparable generosity in land, he got the prayers of the priests and monks, the services of a clerical bureaucracy, and the miraculous power of the relics of an army of martyrs. There was also a hidden advantage that no ruler could have banked on and that the next chapter must disclose. In the last three centuries of the first millennium, Islam, Buddhism, and, to a lesser extent, Christianity played vital and spectacular roles in new forms of environmental management.

PROBLEMS AND PARALLELS

1. What were the four chief ways in which world religions were spread? In which world religions did merchants play a leading role in spreading the faith?

2. What advantages did Buddhism, Christianity, and Islam enjoy over older religions?

3. How did rulers and elites use religion to consolidate and justify their power over societies?

4. Why is Japan a unique example of a world religion coexisting with a traditional native religion? Was such a working compromise possible in other areas of the world? Why or why not?

5. How did differing forms of Christianity arise on the margins of Christendom?

6. How did Christianity and Islam trickle down to the masses after the elites adopted these religions in Eurasia and Africa? How did average citizens benefit from adopting (or not adopting) these religions?

7. Why did monasticism play such a large role in the early history of Buddhism and Christianity? Why was monasticism less important in the Islamic world? What new roles did women acquire?

8. How did the triumph of Buddhism, Christianity, and Islam change the societies and cultures where they triumphed? How were they in turn changed and modified?

DOCUMENTS IN GLOBAL HISTORY

- Ibn Wahab: an Arab Merchant visits Tang China
- from *The Life of St. Nino*
- Xuanzang's descriptions of the caste system
- Ibn Fadlan's journey to Russia
- Eusebius of Caesarea, selections from *The Life of Constantine*

- Isidore of Seville's T-O map of the world
- The Rule of St. Benedict
- from *The Confession of St. Patrick*
- Rabia al-Adawiyya, "Brothers, My Peace Is in My Aloneness"

Please see the Primary Source DVD for additional sources related to this chapter.

READ ON

To understand the problems of what conversion means, A. D. Nock, *Conversion: The Old and the New in Religion from Alexander the Great to Augustine of Hippo* (1933) is an indispensable classic, and K. F. Morrison, *Understanding Conversion* (1992) is an up-to-date introduction.

On Buddhism H. Bechert and R. Gombrich, eds., *The World of Buddhism: Buddhist Monks and Nuns in Society and Culture* (1984) is a superb survey, much wider in scope than the title implies. Works that deal with the reception of Buddhism in particular cultures are E. Zürcher, *The Buddhist Conquest of China* (1959), which is a work of outstanding scholarship; K. Lal Hazra, *Royal Patronage of Buddhism in Ancient India* (1984); M. T. Kapstein, *The Tibetan Assimilation of Buddhism* (2000); and the collections of essays edited by L. R. Lancaster and C. S. Yu, *Introduction of Buddhism to Korea* (1989); *Assimilation of Buddhism in Korea* (1991); and (with K. Suh) *Buddhism in Koryo* (1996). The Cambridge History of Japan (1988) deals expertly with all aspects of Japanese history in the period, including the reception of Buddhism. The travels of Xuangzang and other Chinese

monks in search of Buddhist learning are covered in J. Mirsky, *The Great Chinese Travelers* (1964).

On Manichaeanism, P. Mirecki and J. BeDuhn, *Emerging from Darkness: Studies in the Recovery of Manichaean Sources* (1997) is a fascinating insight into the development of current scholarship. C. Mackerras, *The Uighur Empire* (1972) is a masterly survey.

On the spread of Islam it is helpful to consult G. S. P. Freeman-Grenville, *Historical Atlas of Islam* (2002). For the Indian Ocean, K. Chaudhuri, *Asia before Europe* (1990) is again to be recommended, with a word of caution about the demanding nature of this work.

For Africa, T. Insoll, *The Archaeology of Islam in sub-Saharan Africa* (2003) is of great importance. M. Hiskett, *The Course of Islam in Africa* (1994) is a useful introduction. On East Africa, J. Trimingham, *Islam in East Africa* (1964), and M. Horton and J. Middleton, *The Swahili* (2000) (which is a good general history of the coastlands) can be recommended. For West Africa, M. Hiskett, T*he Development of Islam in West Africa* (1984) and J. S. Trimingham, *A History* *of Islam in West Africa* (1962) are standard. For the Turks, an interesting source from the pre-Muslim period is G. Lewis, ed., *The Book of Dede Korkut* (1974). The important work I cite on Persia is R. W. Bulliet, *Conversion to Islam in the Medieval Period: An Essay in Quantitative History* (1979).

On Christianity, W. H. C. Frend, *The Rise of Christianity* (1984); R. MacMullen, *Christianizing the Roman Empire* (1984); and R. Fletcher, *The Barbarian Conversion: From Paganism to Christianity* (1997) are fundamental and between them take the story down to the late Middle Ages. Exemplary case studies can be found in H. R. Mayr-Harting, *The Coming of Christianity to Anglo-Saxon England* (1972), J. Muldoon, ed., *Varieties of Religious Conversion in the Middle Ages* (1997), and B. Sawyer et al., eds., *The Christianization of Scandinavia* (1987).

For works on Constantine, see Chapter 8.

For the rise of Christianity in Ethiopia, S. Munro-Hay, *Aksum* (1991) is vigorous and makes much use of the stela texts; D. W. Phillipson, *Ancient Ethiopia* (2002) is a superb survey based on archaeological evidence; G. W. B. Huntingford, *The Historical Geography of Ethiopia* (1989) is a basic and classic work.

For the Caucasus, N. Garsoian, *Church and Culture in Early Medieval Armenia* (1999), and *Armenia Between Byzantium and the Sasanians* (1985) are collections of significant essays. C. Toumanoff, *Studies in Christian Caucasian History* (1963), and D. Braund, *Georgia in Antiquity* (1994) are also useful and important.

On Vladimir, F. Butler, *Enlightener of the Rus* (2000) is an interesting work, tracing the subject's historical reputation. The work of S. Franklin is fundamental.

On the origins of monasticism, G. Gould, *The Desert Fathers on Monastic Community* (1993), and W. Harmless, *Desert Christians* (2004) are highly instructive; and M. Dunn, *The Emergence of Monasticism* (2000) is a good introduction. There are many editions of *The Rule of St. Benedict*.

On Sufism, F. Meier, *Essays on Islamic Piety and Mysticism* (1999) contains many interesting pieces, while A. D. Knysh, *Islamic Mysticism* (2000) surveys the whole history of the subject efficiently. For Buddhist monasticism, the already-cited work edited by Bechert and Gombrich is excellent.

The account of human sacrifice among the Rus is from S. H. Gross and O. P. Sherbowitz, eds., *The Russian Primary Chronicle: Laurentian Text* (1953), p. 111.

10 Remaking the World: Innovation and Renewal on Environmental Frontiers in the Late First Millennium

The small castle of Qusayr Amra dates from the reign of Caliph Walid I (ca. 705–715). It contains his spectacular bathhouse, lavishly decorated with paintings, including portraits of the monarchs he considered his rivals: the rulers of Byzantium, Ethiopia, Persia, and Visigothic Spain.

One of the oddest monuments of the early Islamic world is the bathhouse of a caliph's hunting lodge in the Jordanian desert. Here Muhammad's successor could relax unseen. He could also relax Islamic condemnations of art that depicted the human form, for Muhammad was supposed to have exempted bathhouses specifically from such bans. Mosaics smother the walls and ceilings. One wall was decorated with six portraits of failed enemies of Islam. Two of the images are too decayed to be recognizable. The others show a Visigothic king from Spain, Roman and Persian monarchs, and an Ethiopian emperor, depicted as the equal of the other great rulers of the world.

JORDAN

ETHIOPIA

• • • • •

In the eighth century, Ethiopia was not yet in the state of collapse that had overcome the Roman and Persian realms, but it was in trouble. Nomadic "barbarians" infiltrated from the north. No coinage was issued. Monumental building stopped. Squatters were taking over abandoned mansions in the capital. At the port of Adulis on the Red Sea, eighth-century ash lies thickly over ruined buildings, evidence that fire had wrecked the city. By the ninth century, central political control was hard or impossible to maintain. Later writers remembered shadowy, allegedly demonic female rulers, who seized power in the tenth century. "God has become angry with us," wrote a fugitive king. "We have become wanderers. ... The heavens no longer send rain and the earth no longer gives its fruits."

Environmental influences played a big part in Ethiopia's eclipse. Trees vanished from hills overexploited for wood and charcoal. Intensive farming exhausted the soil. Heavy rains aggravated erosion. Mudslides buried buildings. Below volcanic hills, once-rich earth turned to dust. To renew the state and resume expansion, Ethiopians had to find new resources, new frontiers, new techniques.

From around 700 to 1000, states all over the world responded to similar problems. New ways to manage the environment multiplied. They constitute something like a global story—or at least, a story that spans most of the world. Outcomes, however, continued to vary, and in some regions, such as the Islamic world, China, and Japan, the innovations of the period proved more durable than in others. What we might call the **axial zone** of the world expanded. The densely populated central belt of Eurasia, stretching from China to Europe and North Africa—the region that had seen so many experiments in civilization for so long—incorporated new frontiers within it. In the Americas, sub-Saharan Africa, and the Pacific, similar but smaller zones began to take shape but remained fragile.

FOCUS questions

- HOW DID geography influence the transmission of culture in sub-Saharan Africa and the Americas?
- WHAT WERE the environmental consequences of the Islamic conquests?
- HOW DID Japan, China, and the states of southeast Asia seek to stimulate economic growth?
- HOW DID Pacific Islanders succeed in colonizing the Pacific?
- WHERE DID Christendom expand in the eighth and ninth centuries?
- WHERE—if anywhere—did civilizations experience "dark ages" in this period?
- HOW WIDESPREAD during the history of this period was ecological experiment?

ISOLATION AND INITIATIVE: SUB-SAHARAN AFRICA AND THE AMERICAS

African Geography

Geography is often said to imprison sub-Saharan peoples. While great axes of communication cross-fertilize much of the Old World, the Sahara and the Indian Ocean separate most of Africa from those highways of cultural exchange. Except on the Mediterranean and along the coast north of the Mozambique Channel in East Africa, shores exposed to the wind make communication difficult by sea. Rivers are hard to navigate. Dense, malarial forest impedes communications. Some of the flows of culture, such as the spread of farming and of Bantu languages (see Chapter 5), took centuries longer than comparable transmissions in Eurasia.

THE EMERGENCE OF GHANA AND GAO Still, it is surprising that there has never been much exchange along the obvious axis of transcontinental communication in Africa: the Sahel, the belt of grassland that links East Africa, where Ethiopian civilization took shape, to another precocious region in the Niger valley in West Africa. Here, urban life, commerce, and industry show up in the archaeological record of the third century B.C.E. onward. By the first century C.E., at Jenne-Jeno, where floods fed the soil, farmers and ironworkers grew millet and rice. The population was reputedly so dense that royal proclamations could be "called out from the top of the city's walls and transmitted by criers from one village to the next."

The region was a natural crossroads, where traders could deal in slaves, desert salt, local copper, and gold from the mines of Senegambia and the middle Volta River. Toward 1000, two states impressed Arab visitors: Ghana and Gao (gow). Ghana was in the territory of the Soninke (son-in-KAY) people, west of the middle Niger River. Its capital at Kumbi-Saleh had houses of stone and wood, and a royal compound, where a sacred snake with a sensitive snout supposedly sniffed out royal quality from among the contenders for the throne. Enriched by taxes on trade, the monarchs of Ghana and Gao attracted the reverence paid to sacred beings. Subjects prostrated themselves and covered their heads with dust. When the king of Gao ate, all business in the town was suspended, until shouts announced he had finished.

Sacred kingship spread along the Sahel. The Zaghawa of the Chad region in the late ninth century had "no towns," according to an Arab traveler's report, but "they worshipped their king as if he were Allah." In Yoruba (YOU-roo-bah) territory on the lower Niger River, evidence of divine kingship appears from the tenth century in clay portraits of men and women with elaborate headgear and hairstyles. Had contacts developed across the Sahel between West African realms and Ethiopia, rather in the way that the steppeland linked Europe to China, African history might have, in the long run, more closely resembled that of Eurasia. But the West African kingdoms remained focused on relations north across the Sahara, while Ethiopia's avenues of approach to the rest of the world led every direction but westward: north to the Nile, east to the Indian Ocean, south along the Rift valley (see Map 10.1).

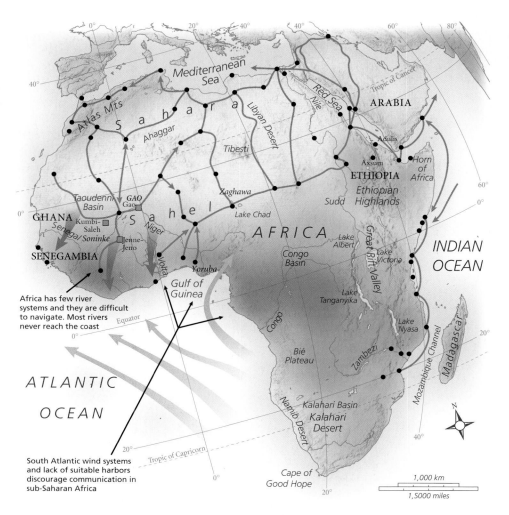

MAP 10.1

African Geography

— trade route
▪ city described on pages 301–302
● other city/town/village
GAO state
Yoruba people
⟹ South Atlantic trade winds
⟹ African wind systems

Africa has few river systems and they are difficult to navigate. Most rivers never reach the coast

South Atlantic wind systems and lack of suitable harbors discourage communication in sub-Saharan Africa

1,000 km
1,5000 miles

American Geography

It is tempting to use similar arguments about the geography of the Americas to explain why the Old World developed differently from the New. The shape of the American hemisphere slowed diffusion of new culture and new crops, which had to travel across climate zones through the narrow, central continental funnel. Most of the great rivers flow east and west from the mountain spines that run up and down North and South America, and only the Mississippi River traverses much distance from north to south.

Still, isolation did not prevent civilizations from developing in the Andean region, in parallel with those of Mexico and Central America, taking advantage of the different ecosystems that a world of slopes and valleys, microclimates, and diverse plants and animals provided. The highlands of North America, on the other hand, housed nothing comparable. This may have been, in part, because the Andes and the Sierra Madre in Central America and Mexico are better placed than the mountains of the north: close to rain forests, seas, and swamps for maximum biological diversity.

MOCHE AND NAZCA Similarly, though North and South America both have arid deserts, the effort to civilize them encountered earlier success in the south (see Map 10.2). One of the strangest deserts in the world is in northern Peru.

Gulf of Mexico

Tropic of Cancer

Sierra Madre

MEXICO

Mesoamerica

see inset map

GUATEMALA

HONDURAS

CENTRAL AMERICA

Caribbean Sea

PACIFIC OCEAN

N

Andes

Amazon

Marajó Island

SOUTH AMERICA

BRAZIL

Ayacucho Valley

Lake Titicaca

BOLIVIA

Tropic of Capricorn

Tropic of Capricorn

ATLANTIC OCEAN

CHILE

Andes

1,000 km

1,000 miles

Inset (Mesoamerica):

Tula

Plateau

Yucatán Peninsula

Palenque

Tikal

Lowlands

Copán

Highlands

Inset (Andes):

Moche

Huari

Nazca

Tiahuanaco

Legend:

MAP 10.2

Mesoamerica and the Andes, 300 C.E. to 1000 C.E.

Maya cultural area
Moche cultural area
Tiahuanaco cultural area
Nazca cultural area
Huari cultural area
maize
beans
squash
cacao
turkeys
guinea pigs
peanuts
peppers
potatoes
irrigated river valleys
underground aqueduct
HONDURAS modern-day country

Except when El Niño drenches the land, almost no rain falls. The region is cool, although dank with ocean fog. Little grows naturally, but modest rivers create an opportunity to irrigate. The sea is at hand, with rich fishing grounds, and guano provides fertilizer to turn desert dust into cultivable soil. From the third century to the eighth, the civilization known as Moche (MOH-cheh) made this desert rich with corn, squash, peppers, potatoes, and peanuts.

Under platforms, built as stages for royal rituals, their rulers' graves lie: divine impersonators in golden masks, with earspools decorated with objects of the hunt, scepters and bells with scenes of human sacrifice, necklets with models of shrunken heads in gold or copper, and portraits of a divine sacrificer wielding his bone knife. At San José de Moro, a woman was buried with limbs encased in plates of precious metals. In 2006, archaeologists in southern Peru found another female Moche mummy with gold jewelry and weapons. Farther south, in the same period, in the even more inhospitable desert of northern Chile, the people known as the Nazca built underground aqueducts to protect irrigation water from the sun. Above ground, they created some of the most ambitious works of art in the world: stunning representations of nature—a hurtling hummingbird, a cormorant spread for flight, sinuous fish—and bold abstract lines, triangles, and spirals, scratched in the rock. Some of the images are 1,000 feet wide, too vast to be visible except from a height the artists could not reach, capable of permanently arousing the imagination.

Despite these achievements, the desert remained a fragile environment for ambitious ways of life. The Moche survived repeated droughts, which archaeologists have inferred from cores sampled from nearby mountain glaciers. El Niño events periodically drove away the fish and washed away the irrigation works. These were occurrences frequent enough for the locals to learn to live with. After the mid–eighth century, however, no mounds were built, no great artworks made, and the irrigated land dwindled. No one knows why, though most scholars speculate that the people overexploited their environment, or an unusually protracted drought may have defeated them.

ANDEAN DEVELOPMENTS The center of gravity of large-scale innovation shifted to the high Andes, though with little long-term gain in security. The city of Huari, 9,000 feet up in the Ayacucho valley in Peru, lasted as a metropolis only from the seventh century to the ninth. It had garrison buildings, dormitories for the elite, and communal kitchens, with a population of at least 20,000 clustered around it. It also seems to have had satellite towns dotted about the area.

At over 12,000 feet above sea level, potatoes fed the city of Tiahuanaco (tee-ah-wahn-AH-koh) in Bolivia because its altitude was hostile to growing grains. The tillers built stone platforms topped with clay and silt. They drew water from Lake Titicaca through channels to irrigate their mounds and protect them from violent changes of air temperature. Beds in this form stretched more than nine miles from the lakeside and could produce up to 30,000 tons of potatoes a year. By about 1000, building had ceased, and the site was becoming abandoned—again for unknown reasons, but perhaps because of overexploitation of the soil, or a shift in the balance of power. Tiahuanaco, as it gradually subsided into ruins, became a source of inspiration for all subsequent efforts to cultivate and build in the Andes.

THE MAYA No case has excited more curiosity than that of the Maya. They inhabited—their descendants still inhabit—three contrasting environments: the abrupt, volcanic highlands of Guatemala, where microclimates create diverse eco-niches at different altitudes; the dry, hilly, limestone plateau of

The Dresden codex. The Maya almanac known as the Dresden Codex contains a wealth of data on agriculture, divination, and religion. But its most remarkable contents, perhaps, are the detailed astronomical observations and predictions, especially the table recording the cycle of Venus, one page of which is shown here. The red bars and dots at bottom right are numbers, adding up to 584—the average number of days between the dates on which Venus rises with the sun. Such dates were favorable for war and sometimes foretold drought and death. The gods depicted represent, from top to bottom, the Morning Star, Venus as bringer of war, and Venus demanding sacrifice.

Yucatán (yoo-kah-THAN), the peninsula on Mexico's Caribbean coast, where agriculture depends on irrigation from pools and wells; and tropical lowlands in Central America, with dense forests of heavy seasonal rain. There is bound to be cultural diversity across such varied environments, and among these regions, the chronology of Maya civilization varied considerably. The lowlands experienced a Classic Age of monumental building and art from about the third to about the tenth centuries, whereas the plateau "peaked" later in these respects. But Maya civilization has some surprisingly uniform features.

The Maya demonstrated, in spectacular ways, common threads of Native American civilizations seen from the Olmecs onward (see Chapter 4). Maya rulers had three areas of responsibility: war, communication with the gods and the dead, and building and embellishing monumental ceremonial centers. Royal portraits, often engraved on stone and displayed in the grand plazas where their subjects assembled, show rulers in roles similar to those of professional shamans, wearing divine disguises, or engaged in rituals of bloodletting designed to induce visions. We can still confront the images of many kings. At Palenque (pa-LEHN-keh), in the rain forest of southern Mexico, the seventh-century King Pacal (pa-KAL) is depicted on his tomb—dead, but refertilizing the world. A sacred ceiba tree springs from his loins. In Copán (koh-PAN) in Honduras, the kings of the Macaw dynasty from the fifth century to the ninth, are shown communing together, as if at a celestial conference. At Tikal, when the sun is in the west and gilds the huge temple where he was buried, you can still pick out the vast outline of the fading image of King Jasaw Chan Kaui'il (ha-SA-oo chan kah-wee-EEL), molded onto the temple facade.

Politically, the Maya world was divided among city-states. They were perhaps too equally matched for imperialism to succeed. They were competitive in trade and war, which, for most of them, seem to have been almost constant. Boasts of captives sacrificed are common in the texts. Mayan art often depicts scenes of sacrifice—including torturing to death and dismemberment while the victim was still alive.

Everything the Maya thought important—everything on Earth that they thought worth recording—happened in and around the ceremonial centers. The countryside was there to support and sustain those centers. Monumental buildings housed elites and displayed rites to appease the gods and promote civic solidarity. Elite dwellings were imposing and built of stone, but the facades of some of them are adorned with carvings of humble dwellings, such as the Maya peasantry still inhabit today, built of reeds and thatch with a single stone lintel. The temples, which often doubled as tombs, always evoked the mounds on which, in the lowlands, farming was practiced: structures with vast, terracelike flights of steps, surmounted by platforms on which rituals were enacted. Typically, especially in the highlands and lowlands, false facades topped them, jutting into the sky, decorated with molded reliefs, displaying the symbols of the city, the portraits of the kings, the records of war, and the rewards of wealth. In their time, for travelers, traders, or would-be aggressors, they carried an unmistakable message of propaganda: an invitation to commerce, a deterrent against attack.

Thousands of peasants' flimsy dwellings surrounded these centers in a landscape adapted for intensive agriculture. Small fields called *milpas* were carved into highland terraces or dredged, in the lowlands, between canals that were used for

The date of the ritual, shown here, was October 26, 709.

The carvings announce that the king and queen are shedding their blood.

ROYAL BLOODLETTING

The reign of Itzamnaaj B'alam ("Shield Jaguar") II of Yaxchilán (681–742), in what is today Mexico, produced some of the finest stone reliefs in which Maya rulers commemorated their performance of important rituals. The most common ritual was royal bloodletting, which was intended to provoke visions. During these bloodlettings, kings communicated with ancestors or gods.

The king wears a sacrificed captive's skull on his headdress and an emblem of the sun on his breast.

The queen draws a spiked thong through her tongue to spill her blood. A king would draw blood from his penis. Bark paper in the bowl below the monarchs absorbed the blood, which was then burned. The monarchs would inhale the smoke to induce a trance.

What does this stone relief tell us about Mayan kingship?

irrigation or fish farming. The fields were sown with the three Native American staples: maize, beans, and squash, supplemented with other foods according to region or locality. Or they were devoted to cash crops, like cacao, which was in high demand for the luxury beverage that accompanied rituals and feasts.

The Maya possessed a singular feature—it is tempting to say, a secret ingredient—because their writing system, the most expressive and complete known in the Native American world before the arrival of Europeans, did not spread to other culture areas. Much more common in lowland regions than in the plateau and highlands, these writings were carved in stone. Virtually all the writing falls into two categories: first, records of astronomical observations and priestly timekeeping —a vital area of interest in Maya efforts to communicate with the gods and appease nature; second, dynastic records, genealogies of kings, records of their conquests, sacrifices, and acts of communion with their ancestors.

Of course, all the surviving written evidence is propaganda, produced under the patronage of states. Claims and counterclaims of conquests and captures are evidence not of what the kings actually did but what they thought important. The central drama of kingship—the ritual the inscriptions most often commemorate—was the spilling of royal blood. A king would use a bone needle or spike to draw blood from his penis or scatter it from his hand. A queen might perform the ceremony by dragging a knotted thong, studded with sharp bones or spines, through a perforation in her tongue. Blotted onto bark, the blood would burn with hallucinatory drugs in an open fire. Enraptured by the fumes and by blood-loss, the monarch would succumb to a vision, characteristically depicted as a serpent rising from the smoke. The serpent was the mouthpiece of the ancestors. Their message usually justified war.

Maya civilization largely abandoned the lowlands in the ninth and tenth centuries. New building in ceremonial centers ended. Inscriptions ceased. The royal cult disappeared. Evidence vanished of rich elites and professions specialized in learning and the arts. Squatters occupied the ruins of decaying ceremonial centers. Traditional scholarship has dramatized and mystified these events as the collapse of classic Maya civilization—an echo of the decline and fall of the Eurasian civilizations of the axial age. It seems more helpful to see what happened as the displacement of the centers of the Maya world from the lowlands to the plateau. Still, it is mysterious. None of the explanations scholars suggest fit the chronology or the evidence. War is unlikely to have put an end to the lowland tradition. The Maya practiced wars so constantly that warfare must have served a useful purpose in their society. Spells of severe and prolonged drought certainly overlapped with the period of decline but do not seem to have matched it. Political revolutions—rebellions of the masses or struggles within the elite—might have overthrown the regimes. But even if there were direct evidence of such upheavals, we would still need to explain why they occurred at roughly the same time in so many states.

That elite activities ended only in one eco-zone suggests that an environmental explanation should help us understand what happened. The lowlands were always hostile to intensive agriculture and monumental building. In some ways, it is more surprising that such practices should have happened at all, and attained such impressive achievements, than that they should ultimately have failed. To sustain hundreds of cities and what were evidently dense populations, the Maya probably had to exploit their environment close to the limit of its possibilities.

Civilizations of the Americas, ca. 200–1100

ca. 200–900	Flourishing of Moche and Nazca civilizations
ca. 200–1100	Maya Classic Age (lowlands)
1000	Andean city of Tiahuanaco abandoned
ca. 1106–1200	Tula abandoned

TULA For a while, the influence and, in some degree, the power of the central Mexican empire of Teotihuacán stretched into the Maya world. Yet, as we saw in Chapter 8, Teotihuacán itself withered in the eighth and ninth centuries. This vast metropolis—once the center of a population that could probably be numbered in six figures—was never reoccupied, but became something like what we today would call a heritage site: revered and remembered by peoples who imitated its art and recalled its grandeur in their poetry. A new metropolis arose, well to the northwest, at Tula, the "garden of the gods," where blood sacrifices irrigated groves of stone pillars and ceremonial enclosures. The region already had a history of unstable settlement and, by comparison with most earlier Maya cities or with Teotihuacán, Tula did not last long. Its site was abandoned in the twelfth century, but the ruins continued to inspire experiments in urbanization.

The Maize Frontiers

We can sum up all these New World histories of the late first millennium as efforts to open up frontiers of exploitation for intensive agriculture, state formation, and city-building—activities formerly confined to narrowly limited areas and vulnerable to periodic extinction. Hunter–gatherers, too, could engage with their environment in more productive ways. On the northwest coast of North America, houses got bigger as fishhooks got more plentiful and became more specialized. Along the northern edge of America, whale hunters were working their way along the Arctic coast, spreading new hunting and fishing techniques as they went, reaching Greenland by about 1000.

In other parts of the Americas, new crops and new technologies extended farmers' frontiers, sometimes with transforming effects. Between the Missouri and Ohio River valleys, for instance, a large trading network flourished among peoples of similar material culture from about 200 to about 400. They buried their dead with copper earrings and breastplates, clay figures and smoking pipes, and ornaments carved from flat sheets of copper ore in the shape of leaves and claws. They built tombs into mounds of elaborate design: one in Ohio is in the shape of a long, coiling serpent—identifiable from a practically unattainable height, like the artworks of the Nazca in Chile. Sometime after 500, these practices ended; as leadership of society changed, maize cultivation spread through the region, and population grew.

This was the period of the great extension of maize cultivation into regions of North America formerly inhabited almost exclusively by hunter–gatherers, displacing former power groups, coaxing chiefdoms into existence and existing chiefdoms toward statehood. Farmers brought maize and beans into the central plains and, in some places from the Dakotas to the Red River in Canada, built burial mounds and earthworks similar to those found earlier along the Ohio and Missouri Rivers. In some respects, this process looks like another case of a culture not extinguished, but changed and displaced from its former heartland. Maize farming reached the Great Basin of the North American plains, at sites where pottery and rock art were also made for the first time in this period. Beginning after 700, in the North American southwest, where maize had been long established (see Chapter 5), large dwellings of adobe or stone displaced the semiunderground houses in which people formerly sheltered. Villages got larger, building toward the urban network that emerged around 1000 and that is

Bird claw. Cut from a sheet of mica, this sublime representation of the claw of a hawk or eagle was buried in a chief's grave in what is now Ross County, Ohio, in about 400 C.E. Hands and birds of prey were the symbols most often placed in the graves of the region's chieftains in this period.

○ MAKING CONNECTIONS ○

EXPANDING STATES OF THE AMERICAS, 200–900

REGION / CULTURE →	ENVIRONMENT →	POLITICAL ORGANIZATION →	ACHIEVEMENTS
South America Moche and Nazca	Desert; adjacent to Pacific Ocean; cool weather; little precipitation; abundant fish; small rivers	Communities governed by elites	Highly developed ceramics, gold/silver work; pottery; elaborate irrigation systems, some underground
Andean highlands (Huari)	Mountainous; glacier-fed streams and lakes; cultivable soil	Empire governing highlands and coast after decline of Moche; administrative centers; satellite towns	Intensive mound agriculture (potatoes); religious centers; road networks
Mesoamerica Maya	Contrasting environments: volcanic highlands of Guatemala; limestone plateau of Yucatán; tropical lowlands	City-states with rulers responsible for war, communication with gods; numerous ceremonial sites	Large-scale cities with monumental architecture; writing system and literature; long-distance trade networks; intensive agriculture, industry fueling population growth
Tula	Highlands with access to rivers, trade routes	City-states with ceremonial enclosures; use of blood sacrifice	Successor to Teotihuacán, largest city-state in Mesoamerica; monumental architecture; intensive irrigation
North America	Wide range of environments from mountains, to forests, deserts, open plains	Primarily chiefdoms, with larger-scale communities in Mississippi, Missouri, Ohio River valleys	As maize agriculture spreads, agricultural populations increase, displacing hunter–gatherer groups; large-scale mounds, tombs mark large population centers

a subject for the next chapter. Meanwhile, in the southeast, the arrival of maize and, by around the year 1000, beans fed the ancestors of the large-scale builders of the early part of the next millennium.

On Marajó Island, in the mouth of the Amazon in Brazil, although there is no evidence of new crops or techniques, people were practicing traditional agriculture with enhanced efficiency in an expanded area. Clusters of villages got denser after the middle of the first millennium, with mounds raised for ceremonies and agriculture. Here, the bones of the elite, boiled of their flesh, were buried in pots with clay representations of female genitals and gifts of beads, axes, and other valuables dependent on rank. Richly decorated burial urns grant glimpses of the creatures of their myths: turtles, scorpions, serpents, and almond-eyed humans.

THE ISLAMIC WORLD AND THE ENVIRONMENT

So cultures widely scattered around the New World showed how basic tool kits or limited new crops could have profound effects. This feature of the period was paralleled in the Old World—especially in the Islamic world. Though Islamic conquests slowed in the eighth century, an even more significant kind of expansion followed it: ecological expansion, as cultivators developed new crops and introduced them to new environments (see Map 10.3). For the desert pastoralists who bore Islam abroad, every frontier was a revelation. When, for example, the follow-

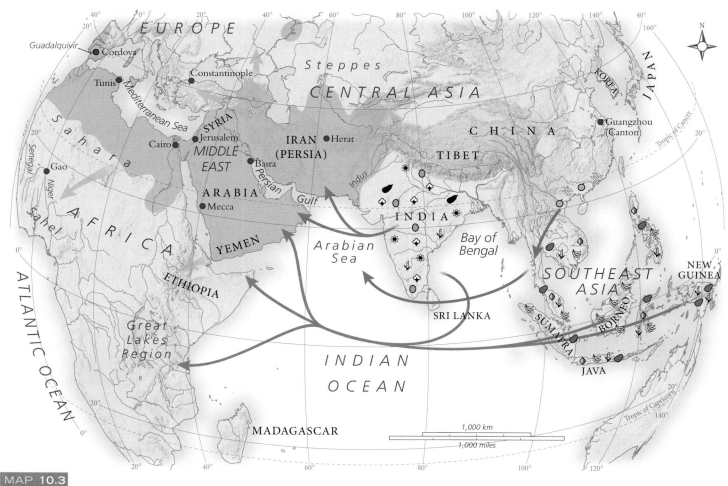

MAP 10.3

Transmission of New Crops to the Islamic World, ca. 1000

	Islamic world, ca. 1000		eggplant		sugarcane
	spread of crops from India		safflower		bananas
	spread of crops from South and southeast Asia		mung bean		taro
	spread of crops from China (by way of southeast Asia/Indian Ocean		cotton		orange
	Transmission of crops beyond Islamic frontier		lemon/lime		rice

ers of Muhammad captured Basra on the Persian Gulf in what is today Iraq in 637, an eyewitness reported how they found two food baskets that the retreating Persians had abandoned. They ate the basket of dates but assumed the other contained poison, until a horse ate its contents without ill effects. "And their commander said, Pronounce the name of Allah over it and eat. And they ate of it and they found it a most tasty food." It was the Arabs' first taste of rice.

The outreach of Islam was a process of discovery and renaissance in which a great array of new foods was gathered, adapted, and transplanted. The Islamic world extended over the Mediterranean, and touched Sahel, savanna, and tropical forests in sub-Saharan Africa, as well as monsoon lands in Yemen and northwest India, and regions of severe continental climate in Central Asia. The result was an unparalleled opportunity to exchange useful plants and animals among diverse environments.

Rulers encouraged new introductions, employing agronomists to manage their gardens, enhance their collections of medicinal plants, supply their tables, and improve their estates. For example, between 775 and 785, Yahya ibn Khalid led a mission on the caliph's behalf to India to study medicinal drugs. Abd al-Rahman, ruler of Muslim Spain in the mid–eighth century, sent plant collectors to Syria. By the tenth century, Cordova his capital, had, in effect, a special garden to grow exotic plants with fields for cuttings and seeds from abroad.

Plants from the tropics made a new summer growing season possible in the Middle East. Sugarcane, for instance, originated in south or southeast Asia. From India, "a reed that produced honey without bees" had reached Persia. The Arabs extended its cultivation to the Mediterranean. Eggplant, too, was unknown in the Mediterranean or Middle East before this period. The tenth-century geographer, Ibn Hawqal, tells of a landowner in northern Iraq who doubled his revenues by planting cotton and rice. The most important development to improve mass nutrition was of hard durum wheat in the Middle East. Some crops were transmitted onward, beyond the frontiers of the Muslim world. West Africa got cotton, taro, bananas, plantains, sour oranges, and limes in this period, probably across the Sahara. Christian Europe, by contrast, was slow to receive the benefits of Muslim agronomy. Spinach and hard wheat were not cultivated there until the thirteenth century, rice not until the fifteenth.

The new crops required watering during summer, stimulating irrigation by underground tunnels and wells, which led, in turn, to the adoption for agriculture of marginal land. Forest clearance increased. The use of fertilizer multiplied crop yields. Fertile land left uncultivated seems to have been rare in the Muslim world.

Islamic law favored farmers. Landowners could use and dispose of their land as they liked. The enforcement of a free market in land meant that farms tended to fall into the hands of owners who used them most productively. Tenants acquired farms, as conquest broke up big holdings that had stagnated under the previous regimes. Tax rates in regions under the rule of the caliphs in Baghdad (bag-DAD) were low after reforms in the late eighth century—commonly a tenth of output, with summer crops often being exempted. Villages thrived. There were 12,000 villages along the Guadalquivir (gwahd-ahl-kee-BEER) River in Muslim Spain by the tenth century. Forty-eight thousand square miles were subject to land tax in seventh-century Sawad (sah-WAD) in Syria—virtually the entire cultivable area.

Watermill. Increased agricultural output caused demand for more and bigger mills to grind grain. Most have not survived, but a fine example of medieval watermill technology, pictured here, is on the Orontes River at Hama, Syria. Waterwheels on this scale also hoisted water from riverbeds to aqueducts and irrigation channels.

FRONTIER GROWTH IN JAPAN

The vast extent of the Islamic world made this rich environmental history possible. But on a smaller scale, a similar program was possible even in relatively small and isolated Japan. Here, bureaucrats carefully totted up the hostility of the natural world. Between 806 and 1073, official records list 653 earthquakes, 134 fires, 89 cases of damage to crops, 91 epidemics, 356 supernatural warnings (including volcanic eruptions), and 367 appearances by ghosts. They recorded only 185 favorable events in the same period. In the *Nihongi* of the early eighth century, one of the earliest native Japanese chronicles, the rise of the imperial dynasty is linked with the overthrow of Susa-no-o, a god who "brought many people to an untimely end" by "making green mountains wither" and wrecking rice fields. Japanese rulers took seriously their responsibility to regulate their subjects' relations with the natural world. Unlike their counterparts in most other cultures, they did not limit themselves to acts and sacrifices intended to appease the forces of nature. From the early eighth century, they had ambitious environmental policies.

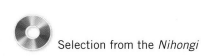

Selection from the *Nihongi*

Some growth in the yield of agriculture would have happened even without state guidance. Rice yields improved thanks to new, labor-intensive techniques in which whole communities cooperated: growing seedlings in nurseries and transplanting them to the fields. Heavy plows arrived from Korea in the fifth century. It is doubtful, however, whether they made much impact until the ninth or tenth century because Japan had little iron to make plows, and most cultivation was on wetlands. Meanwhile, barley gradually replaced millet as the country's second most important crop after rice, with some benefits for nutrition. Population was growing. Census returns show—by global standards—exceptionally large households of an average of ten persons each. Family customs helped. Young mothers commonly spent the first 5 to 15 years of married life in their parents' home, where their husbands visited them. This spread the burden of child care.

The government drive to boost food production was under way by 711, when a decree authorized aristocrats to apply to provincial governors for permission to cultivate virgin land at their own expense. The aim, according to a proclamation of 722, was to add 2.5 million acres to the area devoted to rice production. In the following year, farmers became eligible to inherit newly cultivated fields for three generations if they irrigated those fields from new ditches or ponds. In 743, farmers acquired absolute ownership of such lands.

As well as a state-sponsored, aristocratic enterprise, the conquest of new environments was a preserve of freelance holy men. The most effective of them was the Buddhist monk Gyoki. Traditionalists accused him of embezzling alms, impiously burning the bodies of the dead, and aggressively pursuing converts. But everyone approved of the way he organized his followers to perform public works—building bridges and roads, digging ponds and embankments. The state contracted Gyoki's workers to undertake official projects.

Frontier expansion at the expense of the "barbarians" of Japan's northeast Honshu island increased available land (see Map 10.4). The native Emishi (ah-MEE-shee) were described in terms that seem almost universal among imperial peoples who want to conquer, dispossess, or exterminate others. They were "fierce and wild," dangerous, lacking a recognizable political or legal system. Without chiefs, they "all rob each other. . . . In winter they lodge in holes, in summer they dwell in nests." By 796, the state had settled 9,000 colonists on Honshu to cultivate conquered lands.

By the early ninth century, the state was growing more confident about its ability to manage the environment and keep disaster at bay. After performing a successful rainmaking rite, the hermit Kukai began his song of self-praise with a conventional reflection. Nature, he said, responded to human decadence. "And thus," he continued, "even though it is time for rain to fall, the four horizons are blazing with heat." In such circumstances, the emperor intervenes. He fasts, and orders appropriate rites in all temples. "As the venerable monks chant the sacred scriptures . . . waterfalls gush forth from high peaks and soak wild animals, while rain fills the fields enough to drown water buffaloes. . . . Peasants! Do not lament any more. . . . See the storehouses, where grain piles up like islands, like mountains."

Indian land grants, 753 C.E.

CHINA AND SOUTHEAST ASIA

In Japan, as in the Islamic world, the human assault on the natural frontier had growing state power to back it. But in the same period, similar developments occurred even in politically unstable conditions in China and India. After the collapse of the Gupta empire (see Chapter 9), kingdoms in south India and the Deccan boosted their revenues, reach, and power by granting wasteland to priests, monks, and warriors to promote agriculture. In land grants recorded in forest areas acquired by conquest in the sixth century, monks and holy men are the biggest beneficiaries. This should not be seen merely—or perhaps at all—as evidence of kings' religious priorities but of monasteries' ability to transform the environment.

An inscription on copper, dated 753, shows what happened when a priest received a royal land grant. "We the inhabitants went to the boundaries which the headman of the district pointed out, circumambulated the village . . ., and planted milk-bushes and placed stones around it. . . . The donee shall enjoy the wet land and the dry land included within these four boundaries, wherever the iguana runs and the tortoise crawls, and shall be permitted to dig river channels and inundation channels." The king would receive taxes on these facilities. The inscription also reveals the full range of collective activities that community contributions supported. The settlers made and operated oil presses and looms. They dug wells. They paid taxes to support the king, the district administration, and the priestly caste out of the yield of crops, including water lilies, "the share of the potter," the price of butter and cloth. To the royal court they sent huntsmen, messengers, dancing girls, servants, fodder, cotton, molasses, "the best cow and the best bull," and "the fourth part of the trunks of old trees." Irrigation and double cropping appear in many Indian inscriptions of the following two centuries. Marginal land was coming under the plow.

In China, although the emperors of the early seventh century were unable to sustain a lasting dynasty, they did build a canal system that crisscrossed the country, stimulating the grain trade and improving irrigation. In 624, in Shaanxi province, imperial waterworks irrigated more than 80,000 acres. Meanwhile, large-scale land reclamation proceeded by drainage, as population growth and improving food supply stimulated each other. The policy of the Tang dynasty (see Chapter 8) was usually to break up large landholdings and distribute them among taxpayers. A major land reform of 737 divided great estates among their workers. This encouraged cultivation because peasants farmed their holdings more intensively than large landowners did. It was part of an ideology of imperial benevolence that also established price-regulating granaries where food stocks accumulated at government expense when prices were low for redistribution at a discount when prices were high. The resulting stocks helped cushion disaster in the plague-ravaged, famine-fraught 730s through 740s. Improved rice strains, adapted from varieties of rice that Tang armies brought back from campaigns in Vietnam, helped.

Imperial policy also stimulated the southward shift of settlement into regions, far from the threat of steppeland invasion, where rice grew, with beneficial effects on nutrition and therefore on levels of population. In 730, vagrant families were ordered to agricultural colonies under military discipline. Such proclamations often failed to produce results, but some colonies did take shape under this program, cultivating rice on the Huai River in 734. Although Confucians tended to despise Buddhism and Daoism as superstitious, monasteries were generally encouraged because they could kick start development in underexploited areas. By the mid–eighth century, a third of China's people lived in the Huai and Yangtze River valleys and, by the eleventh century, over half did. As colonization proceeded,

Chinese villages replaced aboriginal populations, which were exterminated, assimilated, or driven into marginal areas. Population figures—statistics untrustworthy anywhere at the time except in China—suggest Tang environmental policies paid off. China had about 50 million people after An Lushan's rebellion in the 750s (see Chapter 8). Its population had grown to 60 million by the year 1000.

The extension of the frontier of settlement and of rice cultivation in southern China was part of a bigger phenomenon, extending over the moist, hot, dense forests of mainland southeast Asia (see Map 10.4). In the sixth century, Chinese geographers located a state they called Chen-la in the interior of what is now Cambodia. This was the first sign we get of an important change under way in the region. Alongside the maritime states, founded on trade that lined the routes from China to India, agrarian kingdoms were growing up, based on rice production.

For centuries small chiefdoms and aspiring states had dotted the lower Mekong River valley, but in the eighth century, the people of the region, the Khmer (k-MER), began to coalesce into a single kingdom, centered at the new city of Angkor (AHNG-kor), on the north shore on the Tonle Sap—a natural reservoir of monsoonal rains. This region had no mines, no great commercial fleets, and no great industries. The wealth of the Khmer derived from a peculiar feature of the Mekong. Swollen by the monsoon, the river becomes, in effect, too heavily charged to empty into the sea through its own delta. The water begins to flow backward, flooding the plain of the Tonle Sap. The soil there is so rich that, provided the waters are well managed and channeled into reservoirs, it yields three rice crops a year. In 802, Angkor became a capital with explicitly imperial pretensions, when King Jayavarman II proclaimed himself monarch of the universe, and priests in his employ performed a ceremony nullifying all former oaths of loyalty.

Similar experiments occurred all over southeast Asia. The growth of the Viet and Cham kingdoms—the other big states that took shape in Indochina in the period—owed something to the traditional wealth of the region in ivory, rhinoceros horn, and aromatic woods, and much to the bureaucracy that arrived with Buddhism. But it was based mainly on taxes from lumber and food, as new fields replaced forests. By the year 1000, a comparable transformation was taking shape in the northwest corner of the region. Here, in the Irawaddy valley on the borders between India and Bangladesh, dry rice cultivation began to transform a near-desert. Meanwhile, offshore, maritime state building shifted toward the Indonesian islands.

Here, in the seventh century, the realm of Srivijaya (sree-vee-JEYE-ah), on the Sumatran coast, impressed the first Chinese sources to notice it. When the pilgrim I-ching (yee-jing) stopped there in 671, the capital had a community of 1,000 Buddhist monks. The court employed Hindu and Buddhist scholars. But the maharajah (mah-ha-RAH-jah), as the sources called the king of Srivijaya, was said to use magic to control the sea, with enchanted crocodiles to guard the mouth of his river.

Srivijaya's economy relied on harbor tolls and the profits of piracy. A river-linked domain behind it supplied it with soldiers and rice, because even trading states needed their own food supplies. Srivijaya had big commercial resources in the form of spices and aromatic woods, but the inhabitants still worked to expand rice production. According to a legend of the foundation of Palembang, the fathers of the city chose its site by weighing the waters of Sumatra's various rivers for silt and finding that those of the Musi would be best for irrigating rice lands. Palembang's earliest inscription, dated 685,

Population of China, 730–1000

730	Vagrant families ordered to resettle in agricultural colonies
734	Rice cultivation on the Huai River
750	China's population is 50 million
Mid–eighth century	One-third of China's population lives in the Huai and Yangtze valleys
1000	China's population is 60 million
Eleventh century	Half of China's population lives in the Huai and Yangtze valleys

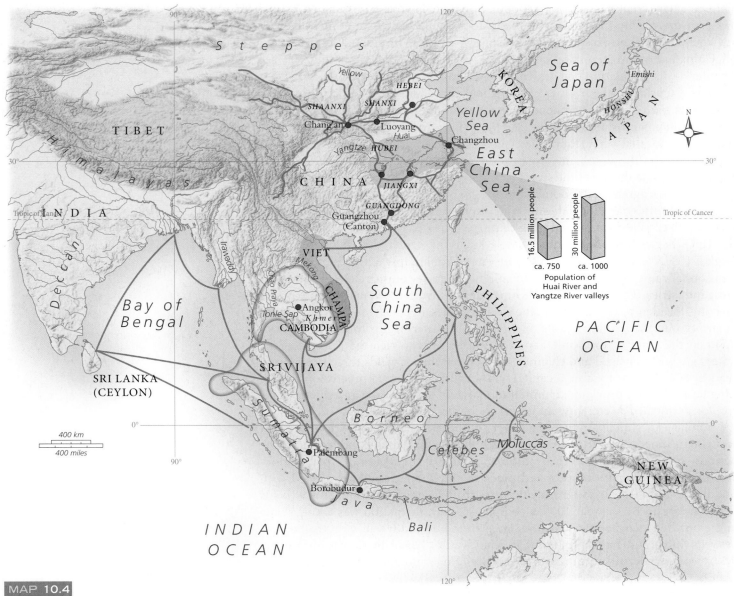

MAP 10.4

China, Japan, and Southeast Asia, ca. 1000

Huai River and Yangtze River valley

Champa

Viet

Cambodia

Srivijaya

— maritime trade route

— canal

Khmer people

expresses a king's concern that "all the clearances and gardens his people made should be full, that the cattle of all species raised by them and their bondsmen should prosper."

The capital, where even the parrots spoke four languages, attracted merchants. The maritime strength of Srivijaya was concentrated in the ragged east coast of Sumatra, with its fringe of islands and mangrove swamps, its deep bays and shelters for shipping, its natural coral-reef defenses, its abundant fish and turtles. Its greatness and survival depended on Chinese commerce, especially for its sandalwood and frankincense.

In eighth-century Java, the Sailendra dynasty rivaled Srivijaya. Their huge temple, Borobodur, seemed to proclaim their patrons' privileged access to heaven. Built of half a million blocks of stone, it arose between about 790 and 830. The maritime economy of Sailendra comes to life in the carvings. One of the most famous depicts a legendary voyage to a promised land that Hiru, the faithful minister of a mythical monk-king, made. Hiru earned the goodwill of heaven by intervening with the king's wicked son and successor, who proposed, among other evil acts, to bury his father's spiritual counselor alive. Miraculously advised to flee in advance of a sandstorm that would smother the court, Hiru fled by sea in a windborne ship to a happy shore. He found granaries, peacocks, varied trees, and hospitable inhabitants. The artist who carved the story had seen such scenes. He knew what a ship looked like and how it worked. The kind of art he produced—evidence, too, of a kind of spirituality—could only come from a world in which travel and trade were regarded as noble, virtuous activities.

According to later inscriptions—in which we must make allowance for mythical distortions or propagandistic exaggerations—a rival kingdom to the Sailendras arose in regions of Java where forest had been newly converted to rice cultivation on the plains of the Solo and Brantas Rivers. Inscriptions credit the expulsion of the Sailendras from these regions in the mid–ninth century to Pikatan, an ascetic king who doubled as a holy man, forest clearer, and temple builder.

The temple of Borobodur on the Indonesian island of Java began to receive pilgrims in the early ninth century. Visitors, emerging from the dense tropical forest that surrounded the site, would ascend through four galleries, where stories of virtuous Buddhists were carved in relief (and, in their day, plastered and brilliantly painted), eventually reaching the realm of Enlightenment—the circular platform, guarded by statues of Bodhisattvas.

THE PACIFIC

An even more impressive drive to colonize new lands and exploit new resources occurred deep in the Pacific, where, as far as we know, the commerce of the monsoonal seas barely reached.

To judge from the currently available archaeological evidence, the Caroline Islands in Micronesia were probably first colonized about 2,000 years ago from the southeast, in the Solomon Islands and New Hebrides, by people who made distinctive round pots and whose houses were raised on stilts. This culture changed at vastly different rates on different islands. The most precocious island was Pohnpei, at the Carolines' eastern end. It is small—probably incapable of supporting more than 30,000 people—but it was a center of ambitious activity toward the year 1000. Large-scale labor was mobilized to carve out artificial islets with increasingly monumental ceremonial centers—for tombs and rites including turtle sacrifices and the nurture of sacred eels. On nearby Kosrae island, a similar history began soon after. Within a couple of hundred years, cities were arising around paved streets within high walls of massive construction.

Beyond the Carolines, in the South Pacific, lay one of the world's most daunting frontiers: an ocean, too big to traverse with the technology of the time, where the winds blew almost without stop from the southeast, and where vast distances separate islands that can support human life. Speakers of Polynesian languages conquered this environment mainly after 500. They grew taro and yams, supplemented with coconut, breadfruit, and bananas. They kept chickens and pigs. They exploited fish for tools—files made of sea-urchin spines, fishhooks from oyster shells. They consumed kava, a fermented drink, to induce trances and celebrate rites. We can infer their notions of the sacred from language and later evidence. **Mana**—a ubiquitous life force—regulated their world, making, for example, nets catch fish or herbs heal.

The Polynesians' was a frontier culture in origin. It grew up in the central Pacific, probably in the islands of Tonga and Samoa, beginning about 2,000 to

 Nineteenth-century description of Lelu, Caroline Islands

◯ MAKING CONNECTIONS ◯

ENVIRONMENTAL/GEOGRAPHIC OBSTACLES TO DEVELOPMENT OF STATES

REGION →	ENVIRONMENTAL /OBSTACLES →	ADAPTIVE STRATEGIES
Sub-Saharan Africa	Isolation—desert in north and lee winds offshore impede communication; widely separated river basins; lack of navigable rivers near coasts; dense forests, malarial jungles	Exploitation of agricultural, mining resources near Sahel grassland; West Africa; trans-Sahara trade routes focusing on copper, salt, gold
North and South America	Bounded by vast oceans—Atlantic and Pacific Oceans; most rivers flow east–west preventing north–south contacts; mountainous terrain	Taking advantage of South/Mesoamerican highlands' proximity to rain forests, seas, swamps for resource exploitation; intensive development of fishing/hunting techniques in North America; introduction of new crops and technologies aided by trade networks from Mesoamerica to Mississippi River basin
Japan	Isolated geography; few navigable rivers; poor soil; earthquake prone	Labor-intensive wetland agricultural techniques; highly regulated society; systematic exploitation of animals as sources of power
Pacific	Vast and isolated region; few food crops, little cultivable soil on many islands	Skillful development of navigational, boat-building techniques; unsurpassed knowledge of ocean and night sky; introduction of basic "tool kit" (fishhooks, taro, coconut, breadfruit, kava, banana plants, chickens, pigs) to uninhabited islands

Polynesian reed map. Traditional Polynesian maps of the Pacific show routes across the ocean in the form of linked reeds between islands symbolized by small shells. The patterns of the reeds enable navigators to identify changes in the ocean swell. © The Trustees of the British Museum

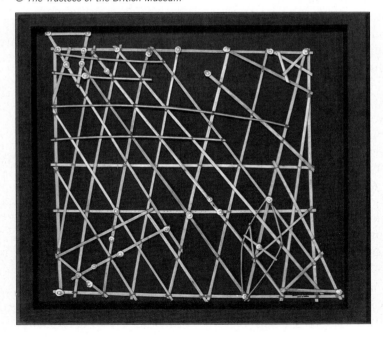

3,000 years ago. From their first emergence in the archaeological record, Polynesians ventured ever farther into the paths of the southeast trade winds, which restricted the range of navigation but which at least promised explorers a good chance of getting home. Around 600, there was a period of "takeoff," from which archaeological finds multiply across the ocean as far as Easter Island (see Chapter 14). In further phases of expansion, Polynesians colonized northward as far as Hawaii, by about 800, and ultimately settled New Zealand and the Chatham Islands.

To colonize so many islands, many of which seemed dauntingly far apart, was such a surprising achievement that scholars who investigated it long assumed that it must have happened by accident—as a result of seafarers or regional traders drifting off course or being blown to new lands. But long-range navigation is part of the logic of life on small islands—a characteristic way to maximize resources, extend economic opportunities, diversify the ecosystem. The Polynesians, in common with other sailors of the northern and western Pacific, had impressive maritime technology: double-hulled canoes big enough to carry 200 people, or smaller vessels with outriggers for longer journeys, rigged with claw-shaped sails that kept the mast and rigging light. Their direction-finding techniques were the best in the world. Chants helped navigators remember the complex guidance of the stars in a hemisphere where no single polestar is available to guide voyagers, as it is north of the equator. Navigation was like "breadfruit-picking," star by star. They mapped the ocean's swells—mentally or perhaps with maps made of reeds, of which later examples survive. Eighteenth-century European observers noted that Caroline and Polynesian navigators could literally feel their way around the ocean, identifying their position by the way that waves felt on their own bodies.

By about the year 1000, the Polynesians may have gotten close to the limits of navigation accessible to them with the technology at their disposal. Oral traditions recall and presumably embellish their history. The most heroic tale is perhaps that of Hui-te-Rangiora, whose journey from Raratonga in the Cook Islands in the remote Pacific in the mid–eighth century took him through bare white rocks that towered over a monstrous sea, to a place of uninterrupted ice. Myths ascribe the discovery of New Zealand to the godlike Maui, who baited giant stingray with his own blood. A less shadowy figure is the indisputably human Kupe, who claimed that a vision of the supreme god Io guided him to New Zealand from Raratonga. Maybe, however, he just followed the migration of the long-tailed cuckoo birds. His sailing directions were: "Let the course be to the right hand of the setting sun, moon, or Venus in the second month of the year."

Polynesian Expansion	
3,000–2,000 years ago	Origins of Polynesian civilization
600	"Takeoff" of Polynesian expansion
ca. 800	Settlement of Hawaii
ca. 1000	Colonization of New Zealand

THE EXPANSION OF CHRISTENDOM

At the opposite end of Eurasia, in the eighth century, Christendom began to outgrow the frontiers of the Roman Empire. Here conquest was the main agent of change. Christendom developed no new crops or technologies. The heavy plow had long been in use. Rye and barley—the grains suitable for the frost-rimed, dense soils of northern Europe—were ancient crops.

Beyond Rome's farthest northern frontiers, monastic exiles took memories of antiquity into Scotland and Ireland, like the monk Columba, longing to compose his hymns "on a rocky outcrop, overlooking the coiling surface of the sea." A similar—more dangerous—enterprise flickered in Germany, where Boniface traveled from England in 719 to share the gospel with the Saxons. Boniface was martyred around 754, but the task of converting the Saxons was taken up 30 years later, from inside the most dynamic spot on the frontier of Christendom: the kingdom of the Franks.

Two events transformed its ruler, Charlemagne, into the self-styled renovator of Rome. His journey to Italy in 774 opened his eyes to ruined splendors and enabled him to gather books and scholars. From the 790s, he could afford unprecedented ambitions when he captured the treasure of invading steppelanders, the Avars. Taking advantage of the fact that Irene, an empress of dubious legitimacy, ruled in Constantinople, he now proclaimed himself successor of the ancient Roman emperors. While remaining first and foremost a Frankish king, Charlemagne affected what he thought was Roman taste. He appeared on coins in a laurel crown. His seals were stamped with slogans of imperial revival. His court writers, who must have known what he wanted to hear, compared him to Constantine and Justinian (see Chapter 8). The manuscript painters, scribes, and ivory carvers of his palace copied ancient models.

Even before Charlemagne came to the throne, the Frankish realm had incorporated lands beyond the margins of the old empire, especially along the North Sea and in central Germany. Charlemagne's conquest of Saxony in 802, which took 18 years to complete, was the first annexation of a large new

Irish cross. Outside the Roman Empire, Christianity was slow to take root in Europe—except in Scotland and Ireland. Isolation made Irish Christian art highly distinctive. This eighth-century bronze crucifix was probably made to adorn the cover of a gospel book. The artist was apparently concerned to represent scripture authentically—hence, the soldiers who pierce Jesus' side and hoist a sponge to his lips. The angels who perch on the arms of the cross display fragments of what may be intended to represent Christ's shroud, or the cloth used to wipe his face.

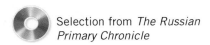

Selection from *The Russian Primary Chronicle*

province in Europe by a selfconsciously "Roman" empire since the Emperor Trajan had conquered Dacia in the early second century. Saxony became a parade ground of Christendom, converted from an insecure frontier into an imperial heartland.

On Christendom's other exposed flanks, similar expansion made slow progress. In the early ninth century, Mojmir I established a Slav state patterned on Charlemagne's monarchy in Bohemia. In 864, the Bulgar Tsar Boris decided to accept Christianity and impose it on his people. The Bulgars rapidly became like the Franks, rival claimants to the mantle of Rome, under a ruler who called himself "emperor of all the Greeks and Bulgars." Yet if the Bulgar Empire was a threat to Constantinople, it was a bulwark for Christendom against pagan steppelanders from farther east.

Despite an isolated position and scant resources, Asturias in northern Spain in the ninth century successfully defended Christendom's frontier at the opposite end of the Mediterranean. Part of the sacred armory of its kings lies in Oviedo Cathedral—vessels of gold, housing relics from the saints who could have a magical effect on the battlefield. On a hill above the town, Ramiro I could look out on his kingdom from his summer palace, or receive ambassadors in a hall decorated with carvings molded after Persian silverwork from some Roman hoard. By the end of the century, the kingdom began to expand beyond the mountains that screened it to the south.

Exploitation of the shrine attributed to the Apostle James the Great at Compostela gave Asturias advantages over other Christian states in Spain—in pilgrim wealth, monastic colonization, and the chances of recruiting knightly manpower. But a frontier position generally was good for state-building. In the 890s, Wilfrid the Hairy, Count of Barcelona, conquered almost all counties around his own, south of the Pyrenees. Laborious settlement of underpopulated areas is the subject of all the documents that survive from his time. Wilfrid's story was typical of the edges of Christendom. In lands reclaimed from pagan conquest on the northern frontier, in England, Alfred the Great was securing a similar reputation as a state builder by lavish generosity to monks, the custodians of the historical record. By 924, Alfred's heirs had completed their reconquest of northern and eastern England. The extension or restoration of the frontier of Christendom was pushing Europe outward.

At the same time, a secular political tradition was being spread even farther afield. Christianity, as we saw in the last chapter, was barely beginning to penetrate Scandinavia, which—in terms of the colonists it generated, the new lands it explored—was the most dynamic part of Europe. A letter from the northern Russian city of Novgorod is said to have reached a Viking prince in 862. "Our land," it read, "is great and rich. But there is no order in it. Come and rule us." In response, he founded the state that eventually became Russia. The story shows how territorial statehood was exported, far beyond the limits of the old Roman Empire, to northern and eastern Europe. Meanwhile, Scandinavian expansion was also going on northward, spreading the frontiers of farming and statehood within its own peninsula, and turning seaward, colonizing Iceland.

IN PERSPECTIVE: The Limits of Divergence

On the face of it, sub-Saharan Africa and the Americas seem to diverge from Eurasia and North Africa from the eighth century to the end of the millennium. In Christendom, Islam, China, southeast Asia, and the western and central Pacific, states came and went, but economies and civilizations were robust—extending frontiers, colonizing new areas, founding new states and empires, or reviving old ones. These regions seem to have bucked the patterns detected by traditional historiography: to have endured beyond periods of decline and fall. At first glance, the contrast with sub-Saharan Africa looks glaring. Ethiopia's dark age really was dark, in the sense that we know virtually nothing about it. Ghana's frustration, and the absence of any evidence of comparable state-building initiatives elsewhere, confirm the traditional picture of a region—like far northern Asia or Australia—about which historians of the period can find almost nothing to say. The myth of Maya collapse has long dominated the way we conventionally think of the Americas in this period as a hemisphere where it was more usual for civilizations to perish than to grow outward or renew themselves. This is an exaggeration—perhaps even a caricature. But there is something in it. Teotihuacán, the Moche, the Nazca, the lowland Maya, Huari, Tiahuanaco—these casualties of the era were replaced, if at all, by unstable successors.

Nevertheless, a theme that, if not quite global, genuinely embraces the Old and New Worlds underlies the apparent differences between them. Broadly stated, this was a period of unusual ecological experiment: the exploration or conquest of new environments. In some cases, new frontiers were breached by expansion into neighboring regions and already-familiar environments, like those of the Islamic world or southeast Asia or most of Christendom. In others, like the Caroline Islands or the Scandinavian expansion, apparently unprecedented adventures were launched from origins that present knowledge cannot adequately explain. In others again, as in China and Japan, internal colonization adapted and transformed previously underexploited wastelands. In others, such as the Andes, central Mexico, and the Maya world, the centers of activity were displaced to new environments—the limestone hills of Tula or Yucatán, the almost incredibly high altitude of Tiahuanaco. In others, which remain necessarily underrepresented in history books because of the absence of evidence, the business of locating resources, developing foodstuffs, and improving production techniques continued without leaving much trace in the record. In the 800s and 900s, for instance, all we have is linguistic evidence for two enormously important developments in the ecology of East Africa. An explosion of new terms shows that banana cultivation and cattle breeding spread inland from the Indian Ocean coast to the Great Lakes of Central Africa. Against this background, the history of the next three centuries, which is the subject of the next part of the book, becomes intelligible. Vibrancy and innovativeness, which became characteristic of most of these regions—and of others where

CHRONOLOGY

(All dates are C.E.)

200–400	Flourishing of mound-building culture in eastern North America
600	"Takeoff" of Polynesian expansion
750	China's population reaches 50 million
754	Martyrdom of Boniface
Third through tenth centuries	Maya Classic Age
Seventh through tenth centuries	Ecological expansion of Islam
Eighth century	Government drive to boost food production in Japan
Eighth through ninth centuries	Decline of Ethiopia
790–830	Construction of Borobodur temple, Java
ca. 800	Settlement of Hawaii
ca. 802	Charlemagne completes conquest of Saxony
ca. 860	Scandinavians begin colonization of Iceland
ca. 1000	Andean city of Tiahuanaco abandoned; China's population reaches 60 million
1100s	Tula abandoned

the evidence only begins to mount up from this point onward—grew out of painstaking efforts to find new, more productive ways to exploit the environment.

The story of the last few centuries of the first millennium C.E. suggests an important point about how history happens. In the past, the search for patterns that help to explain it has driven historians to grotesque oversimplifications: seeing history as a continuous story of "progress" or decline; or representing it as a kind of swing between revolutions and counterrevolutions, or between decadence and dynamism, or between dark ages and rebirths. The reality, it seems, as we get to learn more about the past, is much more subtle and intriguing. At one level, the slow growth of compatible changes—what historians' jargon sometimes calls "structures"—gradually gave the world a new look. Simultaneously, and often with contradictory effect, random or short-term changes stimulate, impede, interrupt, or temporarily reverse those trends, and—sometimes—permanently deflect or end them. So both continuity and discontinuity tend to be visible in the story, pretty much all the time. A picture that omits either is almost certain to be distorted.

In these respects, history is like climate, in which many cycles of varying duration all seem to be going on all the time, and where random or almost-random changes frequently intervene. With increasing intensity in recent years, historians have struggled to match changes in the human record to knowledge of how these cycles and changes have interacted since the end of the Ice Age. As we are about to see, some of the most remarkable insights to have emerged from this quest illuminate worldwide changes that began—or that we can first begin to detect—around 1,000 years ago.

PROBLEMS AND PARALLELS

1. What were new ways of managing the environment during the late first millennium? How did societies exploit new resources and colonize new lands?

2. What role did geography play in impeding the diffusion of culture and crops in sub-Saharan Africa and the Americas?

3. What factors contributed to the flourishing of South American and Mesoamerican cultures and states?

4. What were the effects of environmental expansion under Islam?

5. How were monks and holy men important to the conquest of new environments and the expansion of states?

6. What was the importance of ecological experiment and the conquest of new environments in Christendom, China, southeast Asia, and the Pacific in the late first millennium?

DOCUMENTS IN GLOBAL HISTORY

- Selection from the *Nihongi*
- Indian land grants, 753 C.E.

- Nineteenth-century description of Lelu, Caroline Islands
- Selection from *The Russian Primary Chronicle*

Please see the Primary Source DVD for additional sources related to this chapter.

READ ON

The written sources on West Africa are collected in J. F. P. Hopkins and N. Levtzion, eds., *Corpus of Early Arabic Sources for West African History* (2000).

J. Diamond, *Guns, Germs, and Steel* (2003) sets out the case for the isolating effects of American geography.

On the Moche, G. Bawden, *The Moche* (1996) is standard. For the Nazca, A. F. Aveni, *Nazca: Eighth Wonder of the World* (2000) is useful. B. Fagan, *Floods, Famines, and Emperors* (1999) is a lively romp through the history of the effects of El Niño. For Tiahuanaco, A. Kolata, *Tiwanaku and Its Hinterland* (1996), 2 vols., is exhaustive. R. Keatinge, ed., *Peruvian Prehistory* (1988) collects important essays on the Andean background. On the Maya, M. Coe, *The Maya* (2005), and N. Hammond, *Ancient Maya Civilization* (1982) are the most useful overviews. The exhibition catalog by L. Schele and M. Miller, *The Blood of Kings* (1992), is important for understanding royal rituals. D. Webster, *The Fall of the Ancient Maya* (2002) is a brilliant and provocative study of the crisis of the ninth and tenth centuries. On Copán in particular, W. Fash, *Scribes, Warriors, and Kings* (1993) is a vivid and engaging study. On Tula, R. A. Diehl, *Tula* (1983) is authoritative. On Marajó and related topics, the exhibition catalog by C. McEwan et al., *Unknown Amazon* (2001), contains a wealth of exciting data.

For maize, see W. C. Gallinat, "Domestication and Diffusion of Maize," in R. I. Ford, ed., *Prehistoric Food Production in North America* (1985).

A. M. Watson, *Agricultural Innovation in the Early Islamic World* (1983) is the standard work on Islam's agrarian revolution in this period. K. W. Butzer, *Archaeology as Human Ecology* (1982) is classic, and D. W. Phillipson, *African Archaeology* (1994) is a survey by the leading living expert on Ethiopia.

The Cambridge History of Japan (1993) is unsurpassed on Japanese environmental history in this period.

R. Thapar, *Early India* (2004) and B. Chattopadhyaya, *Aspects of Rural Society and Settlements in Early Medieval India* (1990), and *The Making of Early Medieval India* (1994) are the best works to consult on environmental aspects of Indian history at the time.

M. Elvin, *The Retreat of the Elephants* (2004) is a sparkling historical study of the Chinese environment, focusing on the history of deforestation, about which there is much, too, in N. K. Menzies, "Forestry," in J. Needham, ed., *Science and Civilisation in China*, vi (2000). *The Cambridge History of China*, iii (1979) is fundamental for Chinese history generally in this period.

On Angkor, the classic by G. Coedes, *Angkor, An Introduction* (1986) remains fundamental, supplemented now by the ingenious work of E. Mannika, *Angkor Wat: Time, Space, Kingship* (1996). M. D. Coe, *Angkor and the Khmer Civilization* (2005) is of special interest from a comparative point of view, as the author is a Mayanist. On southeast Asia generally, D. G. E Hall, *A History of South-East Asia* (1981) and the same author's contribution to *The Cambridge History of South-East Asia*, i (2000) are important.

On the Pacific, important contributions are collected in P. V. Kirch and T. L. Hunt, eds., *Historical Ecology in the Pacific Islands* (1997). P. V. Kirch, *On the Road of the Winds* (2001) is immeasurably helpful. P. Bellwood, *The Polynesians* (1987) is a useful introduction. The classic by B. Malinowski, *Argonauts of the Western Pacific* (1984) can still be read for pleasure and profit.

On Christendom, useful essays are collected in the forthcoming series, edited by F. Fernández-Armesto and J. Muldoon, *The Expansion of Christendom: The Middle Ages*, especially in my volume, "The Internal Frontier." C. Wickham, *The Mountains and the City* (1988), and R. Bartlett, *The Making of Europe* (1994) are fundamental.

PART
Five

Contacts and Conflicts, 1000 C.E. to 1200 C.E.

The World Map of Al-Idrisi, a Muslim geographer who ▶ worked in Christian-ruled Sicily in the mid–twelfth century. He tried to follow the advice of the ancient Greek geographer, Ptolemy, and constructed his map on a grid. South is at the north. The shape of Arabia is clearly recognizable to a modern eye (upper center), as is that of Spain at the extreme right.

ENVIRONMENT

1000–1300
North Atlantic warm spell

1000–1200
Transfer of crops
from south and southeast
Asia to Islamic world

CULTURE

ca. 1000
Tale of Genji (Japan)

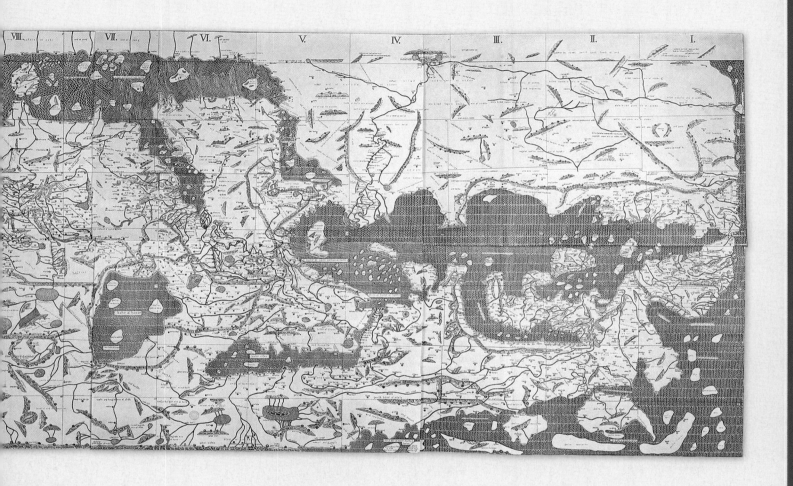

1040s–1090
Increased steppelander
migrations into Middle East

ca. 1070–1122
Chola maritime expansion

900–1200
Growing population,
especially in Europe and China

1098
First Crusade

ca. 1125
Angkor Wat

1000–1200
Spread of Islam
to West Africa

ca. 1200
Cahokia, height of Mississippian
mound building

The pilgrimages of Buddhist monks inspired Japanese stories about the ferocity of the sea. One of the most popular tales in the late twelfth and early thirteenth centuries was about Gisho, a monk who renounced the love of a beautiful woman and set sail for Korea. But in the incident depicted here, she followed him and flung herself into the sea, where, transformed into a dragon, she protected him from storms.
Tokyo National Museum, Photographer: Kanai Morio/DNP Archives.

The farewells lasted "all day and into the night." Aboard ship, the travelers prayed for a peaceful crossing. When the clouds cleared, before dawn, "oars pierced the moon's reflection." Winds lashed. Typhoons threatened. Pirates lurked. The voyagers appealed to the gods by flinging tokens, charms, and cupfuls of rice wine into the sea. They even sacrificed jewels and precious mirrors. It was a routine journey along the coast of Japan in the year 936. The governor of Kochi was on his way home to the capital city of Kyoto.

A journal that the governor's wife, the "Tosa lady," supposedly wrote recorded the journey. Despite dramatizations and fictional conventions, the sailing conditions she described were true to life. The coast was so strewn with dangers that sailors dared not sail at night, except to elude pirates. Unpredictable head winds kept the voyagers cowering in harbor. The journey from Tosa to the port of Osaka can hardly have covered more than 400 miles, yet it took nearly three months. Hostile seas penned in the Japanese, despite their skill in nautical technology. This fact helps to explain why, for most of their history, the Japanese have been confined in their own islands, despite considering themselves an empire.

• • • • •

In other parts of the world, however, long-range navigations were leaping oceans. In the time the Tosa Lady took to sail to Osaka, an Indian Ocean trader, with the benefit of the reversible wind system, could get from the Persian Gulf to Sumatra: a distance of more than 5,000 miles. One Persian captain made the journey to China and back to Persia seven times. The Japanese could only imagine such journeys. Not long after the Tosa diarist wrote, a fanciful Japanese sea story told of a ship—a "hollow tree"—blown by accident nonstop from Japan to Persia.

Pilgrim traffic to Mecca also stimulated Indian Ocean navigation, as Muslim merchant communities spread across Asia and Muslim holy men made converts. Meanwhile, beyond the range of the monsoon, migrants from what is now Indonesia crossed the ocean across the path of the southeast trade winds and colonized Madagascar, off the east coast of Africa. Meanwhile, Polynesian navigators were penetrating deep into the Pacific Ocean with the aid of some of the world's most regular long-range winds (see Chapter 10). Even more remarkably, around the year 1000, Thule Inuit from the Pacific and Norse from Scandinavia crossed the Arctic and Atlantic Oceans from opposite directions and met in Greenland.

FOCUS questions _____

- HOW DID geography influence the spread of culture and state-building in North America and Mesoamerica?
- WHY WAS the Indian Ocean so important for the spread of culture?
- WHY WERE the land routes across Eurasia less significant than the sea routes across the Indian Ocean?
- WHICH AREAS of India were most prosperous in the tenth and eleventh centuries and what was the basis of their prosperity?
- HOW DID their relative cultural isolation affect Japan and Western Europe during these centuries?

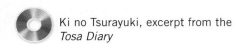

Ki no Tsurayuki, excerpt from the *Tosa Diary*

These extraordinarily long-range migrations were part of a double dynamic, as people stretched the resources available to them to explore for new resources and exploit existing opportunities in new ways. Region by region, culture by culture, in this chapter and the next, we can see people in widely separated parts of the world using similar strategies: felling forests, extending areas of cultivation and pasture, expanding into new terrain, enhancing muscle power with new technologies.

In the eleventh and twelfth centuries, these forms of expansion were widespread themes of world history, but they followed divergent courses in different regions. As was so often the case, relative isolation was usually the key to the difference between long-lasting innovation and faltering, short-lived change. Cultures that exchanged information and artifacts were relatively robust. Peoples isolated from fruitful contacts found it much harder. In the Americas, therefore, as so often before, experiments in new ways of life were arrested by checks, frustrated by failures, interrupted by discontinuities. Meanwhile, however, some parts of the Old World, where long-range contacts were easier and more frequent, experienced enduring transformations.

The new opportunities arose partly from the environmental changes of the preceding centuries, described in the last chapter. To see how people responded, we can devote this chapter to a world tour of some of the regions most affected—starting in the Americas, before turning to the shores of the Indian Ocean, including the parts of East Africa that face that ocean, and ending with the extremities of Eurasia in Japan and Western Europe. In these parts of the world, societies struggled against isolation with varying degrees of success.

In other regions of Africa and Eurasia—China, Central Asia, West Africa, the Byzantine Empire, and the Islamic world—the single most important source of new pressures for change arose from the stirrings of nomadic peoples. These are the subject of the next chapter.

AMERICAN DEVELOPMENTS: FROM THE ARCTIC TO MESOAMERICA

The history of the Americas in the eleventh and twelfth centuries is scattered with stories of new frontiers, developed by new migrations or new initiatives.

Greenland and the North

About 1,000 years ago, a relatively warm spell disturbed the lives of ice hunters along North America's Arctic edge. Taking advantage of improved conditions for hunting and navigating, migrants worked their way across the southern edge of the Arctic Ocean. The Thule (TOO-lee) Inuit, as archaeologists call them, traveled in vessels made of walrus hides stretched across wooden ribs that were so shallow they could hug the shore, and so light that the voyagers could lift them from between ice floes.

The Thule hunted at sea for whales and polar bears. They mounted their harpoons on floats made from seal bladders, which they blew up like balloons. Game

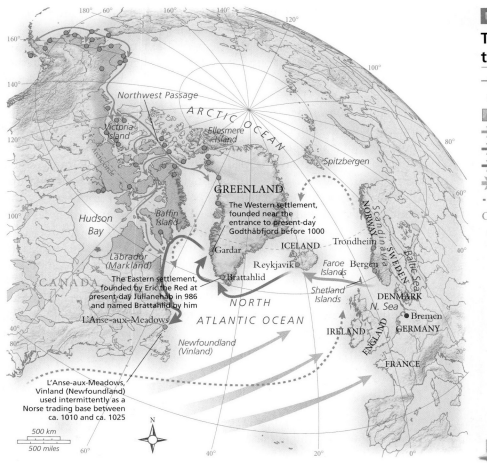

MAP EXPLORATION
www.prenhall.com/armesto_maps

MAP 11.1

Thule Inuit and Norse Migrations to ca. 1200

→	Thule Inuit migrations to ca. 1000
●	Thule Inuit settlements
▨	extent of Inuit, ca. 1200
➡	assumed route of Norse settlement, late 9th century
➡	assumed route of Eric the Red, late 10th century
➡	conjectural route of Leif Eriksson, late 10th century
➡	westerlies
┄►	ocean current
CANADA	modern-day country
●	Norse settlement/town

could then be towed home. On land, they hunted with dogs of a breed new to North America. For warfare against human enemies, they reintroduced the bow and arrow (see Chapter 1). By about 1000, they had reached Greenland and the western extremities of North America (see Map 11.1). The navigation of the Arctic was an astonishing feat, not repeated until the twentieth century.

At the same time, almost equally heroic migrations were under way in the opposite direction, toward the same destinations, across the North Atlantic. Exploitable currents helped navigators from Scandinavia cross the ocean, via Iceland, below the Arctic Circle. It seems extraordinarily daring to risk such a long journey across the open sea, without chart or compass, but the Scandinavians knew that the prevailing winds blew from the west in the latitudes they inhabited. So they could always hope to get home. The voyagers probably judged their latitude by observing the polestar with the naked eye on cloudless nights. By day, the only technical aid they had, as far as we know, was a stump of wood with a protruding stick. The shadow it cast would tell the navigator whether his latitude had changed.

Whereas the Thule Inuit were drawn by the fat-rich foods of the Arctic, the Norse—or Northmen—as the Atlantic voyagers are called, were usually escapees or exiles from poverty or restricted social opportunity. "As to your enquiry what people go to seek in Greenland and why they fare thither through such great perils," said a medieval

Excerpt from *Speculum Princips*, "The Animal Life of Greenland and the Character of the Land in Those Regions"

The Norse and Thule Inuit

900–1100	Warm spell in Arctic
ca. 986	Founding of Brattahlid
ca. 1000	Thule Inuit reach Greenland
1189–1200	Construction of cathedral at Gardar

Inuit seacraft European technology was unable to make a ship that could sail around the Arctic coast of North America between the Atlantic and the Pacific until 1904. But the Thule Inuit accomplished the task with hide-covered craft by about 1000 C.E. Their boats were shallow enough to hug the shore, light enough to hoist onto the ice, and buoyant enough to avoid being crushed by ice floes.

Norwegian book, the answer is "in man's threefold nature. One motive is fame, another curiosity, and the third is lust for gain."

In the early years of their settlement, the environment, harsh as it was, had a lot to offer the newcomers: fish and game, including luxury items valuable as potential exports to Europe, such as hunting falcons and walrus ivory. The Norse, however, changed the environment of Greenland profoundly. They introduced grain and European grasses for grazing. They developed sheep whose wool was prized. The big wooden ships the Norse used, held together with iron nails, in a land with little timber or iron, must have seemed wildly extravagant to the Inuit in their skin canoes. The Norse town of Brattahlid in western Greenland—the remotest outpost of medieval Christendom—had 17 monasteries and churches of stone with bells of bronze. The cathedral at Gardar was built between 1189 and 1200, of red sandstone and molded soapstone, with a bell tower, glass windows, and three fireplaces. The largest farms supported an aristocratic way of life, with big halls in which to feast dependents. But the colony remained precarious and isolated. Adam of Bremen, a learned geographer of the late eleventh century, confided what little he knew: "Greenland is situated far out in the ocean. . . . The people there are greenish from the saltwater, whence, too, that region gets its name."

The North American Southwest and the Mississippi Region

The shore station that Greenlanders or Icelanders set up in Newfoundland in about 1000 did not last. There were not enough wealthy or settled communities in the area with which the Norse could establish trade and cultural exchange. A glance at the map of North America at the time shows similar cases, deep inland, of peoples struggling with isolation. The new way of life traveled along two routes: from the heartlands of maize in what is now Mexico, into the arid lands of the North American Southwest; and from the Gulf of Mexico into the wetlands of the Mississippi valley and the United States' Deep South. The results included the rise of cultures with similarities to predecessors in Mesoamerica (see Chapter 4), with urban life, irrigation, elaborate ceramics and shellcraft, gold and copper work, ball games, and unmistakable signs of statehood (see Map 11.2).

In parts, for instance, of what are now Colorado, New Mexico, and Arizona, evidence of a political network is spread over 57,000 square miles: from high in the drainage area of the San Juan River in the north to beyond the Little Colorado River in the south, and from the Colorado River to the Rio Grande. A system of roadways, up to 12 yards wide, radiated from a cluster of sites around the great canyon near the source of the Chaco River. Only two needs can account for such an elaborate network. Either some ritual was being enacted, demanding close ties between the places linked; or the roads were there to move armies.

The environment is parched and—one would think—unsuitable for settled life. Apart from turquoise, which became the basis of trade, natural wealth was scarce. But the region was densely settled, at least in patches. The canyon people built ambitious cities or ceremonial centers around irregular plazas, surrounded by massive outer walls. The main buildings were of stone, faced with fine masonry. Roofs were made of great timbers from pine forests in the hills—a dazzling show of wealth and power in a treeless desert. To construct the ceremonial center at Chaco Canyon, 200,000 trees were felled. We do not know what the political system was.

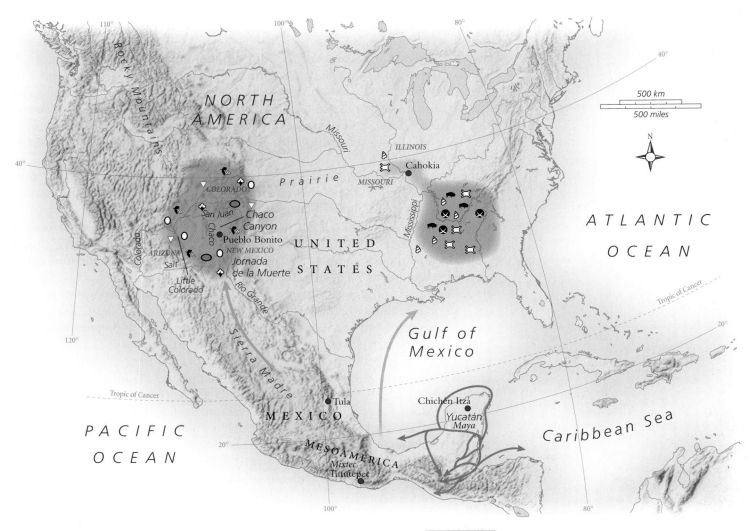

MAP 11.2

North America and Mesoamerica to ca. 1200

▨	canyon cultures
●	major city or ceremonial center
▨	Mississippian cultures
⌂	city associated with Mississippian peoples
➤	roads leading north from Mesoamerica
➤	sea route from Mesoamerica to Mississippi River valley
➤	Mayan trade route
Mixtec	peoples
ARIZONA	modern-day state

Economic Basis of Canyon People

🌽	maize
O	beans
♠	cotton
▽	irrigation
⬭	turquoise

Mississippian Trade Goods

ẟ	seashells
⋈	deerskins
🐗	bison pelts
✹	horn

But we know it was tough. Mass executions have left piles of victims' bones, crushed, split, and picked as if at a cannibal feast.

The economic basis of this civilization was fragile. If water could be delivered to the fields, cotton, maize, and beans would grow predictably, without danger from the fluctuating temperatures that threatened at higher altitudes. Long irrigation canals did the job.

But from the twelfth century onward, the climate got drier, putting the irrigation system under constant strain. The rulers of the canyon people responded by expanding into new zones, building more ambitiously, organizing labor more ferociously. But decline, punctuated by crisis, shows through a series of periodic contractions of the culture area and reorganizations of the settlements. Meanwhile, the harsh peacekeeping methods seem to have stopped working. Settlements withdrew to defensible locations. The problems of isolation defeated or limited all attempts to revive a similar way of life until the nineteenth century.

The canyon cultures were as remote from Mesoamerican civilizations as the Norse of Greenland were from Europe. Roads north from Mesoamerica led across dangerous territory. Nomadic peoples

Canyon de Chelly

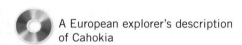

A European explorer's description of Cahokia

North America and Mesoamerica, 10th to 13th Centuries

Tenth century	Flourishing of canyon culture in American Southwest; founding of Cahokia in Mississippi River valley; founding of Chichén Itzá in Mesoamerica
Eleventh century	Mixtec first appear in historical record
1063–1125	Life of Eight-Deer Tiger-Claw
ca. 1100	Climate in American Southwest gets progressively drier
Eleventh–twelfth centuries	Maya intensively exploit Yucatán peninsula
ca. 1150	Canyon settlements withdraw to higher ground
1200	Cahokia population reaches 10,000
ca. 1300	Decline of upper Mississippi valley culture sites

patrolled the northern edges of the Mesoamerican culture area, practicing raids and conquests, like those launched from the steppes into China or Europe. The high road north from what is now Mexico to the nearest patch of easily cultivable soil led through a 61-mile pass known in modern times as the *Jornada de la Muerte*: the "march of death," through rocky defiles and dunes where the glare was so fierce that a traveler's eyes seemed to burst from their sockets, and men "breathed fire and spat pitch."

It was hard to travel that road—harder still to transmit Mesoamerican crops and traditions beyond the world of Chaco Canyon. The prairie, though flat, was an ecological barrier, where few patches could sustain sedentary life. It is more likely that Mesoamerica's tool kit, food, and ways of life and thought traveled across the Gulf of Mexico, by seaborne trade, to reach the North American Southeast. In parts of this region, the environment was promising. In the Mississippi valley and other riverside floodplains, natural ridges accumulated over centuries, wherever the floods dumped soil. These ridges were the nurseries of the farmers' crops and the inspiration for mounds dredged from the swamps to provide gardens. A hinterland of pools and lakes provided ideal centers for fish farming to supplement the field plants, among which maize was increasingly dominant.

In this region, between the ninth and thirteenth centuries, people laid out ceremonial centers in patterns like those of Mesoamerica. Platforms, topped with chambered structures, were grouped around large plazas.

The most spectacular site, Cahokia, east of St. Louis, stands almost at the northwestern limit of the reach of the culture to which it belongs. Its frontier position may have allowed it to act as a commercial gateway between zones of interrelated environments and, therefore, of interrelated products: shells from the Gulf, deerskins from the eastern woodlands, bison pelts and horn from the prairies. It probably covered 5.5 square miles. Cahokia's central platform is over 100 feet high, and at about 13 acres, the base of the great mound is as big as that of the biggest Egyptian pyramid.

The city arose in the tenth century. At its height, in about 1200, Cahokia probably had about 10,000 inhabitants in its built-up area. It was the most intensely and elaborately constructed of a great arc of mound clusters from St. Louis to the easternmost edges of the Mississippi floodplain. Smaller, similar sites extend from the riverbanks to the uplands of Illinois and Missouri. Cahokia's size and air of importance tempt some scholars to think of it as something like the capital of something like a state, or, at least, a cultural center from which influence radiated.

Graves at Cahokia have given up honored dead. Their treasures included tools and adornments of copper, bones, and tortoiseshell covered in copper. One grave had gold and copper masks. Thousands of seashells from the Gulf of Mexico must have possessed the highest imaginable status in this inland place. As time went on, finely made stone arrowheads were buried in elite graves. This is a precious clue to how Cahokian culture changed but is hard to interpret. Were the arrows trophies of success in war or hunting, or simple counters of wealth? In any case, the arrows were aristocratic possessions in a society graded for status and equipped for conflict. When Cahokia lost political power in the thirteenth century, the place retained a sacred aura: Its manufactures—pots, shell work, soapstone carvings, and small axe heads—circulated for centuries after the mound dwellers died out or dispersed.

When objects of great value are concentrated without evidence of a dwelling, grave, or warehouse, it is tempting to talk of a temple. An impressive cache of this type, found at a site southeast of Cahokia, contains carvings that give us glimpses into a mythic history or symbolic system that attached a high value to two themes: fertility and farming, and especially to maize and squash. One female figure tames a snake with multiple tails in the form of squash plants. Another female holds maize. Images and fragments from other sites repeat some of these themes: female guardians of corn and serpents, some of whom also hold dishes as if offering a sacrifice.

The people who built Cahokia inaugurated a way of life that was economically successful and artistically productive for not much more than 200 years—not bad for its place and time, but much shorter than the span major cities in Eurasia achieved. After a spell of stagnation or decline, their inhabitants deserted the upper Mississippi valley culture sites over a period of about four generations around the thirteenth and fourteenth centuries.

Yet culture of the kind that climaxed at Cahokia did not disappear. Rather, it was displaced and some of its more ambitious features—the huge mounds, the vast reach of trade—were abandoned. Mound building continued on a smaller scale, in the lower Mississippi valley and the North American Southeast. Here, traditions of burying chiefs, with rich grave goods and sometimes with large-scale sacrifices, were also maintained.

Mesoamerica

In a similar way in Mesoamerica, the collapse of the cities of the classic Maya in the ninth and tenth centuries in Central America and southern Mexico (see Chapter 10) did not end Maya civilization. Maya city life and state-building continued in a new environment on the Yucatán peninsula in eastern Mexico. Here, unlike the old lowland heartlands of the Maya, the climate was dry, and irrigation relied on pools and wells. But it was possible to reconstruct the old Maya way of life. In Yucatán, lowland tradition met links with central Mexico, which was accessible through seaborne and overland routes (see Map 11.2).

Mixtec creation myth. This Mixtec manuscript about the origins of the Earth predates the fifteenth century. Known as the Vienna Codex and painted on deerhide, it depicts Lord and Lady One-Deer, the legendary ancestors of all the Mixtec rulers, offering sacrifices to the gods of incense and tobacco.

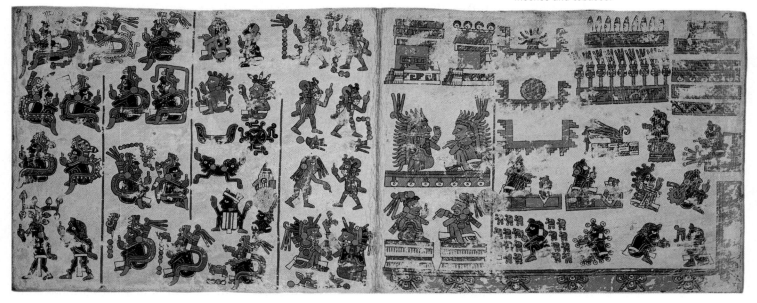

Continuities with the former Maya world are evident in the way the buildings are arrayed in the cities of Yucatán, in layouts that reflect an abiding interest in observing the movements of the stars and planets, and in facades decorated with curl-nosed gods, the jaws of feathered serpents, or scenes of human sacrifice. The greatest Yucatán city, Chichén Itzá (chee-CHEIN eet-SAH), arose in the tenth century, at about the time the lowland Maya culture withered. If traditions recorded later are reliable, a dynasty with imperial ambitions, the Cocom, ruled in this city, and their wars dominated the region for centuries.

Yucatán was a new frontier for the Maya: a region of unprecedentedly intense exploitation in the eleventh and twelfth centuries. It was not the only such area in Mesoamerica. In the Pacific-facing regions of Mexico, beyond the Sierra Madre, the people known as Mixtec (MEESH-tahk) lived, in relatively small communities that were densely settled and famed for their elite craftsmen, especially in gold work and books made of bark. One of the greatest Mesoamerican heroes came from here: Eight-Deer Tiger-Claw (ca. 1063–1125). His activities show what was expected of a Mesoamerican king. He married frequently and had many children. He visited shrines, mediating between gods and men, offering sacrifices, consulting ancestors. He sent and received ambassadors, played the ball game against rival kings, and—above all—made war. He died as he had lived. This model of Mesoamerican kingship was defeated, sacrificed, and dismembered by his enemies—entombed with his royal symbols in an episode vividly recorded in the genealogy of the kings of two Mixtec towns, who wanted to be remembered as his descendants.

AROUND THE INDIAN OCEAN: ETHIOPIA, THE KHMER, AND INDIA

In the Americas, poor communications kept peoples apart and made it hard to exchange wealth and ideas. The Indian Ocean, by contrast, was the world's great arena of exchange, crossed by trade routes and rimmed with rich societies.

East Africa: The Ethiopian Empire

Links across the Indian Ocean lessened East Africa's isolation. By the twelfth century, important changes were occurring there. Arabic-speaking geographers recorded the names of places along the East African coast and knew of Muslim communities as far away as the island of Zanzibar. By 1200, Muslims from the Persian Gulf ruled Mogodishu in modern Somalia. Muslim geographers mentioned Mogadishu's transoceanic trade, bound for India and China, and East Africa is well marked on thirteenth-century Chinese maps.

The increased trade of coastal kingdoms and cities could affect state-building far inland. This is important, because state-building is a measurable indicator of thoroughgoing, long-term change. In twelfth-century Ethiopia, a new dynasty recovered political unity and began a modest recovery. In this land, which had now been predominantly Christian for over 700 years (see Chapter 9), a time of internal crusade began, recorded in the lives of frontier saints. On tireless pilgrimages, for instance, Takla Haymanyot made converts, dethroned idols, and chopped down "devils' trees" to build churches. An ideology of holy war seems to have taken hold.

On the Ethiopian frontier, the monastery churches of Lalibela began to emerge from the rocks: literally so, for they are hewn out of the ground. King Lalibela, after whom their location is named, and who is credited with building most of them, is known only from semilegendary sources. But the traditional tales are revealing:

After showing him what churches are like in heaven, God said to Lalibela, "It is not for the passing glory of this world that I will make you king, but that you may construct churches, like those you have seen, ... out of the bowels of the earth." Stories of angels who worked on the buildings reflect the superiority of the craftsmanship. The monks who wrote Lalibela's life story emphasized that he used wage labor to supplement angelic work. Hatred of slavery was common in the writings of Ethiopian monks.

The Zagwe (ZAHG-way), as the kings of Lalibela's dynasty were called, were frontiersmen. The elites of the central highland region around Axum despised them. Nor perhaps did the Zagwe carry total conviction when they claimed to be heirs of Solomon. Everyone knew that they were upstarts. Propaganda increasingly identified Ethiopia with the realm of the biblical Queen of Sheba, Solomon's concubine. Ethiopia was even proclaimed as "the new Israel." These claims to ancient roots favored rivals for the throne, who emerged in the second half of the thirteenth century, representing themselves as the rightful heirs of the Axumite monarchs or claimed to be descended from King Solomon. In 1270, they seized power. The state was organized for war. The monasteries of Debra Hayq and Debra Libanos, on the islands of Lake Tana, became schools of missionaries whose task was to consolidate Ethiopian power in the conquered pagan lands of Shoa and Gojam.

Rock-cut church. Perhaps because of its relative isolation in a mountainous region, Ethiopian civilization has always shown great originality. The political and cultural revival of Ethiopia in the late twelfth and early thirteenth centuries is associated with King Lalibela, who began to build a new sacred capital in a frontier region, where masons dug churches out of the rock. Lalibela seems to have conceived this work as a place of pilgrimage, a "New Jerusalem," and an embodiment of what he claimed was a vision of heaven.

Ethiopia remained primarily an agrarian state, a mountain kingdom, with an ideology of defiance against neighboring states and peoples. But the multiplication of contacts across the Indian Ocean enabled Ethiopia to struggle against the effects of isolation with increasing success.

Southeast Asia: The Khmer Kingdom

At the opposite end of that ocean in southeast Asia, the same context helps to explain the wealth and power of another inland, agrarian kingdom: that of the Khmer in Cambodia. As we saw in Chapter 10, the fertility of the soil of the Khmer homeland nourishes three rice harvests a year. That productivity was the foundation of the kingdom's greatness. The rhythms of its rise, however, matched the growth of Indian Ocean trade, which opened outlets for the Khmer farmers' surplus. The ascent of the kingdom is documented in the growth and embellishment of its great city of Angkor.

The plan of the city reflects influences from India. Angkor was laid out to evoke the divine design of the world common to both Hindu and Buddhist beliefs: the central mountain or *Meru*, the mountains that ring it, the outer wall of rock, the seas flowing beyond in circle-like patterns. The royal palace built in the eleventh century centered on a tower that bore the inscription: "He thought the center of the universe was marked by Meru, and he thought it fitting to have a Meru in the center of his capital."

The architecture of the twelfth-century King Suryavarman II proclaims a new era. He had himself carved in the walls of his greatest foundation, the biggest temple in the world, Angkor Wat. Previously, monumental sculptures had only honored dead monarchs or royal ancestors. Suryavarman appears repeatedly in one of

Angkor Wat. By the time of King Suryavarman II (r. 1113–1150), the great central temple of Angkor Wat, rising like the sacred mountain Hindus and Buddhists imagined at the center of the world, already dominated the skyline of Angkor. Thanks to silt deposited by the Mekong River, intensive rice cultivation generated huge food surpluses, making possible the investment of work and wealth required to build the stupendous city.

the temple galleries, surrounded by environment-defying goods: umbrellas against the sun, fans against the humidity. A dead snake dangles from his hand, perhaps in allusion to an anecdote about his accession. He seized the throne by leaping on the royal elephant and killing his aged predecessor, like a god, who, "landing on the peak of a mountain, kills a serpent." Carvings reenact the creation of the world, as if his reign were the world's renewal. They show the cosmic tug of war between good and evil gods. Scenes of the churning of the magic potion of life from the ocean suggest that the fortunate age of the world is about to begin. According to Hindu myth, peace and unity will prevail in the new age, and the various ranks of society will willingly perform their roles.

Hindu tradition predicted that this new age would last 1,728,000 years. Suryavarman's was over by 1150. But his ambitious building programs continued, especially under King Jayavarman VII later in the century. Jayavarman surrounded Angkor with shrines and palaces, way stations, and—it was said—more than 100 hospitals. A proclamation of his public health policy reads:

> He felt the afflictions of his subjects more than his own. . . . May all the kings of Cambodia, devoted to the right, carry on my foundation, and attain for themselves and their descendants, their wives, their officials, their friends, . . . deliverance in which there will never be any sickness.[1]

The allocation of resources for the hospitals hints at both the scale and the basis of Khmer wealth. Over 80,000 tributaries provided rice, healing spices, 48,000 varieties of fever medicines, salve for hemorrhoids, and vast amounts of antiseptics, purgatives, and drugs. From no other realm of the time—not even China—do we have figures of this sort or on this scale.

Even amid all this medication, the favorite remedy for illness was prayer. In 1186, Jayavarman dedicated a temple to house an image of his mother as "the Perfection of Wisdom." Again the statistics recorded in surviving documents are dazzling for their precision—which reveals the participation of meticulous bureaucrats—and the wealth they display. The temple received tribute from over 3,000 villages. Its endowments included vessels made of gold and silver weighing more than 1,100 pounds. The records itemize thousands of precious stones, together with imported and locally produced luxury textiles. Daily provisions for a permanent establishment of 500 residents included rice, butter, milk, molasses, oil, seeds, and honey. Worshippers at the temple required annual supplies of wax, sandalwood, camphor, and clothing for the temple's 260 images of Buddhas. This is all evidence of the penetration of Cambodia by Indian Ocean trade.

The same source adds evidence on a revolution of Jayavarman's reign: the triumph of Buddhism over Hinduism as the court religion. "Doing these good deeds," the inscription concludes,

> the king with extreme devotion to his mother, made this prayer: that because of the virtue of the good deeds I have accomplished, my mother, once delivered from the ocean of transmigration, may enjoy the state of Buddhahood.[2]

Meanwhile, in the inner chamber of the gilded tower that the king added to the city, a Buddha replaced the Hindu images of previous reigns. The triumph of Buddhism in a state rooted in Hinduism was part of a broader trend. Though Buddhism dwindled in India, it spread in east, southeast, and Central Asia.

India: Economy and Culture

The strength of cultural links across the Bay of Bengal, between India and southeast Asia, is a reminder of another problem. India had long exerted influences across Eurasia: Buddhism and Hinduism; the science, logic, and technology of the Indian sages (see Chapter 6). The Indian subcontinent's central position athwart Indian Ocean trade routes guaranteed it against isolation and gave it privileged access to far-flung markets (see Map 11.3). India's long, open coasts could soak up ideas from across the oceans like the pores of a sponge.

Yet from the eleventh century, India's role in originating and recycling cultural influences began to diminish. Whereas earlier Muslim scholars had looked to India as a source of useful learning, Al Biruni, who came from Persia in the 1020s and was regarded as the most learned man of his time, found the Indian sages of his day complacent and uninterested in learning from abroad. Hindu science "presumed on the ignorance of the people."

While his picture may have been distorted by the desire to advocate the superiority of Islam over native Indian religion, there was some truth on Al Biruni's side. At least in the north—the part of India he knew—political dissolution accompanied a decline in the quality and output of works of art and learning. The large states that had filled most of the subcontinent since the early ninth century collapsed under the strain of trying to compete with each other and the impact of invaders and rebellions. Much of central and northern India was divided among competing royal dynasties that found it hard to sustain the loyalties of their followers. The rich Hindu temples of northern India became the prey of Muslim raiders from Afghanistan.

Nevertheless, though states provide the peace commerce requires—and, if the rulers are wise, the infrastructures that help trade thrive—economies can sometimes function well despite political troubles. In some parts of India, the economy was booming. Records of tribute paid to the temples in Rajasthan in northwest India reveal a lively trade in sugar, dyes, textiles, salt, areca nuts, coconuts, butter, salt, sesame oil. A ruler in Shikar in Rajasthan in 973 levied tribute in pearls, horses, "fine garments," weapons, camphor, betel nuts, sandalwood, "and endless quantities of gold and with spirited rutting elephants, huge like mountains, together with their mates." From the eleventh century, we can reconstruct merchant lineages that are astonishing, because they reveal how merchants saw

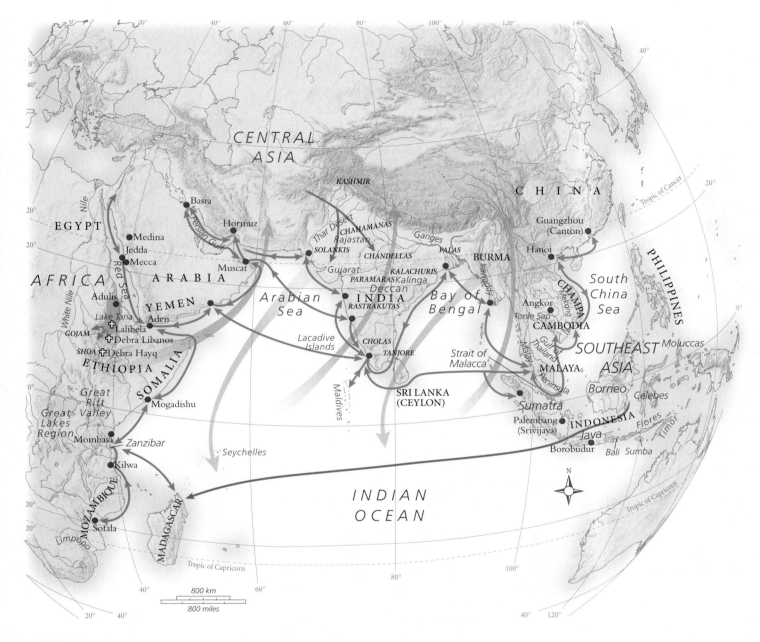

MAP 11.3

The Indian Ocean: From Ethiopia to Cambodia, ca. 1000–1200

- ▨ Zagwe dynasty, Ethiopia
- → Ethiopian expansion under the Solomids
- ✠ monastery
- → maritime trade route
- *CHOLAS* Indian dynasty, 9th–13th centuries
- → colonization route to Madagascar
- ➤ warm monsoon (April to September)
- ➤ cold monsoon (October to March)
- → Muslim raids into northern India, 11th century

themselves. The Pragvata family, for instance, considered themselves warriors in a trade war against Muslim competitors and advanced loans to rulers to fight real wars. Not only the warrior caste, says one inscription, can fight in "the shop of the battlefield." In most societies of the time, merchants would not have dared to liken themselves to the warrior elite. Clearly, the economy was doing well.

The most spectacular effect was the revival of Indian cities after a long period of relative stagnation. This effect was particularly strong in the south, where political troubles were fewer and invasions infrequent. In Karnataka in southwest India, eleventh-century inscriptions mention 78 towns—three times the number recorded for the eighth century. A grant to a temple in northern Karnataka in 1204 reveals how a city was laid out, with streets leading between white-plastered temples, bazaars, water tanks, flower gardens, and food plots, with arterial roads at the city's edges.

India: The Chola Kingdom

Far from the political disorder of the north, states in southern India could enjoy the strength that the wealth of the Indian Ocean made possible. The Chola kingdom was the most remarkable. Like that of the Khmer or of Ethiopia, its heartland lay away from the coasts in rice fields and pastures. The Chola labored to extend their landward frontiers and develop their landward resources by ruthless exploitation, felling forests on a gigantic scale.

The Chola Kingdom	
1070–1122	Reign of Kulottunga I, proponent of seaborne imperialism
Thirteenth century	Decline of Chola

The power, wealth, and ambitions of the Chola kings fused with those of the merchant communities on the coast. In the kingdom's grand ports, gold was exchanged for pearls, coral, betel nuts, cardamom, cottons, ebony, amber, incense, ivory, and rhinoceros horn. Elephants were stamped with the royal tiger emblem before being shipped out for export.

Chola merchants had private armies and a reputation "like the lion's" for "springing to the kill." The imperial itch seemed strongest in kings whose relations with merchants were closest. King Kulottunga I (r. 1070–1122), who relaxed tolls paid to the crown, imagined himself the hero of songs "sung on the further shore of the ocean by the young women of Persia." Most Chola seaborne "imperialism" was probably just raiding, though there were Chola footholds and garrisons on Sri Lanka, the Maldives, and perhaps in Malaya. Its impact, however, crippled Srivijaya in Indonesia (see Chapter 10) and enriched the temples of southern India.

Hindu temples were the allies of the Chola kings in managing the state and the biggest beneficiaries of victories in war. While the seaward drive lasted, the registers of gifts inscribed on temple walls show its effects: dazzling bestowals of exotic goods and cash, especially from about 1000 to about 1070. The treasures of the city temple of Tanjore included a crown with enough gold to buy enough oil to keep 40 lamps alight in perpetuity, and hundreds of precious gemstones and jewels, with plenty of umbrellas and fly whisks for the comfort of the worshippers at ceremonies.

The temples are the best evidence of the grandeur of the Chola Empire and the reach of its power and trade. But they also suggest why, ultimately, the Chola withdrew from overseas ventures. The temples invested heavily in land and in the revenues of farmers whom they supplied with capital to make agricultural improvements. In consequence, they may have contributed to a shift toward agriculture and land-based wealth and, therefore, to weakening Chola maritime imperialism—an enfeeblement that became marked in the thirteenth century. So, although India remained as rich as ever, some forms of Indian enterprise turned inward.

EURASIA'S EXTREMITIES: JAPAN AND WESTERN EUROPE

The Indian Ocean enclosed the main routes of communication around maritime Asia and between Asia and Africa. Of secondary importance were the land roads across Central Asia and the Sahara, which are subjects for the next chapter. For travelers on both the ocean roads and the land roads, Japan and Western Europe—the regions at the easternmost and westernmost extremities of Eurasia—were hard to get to and from. But they were close enough to the major communications routes to tap into the great exchanges of culture. During the eleventh and twelfth centuries, both areas emerged from relative isolation.

Japan

While in much of the world people struggled to overcome isolation, Japanese rulers had tried to make a virtue of it. They were fearful of losing migrants to richer regions and apprehensive of Chinese power. They had suspended diplomacy and trade with China in 838 and with Korea nearly a century later. Permission to trade abroad was hard to obtain. Even Buddhist monks had to get permission to leave the country on pilgrimage. Of course, illicit trade—or "piracy"—went on. But self-sufficiency remained government policy.

The best-known Japanese literature of the tenth and eleventh centuries is focused on a narrow, closed court society in a narrow, closed country. The fiction of Murasaki Shikibu in *The Tale of Genji*, one of the earliest realistic novels ever written, depicts a world in which the supreme values seem to be snobbery and sensitivity. Struggles for precedence dominate court life. The emperor grants his favorite cat the privileges "of a lady of middle rank." A nurse can tell from the sound of a visitor's cough to what level of the nobility he belongs. The court is everything. Even an appointment as governor of a province is a disgrace. Court literature scarcely mentions the peasants, beaten down by famine and plague, whose rice taxes sustained the aristocracy.

Murasaki portrayed the vices of a faction-ridden system. She was a spokeswoman for courtiers excluded from power by the man she hated, whose amorous advances she claimed to have turned down: the all-powerful courtier, Fujiwara no Michizane, who manipulated the political system by marrying his womenfolk into the imperial family and providing an effective bureaucracy from his own household. After three emperors died in factional struggles, he was left as regent of the empire in 1008. He exploited his opportunities so well that, according to one embittered critic, "not a speck of earth was left for the public domain." Emperors were so preoccupied with ritual duties that they could only bid for power by abdicating and attempting to control their heirs.

Provincial rule was left to administrators supported by retinues of hired tough guys. Despised at court for their "badly powdered faces," these local leaders wielded real power and wealth. Many of them were the descendants of imperial princes who had been sent to the provinces for want of employment at court, or who had opted for provincial careers to pursue wealth and authority. Increasingly they became warriors whose authority depended on force. As the court began to lose control of the provinces, these provincial warmongers allied in rival bands.

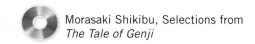

Morasaki Shikibu, Selections from *The Tale of Genji*

Genji. The earliest illustrated manuscripts of *The Tale of Genji* date from the 1120s, more than 100 years after the novel was written. But they demonstrate its enduring popularity and faithfully capture its atmosphere: the leisured opulence of the imperial palace at Heian, the learning and luxury of the court ladies, and the difficulty of leading a private life—let alone conducting the complex love affairs that the story depicts—behind frail partitions that were literally paper-thin.

In the 1070s, courtiers, temples, and merchants succeeded in opening Japan to foreign trade in their own economic interests. Trade with Korea resumed for a while as a result of the initiative of Korea's energetic King Munjon (r. 1046–1083). Direct relations between Japan and China followed. The results were dramatic: Newly rich families became players for power. The greatest profiteers were the Taira clan, who relentlessly, during the twelfth century, built up their power by acquiring provincial governorships and dominating the imperial court. In a series of civil wars, culminating in 1185, their rivals and relatives, the Minamoto clan, replaced them as imperial "protectors" or **shoguns** (shoh-GUNS). From then on the emperors never recovered real power. The renowned monk Mongaku was an adviser to successive shoguns. Invited to pray for a new shogun in 1200, he showed just what he thought of the request: "In the dwellings of those who offend, prayer is of no avail."

As the diary of the Tosa Lady shows, it was hard to get around Japan's home islands—even that relatively small part of the islands the Japanese state occupied. Overseas contacts were difficult, the surrounding seas daunting. Yet Japan's isolation had never shut out Chinese cultural influence. Some of Murasaki's characters showed impatience with "Chinesified" styles, appealing to the "spirit of Japan." And popular literature did depict China as strange and exotic. But educated Japanese were aware of their dependence on China for almost all their models of learning, art, and government. Chinese was the language of the upper administration as well as of serious literature. The elite used quotations from Chinese classics to clinch arguments. Confucian ceremonies and Chinese poetry contests were among the main occupations at court. Murasaki repelled Fujiwara's unwanted attentions by capping his Chinese verses.

Japan: Official Isolation

838	Trade and diplomacy with China suspended
ca. 1000	*The Tale of Genji* written
1070s	Opening of Japan to limited foreign trade; restoration of direct relations with China
1160	Taira clan ascendant
1185	Minamoto replaces Taira as shoguns

Western Europe: Economics and Politics

Nowhere else in the world were there long-range trade routes to match those of the Indian Ocean. But the land routes across Eurasia, from Europe to China, and across the Sahara, between the Mediterranean and the Sahel, were probably carrying increasing amounts of traffic through the eleventh and twelfth centuries. Western Europe lay at or just beyond the western and northern extremities of these land routes.

Its relative isolation always threatened the region with backwardness. The Atlantic clouded Europe's outlook to the west. The Sahara cut it off from much of Africa. Europe's frontier on the east to the great civilizations of Asia was hard to keep open across plains that hostile steppelanders patrolled or forests and vast marshlands obstructed. There was no direct access to the Indian Ocean. Western European merchants rarely went there—and, when they did, they had to undertake epic overland journeys via the Nile valley or across Arabia or what are now Turkey and Iraq.

A Muslim geographer, al-Istakhri, contemplating the world from Persia in 950, hardly noticed Western Europe at all. In his map, the West dangled feebly off the edge of the known world. Meanwhile, Latin Christians who looked out at the world in their own imaginations probably saw something like the version mapped at about the same time by the monks who drew the illustrations in the *Commentary on the Apocalypse* of Beatus of Liébana in northern Spain: Asia and Africa take up most of the space, Europe consists mainly of three peninsulas—Spain, Italy, and Greece, jutting into the Mediterranean—with a thin strip of hinterland above

A Muslim view of the world. The world, mapped by the Muslim geographer al-Istakhri in the tenth century. The map is now in the library of Leiden University in the Netherlands. Persia, the map-maker's homeland, is in the center. Europe is the tiny triangle at the lower right. The Caspian and Aral Seas are represented as two large round blobs in the middle of Asia in the lower portion. West Africa is the landmass at the top.

them. In 1095, urging fellow Christians to new efforts against the Muslims, Pope Urban II expressed the feeling of being under siege:

> The world is not evenly divided. Of its three parts, our enemies hold Asia. . . . Africa, too, the second part of the world, has been held by our enemies for two hundred years and more. . . . Thirdly there is Europe. . . . Of this region we Christians inhabit only a small part, for who will give the name of Christians to those barbarians who live in the remote islands and seek their living on the icy ocean as if they were whales?[3]

Urban wanted Christendom to combine to redress what he saw as an imbalance of power. But disunity fragmented what political scientists call a state system with lots of interlocking territorial states. From 962, the German ruler Otto I called himself—more in hope than in reality—"Roman emperor," and tried to recover a sense of unity. When his grandson, Otto III (r. 982–1002), looked back at the reflection of himself that stared, enthroned in power, from an illustration in his gospel book, he could see lavish images of Germany, Gaul, and the Slav lands humbly bearing their tribute toward him, led by a personification of Rome. These pretensions were hollow. The empire of the Ottos did not cover much more than modern Germany.

Yet disunity can be stimulating, encouraging rival states in competition. Latin Christendom emerged as an expanding world, as it stretched between increasingly remote horizons. As we have just seen with Ethiopia, expansion does not only happen outward. There are often inward cracks and gaps to fill, slack to take up. From the eleventh to the early fourteenth centuries, a process of internal expansion, accompanied by new economic activity, was under way in Western Europe.

Settlement encroached on marginal soils and headed uphill. Forests fell. Bogs were drained. Farmers moved in. This was more than an economic enterprise: It was a sacred undertaking—reclaiming for God the terrain of paganism. The forest was alive with sprites, demons, and "wild men of the woods." The pious felled trees sacred to pagans. The most famous example is the best. Unable to sleep "on a certain night" in 1122, Abbot Suger of Saint-Denis, a monastery near Paris, rose to search the forest for 12 trees mighty enough to frame the new sanctuary he was planning for his abbey church, built—he hoped—to be full of light and "to elevate dull minds to the truth." The foresters wondered if the abbot was "quite ignorant of the fact that nothing of the kind could be found in the entire region"; but he found what he needed "with the courage of faith."

It was a representative incident in a vast project to tame little-exploited and underexploited environments. The Cistercians, one of the most dynamic new monastic orders of the period, directed their efforts into "deserts" where habitation was sparse and nature hostile. They razed woodlands and drove flocks and ox teams into wildernesses where today, all too often, the vast abbeys lie ruined in their turn. Sometimes, in their craving to escape the greedy secular society that put their souls at risk, Cistercians actually drove existing settlers away from their lands, extending the frontiers of colonization even farther as peasants imitated Cistercian practices on even more marginal lands.

Engineering came to the aid of environmental adaptation. Drainage extended the land on which people could dwell. In Holland, rapid population growth seems closely linked with the success of a project Count Floris V (r. 1256–1296) launched to reclaim waterlogged land. New embankments and canals made rivers easier to navigate. Searching out new routes and building roads and bridges were urgent tasks for which monarchs accepted some responsibility and for which—for example—Domingo de la Calzada, who built causeways and bridges for pilgrims to the shrine of St. James at Compostela in northern Spain, was made a saint.

Behind the expanding frontiers, modest technical revolutions were boosting production. Among inventions originating in Europe at this time were windmills, ground lenses, and clocks. Others, brought there thanks to improved communications across Eurasia, were paper mills, the compass, firearms, and—in the fourteenth century—the blast furnace. Large, heavy plows with curved blades enabled farmers to exploit the dense, wet soil of northern Europe. More effective harnesses enabled horses to pull the plows and take over a lot of hard work in the fields. More efficient windmills and water mills, more exact metallurgy and new products, especially in arms and glassware, extended the range of business and the flow of wealth. The advances in agriculture that began in the Islamic world toward the end of the previous millennium (see Chapter 10) spread hesitantly, across Western Europe, improving farming with new strains of wheat and—where it would grow—of rice. More varieties of beans improved nutrition and added nitrates to the soil.

Historians debate who was responsible for extending tillage and coaxing new wealth from the soil. Was it primarily the work of "free peasants"? Or did landowners force peasant dependants into greater productivity? There were many different patterns of landholding, which varied regionally and locally, and the drive to improve efficiency probably happened no matter what form landholding took. In any case, the colonization of new lands created opportunities of enrichment at all social levels. More food meant more people. The population of Europe may have doubled, from about 35 million around the year 1000, while these changes took place.

As production and population increased, so did opportunities for trade. New trade routes knitted Atlantic and Mediterranean seaboards in a single economy. This was important, because Western Europe has two natural economic zones—formed respectively along the Mediterranean and Atlantic coasts. The Strait of Gibraltar separates them, with widely different sailing conditions along the two seaboards. Inland a chain of breakwaters splits the continent, determining the flow of rivers and, therefore, the directions of exchange. Communication between these two zones was not easy. Limited access across France and the Alpine passes kept commerce alive, even when commercial navigation from sea to sea was abandoned.

New kinds of economic activity became possible in growing towns. Lübeck, founded in 1143, was the pioneer city of what became the **Hanseatic League**—a network of allied ports along the North Sea and Baltic coasts that collaborated to promote trade. Soon after, Mediterranean craft, mainly from the Italian city of Genoa, the island of Majorca, and Spain, resumed large-scale ventures along Atlantic coasts, such as had not been recorded since the Western Roman Empire collapsed in the fifth century (see Chapter 8).

Exchange across vast distances made geographical specialization and genuine industrialization possible. For instance, industries served by the trade of Genoa depended on geographical specialization. Textiles depended on concentrating wools and dyestuffs from widely separated places of origin. Food processing relied on matching fresh foodstuffs, such as herring, with salt. Shipbuilding demanded a similar marriage of raw materials—wood, iron, sailcloth, and pitch.

The results included urbanization: the revival of old cities and the building of new ones. The best way, indeed, to measure the economic progress of the period in much of Europe is by the growth of towns—ways of organizing life, which, at the time, were prized as uniquely virtuous. "The order of mankind," according to Gerald

Otto III. The workshop of the Abbey of Reichenau in Germany was one of the finest art studios in tenth- and early eleventh-century Europe, producing the Gospel book of Emperor Otto III on gilded pages. The enthroned emperor grasps the orb of the world, stamped with the cross of Christ (top). He towers over clergy and aristocracy alike, while the regions of Europe, led by Rome, shuffle humbly toward him with their tribute (bottom).

○ MAKING CONNECTIONS ○

CONTENDING WITH ISOLATION, CA. 1000–1200

REGION / PEOPLE OR KINGDOM →	OPPORTUNITIES →	EXPLOITATION STRATEGIES
Arctic/Inuit	Change in climate: warming weather allows for navigation across Canadian Arctic; introduction of new breed of pack dogs for transportation; introduction of bow and arrow	New techniques for constructing walrus-hide boats; new uses for sealskin, other animal hides for transport, hunting, food
Greenland/Norse	Warming climate; wealth of fish and game in almost uninhabited region; availability of export items such as hunting falcons, walrus ivory	Improved navigational techniques; new understanding of prevailing winds, ocean currents to improve chances of successful voyages; introduction of European grains and grasses for grazing animals; development of new breed of sheep
North American Southwest and Mississippi region/ Native Americans	Southwest: introduction of maize from Mexico; defensible canyons with water supply; growing population Mississippi: introduction of Mesoamerican "tool kit," food, way of life, thought; expanded trade routes bring deerskin, shells, bison hides, metals, and minerals	Southwest: irrigation canals to expand agriculture; many ceremonial centers; expansion into new zones; intensive organization of labor; development of multistoried residential structures Mississippi: expansion of trade routes; new forms of agriculture with maize, beans, squash, and fish farming; larger populations lead to more intensive crafts development/industry
Mesoamerica/Yucatán: Maya	Abundant forests, wildlife, coastal resources	New forms of irrigation, wells; new communities lead to expanded sea and land trade routes
East Africa/Ethiopia	Wider access to trade goods	Increased Indian Ocean trade with Arabs, Chinese, Indians helps equip Ethiopian dynasties to expand into new terrain
Southeast Asia: Khmer kingdom (Cambodia)	Growth of Indian Ocean trade opens outlets for Khmer rice surplus; wealth from trade and taxes funds Angkor Wat	Expansion of kingdom coincides with monumental temple complexes at Angkor, complete with expanded amenities for subjects—hospitals, shrines, etc.
India/Chola kingdom	Expansion of frontiers through inland raids brings additional natural resources (forests, agricultural land)	Landward strategy of clearing forests, planting crops and building large temples; coastal merchant communities merge with pirate expeditions sponsored by Chola kings to raid foreign ports
Japan	Provincial warriors break away from imperial court, open Japan to foreign trade; new wealth	Taira and other newly rich families begin to dominate imperial court, develop shogunate system of government to rule more efficiently
Western Europe	Expanding settlements into marginal agricultural areas; new engineering techniques to manage rivers, build infrastructure	Intensive land management—felling forests, draining bogs combines with Christianizing efforts to "civilize" barbarian areas; increased commerce leads to economic specialization, growth of towns and communes

of Wales in the 1180s, "progresses from the woods to the fields and from the fields to the towns and the gatherings of citizens." In Italy, the **commune**—as the citizen body was collectively called—became an institution of civic government in the late eleventh or early twelfth century. In what seems to have been a conscious reaching back to a Roman model, many Italian cities acquired "consuls" in this period. By the mid–twelfth century Otto of Freising regarded autonomous city governments as typical of northern Italy. Instead of deferring to some great protector—bishop, nobleman, or abbot—Italian cities became their own "lords" and even extended jurisdiction into the countryside. In effect, some cities were independent republics, forming alliances in defiance of, or despite, their supposed lords. Others tried unsuccessfully for the same status.

Self-ruling city-states were most common in Italy, where, perhaps, memories of Rome remained most alive. But urban awareness and the numbers and size of towns grew over much of Europe. On the edges of Christendom, planned towns were laid out with the measuring rod and peopled by wagon trains. In Spain, the granting by monarchs of founding documents to tiny new communities marked the progress of settlement on the frontier with the Islamic world. These usually gave the inhabitants some share in judicial or administrative power. All towns of the time were small by modern standards. As few as 2,000 citizens could make a town if it had walls and a charter. "Feelings," it was said, "make the town." If the people felt urban, in other words, they were urban. Thirty thousand inhabitants was a metropolis.

For the sake of comparison, it is worth glancing at the farther edge of Christendom, beyond the reach of the Latin church, in western Russia. Here the cities of Novgorod and Pskov contended against a hostile climate beyond the grain lands on which they relied for sustenance. Famine besieged them more often than human enemies did. Yet control of the trade routes to the river Volga made Novgorod cash rich. It never had more than a few thousand inhabitants, yet its monuments record its progress: its *kremlin* (or palace-fortress) walls and five-domed cathedral in the 1040s; in the early twelfth century, a series of buildings that the ruler paid for; and in 1207, the merchants' church of St. Paraskeva in the marketplace.

From 1136, communal government prevailed in Novgorod. The revolt of that year marks the creation of a city-state on an ancient model—a republican commune like those of Italy. The prince was deposed for reasons the rebels' proclamations specify. "Why did he not care for the common people? Why did he want to wage war? Why did he not fight bravely? And why did he prefer games and entertainments rather than state affairs? Why did he have so many gerfalcons and dogs?" Thereafter, the citizens' principle was, "If the prince is no good, throw him into the mud!"

Western Europe: Religion and Culture

Transformations in art, thought, and worship matched the dynamism of the economy and of political change. New forms of heresy, for instance, were enormously important for the future of Western Christendom. If popular heresy existed in Western Europe before the eleventh century, no one noticed it. After the year 1000, however, it emerged as a threat. A French peasant named Leutard had a vision in which bees—a symbol of supposedly sexless reproduction—entered his body through his penis. The vision drove him to renounce his wife, shatter the images of

Technology and Growth in Europe

Late tenth century	Beginning of warm spell in climate
1000	Population of Europe approximately 35 million
1143	Founding of Lübeck; beginning of Hanseatic League
ca. 1200	Introduction of new technologies: heavy plows, better harnesses, windmills, water mills, ground lenses, clocks

Hell's mouth. The Archangel Michael locks the gate of hell, pictured as a monster's jaws. Note that some of the tortured souls in this thirteenth-century miniature painting are monarchs and monks, with crowns and tonsures. Whatever their wealth or social position, all Christians were equally subject to God's judgment.

Jesus and the saints in the local church, and preach universal celibacy. Among fellow peasants, he attracted a following that survived his death, albeit not for long. In 1015, the first burnings of heretics in the West for over 600 years were kindled. From then on, popular heretical movements were a continuous feature of Western European history.

Two long, slow changes seem to underlie this phenomenon. By the late eleventh century, a movement of Christian renewal and evangelizing fervor (known to historians as the Gregorian Reform, after Pope Gregory VII [r. 1073–1085], its greatest sponsor) was demanding new and exacting standards both of clerical behavior and of lay awareness of the faith, and challenging kings and noblemen for control over appointments in the church. More than a power struggle, it was a drive to purge the church of profanity.

At the same time, the evangelical fervor of the clergy was lowering its sights to include the peasantry, to whom clerics had, up to then, paid little attention. This was the result, in part, of a long build up of dissatisfaction with the shallowness with which Christianity had penetrated popular minds. Among its effects was a new or increased emphasis in saints' lives on how saints could—in today's jargon—"relate" to ordinary people by doing menial jobs. A French count, for instance, who joined a monastery in about 990, was set first to keep the hens, then the sheep, then the pigs, and was astonished at his own delight in each successive task.

On the other hand, the rise of popular dissent bears some signs of a revolution born of prosperity. Lay people were demanding more of their clergy. The really popular heresies of the eleventh and twelfth centuries were those ministered to by men of ferocious sanctity, like the preachers who called themselves "the perfect," and whose fanatical renunciation of worldly pleasures made them seem holier than the church. At the same time, the new security of life, the opportunities to gather harvests without being attacked, the leisure that increased yields from the soil gave to people, all bought time for a luxury unavailable in hard times: time to think about the Christian mysteries and develop a desire to get involved in them. At a relatively high level of education, the church could satisfy these stirrings by providing pilgrimages, private prayers, devotional reading matter, and orders of chivalry for the warrior class. Spiritually minded peasants, like Leutard's enthusiasts, could not be accommodated so easily.

In the struggle to save their souls, European laymen in the Middle Ages were at a disadvantage. The religious life opened heaven's gates; the warrior's life, stained with bloodshed, distracted by the world, closed them. The religious model suggested that obedience to rules—like those of monks and nuns—could sanctify the lay life. The first such rules or "codes of chivalry" in the twelfth century emphasized religious vows of chastity, poverty, and obedience, but lay virtues gathered prominence, redirected against deadly sins: generosity against greed, self-control against anger, loyalty against lies and lust. **Chivalry** became the prevailing disposition among the aristocracy of the age. It did not make warfare any more gentle or moral or all aristocrats good. But it did widen the range of the virtues to which aristocrats aspired.

The art of the West in the eleventh and twelfth centuries reveals a sort of cult of the commoner. Images of peasants and artisans appeared alongside saints and angels around church doorways, engaged in the economic activities that paid for this art. Here were arrayed the members of a peaceful and orderly society, with everyone in their place and doing well out of it. The new mood affected the way artists humanized heaven by evoking piercing emotions. Early in the eleventh century, the painter of the gospel book of Abbess Hilda of Merschede painted a scene of Jesus asleep in a storm on the Sea of Galilee, in which the ship leaps into life and the anxiety of the Apostles burdens their brows. The Jesus carved for Archbishop Gero of Cologne dates from before the end of the tenth century, but no modern master ever chiseled the face of the suffering Jesus with more exquisite agony: drawn lips, taut cheeks, nerveless lids, and a trickle of blood at the brow.

In art, literature, and scholarship, a sense of continuity with ancient civilization shines through. Sculptors and builders copied classical works. Abbot Suger's ideas on the beauty of light were derived from what he thought was a Greek text from the first century. The twelfth-century English historian, Geoffrey of Monmouth, claimed to trace the "British" monarchy back to characters from the ancient Greek poet Homer. Poets in England and Germany tried to write like ancient Romans. Lectures in Paris introduced students to the logic of Aristotle. Abelard (1079–1142), the most renowned teacher of the era in Paris, gave audiences the impression that there was nothing logic could not do. In his book on logic, *Sic et Non* (*Yes and No*) of 1122, he exposed the contradictions in many treasured assumptions of theology and philosophy. The twelfth-century Archbishop of Canterbury, Anselm, too, wrote about God using reason as his only guide—suppressing references to Scripture or the tradition of the church. Indeed, Anselm sought to prove the existence of God—or at least of a real being with the perfection Christianity ascribed to God—by unaided reason. Roughly, his proof says that the most perfect being we can think of must exist, since, if he did not, we should be able to think of another, more perfect being who did.

By the twelfth century, students of nature were beginning to "stand on the shoulders of giants" of antiquity and see farther than they had. In 1092, Walcher of Malvern fixed the difference in time between Italy and England by timing an eclipse. Adelard of Bath noted that light travels faster than sound. He agreed with his younger contemporary, William of Conches, that God likes to work through nature and that miraculous explanations should never be invoked when scientific ones will do. Practical observations piled up: the heights of tides, the habits of volcanoes. Carvers of capitals on pillars in churches imitated natural forms. Sculptors chiseled plants and flowers into monastery cloisters.

IN PERSPECTIVE: The Patchwork of Effects

The great leap of Latin Christendom—the renaissance or rebirth in art and thought that began after the year 1000—was possible because Western Europeans found ways to cope and contend with their relative isolation. Scholars in the late tenth and eleventh centuries went to Muslim Spain to learn science, mathematics, and Arabic. Gerbert of Aurillac—the Emperor Otto III's tutor—sweated to learn mathematics in the Spanish Muslim city of Toledo. Adelard of Bath studied Arabic translations of classical Greek books, lost in the West. In the late eleventh and twelfth centuries, as we shall see in the next chapter, pilgrimages, wars, and trade took Western Europeans in unprecedented numbers eastward, to the eastern Mediterranean, and to contact with the Islamic world and Eastern Christendom at Constantinople. At the same time, the westward trickle of communications with south and east Asia probably increased along the Silk Roads.

For Japan, too, isolation might have been frustrating. But there was just enough contact with Korea and China to stoke Japanese art and learning with Chinese influences. The delicately folded poems written by Genji and his friends and

Romanesque art has a reputation for stylization and formality. But in this early example that Archbishop Gero of Cologne in Germany commissioned before the end of the tenth century, the artist was evidently already interested in anatomical realism and in depicting intense emotion. Instead of a remote, divine, judgmental Christ, we see the sorrow and resignation of Jesus, a suffering human being.

Abelard defends himself, from *The Letters of Abelard and Heloise*

CHRONOLOGY

Tenth century	Flourishing of canyon culture in American Southwest; Chichén Itzá founded
Late tenth century	Norse reach Greenland
ca. 1000	*The Tale of Genji* (Japan); Thule Inuit reach Greenland
1000–1300	Rapid population growth in Europe and development of new technologies; Maya intensively exploit Yucatán peninsula
1000–1100	Flourishing of Chola kingdom (India)
1070s	Opening of Japan to limited foreign trade; restoration of direct relations between China and Japan
Early twelfth century	Building of Angkor Wat (Cambodia) begins
1150	Canyon settlements in American Southwest withdraw to higher ground
1200	Population of Cahokia reaches 10,000
1270	Solomids seize power in Ethiopia
1300	Decline of upper Mississippi valley culture

real-life counterparts were all in Chinese—part of an ancient renaissance, as influential as anything Europeans wrote or sculpted in imitation of antique models.

In the preindustrial world, the size of states and the scope of economies were functions of time as well as distance. Messages, armies, revenues, and cargoes took a long time to travel across broken country or, by sea, through variable winds. Around the Indian Ocean, increased traffic brought areas in East Africa and southeast Asia out of isolation and kept India rich, despite its political troubles. Despite the heroic efforts of the Norse in the Atlantic, the Thule Inuit in the Arctic, and the Polynesians in the Pacific, the wealth-creating effects of sustained transoceanic or interoceanic commerce could not yet be reproduced outside the region of the monsoons around the Indian Ocean.

Even so, India was much less influential in world history—far less productive of ideas and movements that affected the rest of the world—after 1000 than it had been before. This is only one of many ways in which India seems to have reached a "peak" of achievement. According to the best available studies, India's population was over 200 million in 1000 and fell for the rest of what we think of as the Middle Ages. The Chola kingdom was the last Indian empire to exert major influence in southeast Asia, where Hinduism began to decline—ultimately, to survive only in patches outside India itself.

In the Americas and parts of sub-Saharan Africa, the arresting effects of isolation could not be overcome. Cultural contacts between Mesoamerica and parts of North America helped, for a while, to produce spectacular experiments in building states and modifying environments. But the networks were too fragile and temporary for the effects to endure.

In the next century, the thirteenth, changes in the pattern of communications across Eurasia would heighten the differences between the Old and the New Worlds. To understand these events and their effects, we have to turn first to the other great theme of the history of the eleventh and twelfth centuries: the growing contacts and conflicts between sedentary and nomadic peoples in Eurasia and parts of Africa and their effects on the interactions of surrounding regions.

PROBLEMS AND PARALLELS

1. How did societies around the world contend with their relative isolation between 1000 and 1200?

2. How did isolation affect Greenland and the North American cultures from 1000 to 1200?

3. What roles did Cahokia play in central North America? What evidence is there that it was influenced by the civilizations of Mesoamerica?

4. How did Buddhism and Hinduism spread throughout southeast Asia? How did these religious traditions affect parts of Asia outside India?

5. How did the lands on the extremities of Eurasia (Japan and Europe) overcome their isolation and emerge with powerful political, cultural, and economic systems?

6. How did urbanization affect religious, economic, and political life in Europe between 1000 and 1200?

7. How did increased trade across the Indian Ocean affect East Africa during the eleventh century?

8. What are the benefits and drawbacks of cultural and economic isolation?

DOCUMENTS IN GLOBAL HISTORY

- Ki no Tsurayuki, excerpt from the *Tosa Diary*
- Excerpt from *Speculum Princips*, "The Animal Life of Greenland and the Character of the Land in Those Regions"
- Canyon de Chelly

- A European explorer's description of Cahokia
- Morasaki Shikibu, Selections from *The Tale of Genji*
- Abelard defends himself, from *The Letters of Abelard and Heloise*

Please see the Primary Source DVD for additional sources related to this chapter.

READ ON

A convenient version of the Tosa diary is printed in D. Keene, ed., *Anthology of Japanese Travel Literature* (1960). *The Book of the Wonders of India* is available in an edition by G. S. P. Freeman-Grenville (1984). G. R. Tibbetts, *Arab Navigation in the Indian Ocean before the Coming of the Portuguese* (2002) gives the background.

On Greenland, K. Seaver, *The Frozen Echo* (1997), is a brilliant work with contentious conclusions.

On the North American Southwest, S. Lekson et al., *Great Pueblo Architecture of Chaco Canyon* (1986) is outstanding; pages in B. G. Trigger and D. Washburn, eds., *The Cambridge History of the Native Peoples of North America*, v.1, Part I, bring it up to date. The Mississippi sites are covered in T. R. Pauketat and T. E. Emerson, *Cahokia: Domination and Ideology in the Mississippian World* (2000); T. E. Emerson and R. B. Lewis, eds., *Cahokia and the Hinterland* (2000); and T. R. Pauketat, *The Ascent of Chiefs* (1994). On the Mixtec, R. Spores, *The Mixtec Kings* (1967) cannot be bettered.

For Ethiopia under the Zagwe, some sources appear in R. B. Pankhurst, *The Royal Chronicles of Ethiopia* (1967). On Ethiopia and Angkor the works recommended for Chapter 9 are good for the period covered here.

Albiruni's *India*, ed. C. Sawyer is the classic text. M. A. Saleem Khan, *Al-Biruni's Discovery of India* (2001) attempts an interpretation. The works of Chattopadhyaya and Thapar remain fundamental for this period in India. For the Cholas, V. Dehejia, *Art of the Imperial Cholas* (1990) is a breathtaking

work; B. K. Pandeya, *Temple Economy under the Cholas* (1984) is important.

V. K. Jain, *Trade and Traders in Western India* (1990) and B. Stein, *Peasant, State and Society in Medieval South India* (1994) are useful on their subjects.

There are many editions of *The Tale of Genji*. For Japan in this period, *The Cambridge History of Japan*, ii (2002) is comprehensive.

On Western Europe, R. Southern, *The Making of the Middle Ages* (1961) is a classic work, unsurpassed. R. Bartlett, *The Making of Europe* (1994) is fundamental. Classic essays on some of the topics covered here are collected in F. Fernández-Armesto and J. Mudoon, eds., *The Internal Frontier of Christendom* (Forthcoming). A useful little collection of Cistercian sources is in P. Matarasso, ed., *The Cistercian World* (1993). Abbot Suger is best approached through E. Panofsky, ed., *Abbot Suger on the Abbey Church of St Denis and Its Art Treasures* (1979). On technology, J. Gimpel, *The Medieval Machine* (1977) is superb and standard. On peasants, G. Astill and J. Langdon, eds., *Medieval Farming and Technology* (1997) provides an excellent introduction.

On heresy, M. Lambert, *Medieval Heresy* (2002) is spirited and comprehensive. A. Murray, *Reason and Society in the Middle Ages* (1978) is an ingenious work, full of insights. C. H. Haskins, *The Renaissance of the Twelfth Century* (2005) is a classic, once pioneering, now enduring. P. Lasko, *Ars Sacra* (1995) is a good introduction to the art of the period.

CHAPTER 12

The Nomadic Frontiers: The Islamic World, Byzantium, and China, ca. 1000–1200

Scenes of steppeland life in the Middle Ages. Two warriors do their washing. A shaman writhes by the campfire. Weapons are stacked. Horses graze. Starving dogs hope for scraps. A chief mends his saddle.

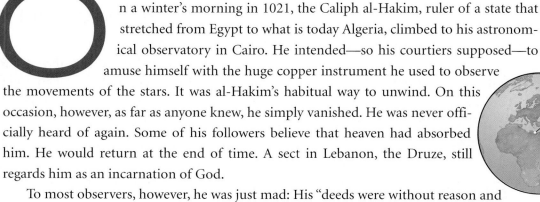

O n a winter's morning in 1021, the Caliph al-Hakim, ruler of a state that stretched from Egypt to what is today Algeria, climbed to his astronomical observatory in Cairo. He intended—so his courtiers supposed—to amuse himself with the huge copper instrument he used to observe the movements of the stars. It was al-Hakim's habitual way to unwind. On this occasion, however, as far as anyone knew, he simply vanished. He was never officially heard of again. Some of his followers believe that heaven had absorbed him. He would return at the end of time. A sect in Lebanon, the Druze, still regards him as an incarnation of God.

To most observers, however, he was just mad: His "deeds were without reason and his dreams without interpretation." At different times, he outlawed dogs, churches, evening traffic, canal trade, and women's shoes. He expected the end of the world—which perhaps explains his personal austerity and reckless almsgiving. His main defect, in his critics' eyes, was that he was a Shiite (see Chapter 9). He saw himself as the fulfillment of Shiite belief in the divine appointment of an infallible **imam,** or holy ruler, to supplement Muhammad's teaching.

The conflict between rival caliphs, the Shiite in Cairo, and the Sunni in Baghdad, divided the Islamic world into roughly equal portions. To make matters worse, from the 920s, a third dynasty, with its court in Cordova in Spain, also claimed to be caliphs. In the tenth and eleventh centuries, Shiites seized Baghdad and humiliated the Sunni caliphs. From 1090, the Shiite sect known as the Assassins occupied Alamut—a mountain fortress in Persia—from where they launched raids and unleashed allegedly drug-crazed fanatics to execute political murders. The word *assassin* comes from "hashish."

●   ●   ●   ●   ●

Threads of cultural unity still linked the Islamic world: veneration of the prophet Muhammad, adherence to the Quran, the use of Arabic as the language of religion and learning, the unifying force of the pilgrimage to Mecca. Mutual obligations among Muslims were strong, even between Shiites and Sunnis. In 1070, for instance, when famine threatened Cairo, the Fatimid caliph sent his womenfolk to Sunni Baghdad to escape starvation. Islamic civilization was still the most widely dispersed civilization the world had ever seen. Muslims ruled a continuous band of territory from Spain, across North Africa, to the Arabian Sea and the Indus River, and into Central Asia (see Map 12.1).

FOCUS questions

- HOW DID the Islamic world deal with its steppeland neighbors?
- WHAT STRENGTHS did the Turks bring to the Islamic world?
- HOW DID Byzantine civilization combine religious and secular values?
- HOW DID Byzantium survive? How far can it be said to have "declined"?
- HOW DID the Crusades affect the Islamic world and Byzantium?
- HOW DID Song China deal with the northern barbarians?
- WHY DO nomads and settled peoples tend to be enemies?

Nonetheless, political disunity disturbed Muslims. Fragmentation weakened the states it created and wasted their strength in wars against each other. The strain told. In the eleventh century, the Spanish caliphate crumbled. In most of Iran and Kurdistan, minor dynasties made the rule of the caliph in Baghdad no more than symbolic. The Fatimid caliphate had reached the limits of its expansion. In Spain, southern Italy, and Anatolia, aggressive Christian states were active.

THE ISLAMIC WORLD AND ITS NEIGHBORS

Both a challenge to and the salvation of Islam came from unlikely directions: the Sahara and the steppes. The Islamic world was caught up in a sweeping Eurasian confrontation. Settled societies faced warlike, pastoral ememies from Central Asia and North Africa. Sometimes the relationship was hostile. It was always tense. In this chapter, we look in turn at the societies most affected—the Islamic world, with its western neighbors in Spain and West Africa, and then the Byzantine and Chinese Empires.

The Coming of the Steppelanders

The steppelands seemed full of threat, as Turkic peoples overspilled the steppeland in waves of migrants and invaders. We do not know what set them off. But once the shifts of population began, they rattled a chain reaction, with some groups pushing others ahead of them.

Pilgrim caravan. "I cling to journeying, I cross deserts, I loathe pride." The freedom and frequency of travel across the Muslim world are among the main themes of one of the most popular Arabic works of the thirteenth century, the *Maqamat* (or *Scales of Harmony*) of al-Hariri, which inspired some of the finest illustrated manuscripts of the time.

In 1055, Seljuk Turks seized Baghdad and turned the caliph into a client—"a parrot in a cage." In Afghanistan, Mahmud of Ghazni, the descendant of a Turkish adventurer, was the self-appointed guard of Islam, whose raids into India gathered so many captives that prices in the slave markets tumbled. Muslims called the Turks "the army of God"—not in approval but in fear. God had unleashed these ferocious pagans to punish Muslims' sins.

Just as the Arabs had destroyed the Persian Empire and the western barbarians had broken Rome, the Turks might have shattered the Islamic world. After stunning conquests, however, they stopped, converted by the culture they had conquered. Seljuk and his sons were among the early converts. The ruins of the capital they built at Konya in Anatolia show how thoroughly they abandoned pastoralism and absorbed urban habits. By the end of the twelfth century, 108 towers enclosed the city. Market gardens on the surrounding plain fed a population of perhaps 30,000. Inns accommodated merchants and their camels. But the Seljuks never entirely forgot the steppe. Their coins showed hero-horsemen with stars and haloes round their heads. Their sultans lay in tombs, shaped to recall the tents in which their ancestors dwelled. Seljuk experience was typical. No one knows how it happened, but the Islamic world transformed most of the Turkic invaders into its strength and shield.

The newly converted Turks conquered Anatolia and Armenia from Christians, Syria and Palestine from Shiites. Success in attracting, converting, and domesticating pastoral peoples—and recycling their violence in Muslim service—is one of the decisive and distinctive features of the history of the Islamic world. Its importance is apparent when one compares the Islamic record with those of other settled agricultural societies in Christendom, China, India, and Africa. Christendom usually dealt with steppelander threats by trying to fight them off or buy them off. The Magyars (MAHG-yahrs) and Bulgars, who settled in Hungary and Bulgaria respectively, were Europe's only successfully absorbed steppeland invaders. China seduced steppeland conquerors to Chinese ways of life, but was unable or unwilling to turn them permanently into a favorable fighting force. In India invading pastoralists sometimes adopted parts of Indian culture but usually remained intruders. In none of these regions did native cultures manage to harness nomad energies for wars of their own.

The Crusades

It is worth comparing the Islamic world's response to the steppeland invaders with the fate of other intruders: the crusaders, who attacked from Christian Europe. Writers of world history usually give the Crusades a lot of attention, seeking signs of the vitality of the West—the capacity of Western Europeans to reach overseas and make war way beyond their frontiers. For the Islamic world, however, the Crusades were a minor nuisance. Crusaders were few. Their states were small and mostly short-lived. Crusaders could not be converted to Islam, but—thanks to the availability of Turkish manpower and leadership—their threat was neutralized.

The Crusading movement started as an outgrowth from pilgrimage. Increasingly in the tenth and eleventh centuries, Christians made pilgrimages as an act of penance for their sins. Pilgrimages—in theory, peaceful journeys, on which the pilgrims relied on the charity of people whose lands they crossed—became armed expeditions. Simultaneously, Christians began to adopt what had formerly been a Muslim notion: holy war. The land where Jesus' feet trod sanctified those who fought and died for it. Warriors could fulfill their vocation for violence and still be saved. "The blood of Muslims," declared a French poet in the twelfth century, "washes out sins." War for the recovery of Jerusalem would also be just, according to Christian theorists: Palestine had once been Christian land—so it was right to try to win it back.

In the 1090s, preachers whipped up collective hysteria that sent thousands of poor, ill-armed pilgrims to their deaths in an effort to get to Jerusalem. Pope Urban II (r. 1088–1099) orchestrated a relatively well-planned military expedition. It is often claimed that the crusaders were younger sons, with inadequate inheritances, and adventurers "on the make." But many crusaders were rich men with a lot to lose. The church is also often thought to have encouraged the Crusades to increase its own wealth. That was one of the effects, as crusaders left property to monasteries and churches to look after in their absence, and, once they got to the east, made grants of conquered land and treasure to religious institutions there.

The early crusaders blundered to success, capturing Jerusalem in 1099 and lining the shores of the Levant with states their own leaders ruled. Muslim divisions made these successes possible. Muslim indifference and infighting prolonged them. The crusader kingdoms got support from Italian merchant-communities, which welcomed access to trade, and, occasionally, received reinforcements from Europe.

Early Turkish history from the *Dede Korkut*

Al-Thalibi, *Recollections of Bukhara*

A medieval tourist-guide. This late twelfth-century guide was made to help English pilgrims find the major tourist attractions and useful spots in and around Jerusalem. The money exchange is in the center, and the food market is to its right. The Temple of Solomon occupies the upper right quarter of the city (surrounded by circular walls), and the Golden Gate "where Jesus entered sitting on a donkey" leads to it. The cross marks Golgotha where Jesus was crucified. The Holy Sepulcher where he was buried is below it.

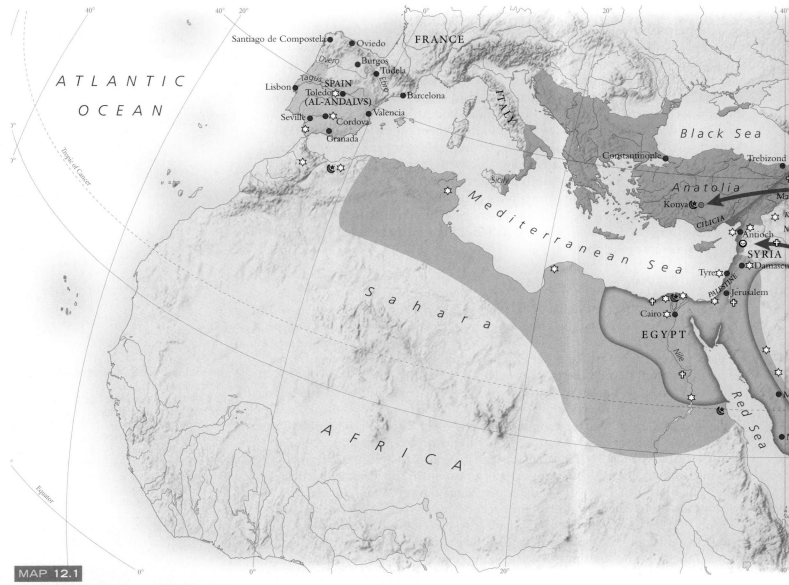

MAP 12.1

The Middle East and the Mediterranean, ca. 900–1100

	extent of caliphate, ca. 900
	area controlled by Ghaznavids, ca. 1000
➤	raids by Mahmud of Ghazni
BUWAYHIDS	Muslim dynasty with dates
➤	Seljuk conquests, ca.1040–1090
●	Seljuk capital (from 1077)
☻	Assassin stronghold
UZBEKISTAN	modern-day country
	Byzantine Empire, ca. 1050
⚔	battle
Karkhanids	people
☆	Jewish communities
☾	Sufi shrines, ca. 1250
✚	Christian communities
	caliphate of Cordova
	Fatimid dynasty

The newcomers from Europe, however, were often zealots who tended to disrupt the delicate tolerance between Christians and Muslims on which the crusader states relied for stability.

In the mid–twelfth century, Zangi (ZAN-gee)—a Turkish chief who dubbed himself "pillar of the faith"—proclaimed a *jihad* against infidels and Shiites. He and his heirs began to reconquer the lands lost to the crusaders. Saladin (SAH-lah-deen), the Kurdish soldier who seized Zangi's empire in 1170, overthrew the crusader kingdom of Jerusalem in 1187, reduced the crusader states to tiny enclaves on the coast, and beat off attempts by new crusaders to recover Jerusalem.

Yet the defeat of the crusaders was a sideshow. More important, in the long run, for the future of the Islamic world was Saladin's extinction of the Fatimid caliphate and the conquest of Egypt for Sunni Islam. Though heresy continued

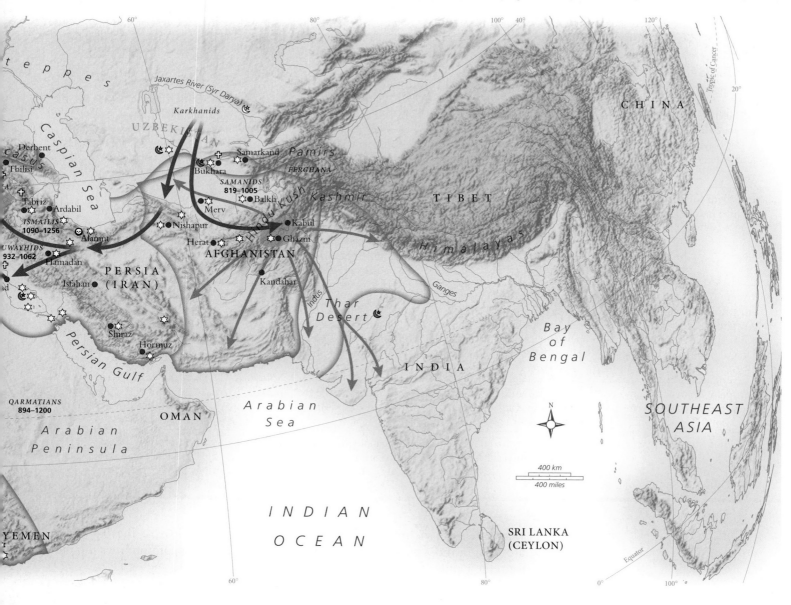

A Muslim view of the Crusaders

to disrupt Islamic uniformity, no such large or menacing Shiite state outside Iran ever again challenged Islamic solidarity. The other legacy of the Zangi and Saladin was Islamic militancy. Jihad remained a way to legitimize upstart dynasties and regimes.

The Crusades, meanwhile, left an equally sad legacy. For most of the Middle Ages, Christian, Muslim, and Jewish communities in the Middle East, Egypt, and Spain lived alongside one another in relative peace. Christians and Muslims intermarried, exchanged culture, and, in some frontier zones, even worshipped at the same shrines. Christian and Muslim states often made alliances against third parties, regardless of religious affiliation. The Crusades, however, fed on religious propaganda and encouraged the two traditions to demonize each other. Crusading fervor also increased hostility in Europe between Christians and Jews, since Jews

○ MAKING CONNECTIONS

THE CRUSADES

HISTORICAL BACKGROUND →	CAUSE FOR ACTION →	EUROPEAN CONSEQUENCES →	CONSEQUENCES IN EASTERN MEDITERRANEAN
Tradition of pilgrimage—Christians go to Jerusalem	By 1050, increased danger, disorder, and occasional persecution in Middle East	Transformation of armed escorts; adoption of Islamic idea of holy war	Transformation of Holy Land into region of continual battle
Jerusalem formerly a Christian and Jewish land	Muslim population, kingdoms control the region	Religious leaders whip up mass movement—disorganized expeditions lead to disastrous results; Pope Urban II organizes a military expedition (First Crusade)	Quick capture of Jerusalem; creation of small "crusader kingdoms"
Roman Catholic Church most important institution in Western Europe	Church needs land, wealth to fund its clerics, infrastructure, and religious activity; new spirituality favors annual pilgrimages as a form of penance	Local bishops and papacy help coordinate, orchestrate Crusades; crusaders left property to monasteries and churches while abroad	Conquered land and treasure often granted to church institutions
European lay aristocracy needs means of salvation	Development of chivralric ethos; founding of knightly orders	Aristocratic violence exported on Crusades	Crusades become ruling elite over large Muslim population
Defeat of Muslims by crusaders	Weak, disorganized Muslim kingdoms in eastern Mediterranean	Initial success of crusaders; occupation of Jerusalem and Holy Land	Proclamation of *jihad* by Zangi, Turkic chief; reconquest completed by Saladin; overthrow of crusader kingdoms

were often the victims of rioting that laments over the loss of the Holy Land aroused. In most places, Jews were the only non-Christian communities the mob found to hand.

The common opinion that the Crusades demonstrated the growing power of Latin Christendom seems—at best—exaggerated. There was dynamism in the Western Europe of the eleventh and twelfth centuries, but most of it was expended on inward development and on expanding the frontiers. If anything, the Crusades' failure helped alert people in Europe to their backwardness and vulnerability compared to the cultures of the Near East.

The Invaders from the Sahara

On their westernmost frontier, in Spain and Portugal, Muslims badly needed new strength. Since the eighth century, Muslim rulers had held territory as far north as the Duero and Ebro River valleys. But **al-Andalus** (ahl-AHN-dah-loos), as they called it, was hard to hold together and defend. The original Muslim settlers—mostly Berbers from North Africa—were few in number, uneasily holding down large Christian populations. Internal communications relied on roads that the Romans had built centuries earlier to link widely scattered communities. Between the rivers Tagus and Duero was a vast frontier, strewn with fortifications. Wealth made al-Andalus viable: wealth gathered from the agricultural surplus of rich soils in the south and east; wealth spent on the luxuries—

ivory work, jewels, palaces, lavish gardens—for which Spanish art of the time is renowned.

In the late tenth century, a general, Almanzor (ahl-mahn-SOHR), kept the potentially mutinous armies and regional aristocracies of the Spanish "caliphate" busy with wars against the Christians. He died in 1002. In 1009, Berber mutineers sacked his headquarters, "wilder now than the maws of lions, bellowing the end of the world." The caliphate dissolved into numerous competing kingdoms. The northern Christian kingdoms took advantage. By the 1080s, the Tagus valley was in Christian hands. In alarm, some of the Spanish Muslim kingdoms called on warrior ascetics from North Africa, the Almoravids (ahl-moh-RAH-vihds), for help.

In Arabic the Almoravids' name suggests both hermits and soldiers. They emerged as an alliance of pastoral bands from the Sahara, whom firebrand preaching aroused into self-dedication to holy war from the mid–tenth century. Nomads whom the Fatimids had expelled from southern Egypt had already wrought havoc in the region. The Almoravids, however, were more numerous and effective.

When they received the summons to Spain, the Almoravids had already created a state that spanned the Sahara. In the tradition of many Saharan tribes, they had—at least at an early stage of their history—a surprisingly egalitarian attitude to women. A woman, Zaynab al-Nafzawiya, dominated: "Some said the spirits spoke to her, others that she was a witch."

In Spain, the Almoravids drove back the Christians but also swept away the rulers of the petty Muslim kingdoms, first denouncing their luxury, then seizing it for themselves. The corruption to which the Almoravids submitted in their turn became a provocation and an enticement to other religiously inspired desert pastoralists. In the 1140s, the Almoravids' empire was conquered by a new ascetic alliance, the Almohads (AHL-moh-hads)—the name means "people of the oneness of God"—who again invaded Spain from North Africa and, for a while, propped up the Islamic frontier (see Map 12.2).

These movements of desert zealots also turned south on Islam's frontier with paganism in Africa. Almoravid efforts focused on Ghana (see Chapter 10). Ghana was gold-rich, for it controlled access to trans-Saharan trade, where gold was exchanged for salt. It was also offensive to the Almoravids as the home of "sorcerers," where, according to reports, people buried their dead with gifts, "made offerings of alcohol," and kept a sacred snake in a cave. Muslims—presumably traders—had their own quarter in or near the Ghanian capital Kumbi Saleh, reportedly with a dozen mosques, but were kept apart from the royal quarter of the town. Ghana fought off Almoravid armies until 1076 when Kumbi fell, and its defenders were massacred. The northerners' political hold south of the Sahara did not last, but Islam was firmly implanted in West Africa.

In the next century, Arab writers regarded Ghana as a model Islamic state, whose king revered the true caliph in Baghdad and dispensed justice with exemplary openness. They admired his palace, with its objects of art and windows of glass; the huge gold ingot that was the symbol of his authority; the gold ring by which he tethered his horse; his silk clothes; his elephants and giraffes. This magnificence did not last. After a long period of stagnation or decline, pagan invaders destroyed Kumbi. But Islam had spread so widely by then in the Sahel that it retained its foothold south of the Sahara for the rest of the Middle Ages.

Christian and Muslim harmony. Songs in praise of the Virgin Mary, written by King Alfonso X of Castile (r. 1252–1284), could be played and enjoyed by both Christian and Muslim musicians. Both traditions upheld—and still uphold—the virginity of Jesus' mother. Food, dress, language, and even some religious practices spanned the frontier between Christian- and Muslim-ruled areas.
A Moor and a Christian playing the lute, miniature in a book of music from the 'Cantigas' of Alfonso X 'the Wise' (1221–84). 13th Century (manuscript). Monasterio de El Escorial, El Escorial, Spain/ bIndex/Bridgeman Art Library.

The Almoravids and Almohads

1076	Kumbi Saleh falls to Almoravid armies
1080s	Muslim kingdoms in al-Andalus call on Almoravids for help
1140s	Almoravid Empire falls to the Almohads

A CORDOVAN IVORY JAR

Richly carved ivory jars for holding rare and costly essences, such as camphor, ambergris, and musk, show how luxurious life was in the palace of Madinat al-Zahra in Cordova in Muslim Spain in the late tenth century. This example was made for a brother of the reigning caliph.

The domed shape suggests the architecture of palaces and mosques. The missing knob would have had the form of a rich fruit, such as a pomegranate.

The inscription reads: "Blessings from God, goodwill, happiness, and prosperity to al-Mughira, son of the Commander of the Faithful, may God's mercy be upon him," with the date, 967.

The scenes depict hunters picking dates, court attendants, boys stealing eagles' eggs, and lions devouring bulls. The exact meaning of the images—if there ever was any—is lost, but all hint at royal power and well-being.

Ivory pyxis of Al–Mughira. Scene of harvesting dates. 968 CE. From Cordoba, Spain. Inv. 4068. Photo: H. Lewandowski/ Musée du Louvre/RMN Reunion des Musées Nationaux, France. Art Resource, NY.

How does this ivory jar reflect the wealth of Muslim Spain around 1000 C.E.?

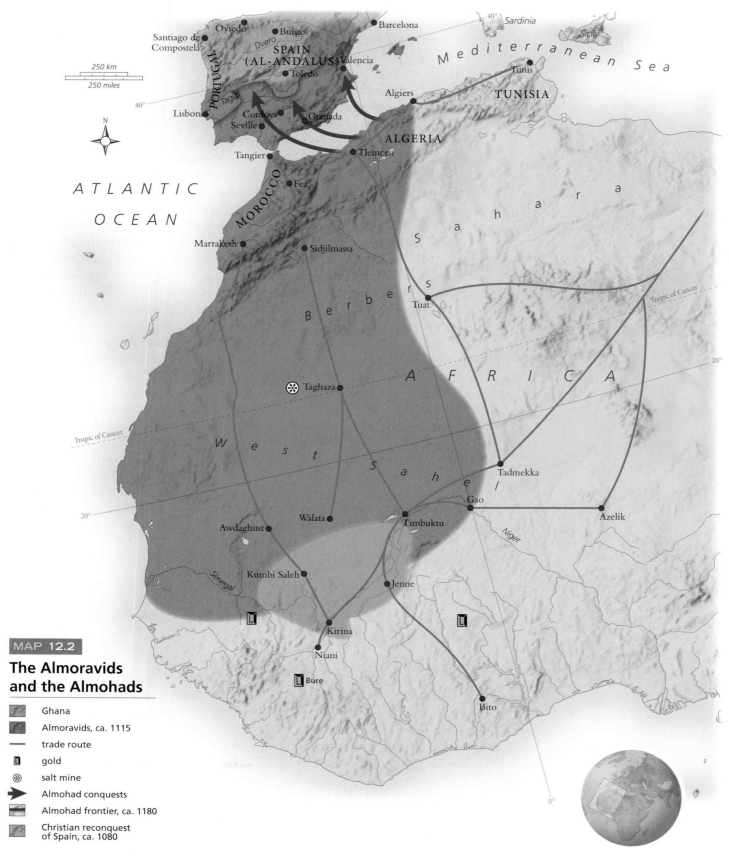

250 km

250 miles

ATLANTIC
OCEAN

Mediterranean Sea

Sardinia

Sicily

Santiago de
Compostela

Oviedo

Burgos

Barcelona

Dvero

SPAIN
(AL-ANDALUS)

Valencia

Toledo

Tunis

Lisbon

Tagus

Cordova

Seville

Granada

Algiers

TUNISIA

Tangier

Tlemcen

ALGERIA

Fez

MOROCCO

Marrakesh

Sidjilmassa

Berbers

Sahara

Tuat

Tropic of Cancer

AFRICA

Taghaza

Tropic of Cancer

West
Sahel

Tadmekka

Gao

Azelik

Walata

Timbuktu

Niger

Awdaghust

Kumbi Saleh

Jenne

Senegal

Kirina

Niani

Bure

Bito

MAP 12.2

The Almoravids
and the Almohads

Ghana

Almoravids, ca. 1115

trade route

gold

salt mine

Almohad conquests

Almohad frontier, ca. 1180

Christian reconquest
of Spain, ca. 1080

The Progress of Sufism

It is doubtful whether war alone could heal the divisions among Muslims and equip the Islamic world to expand. For that, inventive intellectuals were necessary—shapers of a religion that could appeal to a diversity of cultures and engage human sympathies and sensibilities without provoking conflict. Sufism (see Chapter 9) had enormous popular appeal. But most of the Muslim elite rejected it. In the early tenth century, for instance, ordinary people revered the great spokesman of Sufism, al-Hallaj (ahl-hah-LAJ), as a saint, but the Islamic authorities put him to death, because he claimed to have achieved self-extinction and mystical union with God. Gilani (gee-LAH-nee), his successor, who became one of the most popular preachers in mid–eleventh-century Baghdad, offered a simple morality of dependence on God—based on the rule, "Expect nothing from human beings"—as an alternative to the rigid legalism of Islamic scholars.

The divergence between legal-minded and mystic-minded Muslim theologians seemed unbridgeable until al-Ghazali (ahl-ga-ZA-lee) entered the debate. He was blessed or cursed with an "unquenchable thirst for investigation … an instinct and a temperament implanted in me by God through no choice of my own." At the height of a career as a conventional theologian in Baghdad, he experienced a sudden awareness of his ignorance of God. He became a Sufi, retired to his native Persia, and, before his death in 1111, wrote a dazzling series of works reconciling Sufism and Sunni orthodoxy. He was a master of reason and science but demonstrated, to the satisfaction of most of his readers, that human minds could not grasp some truths without direct illumination from God. Study could tell you about God, but only a mystical experience can show you who God is. Al-Ghazali likened the effect of mysticism to the difference between knowing what health is and being healthy. He valued the faith of the poor and uneducated as highly as the learning of the officials of the mosques. His rehabilitation of Sufism was vital for the future of Islam. Because Sufis were indifferent to externals, Sufi mystics could tolerate cultural differences among Muslims and between Muslims and non-Muslims in a way the legal-minded Islamic intellectuals could not. Sufi habits of holiness satisfied ordinary people's craving for saints. They were Islam's most effective missionaries in subsequent centuries.

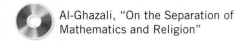

Al-Ghazali, "On the Separation of Mathematics and Religion"

THE BYZANTINE EMPIRE AND ITS NEIGHBORS

If the pastoralists contributed to the salvation of the Islamic world, their attacks were disastrous for the non-Muslim states that proved less skillful at absorbing them or deflecting their power. A dramatic case in point is that of the Byzantine Empire.

Byzantium and the Barbarians

The Roman-ness of Byzantium dwindled by degrees. Under Justinian in the mid–sixth century, the government at Constantinople was still trying to reconstruct the Roman world (see Chapter 8) and ruled substantial parts of the Western Roman Empire as far away as Spain. But events of the seventh and eighth centuries shifted its frontiers and changed its character. The Arab expansion after the death of Muhammad (see Chapter 9) stripped away the empire's territory south of the Mediterranean—Syria, Egypt, and North Africa. Meanwhile, from the sixth century to the eighth, speakers of Slav languages slowly colonized much of the Balkans, including Greece. Arabs, Bulgars, and Russians threatened Constantinople itself.

In defense of the empire, missionaries and diplomats were as important as armies. The church virtually monopolized literacy in the areas of the Balkans and Russia where Byzantine missions were active. Missionaries invented the alphabets in which Slav languages were written. They also helped to spread statehood, legitimating strong rulers, sanctifying weak ones. Many Balkan states slipped and slid between allegiance to the Latin- and Greek-speaking churches, but for a while, thanks to missionary efforts launched from Constantinople, Moravians, Croats, and Hungarians hovered in Byzantium's orbit before finally opting for the Latin church. The greatest success for this religious diplomacy was the conversion of the rulers of much of what is now Russia (see Chapter 9). The policy was most effective when lavish gifts and the hands of Byzantine princesses, who married Bulgar khans and Russian princes, backed it. Instead of an empire like Rome's, a Byzantine "commonwealth" of Christian states was being built up—a diplomatic ring of outer defenses.

Byzantine diplomacy economized on force by intimidating visiting barbarians with elaborate ceremonials. The early tenth-century emperor, Constantine VII, laid down rules for courtly displays that were designed to embody imperial power and, in effect, to wield it. The effect designers aimed for was unashamedly theatrical. When an ambassador arrived at Constantinople in 924, the artificial roar of mechanical lions that guarded the imperial throne surprised him.

Liutprand of Cremona, from *Report of His Mission to Constantinople*

The deftness of Byzantine diplomacy, its rulers' ability to impress or intimidate surrounding "barbarians," is part of the repertoire of strategies with which all successful states managed the surge of migrations of the period. The wealth of the empire underpinned those strategies and paid for vital military backup. The Byzantine economy relied on the productivity of the peasantry of Anatolia and the trade that passed through Byzantine territory, for the empire enjoyed a privileged position where great arteries of trade converged: the Silk Roads, the Volga, the Mediterranean.

Yet the system was rickety. Wealth depended on security, which was hard to guarantee. And the effectiveness of Byzantine diplomacy had its limits. While a zone of Byzantine influence took shape in the Balkans, Russia, and the Caucasus, most steppeland peoples, and the Muslims to the east and south, were indifferent to Byzantine religion and unintimidated by Byzantine methods. Caught between Bulgars and Turks, Byzantium seemed to lie at the eye of the steppelander storm. Byzantines tended to see their predicament as a test of faith—an episode of sacred history. In 980, the miracle at Chonae first appeared in Byzantine writings: the story of how the Archangel Michael diverted a river that evil pagans had turned to threaten his church. It is tempting to read this story as an allegory for the prayed-for escape of the "Roman Empire" from destruction at barbarian hands.

Basil II

The longed-for savior appeared from an unlikely quarter. The emperor Basil II barely survived adolescence. Usurpers allowed him to live on after his father's death until he succeeded to the throne peacefully in 976. His image appears on a page from his prayer book—heavily armed, attended by angels, while barbarians cringe at his feet. This is how he liked to see himself and wished to be remembered.

He ruled intuitively, as if coping with a constant state of emergency, enforcing his own will, administering rough justice, respecting no laws or conventions. In 996, he dealt with a landowner he saw exploiting peasants: "we had his luxurious

The crown of King Geza I of Hungary (r. 1074–1077) received from Byzantium was not a disinterested gift, but an attempt to imply that the king was a subject of the empire and dependent on Byzantium for the legitimacy of his rule. Hungary, however, remained firmly attached to the Church of Rome and to Latin culture.

villa razed to the ground and returned his property to the peasants, leaving him with what he had to begin with and reducing him to the peasants' level." This was an instance of a long conflict between great landowners and the throne. Emperors needed prosperous, independent peasants to provide taxes and manpower for the armies. Landowners wanted to control the peasants themselves. Aristocratic revolts and resistance to taxation were commonplace.

Basil dealt with the most troublesome of Byzantium's satellite peoples, the Bulgars, by blinding—so it was said—14,000 of their captured warriors and cowing them into submission. He incorporated Bulgaria into the empire in 1018. On the southern front, he made peace with the Arabs. In consequence, he gave the empire virtually ideal borders. In Bulgaria he followed up his terror stroke with conciliation, cooperating with the native elite, appointing a Bulgar as the local archbishop. In Greece he relied on repression, forcing the empire's religion and language on the immigrant Slavs. In Armenia, his successors lost patience with diplomacy and reconquered the region (see Map 12.3).

Force was expensive by comparison with the waiting game, bribes, and tricks of traditional Byzantine policy. Basil paid for a professional army by heavily taxing the aristocracy. When he died in 1025, his treasury was fuller than any emperor's since the sixth century. Prayers cited his name in Russia and Armenia. As late as the 1070s, a Hungarian king accepted a crown from Constantinople. The so-called crown of St. Stephen depicts the king reverencing the rulers of the Byzantine Empire.

The Era of Difficulties

Basil's legacy, however, was unsustainable. His methods of government were personal and arbitrary. The aristocracy could afford his taxes only while his power protected their lands from invaders. As Turkish migrations and invasions began to roll over Byzantine Anatolia, the revenues failed. The succession to the throne was problematic. Basil had no children, and his brother, who succeeded him, had only daughters. These were unusual circumstances: an opportunity for strong women to come to the fore. In the background, deeper social changes were under way. The family—formerly, in theory, a second-best lifestyle to monastic chastity—rose in Byzantine esteem in the tenth century. Women began to be admired for fertility as well as virginity.

In the eyes of influential classes—clergy, landowners, courtiers—eleventh-century experiments did not seem to justify the empowerment of female rulers. Princesses spent their lives confined to the palace, and though they got the same formal education as men, they were denied the opportunity to accumulate useful experience of the world. Basil's niece, Zoe, regarded the throne as a family possession and responsibility. Her "family album" is laid in mosaic in her private enclosure in the gallery of Constantinople's cathedral. Her third husband's portrait smothers that of her second, who murdered his predecessor, at Zoe's behest. Zoe outraged Constantinople's snobbish elite by adopting a workman's son as her heir—an upstart "pygmy playing Hercules," said the snobs. Zoe's sister Theodora ruled alone in 1055–1056, "shamefully" and "unnaturally"—according to her opponents—refusing to marry. These judgments lack objectivity, but show the outrage the sisters provoked among the elite.

Meanwhile, relations between the Latin- and Greek-speaking churches broke down. Differences had been growing over rites, doctrines, language, and discipline between the sees of Constantinople and Rome for centuries. Underlying the theo-

MAP 12.3

Byzantium and Its Neighbors, ca. 1050

- Byzantine empire, ca. 1050
- ✂ battle of Manzikert, 1071
- maximum extent of crusader kingdoms, 1144
- - - - frontier with Seljuks of Rum after 1077
- *Croats* people

logical bitterness were deep cultural differences. Language was in part to blame. The Greek-speaking Byzantine Empire could not share the common culture of the Latin-speaking elites of Western and Central Europe, while few in the Latin West could speak or read Greek with fluency. Subtle theological distinctions, inexpressible in Latin, came easily in Greek.

Dogmas supposed to be universal turned out differently in the two tongues. For most people, religion is more a matter of conduct than creed. In this respect, differences between the Roman and Byzantine traditions built up over centuries of

Empress Zoe. The gallery of the great church of Hagia Sophia in Constantinople functioned as a private enclosure for members of the imperial family and was decorated with portraits of rulers and their spouses in pious attitudes. The mosaic dedicated to the Empress Zoe (980–1050) betrays the questionable complexities of her sex life. The face of Constantine IX Monomachus, her third husband, shown offering gold to Christ, was remodeled to replace the likeness of her second spouse, Michael IV, whom she had first employed to murder his predecessor, then banished to a monastery in 1041 when she tired of him. The squashed lettering above Constantine's halo to the left is clear evidence of a botched job.

relative mutual isolation. The process began as early as the mid–sixth century, when the Eastern churches resisted or rejected the supremacy of the pope. The effects were gradual but great. From the 790s, Greek and Latin congregations recited slightly different versions of the creed, the basic statement of Christian belief. By about 1000, the pope was the supreme authority regarding doctrine and liturgy and the source of patronage in the church throughout Western Europe. The Western church still enclosed tremendous local diversity, but it was recognizably a single communion. Eastern Orthodox Christians felt no particular allegiance to the pope. In the West, moreover, the popes generally maintained, with difficulty, their own political independence. In the East, the patriarchs of Constantinople, as that city's bishops were titled, were the emperor's subjects and generally deferred to imperial power.

It might have been possible to restore Christian unity in the mid–eleventh century. Constantinople and Rome faced common enemies. Norman invaders threatened the pope's political independence and the last Byzantine possessions in southern Italy and Sicily. On June 17, 1053, a Norman army cut the pope's German guard to pieces and, imploring the pope's forgiveness, took him hostage.

Eventually, the papacy would turn the Normans into its sword bearers. At first, however, the pope turned to the Byzantines for help. Meanwhile, in 1054 in Constantinople, the patriarch, who was the head of the Byzantine church, saw an opportunity to exploit the pope's weakness. He closed the churches of the city's Latin-speaking congregations. The pope sent an uncompromising mission to Constantinople. His representative, Cardinal Humbert, after weeks of bitter insults, served notice of excommunication on the "false patriarch, now for his abominable crimes notorious." The patriarch responded by excommunicating the pope. At the time, most people assumed this was just a political maneuver, soon to be rescinded or forgotten. In fact, relations between the Eastern and Western churches never fully recovered. A cultural fault line was opening across Europe.

The shenanigans of the imperial family and the quarrelsome habits of the church have given Byzantium a bad name as a society doomed by its own decadence. But it was not doomed. There are no irreversible trends in history. Nor, even when beset by difficulties, was the Byzantine Empire particularly decadent. On the contrary, the most unsuccessful emperor of the era was a model of energy and courage. Becoming emperor in 1068, Romanus IV Diogenes had to cope with aristocratic unrest while fighting on two fronts. In the west, the Normans threatened Byzantium's last possessions in Italy. In the east, Turks were penetrating Armenia and Anatolia, stealing the empire's vital food-producing zone. Romanus's military record made him look insuperable, but his generalship proved unequal to the task. In 1071, at the battle of Manzikert, the Turks forced the emperor to kiss the ground before the feet of their leader, Alp Arslan—a great-grandson of Seljuk's. Romanus was deposed by a coup. Feuding at Constantinople between aristocratic factions allowed the Turks to overrun much of Anatolia.

Byzantium and the Crusaders

In 1097, crusaders arrived at Byzantium, ostensibly to help. But by then, the Byzantines had already begun to recover the lost ground on their own. The Byzantine princess Anna Comnena considered the newcomers more of a hindrance. Superbly

Anna Comnena, from the *Alexiad*

educated in the classics, she was the official biographer of her father, the emperor. To her, the crusaders were lustful drunkards, enemies whose object was "to dethrone the emperor and capture the capital."

The tense cooperation between Byzantium and the crusaders, which characterized the First Crusade, broke down completely in the twelfth century. The crusaders failed to return to the empire most of the Byzantine territory they recaptured from the Muslims. Instead, they kept it for themselves. Byzantines were convinced of their own moral and cultural superiority over impious, greedy Westerners, while crusaders blamed "Greek treachery" for their failures. The crusades might have saved Byzantium, as the Turks saved the Islamic world. Instead, they undermined the empire.

Byzantium's difficulties multiplied. Agriculture was stagnant, despite the boom in other parts of Eurasia. The empire's hinterland beyond Constantinople was too insecure to prosper. In the twelfth century, in a reversal of earlier emperors' policy of nurturing the peasants at the landowners' expense, emperors tried to revive their rural revenues by granting control of peasant lands to great lords and encouraging monastic colonization of new lands. To some extent, this was another case of the attempt to exploit new resources, familiar in other societies of the time. The emperor Isaac II Angelus (r. 1185–1195), for instance, gave a port to a monastery that settled a site in Thrace, formerly "devoid of men and dwellings, a haunt of snakes and scorpions, just rough ground, overgrown with spreading trees." Measures like these—which so dramatically increased the farmland of Western Christendom, Ethiopia, or, as we shall see, of China—were of limited usefulness in a state whose territory was much diminished. Byzantium never recovered most of inland Anatolia from the Turks.

Increasingly, the empire was obliged to look to trade and industry for its wealth. There were, as a Byzantine poet observed, "big merchants" who "for large profits disdain terrors and defy seas." Self-made upstarts coveted money "as a polecat gazes at fat." The huge city of Constantinople benefited from its uniquely favorable position for trade, where Mediterranean and trans-Asian routes met. The Jewish merchant, Benjamin of Tudela, who visited in about 1170, celebrated "a busy city" with inhabitants so rich they "they look like princes" where "merchants come from every country by sea and land." With revenues of 20,000 gold pieces a year from rents, market dues, and the tolls on passing trade, "Wealth like that of Constantinople," Benjamin wrote, "is not to be found in the whole world. Here also are men learned in all the books of the Greeks, and they eat and drink, every man under his vine and his fig tree." For William of Tyre, a Latin bishop who visited at about the same time, the city seemed equally splendid on the surface. But William was more aware of underlying squalor and inequalities of wealth. "The wealthy overshadow the streets," he wrote—alluding to the mansions of the rich—"and leave dark, dirty spaces to the poor and to travelers." William's prejudices are obvious, but, precisely because he was so keen to criticize the city, we can trust his witness to its wealth.

 Benjamin of Tudela, *Book of Travels*

A special relationship developed between Byzantium and Venice, a maritime republic near the northernmost point of the Adriatic Sea, where trade routes across the Alps converged with the main axis of north Italian commerce, the river Po. Venice's position on marshy, salty islands allowed little scope to accumulate wealth except by piracy, which Venetians practiced, mainly at the expense of Muslim shipping. In the ninth and tenth centuries, however, they began to build up enough capital to become major traders, channeling toward Europe a share of the valuable

Byzantium

527–565	Reign of Justinian
Sixth to eighth centuries	Colonization of Balkans by Slavs
Seventh and eighth centuries	Loss of territory as a result of Arab expansion
Ninth century	Missions to convert Balkans and Central Europe to Byzantine Christianity
1018	Bulgaria incorporated into Byzantine Empire
1054	Schism between Orthodox and Latin churches
1071	Battle of Manzikert; Byzantine army routed by Seljuk Turks
1095	Launch of First Crusade
1204	Sack of Constantinople

The Veroli casket. Classical stories with an erotic edge decorated Byzantine trinket boxes in the twelfth century. The panels visible in this picture of a famous example, the Veroli casket, finely carved in ivory, show Helen of Troy, Bellerophon with his winged horse, and the chaste Hippolytus on the right resisting the sexual advances of his wicked stepmother. Such were the subjects that entertained a rich lady's mind while she donned her jewels.

trade in silks and spices that was concentrated at Byzantium. Culturally, as well as economically, Venice was close to Byzantium. Though Venetians belonged to the Latin church and spoke a language derived from Latin, Byzantine models saturated their taste in art and buildings. It could not be otherwise. They knew Byzantium well, and so they had to admire it—and covet what they saw there.

Byzantium's wealth was a magnet and its weakness a motive. Toward the end of the 1190s, in Western Europe, popular enthusiasm revived for a new effort to launch a Crusade to recapture Jerusalem. The Venetians agreed to ship the crusading army out at what was to prove an unaffordable price. While the army gathered, an embassy arrived from the pretender to the Byzantine throne, Alexius IV, proposing a detour. If the crusaders put Alexius on the throne, he would help them against the Turks. Faced with their inability to pay the Venetians' bill, most of the crusaders agreed to a diversion. The Fourth Crusade, launched in 1202 to recapture Jerusalem, ended by shedding Christian blood in 1204 by capturing and sacking Constantinople and dividing most of what was left of the Byzantine Empire in Europe among the victors. Venice seized—in the words of the treaty that divided the empire—"one quarter and one half of one quarter" of Byzantine territory, achieving virtual monopoly rights in Byzantine trade and suddenly becoming an imperial power in the eastern Mediterranean. Meanwhile, in the remnants of Byzantine Anatolia, rival dynasties disputed claims to the imperial title.

Byzantine Art and Learning

Throughout the period this chapter covers, even amid the most severe difficulties of the twelfth century, Byzantium remained a beacon of learning and art. It is easy to get starry-eyed about the excellence of Byzantine culture. The most constant and careful Byzantine work in copying and analyzing the texts of classical authors and of the fathers of the Church was probably over by the tenth century. Mystics, represented by Saint Symeon the New Theologian (as he is called), who died in 1022, proposed an alternative route to learning, through divine illumination. "Orators and philosophers" could not access the wisdom of God. Painters

developed a tradition that abandoned realism in favor of stylized, formal figures, usually set against abstract or sketchy backgrounds, more indebted, perhaps, to the mosaics, in which Byzantine artists excelled, than to classical painting or sculpture. Most painters worked only on religious commissions and accepted the artistic vocation as a sacred obligation, aiming at work that captured the spirit of its subject and would be revered as holy in itself. Innovation happened slowly and subtly, for artists had to treat every subject strictly in accordance with tradition and church dogma.

Nonetheless, in most arts, and in learning, Byzantium preserved the classical legacy, and more. In the eleventh and twelfth centuries, it was revived in an intellectual movement comparable with the renaissance of the same period in the West (see Chapter 11). The historian and biographer Michael Psellus (1018–1078), for instance, wrote in an antique style based on classical Greek models, interpreted the meanings of ancient art, and lectured on Plato and Aristotle (see Chapter 6). Anna Comnena's historical work was saturated in knowledge of Homer, and she commissioned commentaries on neglected works of Aristotle. A renaissance of classical pagan themes in art followed in the twelfth century. The recovery of classical traditions in the West would probably have been impossible without cross-fertilization with the Islamic world and Byzantium.

CHINA AND THE NORTHERN BARBARIANS

Beyond the limits of the Turkish steppe, other steppeland peoples were even harder to deal with. Not even the Seljuks seemed able to win battles against them. Fortunately, however, for the Islamic world, none of these remoter nomads yet seemed willing to extend their conquests beyond the steppeland. Their critical relationships lay to the east, with China. We thus need a brief account of what had happened in China in the ninth and tenth centuries at this point.

The End of the Tang Dynasty

The history of China, in the 800s and 900s, looks like a series of disasters. An era of political disintegration began in the ninth century. Eunuchs controlled the succession to the imperial throne. The Xuantong (shoo-ehn-tuhng) emperor, who died in 859, never named an empress or an heir lest he be "made idle," that is, murdered. Steppelander incursions continued. In 840, in a typical incident, 10,000 Uighurs (see Chapter 9), driven from their Central Asian homeland by rival nomads, arrived on the Yellow River proposing to garrison the Chinese frontier. A new menace was the rise of banditry. In a land as densely populated as China's, every invasion, war, or natural disaster had profound environmental consequences, impoverishing many peasants and driving them to survive by any available means. In the late ninth century, bandit gangs grew into rebellious armies led by renegade members of the elite—students who had failed to pass the examinations for the civil service, Buddhist clergy forced out of monasteries the government had confiscated.

An imperial decree of 877 complained that the bandit forces "come and go just as they please." In 879, the bandit leader, Huang Chao (hwang chow), took Chang-an, the seat of the court, with effects described in one of the most striking poems of the time, the *Lament of Lady Qin*: rape, pillage, and bloodshed. Huang's successor, Zhu Wen (joo when), emerged as the most powerful man in China, effectively replacing the Tang dynasty in 907. His state fell in turn in 923 to Turkic nomads, and the Chinese Empire dissolved into "ten kingdoms."

China's situation recalls that of Western Europe, striving to maintain the ancient sense of unity and—for some rulers—even actively seeking to recover it in times of political dissolution. The Chinese predicament also parallels those of the Islamic world and Byzantium, beset by nomadic migrants and invaders. Chinese responses, as we shall see, were also similar. They tried to fend off the "barbarians" by methods akin to those of the Byzantines: diplomacy, bribery, intimidation, displays of cultural superiority. As in the Islamic world, Chinese worked to convert invaders to their own culture, usually successfully. As in all the states we have looked at, the reexploitation of internal resources—especially by converting forest to farmland—made an important contribution.

For China, however, the outcome was different from those of other comparable regions. Throughout the period this chapter covers, the reconstruction of unity never seemed perfect or stable, but unity remained an actively pursued and—as we shall see—ultimately recoverable ideal. Divisions over religion, which deepened disunity in Christendom, or in the world of al-Hakim, had no parallel in China. China survived the invaders from the steppes but surrendered much territory to them. And, unlike the Islamic world, China never wholly succeeded in turning invading warriors into a force it could use for its own expansion.

The Rise of the Song and the Barbarian Conquests

The fight for unity after the collapse of the 920s began in 960, when a mutinous army proclaimed its general as emperor. The dynasty he founded, the Song (soong), lasted until 1279, but it always had to share China's traditional territory with steppeland invaders who created empires and dynasties of their own in the north. These barbarian states adopted Chinese political ideas and bureaucratic methods and claimed the mandate of heaven—or, at least, a share in it—for themselves. But none of them were able to extend their conquests south of the Huai River, into the lands of rice paddies and dense population the Song retained.

First, from the early tenth to the early twelfth centuries, the Khitan state of Liao (lee-ow) loomed over China from Mongolia and Manchuria. In the tenth century, mainly under warrior-empresses, the Liao state acquired a southern frontier across the Yellow River valley. The Khitans remained faithful to their pastoral traditions, but they split their empire into two spheres, creating a Chinese-style, Chinese-speaking administration for their southern provinces. They began to build cities, following Chinese urban planning models, apparently to attract migrants. The Khitan Empire had its own civil service, selected on Confucian principles. In a treaty of 1004, the Song conceded equality to Liao, which became known as the Northern Kingdom, alongside the Southern Kingdom of the Song. The two states lived together in uneasy equilibrium.

Toward the end of the 1030s, a second steppeland state proclaimed itself an empire—the realm of Xia (hsia). The axis of the state was a strip of grazing land, 900 miles long, squeezed between Tibet and the southern Gobi Desert. In 1044 Xia arrogated the status of a kingdom superior to all others except Song and Liao. It had its own system of writing, its own bureaucracy, and an iron coinage much used along the Silk Roads. It also had a scholarly establishment, largely devoted to acquiring and commenting on Buddhist scriptures.

The last state builders to intrude into the region were the Jurchen (juhr-chehn), who from 1115 began to build up conquests that eventually included the whole Liao Empire and covered northern China as far as the Huai River (see Map 12.4). Their homeland was in the forests of northern Manchuria. Their traditional economy

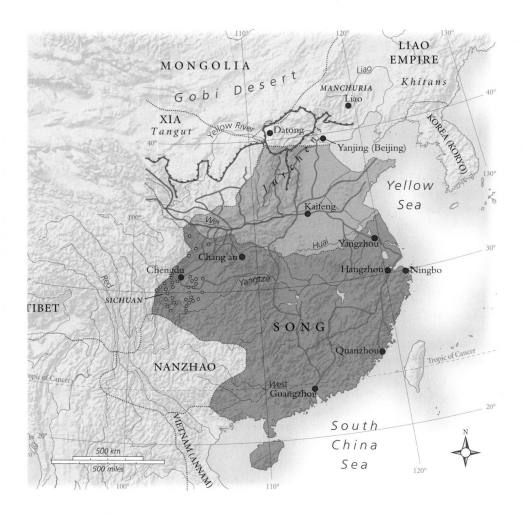

MAP 12.4

Song Empire, ca. 1150

- Song empire, ca. 1050
- Song empire, 1127–1234
- Silk Road
- Great Wall
- salt mine
- imperial highways
- *Jurchens* people

relied on hunting rather than herding. They were "sheer barbarians," Chinese envoys reported, "worse than wolves or tigers."

The Jurchen wars forced the Chinese to acknowledge Jurchen claims to the mandate of heaven. A treaty of 1127 imposed heavy annual tribute on the Song in silver, copper, and silk. Jurchen campaigns penetrated far into the south of China. In 1161, however, the invaders despaired of creating a river navy strong enough to dominate the Yangtze. The Song and Jurchen states learned to live with each other.

Meanwhile, the Jurchen adopted Chinese habits and traditions more fully than even the Khitans and Xia had. The Jurchen emperors were uncertain about this trend. On the one hand, they were quick to adopt Chinese bureaucracy and courtly customs themselves. On the other, they were afraid that the Jurchen would lose their warlike strength and will to dominate. The Jurchen, after all, were few in number—perhaps a few hundred thousand—compared with their more than 50 million Chinese subjects recorded in a census of 1207. Despite legislation forbidding Jurchens to adopt Chinese language or dress, distinctive Jurchen culture largely vanished.

Chinese thinkers found it hard to adjust to a world in which "barbarians" seemed their equals. On the whole, the Song accepted the reality of the new distribution of power, bribing and coaxing the foreigners into remaining quiet. One of the most supple intellects of the Song era was that of the early eleventh-century palace official, Ouyang Xiu (oh-yahng shoo). Earlier barbarian attacks, he thought, had been like "the sting of gadflies and mosquitoes." Now they were more serious and could not merely be brushed aside. He advised,

> Put away ... armor and bows, use humble words and ... generous gifts. ... Who would exhaust China's resources ... to quarrel with serpents and swine? ... Now is the moment for binding friendship. ... If indeed Heaven causes the rogues to accept our humaneness and they ... extinguish the beacons on our frontiers, which will be a great fortune to our ancestral altars.[1]

Civilization, he believed, would always win encounters with savagery. Barbarians might be invincible in battle, but in the long run, they could be shamed into submission. There was a lot to be said for this point of view. China always survived. Barbarian invaders were always seduced by culture. But the adoption of Chinese ways by barbarians usually followed bloody wars and destruction.

In their way, Ouyang Xiu's arguments simply rewrote the old script—Chinese superiority would ultimately prevail. This kind of thinking made defeat by the Jurchen even harder to bear. The traumas the victims of the wars suffered come to life in pages by the poet Li Qingzhao (lee ching-jhao): a memoir of her life with her husband, whom she had married for love when he was a student and she was a teenager. The couple played intellectual games at teatime, rivaling each other in being able to identify literary quotations. Their books were their most cherished possessions. When the Jurchen invaded in 1127, the fleeing couple "first gave up the bulky printed volumes, the albums of paintings, and the bulkiest ornaments." They still had so many books that it took 15 carts to bear them and a string of boats to ferry them across the Yangtze. Another Jurchen raid scattered more of the collection "in clouds of black smoke." When Li Qingzhao finally got beyond danger, after the couple's parting and her husband's death, only a few baskets of books were left—and most of those were later stolen.

Economy and Society Under the Song

Under pressure from the barbarian north, Song rule shrank toward the south. The Yangtze became the axis of the Song Empire. This amputation of the ancient Yellow River heartlands was bearable because population, too, had shifted southward. About 60 percent of Chinese lived in the Yangtze valley by the end of the tenth century.

Away from the steppeland frontier, Chinese expansion continued. Loss of traditional territory, combined with the growth of population, stimulated colonization in new directions. The census of 1083 reported 17,211,713 families. By 1124, the number had grown to 20,882,258. Censuses tended to underestimate numbers because tax evaders eluded the count. The Jurchen wars brought the growth of population to an end, but by then, Song China must have had well over 100 million inhabitants—perhaps about half as many again as the whole of Europe. The state had the most basic resource: labor. It needed food and space.

The founder of the Song dynasty, known as the Taizu (teye-tzoo) Emperor, realized that China's new opportunities lay in a further shift to the southwest: the vast, underpopulated region of Sichuan (seh-chawn). Colonization needed peaceful conditions. So the native tribes had to be suppressed. In a heavily forested, mountainous region, where tribal chiefs had a demonic reputation, this was not easy. By repute, the wildest inhabitants were the Black Bone Yi, led by a chief the Chinese called the "Demon Master." In 1001, the Song divided the region into two administrative units called "routes." A campaign in 1014 began the pacification. In 1036, the Demon Master became a salaried state official. The "forbidden hills" of

Lu Yu, from *Diary of a Journey to Sichuan*

Sichuan were stripped of forests and planted with tea and mulberries for silk production. The salt mines became resources of the Chinese Empire. A land poets formerly praised as a romantic wilderness became China's "heavenly storehouse."

Alongside the colonization of new land, new methods of exploitation enriched China, in a process of internal expansion reminiscent of what was going on at the same time in other regions, notably in Europe and Ethiopia (see Chapter 11). Environmental change fed the growing population. Wetlands were drained. New varieties of rice arrived from Vietnam. Planting and harvesting two crops a year effectively doubled the capacity for food production in the Yangtze valley. From the 1040s, the state promoted agriculture by making loans to peasants for seed grain at favorable rates. Deforestation continued, stimulated by a tax on unharvested timber. By the end of the eleventh century, the forests around the city of Kaifeng (keye-fung) had disappeared, sacrificed to huge iron-smelting works, employing 3,000 men. In 1132, a new palace at Kaifeng was built with timber from the Qingfeng (chihng-fung) Mountains, reputedly inaccessible for centuries, like the enchanted forests of fairy tales.

Meanwhile, the money economy boomed. Song mints were always pumping out new coins—a million strings of coins a year in the early eleventh century, 6 million in 1080—and always devaluing the currency by putting less gold and silver into coins. Paper money became a state monopoly from 1043. Towns grew spectacularly. Until the Jurchen captured it, Kaifeng was not just a seat of government but a thriving place of manufacture and trade. A famous twelfth-century painting by Zhang Zeduan (jwang tzeh-dwan) depicts the bustling life of the city: craftsmen, merchants, peddlers, entertainers, shoppers, and gawking crowds; groaning grain ships bring the extra food; diners enjoy their meals in some of Kaifeng's 72 large restaurants, each of up to five pavilions, three storeys high, and connected by delicate bridges. In 1147, the poet Master Meng (mung) recalled in his *Dream of the Eastern Capital's Splendor* how in Kaifeng the entertainers' din "could be heard for miles."

Women rarely appear in Meng's verses or on Zhang's scroll. They never enjoyed the same status in China as among the pastoral cultures of the steppeland, where women were always important partners in managing the herds. Increasingly, in China, women were traded as commodities, and as young girls, their feet were tightly bound with cloth, so that they became permanently deformed, in a practice perhaps originally designed to hobble them against escape.

Despite the troubled relationship with the nomads and the loss of the northern provinces, the late Song Empire brimmed with wealth. In 1170, an official set off up the Yangtze to his job in Sichuan. He admired everything he saw: the new bridges, the flourishing commerce, the boats crowded together "like the teeth of a comb." The war readiness of 700 river galleys, with their "speed like flight," excited him. He celebrated ample signs of prosperity. Sichuan possessed enviable wealth. Two districts there had between them 22 centers of population producing annual tax revenue of between 10,000 and 50,000 strings of cash—more than any other district of the Song Empire outside the lower Yangtze. The frontier had been drawn into the empire.

Rice cultivation. In the second half of the thirteenth century, Zhen Ji illustrated poems on rice cultivation in a long series of paintings, all copied—like the poems—from twelfth-century originals. His art demonstrates the continuity of Chinese agriculture. Even after revolutionary new strains of rice were introduced in China, older varieties of the crop were still cultivated in traditional ways.

Song Art and Learning

The era left an enduring intellectual and artistic legacy. To the eleventh-century elite, philosophy was the basis and business of government. On one side of the debate, Ouyang Xiu aimed to restore "the perfection of ancient times"—an ideal age "when rites and music reached everywhere." Wang Anshi (wahng ahn-sheh), who led the party on the other side of the debate, thought life was like a dream and valued "dreamlike merits" equally with practical results. He carried the notion of socially responsible government to extremes and consulted "peasants and serving girls" rather than relying on Confucian principles and ancient precedents. His policies when he was in charge of the government in the 1070s included progressive taxation, the substitution of taxes for forced labor, cheap loans for farmers, and state-owned pawnshops. Wang mistrusted Confucian confidence in China's ability to tame the steppelanders—he introduced universal conscription. To combat banditry, he organized village society in groups of ten families, so that each family was held responsible for the good behavior of the others.

Both parties supported reform of the examination system that produced the imperial officials with two objectives in mind: to encode in it an ethic of service to society, and to recruit the state's servants from as wide a range of social backgrounds as possible. The old examination tested only skill in composition, especially in verse, and in memorizing texts. The new test asked questions about ethical standards and about how the state could serve the people better. It was a conservative revolution.

While Wang's agenda shaped policy, Ouyang Xiu's dominated the intellectual mainstream. The dominant trend in philosophy for the rest of the Song era was the effort to reinterpret the Confucian classics for the readers' own times. Zhu Xi (joo shi) (1130–1200) summarized and synthesized all previous thinking on this subject. In some ways, he was what we would now call a secular humanist. He upheld the doctrine of the natural goodness of human beings. He doubted whether "there is a man in heaven judging sin" and dismissed prayer in favor of self-examination and study of the classics. Morality, he thought, was a matter of individual responsibility, not heavenly regulation. But he did accept the tradition on which the Chinese state was based: "Heaven" decreed the fortunes of society according to the merits of its rulers. Zhu's synthesis defined what subsequent ages called Confucianism.

The intellectual and economic environment of the Song Empire was favorable to the arts. There was money and enthusiasm for patronage of artists. The painting of the era has always attracted admiration, not just because it was technically excellent, but also because it specialized in scenes from the natural world. Admiration for the beauty of nature, untouched by human hands, is, perhaps, a measure of the maturity of a civilization. It is doubtful, however, whether Song artists painted nature, as modern romantics do today, for its own sake. To them, the natural world was a book of lessons about humankind. Su Dongpo (soo dohng-pwoh) (1036–1101) painted virtually nothing but bamboo, because its fragility suggested human weakness. Li Longmian (lee lung-mee-en) (1049–1106) favored gnarled trees, defying weather, as symbols of the resilience of the sages. Mi Fei (mee fay) (1051–1107) perfected the representation of mist—which is the breath of nature, with power to shape the image, like the spiritual dimension of human beings. With other Song painters, they produced some of the world's most influential, most imitated images.

Chinese night revels. A female musician entertains members of the scholar-gentry in *The Night Revels of Han Xizai,* painted in the tenth century by Gu Hongzhong. Chinese paintings rarely show men and women together in this kind of interior setting. The elaborately laid and decorated table, the porcelain ware, and the luxury and sexual appeal of female entertainment provide an intimate glimpse of courtly life during the Song dynasty.

IN PERSPECTIVE: Cains and Abels

The North African Muslim Ibn Khaldun (ihb-ihn hahl-DOON), one of the world's best historians, looking back from the late fourteenth century, saw history as a story of struggle between nomads and settled people. To some extent, he based his view on the experience of his native region in the eleventh and twelfth centuries, when, as far as he could make out, pastoralist invaders wrecked its peace and prosperity: first, Arab herders whom the Fatimids released or expelled from southern Egypt; then the Almoravids and Almohads from the Sahara. Modern historians have challenged his interpretation. The mutual disdain between tillers and herders was neither as deep nor destructive as Ibn Khaldun thought. But the tension he perceived was real. The biblical story of Cain and Abel traces the origins of human conflict to the mutual hatred and murderous rivalry of a tiller of the soil and a keeper of flocks.

Ibn Khaldun, from *The Muqaddimah*

Nomads threatened their farming neighbors in various ways. The nomadic way of life demanded immeasurably more land per head of population than the intensive agriculture that fed dense farming populations. Nomads were ill equipped for some economic activities, including mining and silk manufacture, and the production of commodities, such as tea, fruit, and grain. For these things, therefore, they depended on theft, tribute, or trade from farming communities. The nomads were better equipped for war. Horsemanship made their way of life a preparation for battle. Sedentary peoples had not yet developed firearms or fortifications good enough to tilt the balance in their own favor. The nomads tended to cherish ideologies of superiority—of jihad or of divine election for empire—that clashed with the opposite convictions of the settled peoples. Nomads could exploit farmers' lands, but agricultural communities did not yet have the technology—steel plows, mechanical harvesters—to turn the soils of the grasslands into farmland.

Yet the hostility of nomads and farmers arose less, perhaps, from conflicts of interest than from mutual misunderstanding: a clash of cultures, incompatible ways of seeing the world and coping with it. There is no moral difference between settled and nomadic lifeways. Yet each type of community tended to see the other as morally inferior. This was probably because for followers of each way of life, those of the other represented all that was alien. Their mutual descriptions were full of incomprehension and disgust.

Real differences underpinned this mutual revulsion. Pastoralist diets were, for farmers, literally stomach churning. Pastoralists relied on dairy foods, which most

● MAKING CONNECTIONS

NOMADIC THREATS TO SEDENTARY PEOPLES

CHARACTERISTICS OF NOMADS	CONSEQUENCES
Nomadic way of life requires extensive land →	Constant threat of attack on sedentary peoples
Nomads ill equipped for certain economic activities and the manufacture of favored commodities →	Dependence on theft and tribute from or trade with sedentary peoples
Nomads expert horsemen →	Until development of firearms and fortifications, sedentary peoples at a disadvantage in war
Nomads cherish ideologies of superiority →	Clash between nomads and settled peoples
Nomads can easily exploit farmers' lands →	Until development of steel plows and mechanized harvesters, farmers could not exploit grasslands

CHRONOLOGY

907	End of Tang dynasty
960	Beginning of Song dynasty; conversion of Karkhanid Turks to Islam
1054	Schism between Latin and Orthodox Christianity
1071	Battle of Manzikert; end of Byzantine dominance in Anatolia
1076	Kumbi Saleh falls to Almoravid armies
1080s	Muslim kingdoms in al-Andalus call on Almoravids for help
1095	Pope Urban II calls for crusade to capture Jerusalem
1099	Jerusalem falls to crusaders
1111	Death of al-Ghazali, Sufi mystic and theologian
1140s	Almoravid Empire falls to the Almohads
1187	Crusader kingdom of Jerusalem falls to Saladin
1204	Sack of Constantinople by crusaders

farmers rejected, because after early childhood they did not naturally produce lactase—the substance that makes milk digestible. It was also normal for herders to open their animal's veins for fresh blood to drink. This practice enabled nomad armies to take nourishment without halting on the march. Nomad diets tended to be short on plant foods. So to balance their intake, nomads would usually eat the raw organ meats of dead animals, which contain relatively high levels of vitamin C, which, in other cultures, people get from fruit and vegetables. Indeed, meat processed without cooking was important in the treeless environments of the steppe and the desert, where the only cooking fuel was dried animal dung. One of the great resources of the Eurasian steppe was the fat-tailed sheep, specially bred to drag its broad tail behind it. Its fat is wonderfully soft. Even if nomads have no time to heat this fat, or no kindling with which to cook it, they can eat it raw and digest it quickly. These were all elements of a rational food strategy for the nomadic life, but they inspired denunciations of the "barbaric" customs of eaters of raw meat and drinkers of blood. The nomads responded with equal contempt. For them, the settled life was soft and corrupt. Farming involved grubbing and groveling in mud. Cities and rice paddies were cramped and unhealthy.

After successful conquests, the nomads could usually be absorbed and induced to adopt or tolerate settled ways of life; but the conquerors kept coming. The relative success of the Islamic world in absorbing and converting the invaders of the tenth and eleventh centuries was a decisive feature of the history of the period. Byzantium, by contrast, failed to tame the intruders, while Western Christendom could recruit no more pastoralists after the Magyars. China developed no strategy to cope with the nomads, except to retreat and wait for them to adopt Chinese ways. Unprecedented changes in the steppeland, however, were about to upset the balance between nomads and settled peoples and unleash the most formidable steppeland conquerors of all, the Mongols. The outcome would transform the history of Eurasia.

PROBLEMS AND PARALLELS

1. Was the Islamic world's disunity an inevitable outcome of its vast geographic expansion by 1000? What parallels, if any, are there to earlier empires?

2. What was the influence of steppeland invaders on the Islamic world? Why was the Islamic world more successful in absorbing nomads than was Christian Europe?

3. The Crusades started as an outgrowth of the tradition of pilgrimage. How was a religious process transformed into a series of violent military campaigns? What were the ultimate effects of the Crusades?

4. Did the Almoravids' and Almohads' involvement in Spain in the twelfth century ultimately hinder or help Islamic power there? Why is the conversion of Ghana to Islam ultimately of more historical significance?

5. Why did most Muslim elites and clerics reject the Sufis? Why were the Sufis more popular with ordinary Muslims than with the Islamic elite?

6. Why was it important for the Byzantines to claim to be the Roman Empire? Why was it strategically important for the rulers of Constantinople to build a Byzantine "commonwealth"? What were the consequences of the rupture in relations between Latin and Orthodox Christianity?

7. How did China under the Tang deal with nomadic invaders? Were the Chinese more or less successful than their European and Muslim contemporaries?

8. Why does the hostility between pastoralists and sedentary peoples have less to do with conflicts of interest than with a clash of cultures?

DOCUMENTS IN GLOBAL HISTORY

- Early Turkish history from the *Dede Korkut*
- Al Thalibi, *Recollections of Bukhara*
- A Muslim view of the Crusaders
- Al-Ghazali, on "On the Separation of Mathematics and Religion"
- Liutprand of Cremona, from *Report of His Mission to Constantinople*

- Anna Comnena, from the *Alexiad*
- Benjamin of Tudela, *Book of Travels*
- Lu Yu, from *Diary of a Journey to Sichuan*
- Ibn Khaldun, from *The Muqaddimah*

Please see the Primary Source DVD for additional sources related to this chapter.

READ ON

B. Lewis, *The Middle East* (1997) is a broad introductory narrative. M. S. Hodgson, *The Venture of Islam* (1977) is as always fundamental for anything in Islamic history. L. Yaacov, *State and Society in Fatimid Egypt* (1991) is an important collection of studies on the background to the caliphate of al-Hakim. T. Talbot-Rice, *The Seljuks in Asia Minor* (1960) is important for understanding the assimilation of the Turks. The *Dede Korkut* (1974) is available in an excellent edition by G. Lewis.

T. Asbridge, *The First Crusade* (2005) is a vigorous, up-to-date account. C. Tyerman, *God's War* (2006) is an efficient general introduction, as is J. Riley-Smith, *The Crusades* (2005). J. Riley-Smith, *Atlas of the Crusades* (1990) is a useful standby. K. M. Setton, ed., *A History of the Crusades* (1969) is exhaustive.

H. Kennedy, *Muslim Spain and Portugal* (1997) and R. Fletcher, *Moorish Spain* (1993) are helpful as introductions. D. Wasserstein, *The Rise and Fall of the Party Kings* (1985) deals with the dissolution of the caliphate of Cordova and its successor states. For the Spanish background, R. Fletcher, *The Quest for El Cid* (1991) is scintillating and highly readable. E. W. R. Bovill, *The Golden Trade of the Moors* (1992) and *Saharan Myth and Legend* (1959) are classic works that unfold the background to the Almoravids. N. Levtzion, *Ancient Ghana and Mali* (1980) is an authoritative and concise study. J. S. Trimingham, *The Sufi Orders in Islam* (1998) is the great classic treatment of its subject.

On Byzantium, as well as works recommended in earlier chapters, C. Mango, *Byzantium and Its Image* (1984) is par-

ticularly good on cultural aspects, and D. Obolensky, *The Phoenix: The Byzantine Commonwealth* (2000), which is particularly good on diplomacy, are helpful. B. Hill, *Imperial Women in Byzantium* (1999) is an indispensable modern study. A. J. Toynbee, *Constantine Porphyrogenitus and His World* (1973) is a timeless classic by one of the great historians of the last century. Among the texts referred to in this chapter, *The Embassy to Constantinople and Other Writings of Liutprand of Cremona*, ed. J. J. Norwich is instructive and there are many editions of the *Alexiad* of Anna Comnena and *The Itinerary of Benjamin of Tudela* (many editions). On relations with the Latin church, S. Runciman, *The Eastern Schism* (1955), though now half a century old, is concise and readable. J. J. Norwich, *A History of Venice* (1982) is a richly detailed narrative. D. E. Queller, *The Fourth Crusade* (1999) nicely blends narrative and analysis. There are many editions of the most engaging source: G. de Villehardouin, *The Conquest of Constantinople* (2006). N. Wilson, *Scribes and Scholars* (1991) is a lively account of Byzantine learning.

On Liao, J. S. Tao, *Two Sons of Heaven* (1988) is valuable; for the Jurchen, Y. S. Tao, *The Jurchen in Twelfth-Century China* (1977) is particularly good on sinicization. R. von Glahn, *The Country of Streams and Grottoes* (1988) is scholarly and well written, bringing the internal frontier of China to life. R. Egan, ed., *The Literary Works of Ou-yang Hsiu* (1984) is an invaluable source. J. T. C. Liu, *Reform in Sung China*, which originally appeared in the 1950s, has not been replaced as far as I know.

PART

Six

The Crucible: The Eurasian Crises of the Thirteenth and Fourteenth Centuries

This Korean world map, from about 1402, known ▶ as the Kangnido, is the earliest known map of the world from east Asia. It is also the oldest surviving Korean map. Based on Chinese maps from the fourteenth century, the Kangnido clearly shows Africa (with an enormous lake in the middle of the continent) and Arabia on the lower left. The Indian subcontinent, however, has been merged into a gigantic landmass that represents China. The Korean peninsula, on the upper right, is shown as much bigger than it actually is, while Japan, on the lower right, is placed much farther south than where it is actually located.

ENVIRONMENT

1300–1800
Little Ice Age

● **since mid-1200s**
Lenses and clocks in Europe

CULTURE

1206–1360s
Mongol hegemony

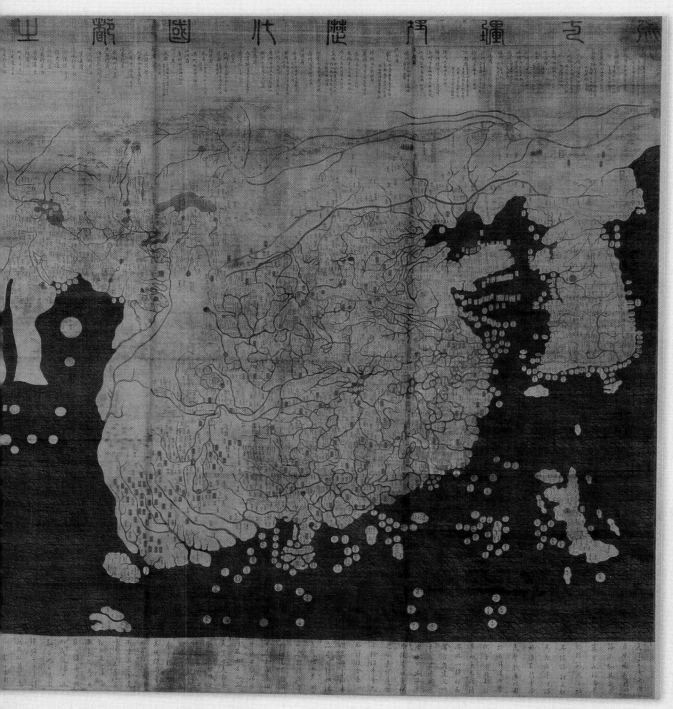

山巖區代歷搏疆古燕

1330s–mid–1400s
(and sporadically to 1700s)
Plague in Eurasia

since mid–1400s
Growth of Atlantic navigation

from 1350s
Rise of the Ottomans

1368–1644
Ming Dynasty (China)

from 1440s
Rise of Muscovy

from mid–1400s
Rise of Incas, Aztecs
Beginnings of oceanic imperialism

FRONT

BACK

FRONT

BACK

The Mongols arrive in Georgia. Two coins from the kingdom of Georgia, minted less than two decades apart, show that the Mongols had conquered that Caucasian state. The front of the top coin, minted by Queen Rusudan of Georgia in 1230, features a bust of a bearded Jesus Christ, draped in a mantle and backed by a cross-shaped halo. The Greek abbreviations for the words "Jesus" and "Christ" flank his right and left shoulders respectively. A Georgian inscription runs along the border. The back of the coin shows inscriptions in both Georgian and Arabic. In contrast, on the bottom coin, minted by King David in 1247, a figure on horseback has replaced the image of Jesus Christ (front), while the inscription on the back of the coin is exclusively in Arabic and identifies the king as "the slave of the Great Khan."

© The Trustees of the British Museum.

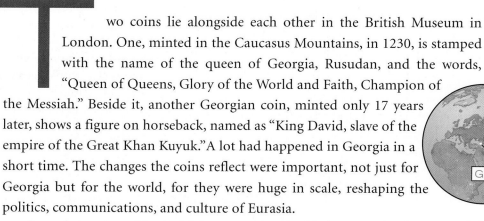

GEORGIA

Two coins lie alongside each other in the British Museum in London. One, minted in the Caucasus Mountains, in 1230, is stamped with the name of the queen of Georgia, Rusudan, and the words, "Queen of Queens, Glory of the World and Faith, Champion of the Messiah." Beside it, another Georgian coin, minted only 17 years later, shows a figure on horseback, named as "King David, slave of the empire of the Great Khan Kuyuk." A lot had happened in Georgia in a short time. The changes the coins reflect were important, not just for Georgia but for the world, for they were huge in scale, reshaping the politics, communications, and culture of Eurasia.

Georgia, protected by its high mountains, had been remarkably successful in resisting the nomad armies of the eleventh and twelfth centuries. Though the Seljuk Turks (see Chapter 12) had briefly terrorized the kingdom and exacted tribute, the Georgians fought back. They refused to pay tribute, recovered their lost possessions, and extended their frontiers over parts of neighboring Armenia. In the early thirteenth century, Georgia was a formidable state, capable of imposing rulers as far afield as the Byzantine city of Trebizond (TREH-bih-zahnd) on the Black Sea and the Muslim city of Ahar in Azerbaijan (ah-zehr-bay-ZHAHN) on the Caspian. In the 1220s, James of Vitry, a Catholic bishop and historian of his own times, admired Georgian pilgrims he saw in Jerusalem, who "march into the holy city with banners displayed, without paying tribute to anyone, for the Muslims dare in no way molest them".

As James of Vitry noted, Georgia was "surrounded by infidels on all sides". That did not seem to matter. The Georgians even wrote to the pope promising assistance in a new crusade. Suddenly, however, in 1224, letters from Georgia arrived in Rome, withdrawing the promise. "A savage people of hellish aspect has invaded my realm," wrote Rusudan, "as voracious as wolves in their hunger for spoils, and as brave as lions." In the next decade, her letters got increasingly desperate. The Mongols were coming. The world would never be the same again.

● ● ● ● ●

FOCUS questions

- WHY WERE the Mongols able to conquer such a vast empire?
- WHAT WERE the positive and negative effects of the Mongol conquests?
- WHY DID the Mongols fail to conquer Egypt, India, and Japan?
- HOW DID Kubilai Khan's reign blend Mongol and Chinese traditions?
- WHAT TECHNOLOGIES did the West develop in the thirteenth century and what were the consequences?
- WHY DID nothing comparable to the Mongol Empire develop in Africa or the Americas?

The effects of the events of the rest of the century refashioned Eurasia, destroying old states, creating new ones, disrupting existing communications and reforging stronger, wider-ranging links. Though at first the Mongols razed cities, destroyed crops, slaughtered elites, and depleted peoples, it looked for a while as if a safer, richer, more interconnected, more dynamic, more expanding, and more enlightened world might emerge—as if something precious were to form in an alchemist's crucible, out of conflicting ingredients, flung at random and stirred with violence. Then a century of environmental disasters arrested these changes in most of Eurasia. Catastrophes reversed the growth of populations and prosperity. But previously marginal regions began to be drawn more closely into a widening pattern of contacts and cultural exchange. Some peoples, in Africa and southeast Asia, for example, looked outward because they escaped disaster. Others, especially in Europe, did so because their reverses were so enormous that there was nothing else they could do.

THE MONGOLS: RESHAPING EURASIA

The earliest records of Mongol-speaking peoples occur in Chinese annals of the seventh century, when they emerged onto the steppes of Central Asia, from forests to the north, and became horse-borne nomads and sheepherders. In the early twelfth century, the bands or alliances they formed got bigger, and their raids against neighboring sedentary peoples became more menacing. In part, this was the effect of the growing preponderance of some Mongol groups over others. In part, it was the result of economic change.

Contact with richer neighbors enriched Mongol chiefs as mercenaries or raiders. Economic inequalities arose in a society in which blood relationships and seniority in age had formerly settled every person's position. Prowess in war enabled particular leaders to build up followers in parallel with—and sometimes in defiance of—the old social order. They called this process "crane catching"—comparing it to caging valuable birds. Successful leaders enticed or forced rival groups into submission. The process involved peoples who were not strictly Mongols, including many who spoke Turkic languages. In 1206, Temujin (TEH-moo-jeen), the most dynamic leader, proclaimed himself ruler "of all those who live in felt tents"—staking a claim to a steppe-wide empire. He was acclaimed by a title of obscure meaning that is traditionally rendered in the Roman alphabet as "Genghis Khan" (GEHN-gihs hahn).

Today, his memory is twisted between myths. When Mongolia was a communist state between 1921 and 1990, he was an almost unmentionable figure, inconsistent with the "peace-loving" image the communists tried to project. Now he is Mongolia's national hero. In his own day, he addressed different audiences with conflicting messages. To Muslims, he was sent by God to punish them for their sins. To Chinese, he was a candidate for the mandate of heaven. To Mongols, he was a giver of victory and of the treasure it brought. To monks and hermits, he stressed his own asceticism. "Heaven is weary of the inordinate luxury of China," he declared. "I have the same rags and the same food as cowherds and grooms, and I treat the soldiers as my brothers."

The violence endemic in the steppes now turned outward to challenge neighboring civilizations. Historians have been tempted to speculate about the reasons. One explanation is environmental. Temperatures in the steppe fell. People farther west on the Russian plains complained that a cold spell in the early thirteenth century caused crops to fail. So declining pastures might have driven the Mongols to expand from the steppes. Population in the region seems to have been relatively high, and the pastoral way of life demands large amounts of grazing land to feed relatively few people. So perhaps the Mongol outthrust was a consequence of having more mouths to feed. Yet the Mongols were doing what steppelanders had always sought to do: dominate and exploit sedentary peoples. The difference was that they did it with more ambition and efficiency than their predecessors.

Genghis Khan enforced or induced unity over almost the entire steppeland. A single ideology came to animate, or perhaps reflect, his program: the God-given right of the Mongols to conquer the world. Mongol-inspired sources constantly insist on an analogy between the overarching unity of the sky and God's desire for the Earth to echo that unity through submission to one ruler. This imperial vision probably grew on Genghis Khan gradually, as he felt his way from raiding, tribute gathering, and exacting ransom to constructing an empire, with permanent institutions of rule. Tradition alleges a turning point. When one of his generals proposed to exterminate 10 million Chinese subjects and convert their fields into pasture for Mongol herds, Genghis Khan realized that he could profit more by sparing the peasants and taxing them to the tune of 500,000 ounces of silver, 400,000 sacks of grain, and 80,000 bolts of silk a year.

The process, however, that turned him from destroyer to builder was tentative. The khan himself may have been only dimly aware of it. His initially limited ambitions are clear from the oath Mongol chiefs swore to him at his election. "If you will be our khan, we will go as your vanguard against the multitude of your enemies. All the beautiful girls and married women that we capture and all the fine horses we will bring to you." The khan acquired an unequaled reputation for lust and bloodlust. "My greatest joy," he was remembered for saying, "is to shed my enemies' blood, wring tears from their womenfolk and take their daughters for bedding." Meanwhile, he made the streets of Beijing (bay-jeeng)—according to an admittedly imaginative eyewitness—"greasy with the fat of the slain." His victims in Persia amounted, believably, to millions. Even after Genghis Khan had introduced more constructive policies, terror remained an instrument of empire. Mongol sieges routinely culminated in massacre.

Wherever Mongol armies went, their reputation preceded them. Armenian sources warned Westerners of the approach of "precursors of Antichrist ... who rush with joy to carnage as if to a wedding feast or orgy." The invaders looked like monkeys, it was said, barked like dogs, ate raw flesh, drank their horses' urine, knew no laws, and showed no mercy. Matthew Paris, the thirteenth-century English monk who, in his day, probably knew as much about the rest of the world as any of his countrymen, summed up the Mongols' image: "They are inhuman and beastly, rather monsters than men. ... And so they come, with the swiftness of lightning to the confines of Christendom, ravaging and slaughtering, striking everyone with terror and with incomparable horror."

The Mongol conquests reached farther and lasted longer than those of any previous nomad empire (see Map 13.1). At its fullest

Genghis Khan. Rashid al-Din (1247–1318) was a former Jewish rabbi, converted to Islam, who became the chief minister of the Mongol rulers of what is now Iran. His *Compendium of Chronicles* was propaganda that depicted Mongol rulers in Persian style. This is the image of Genghis Khan his successors liked to project—a lone, simple tent-dweller who was the arbitrator and lawgiver to petitioners from many nations.

The Rise of the Mongols

Seventh century	Earliest records of the Mongol people
Early twelfth century	Larger Mongol bands attack sedentary peoples
1206	Temujin proclaims himself khan

HOLY ROMAN EMPIRE

Venice

POLISH STATES

Esztergom
Pest
Cracow
Sandomierz
Vladimir
Galich
Kamenets

HUNGARY

SERBIA

BULGARIA

Lithuanians

Oder
Vistula

Novgorod

RUSSIAN PRINCIPALITIES

Torzhok
Tver'
Yaroslavl'
Pereyaslavl'
Moscow
Suzdal
Kolomna
Vladimir
Ryazan'

Chernigov

Kiev
Pereyaslav

Danube

Dniester

Dnieper

VOLGA BULGARIA

Bulgar

Volga

Ural Mountains

LATIN EMPIRE

EMPIRE OF NICAEA

Soldaia
Constantinople

Black Sea

Anatolia

EMPIRE OF TREBIZOND

SELJUK SULTANATE OF RUM

CILICIA

Sivas
Kayseri

Caucasus

GEORGIA

Thilisi

Derbent

Don

Saray

Astrakhan

Caspian Sea

Ural

S t e p p e

Aral Sea

Syr Darya

Yanikant
Jand
Signak

TRANSOXIANA

Lake Balkhash

Ili

TURK

Mediterranean Sea

CRUSADER STATES

Alexandria

Cairo

EGYPT (MAMLUKS)

Aleppo

Homs
Damascus
Jerusalem
Ain Jalut

Euphrates

Tigris

Mosul
Maragheh

IRAQ

Baghdad
Hamadan

ABBASID CALIPHATE

AZERBAIJAN

Tabriz

Qazvin
Alamut
Amol
Qum
Rayy

Nishapur

Urgench

Amu Darya

Bukhara

Zarnuq
Nur

Otrar

Banakat

Tashkent

Balasaghun

Samarkand

Balkh

Herat

Pamirs

Red Sea

PERSIA (IRAN)

Iranian Plateau

Persian Gulf

Arabian Peninsula

Hindu Kush

AFGHANISTAN

Ghazni

Parwan
Kabul

Indus

Multan

PUNJAB

OMAN

Arabian Sea

N

4,445 km (2,764 miles)

8,372 km (5,224 miles)

Scale varies with perspective

N

1200: Cold spell throughout Eurasian steppe

1211: First invasion of northern China

1237: Beginning of conquest of Russia

1242: Mongols reach Elbe River (Germany)

1260: Battle of Ain Jalut; Mongols invasion of Egypt repulsed

1276: Conquest of Song China complete

1292: Mongols raid Java

1200   1220   1240   1260   1280   1300

1206: Mongols united under Genghis Khan

1227: Death of Genghis Khan

1240: Kiev sacked

1258: Sack of Baghdad; last Caliph put to death

1274: First failed attempt at invading Japan

1281: Second failed invasion of Japan

1295: il-Khans adopt Islam

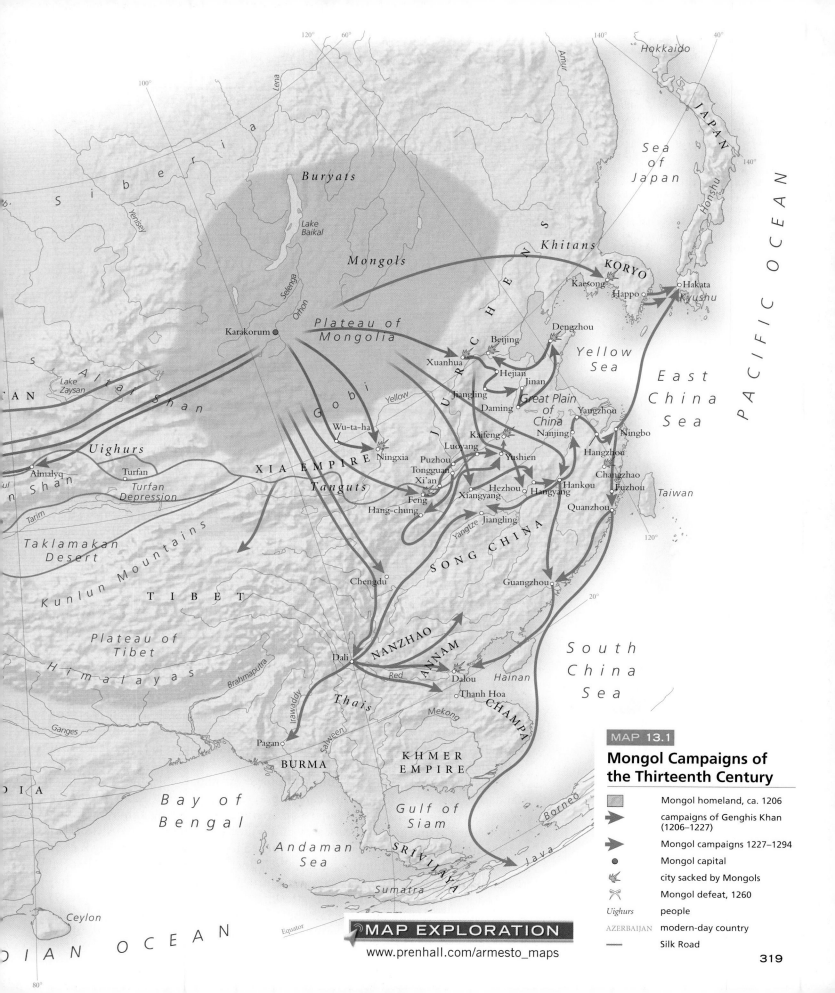

Siberia

Buryats

Lake
Baikal

Mongols

Plateau of
Mongolia

Karakorum

Khitans

Sea
of
Japan

KORYO

Kaesong

Happo

Hakata
Kyushu

Beijing

Xuanhua

Dengzhou

Yellow
Sea

East
China
Sea

PACIFIC OCEAN

Altai Shan

Uighurs

Almalyq

Shan

Turfan

Turfan
Depression

Lake
Zaysan

Gobi

Yellow

Wu-ta-ha

XIA EMPIRE

Tanguts

Ningxia

Hejian

Jinan

Jiangling

Daming

Great Plain
of
China

Yangzhou

Nanjing

Ningbo

Kaifeng

Luoyang

Puzhou

Yushien

Hangzhou

Changzhao

Tarim

Taklamakan
Desert

Kunlun Mountains

TIBET

Tongguan
Xi'an
Feng

Hang-chung

Xiangyang

Hezhou

Hankou
Hangyang

Fuzhou

Quanzhou

Taiwan

SONG CHINA

Yangtze Jiangling

Plateau of
Tibet

Himalayas

Brahmaputra

Chengdu

Guangzhou

Ganges

NANZHAO

Dali

ANNAM

Red

Dalou

Hainan

South
China
Sea

Irrawaddy

Thais

Thanh Hoa

CHAMPA

Pagan

BURMA

Salween

KHMER
EMPIRE

Mekong

Bay of
Bengal

Gulf of
Siam

Borneo

Java

Andaman
Sea

SRIVIJAYA

Sumatra

Ceylon

Equator

OCEAN

MAP 13.1

**Mongol Campaigns of
the Thirteenth Century**

▢ Mongol homeland, ca. 1206

➤ campaigns of Genghis Khan
(1206–1227)

➤ Mongol campaigns 1227–1294

● Mongol capital

🗲 city sacked by Mongols

✕ Mongol defeat, 1260

Uighurs people

AZERBAIJAN modern-day country

— Silk Road

"Exceptionally adaptable warmongers". This fourteenth-century Muslim painting shows the Mongols capturing Baghdad in 1258, with the help of siegecraft and specialist engineers as well as their traditional cavalry. The last caliph appears behind a screen in his palace in the left background. In the center background, he emerges on a white horse to meet the Mongol leader, Hülegü. The painting seems to show the Mongols respecting the sacredness of the city and its ruler. Indeed, they showed their respect by putting the caliph to death without spilling his blood—a sign of reverence for the condemned in their culture

extent, the empire encompassed the whole of Russia, Persia, China, the Silk Roads, and the steppes. It was the largest empire, in terms of territorial extent, the world had seen. Efforts to explain this success appeal to Genghis Khan's military genius, the effectiveness of the Mongols' curved bows and inventive tactics, the demoralizing psychological impact of their ruthless practices. Of course, they had the usual steppelander advantages of superior horsemanship and unrivaled mobility. It is likely that they succeeded, in part, through sheer numbers. Though we call it a Mongol army, Genghis Khan's was the widest alliance of steppelander peoples ever. And it is probable that, relatively speaking, the steppeland was more populous in his day than ever before.

Above all, the Mongols were exceptionally adaptable warmongers. They triumphed not only in cavalry country, but also in environments where previous steppelander armies had failed, pressing into service huge forces of foot soldiers, mobilizing complex logistical support, organizing siege trains and fleets, appropriating the full potential of sedentary economies to finance further wars. The mountains of Georgia could not stop them. Nor, in the long run, could the rice paddies and rivers of southern China where the Mongols destroyed the Song dynasty in the 1270s. Toward the end of the century, when another supreme khan wanted to conquer Java and Japan, they were even willing to take to the sea. But both attempts failed.

As well as for extent, the Mongol Empire was remarkable, by steppelander standards, for longevity. As his career progressed, Genghis Khan became a visionary lawgiver, a patron of letters, an architect of enduring empire. His first steps toward acquiring a bureaucracy and a judicial system more or less coincided with his election as khan. He then turned to lawmaking. Gradually, a code took shape, regulating hunting, army discipline, behavior at feasts, and social relationships, with death the penalty for murder, serious theft, conspiracy, adultery, sodomy, and witchcraft. Initially, the khan relied on Uighurs (see Chapter 9) for his administrators and ordered the adoption of the Uighur script for the Mongols' language. But he recruited as and where he conquered, without

Mongol defeat. Japanese screen painters recorded the defeat of Mongol invaders. Though the Mongols adapted successfully to every kind of terrain, they were unable to continue their conquests overseas. The "divine winds"—kamikaze, as the Japanese called them—protected Japan by making it impossible for the Mongols adequately to supply or reinforce their task force. *Copyright Museum of Imperial Collections, Sanno-maru Shozo kan. Photographs through courtesy of the International Society for Educational Information, Inc.*

favoritism for any community or creed. His closest ministers included Muslims, Christians, and Buddhists.

In 1219, a Chinese Daoist sage, Changchun (chahng-chwauhn), answered the khan's call for wise experts. At age 71, he undertook a three-year journey from China to meet the khan at the foot of the Hindu Kush mountains. There were sacrifices of principle he would not make. He would not travel with recruits for the imperial harem, or venture "into a land where vegetables were unavailable"—by which he meant the steppe. Yet he crossed the Gobi Desert, climbed "mountains of huge cold," and braved wildernesses where his escort smeared their horses with blood to ward off demons. Admittedly, Changchun's meeting with the khan was disappointing. The question the conqueror was most eager to put was not about the art of government, but about a potion to confer longevity on himself.

The Mongol Steppe

Still, many lettered and experienced officials from conquered states took service at the khan's court. The result was an exceptional, though short-lived, era in steppeland history: the **Mongol peace**. A European, who witnessed it in the 1240s, described it to reproach his fellow Christians with the moral superiority of their enemies: "The Mongols are the most obedient people in the world with regard to their leaders, more so even than our own clergy to their superiors. ... There are no wranglings among them, no disputes or murders." This was obviously exaggerated, but Mongol rule did make the steppeland safe for outsiders. This was new. A previously inaccessible road through the steppes opened across Eurasia north of the Silk Road. The Mongols became its highway police. Teams of Mongol horses, for instance, took the pope's ambassador, John of Piano Carpini, 3,000 miles in 106 days in 1246. Missionaries, spies, and craftsmen in search of work at the Mongol court also made the journey in an attempt to forge friendship between the Mongols and the Christian West, or, at least, to gather intelligence (see Map 13.2).

William of Rubruck, a Franciscan envoy, recorded vivid details of his mission to Genghis Khan's grandson in 1253. After taking leave of the king of France, who hoped for an alliance with the Mongols against the Muslims, William crossed the Black Sea in May and set out across the steppe by wagon, bound for Karakorum (kah-rah-KOH-ruhm), the new city in Mongolia where the khan held court. "After three days," he recorded, "we found the Mongols and I really felt as if I were entering another world."

John of Piano Carpini on the Mongols

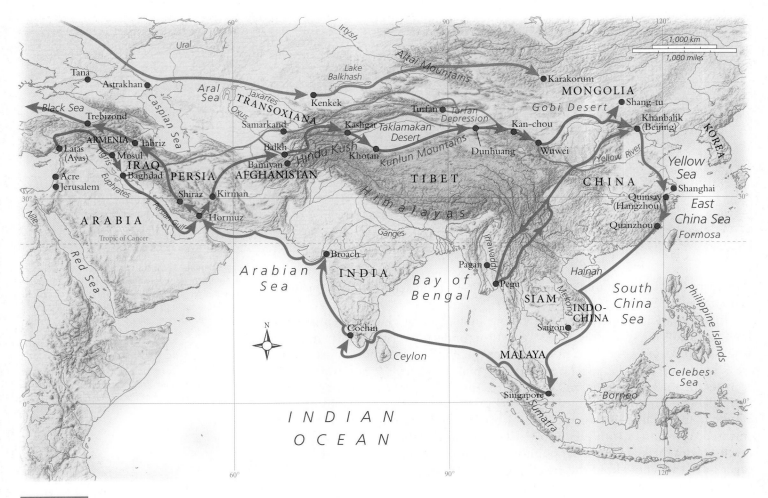

MAP 13.2

European Travelers of the Mongol Roads, 1245–1295

➤ John of Piano Carpini 1245–1247 and
William of Rubruck 1253–1254

➤ Marco Polo 1271–1275

➤ Marco Polo 1275–1295

— Silk Road

By November, he was in Transoxiana, "famished, thirsty, frozen, and exhausted." In December, he was high in the dreaded Altai Shan, the mountains. Here he "chanted the creed, among dreadful crags, to put the demons to flight." At last, on Palm Sunday, 1254, he entered the Mongol capital.

Friar William always insisted that he was a simple missionary, but he was treated as an ambassador and behaved like a spy. And, indeed, he had more than one objective. The Mongols might adopt Christianity or at least make an alliance against common enemies in the Muslim world. On the other hand, they were potential enemies, who had invaded the fringes of Europe and might do so again. Intelligence about them was precious. William realized that the seasonal migrations of Mongol life had a scientific basis and were calculated for military efficiency. "Every commander," he noted, "according to whether he has a greater or smaller number of men under him, is familiar with the limits of his pasture lands and where he ought to graze in summer and winter, spring and autumn."

Little useful intelligence escaped William. But he also showed interest in the culture he tried unsuccessfully to convert to Christianity. His description of a Mongol tent dwelling still holds good. The layout, social space, and way of life William saw have not changed much since his day. A frame of interlaced branches stretched and converged at the top. The covering was of white felt, "and they decorate the felt with various fine designs." Up to 22 oxen hauled houses on wagons 20 feet broad.

A MONGOL PASSPORT

Although they were in use in China before the Mongols arrived, documents called *paizi*, such as the one depicted here, were used as passports to regulate communication and administration in the vast Mongol empire. Their use, the way they were designed, and the language in which they were written help us understand the massive movements of people and the rapid exchange of ideas and technology that occurred across Eurasia during the thirteenth and fourteenth centuries when Mongol rule was at its height. William of Rubruck and Marco Polo would have carried one of these passports on their return journeys from Mongol courts in Asia to Europe.

This passport is made of iron. Thick silver bands on it form characters in the script that the Tibetan monk Phagspa, a close advisor to Kubilai Khan (r. 1260–1294), devised for writing the Mongol language in 1269.

Above the inscription is a handle with a silver lion mask inlaid on it that shows the influence of Tibetan and Indian art.

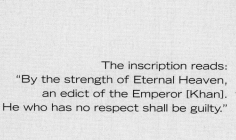

Most *paizi* were circular or rectangular in shape and were either fastened on an item of clothing or suspended from the neck, so that customs officers could easily see them.

The inscription reads: "By the strength of Eternal Heaven, an edict of the Emperor [Khan]. He who has no respect shall be guilty."

The Metropolitan Museum of Art, Purchase, Bequest of Dorothy Graham Bennet, 1993 (1993.256) Photograph © The Metropolitan Museum of Art.

● What does this passport reveal about the Mongol peace?

Yurt. The shape and decoration of a Mongol tent dwelling—known as a *yurt* or *ger*—has not changed since William of Rubruck described those he saw in the thirteenth century. In the background of this photograph are the Pamir Mountains, which travelers westward on the Silk Roads had to cross when they emerged from the Taklamakan Desert.

William of Rubruck's account of the Mongols

Each wife of the master of the household had her own tent, where the master had a bench facing the entrance. In an inversion of Chinese rules of precedence, the women sat on the east side, the men to the right of the master, who sat at the north end. Ancestral spirits resided in felt bags arrayed around the walls. One each hung over the heads of master and mistress, with a guardian image between them. Others hung on the women's and men's sides of the tent, adorned with the udders of a cow and a mare, symbols of life for people who relied on dairy products for their diet. The household would gather to drink fermented mare's milk in the tent of the chosen wife of the night. "I should have drawn everything for you," William assured his readers, "had I known how to draw."

Shamans' trances released the spirits from the bags that held them. Frenzied drumming, dancing, and drinking induced the shamans' ecstasies. The power of speaking with the ancestors' voices gave **shamans** enormous authority in Mongol decision making, including the opportunity to interfere in making and unmaking khans. This was a point William missed. The Mongols leaders' interest in foreign religions, and their investment in the cult of heaven, were, in part at least, strategies to offset the power of the native priests.

Outside the tent, William vividly captured the nature of the terrain—so smooth that one woman could pilot 30 wagons, linked by trailing ropes. He described a way of life that reflected steppeland ecology. The Mongols had mixed flocks of various kinds of sheep and cattle. Mixed pastoralism is essential in an environment in which no other source of food is available. Different species have different cycles of lactation and fertility. Variety ensures a reliable food supply.

The horse was the dominant partner of life on the steppe. Mare's milk was the Mongols' summer food. By drawing blood from the living creatures, Mongols on campaign could refresh themselves without slowing the herds. This was the basis of their reputation for blood-sucking savagery among their sedentary neighbors. Fermented mare's milk was the favorite intoxicating drink. The Mongols revered drunkenness and hallowed it by rites: offerings sprinkled over the bags of ancestral spirits, or poured out toward the quarters of the globe. Drinking bouts were a nightly entertainment.

William's conversations with the habitually drunken Möngke Khan, (MOHNG-keh hahn), grandson of Genghis Khan, revealed some of the qualities that made the Mongols of his era great: tolerance, adaptability, respect for tradition. "We Mongols believe," Möngke said, "that there is but one God, in Whom we live and in Whom we die, and towards him we have an upright heart." Spreading his hand, he added, "But just as God has given different fingers to the hand, so He has given different religions to people."[1] Later in the thirteenth century, Kubilai Khan (KOO-bih-la-yee hahn), another of Genghis Khan's grandsons, expressed himself to the Venetian traveler, Marco Polo, in similar terms.

THE MONGOL WORLD BEYOND THE STEPPES: THE SILK ROADS, CHINA, PERSIA, AND RUSSIA

The steppeland route was ideal for horseborne travelers. Trading caravans, however, still favored the traditional **Silk Roads**, which crossed Eurasia to the south of the steppe through the Taklamakan (tahk-lah-mah-KAHN) Desert. These routes had developed over centuries, precisely because high mountains protected them from steppeland raiders. But the security of the Mongol peace boosted the amount of traffic the roads carried. Mongol partiality for merchants also helped. Mongols encouraged Chinese trade, uninhibited by any of the traditional Confucian prejudices against commerce as an ignoble occupation. In 1299, after the Mongol Empire had been divided among several rulers, a Persian merchant was made the ambassador of the Supreme Khan to the court of the subordinate Mongol **Il-khan** (EEL-hahn) in Persia—an elevation unthinkable under a native Chinese dynasty, which would have reserved such a post for an official educated in the Confucian classics. The khans gave low-cost loans to Chinese trading companies. Chinese goods—and with them, patterns and styles—flowed to Persian markets as never before. Chinese arts, under Mongol patronage, became more open to foreign influences.

Geography still made the Silk Roads hard to travel. Marco Polo was a young Venetian who accompanied his father and uncle on a trading mission to Mongol-ruled China in the early 1270s. "They were hard put to it to complete the journey in three and a half years." The Taklamakan Desert was the great obstacle. The normal rule for caravans was the bigger, the safer. But the modest water sources of the desert could not sustain many more than 50 men at a time with their beasts. The key to exploiting the desert routes was the distribution of water, which drains inland from the surrounding mountains and finds its way below the desert floor by underground channels. It was normal to go for 30 days without finding water, though there might be an occasional salt-marsh oasis or an unreliable river. The worst danger was getting lost—"lured from the path by demon-spirits."[2] As a fourteenth-century painter at Persia's Mongol court imagined, the demons were black,

 from *The Travels of Marco Polo*

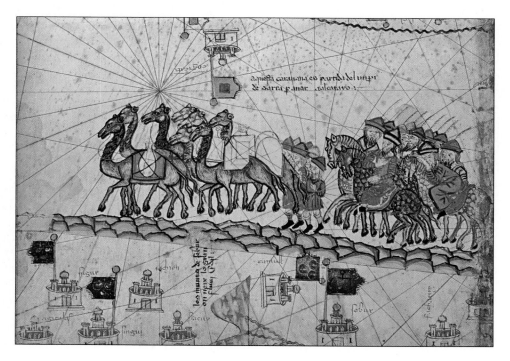

The Silk Roads. Cresques Abraham was the finest mapmaker of his day. He painted this image of a caravan on the Silk Roads in the late 1370s or early 1380s in an atlas probably commissioned for the king of France. By that date the Mongols no longer controlled the whole of the route, though the lances of an armed escort, presumably of Mongols, are visible behind the merchants. The caption says the caravan is bound for China, but it is heading in the opposite direction.

Travelers During the Mongol Peace

1245–1247	John of Piano Carpini
1253–1254	William of Rubruck
1271–1275; 1275–1295	Marco Polo
1275–1288	Rabban Bar Sauma

from Francesco Balducci
Pegolotti's *The Practice of
Commerce.*

from *The History of the Life and
Travels of Rabban Bar Sauma*

athletic, and ruthless, waving dismembered limbs of horses as
they danced. As Friar William had seen, the Mongols recommended warding them off by smearing a horse's neck with blood.

A fourteenth-century guide included tips for Italian merchants
who headed for East Asia to extend the reach of the commerce of
their cities. At the port of Tana (TAH-nah), on the Black Sea, you
should hire a good guide, regardless of expense. "And if the merchant likes to take a woman with him from Tana, he can do so." On
departure from Tana, 25 days' supply of flour and salt fish were
needed—"other things you will find in sufficiency and especially meat." The road
was "safe by day and night" and protected by Mongol police. But it was important to
take a close relative for company. Otherwise, should a merchant die, his property
would be forfeit. The text specified rates of exchange at each stop and recommended
suitable conveyances for each stage of the journey: oxcart or horse-drawn wagon to
the city of Astrakhan (AHS-trah-hahn) where the Don River runs into the Caspian
Sea. Thereafter camel train or pack mule was best, until you arrived at the river system of China. Silver was the currency of the road, but the Chinese authorities would
exchange it for paper money, which—Westerners were assured—they could use
throughout China.

After the deserts, the next obstacles were the mountains on their rims. The Tian
Shan, which screens the Taklamakan Desert, is 1,800 miles long, up to 300 miles wide, up
to 24,000 feet high, and punctuated by deep depressions. Farther north, the Altai Shan
mountains guard the Mongolian heartlands. "Before the days of the Mongols," wrote the
bishop of the missionary diocese the Franciscans had established in China, "nobody
believed that the Earth was habitable beyond these mountains, ... but by God's leave and
wonderful exertion the Mongols crossed them, and ... so did I."

Europeans frequently made the journey to China. That reflects the balance of
wealth and power at the time. China was rich and productive, Europe a needy
backwater. We know of only one subject of the Chinese emperor who found it
worthwhile to make the journey in the opposite direction. Rabban Bar Sauma
(rah-BAHN bahr SAH-no-mah) was a Nestorian Christian who set out from
China on a pilgrimage to Jerusalem. He got as far as Maragha in what is now Azerbaijan, the intellectual capital of the western Mongol world, with a library reputedly of 400,000 books and a new astronomical observatory. Then in 1286 he was
appointed the Mongols' ambassador to the kingdoms of the Christian West, to
negotiate an alliance against Muslim Egypt (see Map 13.3).

When he got to Rome, he was received by the cardinals who had assembled to
elect a pope. In Paris, he recognized the university there as an intellectual power-
house reminiscent of Maragha, with schools of mathematics, astronomy, medicine,
and philosophy. Persian was the only language in which Bar Sauma could communicate with Western interpreters. He mistook diplomatic evasions for assent and
vague expressions of Christian fellowship for doctrinal agreement. But the fact that
he completed the journey at all shows how the Mongols made it possible to cross
Eurasia.

China

The Mongols never ran their dominions as a centralized state. Three main areas of
conquest beyond the steppeland—in China, Persia, and Russia—were added after
Genghis Khan's death. All were exploited in different ways, specific to the Mongols'
needs and the peculiarities of each region.

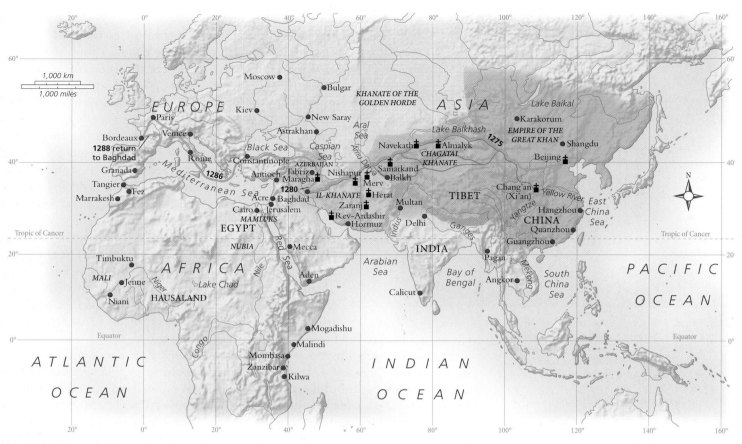

MAP 13.3

The Travels of Rabban Bar Sauma, 1275–1288

—— Silk Road

—— travels of Rabban Bar Sauma, 1275–1288

♦ Nestorian see

The conquest of Song China was long and difficult for two reasons. It was a more powerful state than any the Mongols faced elsewhere, and it was highly defensible: compact, so that its armies could maneuver on interior lines of communication, and scored by terrain inhospitable to Mongol horsemen. But, fueled by resources from the Mongols' other conquests, the conquest unfolded relentlessly bit by bit. Letters from the Chinese court seeped desperation as the Mongols closed in for the kill. In 1274, the Chinese empress mother reflected on where the blame lay.

> The empire's descent into peril is due, I regret, to the instability of our moral virtue. … The sound of woeful lament reverberated through the countryside, yet we failed to investigate. The pall of hunger and cold enveloped the armed forces, yet we failed to console.[2]

Unlike previous steppelander invaders, the Mongols spared no resources to pursue all-out victory and hired the troops and equipment needed to subdue a country of cities, rice paddies, and rivers. Clearly, the size of the Mongols' existing empire helped. Persian engineers built the siege engines that helped overcome southern Chinese cities. The last battle was at Changzhao (chanhg-jeeow)

Kubilai Khan. Liu Guandao was Kubilai Khan's favorite painter. So we can be fairly sure that this is how the khan would like to be remembered: not just in the traditional inert Chinese pose (which Liu also painted), but also active, dressed and horsed like a Mongol ruler, engaged in the hunt. A woman, presumably his influential consort, Chabi, is at his side. The blank silk background evokes the featurelessness of the steppe, while also highlighting the human figures.

in 1275. The Chinese poet Yi Tinggao (yee teen-gow) was there, "smelling the acrid dust of the field," spying "the green irridescence of the dead." The misery could be measured in the grief-stricken literature that survives: the suicide notes, the cries of longing for loved ones who disappeared in the chaos, massacred or enslaved. Years later, Ni Bozhuang (nee bwo-chwang), bailiff of a Daoist monastery, recalled the loss of his wife: "I still do not know if you were taken because of your beauty, or if, surrounded by horses, you can still buy cosmetics." In 1276, with his advisers fleeing and his mother packed for flight, the young Song emperor wrote his abdication letter to the Mongol khan. "The **Mandate of Heaven** having shifted, your Servant chooses to change with it, ... yet my heart is full of emotions and these cannot countenance the prospect of the abrupt annihilation of the ... altars of my ancestors. Whether they be misguidedly abandoned or specially preserved intact rests solely with the revitalized moral virtue you bring to the throne."

For the Mongols, the conquest of China was a logical continuation of the policies of Genghis Khan and a stage in fulfilling the destiny of world conquest heaven supposedly envisaged. But it was also the personal project and passion of Kubilai Khan (1214–1294), Genghis's grandson, who became so immersed in China that he never asserted his supremacy against those Mongol leaders in the extreme west of the Mongol world who resisted his claims to supremacy. Some of his Chinese subjects resented Kubilai's foreign ways: the libations of fermented mare's milk with which he honored his gods, his barbarous banquets of meat, the officials he chose from outside the Confucian elite and even from outside China. Marco Polo reported that all the Chinese "hated the government of the Great Khan, because he set over them steppelanders, most of whom were Muslims, and ... it made them feel no more than slaves." In this respect, the khan indeed broke with Chinese tradition, which was to confine administrative positions to a meritocracy, whose members were selected by examination in the Confucian classics. Kubilai showed his reverence for Confucius by building a shrine in his honor, but he needed to recruit, as Genghis Khan had, from the full range of talent the Mongol Empire supplied.

Kubilai, indeed, remained a Mongol khan. In some respects, he flouted Chinese conventions. He showed traditional steppelander respect for the abilities of women, giving them court posts and, in one case, a governorship. His wife, Chabi, was one of his closest political advisers. Mongols became a privileged minority in China, ruled by their own laws, and resented for it by most Chinese. In defiance of Confucian teachings, Kubilai felt obliged to fulfill the vision of world conquest he inherited from Genghis Khan. But beyond China, he registered only fleeting success. In Java, the Mongols replaced one native prince with another, without making permanent gains. In Vietnam, the Mongols were only able to levy tribute at a rate too low to meet the cost of their campaigns there. So-called *kamikaze* winds—divine typhoons that wrecked the Mongol fleets—drove Kubilai's armies back from Japan.

While upholding Mongol traditions, Kubilai also sought to be a Chinese emperor, who performed the due rites, dressed in the Chinese manner, learned the language, patronized the arts, protected the traditions, and promoted the interests of his Chinese subjects. Marco Polo, who seems to have served him as a sort of professional storyteller, called him "the most powerful master of men, lands, and treasures there has been in the world from the time of Adam until today."

Persia

In Persia, meanwhile, the Mongol rulers were like chameleons, taking on the hues of the culture they conquered. But, as in China, they were anxious to maintain a distinct identity and to preserve their own traditions. The court tended to stay in the north, where there was grazing for the kinds of herds their followers brought with them from the steppe. The Il-khans—"subordinate rulers," so called in deference to Kubilai Khan's nominal superiority—retained nomadic habits, migrating every summer and winter to new camps. In southern Iran and Iraq, the Il-khans tended to entrust power to local dynasties, securing their loyalty by marriages with the ruling family or court nobility. In effect, this gave them hostages for the good conduct of provincial rulers.

Eventually in 1295, the Il-khans adopted Islam, after flirtations with Nestorianism and Buddhism. This marked an important departure from the tradition of religious pluralism Genghis Khan had begun and Kubilai had upheld. From the moment the Il-khan Ghazan (r. 1295–1304) became a Muslim, the state began to take on a militantly religious character, excluding the Christians, Zoroastrians, Buddhists, and Jews formerly admitted to the khan's service. Moreover, the form of Islam the Il-khans finally adopted was Shiism, the prevailing tradition in Iran. Shiites (see Chapter 9) embraced doctrines most Muslims rejected: that Muhammad's authority descended via his nephew Ali; that a divinely selected leader or imam would perfect the Prophet's message; and that in the meantime the clergy had the right to interpret Islam. The Il-khans' option ensured that Persia would be the only officially Shiite state in the Muslim world.

The religious art of the Il-khanate looked unorthodox, full of human figures, especially those of Muhammad and his nephew. Painters even copied Christian nativity scenes to produce versions of the Prophet's birth. The Il-khans' Persia, however, was not isolated from neighboring states. On the contrary, as was usual in the Mongol world, the presence of rulers descended from Genghis Khan promoted trans-Eurasian contacts and exchanges of goods, personnel, and ideas. Persia supplied China, for instance, with engineers, astronomers, and mathematicians, while Persia received Chinese porcelain and paper money, which, however, did not take root in Persia before the twentieth century. Chinese designs influenced Persian weavers, and Chinese dragons appeared on the tiles that decorated Persian buildings. Mongol rule ended in Persia in 1343 when the last Il-khan died without an heir.

Russia

Meanwhile, the Mongols who remained in their central Asian heartlands continued their traditional way of life. So did those who formed the elite in the remaining areas the heirs of Genghis Khan inherited: in Turkestan and Kashgaria in Central Asia, and the steppes of the lower Volga River. From the last of these areas, where the Mongols were known as the Golden Horde, they exercised overlordship over Russia, where they practiced a kind of imperialism different from

Il-Khan art. When Mongols converted to Islam, they did not necessarily accept all the beliefs and conventions of orthodox religion. In this four-teenth-century painting from what is now Iran, the white rooster symbolizes the Muslim call to prayer—but the rooster was also a traditional Zoroastrian symbol of dawn. The prophet Muhammad, moreover, is realistically depicted at bottom right—something most Muslim painters would regard as impious, even today. The other figures are of angels.

Novgorod. The cathedral of St. Sophia in Novgorod in Russia would have presented essentially the same outline in the thirteenth century that it does today. At the time, it was one of relatively few buildings in that mercantile city-state built of stone rather than wood. The tallest gilded dome shows the position of the sanctuary at the heart of the church.

Excerpt from the *Novgorod Chronicle*

those in China and Persia. The Mongols left the Christian Russian principalities and city-states to run their own affairs. But their rulers had to receive charters from the khan's court at Saray (sah-RAY) on the lower Volga, where they had to make regular appearances, loaded with tribute and subject to ritual humiliations. The population had to pay taxes directly to Mongol-appointed tax gatherers—though as time went on, the Mongols assigned the tax gathering to native Russian princes and civic authorities.

The Russians tolerated this situation—albeit unhappily, and with many revolts—partly because the Mongols intimidated them by terror. When the Mongols took the great city of Kiev in 1240, it was said, they strewed the fields "with countless heads and bones of the dead." Partly, however, the Russians were responding to a milder Mongol policy. In most of Russia, the invaders came to exploit rather than to destroy. According to one chronicler, the Mongols spared Russia's peasants to ensure that farming would continue. Ryazan, a Russian principality on the Volga, southeast of Moscow, seems to have borne the brunt of the Mongol invasion. Yet there, if the local chronicle can be believed, "the pious Grand Prince Ingvary Ingvarevitch sat on his father's throne and renewed the land and built churches and monasteries and consoled newcomers and gathered together the people. And there was joy among the Christians whom God had saved from the godless and impious khan." Many cities escaped lightly by capitulating at once. Novgorod, that hugely rich city (see Chapter 11), which the Mongols might have coveted, they bypassed altogether.[3]

Moreover, the Russian princes were even more fearful of enemies to the west, where the Swedes, Poles, and Lithuanians had constructed strong monarchies, capable of sweeping the princes away if they ever succeed in expanding into Russian territory. Equally menacing were groups of mainly German adventurers, organized into crusading "orders" of warriors, such as the Teutonic Knights and the Brothers of the Sword, who took monastic-style vows but dedicated themselves to waging holy war against pagans and heretics. In practice, these orders were self-enriching companies of professional fighters, who built up territorial domains along the Baltic coast by conquest. Between 1242 and 1245, Russian coalitions fought off western invaders, but they could not sustain war on two fronts. The experience made them submissive to the Mongols.

THE LIMITS OF CONQUEST: MAMLUK EGYPT AND MUSLIM INDIA

In the 1200s, Egypt was in chaos because of rebellions by pastoralists from the southern desert and revolt by the slaves who formed the elite fighting force. It seems counterintuitive to arm slaves. But for most of the thirteenth century, the policy worked well for Saladin's heirs, who had ruled Egypt since 1192. The rulers' handpicked slave army, or Mamluks, came overwhelmingly from Turkic peoples that Mongol rebels displaced or captured and sold. These slaves had nowhere else to go and no future except in the Egyptian sultan's service. They were acquired young. They were trained in barracks, which became their substitutes for families and the source of their pride and sense of comradeship. The Mamluks seemed, from the ruler's point of view, ideally reliable: a dependent class. However, in the 1250s, they rebelled "like an unleashed torrent." Their own later propaganda cites the sultan's failure to reward them fairly for their services, and their outrage at the promotion of a black slave to one of the highest offices in the court.

Rise of the Mamluks	
1254	Mamluks depose sultan of Egypt
1260	Mamluk army victorious at the battle of Ain Jalut in Syria
1268–1291	Mamluks overthrow last of the crusader states

In September 1260, the rebels turned back the Mongol armies at one of the decisive battles of the world at Ain Jalut (EYE-in jah-LOOT) in Syria. It was the first serious reversal the Mongols had experienced since Genghis Khan united them. And it gave the slave army's commander, Baybars (BYE-bahrs), the chance to take over Egypt and Syria. He boasted that he could play polo in Cairo and Damascus within the space of a single week. The Mamluks mopped up the last crusader states on the coast of Syria and Palestine between 1268 and 1291. In combination with the effects of the internal politics of the Mongol world, which inhibited armies from getting too far from the centers of power, the Mamluk victory kept the Mongols out of Africa.

Mamluk victory marked a further stage in the Islamization of Africa. The Mamluks levied tribute on the Christian kingdoms of Nubia (see Chapter 9). Then, in the next century, they imposed Islam there. Cairo became a normal stopping place on the pilgrimage route to Mecca for Muslim kings and dignitaries from West Africa. Islam percolated through the region of Lake Chad and in what is today Nigeria.

Muslim India: The Delhi Sultanate

After the disruptions the violent Turkic migrations of the twelfth century caused, it took a long time for a state in the mold of Mahmud's to reemerge in Ghazna (see Chapter 12). By the 1190s, however, a Muslim Turkic dynasty and people, the Ghurids (GOO-rids), had resumed the habit of raiding into Hindu India, where they levied tribute and scattered garrisons. One of their most far-flung outposts—and therefore one of the strongest—was at the city of Delhi in northern India. The adventurer Iltutmish (eel-TOOT-mihsh) took command there in 1211. He was a former slave who had risen to general and received his freedom from his Ghurid masters. He avoided war with Hindus—which was, in essence, his job—in favor of building up his own resources. In 1216 he effectively declared himself independent. Over the next 12 years, he exploited the rivalries of Muslim commanders to construct a state from the Indus River to the Bay of Bengal. Meanwhile, the effects of the Mongol conquests on Central Asia protected this new realm, which became known as the Sultanate of Delhi, against outside attack (see Map 13.4). As one of the early chroniclers of the sultanate said, "Rulers and governors, … and many administrators and notables came to Iltutmish's court from fear of the slaughter and terror of the accursed Mongol, Genghis Khan."

There was no consistent form of administration. In most of the remoter territories, the Delhi sultan was an overlord of small, autonomous states, many of which Hindus ruled. But there was a core of lands that was the sultan's personal property, exploited to benefit his treasury and run by his administrators. Lands the sultan granted in exchange for military service ringed the core. At great

MAP 13.4

The Delhi Sultanate

Delhi Sultanate 1236

area subject to sporadic influence by Delhi Sultanate

border of Ghaznavid Empire 1186

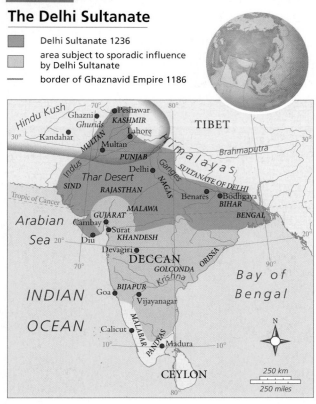

oath-taking ceremonies, the aristocracy—a great diversity of freelance warriors and local rulers whom it was difficult or impossible for the sultan to dismiss—would make emotional but often short-lived declarations of loyalty.

As an ex-slave, Iltutmish was no respecter of conventional ideas of hierarchy. Denouncing his sons for incompetence, he chose his daughter, Radiyya (rah-DEE-ah), as his successor in 1236. In the steppes, women often handled big jobs. In the Islamic world, a woman ruler was a challenge to what was thought to be the natural order of the world. When, in 1250, a little before the Mamluks took over in Egypt, a woman had seized the throne there and applied to Baghdad for legitimation by the caliph, he is supposed to have replied that he could supply capable men, if no more existed in Egypt. Radiyya had to contend both with a brother who briefly ousted her—she put him to death—and male mistrust. Some of her coins emphasize claims to unique feminine virtues as "pillar of women." Others have modest inscriptions, in which all the glorious epithets are reserved for her father and the caliph in Baghdad. Her best strategy was to behave like a man. She dressed in male clothing, refused to cover her face, and "mounted horse like men, armed with bow and quiver." To conventional minds, these were provocations. Accused of taking a black slave as a lover, she was deposed in 1240 in favor of a brother. Her real offense was self-assertion. Those modest coin inscriptions suggest that power brokers in the army and the court were only willing to accept her as a figurehead, not as an active leader of men.

The sultanate had to cope not only with the turbulence of its elite but also with Hindu subjects and neighbors. Dominion by any state over the entire Indian subcontinent remained, at best, a dream. Frontier expansion was slow. Deforestation was an act of state, because, as a Muslim writer of the fourteenth century complained, "the infidels live in these forests, which for them are as good as city walls, … so that they cannot be overcome except by strong armies of men who go into these forests and cut down those reeds." In Bengal, the eastward shift of the Ganges River made Islamization easier. Charismatic **sufis**, with tax-free grants of forest land for mosques and shrines, led the way.

For most of the thirteenth century, the Mongol menace overshadowed the sultanate. The internal politics of the dynasty of Genghis Khan caused dissensions and hesitancies that protected Delhi. Mongol dynastic disputes cut short periodic invasions. Moreover, a buffer state dissident Mongols created in Delhi's western territories absorbed most of the khans' attacks. In the 1290s, however, the buffer collapsed. By what writers in Delhi considered a miracle, the subsequent Mongol attacks failed.

EUROPE

With the scare the Mongol invasions caused and the loss of the last crusader states in Syria to the Mamluks, Latin Christendom looked vulnerable. Attempts to revitalize the crusading movement—especially by Louis IX, the king of France (r. 1226–1270) who became a model monarch for the Western world—all failed. A further reverse was the loss of Constantinople by its Latin rulers to a Byzantine revival. The Mongols destroyed or dominated most of the successor states that claimed Byzantium's legacy, but at the city of Nicaea in western Anatolia, rulers who continued to call themselves "Roman emperors" maintained the court rituals and art of Byzantine greatness. In 1261, they recaptured the old capital from the crusaders "after many failures," as Emperor Michael VIII (r. 1261–1282), admitted, "because God wished us to know that the possession of the city was a grace dependent on his bounty."

Nevertheless, Latin Christendom grew on other fronts, deep into formerly pagan worlds along the Baltic in Livonia, Estonia, Prussia, and Finland. The *Rhyming Chronicle* of the conquest of Livonia recounts with equal pleasure the destruction of native villages and the piety of forced converts. Swedish knights led by Henry of Finland (d. ca. 1160) were said to have wept over the potential converts they slew in the twelfth century.

Between the 1220s and the 1260s, Christian kingdoms seized most of the Mediterranean seaboard of Spain and the Balearic islands from Muslim rulers. Here the existing economy and population were not much disturbed. Conquests Castile and Portugal made over the same period in the Iberian southwest became a sort of wild west, of sparse settlements, tough frontiersmen, and vast cattle and sheep ranches. Meanwhile, traders of the western Mediterranean increased their commerce with northern Europe along the coasts the Spaniards conquered, through the Strait of Gibraltar (see Map 13.5). Toward the end of the century, as they became accustomed to Atlantic sailing conditions, some of them began to think of exploring the ocean for new routes and resources. In 1291, an expedition set off from the Italian city of Genoa to try to find "the regions of India by way of the ocean." The voyagers were never heard of again, but their voyage marked the beginning of a long effort by maritime communities of Western Europe to exploit the ocean at their feet.

The big new opportunities, however, lay to the east, from where transforming technologies reached Europe. Paper was a Chinese invention that had already reached the West through Arab intermediaries, but only in the late thirteenth century was it manufactured in Europe on a large scale. European maritime technology—a prerequisite of the prosperity borne by long-range trade and of the reach of most long-range imperialism—was especially primitive by non-European standards up to this time. Though the compass was first recorded in Europe in about 1190, the West had as yet no maritime charts. The earliest reference to such a device dates only from 1270. Gunpowder and the blast furnace were among the magical-seeming technologies that first reached Europe from China in the thirteenth and fourteenth centuries.

Meanwhile, with consequences for the future that can hardly be overestimated, Western science grew more **empirical**, more committed to observation and experiment. The cosmos came to seem measurable, portrayed between the dividers of Christ the geometer, like a ball of fluff trapped between tweezers. At the University of Paris, scholars cultivated a genuinely scientific way of understanding the world. The work of encyclopedists arrayed in precise categories everything known by experience or report. The greatest intellect of the age, Thomas Aquinas (1225–1274), compiled comprehensive schemes of faith and secular knowledge.

The Qutb Minar. The founder of the Ghurid dynasty began the Qutb Minar, near Delhi, as a monument to his own prowess in battle, toward the end of the twelfth century. Successors continued the project until, by the late fourteenth century, it was the tallest tower in India—much bigger than any minaret designed to hoist the call to prayer. The ridged form and decorative use of sandstone are typical of the stylistic traditions the Ghurids brought to India from Afghanistan.

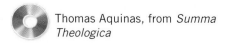

Thomas Aquinas, from *Summa Theologica*

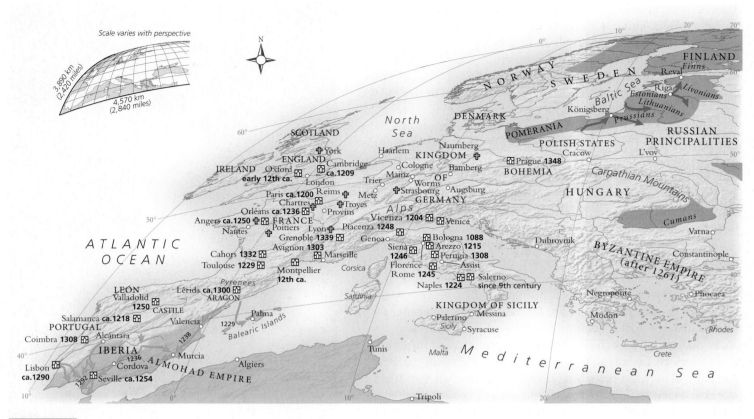

MAP 13.5

Latin Christendom, 1200–1300

- predominantly pagan lands
- → reconquest of Spain in thirteenth century
- ⊞ university, with date of foundation
- ✚ important churches with stained glass
- ➤ campaigns of Teutonic Knights and Sword Brothers

Roger Bacon on experimental science

In the third quarter of the thirteenth century, Parisian teachers pointed out that the doctrines of the church on the creation and the nature of the soul conflicted with classical philosophy and empirical evidence. "Every disputable question," they argued, "must be determined by rational arguments." A professor at the University of Paris, Roger Bacon, said that excessive deference to authority—including ancestral wisdom, custom, and consensus—was a cause of ignorance. He insisted that scientific observations could help to validate holy writ and that medical experiments could increase knowledge and save life. He also claimed—citing the lenses with which Archimedes reputedly set fire to a Roman fleet during the siege of the Greek city of Syracuse in Sicily in 212 B.C.E.—that science could cow and convert infidels. Bacon was a Franciscan friar, a follower of Francis of Assisi (1181–1226), and his enthusiasm for science seems to have owed something to Francis's doctrine that because the world made God manifest, it was worth observing.

Francis was a witness and maker of the new European imagination. He was a rich man's son inspired by Jesus' advice to renounce riches for a life of total dependence on God. In anyone less committed and charismatic, his behavior might have been considered insane or heretical. He launched his mission by stripping naked in the public square of his native city, as a sign that he was throwing himself, unprotected, on God's mercy. He relied for sustenance on what people gave him. He modeled his followers' way of life on the way he thought Jesus and the Apostles lived, refusing to accept property, sharing the alms the brethren received. For a church that relied on immense wealth to keep its operations going, these were dangerous ideas. The very notion of a religious order wandering around the world without the discipline of common life ran counter to everything the church had believed about monasticism for at least 500 years.

Francis, however, could be tamed. He had enough humility to defer to the church's discipline. Bishops who met him—including the pope himself—let him carry on. He made compromises with respectability, ordering his female followers into nunneries, and—in obedience to a vision in which Jesus told him, "Build my Church"—put his efforts into buildings of stone and mortar, as well as spiritual edification. Francis was suspicious of learning. It was a kind of possession—a compromise with poverty. It made men vain. But he accepted that education was part of the church's mission and that friars had to study to equip them to be preachers and confessors.

The Franciscans became the spearhead of the church's mission to the poor and inspired other orders of friars—clergy who combined religious vows of poverty, chastity, and obedience with work in the world. In an age of urbanization, friars could establish bonds of sympathy with the rootless masses, who had lost the familiar companionship of rural parishes. Friars, if they stayed true to their vocations, were also a valuable counter force to heretics who denounced the church for worldliness.

In his attitude to nature, Francis was representative of his time. Against heretics who condemned the world as evil, he insisted on the goodness of God's creation, which was all "bright and beautiful." Even its conflicts and cruelties were there to elicit human love. He tried to enfold the whole of nature in love. He preached to ravens and called creatures, landscapes, sun, and moon his brothers and sisters, eventu-

Francis of Assisi. Franciscan art patronage rewarded painters like Giotto, who were interested in creating vivid versions of sacred scenes in which the actors seemed real rather than abstract. Francis preached to the birds because humans failed to heed his message—but the image suggests, too, how the Franciscans promoted awareness of the natural world. Piety and science coincided in the observation of nature.

Francis of Assisi, selection from *Admonitions*

ally welcoming "Sister Death." He communicated his sensibilities to his followers. As a result, Franciscans were prominent in scientific thinking in the West. Love of nature made them observe it more closely and keenly and scrutinize it for good uses.

Franciscans also became patrons of naturalistic art. The art they commissioned for their churches drew the onlooker into sacred spaces, as if in eyewitness of the lives of Jesus and the saints. The devotion of the rosary, introduced early in the thirteenth century, encouraged the faithful to imagine sacred mysteries, while praying, with the vividness of scenes of everyday life, as if witnessed in person—looking at the world with eyes as unblinking as those of the new scientific thinkers. Considered from one point of view, the realism Western painting increasingly favored was a tribute to the enhanced prestige of the senses. To paint what one's eyes could see conferred dignity on a subject not previously thought worthy of art. So art linked the science and piety of the age.

The revolutionary experiences of the West at the time—the technical progress, the innovations in art, the readjustment of notions of reality through the eyes of a new kind of science—were owed, in part, to influences transmitted along routes the Mongols maintained. None of this experimentation and imagination put Western science abreast of that of China, where observation and experiment had been

Astrolabe. The Syrian instrument maker, al-Sarraj engraved his signature on this fine astrolabe in 1230–1231. The purpose of the astrolabe is to assist in astronomy—one of the many sciences in which the Islamic world excelled at the time. By suspending the instrument at eye level and swiveling a narrow central bar until it aligned with any observed star, the user could read the star's elevation above the horizon, as well as such additional information as the latitude, the date, and even the time of day from the engraved discs.
© National Maritime Museum Picture Library, London, England. Neg. #E5555-3

continuous in scientific tradition since the first millennium B.C.E. (see Chapter 6). In two technologies, however—key technologies for their influence on world history—Western Europe came to house the world's leading centers of development and production.

The first was glassmaking. In the thirteenth century, demand for fine glassware leaped in the West because of the growing taste for using church windows made of stained glass, to illuminate sacred stories and to exhibit the wonders of creation. Glassmakers adapted their skills to meet demand for glass mirrors and optical lenses. These objects were not manufactured on a significant scale anywhere else in the world, though for centuries scholars writing in Arabic had known how to make them and use them in scientific observation. Now Western savants could make the same experiments and even improve on them.

Second, the West drew ahead in the technology of clockwork. Mechanical clocks had a long history in China and the Islamic world. But clockwork never caught on except in Europe, perhaps because it is too regular to match the movements of the heavens. It divides the day into arbitrary hours of equal length that do not match those of the sun. But this way to organize life suited Western monasteries, where, apart from the prayers prescribed for the dawn and nightfall, the services of prayer were best arranged at regular intervals, independently of the sun. For city churches in an age of urban growth, regular timekeeping was also convenient. Clockwork suited the rhythms of urban life. Civic authorities began to invest in town clocks in the thirteenth and fourteenth centuries. This was the beginning of the still-familiar Western convention of an urban skyline dominated by the town hall clock tower.

The combination of lenses and clockwork mattered because eventually—not until the seventeenth century, when telescopes were combined with accurate chronometry—it gave Western astronomers an advantage over Muslim and Chinese competitors. This in turn gave Western scientists the respect of their counterparts and secured the patronage of rulers all over the world in societies interested in astronomy either for its own sake or—more often—because of astrology.

IN PERSPECTIVE: The Uniqueness of the Mongols

Like most great revolutionaries, the Mongols started bloodily and became constructive. The Mongols came to play a unique and constructive role in the history of Eurasia. For 100 years after the initial horror of the Mongol conquests, the steppe became a highway of fast communication, helping transfer culture across two continents. Without the Mongol peace, it is hard to imagine any of the rest of world history working out as it did, for these were the roads that carried Chinese ideas and technology westward and opened up European minds to the vastness of

MAKING CONNECTIONS

EUROPEAN TRANSFORMATIONS AND INNOVATIONS, THIRTEENTH AND EARLY FOURTEENTH CENTURIES

TRADE AND TRANSPORTATION	TECHNOLOGY AND SCIENCE	POLITICS	RELIGION
Increased communication across Eurasia leads to introduction of Chinese and Arabic technology, medicine, and inventions	Imported inventions such as paper, magnetic compasses, gunpowder, and blast furnace combine with focus on empiricism	Christian kingdoms seize Muslim lands in Spain, Mediterranean islands; revival of Crusades, extension of frontier north to the Baltics, Finland, and Scandinavia	Francis and his religious order place new emphasis on observing nature, serving the poor, and renouncing wealth; increased emphasis on sacred mysteries
↓	↓	↓	↓
Increased transportation and trade links within Europe aided by new infrastructure (roads, canals); growth of towns; economic and political stability leads to larger towns and cities; more productive industry	Better maritime technology expands range of sea voyages; demand for elaborate church windows spurs glassmaking and innovation in glass lenses; clocks provide regularized timekeeping for monasteries and cities; availability of paper multiplies books and empowers states with a medium for their messages	Bigger, richer states with more scope to communicate and enforce commands; more church–state competition and conflict	Mendicants prominent in scientific thinking in West; spearhead Church's mission to poor in growing towns

the world. The importance of the Mongols' passage through world history does not stop at the frontiers of their empire. It resonated across Eurasia.

The Eurasian experience was unique. Why did nothing like it happen in Africa or the Americas? Cultural exchanges across the grasslands of prairie, pampa, and Sahel never spread far until the nineteenth century. None of those regions saw conquerors like the Mongols, able to unify the entire region and turn it into a causeway of civilizations, shuttling ideas and techniques across a continent.

In the Americas, geography was an inhibiting influence. The North American prairie is aligned on a north–south axis, across climatic zones, whereas the steppe stretches from east to west. Plants and animals can cross the steppe without encountering impenetrable environments. Seeds can survive the journey without perishing and without finding, at the end of the road, an environment too sunless or cold to thrive in. In North America, it took centuries longer to achieve exchanges on a comparable scale. As we have seen almost whenever the Americas have entered our story, transmissions of culture across latitudes are much harder to effect than those that occur within latitudes, which have relatively narrow boundaries, where climate and conditions are familiar.

Moreover, to function, an avenue of communications needs people at either end of it who want to be in touch. The Eurasian steppe was like a dumbbell, with densely populated zones and productive economies at either end of it (see Map 13.6). People in Europe, southwest Asia, and North Africa wanted the products of south, southeast, and east Asia. The suppliers of spices, drugs, fine textiles, and luxury products in the east liked having customers who paid in silver. In the Americas, there was no chance to reproduce such relationships. The concentrations of

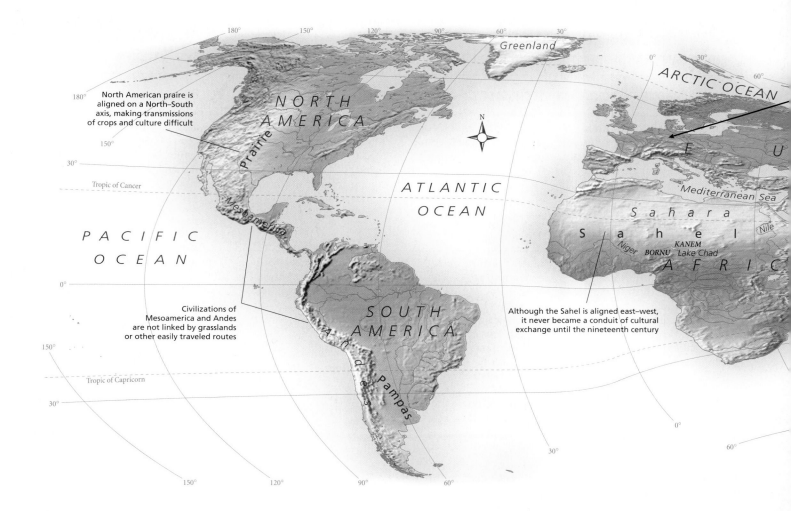

North American praire is aligned on a North–South axis, making transmissions of crops and culture difficult

Civilizations of Mesoamerica and Andes are not linked by grasslands or other easily traveled routes

Although the Sahel is aligned east–west, it never became a conduit of cultural exchange until the nineteenth century

wealth and population were in two regions—Mesoamerica and the Andes—that neither grasslands nor any other easily traveled routes linked. Though societies in other parts of the hemisphere drew lessons, models of life, technologies, and types of food from those areas, the results (see Chapter 11) were hard to sustain because communications between these areas and outlying regions were hard to keep up. Without the horse—extinct in the Americas for 10,000 years—the chances of an imperial people arising in the prairie or the pampa to do the sort of job the Mongols did in Europe were virtually zero. (Much later, as we shall see in Chapter 21, when European invaders reintroduced the horse in the Americas in the 1500s, experiments in grassland imperialism by peoples such as the Sioux followed.)

In Africa, the constraints were different. The **Sahel** might have played a role similar to that of the steppes in Eurasian history. There was a viable corridor of communication between the Nile and Niger valleys. In theory, an imperial people might have been able to open communications across the continent between the civilizations of East Africa, which were in touch with the world of the Indian Ocean, and those of West Africa, which the trade routes of the Sahara linked to the Mediterranean. But it never happened. For long-range empire building, the Sahel was, paradoxically, too rich, compared with the Eurasian steppe. The environment of the Sahel was more diverse. Agrarian or partly agrarian states had more oppor-

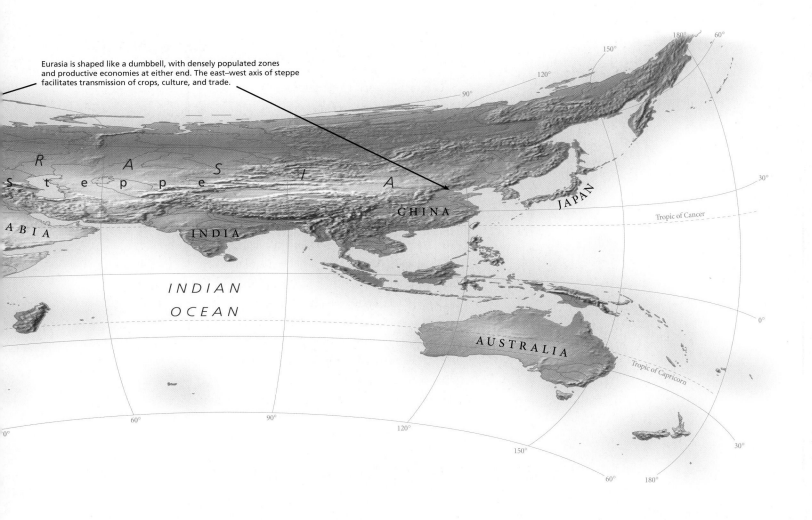

Eurasia is shaped like a dumbbell, with densely populated zones and productive economies at either end. The east–west axis of steppe facilitates transmission of crops, culture, and trade.

MAP 13.6

Grassland Environments Compared

tunity to develop, obstructing the formation of a Sahel-wide empire. Although pastoral peoples of the western Sahel often built up powerful empires, they always tended to run into either or both of two problems. First, as we have seen, and shall see again, invaders from the desert always challenged and sometimes crushed them (see Chapter 12).

Second, while they lasted, the empires of the Sahel never reached east of Lake Chad. Here states grew up, strong enough to resist conquest, but not strong enough to expand to imperial dimensions themselves: states like Kanem and Bornu—which were sometimes separate, sometimes united. Early Muslim visitors reviled the region for its "reed huts … not towns" and people clad only in loincloths. But by the twelfth and thirteenth centuries, Kanem and Bornu commanded respect in Arab geography. Lakeshore floodplains for agriculture enriched them, together with the gold they obtained from selling their surplus millet. According to Arab sources, the region enclosed 12 "kingdoms" around 1300.

The Mongols, after their initial bout of extreme destructiveness, brought peace, and, in the wake of that peace, wealth and learning. But with increased travel, the steppeland also became a highway to communicate disease. The Mongol peace lasted less than 150 years. The age of plague that was about to begin would influence the history of Eurasia, and therefore of the world, for centuries.

CHRONOLOGY

1181–1226	Life of Francis of Assisi
1190	First European recorded reference to a compass
1206	Temujin proclaims himself khan
1211–1236	Reign of Iltutmish, sultan of Delhi
1225–1274	Life of Thomas Aquinas
1234	Mongols conquer Georgia
1241–1242	Mongol armies reach Elbe River, Germany
1253–1254	Mission of William of Rubruck to Mongolian court
1258	Mongols capture Baghdad, last caliph put to death
1260	Mamluks defeat Mongols at battle of Ain Jalut
1261	Byzantine Empire regains Constantinople
1268–1291	Mamluks overthrow last crusader kingdoms
1270	Earliest European reference to maritime charts
1271–1275	Marco Polo's first journey to China
1274, 1281	Failed Mongol attempts to invade Japan
1279	Mongol conquest of China completed
1286	Rabban Bar Sauma appointed Mongol ambassador to Christian West

PROBLEMS AND PARALLELS

1. How did the Mongols transform Eurasia in the thirteenth century? What techniques did the Mongols use to rule neighboring civilizations, and how successful were they?

2. How did Mongol rule affect travel and trade along the Silk Roads?

3. How did the civilizations they conquered affect the Mongols? How did Mongol culture in turn influence the civilizations they ruled?

4. Why did Egypt and India show so much vitality in the thirteenth century?

5. How did Francis of Assisi and the Franciscan order remedy some of the social problems that medieval Europe faced? What was the impact of empirical-based learning on European thinking at this time?

6. How did geography hinder the development of continent-wide empires in Africa and the Americas?

DOCUMENTS IN GLOBAL HISTORY

- John of Piano Carpini on the Mongols
- William of Rubruck's account of the Mongols
- From *The Travels of Marco Polo*
- From Francesco Balducci Pegolotti's *The Practice of Commerce*
- From *The History of the Life and Travels of Rabban Bar Sauma*

- Excerpt from the *Novgorod Chronicle*
- Thomas Aquinas, from *Summa Theologica*
- Roger Bacon on experimental science
- Francis of Assisi, selection from *Admonitions*

Please see the Primary Source DVD for additional sources related to this chapter.

READ ON

D. Morgan, *The Mongols* (1986) is the best history of the Mongols: concise, readable, reliable. R. Grousset, *The Empire of the Steppes* (1970) is a translation of the unsurpassed classic history of steppeland peoples in antiquity and the middle ages. Samuel Adshead, *Central Asia in World History* (1993) is also helpful on this period.

P. Jackson, ed., *The Travels of Friar William of Rubruck* (1990) is an outstanding and informative edition of the most vivid of sources. Extracts from sources of the same kind are in I. de Rachewitz, ed., *Papal Envoys to the Great Khan* (1971) and Dawson, ed., *Mission to Asia* (1980). A. Waley, ed., T*he Secret History of the Mongols* (2002) collects some Mongol sources in lively translation.

M. Rossabi, *Voyager from Xanadu: Rabban Sauma and the First Journey from China to the West* (1992), and *Kubilai Khan* (1989) are the best books on their respective subjects. On the voyage of Chang Chun, J. Mirsky, *Chinese Travellers in the Middle Ages* (2000) translates the main texts.

On the Silk Roads, the exhibition catalog edited by S. Whitfield, *The Silk Roads* (2004) is the best work. R. Latham, ed., *The Travels of Marco Polo* (1958) is a convenient and accessible abridgement in translation.

On China, R. Davis, *Wind against the Mountain: the Crisis of Politics and Culture in Thirteenth-century China* (1996) is an outstanding account written with close reference to the sources. The exhibition catalog edited by M. Rossabi, *The Legacy of Genghis Khan* (1996) is the best guide to the art of the Ilkhanate and other Mongol successor-states. M. Ipsiroglu, *Painting and Culture of the Mongols* (1966) is indispensable.

J. A. Boyle, ed., *The History of the World Conqueror* (1997) and *The Successors of Genghis Khan* (1971) translate some of the most important sources on the Ilkhanate.

On the Mamluks, R. Irwin, *The Middle East in the Middle Ages: The Early Mamluk Sultanate* (1986) is the best account of their rise, and R. Amitai-Preiss, *Mongols and Mamluks* (2005) is superb study of the wars against the Mongols. S. A. El-Banasi, ed., *Mamluk Art* (2001) covers a wide range of revealing objects.

P. Jackson, *The Delhi Sultanate* (2003) is a splendid introduction to the subject. The best edition of Ibn Battuta is by H. W. Gibb and C. F. Beckingham for the Hakluyt Society, *The Travels of Ibn Battuta* (1956).

On the transmission of Chinese technology westward, J. Needham, *Science and Civilisation in China* (1956) is fundamental—but it is a vast work still in progress. An abridged version in two volumes—*The Shorter Science and Civilisation in China* (1980)—is available. For western science in the period, A. Crombie, *Robert Grosseteste and the Origins of Experimental Science* (1971) is controversial and stimulating. D. C. Lindberg, *The Beginnings of Western Science* (1992) gives an efficient and comprehensive account.

Of many studies of St. Francis, none is entirely satisfactory, but J. H. R. Moorman, *St. Francis of Assisi* (1976) can be recommended, first, for its scholarship and brevity and, second, for its vivacity. K. B. Wolf, *The Poverty of Riches* (2003) is good on St. Francis's theology.

On glassmaking, see G. Martin and A. MacFarlane, *The Glass Bathyscape* (2003) and, on clockwork, D. Landes, *Revolution in Time: Clocks and the Making of the Modern World* (1983). On the general background of the thirteenth-century West, D. Abulafia, ed., *The New Cambridge Medieval History*, vol. 5 (1999) is as close as one can get to a comprehensive guide.

14 The Revenge of Nature: Plague, Cold, and the Limits of Disaster in the Fourteenth Century

City of the dead. The fourteenth-century Arab traveler Ibn Battuta described Cairo's Southern Cemetery as "a place of peculiar sanctity" that "contains the graves of innumerable scholars and pious believers." The Mamluk domes and minarets visible here form part of the Sultaniyyah tomb complex that was built around 1360, a little over ten years after the plague known as the Black Death had struck the city.

"**T**he people of Cairo are fond of pleasure and amusement," wrote Ibn Battuta (ih-bihn bah-TOO-tah), when he first visited the Egyptian city in 1325. Wanderlust had made this Muslim pilgrim the world's most traveled man. Yet he had never seen a city so big. Cairo had—he was told—12,000 water carriers, 30,000 donkey-rental businesses, and 36,000 river craft. Among sources of pleasure he noted were "boys and maids with lustrous eyes," and the gardens and buildings peerless in splendor. On his next visit in 1348, plague raged in the city and corpses were piled in its streets. "I was told that … deaths there had risen to 21,000 a day. . . . All the sheikhs I had known were dead. May God Most High have mercy upon them!"

CAIRO

• • • • •

Ibn Battuta was witnessing the most devastating natural catastrophe ever to have hit Eurasia. The Black Death killed millions of people, disrupted states, and checked expansion. Under the impact of a climate that was growing colder, Eurasia's densely populated zone contracted. The growth of trade and states slowed or stopped. Cultural transmissions across the landmass diminished. Isolation from the main routes of trade and travel suddenly became an advantage.

Among the hardest-hit societies were those with the longest and most active records in challenging their environments. It was as if nature had struck back. Indeed, that was how many observers saw it: Muslim theologians argued that plague was a warning from God, "a martyrdom and a mercy" for Muslims, but "a punishment for an infidel." In China, too, conventional wisdom understood natural disasters as examples of what historian Mark Elvin calls "moral meteorology"—the corrections of heaven, unleashed to restore the balance of nature disturbed by human wickedness.

Climate and microbes resist human power. The fourteenth century was exceptional because, in parts of the world, climate change and disease coincided to menace human activities. The loss of life could be made up—eventually. The empires we shall see shaken and states overthrown in this chapter and the next were restored or replaced. The regions and classes that profited from disaster—for there were some, as there always are in every disaster—did not always retain their advantage for long. But the social shake-up that accompanied the changes had, for some of the people affected, irreversible effects. And it was impossible to undo the jarring psychological impact on societies that had accumulated self-confidence over a long period of expansion.

FOCUS
questions

- HOW DID the climate change globally in the fourteenth century?

- WHICH PARTS of the world suffered most from the plagues of the fourteenth century?

- WHAT WERE the social and political effects of the plague in China, the Islamic world, and Europe?

- WHY DID some parts of the world not suffer from plague?

- HOW DID the absence of plague affect Japan, Java, India, Mali, and the cultures around the Pacific Ocean?

The best—or even, because of the evidence available, the only—way to approach the changes of the fourteenth century is to start in those parts of the Northern Hemisphere, especially in Eurasia and North Africa, where the effects of cold and plague combined. We can then turn to areas that escaped plagues or their worst consequences, in India, sub-Saharan Africa, Japan, and southeast Asia. Finally, we shall turn to far-away societies in and around the Pacific to appreciate how isolation—which usually retards change—acted as a form of quarantine against disease. As plagues affected some of the planet's previously most dynamic regions, other parts of the world leaped into the sight lines of global history.

CLIMATE CHANGE

Climate change is full of conflicting shifts. Three levels are detectable. At one level, ice ages, which periodically smother great parts of the globe, alternate with global warming, when some glacier-covered areas reemerge. We are between ice ages now. All the fluctuations of the period this book covers have happened in a relatively warm era on the planet. Meanwhile, at another level, periods of a few hundred years of relative cold and warmth alternate within eras of global warming. But even within these periods, changes in winds and currents can produce spells, lasting from 10 to 50 years or so, of warmer or cooler temperatures (see Figure 14.1). Finally, there are sudden interruptions of normal conditions—occurring irregularly and, from what we know, unpredictably—when the distribution of atmospheric pressure is disturbed for unknown reasons. This produces the notorious **El Niño** effect in the tropics and the Southern Hemisphere (see Chapter 4). In Europe, reversals of normal patterns produce longer spells, often of a decade or so, of extremely cold weather.

Short-term fluctuations are sometimes traceable to particular causes. The middle of the second decade of the fourteenth century, for instance, was a cold period all over the Northern Hemisphere, probably because the explosion of Indonesian volcanoes pumped ash into the atmosphere and clouded the sun. But the fall in temperatures was

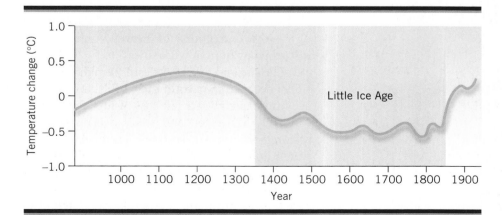

FIGURE 14.1 GLOBAL TEMPERATURE CHANGE, 1000–1900
Source: Hidore, John E., Global Enviornment Change: Its Nature and Impact, (1996). Electronically reproduced by permission of Pearson Education, Inc., Upper Saddle River, New Jersey.

not confined to a few exceptional years. It was part of a general, long-term trend that historians call the "Little Ice Age."

Broadly speaking, from about the tenth century, global temperatures had been relatively warm, with much erosion of natural environments as people converted under-exploited land for farming or grazing (see Chapter 10). Now a cool period—of fluctuating but relatively low temperatures—would last for about 500 years.

The trend began in the Arctic in the thirteenth century. The ice cap crept southward. Glaciers disrupted shipping. Mean annual temperatures in China, which had stayed above freezing from the seventh century to the eleventh, dipped below freezing from the thirteenth century until late in the eighteenth. Glacier growth suggests that North America, too, felt the cold in the four-

"The Frozen Thames," 1677. The Thames River with old London Bridge in the middle distance and Southwark Cathedral on the right. People amuse themselves on the ice. Some shoot, and others skate. The Thames no longer freezes because the arches of the modern bridges across it don't impede the flow of water.

teenth century. Other indicators for the same century include the persistence of pack ice in summer around Greenland and the disappearance of water-demanding plants from the hinterland of Lake Chad in Central Africa. This is important, because glacier growth affects precipitation. When water ices over, less of it evaporates and falls as rain.

The weather of the early fourteenth century seemed hostile to people who had to endure it because temperatures were lower than previously, not because it was cold in any absolute sense (see Map 14.1). The cold was, an English poet wrote, "a new kind of affliction, … not known for a thousand years. . . ." English uplands were abandoned. Glaciers forced Norwegian farmers into retreat.

In 1309–1310 wrote an English chronicler, "bread wrapped in straw or other covering froze and could not be eaten unless it was warmed." During the prolonged cold of 1315–1316, before the ice grew sufficiently to disrupt rainfall, heavy rains all over northern Europe wrecked crops, inflicting famine. Grain "could not ripen, nor had bread such power or essential virtue as it usually has," complained an English chronicler. During 1316, from May to October, cities in Belgium lost 5 to 10 percent of their population. Calamitous flooding and coastal erosion around the North Sea culminated in the "Great Drowning" of 1362, when the sea swallowed vast areas of Holland, Denmark, and England.

Far from the sea, cooling in the Northern Hemisphere brought droughts and famines. In Central Asia, the Mongol world began to contract. China experienced exceptionally severe winters for 36 of the fourteenth century's 100 years. Famines struck China in every year of the reign of the Shun Ti emperor (r. 1333–1368).

At about the same time, climate change seems to have helped destroy an impressive regional system of agriculture and urban life in North America, between the Gila and San Juan Rivers and around present-day Phoenix, Arizona. First the Hohokam people—as archaeologists called them—re-located, from their scattered villages, for closer collaboration in relatively few, dense settlements with huge multi-storey adobe houses. At Paquimé they huddled in a city with the traditional amenities of earlier indigenous civilizations (see Chapter 11): ball courts, carved facades for temples and palaces, wells and irrigation works, workshops for copper workers and jewelers. There was even a macaw hatchery to produce the feathers the elite coveted. It was a splendid effort, but it was clearly a response to stress. Every indicator shows severe population loss throughout the Southwest in the thirteenth and fourteenth centuries. By around 1400, even the new settlements were abandoned. Ruins remain. Casa Grande, in Pinal County, Arizona, leaves

PACIFIC

OCEAN

Lack of rainfall
leads to population
loss throughout the
American Southwest

North American
glaciers increase

Phoenix *ARIZONA*

Casa Grande Paquimé

R o c k y   M o u n t a i n s

M
E
X
I
C
O

NORTH
AMERICA

Mississippi

Hudson
Bay

Greenland

Falling temper...
force abandonm...
settlements in nor...
latitudes and on high g...

Persistence of pack
ice in summer off
coast of Greenland

Iceland

Caribbean Sea

A
n
d
e
s

A
n
d
e
s

A n d e s

Amazon

SOUTH
AMERICA

Thames River
freezes during
the winter of
1309–1310

North
Sea

DEN

ENGLAND

London Bruges

Ypres

Cold, heavy rain and
flooding destroy crops
and erode coastlines
in northern Europe

FRANCE

SPAIN

GERM

ATLANTIC

OCEAN

M e d i t e

MOROCCO

North Africa

S a h a r

Niger

1,000 km

1,000 miles

scale varies with perspective

N

Water demanding
plants disappear from
the Lake Chad region

Equator

Tropic of Cancer

120°

30°

0°

30°

150°

60°

180°

90°

60°

30°

30°

0°

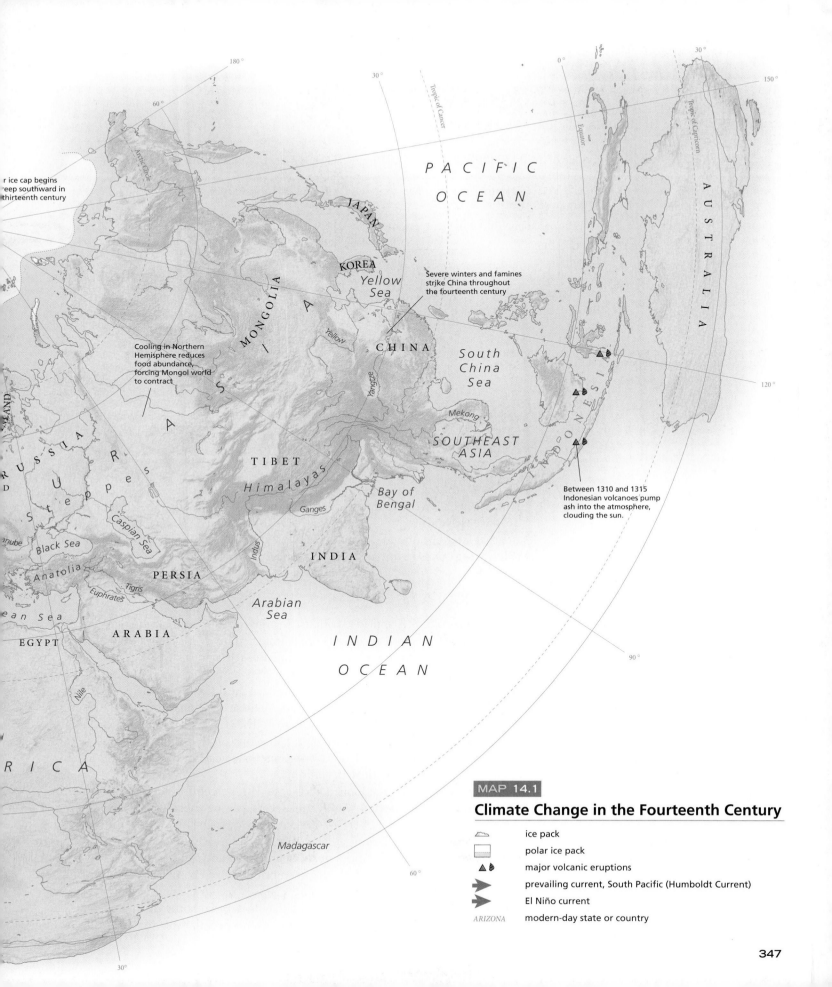

Polar ice cap begins
creep southward in
thirteenth century

Cooling in Northern
Hemisphere reduces
food abundance,
forcing Mongol world
to contract

Severe winters and famines
strike China throughout
the fourteenth century

Between 1310 and 1315
Indonesian volcanoes pump
ash into the atmosphere,
clouding the sun.

PACIFIC
OCEAN

AUSTRALIA

JAPAN

KOREA

Yellow
Sea

MONGOLIA

A S I A

CHINA

Yellow

Yangtze

South
China
Sea

Mekong

SOUTHEAST
ASIA

INDONESIA

Tropic of Cancer

Equator

Tropic of Capricorn

Arctic Circle

RUSSIA

Steppes

Danube

Black Sea

Caspian Sea

TIBET

Himalayas

Ganges

Indus

Bay of
Bengal

ean Sea

Anatolia

PERSIA

Tigris

Euphrates

INDIA

Arabian
Sea

EGYPT

ARABIA

Nile

INDIAN
OCEAN

RICA

Madagascar

180°

60°

30°

30°

0°

30°

150°

120°

90°

60°

30°

MAP 14.1

Climate Change in the Fourteenth Century

⬔   ice pack

▭   polar ice pack

▲🜨   major volcanic eruptions

➤   prevailing current, South Pacific (Humboldt Current)

➤   El Niño current

ARIZONA   modern-day state or country

◯ MAKING CONNECTIONS ◯

CLIMATE CHANGE IN EURASIA, AFRICA, AND THE AMERICAS

REGION/PERIOD →	EVIDENCE AND ENVIRONMENTAL EFFECTS →	EFFECTS ON HUMAN SOCIETY
Arctic / 1200s	Polar ice cap in Northern Hemisphere creeps southward	Glaciers disrupt shipping
North Atlantic, Arctic Ocean / 1300s	Increased evidence of falling temperatures, glaciation	Persistence of pack ice in summer around Greenland disrupts sea voyages
Central Africa / 1300s	Disappearance of water-demanding plants near Lake Chad	Lessened rainfall reduces crop yields
Europe / 1300s	Glaciers encroach in Norway; calamitous flooding and coastal erosion occur around North Sea coasts	Formerly productive agricultural land abandoned in England; famine and mortality increase dramatically throughout northern Europe; numerous coastal villages disappear in flooding
Central Asia, China / 1300s	More severe winters	Abundance of food that fueled Mongol advances runs out; Mongol world begins to contract; famines strike China from mid-1300s
American Southwest /1300s	Evidence of decreasing rainfall, water supplies	Relocation of Hohokam villages in Arizona; severe population loss throughout Southwest including Arizona, New Mexico sites

onlookers amazed at the ambition of the builders and clueless about what befell them. Scholars have speculated that the conditions that crushed the Hohokam may also have driven migrants southward to colonize central Mexico and found the state that later became the kernel of the Aztec world (see Chapter 15). But the only evidence for this is in untrustworthy legends.

THE COMING OF THE AGE OF PLAGUE

In Eurasia the cold spell coincided with the beginning of an age of plague. Starting in the 1320s, unprecedented bouts of pestilence culminated in the Black Death. Innumerable recurrences—less widespread and less intense—of similar or identical diseases remained frequent in Eurasia until the eighteenth century. The age of plague was so unusual and significant that we want to know what the disease was, where it came from, what caused it, and how much damage it did. All these questions are hard to answer.

Most attempts to write the history of disease have foundered on a false assumption: that we can recognize past visitations of identifiable diseases, known to modern medical science, from symptoms historical sources describe. For two reasons, this is an unrealistic expectation.

First, people in the past looked at disease with perceptions different from ours. The symptoms they spotted would not necessarily be those we would note, nor would they use the same sort of language to describe them. Second, diseases change. Many of the microorganisms that cause disease evolve fast because they reproduce rapidly and respond quickly to changing environments.

The plagues of the age of plague need not all have been visitations of a single disease. They may have included some diseases recognizable in today's medical handbooks. But we must be open to the likelihood that some of the diseases that devastated Eurasia in the age of plague were peculiar to that period. New pathogens are deadly, because when they strike, no one has had a chance to build up immunity to them.

Of diseases now known to medical science, bubonic plague—not, perhaps, of the same variety we know today—was most likely to have played a part in the age of plague. Bubonic plague is a rat-borne disease. When they bite, rats' fleas regurgitate the bacillus, ingested from rats' blood, into human victims, or communicate infection by defecating into their bites. In cases of septicemic plague (a systemic disease caused by pathogens in the blood), one of the first symptoms is generally death. Otherwise, swellings appear—small like Brazil nuts or big like grapefruit—over the neck and groin or behind the ears. Jitters, vomiting, dizziness, and pain might follow, often accompanied by an inability to tolerate light.

Fourteenth-century sources describe all these symptoms, together with sudden fainting, before victims, as one observer explained, "almost sleeping and with a great stench eased into death." The trouble is that during the first hundred years of the age of plague, of all the sources that describe the symptoms, fewer than one in six lists symptoms of this kind. Moreover, almost everyone at the time was convinced that plague spread by infection or contagion. Rats—the normal agent for the spread of bubonic plague—play little part in the accounts. Finally, it seems most unlikely that the frequent epidemics reported in China from the 1320s to the 1360s can have been of bubonic plague in the form now familiar to us, which, as we shall see, hit an unimmunized China in the late eighteenth century. The suddenness and virulence of the visitations suggest the arrival of a new and previously unexperienced pathogen, for the Chinese, with their long experience in farming and animal domestication, enjoyed highly developed natural immunities to the familiar diseases that breed in farming environments.

Many accounts of the Black Death include a bewildering variety of symptoms that are not associated with bubonic plague: complications in the lungs, spitting blood, headaches, extremely rapid breathing, strangely colored urine. The emphasis on lung disorders suggests a mixture of bubonic and pneumonic plague, which primarily attacks the lungs. To judge from other descriptions, outbreaks of typhus, smallpox, and various kinds of influenza coincided with some visitations of plague. In the Mediterranean, the plague usually struck in summer. In northern Europe, autumn seems to have been the deadliest season. But, looked at as a whole, the plagues of the period had no seasonal pattern and no obvious connection with any particular weather systems or atmospheric conditions. This again points to the involvement of more than one pathogen.

It seems likely that domestic animals were an essential part of the background—as carriers of disease, as a reservoir of infection, and even as sufferers. Some early plague victims were sure that their domestic animals suffered from the disease, just as they did themselves. A chronicler in the city of Florence in Italy listed "dogs, cats, chickens, oxen, donkeys, and sheep" among the sufferers, with the same symptoms as humans, including swellings in the groin and armpits. At the port of Salona on the Adriatic coast, the Black Death's first victims were "horses, oxen, sheep, and goats." The Egyptian chronicler, al-Maqrizi (ahl-mah-KREE-zee), who was among the most observant and thoughtful witnesses, believed that the disease started, like so many others, among animals before transferring to human hosts. It had spread from grazing flocks on the steppe in 1341, after which "the wind transmitted their stench around the world." He and other Muslim commentators thought wild animals caught it, too. If these sources are correct, the Black Death must have been—or included—a disease unknown today.

Marchione di Coppo Stefani, from *The Florentine Chronicle*

Plague victims. The illustrator of an early fifteenth-century German chronicle imagined the plague of Egypt—sent by God, according to the Book of Exodus in the Bible, to make Pharaoh "let my people go"—with the same symptoms as the Black Death. In the background, Moses brings plague down on Egypt by prayer. By implication, prayer and obedience to the will of God could also be remedies for plague.

An unanswered question is, *How, if at all, were changes in climate and disease patterns linked?* The plague pathogens, as we have seen, struck at different seasons and in climatically different regions of Eurasia, from cold Scandinavia and rain-drenched Western Europe to the hot, dry Middle East. The plagues were less penetrative, however, in hot, moist regions and do not seem to have reached across the Sahara to tropical Africa, even though many potential disease carriers crossed that desert to trade. It is worth bearing in mind, however, that the plague pathogens seem to have included new arrivals in the microbial world that remained active for as long as global cooling lasted.

The Course and Impact of Plague

It is easier to describe the routes by which the plague traveled (see Map 14.2). The Italian chronicler Matteo Villani said the plague came from China and Central Asia, "then through their surrounding lands and then to coastal places across the ocean." Arabic sources specify the same, or a similar, path.

The age of plague indeed seems to have started in China. But that is not the same as saying that subsequent outbreaks elsewhere were the result of communication from China, or even that they were necessarily outbreaks of the same disease or diseases. Repeated occurrences—or, perhaps, a continuous visitation—of massively lethal maladies were recorded in southwest China and central China in the early 1320s. In 1331, mortality rates in parts of northeast China that had endured five reported outbreaks of plague in the previous two decades reputedly reached 90 percent. Two years later, a plague claimed 400,000 lives in the Yangtze and Huai (hway) valleys. In 1353–1354, chroniclers reported that around two-thirds of the population perished from pestilence in eight distinct Chinese districts. Most of those areas experienced repeated bouts of disease of the same sort in the late 1350s or early 1360s.

Doubt persists, however, over whether the diseases rampant in China were the cause of—or even the same as—those found farther west. Most commentators at the time in Europe and the Middle East believed that plague, like the Mongols, was an invader from the steppeland. Many observers noted that the Mongols transmitted plague. Of course, there were multiple points of entry, as a lawyer in Italy acknowledged:

> Almost everyone who had been in the East, or in the regions to the south and north, fell victim. . . . The scale of the mortality ... persuaded ... the Chinese, Indians, Medes, Kurds, Armenians, Cilicians (sih-LEES-see-yahns), Georgians, Mesopotamians, Nubians, Ethiopians, Turks, Egyptians, Arabs, Saracens, and Greeks... that the last judgement has come.[1]

A pandemic on this scale was unprecedented. The pathogens responsible had found an eco-niche as wide as Eurasia.

Chroniclers' estimates of mortality are notoriously unreliable, but verifiable evidence bears out some of the most shocking assessments of the damage. In Barcelona on the Mediterranean coast of Spain, 60 percent of jobs in the church fell vacant. Clerical records in northern England suggest the first visitation of the plague killed 40 percent of clergy there. Clergy were members of a high-risk profession, but the laity suffered just as much. In some manors in England, up to 70 percent of tenants died. Villages in southern France lost four-fifths of their population. Towns ran out of cemetery space. The living had to pile the dead in pits with quicklime to speed decomposition and minimize rot. Half the villages of Sicily were abandoned, as were a third of those around Rome.

When the plague reached the Middle East, Ibn Battuta was there to observe it, on his way back to Cairo. Arriving in Syria in May 1348, he found that deaths in the city of Damascus reached 2,400 a day. In one town, three-quarters of the public officials had died. The plague spread along the coast of North Africa, causing—so people claimed—1,000 deaths a day at its height in Tunis. In Morocco, Ibn Battuta's own mother was among the victims.

In Central Asia, where plagues bred or where microorganisms traveled between the densely populated ends of Eurasia, Arab sources reported that many steppeland dynasties and Mongol warriors succumbed to plague. Nestorian headstones in what is now Russian Central Asia refer to plague as the cause of deaths in 1338 and 1339. In 1345 and 1346, according to Russian chronicles, pestilence devastated cities in the Mongol-ruled parts of southern Russia. Uzbek villages emptied. In 1346–1347, an official in Crimea reputedly counted 85,000 corpses.

In China, there seems little doubt that the population fell in the relevant period. The census of 1393, with adjustments demographers made to compensate for the official habit of underestimating the numbers, suggests a total population of around 80 million—compared with about 120 million in the mid–fourteenth century. The loss of people was by no means uniform. Some regions even seem to have made slight gains.

Moral and Social Effects

Natural disasters always inspire moralizing. Although the Black Death killed the vicious and the virtuous alike, it was tempting, especially for Christians, to see it as a moral agent, even a divine instrument to call the world to repentance and make people good. The plague was a leveler, attacking all sorts and conditions. For many who experienced it, the plague was a test of faith, first eliciting selfish reactions of terror and flight, profiteering and despair, then, as a Florentine chronicler observed, "people … began to help one another, from whence many were cured."

Flagellants. In 1349, the Black Death inspired thousands of penitents to organize processions and cults of self-flagellation across Europe in an attempt to deflect God's wrath. Like many others, the Flemish chronicler whose work is depicted here denounced the flagellants for claiming that their penance was a kind of baptism, that it could wipe out sin, and that it was a sacrifice akin to Christ's death on the cross. The king of France banned flagellation, and the pope outlawed it.

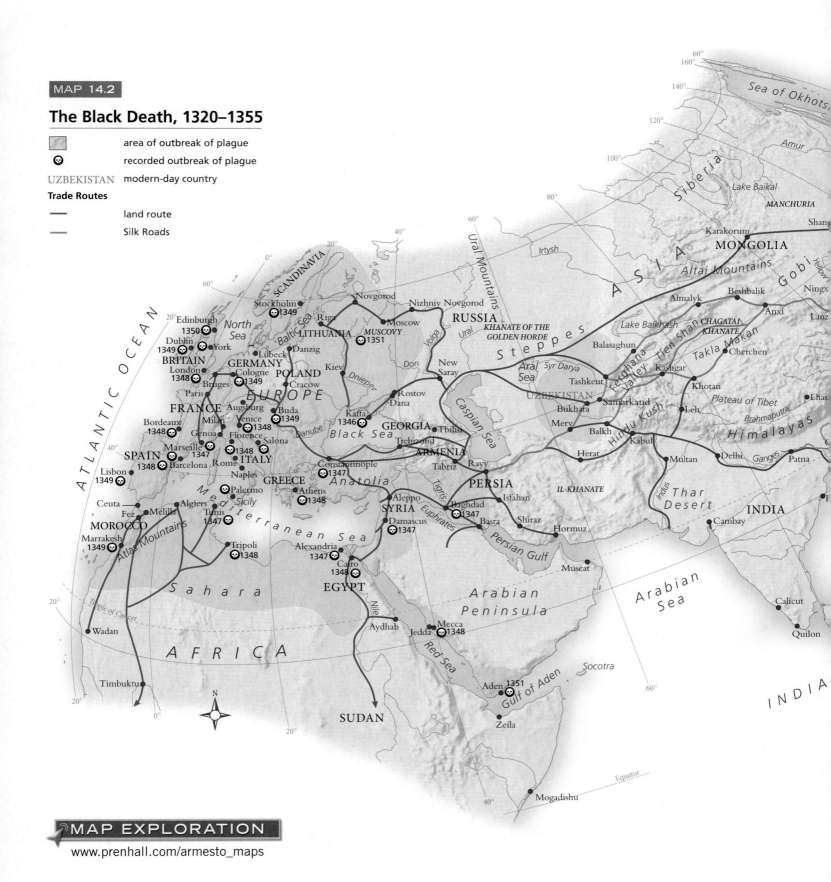

MAP 14.2

The Black Death, 1320–1355

area of outbreak of plague

recorded outbreak of plague

UZBEKISTAN modern-day country

Trade Routes

land route

Silk Roads

MAP EXPLORATION
www.prenhall.com/armesto_maps

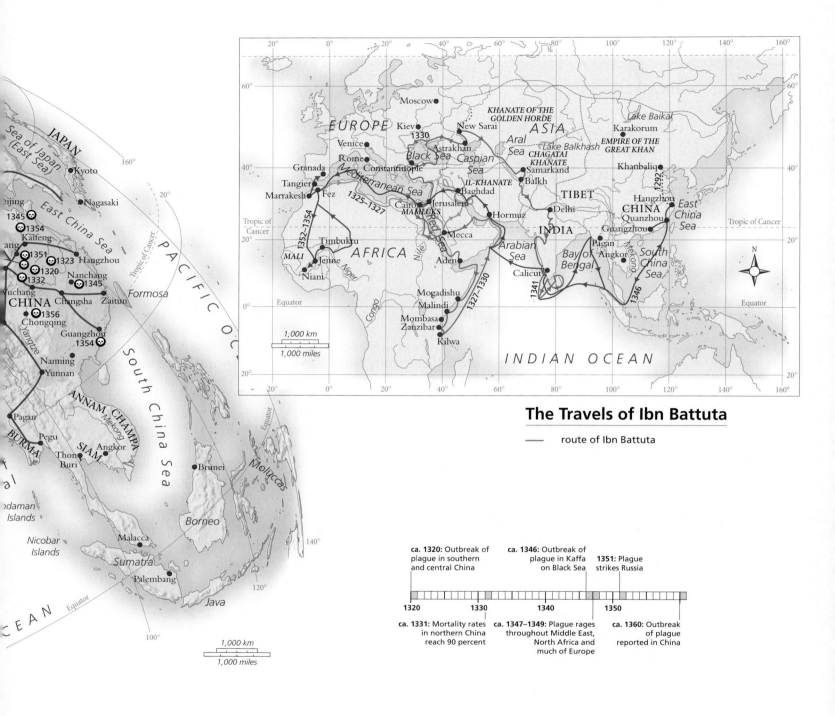

The Travels of Ibn Battuta

—— route of Ibn Battuta

ca. 1320: Outbreak of plague in southern and central China

ca. 1346: Outbreak of plague in Kaffa on Black Sea

1351: Plague strikes Russia

ca. 1331: Mortality rates in northern China reach 90 percent

ca. 1347–1349: Plague rages throughout Middle East, North Africa and much of Europe

ca. 1360: Outbreak of plague reported in China

1320   1330   1340   1350

Dice makers, claimed an abbot in northern France, turned to the manufacture of rosary beads. In China, plague, combined with other natural disasters, helped to stir up religious movements that led to political revolution (see Chapter 15). In the Islamic world, fear of plague stimulated a revival of popular religion: summoning spirits, magical spells, and charms.

Plague also stimulated science as people searched for a cure. It was normal to speak as if sin were the cause of the plague. But most people did not take such talk literally. Moralistic explanations of disease were hardly more convincing in the fourteenth century than they are today, and scientific inquiry soon replaced lamentations. The University of Paris medical faculty blamed "a year of many fogs and damps ... any pestilence proceeds from the divine will, ... but this does not mean forsaking doctors." Astrologers produced fatalistic explanations. "Corrupt air" was widely blamed, perhaps caused by polluted wells or earthquakes. In the Islamic world, too, religious interpretations of the origin of plague never inhibited scientific inquiry into its causes and possible cures. Muslim physicians also blamed corrupt air, caused by irregular weather, decaying matter, and astrological influences.

As for how to treat plague, practices were wildly different. In Cairo, when the Black Death broke out in 1347, healers smeared the swellings with clay. In Spain, the physician Ibn Khatib (ih-bihn khah-TEEB) advised abstention from grains, cheese, mushrooms, and garlic. Barley water and syrup of basil were widely prescribed. In Italy, Gentile of Foligno, who died of the plague in 1348, recommended an ancient medicine, dried snake's flesh. Gabriele de' Mussis favored bloodlettings and plasters of mallow leaves. Turks sliced off the heads of the boils on the bodies of the sick and supposedly extracted "green glands." The medical consensus among both Christians and Muslims saw infection and contagion as the main threats. Where the authorities imposed quarantine, lives were spared.

Where it could not be averted, plague shattered morale. A poet in Cairo described the psychological effect of the disease: "God has not just subdued Egypt, he has made her crawl on her knees." The Florentine poet, Petrarch, raged at his fellow survivors: "Go, mortals, sweat, pant, toil, range the lands and seas to pile up riches you cannot keep. . . . The life we lead is a sleep; whatever we do, dreams. Only death breaks the sleep. ... I wish I could have woken before this."

Plague had winners and losers. In Europe, Jews were among the losers. A skeptical German Franciscan reported the common opinion that Jews started the plague by poisoning wells "and many Jews confessed as much under torture: that they had bred spiders and toads in pots and pans, and had obtained poison from overseas. ... Throughout Germany, and in all places, they were burnt. For fear of that punishment many accepted baptism and their lives were spared." The massacres that ensued, especially in Germany, were nearly always the result of outbreaks of mob violence, which the authorities tried to restrain. In July 1348, Pope Clement VI declared the Jews innocent of the charge of well poisoning and excommunicated anyone who harmed them. In January 1349, the city council of Cologne in the Rhineland warned other cities that anti-Jewish riots could ignite popular revolt. "Accordingly we intend to forbid any harrassment of the Jews in our city because of these flying rumors, but to defend them and keep them safe, as our predecessors did—and we are convinced that you ought to do the same." But massacres continued.

University of Paris Medical Faculty, *Report on the Plague*

Burying the dead. "How come you feel no sadness when you bury a fellow-creature ... that you remain unready for your own graves ... that you pay no heed when warnings of death reach your ears?" The twelfth-century Muslim writer al Hariri asked this question in his Maqamat, a collection of moralistic stories. Al Hariri had no doubt that sickness, besides being a physical affliction, also served a moral purpose. God sent it to test human virtue and compassion. When the Black Death struck in the 1300s, many Muslims and Christians also saw the plague this way and tried to minister to the sick and dying. Yet the number of deaths could overwhelm the living, and many of the dead were dumped in mass graves.

Why did some Europeans victimize Jews? Jewish communities had existed all over the Mediterranean since Roman times (see Map 14.3). Like other migrants from the east, such as Greeks, Syrians, and Arabs, they were an urban and often a commercial people. The twelfth-century Jewish merchant, Benjamin of Tudela, describes their close-knit world, in which a structure of family firms and coreligionists helped Jews to trade between the Christian and Muslim worlds. An isolated reference to Jews in Cologne occurs as early as 321 C.E. when the Rhineland was part of the Roman Empire, but Mediterranean communities

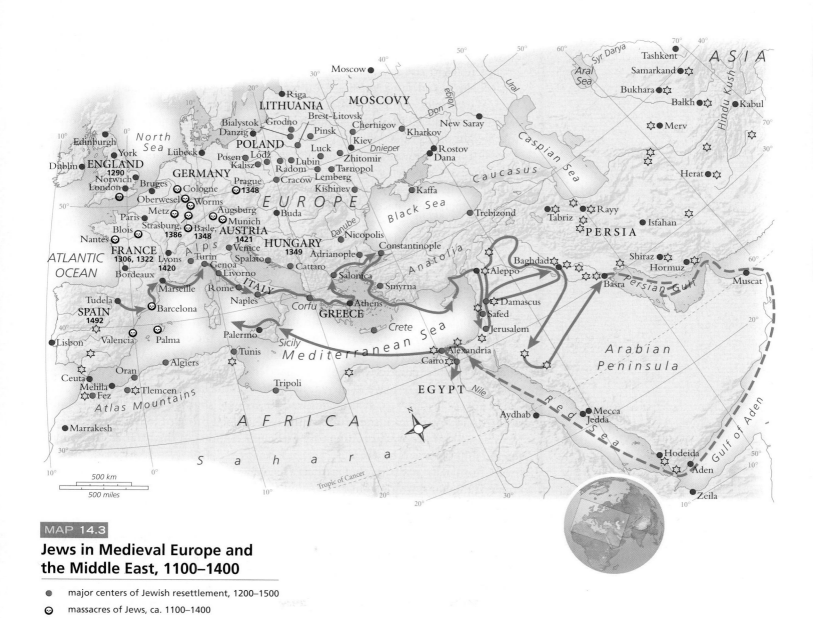

MAP 14.3

Jews in Medieval Europe and the Middle East, 1100–1400

- major centers of Jewish resettlement, 1200–1500
- massacres of Jews, ca. 1100–1400
- **1290** date of expulsion of Jews
- ➤ travels of Benjamin of Tuleda, ca. 1160–1173
- ➤ presumed route of Benjamin of Tuleda
- ☆ Jewish communities in Muslim world

were probably the springboard for Jewish colonization of northern European cities between the sixth and eleventh centuries.

Wherever they went, Jews were alternately privileged and persecuted: privileged, because rulers who needed productive settlers rewarded them with legal immunities; persecuted, because host communities resented intruders who were given special advantages. **Anti-Semitism** has been traced to the influence of Christianity. Indeed, medieval anti-Semitism did exploit Christian prejudices. Gospel texts could be read—as they were, for example, at the time of the First Crusade (see Chapter 12)—to saddle Jews with collective responsibility for the death of Jesus. And Holy Week, when Christians prepare to commemorate Christ's death, was at best an expensive and at worst a fatal time for Jewish communities, who had to buy security from bloody reprisals.

In the Greek world, however, anti-Semitism was older than Christianity. Medieval anti-Semitism, moreover, was just one aspect of society's antipathy for groups it could not assimilate—comparable, for instance, to the treatment of lepers, Muslims, and, later, gypsies. Outbreaks of anti-Jewish hatred are intelligible, in part, as examples of the prejudice outsiders attract. At the time of the Black Death, lepers were also accused of well poisoning. So were random strangers and unpopular neighbors. Similar phenomena occur in almost every culture. The case of the Jews in Europe demands attention not because it is unique, but because it is surprising, given Western society's indebtedness to Jewish traditions and to the individual genius of many Jews.

The increasing pace and intensity of persecution in the fourteenth century drove Jews to new centers. England had already expelled those Jews who did not convert to Christianity in 1290. The Jews were forced out of most of France in the early fourteenth century, and from many areas of Germany in the early fifteenth century. (Spain and Portugal followed suit in the 1490s.) The effect was to shift Jewish settlement toward the central and eastern Mediterranean, Poland, and Lithuania.

Though the evidence relates almost entirely to Europe, there were also people—whole groups of people—who benefited from the effects of plague. In Western Europe, propertied women were among them. The aristocratic marriage market could be fatal to women who married young and faced repeated pregnancies, but it tended to leave many young widows—the last wives of aging husbands. So property law had to ensure widows an adequate share in their dead husbands' estates and reversion of the property the women had brought to their marriages as dowries. More widows burying more husbands could shift the balance of property ownership between the sexes.

Chroniclers, insisting on Death as a leveler, often remarked that the plague carried off men and women alike. But, after the devastations of 1348, contemporaries who noticed a difference in mortality rates between the sexes saw men as the main victims. The plagues of the fourteenth century seem to have hit men harder than women, presumably because women led more secluded, and therefore protected, lives than men. Rich widows, often accumulating property from successive marriages, wielded power in their own right. The same considerations applied lower down the ranks of society. For instance, during the period of high mortality associated with cold and famine in the second decade of the fourteenth century, more than half the weddings among the peasants of the manor of Taunton in southwest England involved rich widows. After the Black Death, the lords of the manor introduced massive license fees for anyone who wanted to make such marriages, ostensibly to protect widows from predatory Romeos. In unprecedented numbers, widows became the administrators of estates. Women of leisure, education, and power played a bigger part in Western society after this. The increased prominence of women in political, literary, and religious life from the fifteenth century onward might not have been possible without the damage plague did to men.

In Western Europe peasants, if they survived the plague, also benefited from it. In the long run, owners could only keep great properties viable after plague had scythed the labor force by splitting the proceeds with their workers, or by breaking the estates up and letting peasants farm the parcels as tenants. Instead of taking orders from the lord's agent or bailiff, tenants paid rent and could manage their landholdings as they liked. The trend toward "free" peasantries started long before the Black Death struck, because it suited landowners, too. Peasants often made the land more productive. It made economic sense to allow them to improve their holdings. In England, where the royal courts encouraged peasant freedom to weaken aristocrats' power, about half the peasants in the south of the country were already free when the plague arrived.

Lords wrote off their rights to labor services because, as a steward on an English estate admitted in 1351, "the lord's interest made it necessary." The contract peasant dependants of an English abbey renegotiated is revealing: "At the time of the mortality or pestilence which occurred in 1349, scarcely two peasants remained on the manor." They threatened to leave unless a new contract were made. Most of their former services—including plowing, weeding, carting, and preparing soil for planting—were commuted for rent "as long as it pleases the lord—and would that it might please the lord for ever," added the scribe, "since the aforesaid services were not worth very much." It is remarkable, however, that the growth of lease-holding and the relaxation of lordly controls over peasant farmers happened on a large scale in the late fourteenth and fifteenth centuries in the parts of Western Europe plague affected. In areas the Black Death bypassed—such as Poland, much of Russia, and parts of Central Europe—the opposite happened. Peasants became tied to their lords' land and subject to the landholders' jurisdiction.

Were the effects on the European peasantry duplicated in other plague-ridden lands? Certainly, the rural population became more restive and mobile in Egypt and Syria. Villages in Egypt often had their tax burdens reduced in acknowledgment of the loss of population. The cost of labor services rose as population fell, creating opportunities for economic mobility among peasants and urban workers, and stimulating a further decline in rural population levels as peasants migrated to towns. But these changes did not disturb landowners' grip on their holdings. Peasants and landowners seem to have suffered together the effects of declining rural productivity.

Moreover, most governments responded to the demographic disaster, loss of revenue, and loss of labor by raising taxes and trying to limit labor mobility. In previous centuries, ecological disasters and political oppression had often driven peasants into religious extremism or rebellion. Now, popular revolt took on a new agenda: revolutionary **millenarianism**—the doctrine that in an imminent relaunch of history, God would empower the poor. This happened independently

The Wife of Bath. "Thanks be to God, who is for aye alive / Of husbands at Church door have I had five." "The Wife of Bath" was a fictional character of about 1400—shown here in a contemporary illustration to the English writer Geoffrey Chaucer's verses about her. But, like all good satire, she was representative of the society of her times: sexually shameless, irrepressibly bossy, and determined to exert "power, during all my life" over any husband "who shall be both my debtor and my slave." *Eileen Tweedy/Picture Desk, Inc./Kobal Collection*

but in strikingly similar ways, in both Europe and China. A popular preacher, who incited peasant rebels in England in 1381, expressed the doctrine of egalitarianism:

> How can the lords say or prove that they are more lords than we—save that they make us dig and till the ground so that they can squander what we produce? But it is from us and our labor that everything comes with which they maintain their pomp.[2]

Prophecies nourished revolt. Some Franciscans (see Chapter 13), with their special vocation to serve the poor, excited expectations that the end of the world was near, and that God would release riches from the Earth and eliminate inequality. In China, a similar doctrine inspired peasant rebels in the 1350s. A new Buddha would inaugurate a golden age and give his followers power over their oppressors (see Chapter 15). According to both movements, a divinely appointed hero would put a bloody end to the struggle of good and evil.

The next chapter describes the politics of the ensuing revolt. According to popular traditions, the leader of the rebellion, the founder of China's Ming dynasty, who claimed to be the prophesied hero, rose to prominence by inventing a medicine that could cure a new plague, "which killed half the people and which no known medicine could combat."

The plagues also helped transform the Mongol world. The region the Mongols dominated spanned the plague's trans-Eurasian corridors of transmission. Though the evidence comes from European observers, it is a safe assumption that Mongol manpower suffered, and that population levels in some regions from which the Mongols levied recruits and taxes also fell. The loss of China in 1368 was, of course, the Mongols' most spectacular forfeiture of power. But Mongol control also slackened in other dominions, and, on the Chinese front, it never recovered.

In general, plague-stricken societies showed more social mobility. Aristocracies, which were always subject to rapid turnover as families died out, thinned and refilled faster than ever. This seems to have applied as much to China's scholar elite, whose hold on power was not fully reasserted until the fifteenth century, as to Western European nobilities, whose composition changed. In Western Europe, the increase in the numbers of free peasants and tenants created a form of rural capitalism. Families formerly restricted to modest social ambitions could accumulate wealth and bid for higher status, buying education, business opportunities, or more land.

THE LIMITS OF DISASTER: BEYOND THE PLAGUE ZONE

How far did the plagues of the fourteenth century reach? The plague changed the history of China, Western Europe, the Middle East, and the steppeland empires. But much of Central and Eastern Europe escaped. So did areas that ought to have been vulnerable, such as southeast Asia, and the parts of West and East Africa that were in touch, via the Indian Ocean or the Saharan caravan routes, with affected regions. Relative isolation protected Japan. Apart from a pestilence in the capital Kyoto in 1342, there were no visitations of any disease on a scale resembling that of the Black Death. The principalities and city-states of central and northern Russia suffered relatively little and late—not before 1350, which is surprising in view of Russia's openness to the steppeland and close contact with the Mongols. India was relatively little affected.

Beyond the reach of the plagues—or, at least, beyond the zone of its most severe effects—the fourteenth century was an era of opportunity in Eurasia (see

Map 14.4). The Mongols were now troubled giants, from whom states in India, Japan, and southeast Asia were safe. We can look at those regions first, before turning to others where, as far as we know, the plagues never penetrated, in sub-Saharan Africa and the Pacific.

India

In India, the sultanate of Delhi profited from the Mongols' decline. Sultan Muhammad Ibn Tughluq (moo-HA-mahd ih-bihn TOOG-look) (r. 1325–1351) was the driving force of a policy of conquest that almost covered the subcontinent with campaigns. Ibn Battuta called him "of all men the most addicted to the making of gifts and the shedding of blood. His gate is never without some poor man enriched or some living man executed." Emphasis on the sultan's generosity reflects Ibn Battuta's own priorities. He was always on the lookout for rich patrons. But Ibn Tughluq's ran his court and army by balancing lavish gifts with intimidating displays of wrath.

His administration was a machine for recycling wealth. Ibn Battuta describes the regular arrival of revenue collectors from villages, casting gold coins into a golden basin: "These contributions amount in all to a vast sum which the sultan gives to anyone he pleases."

MAP 14.4

South and Southeast Asia, ca. 1350

- region where Majapahit claimed tribute
- Delhi sultanate at its greatest extent, ca. 1335
- area subject to sporadic influence by Delhi Sultanate
— main trade route
● important trade centers

Traded Goods

- pepper
- cinnamon
- sandalwood
- nutmeg
- cloves
- mace

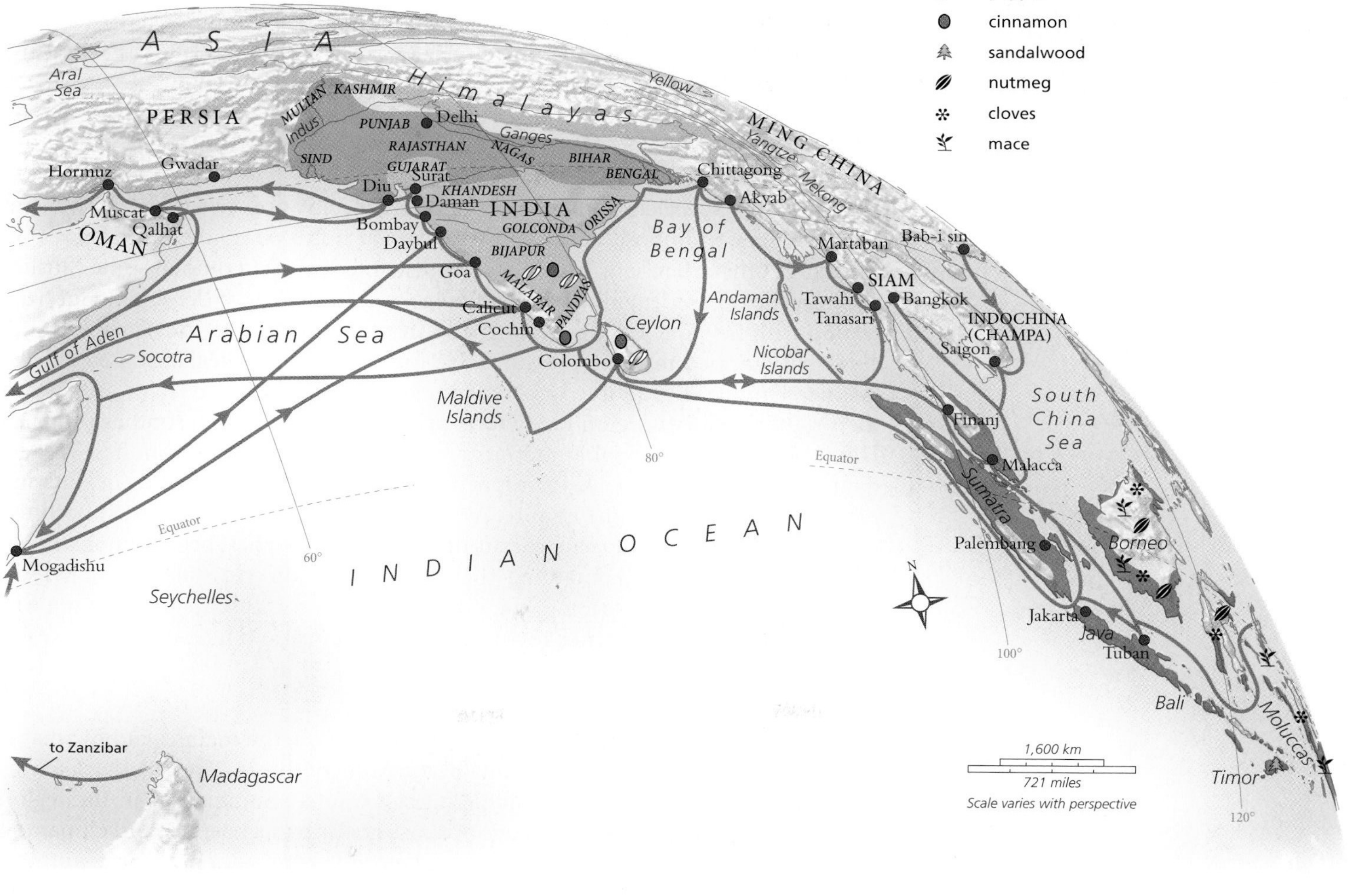

Daulatabad. The Delhi Sultan Ibn Tughluq (r. 1325–1351) transferred his court to the strongest fortress in India, which he called Daulatabad or "City of Riches," near the frontier of his campaigns against Hindu kingdoms in the south. He planned to re-locate the entire population of the city of Delhi to the surrounding slopes. The steep ascent made the place defensible. A narrow gangway was the only approach to the palace complex.

While praising the sultan's sense of justice, Ibn Battuta indicts him for the use of terror, arbitrary abuses of power, and judicial murder. "Every day there are brought to the audience hall hundreds of people, chained, beaten and fettered, and those who are for execution are executed, those for torture tortured, and those for beating beaten." On one occasion, the sultan executed 350 alleged deserters at once. A sheikh who accused him of tyranny was fed with excrement and beheaded. Twice, Ibn Tughluq expelled the classes of Muslim notables whom he suspected of disaffection from Delhi.

Ibn Tughluq's was a personal empire. His own dynamism and a policy of religious toleration held it together—the only policy workable for a Muslim elite in a largely Hindu country. But Ibn Tughluq's state was not built to last. It relied on conquest to fuel the system. The Turkic elite, who provided the muscle for revenue collection and war, demanded constant rewards. When they did not get them, they seceded from the state. This began to happen on a large scale toward the end of Ibn Tughluq's life. Conquest is, in any case, a gambler's game. Military fortunes change, and military systems, even of the most crushing superiority, can fail. Disaster struck Ibn Tughluq, for in stance, when a plague devastated his army. "The provinces withdrew their allegiance," Ibn Battuta reported, "and the outer regions broke away."

Moreover, the Delhi sultans were under constant pressure from the Muslim establishment to impose Islam by force, launch holy war, and ease the taxes on Muslims at the expense of "infidels." The discontent evident among some Muslim notables during Ibn Tughluq's reign owed something to fear of the sultan. But frustration with his policies of toleration also inspired much of it. Ibn Tughluq's successor succumbed to these pressures. He forfeited Hindu allegiance. Beyond the frontier, Hindu states adopted a counter ideology of resistance to Islam—at least in their rhetoric, since religion rarely took priority over politics. In southern India, a Hindu state with imperial ambitions arose at Vijayanagar. The conquest juggernaut of the sultanate of Delhi stopped rolling, and provincial elites in outlying regions dropped out of the empire. As so often before in Indian history, both the difficulties of and the capacity for an India-wide empire had been demonstrated. But the problems of maintaining such a large and diverse state were obvious. Future attempts would run into the same difficulties as those that caused the sultanate's control of the outer edges of the state to unravel and its expansion to cease.

Southeast Asia

Rather as Delhi did in India, a native kingdom in Java, the main island of what is today Indonesia, exploited the waning of the Mongol threat. The islands of southeast Asia produced goods the Chinese market wanted. Some states in the region could threaten or control the passage of those goods by sea: pepper and cinnamon from southern India and Sri Lanka; sandalwood from Timor; timber, nutmeg, cloves, and mace from Borneo and the Moluccas. Control of the strait between

Malaya, Java, and Sumatra was strategically vital for China-bound trade, and the shipping of Java was important for the commerce of the region. That is why Kubilai Khan focused on Java when he tried to extend his empire into southeast Asia (see Chapter 15).

The establishment of a powerful state on Java, centered on the inland city of Majapahit, was the achievement of Kertanagara, who died in 1292. Chroniclers credited him with magic powers or saintly virtues. In fact, he seems to have balanced the rituals of Buddhist, Hindu, and indigenous religions to keep a diverse array of followers together and repulse Kubilai Khan's Mongol invasion.

The king who launched Majapahit on its own imperial career in the mid–fourteenth century was Hayan Wuruk, who died in 1389. He had dazzling ambitions. We know this because one of his chief ministers wrote a poem in his praise that reveals how the king wanted people to think of him. The royal palace at Majapahit had gates of iron and a "diamond-plastered" watchtower. When Hayan Wuruk traveled, his court filled numberless carts. Through the streets of his capital, he paraded, clad in gold, borne on a throne carved with lions, to the sound of music. Ambassadors from foreign courts sang his praises.

He was both "Buddha in the body" and "Shiva incarnate"—worshipful to Buddhist and Hindu subjects alike. Hayan Wuruk's realm, according to the poet, was more famous than any country in the world except India. In reality, the kingdom occupied about half the island of Java. The king, however, aimed to make it bigger. The poet listed tributaries in many islands in what is today Indonesia, and "protectorates" in northern Malaya, Thailand, and Indochina. Even China and India, he claimed, defer to Hayan Wuruk. "Already the other continents," he boasts, "are getting ready to show obedience to the illustrious prince" and a state "renowned for its purifying power in the world."

That was all the exaggeration of propaganda. But a disinterested foreign chronicler left a description of Majapahit that confirms much of the picture:

> The empire grew prosperous. . . . There was a ceaseless coming and going of people from the territories overseas which had submitted to the king . . . . Everywhere one went there were . . . people dancing to the strains of all kinds of loud music, entertainments of all kinds . . . .[3]

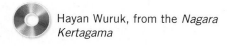

Hayan Wuruk, from the *Nagara Kertagama*

Surviving temple reliefs show what the Java of Hayan Wuruk was like. Wooden houses, perched on pillars over stone terraces, formed neat villages. Peasants grew paddy rice, or coaxed water buffalo over dry fields to break up the soil. Women did the harvesting and cooking. Orchestras accompanied masked dancers. Royal charters fill out the picture of economic activities. Industrial processes included salt making by evaporation, sugar refining, processing water-buffalo meat, oil pressing from seeds, making rice noodles, ironmaking, rattan weaving, and dyeing cloth. More sophisticated ceramics and textiles were imported from China. The same charters reveal the extension of royal power into the hinterland. They establish direct relationships between the royal court and local elites. They favor the foundations of new temples and encourage the spread of communications, the building of bridges, the commissioning of ferries, and the erection of "rest houses, pious foundations, and hospitals."

Majapahit was an expanding realm. As Mongol vigilance relaxed, Majapahit's power increased. In the 1340s, a network of ports in the hands of Majapahit garrisons spread over the islands of Bali and Sumatra. In 1377, Hayan Wuruk launched an apparently successful expedition against Palembang, the major way station on the route from India to China. A struggle was on to profit from southeast Asia's trade.

Japan

Japan, like Java, was a region the plagues spared and the Mongols failed to conquer. Here, however, as the Mongol threat receded, so did pressure to stay united. Rebels could now raise armies with increasing ease. Japan had enjoyed more than a century of stability. The warrior class had been pacified with grants of estates and their revenues. Now people at all social levels were accumulating wealth, and social status was up for grabs. Warriors began to diversify into new occupations, to sell or break up their estate rights, and to resort to violence as a way of life.

At the top of this volatile society, rival branches of the imperial family contested the throne. From 1318, the emperor Godaigo fought to exclude family competitors and take back the power the shoguns exercised in the emperor's name. He found, however, that loyalty was liable to change hands as circumstances changed. "Then was then," proclaimed a saying of the time. "Now is now: rewards are lord!"

Godaigo's army deserted in dissatisfaction over the rewards he could provide. "How," complained one of his officials, "can those who tend to have the outlook of a merchant be of use to the court?" The new disorder was, for some, a social revolution: the result of violations of the proper boundaries of class and rank.

In 1335, the most powerful of the warlords, Ashikaga Takauji, seized the position of **shogun** in defiance of Godaigo's wishes. In 1336, he overwhelmed Godaigo's followers at the Battle of Minato River (see Map 14.5). The Ashikaga dynasty survived as shoguns almost until the end of the century by accepting the realities of the changed world and attempting only modest interventions in the spheres of other major warlords. The Ashikaga also restored the old relationship between shogun and emperor, in which pieties disguised the real displacement of authority into the shogun's hands.

The chaos of the fourteenth century favored the rise of **Zen**, a Buddhist tradition that valued personal extinction as a part of mystical experience. A twelfth-century Japanese text defined it: "a special transmission outside the scriptures, not founded on words or letters, which allows one to penetrate the nature of things by pointing directly to the mind." Zen made progress, partly because of the influx of monks from China, escaping from the Mongols, and partly because Zen ideas suited the warriors and warlords who now ruled Japan. Discipline, self-denial, and willingness to die are martial virtues. The warriors recognized Zen monks as kindred spirits.

For the women of families of warrior and aristocratic rank, the changes of the period were oppressive. Women could attain responsible positions in the emperor's court. Hino Meishi, for instance, was in charge of the sacred imperial symbols in 1331, when the shogun tried to depose Godaigo. But changing marriage customs were unfavorable to women's personal independence. Until the fourteenth century, marriage in Japan was predominantly a private, essentially sexual relationship. Now it became increasingly formalized, as a union of two families. Wives moved into the homes of their husbands' families, instead of remaining in their own homes.

A sign of women's changed circumstances is that they stopped writing fiction and the kind of personal diaries familiar from earlier periods. Self-expression was now considered inappropriate for the female sex. Wives came to be thought of as their husbands' property. It also became common for women aristocrats to receive a life interest in a share of family property, rather than inheriting property out-

A shogun's armor. This armor is believed to have belonged to Ashikaga Takauji who was shogun from 1338 to 1358. The quality and costliness of the gilt copper breastplate and helmet mountings show that the armor could only have belonged to a person of high status such as Ashikaga Takauji. Stenciled in lacquered doeskin, an image of Fudo Myo-o—the god who personified the samurai virtues of outward ferocity and inner calm—adorns the breastplate. Silk ribbons of many colors, symbolizing the fleeting beauty of the rainbow, were used to tie up the skirts of the armor.
The Metropolitan Museum of Art, Gift of Bashford Dean, 1914 (14.100.121) Photograph © 1991 The Metropolitan Museum of Art

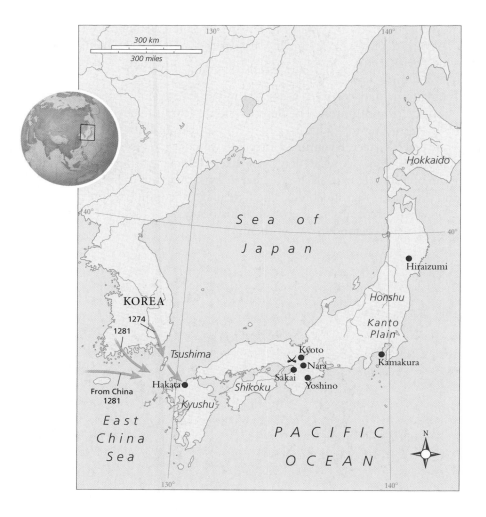

MAP 14.5

Japan, ca. 1350

→ Mongol invasion attempts

⚔ battle of Minato River

right. Property rights were steered toward a single male heir. Among commoners, however, this practice failed to take hold, and women held property and engaged in business in their own right.

The peasants profited from the changes that were transforming the warrior class. Relaxation of central authority freed villagers to get on with improving crop yields as they saw fit. The new regime of rewards for military service meant that the landlords were always changing—dispossessed and replaced as the fortunes of war shifted. The rapid turnover of lords, who were usually absentees, also allowed the peasants to get on with their business. There were no epidemics in the fourteenth-century countryside in Japan, and serious crop failures were rare. Nor were population growth and the extension of cultivated land interrupted. As a result of the successful exploitation of formerly marginal lands, outside the great estates, the numbers of small independent farmers multiplied, though not on anything like the scale discernible at the same time in Western Europe.

Mali

Just as Java and Japan seemed to grow in stature by comparison with the afflictions of China and the Mongols, parts of West Africa projected an image of abundance toward the devastated Mediterranean world. Evidence for West African prosperity is the Catalan Atlas, made

The Ashikaga Shogunate

Fourteenth century	Changing marriage customs diminish women's independence
1318	Emperor Godaigo seeks to regain imperial power
1335	Ashikaga Takauji seizes shogunate in defiance of Godaigo
1336	Last of Godaigo's supporters defeated

in the studio of the finest mapmaker in Europe, Cresques Abraham, in the 1370s or 1380s. The map depicts a black king in West Africa—bearded, crowned, enthroned, surrounded by rich cities—holding a huge nugget of pure gold. "This is the richest king in all the land," says a caption.

His kingdom, Mali, occupied grassland and mixed savanna between the Sahara Desert and the tropical forest. The desert sealed it from the effects of plague (see Map 14.6). According to tradition, a hero known as **Sundiata** founded the kingdom in the early thirteenth century. Horsemen were the strength of its army. Terracotta sculptures show us what they were like. Helmed and armed, with round shields and breastplates over slashed leather jackets, they kept their heads haughtily tilted and their horses on short rein. Their great age of conquest came in the 1260s and 1270s when, according to the Muslim historian Ibn Khaldun, "all nations of the land of the blacks stood in awe of them."

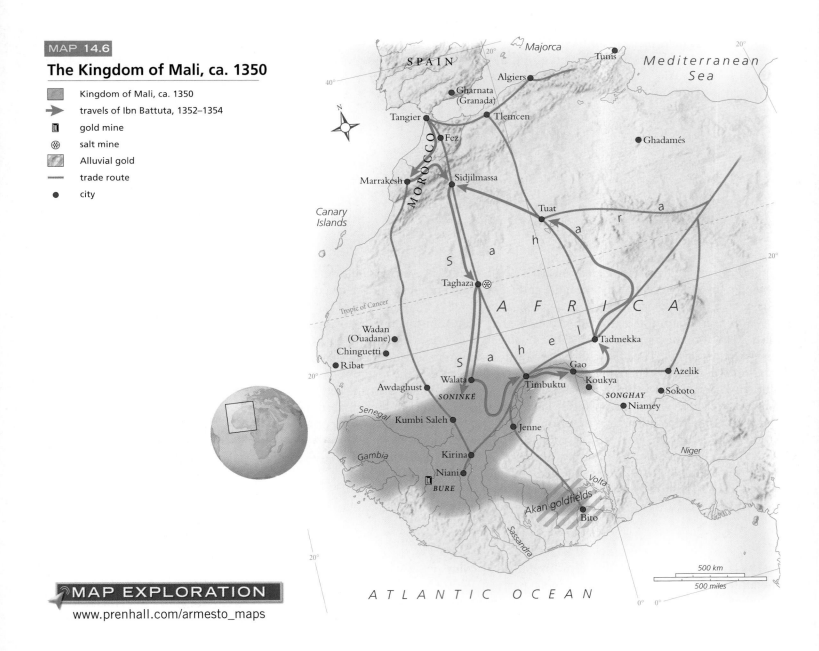

MAP 14.6

The Kingdom of Mali, ca. 1350

- Kingdom of Mali, ca. 1350
- → travels of Ibn Battuta, 1352–1354
- gold mine
- salt mine
- Alluvial gold
- — trade route
- ● city

MAP EXPLORATION
www.prenhall.com/armesto_maps

The "mansas," as the kings of Mali were titled, made pilgrimages to the Muslim holy city of Mecca via Cairo. The mere fact that they dared absent themselves for the year-long journey shows how stable the state must have been. In about 1324, Mansa Musa stayed in Egypt for about three months on his way to Mecca. He gave 50,000 gold coins to the Mamluk sultan and endowed so many mosques and shrines that he caused inflation.

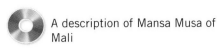
A description of Mansa Musa of Mali

The location of West Africa's gold mines was a closely guarded secret, but it was probably in Bure (BOO-ray), around the upper reaches of the Niger River and the headwaters of the Gambia and Senegal Rivers. The merchants of Mali handled the gold trade but never controlled its production. The mansa took nuggets for tribute—hence, the image on Cresques Abraham's map. The gold bought salt. Mali was so rich in gold and so short of salt that the price of salt reputedly tripled or quadrupled in the kingdom's markets.

In 1352, Ibn Battuta joined a salt caravan across the Sahara. He detested the manners, food, and sexual promiscuity he found in Mali, "and their contempt for white men," but praised the "abhorrence of injustice" he found. The mansa's court impressed him and other visitors in the same period. This consensus is striking, because North African Muslim writers rarely praised black achievements. The

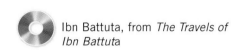
Ibn Battuta, from *The Travels of Ibn Battuta*

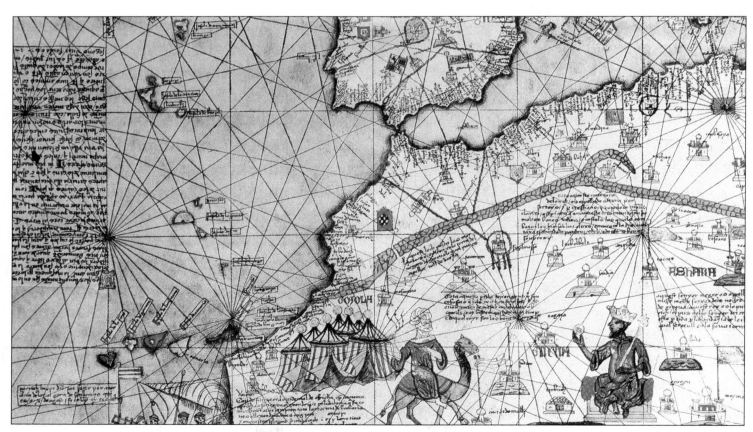

Mansa Musa. "Lord of the blacks of Guinea," reads the legend accompanying the portrait of Mansa Musa (r. ca. 1312–1327), the king of Mali in West Africa, on the fourteenth-century Catalan Atlas. "This lord is the richest and most noble lord of all this region owing to the abundance of gold which is gathered in this land." The Mansa's wealth was said to exceed that of all other kings. His European-style crown and ample beard are compliments bestowed by an artist who had not learned, as Europeans were to do in later centuries, to despise black African kingship.

Mansa. "All the peoples of the land of the Blacks stood in awe of them," wrote Ibn Khaldun of the mounted warriors of the mansas of Mali. Many fired-clay representations of these soldiers survive from the thirteenth to the fifteenth centuries. Nearly all show the same erect posture, proudly uptilted head, and elaborate helmets and bridles.

mansa, according to Ibn Battuta, commanded more devotion from his subjects than any other ruler in the world, though most of the court ceremonial was traditional in West Africa. The ruler, for instance, spoke only through an intermediary, for to raise his voice was beneath his dignity. Supplicants had to prostrate themselves and sprinkle dust on their heads as they addressed him. When his words were relayed to the people, guards strummed their bowstrings and everyone else hummed appreciatively. Sneezing in the mansa's presence was punishable by death. Hundreds of servants attended him with gilded staves. Poets and scholars came to serve the mansa from Muslim Spain and North Africa.

Meanwhile, the gold of West Africa inspired European efforts to get to its source. Western Europe produced only small amounts of silver, and its economies were permanently short of precious metals with which to trade. There was a long-standing adverse trade balance with more productive Silk-Road economies. To keep it going, this trade always needed infusions of cash. So, as Mali's reputation grew, the search for African gold obsessed European adventurers. But the attempts to find a sea route to Mali were hopeless. Mali was landlocked, and the African coasts had little gold until well into the fifteenth century.

THE PACIFIC: SOCIETIES OF ISOLATION

Beyond the world that escaped the Black Death lay regions contagion did not threaten. Isolation, which had arresting effects in so many cases, was a privilege in the fourteenth century. To understand this reversal of the normal pattern of global history, we need to look at some relatively isolated societies. The vastness of the Pacific—which the technology of the time could not cross—ensured that exceptionally isolated cultures lay scattered around that ocean.

For instance, Easter Island lay, at the time, more than 2,000 miles away from any other human habitation. The island covers only 64 square miles of the Pacific Ocean. It is hard to believe that the Polynesian navigators who first colonized the island, possibly over 1,500 years ago, would have stayed if they had been able to continue their journey or go home. Most of the soil is poor. Chickens and the starchy plant called taro came with the first settlers. But not much that was edible was available to them when they arrived. Migrant birds were their renewable source of food.

Yet despite the island's natural poverty and its isolation from other societies, it housed, in the fourteenth century, a people at the height of their ambition. Probably late in the first millennium, they had begun to erect monumental statues called *Moais* for reasons we can no longer determine. These stone statues resemble those other Polynesian peoples erected: tall, elongated, stylized faces. They were originally adorned with red topknots and white coral eyes. The Easter Island statues are unique compared with other Polynesian works of the same sort only because they are so big and there are so many of them—some 600 finished examples survive, most of them more than 20 feet tall.

It took communal effort to make and erect the statues, each carved from a pillar of rock weighing between 30 and 40 tons. A single extended family—say, about 400 people—joining together to provide the labor and feed the workers, would have taken more than a year to complete the task. As time went on, the statues got bigger—a clear case of competition, driving up the costs of the culture, and, perhaps, condemning it to collapse, a century or two later. So an enterprising community could buck the effects of isolation, and even turn isolation to advantage—but, in an extreme case like that of Easter Island, the effort was hard to sustain. Statue building slowed and, in the sixteenth or seventeenth century, stopped.

Moais. Monumental statue making on Easter Island was probably at its most intense in the fourteenth century. For a small population on a poorly provided and remote island, the investment of energy the practice required seems astounding. The images are similar to those of ancestor cults elsewhere in Polynesia, but they are exceptional in being carved from stone, rather than wood, huge, and numerous. Isolation apparently made Easter Island culture distinctive, but still recognizably like that of other Polynesian colonies.

New Zealand was an almost equally remote outpost of the Polynesian world (see Chapter 11), but with infinitely more resources than Easter Island. By the fourteenth century, population had increased, and hunting resources diminished as the fur seal and the moa began to get scarce. The moa was a huge, flightless bird, with eggs as big as a hundred hen's eggs, that was among early settlers' main sources of food until they hunted it to extinction.

As the balance of the way of life shifted from hunting toward farming, mobile colonies settled down. The results included stronger community identification with land and, therefore, more competition for cultivable resources. Part of the farming surplus was invested in war. From the fifteenth century, the number of places where weapons were made grew enormously. So did the number of fortified villages. War was only one of many new or newly intensive activities that favored the power of chiefs. Farming required strong centers of power to organize collective activity and regulate the distribution of food. So did new fishing technologies with gigantic nets that needed many hands to operate them.

Meanwhile, on the Pacific rim of the New World, people experimented with contrasting responses to isolation (see Map 14.7). Good evidence has survived for two different communities. One body of evidence comes from the north of the hemisphere. Probably toward the end of the fifteenth century, a mudslide at Ozette, in Washington State, buried a community of whalers and seal fishers and perfectly preserved the site. This was a hunting culture whose ways of life had not changed significantly for centuries.

MAP 14.7

Societies of the Pacific, ca.1400

☐ area of Polynesian settlement

Economic activities and food resources

🦭 seals

🐟 fishing

⬭ taro

🐦 moa

♀ cotton

🕊 migrant birds

🦃 chickens

🐖 pigs

🥥 coconuts/breadfruit

PERU modern country or state

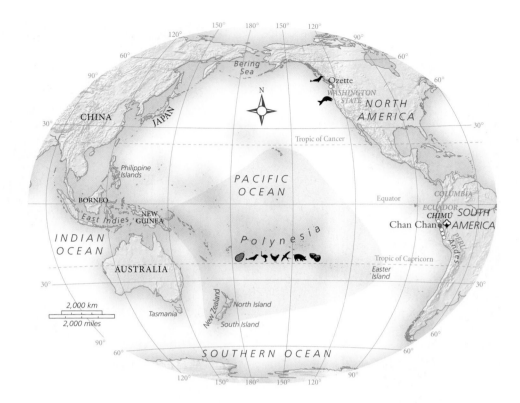

Huaca del Dragón. The date of the stacked platforms of Huaca del Dragón, near the site of Chan Chan in Peru, is much disputed, but the adobe reliefs—of which a recently restored section is depicted here—are probably of Chimú workmanship. Below a frieze of warriors, a divine feast is shown. A double-headed serpent, with a rainbow-like body surrounded by clouds, devours curl-nosed victims, framing similar scenes shown in profile. Food-storage areas were built into the structure, which seems to have been both temple and warehouse—a repository, perhaps, for food of the gods.

The victims of the mudslide lived in cedar buildings, each more than 50 feet long and 30 feet wide. Each building housed about 40 people, divided typically by partitions into half a dozen smaller family units, each with its own hearth. The Ozette people ate almost no vegetable matter except wild berries. Seals provided nearly 90 percent of their meat. For cooking, they boiled or steamed their food in watertight cedar boxes. They hunted and fished in dugouts. Whale images dominated their art, probably because the art had a magical function in bringing good fortune to the whale hunt. Their way of life was, broadly speaking, similar to that of the Thule Inuit centuries earlier (see Chapter 11).

On the Pacific's South American edge, we can trace new activity to roughly the same period. This region was less isolated than New Zealand, Easter Island, or Ozette. The coasts of what are now Peru, Ecuador, and Pacific-side Colombia were always in touch with the cultures of the high Andes and the lowlands beyond. In South America, in and around the fourteenth century, the latest experiment in state-building, intensive agriculture, and city life was under way at Chan Chan. This city was in the coastal desert region of Peru where the Moche had built complex irrigation works and prosperous cities (see Chapter 10) in defiance of a hostile environment. The methods of the Chimú (chee-MOO) people of Chan Chan were dif-

MAKING CONNECTIONS

BEYOND THE PLAGUE ZONE

REGION →	TENTATIVE REASON FOR ABSENCE OF PLAGUE →	CONSEQUENCES
Japan	Protected by relative isolation	Protected from Mongols; new threats emerge from prosperous provincial warlords; in addition, the imperial family divides into rival factions; new dynasty of shoguns emerges; Zen Buddhism expands influence
India	Unknown—although Silk Roads and sea-trade routes were adjacent	Islamic sultanate of Delhi profited from Mongols' decline, initiating policy of conquest; Turkic elite responsible for war and revenue collecting eventually secedes; problems of Hindu/Muslim relations are ever present
Southeast Asia	Unknown—trade routes from China, Europe, Africa should have made the region vulnerable	Establishment of powerful state on Java (Majapahit), to control trade with China and India, creating stable and prosperous society
Pacific	Isolation	Expansion of existing societies; new efforts at developing agricultural resources
Sub-Saharan Africa	Unclear	Control over West Africa's gold trade leads to affluence, European obsession with finding Mali

ferent. They concentrated agriculture in the environs of the city, where 30,000 people lived. Hinterland population was not much bigger than that of Chan Chan itself.

Cotton production was a major economic activity. For protein, the Chan Chan people—or, perhaps, just the elite—relied on llamas, which were farmed in corrals in and around the city. Chan Chan covered almost seven square miles. Its layout shows that the Chimú state was oppressive, with a security-obsessed elite. Fortifications protected the rulers' quarters from their own people. Warehouses were the most vital part of the state because El Niño periodically and unpredictably washed away the irrigation works. Stockpiling enabled the Chimú to recover.

The Chimú elite favored gold for their precious ornaments and ritual objects. But gold did not occur naturally in this part of Peru. Trade or tribute must have brought it to Chimú, for Chimú was evidently an expansionist state. Perhaps it had to be to boost its resources in a difficult environment. Sites of towns built in the style of Chan Chan stretch between the Sana and Supe Rivers.

IN PERSPECTIVE: The Aftershock

Ibn Khaldun left an unforgettable description of the effects of the Black Death on the Muslim world:

> Civilization shrank with the decrease of mankind. Cities and buildings were bared, roads and signposts were abandoned, villages and palaces were deserted. Tribes and dynasties were expunged. It was as if the voice of existence in the world had called out for oblivion, and the world had responded to the call.[4]

But how serious and enduring were the consequences? For Western Europe, many promising initiatives of the preceding period ended. North Atlantic navigation dwindled. The last Icelan7dic voyage to mainland America was in 1347. The Norse Greenland colonies became increasingly isolated. When a bishop's representative sailed to the more northerly of them in the 1340s, he "found nobody, either Christians or heathens. . . ." When the Greenland colony was finally extinguished in the fifteenth century, mysterious raiders of savage ferocity—presumably, the Thule Inuit with whom the Norse had long shared the island— were partly responsible. Exploration of other parts of the Atlantic virtually stopped at the time of the Black Death. In the previous half century preceding the onset of the plague, explorers from maritime communities in Western Europe had made considerable progress. Mapping of the African Atlantic had begun, with the Canary and Madeira Islands, and navigators had begun to investigate the pattern of the northeast trade winds. Few similar voyages were recorded in the second half of the fourteenth century.

Human foes supplemented the plague, famine, and cold. In the northeast, pagan Lithuanians eroded the conquests of the Teutonic Orders along the Baltic (see Chapter 13). Meanwhile, in the parts of Eastern Europe the plague spared, state-building continued, under rulers whose longevity helped bring stability. The period of the Black Death in Western Europe was spanned by the reigns of Charles the Great in Bohemia (r. 1333–1378), Casimir the Great in Poland (r. 1333–1370), and Louis the Great of Hungary (r. 1342–1382). On the whole, the effects of plague favored the state even in the West, because afflicted populations turned to monarchs as potential saviors and were willing to trust them with enhanced powers.

In the Mongol dominions, the case was different. Mongol expansion ceased. Russian principalities began to shake off Mongol control. The Mongol state in Persia fragmented, and the last Il-khan died in 1343. From the ruins of Mongol domination, a new state arose in Anatolia, ruled by a Turkish dynasty, known as the Ottomans. They gradually came to dominate Byzantium and invaded the Balkans (see Map 14.8).

MAP 14.8

The Ottoman State, ca. 1400

▢ Ottoman state, ca. 1400

▢ Byzantine Empire, ca. 1400

In China, as we shall see in the next chapter, the ecological crisis of the mid–fourteenth century contributed to the replacement of the Mongol state by the native Chinese Ming dynasty.

At a deeper level than that of the rise and fall of states and political elites, the coming of the age of plagues, made worse by unpredictable changes in climate, affected the balance of population—and therefore of power—among Eurasian civilizations. Population can recover with surprising speed from natural disasters. But recovery was harder in the wake of the Black Death because, although plagues became less ferocious, and populations built up immunity, plagues affected the same regions for centuries to come, at a rate too rapid to enumerate—more than once on average every four years, for instance, in Egypt in the two centuries following the Black Death. The population of Eurasia probably remained static during the late fourteenth century and most of the fifteenth. In the long run, it looks as if the Islamic world may have been more affected than Christendom or China, both of which seem to have recovered faster and resisted better. This can only be a tentative conclusion, because the evidence is unreliable. It does seem, however, that the populations of Christendom and China recovered to preplague levels by the end of the fifteenth century, while in Egypt, Syria and, perhaps, in other parts of the Islamic world, the recovery did not even begin until then. The increase of population thereafter was generally slower in the Islamic world than in Christendom and China until the twentieth century (see Figure 14.2). This may help to explain one of history's great shifts in wealth, power, and every kind of dynamism—away from the Islamic world. Whereas in what we call the Middle Ages, the Islamic world had contributed far more than Christendom to cultural exchange in Eurasia, and had tended to win out in conflicts with Christendom, Muslim power dwindled over the succeeding centuries. The relative eclipse of the Islamic world and the relative ascent of Europe are major themes of the age of plague and, therefore, of the next two parts of this book.

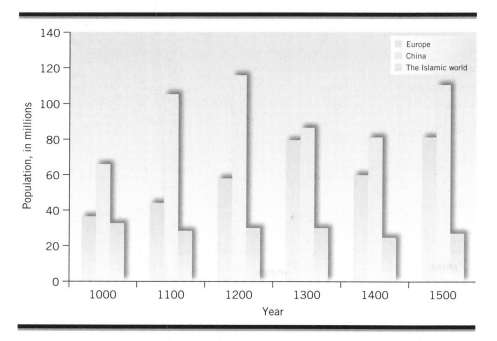

FIGURE 14.2 THE POPULATION OF EUROPE, CHINA, AND THE ISLAMIC WORLD COMPARED

CHRONOLOGY

1290	England expels Jews
Thirteenth and fourteenth centuries	Climate change in Northern Hemisphere
1315–1316	Heavy rains reported all over northern Europe
1320s	Plague epidemics in southwestern and central China
1324	Mansa Musa makes *hajj* to Mecca
1325–1351	Reign of Ibn Tughluq (India)
1326	Ottoman Turks set up capital at Bursa (western Anatolia)
1330s	Mortality rates in northeast China reach 90 percent
1335	Ashikaga Tokauji seizes shogunate (Japan)
1343	Last Il-khan dies in Persia
1346	Plague reported in Crimea (Black Sea)
1347	Last Icelandic voyage to America
1347–1349	Plague rages throughout Europe, Middle East, and North Africa
1350s	Peasant rebellions spread throughout China
1351	Plague strikes southern Russia
1352	Ibn Battuta sets off for Mali
1360	Plague reported in China
1389	Death of Hayan Wuruk (Majapahit)
1400	Settlements in American Southwest abandoned

PROBLEMS AND PARALLELS

1. How might Mongol rule have facilitated the spread of plague during the fourteenth century?

2. What were the long-term effects of the climate change and age of plagues that began during the fourteenth century?

3. What parts of the globe were most adversely affected by plague and climate change during the fourteenth century? Why were some areas of the world hit badly by these phenomena and others hardy at all?

4. Was there a relationship between climate change and plague, and if so, what was it?

5. Who were the "winners" and "losers" in the plague years (other than the immediate survivors and victims)?

DOCUMENTS IN GLOBAL HISTORY

• Marchione di Coppo Stefani, from *The Florentine Chronicle*
• University of Paris Medical Faculty, *Report on the Plague*
• Hayan Wuruk, from the *Nagara Kertagama*

• A description of Mansa Musa of Mali
• Ibn Battuta, from *The Travels of Ibn Battuta*

Please see the Primary Source DVD for additional sources related to this chapter.

READ ON

H. Lamb, *Climate, History and the Modern World* (1995) is the classic work on its subject, complemented by B. Fagan's *The Little Ice Age* (2000). Classic works—now superseded on many points—on the global history of disease are H. Zinsser, *Rats, Lice, and History* (1996), and W. H. McNeill, *Plagues and Peoples* (1998). S. Cohn, *The Black Death* (2003) is indispensable for the plagues in Europe and for the epidemiology of the Black Death. N. Cantor, *In the Wake of the Plague* (2001) has some interesting material on social effects. R. Horrox, *The Black Death* (1994) is a valuable anthology of source material. M. W. Dols, *The Black Death in the Middle East* (1977)—though corrected in some respects by Cohn's work—is invaluable on its subject. As so often, the edition by H. Gibb and C. Beckingham of *The Travels of Ibn Battuta* (1994) is an indispensable guide.

On China, the *Cambridge History of China*, multiple volumes is in preparation; meanwhile, vol. vi is of some help, and the collection of essays edited by P. J. Smith and R. von Glahn, *The Song-Yuan-Ming Transition in Chinese History* (2003) crackles with revisionism. For Europe, M. Jones, ed., *The New Cambridge Medieval History*, vi (2000) is a comprehensive survey. On the problems of the status of women, G. Duby and M. Perrot, eds., *A History of Women* (2000) is the leading work; particularly useful work on the subjects touched on in this chapter includes R. Smith, "Coping with Uncertainty: Women's Tenure of Customary Land in England," in J. Kermode, ed., *Enterprise and Individual in Fifteenth-Century England* (1997), and L. Mirrer, ed., *Upon My Husband's Death* (1992).

For Hohokam, the article by P. Crown, "The Hohokam of the American Southwest," *Journal of World History*, iv (1990) is a good introduction. G. J. Gumerman, ed., *Themes in Southwest Prehistory* (1994) contains some important contributions.

On the Jews, N. Cohn, *Europe's Inner Demons* (2001) is a controversial but gripping attempt to trace the origins of anti-Semitism. P. Johnson, *History of the Jews* (1988)—though superseded in its coverage of the early period—remains the best general history. L. Kochan, *The Jew and His History* (1985) is a good introduction.

On peasant millenarianism, N. Cohn, *The Pursuit of the Millennium* (1970) remains unsurpassed. On Japan, J. Mass, ed., *Origins of Japan's Medieval World* (1997) amounts to a fine history of the fourteenth century. The Delhi sultanate is covered in R. Majumdar, *The History and Culture of the Indian People*, iv (1951). On Java, T. Pigeaud, ed., *Java in the Fourteenth Century* (1960) is a marvelous edition of the poem I cite about Hayan Wuruk. D. G. Hall in N. Tarling, ed., *The Cambridge History of Southeast Asia*, i (1992) provides further help. On Mali, N. Levtzion, *Ancient Ghana and Mali* (1986) is highly accessible, and D. T. Niane covers the subject expertly in *UNESCO History of Africa*, iv (1998), but the classic work by E. W. R. Bovill, *The Golden Trade of the Moors* (1995), can still be read with pleasure. For the Pacific, J. van Tilburg, *Easter Island* (1995) is the only fully reliable work on that island. J. Belich, *Making Peoples* (2002) is insuperable on New Zealand. On Ozette, see R. Kirk and R. D. Dougherty, *Hunters of the Whale* (1998). On the Chimú, R. Keatinge, *Peruvian Prehistory* (1988) is standard.

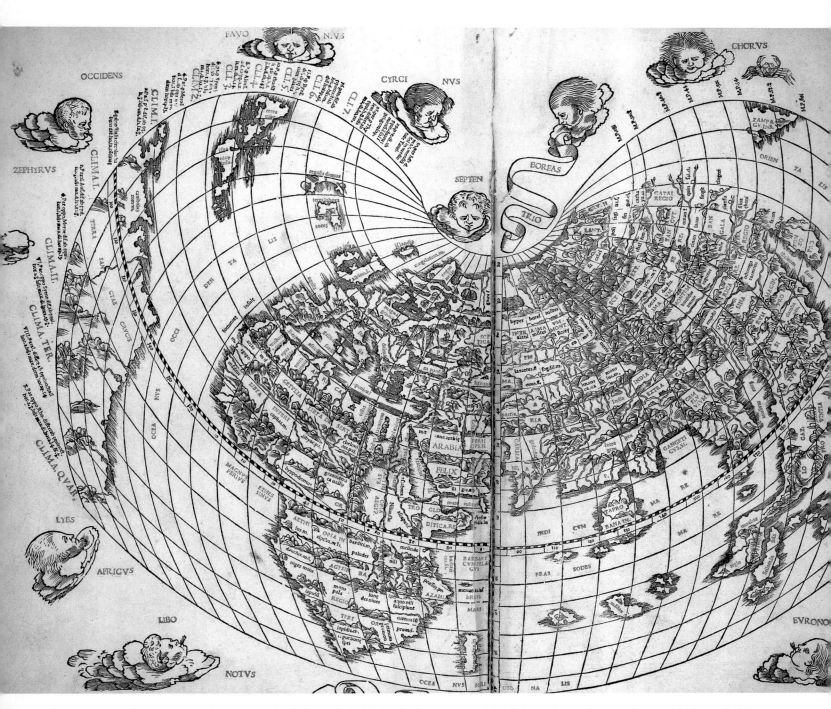

Map of the world. Published in Venice by Bernardus Sylvanus in 1511, this is the first map printed in two colors and represents the earliest period of European exploration of the New World. The islands of Cuba and Hispaniola are identified on the far left side, while Newfoundland is inaccurately shown just to the west of Ireland.

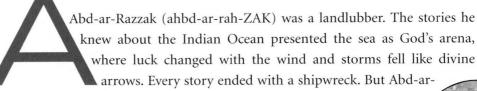

INDIAN OCEAN

Abd-ar-Razzak (ahbd-ar-rah-ZAK) was a landlubber. The stories he knew about the Indian Ocean presented the sea as God's arena, where luck changed with the wind and storms fell like divine arrows. Every story ended with a shipwreck. But Abd-ar-Razzak could not avoid the sea. In 1417, he was appointed Persian ambassador to Vijayanagar (vee-jeh-yeh-NAH-gar), a kingdom in southern India, and there were too many hostile kingdoms between it and Persia for him to cross by land. But his ship sailed late,

> so that the favorable time for departing by sea, that is to say the beginning or middle of the monsoon, was allowed to pass, and we came to the end of the monsoon, which is the season when tempests and attacks from pirates are to be dreaded…. The merchants, who were my intimate friends, cried with one voice that the time for navigation was past, and that everyone who put to sea at this season was alone responsible for his death.

Abd-ar-Razzak's predicament, however, had a positive side. The late monsoon is so fierce that ships speed before it. He made the journey in only 19 days, about two-thirds of the time one might normally expect.

● ● ● ● ●

Abd-ar-Razzak's voyage demonstrates the importance of winds in world history. Most of the planet's surface area is sea. Long-range communications have to traverse wide waters. Throughout the age of sail—for almost the entire history of travel—winds and currents limited what was possible: the routes, the rates, the mutually accessible cultures. More particularly, Abd-ar-Razzak's experience illustrates the paradox of Indian Ocean navigation in his day. The monsoon winds made travel speedy, but the ocean was stormy, unsafe, and hard to get into and out of. Access from the east was barely possible in summer, when typhoons tore into the shores. Fierce storms guarded the southern approaches. No one who knew the reputation of these waters cared to venture between about 10 and 30 degrees south and 60 or 90 degrees east during the hurricane season. Yet the Indian Ocean was the biggest and richest zone of long-range commerce in the world.

FOCUS questions

- WHY WERE some African empires able to expand on such an impressive scale during this period?
- WHAT ROLE did geographic diversity play in the Inca and Aztec Empires?
- WHAT STRONG new empires arose on the Eurasian borderlands?
- WHY DID China turn away from overseas expansion in the fifteenth century?
- WHY DID Europe begin to reach out and cross the oceans in the late 1400s?

By the end of the fifteenth century, European navigators had found a way to penetrate it. Meanwhile, the Atlantic was developing into a rival zone, with transoceanic routes ready to be exploited. Indeed, seafaring on the Atlantic would transform the world by bringing cultures that had been torn apart into contact, conflict, commerce, and cultural and ecological exchange. The divergent, isolated worlds of ancient and medieval times were coming together to form the interconnected world we inhabit today.

How did it happen? How did the world rebound from the plagues and climate changes of the fourteenth century? For one thing, populations gradually acquired immunity against plague, as susceptible people died and those who were naturally most resistant passed on their genes. As for worsening climates, survivors relocated or got used to colder, wetter conditions. To some extent, technological advance made up for—indeed, was a response to—decreased population. Across Eurasia, and in parts of Africa that were in contact with Eurasia, the long period of accelerated exchange in the Song and Mongol eras had equipped expanding economies with improved technology (see Chapter 13). In regions that escaped the catastrophes of the fourteenth century, long-term population growth strengthened states and economies. So it is not surprising that the world of the late fourteenth and fifteenth centuries was a world in recovery and resumed expansion.

From about 1460 on, in states in widely separated parts of the world, expansion speeded up, but the phenomenon was of an expanding world, not, as some historians say, of European expansion. The world did not wait passively for European outreach to transform it, as if touched by a magic wand. Other societies were already turning states into empires and cultures into civilizations. Indeed, in terms of territorial expansion and military effectiveness, some African and American empires outclassed any state in Western Europe until the sixteenth century.

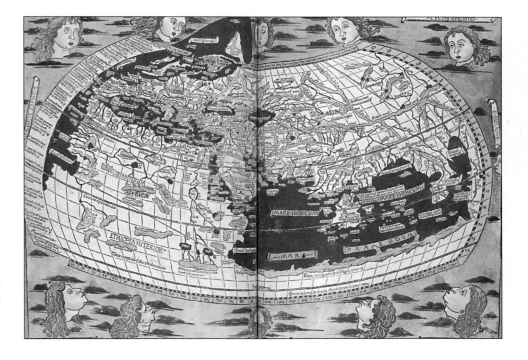

Claudius Ptolemy's Geography, written in Alexandria, Egypt, in the second century, was still the standard source for how educated Europeans saw the world in the fifteenth century. Printed editions, like this one of 1482, usually included attempts to map the world as Ptolemy described it. Common features include a grid of lines of latitude and longitude—the system Ptolemy devised for locating places in relation to one another; the exaggerated size and prominence of Sri Lanka; locating the source of the Nile in mountains beyond large lakes deep in Africa; and showing the Indian Ocean as landlocked, which undermined navigators' confidence that they could reach India and Asia by sea.

As we shall see, European expansion did have unique features—exceptional range, above all, which enabled people from parts of Western Europe to cross unprecedented distances on previously unexplored routes. But we have to see Europe in global context and acknowledge that expansion was a worldwide phenomenon. If we start in Africa and approach Europe only after looking at the Americas and following Abd-ar-Razzak's route in Asia, we can begin to make sense of the peculiar features of the history of Atlantic-side European peoples who launched empires that will take up more and more space in the rest of the book.

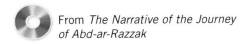

From *The Narrative of the Journey of Abd-ar-Razzak*

FRAGILE EMPIRES IN AFRICA

East Africa

In the late fourteenth century, Ethiopia again began to reach beyond its mountains. Monasteries became schools of missionaries whose task was to consolidate Ethiopian power in the conquered pagan lands of Shoa and Gojam (see Chapter 10). Rulers reopened outlets to the Red Sea and the Indian Ocean. By the time they recaptured the port of Massaweh in 1403, Ethiopian rule stretched into the Great Rift valley. The resulting wealth funded defense of the empire and fueled expansionist ambitions.

Although Ethiopia conquered no more territory after 1469, saints' lives tell of internal expansion. Wasteland was converted to farmland and settled by monks. When Portuguese diplomatic missions began to arrive in Ethiopia in the 1490s, "men and gold and provisions like the sands of the sea and the stars in the sky" impressed them. As we shall see in the next chapter, however, Ethiopia had probably already overreached its resources.

Southward from Ethiopia, at the far end of the Rift valley, lay the gold-rich Zambezi valley and the productive plateau beyond, which was rich in salt, gold, and elephants. Like Ethiopia, these areas looked toward the Indian Ocean for trade with maritime Asia, but their outlets to the sea lay below the reach of the monsoon system and, therefore, beyond the normal routes of trade. Still, adventurous merchants risked the voyage to bring goods from Asia in trade for gold and ivory.

Evidence of the effects of trade lies inland between the Zambezi and the Limpopo Rivers, where fortified, stone-built administrative centers—called **zimbabwes**—had been common for centuries. Now, in the late fourteenth and fifteenth centuries, the zimbabwes entered their greatest age. The most famous, Great Zimbabwe, included a citadel on a hill 350 feet high (see Map 15.1). Near stone buildings, the elite were buried with gold, jeweled ironwork, large copper ingots, and Chinese porcelain.

In the second quarter of the fifteenth century, the center of power shifted northward to the Zambezi valley, with the expansion of a new power. Mwene Mutapa (MWEH-nee MOO-TAH-pah), as it was called, arose during the northward migration of bands of warriors from what are now parts of Mozambique and KwaZulu-Natal. When one of their leaders conquered the middle Zambezi valley, he took the title Mwene Mutapa, or "lord of the tribute payers," a name that became extended to the state. But Mwene Mutapa never reached the ocean. Native merchants, who traded at inland fairs, had no interest in a direct outlet to the sea. They did well enough using middlemen on the coast and had no incentive for or experience of ocean trade. Like Mali (see Chapter 14), Mwene Mutapa was a landlocked empire, sustained by trade in gold and salt.

The Reemergence of Ethiopia

Late fourteenth century	Ethiopia expands into surrounding regions
1403	Recapture of port of Massaweh
1469	End of period of conquest
1490s	First Portuguese diplomatic missions arrive in Ethiopia

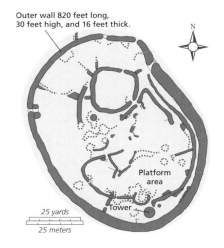

Outer wall 820 feet long, 30 feet high, and 16 feet thick.

Platform area

25 yards
25 meters

Tower

MAP 15.1

Great Zimbabwe

■ stone construction

⋯⋯ walls in ruin

— drain

The turreted walls of Great Zimbabwe surround a 350-foot-high hill, crowned by a formidable citadel, which housed the elite, who ate beef and were buried with gifts of gold, copper, jewels, and Chinese porcelain. Though it was the biggest of the stone-built settlements of the period, Great Zimbabwe was typical, in style and substance, of other buildings in the region south of the Zambezi River during what we think of as the late Middle Ages.

 Leo Africanus on Timbuktu

West Africa

New states emerged in West Africa, too, following the decline of Mali. Like many empires in out-of-the-way places, Mali became a victim of its relative isolation. From about 1360, a power struggle pitted the descendants of Mansa Musa against those of his brother. At about the end of the century, the Songhay (SOHNG-eye), a people from lower down the Niger River, broke away and seized Gao (gow), one of the great trading cities between the rain forest and the desert. Traders could now outflank Mali's trading monopoly. Mali was further weakened in the 1430s when invaders from the Sahara seized its northernmost towns.

By the 1450s, when Portuguese expeditions made the first recorded European contact with Mali, the Mansa's power was virtually confined to the original heartland. The result was a tragedy for the history of the world, for the absence of a strong African state undermined Europeans' views of black Africans as equals. Instead of a great, rich empire, the Portuguese found Mali a ramshackle wreck. Their disappointment prejudiced them, and they wondered if black Africans had any capacity for political greatness. Though some Europeans continued to treat black Africans as equals—and the Portuguese crown, in particular, maintained the affectation that black kings were fellow monarchs on a par with those of Europe—from now on, white people in Africa could nourish convictions of superiority.

Songhay became the most powerful state in the region, but it never controlled as much of the Saharan trade as Mali had. Muhammad Touray Askia, a general who used Islam to justify

The Portuguese in West Africa and the Congo

1450s	First reported Portuguese contact with Mali
1480s	Portuguese make contact with kingdom of Kongo
1482	West African trading post of São Jorge da Mina established

seizing the throne, wrenched Songhay into the Islamic mainstream in the late fifteenth century. In 1497, he undertook a pilgrimage to Mecca on a scale of magnificence calculated to echo that of Mansa Musa in 1324–1325 (see Chapter 14). Askia's ascent to power ensured that the Sahel would be predominantly Muslim. His alliance with the Muslim intelligentsia made Songhay a state "favored by God" in the eyes of religious Muslims—the class on which the state depended for administrators. By imposing peace, he increased Saharan merchants' sense of security. New canals, wells, dikes, and reservoirs scored the land. Cultivated terrain was extended, especially for rice, which had long been known in the region but never previously farmed on a large scale.

Songhay, like Mali before it, benefited from the trade routes of the Sahara that linked the Mediterranean coast to the Niger valley. The river Niger is navigable for almost its entire length, but the Atlantic's adverse winds and currents limited long-range communications by sea. The states and cultures of the tropical forest and coast in the African "bulge" were limited to regional power and wealth. Nevertheless, they have left plenty of evidence of economic expansion and of the wealth and power of their kings in the fifteenth century: the fortifications, for instance, of the city-state of Benin and the splendid metal weapons, adornments, and courtly furnishings of Benin and the Ife.

The whole African coast from Senegambia to the mouth of the Niger impressed Europeans at the time. The trading post that Portugal opened at São Jorge da Mina, on the underside of the African bulge, in 1482, appeared on maps as a fantasy city. It suited the purposes of the Portuguese monarchs to exaggerate the grandeur, but their propaganda reflected the reality of a region of rich kingdoms, commerce, and urban life.

Farther south, too, in the Congo basin, the opportunities for states to reach out by sea were limited. The Kingdom of Kongo dominated the Congo River's navigable lower reaches, probably from the mid–fourteenth century. When Portuguese explorers established contact in the 1480s, Kongo's rulers enthusiastically adopted the religion and technology of the visitors. The kingdom became host to Portuguese missionaries, craftsmen, and mercenaries. The royal residence was rebuilt in Portuguese style. The kings issued documents in Portuguese, and royal princes went to Portugal for their education. One became an archbishop, and the kings continued to have Portuguese baptismal names for centuries thereafter. Portuguese firepower gave the kings a military advantage over their neighbors. They gained territory and slaves, many of whom they sold to the Portuguese for export.

Although Ethiopia, Mwene Mutapa, Songhay, and Kongo were all formidable regional powers, and although many small states of the West African coast expanded commercially and territorially, little of this activity was on an unprecedented scale (see Map 15.2). Ethiopia's sequence of rise and decline had been going on for centuries. Songhay was the latest in a series of empires in the Sahel. Trading states had long studded the underside of the West African bulge. Mwene Mutapa was the successor state of the builders of the zimbabwes. If there was something new out of Africa at this time, it was part of a wider phenomenon. The empires grew at impressive rates and to impressive extents because they were in touch with other phenomena of commercial and political expansion: Songhay across the Sahara, Ethiopia and Mwene Mutapa across the Indian Ocean, the coastal trading cities and Kongo with Portugal. In the Americas, however, in the late fifteenth century, even states that had to contend with isolation could expand on a new scale.

Portuguese soldier. The court art of Benin, in the Niger Delta of West Africa, preserves precious images of Portuguese visitors, as native artists saw them in the sixteenth century. The Obas, as the rulers of Benin were called, frequently asked for Portuguese military help—sometimes offering to adopt Christianity in exchange—and this Portuguese soldier, carved in ivory, is supporting the Oba's saltcellar. Salt was a precious commodity in Benin. The soldier's short spear, feathered straw hat, and sweatband are local touches, but the rest of his clothes, his beard, his sword, and his pectoral cross were exotic emblems to the African artist who carved them.
African, Nigeria, Edo peoples, court of Benin, Saltcellar: Portuguese Figure, 15th–16th century, Ivory; H. 7–1/8 in. (18.1 cm). The Metropolitan Museum of Art, Louis V. Bell and Rogers Funds, 1972. (1972.63ab) Photograph by Stan Reis. Photograph © 1984

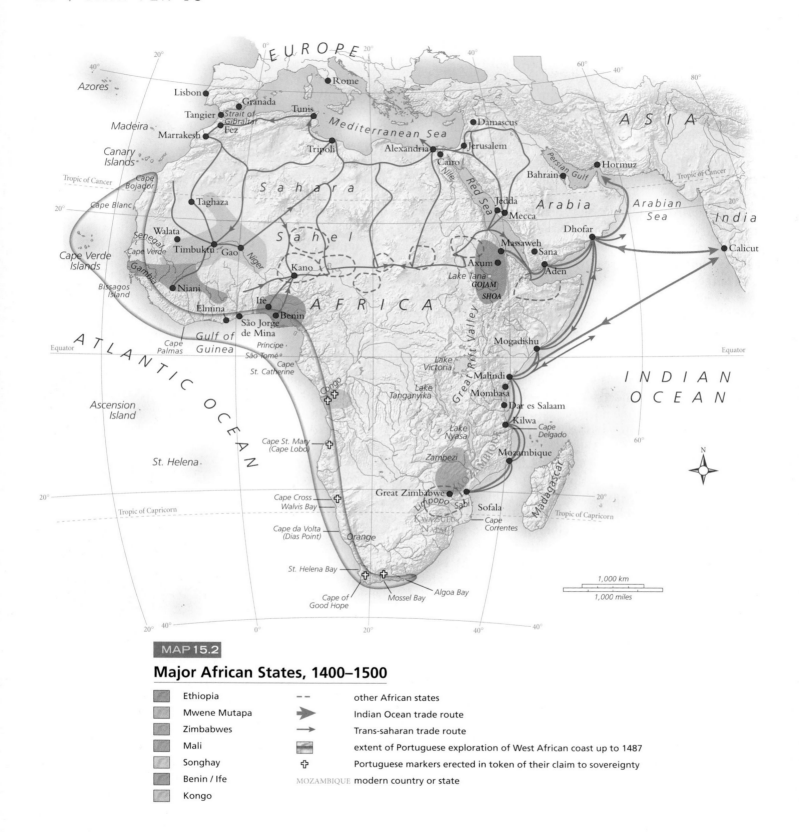

MAP 15.2

MAP 15.2

Major African States, 1400–1500

▨ Ethiopia	––	other African states
▨ Mwene Mutapa	➤	Indian Ocean trade route
▨ Zimbabwes	→	Trans-saharan trade route
▨ Mali	▨	extent of Portuguese exploration of West African coast up to 1487
▨ Songhay	✚	Portuguese markers erected in token of their claim to sovereignty
▨ Benin / Ife	MOZAMBIQUE	modern country or state
▨ Kongo		

ECOLOGICAL IMPERIALISM IN THE AMERICAS

Since Alfred Crosby coined the term **ecological imperialism** in 1972, historians have used it to refer to the sweeping environmental changes European imperialists introduced in regions they colonized. The term also suits Native American empires, especially in Mesoamerica and the Andes, where the key to success in large-scale state-building lay in combining diverse regions and exploiting the complementary products of contrasting ecosystems.

The Inca Empire

In the late fifteenth century, the world's fastest-growing empire was the Inca Empire. The Incas seem to have built their empire during the reigns of three rulers in the late fifteenth and early sixteenth centuries.

Probably early in the second half of the fifteenth century, the founders of the Inca state descended from the highlands to find fertile land. They occupied Cuzco in what is today Peru, which became their biggest city, and began subjugating their neighbors. Their story was typically Andean. They gathered many diverse environments into one state to facilitate exchanging and stockpiling a wide range of products. The Incas, however, took this well-established practice to new lengths. Theirs was one of the most environmentally diverse empires of the time. It was long and thin, with the Andes forming its spine and creating valleys. Abrupt mountains multiplied microclimates, where sun, wind, and rain hit different slopes in different ways (see Figure 15.1). The Inca realm encompassed coastal lowlands and the fringes of rain forest. The tribute system was based on the exchange of products between contrasting zones, as a form of insurance against disaster. When the maize of the lowlands failed, for instance, potatoes from the highlands might still be abundant. The Inca transferred populations to new locations according to the needs of the system.

However, to maintain the state, the Inca had to acquire new territories, leading to hectic and perhaps unsustainable expansion. Moreover, their methods of subjugation were extreme. For example, they extinguished the coastal civilization of Chimú (see Chapter 14) and deported its entire population. An Inca ruler was said to have drowned 20,000 enemy warriors when he conquered the Cañaris (kan-YAR-ees). The survivors became irreconcilable opponents. Many subject-peoples harbored grievances arising from memories of massacred warriors and forced migrations. Even the Incas' allies and elites were dissatisfied. The Checa, for instance, never forgave the Inca for breaking his promise to perform ritual dances at their principal shrine in acknowledgment of their alliance. The Inca never seemed

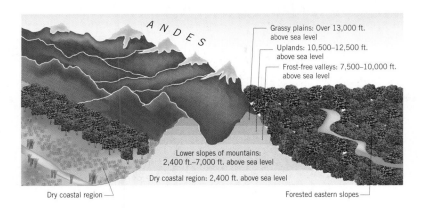

Grassy plains: Over 13,000 ft. above sea level

Uplands: 10,500–12,500 ft. above sea level

Frost-free valleys: 7,500–10,000 ft. above sea level

Lower slopes of mountains: 2,400 ft.–7,000 ft. above sea level

Dry coastal region: 2,400 ft. above sea level

Dry coastal region

Forested eastern slopes

FIGURE 15.1 MICROCLIMATES OF THE ANDES. The Andean environment packs tremendous ecological diversity into a small space, with various climatic zones at different altitudes, contrasting microclimates in the valleys, and tropical forest and the ocean close at hand.

Incas and Aztecs

ca. 1325	Aztecs found city of Tenochtitlán
ca. Mid–fifteenth century	Inca begin period of conquest and expansion
ca. Late fifteenth century	Inca Empire approaches greatest extent
ca. Early sixteenth century	Aztec Empire reaches its peak

to have enough rewards to go around. The cults of dead leaders—who lay, mummified, in expensive shrines maintained by huge pay-rolls—existed to appease key Inca clans and factions, whose resources they boosted at the state's expense because tribute had to be diverted to meet the costs. Toward the end of the fifteenth century, the Inca Empire approached its greatest extent, from Quito (KEE-toh) in what is today Ecuador in the north to what is today Chile in the south—over 1,000 miles. But at its core, the empire was shaky.

The Aztec Empire

In the same period, rapid expansion and environmental diversity characterized Mesoamerica. Here, a dynamic state grew from the city of Tenochtitlán (teh-noch-teet-LAHN) in the valley of Mexico (and some neighboring, allied cities). Tenochtitlán stood in the middle of a lake, some 5,000 feet above sea level. There was too little cultivable soil to grow enough maize and beans to feed the city. Tenochtitlán was too high and the climate too severe for cacao and cotton. Its people, whom we have traditionally called Aztecs, had only two options: poverty or warfare. They chose the latter. At its peak, the Aztec Empire stretched from the Pánuco River in the north to what is now the Mexican-Guatemalan border on the Pacific coast and encompassed hundreds of tributary communities (see Map 15.3).

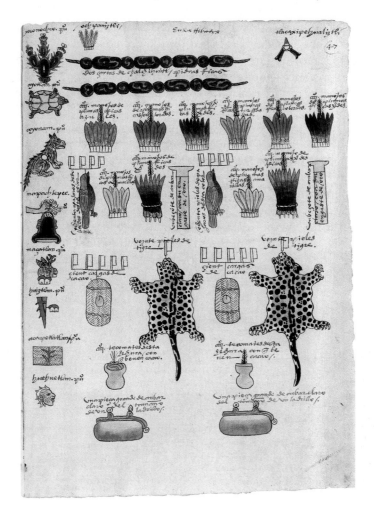

Aztec tribute. Early colonical Spanish administrators were careful to copy tribute records from the archives of the preconquest Aztec state. The records show both the complexity of the tributary networks that linked the Aztec world and the amazing environmental diversity of the regions from which tribute flowed. This folio, from the Codex Mendoza, shows the tribute due to Tenochtitlán—the Aztec capital in central Mexico—from the "hot country" near what is now the Mexican-Guatemalan border. Among the items depicted are ornamental feathers, bird skins, jaguar pelts, and jade beads.

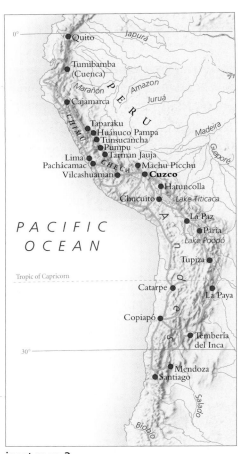

inset map 2

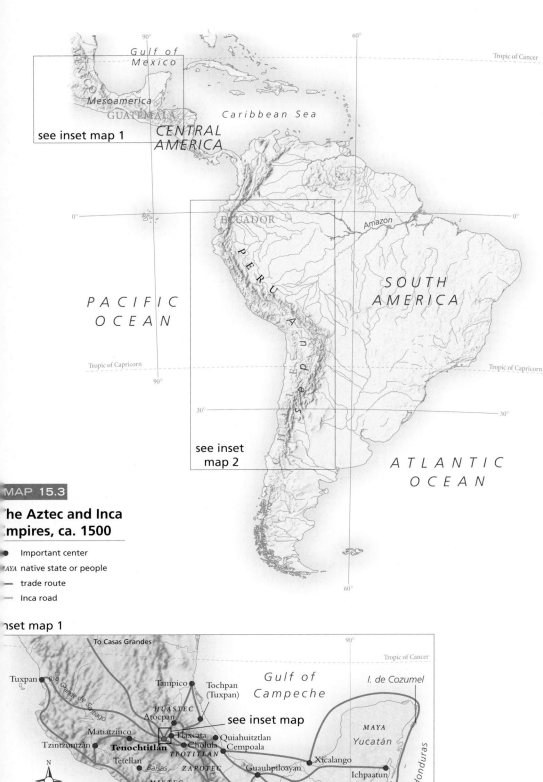

MAP 15.3

The Aztec and Inca Empires, ca. 1500

● Important center

MAYA native state or people

━ trade route

━ Inca road

nset map 1

The Valley of Mexico

○ Aztec town or city   ━ dike

━ aqueduct   marshland

━ causeway

inset map of Tenochtitlán

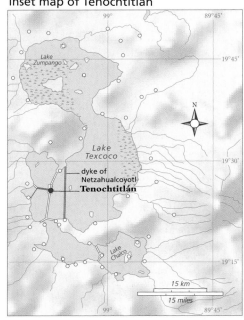

○ MAKING CONNECTIONS ○

EXPANSION AND ITS LIMITS: AFRICA AND THE AMERICAS IN THE FIFTEENTH CENTURY

REGION / STATE OR EMPIRE →	CAUSES FOR EXPANSION →	EVIDENCE / EFFECTS OF EXPANSION →	LIMITATIONS
East Africa / Ethiopia	Access to long-range trading routes to Indian Ocean via Red Sea ports	Recapture of coastal cities in 1400s, increased trade in slaves, ivory, gold, incense; creation of main access road to Indian Ocean	Limited agricultural land; need to control mountainous and lowland areas to access trade routes; major river systems to south and east with large populations; gradually encroaching Portuguese and Muslim influence by sixteenth century
East/Central Africa / Zambezi River valley, Great Zimbabwe	Difficult access to Indian Ocean seaports; large populations with ivory, gold, metal resources	Manufactured goods from Asia (porcelain, silk, etc.) traded for gold, ivory; increasingly large administrative centers in stone, large amounts of coins, jewelry, gold, etc.	Landlocked; altered trade routes; decline in navigability of rivers
West Africa / Songhay Empire	Trade routes of the Sahara, linking Mediterranean and Niger valley; astute leadership (Muhammad Askia) and alliance with Muslim clerics, scholars	Canals, dikes, reservoirs; extension of cultivable land; rich trade with Niger valley goldfields	Limited long-range communication; adverse Atlantic winds/currents
Central Africa / Kongo	Domination of Congo River; alliance with Portuguese; abundant natural resources	Use of Western firearms, Christian religion and symbols to legitimate and maintain control; trading of slaves from conquered territories to Portuguese	Ultimate loss of control over slave trade to Portuguese leads to decline and fall
South America / Inca	Diversity of environments, resources; tribute system allows exchange of products between zones	Quick expansion and use of extreme methods of control; extensive road system; large shrines for dead leaders	Mass executions and other methods of subjugation alienate subject peoples and allies
Mesoamerica / Aztecs	Environmental diversity; hundreds of tributary communities; efficient record-keeping; large array of natural resources	Intensive transformation of environment in/around capital (Tenochtitlán); abundance of commodities, both necessities (food, tools) and luxuries; widespread human sacrifice; monumental architecture	Loose administrative control; fragile alliances; alienation of tributary peoples; excessively rapid expansion

The tribute demonstrated the ecological diversity of the regions. From the "hot countries" in the south came feathers and jaguar pelts, jade, amber, gold, rubber for ritual ball games, incense, and cacao. Ornamental shells arrived from the Gulf Coast and eagles, deerskins, and tobacco from the mountain lands. The tribute system brought necessities as well as luxuries: hundreds of thousands of bushels of maize and beans every year, with hundreds of thousands of cotton garments and quilted cotton suits of armor. Finally, there was the product that best expressed Aztec power and—perhaps in Aztec minds—supplied the blood that fueled the universe: human-sacrifice victims, captured in war or tendered in tribute. In 1487, for instance, at the dedication of a temple in Tenochtitlán, thousands of captives were said to have been slaughtered at once.

Tributary networks were complex. Some communities exchanged tribute, often collecting it from some tributaries to pass part of it on to others. Tenochtitlán was at the summit of the system, but it left most communities to their own devices as long as they paid tribute. This was contrary to the interventionist politics of the Inca. According to records copied in the sixteenth century, Tenochtitlán only garrisoned or directly ruled 22 communities. But like the Incas, the Aztecs relied on fragile alliances, bore the resentment of tributary peoples, and expanded so rapidly that their reach always threatened to outrun available manpower and technology.

The Aztecs and Incas saw themselves as continuing the traditions of earlier empires: Tula and Teotihuacán for the Aztecs, Tiahuanaco for the Incas. The reach of their power seems, however, to have exceeded anything either region had witnessed before. So how did they do it? Long-range exchanges with other cultures helped to propel empires in Eurasia and Africa into expansion, but these advantages did not apply in the Americas. They did not benefit from new technology. Nor, as far as we know, were people in either region bouncing back from anything resembling the demographic catastrophe of parts of the Old World in the previous century. There was no momentum of recovery behind the enormous extensions of Aztec and Inca power. The most likely explanation is that demographic growth crossed a critical threshold in both areas. Probably, only imperial solutions could command the resources and compel the exchanges of goods needed to sustain the growing cities in which the Aztecs and Incas lived. In any case, both empires, as we shall see in the next chapter, were short-lived. They were empires of types traditional in the region and overreached the realistic limits of their potential.

The founding of Tenochtitlán

NEW EURASIAN EMPIRES

The expanding states of fifteenth-century Africa and the Americas proved relatively fragile. In the sixteenth century, European conquerors swallowed the Aztec and Inca states almost at a gulp; Ethiopia barely endured, eroded by Muslim invaders and waves of pagan, pastoralist immigrants; and Songhay fell to invaders from Morocco. Finally, though Mwene Mutapa fought off would-be conquerors from Europe, it dissolved in the 1600s into numerous petty states. It was the borderlands that straddle Europe and Asia that nurtured the really big, enduring new or resumed empires of the age, those of Turks and Russians.

The Russian Empire

The rise of a powerful Russian state was without precedent. Previously, the geography of the region produced unstable empires. Open, flat lands and scattered populations contributed to an environment in which states formed with ease but survived with difficulty. Most came and went quickly, vulnerable to external attack and internal rebellion.

In the fifteenth century, however, the rulers of Moscow established a state of imperial dimensions. Muscovy—as the early Russian Empire was called—has been exceptionally enduring. One of the features that made Muscovy different was the shape of its heartland, based on control of the Volga River, a north–south axis of trade. Earlier empires, including the Mongol, were based on the east–west axis of the steppes, which served as highways for horse-borne armies.

Muscovy's sudden take-off in the second half of the fifteenth century, when territorial conquests of neighboring peoples turned it into an imperial state, overshadowed early efforts at expansion. Indeed, when Constantinople fell to the Turks in 1453, Muscovites could see their city as, potentially, the "Third Rome," replacing Constantinople as Constantinople had replaced Rome (see Chapter 9). By the 1470s, Ivan the Great (r. 1462–1505) had absorbed most of Russia's other surviving principalities. He married a Byzantine princess, incorporated an imperial eagle into his coat of arms, forged a genealogy that traced his family back to the Roman Caesars, imported Italian technicians to fortify his palace, and dismissed an offer from the German emperor to invest him as king. "We have been sovereign in our land from our earliest forefathers," he replied, "and we hold our sovereignty from God."

During his reign, Ivan the Great more than trebled the territory he ruled—to over 240,000 square miles (see Map 15.4). His realm also took a new shape around most of the length of the Volga, uniting the fur-rich north and the cash-rich fringes of Asia. Fur was the "black gold" of the north, inducing Russians to conquest and colonization, just as gold and spices lured other European peoples to Africa and the East.

War parties gathered pelts as tribute along a northern route that missionaries pioneered in the late fourteenth century. Repeatedly from 1465, Ivan sent expeditions to the rivers Perm and Ob to levy tribute. The expedition of 1499 numbered 4,000 men, equipped with sleds drawn by reindeer and dogs. They crossed the Ob in winter, returning with 1,000 captives from the forest-dwelling peoples who hunted for the furs. Ivan's ambassador to the rich Italian duchy of Milan boasted that his master received 1,000 gold ducats' worth of tribute annually in furs—five or six times an Italian nobleman's income.

Timurids and the Ottoman Empire

In the early fifteenth century, Turkish—and therefore Muslim—expansion resumed in southern Europe and Asia, under the leadership of the Ottoman dynasty. The Mongol supremacy had shattered the reputation of Muslim armies and inspired the religious minded to withdraw from the world in a spirit of resignation. The Black Death had also battered the Islamic world. Muslims' numerical preponderance over Christians never got back to earlier levels. But, for global history, the Islamic recovery is a much bigger story than the temporary setback.

To understand recovery, we turn to one of its most brilliant Muslim observers after the Black Death, the historian Ibn Khaldun (ihb ihn-hahl-DOON). In 1377, he began to write one of the most admired works of all time on history and political philosophy, the *Muqaddimah*. Its theme was the counterpoint of herder and tiller, which Ibn Khaldun saw as the motivating force of historical change. Everywhere in his day, Islamic survival and success depended on Muslims' ability to tame the invaders from the deserts and the steppes, and turn their power to the service of Islam. Most Turkic peoples and many Mongols were converted into warriors for Islam. Consequently, Central Asia stayed Muslim, and the Indian Ocean linked mainly Muslim shores. In other words, the Silk Roads and maritime routes of Eurasia had to pass through Muslim-ruled territory. Human fuel also renewed the Islamic world's capacity to wage war and expand its frontiers.

 from the *Muqaddimah* by Ibn Khaldun

MAP 15.4

The Russian Empire, ca. 1505

Russian Empire

routes used by fur traders

fur

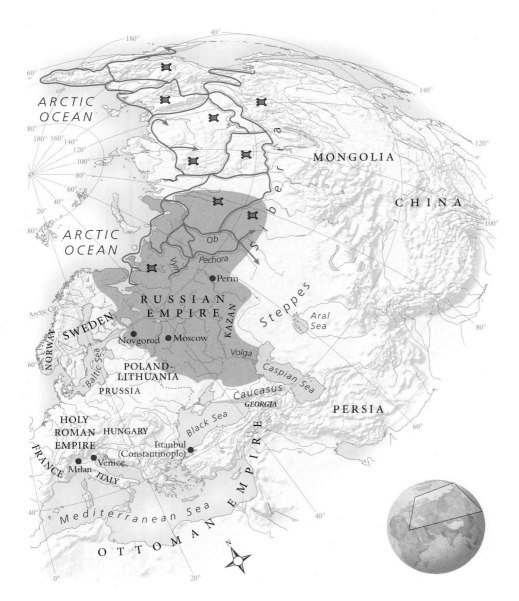

The most conspicuous mobilizer of steppeland manpower in Muslim service in the late fourteenth and early fifteenth centuries was the self-proclaimed "world conqueror," Timur (tee-MOOR) the Lame. His court historian represented him as "the being nearest to perfection" and a pious devotee of holy war, but his role models were Alexander the Great (see Chapter 5) and Genghis Khan.

When Turkic nobles rebelled against their Mongol masters in his homeland, Timur emerged as their leader. By the time he died in 1406, he had conquered Iran, halted the Ottomans, invaded Syria and India, and planned the conquest of China (see Map 15.5). Wherever he went, he heaped up the skulls of citizens unwise enough to resist his sieges. But this destruction was for efficiency, not for its own sake. It made most conquests submit cheaply. His success seemed decreed by God: "Almighty God has subjugated the world to my domination, and the will of the Creator has entrusted the countries of the Earth to my power."

The day after his death, as his heirs turned on one another, his achievements seemed transitory. Even today, Timur's impact on the Islamic world is usually seen as

 A contemporary describes Timur

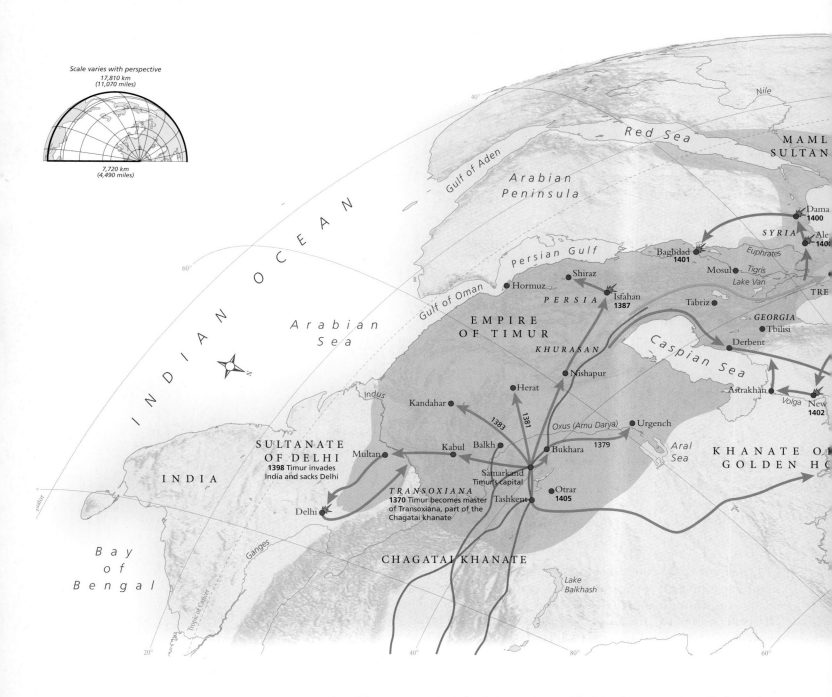

Scale varies with perspective
17,810 km
(11,070 miles)

7,720 km
(4,490 miles)

Nile

Red Sea

MAML
SULTAN

Gulf of Aden

*Arabian
Peninsula*

Dama
1400

SYRIA

Ale
140

Persian Gulf

Baghdad
1401

Euphrates

Shiraz

Mosul

Tigris
Lake Van

Hormuz

PERSIA

Isfahan
1387

Tabriz

TRE

GEORGIA

Tbilisi

I N D I A N   O C E A N

Gulf of Oman

EMPIRE
OF TIMUR

KHURASAN

Derbent

Caspian Sea

*Arabian
Sea*

Nishapur

Astrakhan

Indus

Herat

Volga New
1402

Kandahar

1383

1381

Oxus (Amu Darya) Urgench

*Aral
Sea*

KHANATE O
GOLDEN HO

SULTANATE
OF DELHI
1398 Timur invades
India and sacks Delhi

Multan

Kabul

Balkh

Bukhara

1379

I N D I A

Samarkand
Timur's capital

TRANSOXIANA
1370 Timur becomes master
of Transoxiana, part of the
Chagatai khanate

Tashkent

Otrar
1405

Delhi

*B a y
o f
B e n g a l*

Ganges

CHAGATAI KHANATE

*Lake
Balkhash*

negative. His success against the Ottomans gave Christendom a reprieve. By humbling
the Mongols, he encouraged Christians in Russia. By weakening the Muslim sultans of
Delhi, he liberated millions of Hindus. These reflections, however, overlook his psychological legacy. He was a champion of Islamic orthodoxy and exerted great influence
as a patron of Muslim education. He is also an example of the process that converted
pastoralists. Having been the scourge of the Islamic world, they became its sword.

MAP 15.5

Timur and the Ottomans, ca. 1370–1500

- Empire of Timur, 1405
- Ottoman Empire, 1500
- Mamluk Sultanate
- Silk Road
- ROMANIA modern-day country

Campaigns of Timur: 1379–1405

- against Persia 1379–1388
- against Golden Horde 1388–1391 and 1395
- against sultanate of Delhi 1398–1399
- against Mamluk Sultanate and Baghdad 1399–1401
- against Ottomans 1402
- city sacked by Timur, with date

Timur was like a hurricane—his force soon spent. The Ottomans were more like a monsoon—their armies returned and receded as each season came and went, but they constantly made new conquests. The fate of the Mongols—expelled from China, retreating from Russia—shows how hard it was for a great Eurasian empire to survive in the aftermath of the Black Death, which jarred economies and felled manpower. Yet, the Ottoman Empire managed to do so.

A Turkish fleet at anchor off Toulon, in southern France, in 1543, from a chronicle written to celebrate the wide-ranging campaigns of Sultan Suleiman the Magnificent (r. 1520–1566). The Ottomans were able to wage naval war in the western Mediterranean, thanks to the many harbors along the North African coast controlled by Muslim chiefs who were subjects of the sultans.

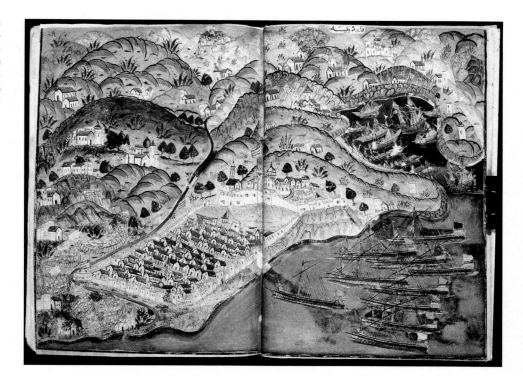

The Ottomans' great advantage was location. The heartlands of the empire were at the crossroads of some of the world's great trade routes, where the Silk Roads, the Indian Ocean routes, the Volga, the Danube, and the Mediterranean almost converged (see Map 15.5). The history of the Byzantine Empire showed the importance of holding on to this location. Byzantium flourished while it occupied these lands, faltered when its control there slackened and ceased (see Chapter 12). From their own past, the Ottomans inherited the traditions of steppeland imperialism. They were content, at first, to levy tribute and allow their tributaries to govern themselves or to exist as puppet states, manipulated according to Ottoman needs.

Gradually, they adapted to the environments they conquered, agrarian, urban, and maritime. Other empires of nomadic origins failed when required to adapt to new military technologies, but the Ottomans' readily became a gunpowder empire. Their forces could blow away cavalry or batter down city walls. They even took to the sea. In the 1390s, the sultans began to build fleets, and by the end of the fifteenth century, the Ottomans had overturned the 400-year-old Christian maritime supremacy in the Mediterranean. Never since Rome defeated Carthage (see Chapter 7) had such an unlikely candidate become a naval power.

Like other steppeland imperialists, the Ottomans mastered the art of keeping subjects of diverse religions loyal to them. They tolerated Jews, Christians, and Shiites but levied punitive taxes on these minorities. On Christians, they imposed a levy of male child slaves, who were brought up as Muslims to form the **Janissaries**, an elite corps of the armed forces, and staff the ranks of the administration. The system provided servants for the state and converts for Islam, while keeping Christian communities in submission. From the 1420s, the sultan functioned as head of two linked systems of law and justice. The first consisted of secular laws and customs that the sultan's appointees administered. The second was enshrined in the Quran and the traditions of Islamic law, with a body of experts to run it, who met in the sultan's palace.

In 1451, Mehmet (MEH-meht) II became sultan at the age of 19. His predecessors had prudently allowed self-rule to continue in the city of Constantinople and its few surviving dependencies—the last fragments of the Byzantine Empire that still proclaimed itself the heir of Rome. The Ottomans controlled what happened in Constantinople with threats and bribes. But some factions in the city were determined to challenge the Turks and formed an alliance with Western Christendom. Mehmet laid siege to Constantinople. He built huge forts to command the sea approaches to the city and fired the heaviest artillery ever made at its walls. He transported ships overland to elude Byzantine defenses. In the end, weight of numbers was decisive. The last Byzantine emperor fell fighting.

With the fall of Constantinople in 1453, Mehmet II could see his empire as a continuation of Rome. He chose Italians to paint his portrait, sculpt his medals, and write some of his propaganda. The direction of Ottoman conquests tilted toward Europe as Mehmet extended his territory into most of what are now Greece, Romania, and Bosnia, seeking to control the shores of the Adriatic and Black Seas.

THE LIMITATIONS OF CHINESE IMPERIALISM

So Ottoman imperialism in the fifteenth century resumed its former course after setbacks caused by the Black Death and the rise of Timur. An observer at the time might have predicted that China, too, would resume expansion and bid for a maritime empire. The best way to understand why such developments seemed likely—and why they were frustrated—is to look back at China's recovery from the mid–fourteenth-century plagues. Like so many decisive episodes of Chinese history, the story begins among the people on whose labor and manpower the empire depended: peasants.

The Yellow River. This pictorial map of the Yellow River is both an artistic masterpiece and a scientific source of information. Ten famous painters representing China's northern and southern schools of art worked on it. Ordered by the first emperor of the Ming Dynasty (1368–1644), the map was drawn to an exact scale and was an invaluable tool to assess the impact of the frequently flooded Yellow River. The houses in the map indicate the population of cities, with each house representing 100 families.

Peasants sometimes defer hope and waiting for the millennium—a fabled future, when divine intervention will either perfect the world or end it. Often, however, in times of extreme disaster, peasant movements arise to try to trigger the millennium. One of the most explosive of all such movements began among Chinese canal workers in 1350.

In mid–fourteenth-century China, peasants were the victims of the slow-grinding effects of economic misery and the survivors of environmental disasters. The plagues that began in the 1320s kept on returning. Not until well into the 1350s did the plagues begin to lose their virulence or to encounter naturally immunized populations. In 1344, the Yellow River flooded. Droughts followed. In this setting, peasants were forced to repair the Grand Canal, which carried essential food supplies from southern and central China to Beijing.

The peasants' hope of deliverance was based on a Buddhist myth. The lord Maitreya, the last of the earthly Buddhas, would come to prepare the world for extinction. Now, however, given the peasants' miserable lives, the myth acquired a political edge. Maitreya would put a triumphant end to the struggle of good against evildoers and give his followers power over their oppressors. A similar movement was current at the same time in Western Europe, where the Fraticelli, a group of Franciscans, identified with the needs of the wretched of the Earth. Fulfilling the biblical prophecy uttered by the mother of Jesus, which the prayers of the church repeated every day, a cosmic hero would put down the mighty from their seat and exalt the humble and meek.

In China, along with their desire for deliverance, peasants harbored a folk memory of the Song dynasty (see Chapter 12) and a hankering for the good times supposed to have preceded the Mongol invasions of a century before. Peasant revolts are often revolutionary in the most literal sense of the word, wanting to turn the world back, "revolve" it full circle, to an imagined or misremembered golden age. Therefore, when the Mongol rulers executed a pretender to the throne who claimed to be the heir of the Song in 1351, his followers rebelled and recruited thousands to their cause.

The leader who emerged from the rebellion was Zhu Yuanzhang (joo yoo-ehn-jhang). By the end of the 1350s, the empire in the Yangtze region had dissolved into a chaos of small states run by similar upstarts. In river warfare of reckless daring, Zhu conquered his rivals and proclaimed a new dynasty in 1368.

Zhu cleverly managed the coalition that had brought him to power. To please the Confucian establishment, he restored ancient ceremonies and the examinations for public service. He kept the military command structure. He renounced the cult of Maitreya, but only after making it clear that he had fulfilled it in his own person by adopting the name "Ming" for his dynasty. The word, which means bright, was traditionally used to describe the lord Maitreya.

Zhu had the self-educated man's contempt for academics. But he recognized that the Confucian bureaucrats had expertise he could use. He therefore kept the traditional power centers of his court in balance: the military top brass, the eunuchs who ran the imperial household, the foreign and Muslim advisers and technicians, the Buddhist and Daoist clergies, and the merchant lobby. Combined, they limited the power of the Confucian elite.

The result was a brief period when expansionist policies prevailed over Confucian caution. Zhu's son, the Yongle (yuhng-leh) emperor (r. 1402–1424), sought contact with the world beyond the empire. He meddled in the politics of China's southern neighbors in Vietnam and enticed the Japanese to trade.

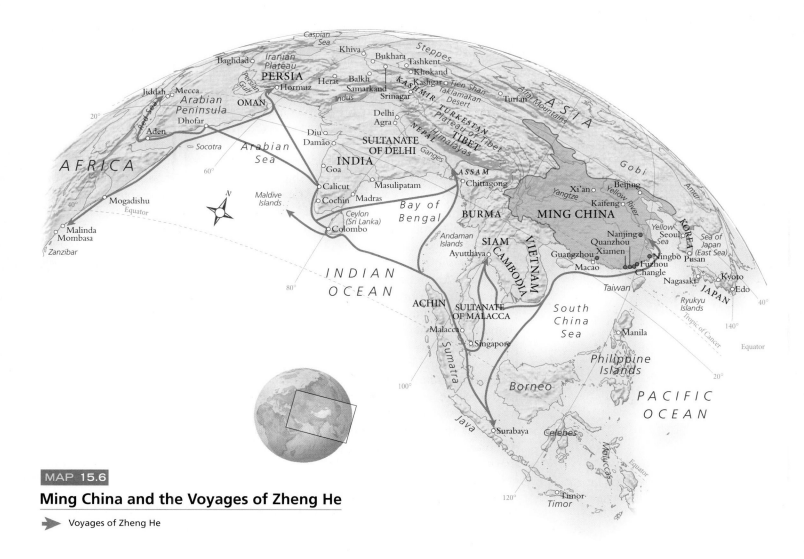

MAP 15.6

Ming China and the Voyages of Zheng He

➤ Voyages of Zheng He

The most spectacular manifestation of the new outward-looking policy was the career of the Muslim eunuch-admiral, Zheng He (jehng heh). In 1405, he led the first of a series of naval expeditions, which was intended in part, at least, to show China's flag all over the Indian Ocean (see Map 15.6). He replaced unacceptable rulers in Java, Sumatra, and Sri Lanka, founded a puppet state on the commercially important strait of Malacca, and gathered tribute from Bengal. He displayed Chinese power as far away as Jiddah, on the Red Sea coast of Arabia and as far south as the island of Zanzibar in East Africa.

Can Zheng He's voyages be called an imperial venture? Their official purpose was to pursue a fugitive pretender to the Chinese throne—but that would not have required such vast expeditions to such distant places. The Chinese called the vessels treasure ships and emphasized what they called tribute gathering (in the more distant spots Zheng He's ships visited, what happened was more like an exchange). Commercial objectives may have been involved. Almost all the places Zheng He visited had long been important in Chinese trade. In part, the voyages were scientific missions:

The Early Ming Dynasty

1350s	Yangtze region dissolves into small warring states
1368	Zhu Yuanzhang founds Ming dynasty
1405	Zheng He leads first naval expedition
1425	Hongxi emperor succeeds to throne; Zheng He's voyages cancelled; Confucian values ascendant

From Ma Huan, *The Overall Survey of the Ocean's Shores*

Ma Huan, Zheng He's interpreter, called his own book on the subject *The Overall Survey of the Ocean's Shores*, and improved maps and data on the plants, animals, and peoples of the regions visited were among the expeditions' fruits. But flag showing is always, to some extent, about power or, at least, prestige. And the aggressive intervention Zheng He made in some places demonstrates that the extension or reinforcement of China's image and influence was part of the project.

Indeed, it is hard to see how else the huge investment the state made in his enterprise could have been justified. Zheng He's expeditions were on a crushing scale. His ships were much bigger than anything European navies could float at the time. His first fleet was said to comprise 66 junks of the largest ever built, 225 support vessels, and 27,870 men. The seventh voyage—probably the longest in reach—sailed 12,618 miles. The voyages lasted on average over two years each. Silly claims have been made for Zheng He's voyages. Ships of his fleet did not sail beyond the limits of the Indian Ocean—much less discover America or Antarctica. His achievements, however, demonstrated China's potential to become the center of an enormous maritime empire.

But the Chinese naval effort could not last. Historians have debated why it was abandoned. In many ways, it was to the credit of Chinese decision makers that they pulled back from involvement in costly adventures far from home. Most powers that have undertaken such expeditions and attempted to impose their rule on distant countries have had cause to regret it. Confucian values included giving priority to good government at home. "Barbarians" would submit to Chinese rule if and when they saw the benefits. Attempting to beat or coax them into submission was a waste of resources. By consolidating their landward empire and refraining from seaborne imperialism, China's rulers ensured the longevity of their state. All the maritime empires founded in the world in the last 500 years have crumbled. China is still there.

Part of the context of the decision to abort Zheng He's missions is clear. The examination system and the gradual discontinuation of other forms of recruitment for public service had serious implications. Increasingly scholars, with their indifference to expansion, and gentlemen, with their contempt for trade, governed China. In the 1420s and 1430s, the balance of power at court shifted in the bureaucrats' favor, away from the Buddhists, eunuchs, Muslims, and merchants who had supported Zheng He. When the Hongxi (huhng-jher) emperor succeeded to the throne in 1425, one of his first acts was to cancel Zheng He's next voyage. He restored Confucian office holders, whom the Yongle emperor had dismissed, and curtailed the power of other factions. In 1429, the shipbuilding budget was cut almost to extinction. The scholar-elite hated overseas adventures and the factions that favored them so much that they destroyed all Zheng He's records to obliterate his memory. Moreover, China's land frontiers became insecure as Mongol power revived. China needed to turn toward the new threat. The state never resumed overseas expansion. Trade and colonization in southeast Asia were left to merchants and migrants. China, the empire best equipped for maritime imperialism, opted out. Consequently, lesser powers, including those of Europe, were able to exploit opportunities in seas that Chinese power vacated.

By the late fifteenth century, the scholars' position seemed unshakable, and the supremacy of Confucian values could not be challenged. The Hongxi emperor aspired to Confucian perfection. He ordered the slaughter or expulsion of court magicians and exiled 1,000 Buddhist and Daoist monks. He resumed a Confucian priority: study of the penal code, which previous Ming emperors had neglected. He reintroduced the palace lectures, during which Confucian professors instructed the emperor. He endowed a library alongside the Confucian temple at the sage's birthplace in Qufu (shoo-foo) and patronized artists whose work radiated Confucian serenity.

THE BEGINNINGS OF OCEANIC IMPERIALISM

Even under the Yongle emperor, China confined its seaward reach to the monsoonal seas of maritime Asia and the Indian Ocean—seas of terrible hazards and fabulous rewards. As we have seen, the Indian Ocean was relatively easy to cross but relatively hard to enter or exit. For most of history, therefore, it was the preserve of peoples whose homes bordered it or who traveled overland—like some European and Armenian traders—to become part of its world. Moreover, all the trade was internal. Merchants took no interest in venturing far beyond the monsoon system to reach other markets or supplies.

From Europe, however, access to the Indian Ocean was well worth seeking. Merchants craved a share of the richest trades and most prosperous markets in the world, especially the spices, drugs, and aromatics that came from Sri Lanka, India, and what is now Indonesia. These products, sold to rich buyers in China, southwest Asia, and Europe, were the most profitable in the world. Many Europeans sought to find out where they came from and take part in the trades. But the journey was too long, laborious, and hazardous to generate much profit. From the Mediterranean, merchants had either to travel up the Nile and proceed by camel caravan to a Red Sea port, or negotiate a dangerous passage through the Ottoman Empire to the Persian Gulf. In either case, they obviously could not take ships with them. This was a potentially fatal limitation because Europeans had little to offer to people in the Indian Ocean basin except shipping services. Until the 1490s, Europeans were unsure whether it was possible to approach the Indian Ocean by sea at all.

Europe's only effective access by sea to the rest of the world is along its western seaboard, into the Atlantic. For the Atlantic to become Europe's highway to the rest of the world, explorers had to discover the winds that led to commercially important destinations. There were, first, the northeast trade winds, which led to the resource-rich, densely populated regions of the New World, far south of the lands the Norse reached. There was also the South Atlantic wind system, which led, by way of the southeast trade winds and the westerlies of the far south, to the Indian Ocean (see Map 15.7).

The technology to exploit the Atlantic's wind systems only gradually became available during a period of long, slow improvements to hulls, rigging, and water casks in the thirteenth, fourteenth, and fifteenth centuries. Historians have emphasized the contribution of formal science in developing maritime charts and instruments for navigating by the stars. Now it seems that these innovations were irrelevant. No practical navigator of this period in Europe seems to have used them.

Only the long accumulation of information and experience could make a breakthrough possible. Several attempts were made during the fifteenth century to explore Atlantic space, but most doomed themselves to failure by setting out in the belt of westerly winds. Presumably explorers chose this route because they wanted to be sure that they would be able to get home. Shortly after 1450, the westernmost islands of the Azores were reached. Over the next three decades, the Portuguese crown often commissioned voyages of exploration farther into the Atlantic, but none is known to have made any further progress.

Not only was exploitation of the Atlantic slow, it yielded, at first, few returns. In the 1480s, however, the situation changed, and Atlantic exploration began to

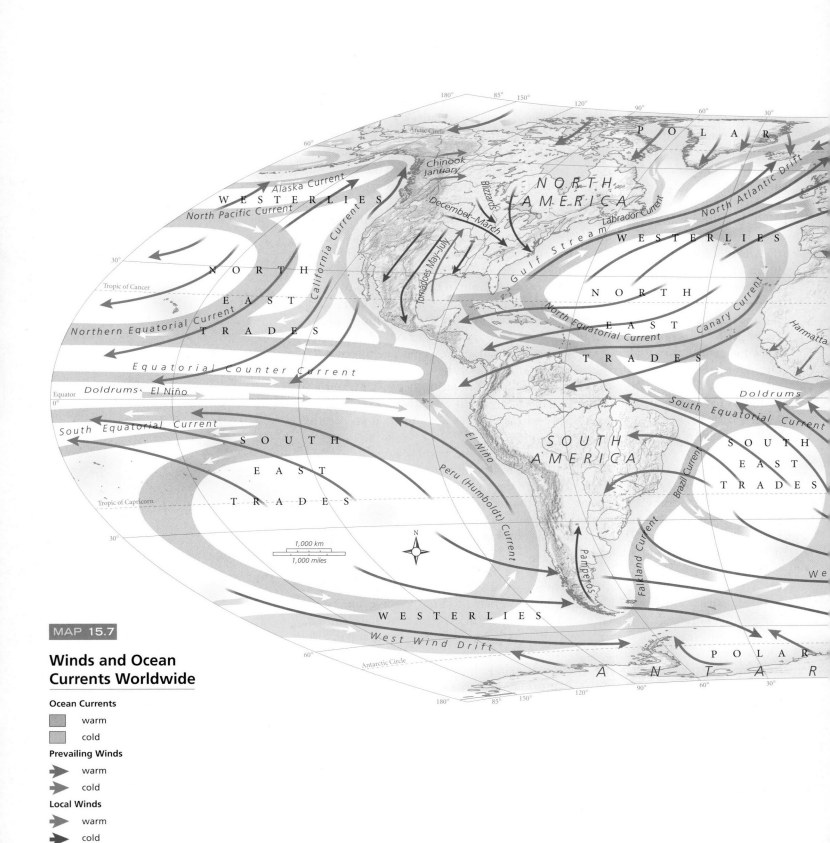

MAP 15.7

Winds and Ocean Currents Worldwide

Ocean Currents
warm
cold

Prevailing Winds
warm
cold

Local Winds
warm
cold

POLAR

NORTH AMERICA

Arctic Circle

Chinook January

Blizzards

December–March

Tornadoes May–July

WESTERLIES

Alaska Current

North Pacific Current

NORTH

EAST

TRADES

Tropic of Cancer

Northern Equatorial Current

Equatorial Counter Current

Doldrums · El Niño

Equator 0°

South Equatorial Current

SOUTH

EAST

TRADES

Tropic of Capricorn

30°

60°

1,000 km

1,000 miles

N

WESTERLIES

West Wind Drift

Antarctic Circle

California Currents

Gulf Stream

Labrador Current

North Atlantic Drift

WESTERLIES

NORTH

EAST

TRADES

North Equatorial Current

Canary Current

Harmatta

Doldrums

South Equatorial Current

SOUTH

EAST

TRADES

SOUTH AMERICA

El Niño

Peru (Humboldt) Current

Pamperos

Falkland Current

Brazil Current

We

POLAR

ANTAR

ANTAR

180° 85° 150° 120° 90° 60° 30°

60°

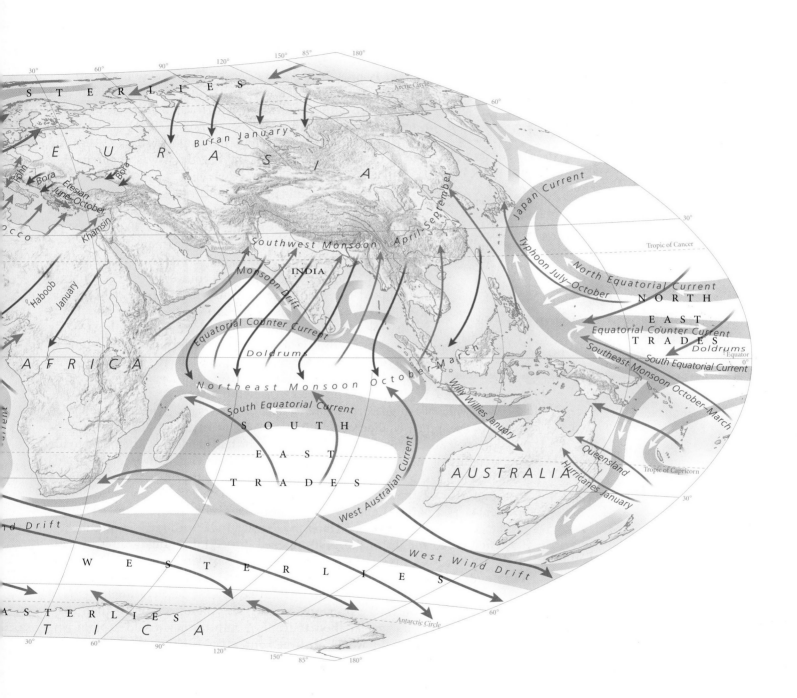

STERLIES
EURASIA
Arctic Circle
60°
30°
60°
90°
120°
150°
85°
180°
Buran January
Japan Current
ohn
Bora
Bora
Eresian
June–October
occo
Khamsin
Southwest Monsoon
April–September
Tropic of Cancer
Typhoon July–October
North Equatorial Current
NORTH
Haboob
January
Monsoon Drift
INDIA
EAST
Equatorial Counter Current
Equatorial Counter Current
TRADES
Doldrums
AFRICA
Doldrums
Equator
Northeast Monsoon October–March
South Equatorial Current
Southeast Monsoon October–March
South Equatorial Current
SOUTH
Willy Willies January
EAST
West Australian Current
AUSTRALIA
Tropic of Capricorn
TRADES
Queensland
Hurricanes January
30°
d Drift
West Wind Drift
WESTERLIES
WESTERLIES
Antarctic Circle
60°
ASTERLIES
TICA
30°
60°
90°
120°
150°
85°
180°

The Beginnings of European Oceanic Imperialism

Tenth and eleventh centuries	Norse explore North Atlantic
Thirteenth and fifteenth centuries	Europeans make advances in maritime technology and knowledge
1430s	Portuguese establish way stations in Azores
1440s	Portuguese begin to obtain West African slaves
1450–1480	Portuguese crown commissions voyages of exploration of the Atlantic
1482	Portuguese found trading station of Saõ Jorge da Mina on West African coast
1484	Sugar production begins in Canary Islands
1492–1493	First voyage of Christopher Columbus
1496	John Cabot discovers direct route across North Atlantic
1497–1498	Vasco da Gama rounds Cape of Good Hope
1500	Vasco da Gama reaches India

pay off. In the North Atlantic, customs records of the English port of Bristol indicate that quantities of whaling products, salt fish, and walrus ivory from the ocean increased dramatically. In West Africa, in 1482, Portuguese traders opened a new post at São Jorge da Mina that was close to goldfields in the Volta River valley. Large amounts of gold now began to reach European hands. In 1484, sugar production at last began in the Canary Islands. In the same decade, Portuguese made contact with the Kingdom of Kongo. Although voyages toward and around the southernmost tip of Africa encountered unremittingly adverse currents, they also showed that the far south of the Atlantic had westerly winds that might at last lead to the Indian Ocean. By the end of the decade, it was apparent that Atlantic investment could yield dividends.

As a result of gains made in the 1480s, the 1490s were a breakthrough-decade in Europe's efforts to reach out across the ocean to the rest of the world (see Map 15.8). In 1492–1493, Christopher Columbus, with finance from Italian bankers in Seville and political backing from the Spanish monarchs, discovered fast, reliable routes across the Atlantic that linked the Mediterranean and the Caribbean. In 1496, John Cabot, another Italian adventurer, backed by merchants in Bristol and the English crown, discovered a direct route across the North Atlantic, using variable springtime winds to get across and the westerlies to get back. His route, however, was not reliable and, for over 100 years, was mainly used to reach the cod fisheries of Newfoundland.

Meanwhile, Portuguese missions sought to determine whether the Indian Ocean was genuinely landlocked. In 1497–1498, a Portuguese trading venture, commissioned by the crown and probably financed by Italian bankers, attempted to use the westerlies of the South Atlantic to reach the Indian Ocean. Its leader, Vasco da Gama, turned east too early and had to struggle around the Cape of Good Hope at the tip of Africa. But he managed to get across the Indian Ocean anyway and reach the pepper-rich port of Calicut at the tip of India. The next voyage, in 1500, managed to avoid the Cape of Good Hope and to reach India without a serious hitch.

The breakthroughs of the 1490s opened direct, long-range routes of maritime trade across the world between Europe, Asia, and Africa. Success may seem sudden, but not if we view it against the background of slow developments in European chronology and knowledge and the accelerating benefits of Atlantic exploration in the previous decade. Was there more to it than that? Was there something special about European culture that would explain why Europeans discovered the world-girdling routes, linking the Old World to the New and the Indian Ocean to the Atlantic, rather than explorers from other cultures? Some European historians have argued just that—that Europeans had something others lacked.

Such a suggestion, however, seems ill conceived. Compared to the peoples of maritime Asia, Europeans were slow to launch long-range voyages. Moreover, the breakthrough explorations were not the work of "Europe" but of people from a few communities on the Atlantic seaboard and in the Mediterranean. What distinguishes them is not that they set off with the right kind of culture, but that they set off from the right place.

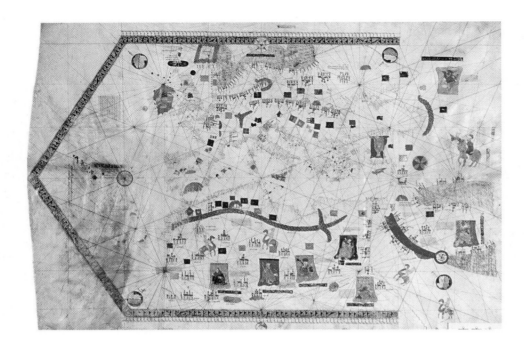

The Azores. The Atlantic voyage of Diogo de Silves of 1427 was unrecorded, except on this map, made in Majorca in 1439. The Azores, which Silves sailed around, can be seen on the extreme left, alongside the traces of a stain made when the famous French novelist, George Sand, spilled an ink pot when examining the map while on a vacation on Majorca with her lover, the composer Frédéric Chopin, in 1838–1839.

THE EUROPEAN OUTLOOK: PROBLEMS AND PROMISE

Western Europe in the fifteenth century was beset with problems. Recovery from the disasters of the fourteenth century was slow. Plagues remained frequent. Though used to the more severe climate, Western Europeans did not reoccupy the high ground and distant colonies that they had vacated in the fourteenth century. In most places, population probably had not reached levels attained before the Black Death. Food supplies were unreliable. Harvests frequently failed.

But hard times created opportunities for those with the skill or luck to exploit them. High mortality opened gaps in elites, which bureaucrats could fill, thanks, in part, to a revolution in government. To legitimize the newcomers' power, Western moralists redefined nobility as the product of virtue or education rather than ancestry.

New economic divisions appeared. The line of the Elbe and northern Danube Rivers and the lands between became a cultural fault line. To the west of this line, underpopulation boosted the value of labor. The effects were to liberate peasants and urban communities from landowners' control, split up landholdings, encourage tenancies, and convert cropland to pasture. In the east the opposite occurred. Landholders responded to the loss of manpower and revenue by clamping down on peasants' rights and forcing towns into submission. New definitions of nobility were rejected. East of the Bohemian forest, nobility was ancient blood or acquired "by martial discipline," and that was that.

Nevertheless, Western Europe showed signs of self-confidence and optimism. Scholars and artists pursued, with renewed vigor, the project of recovering the legacy of the cultural achievements of ancient Greece and Rome. The movement is commonly called "**the Renaissance**" on the grounds that the civilization of classical antiquity was reborn—but scholarship has now identified renaissances in almost every century for the previous 1,000 years. No radically new departure occurred in the fifteenth century from what had gone before—merely

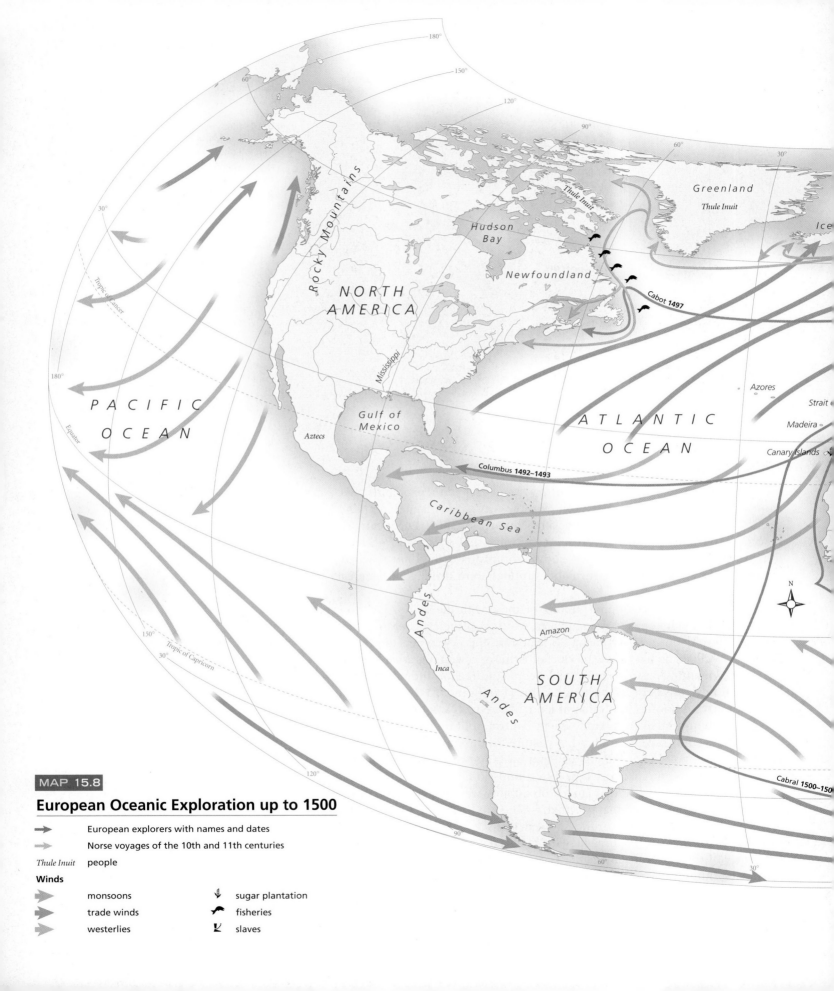

Greenland

Thule Inuit

Thule Inuit

Ice[

Hudson
Bay

Newfoundland

Cabot 1497

Rocky Mountains

NORTH
AMERICA

Mississippi

Gulf of
Mexico

Aztecs

Caribbean Sea

Columbus 1492–1493

PACIFIC
OCEAN

Equator

Tropic of Cancer

ATLANTIC
OCEAN

Azores

Strait

Madeira

Canary Islands

Andes

Amazon

Inca

SOUTH
AMERICA

Andes

Tropic of Capricorn

N

Cabral 1500–150

MAP 15.8

European Oceanic Exploration up to 1500

→ European explorers with names and dates

→ Norse voyages of the 10th and 11th centuries

Thule Inuit people

Winds

→ monsoons   ⚓ sugar plantation

→ trade winds   🐟 fisheries

→ westerlies   ⚒ slaves

an accentuation of long-accumulating tendencies. Humanist students adopted a predominantly secular curriculum: grammar, rhetoric, poetry, history, and moral philosophy, imbibed mainly from classical texts. The classics as well as—even, instead of—Christianity came to inform common ideas of morality, politics, and taste. Spreading, at first, from a few French and north Italian schools, **humanism** gradually became Europe's most prestigious form of learning. Political thinkers turned back to Greek and Roman history for instruction. Religious innovators modeled their ideas on evidence from early Christianity. Artists adopted realism and perspective from what they thought were Greek and Roman models.

Florence demonstrates humanism's power and limitations. In the fifteenth century, classical taste transformed the art and architecture of this Italian city. Comparisons with the Roman republic inspired its citizens to think of themselves as free and self-governing. Yet power gradually fell into the hands of a single family, the Medici, who patronized art in the classical tradition but who actually spent more on jewels and artworks that could display their wealth. When they were temporarily overthrown in 1494, after their banking business collapsed, the state that replaced them was no Roman-style republic. Rather, it was the rule of a "godly" clique, inspired by a hell-fire preacher, who preferred piety to humanism. Botticelli (1444–1510), the great artist who had painted pagan erotica for a Medici villa, turned to biblical subjects.

Still, across Europe, the rise of humanism had lasting consequences. Humanists painstakingly scrutinized the Bible and the historical traditions of the church, exposing incorrect translations and departures from the practices of early Christianity. New styles in church architecture reflected classical taste and, more deeply, arose from the desire to create a setting for the kind of devotion that humanism inspired. Open sanctuaries, brilliantly lit and approached through wide naves and aisles, allowed worshippers to see and take part in events at the altar.

Humanism also helped arouse European interest in the wider world. In the early fifteenth century, the work of the ancient Greek scholar Ptolemy, originally written in Alexandria in the second century, invited intense speculation about geography, mapping the world, and the limits of exploration. The first-century B.C.E. work of Strabo, a Greek geographer, prompted questions about finding unknown continents. Humanists' fascination with the history of language reinforced the search for "primitive" peoples who might cast light on the question of how language originated.

Chivalry, however, was more important than humanism in stimulating overseas exploration. **Chivalry** could not, perhaps, make men good, as it was supposed to do. It could, however, win wars. In 1492, for instance, the monarchs of the Spanish kingdom of Castile extended the frontier of Christendom by conquering Granada, the last Muslim kingdom in Spain, in "a beautiful war," said the Venetian ambassador. "There was not a lord present who was not enamored of some

The four elements. In the fourth century B.C.E., Aristotle proposed that all matter is composed of four elements—earth, water, air, and fire—and exhibits different combinations of four qualities—moist, dry, hot, and cold. Over 1,800 years later, as this fifteenth-century illustration demonstrates, people in the West still believed in this theory. The artist shows the Earth as a sphere, with one large landmass emerging from an encircling ocean. Earth, "cold and dry," is surrounded by water, "cold and moist," and air, "hot and moist." The fourth element, fire, "hot and dry," forms an outer ring.

lady," who "often handed warriors their weapons ... with a request that they show their love by their deeds." The queen of Castile died uttering prayers to the Archangel Michael as "prince of the chivalry of angels."

The typical chivalrous hero of the time took to the sea, conquered an island, married a princess, and became a ruler. Explorers—often men of humble social origins—tried to embody these fictions in real life. Adventurers in the service of the Portuguese Prince Henry (1394–1460) included former pirates and violent criminals. They indulged in chivalric rituals and gave themselves storybook names, like Lancelot and Tristram of the Island. They also colonized the Madeira Islands and parts of the Azores, and explored the coast of West Africa as far as Sierra Leone. The commercial sector that helped to back overseas adventures was looking for new opportunities—especially the Genoese, whose role in the eastern Mediterranean at this period was largely confined to high-bulk, low-profit shipping and trading. Marginal noblemen, shut out from advancement at home and imbued with chivalric ideas, were willing to take amazing risks. That, plus the availability of high-risk investment, helps to explain many early forays in Atlantic exploration.

Prince Henry himself—traditionally misrepresented as a navigator motivated by scientific curiosity—imagined himself a romantic hero, destined to win a kingdom of his own. The truth is that he never went exploring, and his desperate efforts to make enough money to pay his retainers included slave raiding and a soap monopoly. His followers included the father-in-law of Christopher Columbus, a weaver by training who reinvented himself as a "captain of cavaliers and conquests," and who took to exploration to escape the restricted social opportunities of home.

Alongside chivalry, millenarian fantasies may have influenced overseas expansion. The first king of Portugal's ruling dynasty was actually called "Messiah of Portugal." Columbus claimed that the profits of his discoveries could be used to conquer Jerusalem and help complete God's plans for a new age. Franciscan friars who supported Columbus believed that an "Age of the Holy Spirit," which would precede the end of the world, was coming soon, and some of them came to see the New World as the place where such an age might begin.

Europe's outreach into the Atlantic was probably not the result of science or strength as much as of delusion and desperation. This was a space race where it helped to come from behind. The prosperous cultures with access to the Indian Ocean felt no need to explore remote lands and seas for new resources. For cash-strapped Europe, however, the attempt to exploit the Atlantic for new products was like the efforts of underdeveloped countries today, anxiously drilling for offshore wealth from oil or natural gas. In some ways, it paid off.

IN PERSPECTIVE: Beyond Empires

The imperial habit was spreading, and new empires were forming in environments that had never experienced imperialism before. Russia, for example, extended empire to the Eurasian far north. Mwene Mutapa introduced it in sub-Saharan East Africa. The Aztecs and Incas practiced it in the Americas on an unprecedented scale. Nonetheless, most of Africa and the Americas, as well as the whole of Australia and most of the Pacific island world, as far as we know, had still not experienced anything like empire. Most of the world remained in the

Vijayanagar. The steep, gleaming dome that dominates the ruins of Vijayanagar surmounts a shrine nearly 500 years older than the city itself, which arose in the fourteenth century as a focus of resistance against Muslim invaders from the north, on the rocky, easily defended site. By the early fifteenth century, Vijayanagar was the capital of a large state, formed by conquest and controlling much of southern India.

hands of communities with modest political ambitions—kinship networks, chiefdoms, or small states. More remarkably, perhaps, some regions with an imperial past, or under imperialist threat, shied away. Instead, they developed systems in which independent states coexisted with varying degrees of mutual hostility.

In North Africa, for instance, Mamluk Egypt was an immensely rich and productive state but remained confined to the Nile valley, unable to expand beyond the deserts that fringed it. Westward, along Africa's Mediterranean coast, lay numerous small states, founded on the profits of trade or piracy, where Mediterranean and Saharan trade routes met. At the western end of North Africa, Morocco emerged as a kingdom on the edge of the Islamic world, holding Christendom at bay.

South and southeast Asia also housed state systems. In India, the sultanate of Delhi never recovered from the setbacks of the mid–fourteenth century. Hindu states proliferated, some warlike, specifically, toward Islam. The most militaristic, perhaps, was Vijayanagar—the name means "City of Victories"—Abd-ar-Razzak's destination on his ocean voyage from Iran in 1417. Chinese expansion nibbled at the edges of southeast Asia, but China's renunciation of imperialism left the native states of the region free to try one another's strength. The Thai—founders of what is now called Thailand—certainly had expansionist ambitions. In the early fifteenth century, they created the region's largest state at the expense of the Burmese, Khmer, Mons, and Malays. Nonetheless, the region lacked a dominant empire and remained home to a state system in which a number of regional states contended with each other.

Most of Europe, too, continued to enclose a state system. East of the Vistula River, where geography favored the formation of large states, Russia, as we have seen, undertook a massive imperial enterprise. A brief union of the Polish and Lithuanian states in 1386 created what, on the map, at least, also looked like an empire from the Baltic to the Black Sea. Farther west, however, small or middling states got stronger, and the dream of reuniting them and recreating the old Roman Empire faded—or began to look unrealistic. Something like what we now call national feeling emerged where people's mutually intelligible speech and a common sense of identity, defined by birth, caused them to merge into a single community. National communities adopted patron saints. At international gatherings, such as universities and church councils, people defined themselves according to the nation to which they belonged and engaged in ferocious disputes over precedence. States increasingly asserted absolute sovereignty, rejecting any obligation to defer to such traditionally supranational authorities as the church or the Holy Roman Emperor. When, for instance, the Emperor Sigismund visited England in 1415, a knight rode into the sea to challenge him to renounce all claim to authority in England before he was allowed to disembark. Kings of France called themselves "emperors in their own realm" and those of Castile in Spain asserted "my sovereign absolute power."

Some rulers developed ideological grounds for their claims to absolute sovereignty. French kings were supposedly endowed with divine powers to heal. Richard II of England (r. 1377–1399) had himself painted attended by angels, opening his hands to receive the body of Christ from the hands of the Virgin Mary herself.

Meanwhile, the power of the state really did increase. One reason was improved

CHRONOLOGY

ca. 1325	Aztecs found city of Tenochtitlán, according to legend
1368	Beginning of Ming dynasty
1370–1406	Reign of Timur
Late fourteenth century	Ethiopia expands into surrounding regions
1405	First voyage of Zheng He
1417	Voyage of Abd-ar-Razzak to Vijayanagar (India)
1430s	Portuguese establish way stations in Azores
1440s	Portuguese begin to obtain slaves from West Africa
ca. 1450	Inca begin period of expansion and conquest
1453	Ottomans capture Constantinople
1462–1505	Reign of Ivan the Great
ca. 1475	Center of power in southern Africa shifts from Zimbabwe to Mwene Mutapa
1480s	Portuguese make contact with Kingdom of Kongo
1482	Portuguese establish trading post of São Jorge da Mina on West African coast
1484	Sugar production begins in Canary Islands
1490s	First Portuguese diplomatic missions arrive in Ethiopia
1492–1493	First voyage of Christopher Columbus; Spanish kingdom of Castile captures Granada, last Muslim kingdom in Spain
1496	John Cabot discovers direct route across North Atlantic
1497	Pilgrimage of Muhammed Touray Askia, ruler of Songhay, to Mecca; first voyage of Vasco da Gama
1500	Vasco da Gama reaches India; Aztec Empire at its peak

communications. As paper replaced parchment, increasing the output of documents, royal bureaucracies reached more people in more parts of the realm. Changes in the concept of law also strengthened the state. Traditionally, the law was a body of wisdom handed down from the past. Now it came to be seen as a code that kings and parliaments could endlessly change and recreate. The state's power also expanded over vast new areas of public life and common welfare: labor relations, wages, prices, land tenure, markets, the food supply, livestock breeding, and even what people could wear.

Meanwhile, the power of the church declined. Between 1378 and 1415, rulers in Latin Christendom could not agree whom to recognize as pope. The power vacuum eroded what little unity Christendom still had. Secular states became stronger as heresies arose. Under the influence of reformers who demanded—among other changes—lay control of appointments in the church and worship in everyday language, Bohemia for a time refused to recognize papal authority. Reformers known as conciliarists argued that the church should become a kind of republic, with power transferred from Rome to bishops who would meet periodically.

How much difference did the state system make to Europe's prospects? On the one hand, the state system deprived Europeans of unified command of the sort found, for instance, in the Chinese or Ottoman Empires. On the other hand, it stimulated competition among rulers, multiplying the possible sources of patronage available to innovators. For European maritime expansion, the state system was not decisive in launching most initiatives. Explorers and would-be empire builders relied on private enterprise, with little or no state backing. Columbus, for instance, got no direct financial support from the Spanish crown—the myth that Queen Isabella of Castile pawned her jewels for him is nonsense. Prince Henry's Atlantic enterprise was a private venture. Furthermore, as the example of southeast Asia shows, a state system was not in itself sufficient to produce overseas imperialism. For that, the stimulus of coming from behind was necessary. Asian states were at the nodes of the world's richest trades. They had no need to explore new markets or conquer new centers of production, because everything came to them anyway. Europeans, on the other hand, had to expand to gain access to anything worth exploiting.

For all its hesitations and limitations, fifteenth-century expansion was new and potentially world changing. The new routes pioneered in the 1490s linked the populous central belt of Eurasia to the Americas and Africa, and Europe to Asia by sea. We can see the beginnings of a framework of an interconnected globe—a **world system** able to encompass the planet. The expanding empires of the age were reaching toward each other. Where they made contact, they became arenas of unprecedented scale for trade and for transmitting technology, ideas, sentiments, and ways of life. The consequences would transform the world of the next three centuries: worldwide encounters, commerce, conflict, contagion, and cultural and ecological exchange.

PROBLEMS AND PARALLELS

1. Why can the last half of the fifteenth century be considered an age of expansion? How did the beginnings of a world system emerge around 1500?

2. Why were African states fragile in this period?

3. What is meant by the term ecological imperialism? How did the Inca exploit the many different ecosystems of their empire? What was the role of tributary networks in the Aztec Empire?

4. How did the Russian and Turkish worlds expand in the fourteenth and fifteenth centuries?

5. Why did the Chinese turn away from maritime expansionism in the fifteenth century? Why was frontier stability more important than expansion?

6. How do the developments discussed in this chapter demonstrate the importance of winds in world history? Why did the beginnings of European oceanic imperialism have as much to do with geography as with culture?

DOCUMENTS IN GLOBAL HISTORY

- From *The Narrative of the Journey of Abd-ar-Razzak*
- Leo Africanus on Timbuktu
- The founding of Tenochtitlán

- From the *Muqaddimah* by Ibn Khaldun
- A contemporary describes Timur
- From Ma Huan, *The Overall Survey of the Ocean's Shores*

Please see the Primary Source DVD for additional sources related to this chapter.

READ ON

The material on Abd-ar-Razzak comes from R. H. Major, ed., *India in the Fifteenth Century* (1964). D. Ringrose, *Expansion and Global Interaction*, 1200–1700 (2001) gives the background.

On Ethiopia, S. C. Munro-Hay, *Ethiopia: the Unknown Land* (2002), and R. Pankhurst, *The Ethiopians: A History* (2001) are valuable general histories. W. G. Randles, *The Empire of Monomotapa* (1975) is excellent on Mwene Mutapa. On West Africa in this period, E. W. R. Bovill, *The Golden Trade of the Moors* (1995) is a readable classic. Songhay is not well served by books in English but a useful collection of sources is J. O. Hunwick, ed., *Timbuktu and the Songhay Empire: Al-Sa'di's Ta'rîkh al-Sudan Down to 1613, and Other Contemporary Documents* (1999). Anne Hilton, *The Kingdom of Kongo* (1985) is outstanding.

Of histories of the Inca and Aztecs, J. V. Murra, *The Economic Organization of the Inca State* (1980), T. N. D'Altroy, *The Incas* (2003), and M. Smith, *The Aztecs* (2002) are particularly strong on ecological aspects.

My material on the White Sea comes from R. Cormack and D. Gaze, eds., *Art of Holy Russia* (1998). J. Martin, *Treasures of the Land of Darkness* (2004) is enthralling on the economic background to Russian expansion. I. Gray, *Ivan III and the Unification of Russia* (1972) is a businesslike introduction. Ibn Khaldun's great work is *The Muqaddimah: An Introduction to History*, tr. Franz Rosenthal (1969). B. F. Manz, The Rise and Rule of Tamerlane (1999) is the outstanding work on its subject.

For the Ottomans, see H. Inalcik, *The Ottoman Empire: The Classical Age* (2001). E. L. Dreyer, Early Ming China (1982), and *Zheng He: China and the Oceans in the Early Ming Dynasty* (2006) cover the Chinese topics of this chapter admirably. L. Levathes, *When China Ruled the Seas* (1997) is readable and reliable.

On Europe C. Allmand, ed., *The New Cambridge Medieval History, VII* (2005) is comprehensive, while M. Aston, *The Prospect of Europe* (1968) offers a short introduction. On Portuguese expansion, P. E. Russell, *Henry the Navigator* (2001) is admirable, and F. Bethencourt and D. Curto, eds., *The Portuguese Empire* (1998) provides a broad survey. P. O. Kristeller, *The Cambridge Companion to Renaissance Humanism* (1996) is an unsurpassed classic on its topic, and M. H. Keen, *Chivalry* (1986) is on the way to attaining the same status.

Epilogue:
Taking Stock

A popular way of looking at history in ancient Greece was to see it as a thread spun by three goddesses called the Fates: a line you can grasp and feel and follow. But when we look back at the past, the thread seems tangled, or woven into a fantastic tapestry, so rich and crowded with images that no clear line is visible. In the weave of facts, sources, reflections, debates, and unfamiliar names that make up human history, it is hard to keep the central stories of this book in sight: the stories of human societies' relationships with each other and with the rest of nature.

A striking fact is that the whole history of early humankind, almost the entire 150,000-year story of the descendants of Eve, our common African ancestor, would fit into a few pages. This is not because we lack evidence. Archaeology has already unearthed more evidence of our human past than any mind can fully master. In alliance with anthropology and readings of works of art, it can give us vivid insights and provoke worthwhile speculations.

Nor would our coverage of early humankind be brief because nothing much happened during those tens of thousands of years. On the contrary, it was a dynamic period, when humankind changed in definitive ways. Spectacular migrations and colonization took humans to almost every habitable environment around the globe. The huge, hard-to-explain growth in human numbers that began 130,000 years ago helped people the Earth. Social and political changes—including, for instance, sexual specialization between men and women and the rise of chiefs—happened independently all over the world. New hunting technologies and food-gathering strategies came and went, waxed and waned, as communities adapted to new environments and new circumstances. Some sort of seafaring technology emerged (or reemerged, if it is true that prehuman hominids had it). The development of religions and of ways to explain the universe that we can only dimly understand, and of the art that reflects them, reveals minds and thoughts among the "cave men" that were as productive and, at times, as changeable as our own.

Above all, if there was a single human story at work in the Ice Age, it was of divergence—the emergence of different ways of living and of organizing societies and cultures. Societies became physically distant from one another as they spread out of Africa across the globe. They began to develop differences of culture, as they lost touch with one another and adapted to different environments. To some extent, people in widely separated locations even began to look different from one another, although the human gene pool barely altered by a sliver of a fraction of a margin from place to place. Cultures certainly diverged, as languages and ways to obtain and prepare food multiplied and as people devised diets and dwellings and techniques of artistic expression that were appropriate to their different environments.

On the other hand, the world still embraced surprising cultural continuities. Everywhere, people foraged for food rather than producing it themselves. Everywhere, despite increasing variation in hunting technologies, they used similar methods, targeting, on land and increasingly by sea, large, fat-rich animals that they drove to their deaths, at least as much by exhausting or trapping them as by felling them with blows, rocks, or spears. Religious features also had much in common around the world: reliance on shamans to communicate with gods and spirits, worship of big-hipped or big-bellied goddesses. And although differences grew from region to region, the artistic symbols, themes, media, and materials that most early societies produced still had a lot in common. All the people of the

Fates spin the thread of a life. One holds a ball of yarn, the other a spindle. The subject was popular for funeral caskets in ancient times—like the example shown here from the third-century C.E.—because the Fates, three goddesses in Greek and Roman mythology, supposedly spun each individual's life-strand at birth.

time had, as far as we can tell, more or less the same concept of nature. They were part of it. Their relationship with other species was intimate. They were not ecologists. They exploited the environment for what they could get out of it—as all societies have done ever since—and sometimes they hunted species to extinction. They modified their environments, by fashioning dwellings, by using fire, by manipulating grazing, and by corralling herds. But they inhabited the landscapes they found, without feeling the need to change them. If they disliked their habitats, they moved on to a new area that better suited their needs.

The Ice Age was a dynamic time. But to us, who live amid convulsive change, it seems like an age of remarkable stability, continuity, and equilibrium. The retreat of the ice 20,000 years ago ended all that.

As the ice melted, the pace and range of colonization quickened. Cultures became more sharply divided, as some communities opted to continue their hunter-gatherer way of life by following their prey and harvesting wild plants, while others began to grow the food on which they relied. From this point on, societies could be classified in three types: hunters, herders, and tillers who raised livestock and grew crops. If continuity was the common aim, hunters were the most successful because they maintained the essential features of their way of life relatively unchanged.

By contrast, tillers (and to a lesser extent herders) found themselves—whether they willed it or not—committed to dynamic change: political change, because they needed strong leaders to organize production and distribution of food; social and economic change, because they needed large workforces and growing populations; changes in economic specialization and styles of living, because ever larger populations needed to be concentrated in relatively small spaces; changes in health and nutrition, because of the need to survive on limited diets in a new disease-environment; changes in warfare because they had to defend their flocks and fields, or enlarge them at others' expenses. In particular, hostility became routine between societies that relied mainly on tilling the soil and those that had to move frequently from one place to another with the herds they lived off, because grazing needs a lot of space to produce each unit of nutrition—meat, dairy products—from an animal. So practitioners of the two types of culture became competitors for land. And their differences of culture were so marked that farmers and nomad herders found it easier to hate than to understand each other.

Over time, the pace of divergence increased. Because they developed at first in isolation from each other—as agriculture emerged independently in many places around the world and different crops were grown in contrasting environments—farming societies were much more diverse than hunter societies. Both herders and tillers found that the demands of food production and war drove them to new political expedients. Different kinds of states and then bigger states—empires—emerged and grew. Just as cities were relatively unstable environments, so states and empires were relatively unstable and mutually hostile forms of political organization. Though some states lasted for centuries or even thousands of years, their internal histories were full of the changes that tended as time went on to make them more unlike each other. Conflicting ideologies arose. States and empires adapted religions to justify the differences between them and competing states, and, in their turn, religions stoked hostility and helped to cause wars.

Meanwhile, the ambition to modify nature grew in the minds of the world's farmers. Across the globe—in east, southwest, and southeast Asia; in the Indian subcontinent; in parts of the Americas, Africa, and Europe; and around the Pacific—farmers recarved landscape into fields and scored it with irrigation ditches. In extreme cases they smothered it with towns and cities, environments of their own building. Urban environments are ecologically fragile, and the societies that lived in them began to experience the turbulent history—full of declines and falls, crises and collapses, confrontations and conflicts—that makes the broad outline of history so hard to discern and crowds the relatively stable hunting peoples out of the story.

One trend, however, has been irreversible since the first farmers began to till the soil over 10,000 years ago. More and more societies followed their example or adopted it independently, abandoning hunting or restricting it to elites. Peoples that remained loyal to hunting began to retreat into ever more marginal environments, to tundra, forests, and arid grasslands. The reasons for this are hard to understand. To some extent, it was a simple matter of diminishing resources. As farming expanded, less game and land were available for hunting cultures. At another level, it was an effect of relative power. Farming, for all its disadvantages, feeds more people than hunting does and generates more resources for war. Though farming disrupted almost every society that adopted it, and often led to failure and collapse, it worked—or has worked so far—in the long term for most people.

Once most peoples around the world adopted agriculture, divergence became dominant. Until the late 1400s, oceans still divided many of the world's peoples from each other. Some—especially in Australia and New Guinea and in dense forest environments elsewhere—were isolated from contact with outsiders except for their immediate or near neighbors. Poor communications tended to keep peoples apart in most of sub-Saharan Africa and the Americas and to inhibit long-range exchanges of culture and ideas. In consequence, although some of those parts of the world independently experienced changes similar to those we can see elsewhere—including the rise of agriculture, cities, states and empires—the pace of change in these isolated societies was slower and the scale less widespread than in Eurasia and North Africa.

Even within Eurasia, across the great axis of communications that made exchanges of influence, ideas, and technologies possible between regions as widely separated as Europe and China, the effects were markedly different from place to place. Although the sages of ancient China, India, Iran, Palestine, and Greece shared many of the same thoughts, the results of their ideas were so different that they stimulated conflict: mutually hostile religions, mutually antagonistic world visions.

There were few signs by the 1400s C.E. that the era of divergence was reaching its end. But it was. This was partly because the huge states we call empires acted as arenas for transmitting culture. Some empires had functioned in this way for a long time. The Roman Empire transmitted Greek learning and the Christian religion from the eastern Mediterranean to as far away as the Atlantic edge of Europe. In Mesoamerica, the great city of Teotihuacán had influenced fashion and politics in the Maya world. Over many centuries, China had forged a common identity in a vast domain, and the influence of its arts, learning, and political thinking had spilled over into Korea, Japan, and other parts of Asia. China had also been the conduit by which Buddhism spread from India to Korea and Japan. The most spectacular cases were relatively recent. In the seventh, eighth, and ninth centuries, Muslim empire-builders had spread Islam across a great swath of the Old World from Spain to the borders of India and deep into Africa. With Islam came scholars and texts that put the learning of India and of the former Roman world back in touch with one another. Muslim rulers and the gardeners and agriculturalists they patronized exchanged unfamiliar crops back and forth across Eurasia and North Africa. In the thirteenth century, the Mongol Peace that followed the spectacular conquests of Genghis Khan exceeded all previous empires as a stimulus to the migration of ideas and technologies across Eurasia. Individuals, moreover, were effective beyond the reach of empires. Merchants, missionaries, and pilgrims were pioneers of ever more intensive long-range communications across the Eurasian Silk Roads, the trans-Saharan routes, and the wind corridors of maritime Asia and the Indian Ocean that bound together Eurasia and parts of Africa.

After so many thousands of years of human divergence, it seems amazing that the process should have been halted and reversed. But that was what happened next. Gradually, with increasing pace in the fifteenth century and dramatic acceleration from the sixteenth century onward, convergence began to replace divergence as the dominant theme in the history of human cultures. Explorers found routes across the Atlantic, which for the first time linked Europe and Africa to the Americas. They sailed around Africa to connect by sea the lands around the Indian Ocean, the world's richest zone of commerce, to what had been the relatively isolated and backward peoples of Western Europe. Empires and trade overleaped oceans, taking people, animals, plants, and forms of culture with them. Parts of the globe that had for tens of thousands of years grown increasingly unlike one another now began, slowly and selectively at first, to resemble each other once again as they had before the continents had drifted apart millions of years ago.

Abolitionism Belief that slavery and the slave trade are immoral and should be abolished.

Aborigine A member of the indigenous or earliest-known population of a region.

Aborigines Indigenous people of Australia.

Afrikaans An official language of South Africa, spoken mostly by the Boers. It is derived from seventeenth-century Dutch.

Age of Plague Term for the spread of lethal diseases from the fourteenth through the eighteenth centuries.

Ahriman The chief spirit of darkness and evil in Zoroastrianism, the enemy of Ahura Mazda.

Ahura Mazda The chief deity of Zoroastrianism, the creator of the world, the source of light, and the embodiment of good.

Al-Andalus Arabic name for the Iberian Peninsula (Spain and Portugal).

Alluvial plains Flat lands where mud from rivers or lakes renews the topsoil. If people can control the flooding that is common in such conditions, alluvial plains are excellent for settled agriculture.

Almoravids Muslim dynasty of Berber warriors that flourished from 1049 to 1145 and that established political dominance over northwest Africa and Spain.

Alternative energy Energy sources that usually produce less pollution than does the burning of fossil fuels, and are renewable in some cases.

Alternative medicine Medicines, treatments, and techniques not advocated by the mainstream medical establishment in the West.

Americanization The process by which other cultures, to a greater or lesser degree, adopt American fashions, culture, and ways of life.

Anarchists Believers in the theory that all forms of government are oppressive and undesirable and should be opposed and abolished.

Animal rights Movement that asserts that animals have fundamental rights that human beings have a moral obligation to respect.

Anti-Semitism Hostility or prejudice against Jews or Judaism.

Arthasastra Ancient Indian study of economics and politics that influenced the Emperor Asoka. The *Arthasastra* expresses an ideology of universal rule and emphasizes the supremacy of "the king's law" and the importance of uniform justice.

Artificial intelligence The creation of a machine or computer program that exhibits the characteristics of human intelligence.

Arts and Crafts Movement Nineteenth-century artists and intellectuals who argued that the products produced by individual craftsmen were more attractive than and morally superior to the mass, uniform goods produced by industry.

Assassins A secret order of Muslims in what is today Syria and Lebanon who terrorized and killed its opponents, both Christian and Muslim. The Assassins were active from the eleventh to the thirteenth centuries.

Atlantic Slave Trade Trade in African slaves who were bought, primarily in West Africa, by Europeans and white Americans and transported across the Atlantic, usually in horrific conditions, to satisfy the demand for labor in the plantations and mines of the Americas.

Atomic theory The theory that matter is not a continuous whole, but is composed of tiny, discrete particles.

Australopithecine ("southern ape-like creatures") Species of hominids that occurred earlier than those classed under the heading "homo." Most anthropologists date australopithecines to 5 million years ago.

Axial Age A pivotal age in the history of world civilization, lasting for roughly 500 years up to the beginning of the Christian era, in which critical intellectual and cultural ideas arose in and were transmitted across the Mediterranean world, India, Iran, and East Asia.

Axial zone The densely populated central belt of world population, communication, and cultural exchange in Eurasia that stretches from Japan and China to Western Europe and North Africa.

Aztecs People of central Mexico whose civilization and empire were at their height at the time of the Spanish conquest in the early sixteenth century.

Balance of trade The relative value of goods traded between two or more nations or states. Each trading partner strives to have a favorable balance of trade, that is, to sell more to its trading partners than it buys from them.

Bantu African people sharing a common linguistic ancestry who originated in West Africa and whose early agriculture centered on the cultivation of yams and oil palms in swamplands.

Big bang theory Theory that the universe began with an explosion of almost infinitesimally compressed matter, the effects of which are still going on.

Black Death Term for a lethal disease or diseases that struck large parts of Eurasia and North Africa in the 1300s and killed millions of people.

Boers Dutch settlers and their descendents in southern Africa. The first Boers arrived in South Africa in the seventeenth century.

Bon Religion that was Buddhism's main rival in Tibet for several centuries in the late first millennium C.E.

Brahman A member of the highest, priestly caste of traditional Indian society.

British East India Company British trading company founded in 1600 that played a key role in the colonization of India. It ruled much of the subcontinent until 1857.

Bureaucratization The process by which government increasingly operates through a body of trained officials who follow a set of regular rules and procedures.

Business Imperialism Economic domination and exploitation of poorer and weaker countries by richer and stronger states.

Byzantine Empire Term for the Greek-speaking, eastern portion of the former Roman Empire, centered on Constantinople. It lasted until 1453, when it was conquered by the Ottoman Turks.

Cahokia Most spectacular existent site of Mississippi Valley Native American civilization, located near modern St. Louis.

Caliph The supreme Islamic political and religious authority, literally, the "successor" of the Prophet Muhammad.

Canyon cultures Indigenous peoples of the North American Southwest. The canyon cultures flourished between about 850 and 1250 C.E.

Capitalism An economic system in which the means of production and distribution are privately or corporately owned.

Caste system A social system in which people's places in society, how they live and work, and with whom they can marry are determined by heredity. The Indian caste system has been intertwined with India's religious and economic systems.

Centralization The concentration of power in the hands of a central government.

Chaos theory Theory that some systems are so complex that their causes and effects are untraceable.

Chicago economics The economic theory associated with economists who taught at the University of Chicago that holds that low taxes and light government regulation will lead to economic prosperity.

Chimú Civilization centered on the Pacific coast of Peru that was conquered by the Inca in the fifteenth century.

Chinese Board of Astronomy Official department of the Chinese imperial court created in the early seventeenth century that was responsible for devising the ritual calendar.

Chinese diaspora The migration of Chinese immigrants around the world between the seventeenth and nineteenth centuries.

Chivalry The qualities idealized by the medieval European aristocracy and associated with knighthood, such as bravery, courtesy, honor, and gallantry.

Chola Expansive kingdom in southern India that had important connections with merchant communities on the coast. Chola reached its height around 1050 C.E.

Christendom Term referring to the European states in which Christianity was the dominant or only religion.

Cistercians Christian monastic order that built monasteries in places where habitation was sparse and nature hostile. Cistercians practiced a more ascetic and rigorous form of the Benedictine rule.

Citizen army The mass army the French created during the Revolution by imposing mandatory military service on the entire active adult male population. The army was created in response to the threat of invasion by an alliance of anti-Revolutionary countries in the early 1790s.

Civilization A way of life based on radically modifying the environment.

Civilizing mission The belief that imperialism and colonialism are justified because imperial powers have a duty to bring the benefits of "civilization" to, or impose them on, the "backward" people they ruled or conquered.

Clan A social group made up of a number of families that claim descent from a common ancestor and follow a hereditary chieftain.

Class struggle Conflict between competing social classes that, in Karl Marx's view, was responsible for all important historical change.

Climacteric A period of critical change in a society that is poised between different possible outcomes.

Code Napoleon Civil code promulgated by Napoleon in 1804 and spread by his armies across Europe. It still forms the basis for the legal code for many European, Latin American, and African countries.

Cold war Post–World War II rivalry between the United States and its allies and the Soviet Union and its allies. The cold war ended in 1990–1991 with the end of the Soviet Empire in Eastern Europe and the collapse of the Soviet Union itself.

Columbian Exchange Biological exchange of plants, animals, microbes, and human beings between the Americas and the rest of the world.

Commune Collective name for the citizen body of a medieval and Renaissance Italian town.

Communism A system of government in which the state plans and controls the economy, and private property and class distinctions are abolished.

Confraternities Lay Catholic charitable brotherhoods.

Confucianism Chinese doctrine founded by Confucius emphasizing learning and the fulfillment of obligations among family members, citizens, and the state.

Constitutionalism The doctrine that the state is founded on a set of fundamental laws that rulers and citizens make together and are bound to respect.

Consumerism A system of values that exalts the consumption and possession of consumer goods as both a social good and as an end in themselves.

Coolies Poor laborers from China and India who left their homelands to do hard manual and agricultural work in other parts of the world in the nineteenth and early twentieth centuries.

Copernican revolution Development of a heliocentric model of the solar system begun in 1543 by Nicholas Copernicus, a Polish churchman and astronomer.

Council of Trent A series of meetings from 1545 to 1563 to direct the response of the Roman Catholic Church to Protestantism. The council defined Catholic dogma and reformed church discipline.

Counter Reformation The Catholic effort to combat the spread of Protestantism in the sixteenth and seventeenth centuries.

Countercolonization The flow of immigrants out of former colonies to the "home countries" that used to rule them.

Country trades Commerce involving local or regional exchanges of goods from one Asian destination to another that, while often handled by European merchants, never touched Europe.

Covenant In the Bible, God's promise to the human race.

Creoles People of at least part-European descent born in the West Indies, French Louisiana, or Spanish America.

Crusades Any of the military expeditions undertaken by European Christians from the late eleventh to the thirteenth centuries to recover the Holy Land from the Muslims.

Cubism Artistic style developed by Pablo Picasso and Georges Braque in the early twentieth century, characterized by the reduction and fragmentation of natural forms into abstract, often geometric structures.

Cultural relativism The doctrine that cultures cannot be ranked in any order of merit. No culture is superior to another, and each culture must be judged on its own terms.

Cultural Revolution Campaign launched by Mao Zedong in 1965–1966 against the bureaucrats of the Chinese Communist Party. In lasted until 1976 and involved widespread disorder, violence, killings, and the persecution of intellectuals and the educated elite.

Culture Socially transmitted behavior, beliefs, institutions, and technologies that a given group of people or peoples share.

Cuneiform Mesopotamian writing system that was inscribed on clay tablets with wedge-shaped markers.

Czars (Trans.) "Caesar." Title of the emperors who ruled Russia until the revolution of 1917.

Dada An early twentieth-century European artistic and literary movement that flouted conventional and traditional aesthetic and cultural values by producing works marked by nonsense, travesty, and incongruity.

Dahomey West African slave-trading state that began to be prominent in the sixteenth century.

Daimyo Japanese feudal lord who ruled a province and was subject to the shoguns.

Daoism Chinese doctrine founded by Laozi that identified detachment from the world with the pursuit of immortality.

"Declaration of the Rights of Man and Citizen" Declaration of basic principles adopted by the French National Assembly in August 1789, at the start of the French Revolution.

Decolonization The process by which the nineteenth-century colonial empires in Asia, Africa, the Caribbean, and the Pacific were dismantled after World War II.

Deforestation The process by which trees are eliminated from an ecosystem.

Democracy Government by the people, exercised either directly or through elected representatives.

Demokratia Greek word signifying a state where supreme power belonged to an assembly of citizens (only privileged males were citizens).

Devsirme Quota of male children supplied by Christian subjects as tribute to the Ottoman Sultan. Many of the boys were drafted into the janissaries.

Dharma In the teachings of Buddha, moral law or duty.

Diffusion The spread of a practice, belief, culture, or technology within a community or between communities.

Dirlik (Trans.) "Wealth." The term applied to provincial government in the Ottoman Empire.

Divine love God's ongoing love for and interest in human beings.

Dominicans Order of preaching friars established in 1216 by Saint Dominic.

Druze Lebanese sect that regards the caliph al-Hakim as a manifestation of God. Other Muslims regard the Druze as heretics.

Dualism Perception of the world as an arena of conflict between opposing principles of good and evil.

Dutch East India Company Dutch company founded in 1602 that enjoyed a government-granted monopoly on trade between Holland and Asia. The company eventually established a territorial empire in what is today Indonesia.

Dutch East Indies Dutch colonies in Asia centered on present-day Indonesia.

The Encyclopedia Twenty-eight volume compendium of Enlightenment thought published in French and edited by Denis Diderot. The first volume appeared in 1751.

East India Trade Maritime trade between Western Europe and New England and Asia (predominantly India and China) between 1600 and 1800. Westerners paid cash for items from Asia, such as porcelain, tea, silk, cotton textiles, and spices.

Easterlies Winds coming from the east.

Ecological exchange The exchange of plants and animals between ecosystems.

Ecological imperialism Term historians use for the sweeping environmental changes European and other imperialists introduced in regions they colonized.

Ecology of civilization The interaction of people with their environment.

Economic liberalism Belief that government interference in and regulation of the economy should be kept to a minimum.

Edo Former name of Tokyo when it was the center of government for the Tokugawa shoguns.

El Niño A periodic reversal of the normal flow of Pacific currents that alters weather patterns and affects the number and location of fish in the ocean.

Elan vital The "vital force" hypothesized by the French philosopher Henri Bergson as a source of efficient causation and evolution in nature.

Empirical Derived from or guided by experience or experiment.

Empiricism The view that experience, especially of the senses, is the only source of knowledge.

Emporium trading Commerce that takes place in fixed market places or trading posts.

Enlightened despotism Reforms instituted by powerful monarchs in eighteenth-century Europe who were inspired by the principles of the Enlightenment.

Enlightenment Movement of eighteenth-century European thought championed by the *philosophes*, thinkers who held that change and reform were desirable and could be achieved by the application of reason and science. Most Enlightenment thinkers were hostile to conventional religion.

Enthusiasm "Religion" of English romantics who believed that emotion and passion were positive qualities.

Epistemology The branch of philosophy that studies the nature of knowledge.

Equilibrium trap Term coined by the historian Mark Elvin to refer to China in the eighteenth century, when industries were meeting demand with traditional technologies and had no scope to increase output.

Eugenics The theory that the human race can be improved mentally and physically by controlled selective breeding and that the state and society have a duty to encourage "superior" persons to have offspring and prevent "inferior" persons from reproducing.

Eunuchs Castrated male servants valued because they could not produce heirs or have sexual relations with women. In Byzantium, China, and the Islamic world, eunuchs could rise to high office in the state and the military.

European Union (EU) Loose economic and political federation that succeeded the European Economic Community (EEC) in 1993. It has expanded to include most of the states in Western and Eastern Europe.

Evolution Change in the genetic composition of a population over successive generations, as a result of natural selection acting on the genetic variation among individuals.

Examination system System for selecting Chinese officials and bureaucrats according to merit through a series of competitive, written examinations that, in theory, any Chinese young man could take. Success in the exams required years of intense study in classical Chinese literature. The examination system was not abolished until the early twentieth century.

Existentialism Philosophy that regards human existence as unexplainable, and stresses freedom of choice and accepting responsibility for the consequences of one's acts.

Factories Foreign trading posts in China and other parts of Asia. The chief representative of a factory was known as a "factor." Though the earliest trading posts were established by the Portuguese in the sixteenth century, the number of factories grew rapidly in the eighteenth and nineteenth centuries, with European and American merchants trading for silk, rhubarb, tea, and porcelain.

Fascism A system of government marked by centralization of authority under a dictator, stringent socioeconomic controls, and suppression of the opposition through terror and censorship.

Fatimids Muslim dynasty that ruled parts of North Africa and Egypt (909–1171).

Feminism The belief that women collectively constitute a class of society that has been historically oppressed and deserves to be set free.

Final Solution Nazi plan to murder all European Jews.

Fixed-wind systems Wind system in which the prevailing winds do not change direction for long periods of time.

Fossil fuels Fuels including peat, coal, natural gas, and oil.

Franciscans Religious order founded by Francis of Assisi in 1209 and dedicated to the virtues of humility, poverty, and charitable work among the poor.

Free trade The notion that maximum economic efficiency is achieved when barriers to trade, especially taxes on imports and exports, are eliminated.

French Revolution Political, intellectual, and social upheaval that began in France in 1789. It resulted in the overthrow of the monarchy and the establishment of a republic.

Fulani Traditional herdsmen of the Sahel in West Africa.

Fundamentalism Strict adherence to a set of basic ideas or principles.

Futurism Artistic vision articulated by Emilio Filippo Marinetti in 1909. He believed that all traditional art and ideas should be repudiated, destroyed, and replaced by the new. Futurists glorified speed, technology, progress, and violence.

Gauchos Argentine cowboys.

General will Jean-Jacques Rousseau's concept of the collective will of the population. He believed that the purpose of government was to express the general will.

Genetic revolution Revolution in the understanding of human biology produced by advances in genetic research.

Genocide The systematic and planned extermination of an entire national, racial, political, or ethnic group.

Ghana A medieval West African kingdom in what are now eastern Senegal, southwest Mali, and southern Mauritania.

Global gardening The collecting in botanical gardens of plants from around the world for cultivation and study.

Globalization The process through which uniform or similar ways of life are spread across the planet.

Glyph A form of writing that uses symbolic figures that are usually engraved or incised, such as Egyptian hieroglyphics.

GM Crops that have been *genetically modified* to produce certain desired characteristics.

Golden Horde Term for Mongols who ruled much of Russia from the steppes of the lower Volga River from the thirteenth to the fifteenth century.

Grand Vizier The chief minister of state in the Ottoman Empire.

Greater East Asia Co-Prosperity Sphere Bloc of Asian nations under Japanese economic and political control during World War II.

Green revolution Improvements in twentieth-century agriculture that substantially increased food production by developing new strains of crops and agricultural techniques.

Greenhouse effect The increase in temperature caused by the trapping of carbon in the Earth's atmosphere.

Guardians Self-elected class of philosopher-rulers found in Plato's *Republic*.

Guomindang (GMD) Nationalist Chinese political party founded in 1912 by Sun Yat-Sen. The Guomindang took power in China in 1928 but was defeated by the Chinese Communists in 1949.

Habsburgs An Austro-German imperial family that reached the height of their power in the sixteenth century under Charles V of Spain when the Habsburgs ruled much of Europe and the Americas. The Habsburgs continued to rule a multinational empire based in Vienna until 1918.

Haj The pilgrimage to Mecca that all faithful Muslims are required to complete at least once in their lifetime if they are able.

Han Dynasty that ruled China from ca. 206 B.C.E. to ca. 220 C.E. This was the period when the funda-mental identity and culture of China were formed. Chinese people still refer to themselves as "Han."

Hanseatic League Founded in 1356, the Hanseatic League was a powerful network of allied ports along the North Sea and Baltic coasts that collaborated to promote trade.

Harem The quarters reserved for the female members of a Muslim household.

Herders Agriculturalists who emphasize the raising of animals, rather than plants, for food and products, such as wool and hides.

High-level equilibrium trap A situation in which an economy that is meeting high levels of demand with traditional technology finds that it has little scope to increase its output.

Hinduism Indian polytheistic religion that developed out of Brahmanism and in response to Buddhism. It remains the majority religion in India today.

Hispaniola Modern Haiti and the Dominican Republic.

Hohokam People Native American culture that flourished from about the third century B.C.E. to the mid–fifteenth century C.E. in south-central Arizona.

Holocaust Term for the murder of millions of Jews by the Nazi regime during World War II.

Holy Roman Empire A loose federation of states under an elected emperor that consisted primarily of Germany and northern Italy. It endured in various forms from 800 to 1806.

Homo erectus (Trans.) "Standing upright." Humanlike tool-using species that lived about 1.5 million years ago. At one time, Homo erectus was thought to be the first "human."

Homo ergaster (Trans.) "Workman." Humanlike species that lived 800,000 years ago and stacked the bones of its dead.

Homo habilis (Trans.) "Handy." Humanlike species that lived about 2.5 million years ago and made stone hand axes.

Homo sapiens (Trans.) "Wise." The species to which contemporary humans belong.

Human rights Notion of inherent rights that all human beings share. Based in part on the assumption that being human constitutes in itself a meaningful moral category that excludes nonhuman creatures.

Humanism Cultural and intellectual movement of the Renaissance centered on the study of the literature, art, and civilization of ancient Greece and Rome.

Hurons A Native American confederacy of eastern Canada. The Huron flourished immediately prior to contact with Europeans, but declined rapidly as a result of European diseases such as smallpox. They were allied with the French in wars against the British, the Dutch, and other Native Americans.

Husbandry The practice of cultivating crops and breeding and raising livestock; agriculture.

Ice-Age affluence Relative prosperity of Ice-Age society as the result of abundant game and wild, edible plants.

Icon A representation or picture of a Christian saint or sacred event. Icons have been traditionally venerated in the Eastern, or Orthodox, Church.

Il-Khanate A branch of the Mongol Empire, centered in present-day Iran. Its rulers, the Il-Khans, converted to Islam and adopted Persian culture.

Il-khans ("subordinate rulers") Viceroys of the Mongols who ruled Persia and environs in the thirteenth and early fourteenth centuries.

Imam A Muslim religious teacher. Also the title of Muslim political and religious rulers in Yemen and Oman.

Imperator A Latin term that originally meant an army commander under the Roman Republic and evolved into the term *emperor*.

Imperialism The policy of extending a nation's authority and influence by conquest or by establishing economic and political hegemony over other nations.

Incas Peoples of highland Peru who established an empire from northern Ecuador to central Chile before the Spanish conquest in the 1530s.

Indian National Congress Political organization created in 1885 that played a leading role in the Indian independence movement.

Indirect rule Rule by a colonial power through local elites.

Individualism Belief in the primary importance of the individual and in the virtues of self-reliance and personal independence.

Indo-European languages Language family that originated in Asia and from which most of Europe's present languages evolved.

Inductive method Method by which scientists turn individual observations and experiments into general laws.

Industrial Revolution The complex set of economic, demographic, and technological events that began in Western Europe and resulted in the advent of an industrial economy.

Industrialization The process by which an industrial economy is developed.

Information technology Technology, such as printing presses and computers, that facilitates the spread of information.

Inquisition A tribunal of the Roman Catholic Church that was charged with suppressing heresy and immorality.

Iroquois Native American confederacy based in northern New York State, originally composed of the Mohawk, Oneida, Onondaga, Cayuga, and Seneca peoples, known as the Five Nations. The confederation created a constitution sometime between the mid-1400s and the early 1600s.

Isolationism Belief that, unless directly challenged, a country should concentrate on domestic issues and avoid foreign conflicts or active participation in foreign affairs.

Jainism A way of life that arose in India designed to free the soul from evil by ascetic practices: chastity, detachment, truth, selflessness, and strict vegetarianism.

Janissaries Soldiers in an elite Ottoman infantry formation that was first organized in the fourteenth century. Originally drafted from among the sons of the sultan's Christian subjects, the janissaries had become a hereditary and militarily obsolete caste by the early nineteenth century.

Jesuits Order of regular clergy strongly committed to education, scholarship, and missionary work. Founded by Ignatius of Loyola in 1534.

Jihad Arabic word meaning "striving." Muhammad used the word to refer to the inner struggle all Muslims must wage against evil, and the real wars fought against the enemies of Islam.

Joint-stock company A business whose capital is held in transferable shares of stock by its joint owners. The Dutch East India Company, founded in 1602, was the first joint-stock company.

Kaaba The holiest place in Islam. Formerly a pagan shrine, the Kaaba is a massive cube-shaped structure in Mecca toward which Muslims turn to pray.

Keynesianism Economic policy advocated by J. M. Keynes, based on the premise that governments could adjust the distribution of wealth and regulate the functioning of the economy through taxation and public spending, without seriously weakening free enterprise or infringing freedom.

Khan A ruler of a Mongol, Tartar, or Turkish tribe.

Khedive Title held by the hereditary viceroys of Egypt in the nineteenth century. Although nominally subject to the Ottoman sultans, the khedives were, in effect, sovereign princes.

Khmer Agrarian kingdom of Cambodia, built on the wealth produced by enormous rice surpluses.

Kongo Kingdom located in west central Africa along the Congo River, founded in the fourteenth century. The Portuguese converted its rulers and elite to Catholicism in the fifteenth century.

Kulturkampf (Trans.) "The struggle for culture." Name given to the conflict between the Roman Catholic Church and the imperial German government under Chancellor Otto von Bismarck in the 1870s.

Laissez-faire An economic policy that emphasizes the minimization of government regulation and involvement in the economy.

Latin Church Dominant Christian church in Western Europe.

Latitude The angular distance north or south of the Earth's equator, measured in degrees along a meridian.

Law of nations Political theory that serves as the foundation for international law, first theorized by Thomas Aquinas in the thirteenth century and further developed by the Spanish theologion Francisco Suarez (1548–1617).

League of Nations International political organization created after World War I to resolve disputes between states peacefully and create a more just international order.

Legalism Chinese philosophical school that argued that a strong state was necessary in order to have a good society.

Levant The countries bordering on the eastern Mediterranean from Turkey to Egypt.

Liberation theology Religious movement in Latin America, primarily among Roman Catholics, concerned with justice for the poor and oppressed. Its adherents argue that sin is the result not just of individual moral failure but of the oppressive and exploitative way in which capitalist society is organized and functions.

Little Ice Age Protracted period of relative cold from the fourteenth to the early nineteenth centuries.

Logograms A system of writing in which stylized pictures represent a word or phrase.

Longitude An imaginary great circle on the surface of the Earth passing through the north and south poles at right angles to the equator.

Lotus Sutra The most famous of Buddhist scriptures.

Low Countries A region of northwest Europe comprising what is today Belgium, the Netherlands, and Luxembourg.

Magyars Steppeland people who invaded Eastern Europe in the tenth century and were eventually converted to Catholic Christianity. The Magyars are the majority ethnic group in present-day Hungary.

Mahayana One of the major schools of Buddhism. It emphasizes the Buddha's infinite compassion for all human beings, social concern, and universal salvation. It is the dominant branch of Buddhism in East Asia.

Mahdi A Muslim messiah, whose coming would inaugurate a cosmic struggle, preceding the end of the world.

Maize The grain that modern Americans call "corn." It was first cultivated in ancient Mesoamerica.

Mali Powerful West African state that flourished in the fourteenth century.

Malthusian Ideas inspired by Thomas Malthus's theory that population growth would always outpace growth in food supply.

Mamluks Egyptian Muslim slave army. The mamluks provided Egypt's rulers from 1390 to 1517.

Mana According to the Polynesians, a supernatural force that regulates everything in the world. For example, the mana of a net makes it catch a fish, and the mana of an herb gives it its healing powers.

Manchurian Incident Japanese invasion of Manchuria in 1931, justified by the alleged effort of the Chinese to blow up a Japanese train. In fact, Japanese agents deliberately triggered the explosion to provide a pretext for war.

Manchus A people native to Manchuria who ruled China during the Qing dynasty.

Mandarins A high public official of the Chinese empire.

Mandate of heaven The source of divine legitimacy for Chinese emperors. According to the mandate of heaven, emperors were chosen by the gods and retained their favor as long as the emperors acted in righteous ways. Emperors and dynasties that lost the mandate of heaven could be deposed or overthrown.

Manichaeanism A dualistic philosophy dividing the world between the two opposed principles of good and evil.

Manifest destiny Nineteenth-century belief that the United States was destined to expand across all of North America from the Atlantic to the Pacific, including Canada and Mexico.

Manila Galleons Spanish galleons that sailed each year between the Philippines and Mexico with a cargo of silk, porcelain, and other Asian luxury goods that were paid for with Mexican silver.

Maori Indigenous Polynesian people of New Zealand.

Marathas Petty Hindu princes who ruled in Maharashtra in southern India in the eighteenth century.

Maritime empires Empires based on trade and naval power that flourished in the sixteenth and seventeenth centuries.

Maroons Runaway slaves in the Americas who formed autonomous communities, and even states, between 1500 and 1800.

Marshall Plan Foreign-aid program for Western Europe after World War II, named after U.S. Secretary of State George C. Marshall.

Marxism The political and economic philosophy of Karl Marx and Friedrich Engels in which the concept of class struggle is the determining principle in social and historical change.

Material culture Concrete objects that people create.

Matrilineal A society that traces ancestry through the maternal line.

Maya Major civilization of Mesoamerica. The earliest evidence connected to Maya civilization dates from about 1000 B.C.E. Maya civilization reached its peak between 250 and 900 C.E. Maya cultural and political practices were a major influence on other Mesoamericans.

Mercantilism An economic theory that emphasized close government control of the economy to maximize a country's exports and to earn as much bullion as possible.

Mesoamerica A region stretching from central Mexico to Central America. Mesoamerica was home to the Olmec, the Maya, the Aztecs, and other Native American peoples.

Messiah The anticipated savior of the Jews. Christians identified Jesus as the Messiah.

Mestizos The descendents of Europeans and Native Americans.

Microbial exchange The exchange of microbes between ecosystems.

Militarization The trend toward larger and more powerful armed forces and the organization of society and the economy to achieve that goal.

Military revolution Change in warfare in the sixteenth and seventeenth centuries that accompanied the rise of fire-power technology.

Millenarianism Belief that the end of the world is about to occur, as foretold in the biblical Book of Revelation.

Minas Gerais (Trans.) "General Mines." Region of Brazil rich in mineral resources that experienced a gold rush in the early eighteenth century.

Ming Dynasty Chinese dynasty (1368–1644) noted for its flourishing foreign trade and achievements in scholarship and the arts.

Mongol peace A period of history, from about 1240 C.E. to about 1340 C.E., when peace and order, imposed by the Mongols, fostered trade, communication, and cultural exchange across the Eurasian steppes.

Mongols Nomadic people whose homeland was in Mongolia. In the twelfth and thirteenth centuries, they conquered most of Eurasia from China to Eastern Europe.

Monocultures The cultivation of a single dominant food crop, such as potatoes or rice. Societies that practiced monoculture were vulnerable to famine if bad weather or disease caused their single food crop to fail.

Monroe Doctrine The policy enunciated by President James Monroe in 1823 that the United States would oppose further European colonization in the Americas.

Monsoons A wind from the southwest or south that brings heavy rainfall each summer to southern Asia.

Mound agriculture Form of agriculture found in pre-Columbian North America.

Mughals Muslim dynasty founded by Babur that ruled India, at least nominally, from the mid–1500s until 1857.

Multiculturalism The belief that different cultures can coexist peacefully and equitably in a single country.

Napoleonic Wars Wars waged between France under Napoleon and its European enemies from 1799 to 1815. The fighting spilled over into the Middle East and sparked conflicts in North America and India and independence movements in the Spanish and Portuguese colonies in the Americas.

Nationalism Belief that a people who share the same language, historic experience, and sense of identity make up a nation and that every nation has the right to assert its identity, pursue its destiny, defend its rights, and be the primary focus of its people's loyalty.

Natural selection The process by which only the organisms best adapted to their environment pass on their genetic material to subsequent generations.

Nature versus nurture Debate over the relative importance of inherited characteristics and environmental factors in determining human development.

Nazis Members of the National Socialist German Workers' Party, founded in Germany in 1919 and brought to power in 1933 under Adolf Hitler.

Neanderthal Humanlike species, evidence for whose existence was found in the Neander River valley in northern Germany in the mid–nineteenth century. Neanderthals disappeared from the evolutionary record about 30,000 years ago.

Negritude The affirmation of the distinctive nature, quality, and validity of black culture.

Nestorianism The Christian theological doctrine that within Jesus are two distinct and separate persons, divine and human, rather than a single divine person. Orthodox Christians classed Nestorianism as a heresy, but it spread across Central Asia along the Silk Roads.

New Europes Lands in other hemispheres where the environment resembled that of Europe and where immigrants could successfully transplant a European way of life and European culture.

New Rich Rich people whose wealth was acquired in the recent past, often in industry or commerce.

New World Term Europeans applied to the Americas.

Nirvana The spiritual goal of Buddhism, when a person ends the cycle of birth and rebirth and achieves enlightenment and freedom from any attachment to material things.

Noble savage Idealized vision that some people in the West held about certain non-Europeans, especially some Native Americans and Polynesians. It was based on the notions that civilization was a corrupting force and that these peoples lived lives more in tune with nature.

Northwest Passage Water route from the Atlantic to the Pacific through the Arctic archipelago of northern Canada and along the northern coast of Alaska. For centuries, Europeans sought in vain for a more accessible route to the Pacific farther south in North America.

Obsidian Volcanic glass used to make tools, weapons, and mirrors.

Old regime Term for the social, economic, and political institutions that existed in France and the rest of Europe before the French Revolution.

Old World Term for the regions of the world—Europe, parts of Africa and Asia—that were known to Europeans before the discovery of the Americas.

Ongons Tibetan images in which spirits are thought to reside. Shamans claimed to communicate with the ongons.

OPEC The Organization of Petroleum Exporting Countries, an alliance of the world's major oil producers.

Oracle A person or group that claims to be able to have access to knowledge of the future by consulting a god. Ancient rulers often consulted oracles.

Oriental despotism Arbitrary and corrupt rule. Eighteenth-century Europeans saw it as characteristic of Asian or Islamic rulers.

Orthodox Church Dominant Christian church in the Byzantine Empire, the Balkans, and Russia.

Ottoman Empire Islamic empire based in present-day Turkey, with its capital at Istanbul. At its height in the sixteenth century, the Ottoman Empire stretched from Iraq across North Africa to the borders of Morocco and included almost all the Balkans and most of Hungary. The empire gradually declined, but endured until it was dismembered after World War I.

Pampas A vast plain of south-central South America that supports huge herds of cattle and other livestock.

Pan-African Congress A series of five meetings held between 1919 and 1945 that claimed to represent all black Africans and demanded an end to colonial rule.

Pangaea A hypothetical prehistoric supercontinent that included all the landmasses of the Earth.

Partition of India The division in 1947 along ethnic and religious lines of the British Indian Empire into two independent states: India, which was largely Hindu, and Pakistan, which was largely Muslim. The division involved widespread violence in which at least 500,000 people were killed.

Paternalism A social or economic relationship that resembles the dependency that exists between a father and his child.

Patrilineal A society that traces ancestry through the paternal line.

Philosopher's stone A substance that was believed to have the power to change base metals into gold.

Physiocrats Eighteenth-century French political economists who argued that agriculture was the foundation of any country's wealth and recommended agricultural improvements.

Plantation system System of commercial agriculture based on large landholdings, often worked by forced labor.

Polestar Bright star used for navigation.

Positivism Doctrine that asserts the undeniability of human sense perception and the power of reason to prove that what our senses perceive is true.

Pragmatism Philosophy advocated by William James that holds that the standard for evaluating the truth or validity of a theory or concept depends on how well it works and on the results that arise from holding it.

Proletariat The working class, which according to Karl Marx, would overthrow the bourgeoisie.

Protectorate A country or region that, although nominally independent and not a colony, is in fact controlled militarily, politically, and economically by a more powerful foreign state.

Protestantism The theological system of any of the churches of Western Christendom that separated from the Roman Catholic Church during the Reformation. The advent of Protestantism is usually associated with Martin Luther's break from the Catholic Church in the 1520s.

Psychoanalysis Technique developed by Sigmund Freud to treat patients suffering from emotional or psychological disorders by making them aware of their subconscious conflicts, motivations, and desires.

Public sphere Sites for the public discussion of political, social, economic, and cultural issues.

Qing dynasty Last imperial Chinese dynasty (1644–1912), founded when the Manchus, a steppeland people from Manchuria, conquered China. It was succeeded by a republic.

Quantum mechanics Mechanics based on the principle that matter and energy have the properties of both particles and waves.

Quran The sacred text of Islam dictated from God to the Prophet Muhammad by the Archangel Gabriel. Considered by Muslims to contain the final revelations of God to humanity.

Rape of Nanjing Atrocities committed by the Japanese during their occupation of the city of Nanjing, China, in 1937.

Rastafarianism A religious and political movement that began among black people in Jamaica in the 1930s. Its adherents believe that former Emperor Haile Selassie of Ethiopia (r. 1930–1974) was divine and the Messiah whose coming was foretold in the Bible.

Rationalism The doctrine that reason by itself can determine truth and solve the world's problems.

Realpolitik Political doctrine that says that the state is not subject to moral laws and has the right to do whatever safeguards it and advances its interests.

Reformation The Protestant break from the Roman Catholic Church in the sixteenth century.

Renaissance Humanistic revival of classical art, architecture, literature, and learning that originated in Italy in the fourteenth century and spread throughout Europe.

Renewable energy Energy that is not derived from a finite resource such as oil or coal.

Rig Veda A collection of hymns and poems created by a sedentary people living in the area north of the Indus valley where northern India and Pakistan meet. The *Rig Veda* provides evidence for the theory that invaders destroyed Harappan civilization.

Romanticism Intellectual and artistic movement that arose in reaction to the Enlightenment's emphasis on reason. Romantics had a heightened interest in nature and religion, and emphasized emotion and imagination.

Rus A Slavic-Scandinavian people who created the first Russian state and converted to Orthodox Christianity.

Safavids Shiite dynasty that ruled Persia between 1501 and 1722.

Sahel A semiarid region of north Central Africa south of the Sahara Desert.

Saint Domingue A French colony on Hispaniola that flourished in the eighteenth century by cultivating sugar and coffee with slave labor. It became the modern republic of Haiti after a protracted struggle that began in the 1790s.

Samurai The hereditary Japanese feudal-military aristocracy.

Sati In Hinduism, the burning of a widow on her husband's funeral pyre.

Satyagraha (Trans.) "The force of truth." Nonviolent movement launched by Mohandas K. Gandhi, with the goal of achieving Indian independence.

Savanna (or "Savannah") A flat grassland of tropical or subtropical regions.

Scientific revolution The sweeping change in the investigation of nature and the view of the universe that took place in Europe in the sixteenth and seventeenth centuries.

Scientism The belief that science and the scientific method can explain everything in the universe and that no other form of inquiry is valid.

Scramble for Africa Late nineteenth-century competition among European powers to acquire colonies in Africa.

Sea Peoples Unknown seafaring people that contributed to the instability of the eastern Mediterranean in the twelfth century B.C.E., attacking Egypt, Palestine, Mesopotamia, Anatolia, and Syria.

Second Vatican Council Council of the Roman Catholic Church that convened at intervals in the 1960s and led to major changes in church liturgy and discipline.

Secularism Belief that religious considerations should be excluded from civil affairs or public education.

Self-determination Principle that a given people or nationality has the right to determine their own political status.

Self-strengthening Mid–nineteenth-century Chinese reform movement initiated in response to Western incursions.

Seljuks A Turkish dynasty ruling in Central and western Asia from the eleventh to the thirteenth centuries.

Serf Agricultural laborer attached to the land owned by a lord and required to perform labor in return for certain legal or customary rights. Unlike slaves, serfs could not usually be sold away from the land.

Shaman A person who acts as an intermediary between humans and spirits or gods. Such a person functions as the medium though which spirits talk to humans.

Sharia Islamic law. The word *sharia* derives from the verb *shara'a*, which is connected to the concepts of "spiritual law" and "system of divine law."

Shiites Members of the most important minority tradition in the Islamic world. Shiites believe that the caliphate is the prerogative of Muhammad's nephew, Ali, and his heirs. Shiism has been the state religion in Iran since the sixteenth century.

Shinto A religion native to Japan, characterized by veneration of nature spirits and ancestors and by a lack of formal dogma.

Shogun A hereditary military ruler of Japan who exercised real power in the name of the emperor, who was usually powerless and relegated to purely ceremonial roles. The last shogun was removed from office in 1868.

Sikhism Indian religion founded by Nanak Guru in the early sixteenth century that blends elements of the Hindu and Muslim traditions.

Silk Roads Key overland trade routes that connected eastern and western Eurasia. The route first began to function in the aftermath of Alexander the Great's expansion into Central Asia at the end of the fourth century B.C.E.

Sioux A nomadic Native American people of central North America who, with the benefit of horses introduced to the Americas by the Spanish, formed a pastoralist empire in the late eighteenth and mid–nineteenth centuries.

Social Darwinism The misapplication of Darwin's biological theories to human societies, often to justify claims of racial superiority and rule by the strong over the weak.

Socialism Any of various theories or systems in which the means of producing and distributing goods is owned collectively or by a centralized government.

Socialist realism An artistic doctrine embraced by many communist and leftist regimes that the sole legitimate purpose of the arts was to glorify the ideals of the state by portraying workers, peasants, and the masses in a strictly representational, nonabstract style.

Sociobiology The study of the biological determinants of social behavior.

Solidarity Polish trade union founded in 1980 that played a key role in bringing down Poland's communist regime.

Solomids Dynasty that seized power in Ethiopia in 1270 C.E. and claimed descent from the Biblical King Solomon.

Song dynasty Dynasty (960–1279) under which China achieved one of its highest levels of culture and prosperity.

Songhay An ancient empire of West Africa in the present-day country of Mali. It reached the height of its power around 1500 C.E.

Soninke West African kingdom on the upper Niger River.

Soviet Russian term for a workers' collective.

State system Organization of early modern Europe into competing nation-states.

Steppe A vast semiarid, grass-covered plain, extending across northern Eurasia and central North America.

Stoicism Philosophy founded on the belief that nature is morally neutral and that the wise person, therefore, achieves happiness by accepting misfortune and practicing self-control.

Stranger effect The tendency some peoples have to esteem and defer to strangers.

Stream of consciousness A literary technique that presents the thoughts and feelings of a character in a novel or story as they arise in the character's mind.

Subsidiarity Doctrine that decisions should always be made at the level closest to the people whom the decisions most affect.

Suez Canal Canal linking the Mediterranean and the Red Sea. It was built by French engineers with European capital and opened in 1869.

Sufis Members of Islamic groups that cultivate mystical beliefs and practices. Sufis have often been instrumental in spreading Islam, but Muslim authorities have often distrusted them.

Sundiata Legendary hero said to have founded the kingdom of Mali in West Africa.

Sunnis Members of the dominant tradition in the Islamic world. Sunnis believe that any member of Muhammad's tribe could be designated caliph.

Surrealism Literary and artistic movement that attempts to express the workings of the subconscious.

Syllogisms A form of argument in which we can infer a necessary conclusion from two premises that prior demonstration or agreement has established to be true.

Syncretic Characterized by the reconciliation or fusion of differing systems of belief.

Taiping Rebellion Rebellion (1852–1864) against the Qing Empire that resulted in tens of millions of deaths and widespread destruction in southern China.

Tang dynasty Chinese dynasty (618–907) famous for its wealth and encouragement of the arts and literature.

Taro a fibrous root indigenous to New Guinea, first cultivated 9,000 years ago in swamplands.

Tengri "Ruler of the sky." The supreme deity of the Mongols and other steppeland peoples.

The Mongol Peace Era in the thirteenth and fourteenth centuries when Mongol rule created order and stability in Central Asia and enabled goods and ideas to flow along the Silk Roads.

Theory of value The theory that the value of goods is not inherent, but rather determined by supply and demand.

Theravada A conservative branch of Buddhism that adheres to the nontheistic ideal of self-purification to nirvana. Theravada Buddhism emphasizes the monastic ideal and is dominant in present-day Sri Lanka and southeast Asia.

Third Rome Term Russians used for Moscow and Russian Orthodox Christianity. It expressed the belief that the Russian czars were the divinely chosen heirs of the Roman and Byzantine emperors.

Thule Inuit Indigenous Native American people who crossed the Arctic and arrived in Greenland around 1000 C.E.

Tillers Agriculturalists who emphasize the cultivation of plants for food and products, such as timber and cotton.

Tokugawa A family of shoguns that ruled Japan in the name of the emperors from 1603 to 1868.

Trading-post empires Term for the networks of imperial forts and trading posts that Europeans established in Asia in the seventeenth century.

Treasure Fleets Spanish fleets that sailed from the Caribbean each year to bring gold and silver from mines in the Americas back to Europe.

Tundra A treeless area between the ice cap and the tree line of Arctic regions.

Turks A member of any of the Turkic-speaking, nomadic peoples who originated in Central Asia. The Turks eventually converted to Islam and dominated the Middle East.

Uncertainty principle Niels Bohr and Werner Heisenberg's theory that because observers are part of every observation their findings can never be objective.

United Nations International political organization created after World War II to prevent armed conflict, settle international disputes peacefully, and provide cultural, economic, and technological aid. It was the successor to the League of Nations, which had proved to be ineffectual.

Universal love Love between all people, regardless of status, nationality, or family ties.

Upanishads The theoretical sections of the Veda (the literature of the sages of the Ganges civilization). The Upanishads were written down as early as 800 B.C.E.

Urbanization The process by which urban areas develop and expand.

Utilitarianism System of thought devised by Jeremy Bentham, based on the notion that the goal of the state was to create the greatest happiness for the greatest number of people.

Utopianism Belief in a system or ideology aimed at producing a perfect or ideal society.

Vaccination Inoculation with a vaccine to produce immunity to a particular disease.

Vernacular languages The languages that people actually spoke, as opposed to Latin, which was the language used by the Roman Catholic Church and was, for a long time, the language of scholarship, the law, and diplomacy in much of Europe.

Virtual reality A computer simulation of a real or imaginary system.

Wahhabbism Muslim sect founded by Abdul Wahhab (1703–1792), known for its strict observance of the Quran. It is the dominant form of Islam in Saudi Arabia.

Westerlies Winds coming from the west.

Westernization The process by which other cultures adopt Western styles or ways of life.

World system The system of interconnections among the world's population.

World War I Global war (1914–1918) sparked by the assassination of Archduke Francis Ferdinand of Austria by a Serb terrorist in June 1914.

World War II Global conflict that lasted from 1939 to 1945 and ended with the defeat and occupation of Fascist Italy, Nazi Germany, and Japan.

Zen A school of Mahayana Buddhism that asserts that a person can attain enlightenment through meditation, self-contemplation, and intuition.

Ziggurat A tall, tapering Mesopotamian temple. Ziggurats were the physical and cultural centers of Mesopotamian cities.

Zimbabwes Stone-built administrative centers for rulers and the elite in southern Africa. The zimbabwes flourished in the fifteenth century.

Zoroastrianism Iranian religious system founded by Zoroaster that posited a universal struggle between the forces of light (the good) and of darkness (evil).

A NOTE ON DATES AND SPELLINGS

In keeping with common practice among historians of global history, we have used B.C.E. (before the common era) and C.E. (common era) to date events. For developments deep in the past, we have employed the phrase "years ago" to convey to the reader a clear sense of time. Specific dates are given only when necessary and when doing so improves the context of the narrative.

Recognizing that almost every non-English word can be transliterated in any number of ways, we have adopted the most widely used and simplest systems for spelling names and terms. The *pinyin* system of Chinese spelling is used for all Chinese words with the exceptions of *Hong Kong* and *Yangtze*, which are still widely referred to in their Wade-Giles form. Following common usage, we have avoided using apostrophes in the spelling of Arabic and Persian words, as well as words from other languages—thus, *Quran* and *Kaaba* instead of *Qu'ran* and *Ka'ba*, and *Tbilisi* instead of *T'bilisi*. Diacritical marks, accents, and other specialized symbols are used only if the most common variant of a name or term employs such devices (such as *Çatalhüyük*), if they are part of a personal noun (such as *Nicolás*), or if the inclusion of such markings in the spelling of a word makes pronouncing it easier (*Teotihuacán*).

Throughout the text the first appearance of important non-English words whose pronunciation may be unclear for the reader is followed by phonetic spellings in parentheses, with the syllable that is stressed spelled in capital letters. So, for example *Ugarit* is spelled phonetically as "OO-gah-riht." Chinese words are not stressed, so each syllable is spelled in lowercase letters. Thus, the city of Hangzhou in China is rendered phonetically as "hahng-joh." For monosyllabic words, the phonetic spelling is in lowercase letters. So *Rus* is spelled as "roos." The table below provides a guide for how the vowel sounds in *The World: A Brief History* are represented phonetically.

a	as in *cat, bat*
ah	as in *car, father*
aw	as in *law, paw*
ay	as in *fate, same*
eh	as in *bet, met*
ee	as in *beet, ease*
eye	as in *dine, mine*
ih	as in *if, sniff*
o	as in *more, door*
oh	as in *row, slow*
oo	as in *loop, moo*
ow	as in *cow, mouse*
uh	as in *but, rut*

CHAPTER 2

1. J. L. Harlan, *Crops and Man* (1992), p. 27.

2. Charles Darwin, *The Variation of Plants and Animals under Domestication*, 2 vols (1868), i, pp. 309–310.

CHAPTER 11

1. G. Coédès, *Angor: An Introduction* (1963), pp 104–105.

2. G. Coédès, *Angor: An Introduction* p. 96.

3. Patrologia Latina, cli, col. 0572; William of Malmesbury, *Chronicle of the Kings of England*, 68 IV, ch. 2 (ed. J. A. Giles [1857], p. 360).

CHAPTER 12

1. J. T. C. Liu, *Reform in Sung China: Wang An-Shih and His New Policies* (Cambridge, MA: Harvard University Press, 1957), p. 54.

CHAPTER 13

1. P. Jackson, ed., *The Travels of Friar Willam of Rubruck* (London, 1981), pp. 113–114.

2. R. Latham, ed., *The Travels of Marco Polo* (Harmondsworth, 1972), p. 85.

3. J. Fennell, *The Crisis of Medieval Russia* (Longman Publishing Group, 1983), p. 88.

CHAPTER 14

1. R. Horrox, *The Black Death* (Manchester University Press, 1994), p. 16.

2. N. Cantor, *In the Wake of the Plague* (New York: Perennial/Harper Collins, 2002), p. 199.

3. D. Hall in *Cambridge History of Southeast Asia*, ed. N. Tarling (Cambridge University Press, 1992), i, 218.

4. F. Rosenthal ed. *The Muqaddimah*, 3 vols. (New York: Pantheon Books, 1958), i, 64–65.

CHAPTER 16

1. T. Armstrong, ed., *Yermak's Campaign in Siberia* (London, 1975), pp. 38–50, 59–69, 108, 163; B. Bobrick, *East of the Sun: The Epic Conquest and Tragic History of Siberia* (London, 1993), p. 43.

CHAPTER 18

1. *Principes de la philosophie*, Bk I, 8,7; Discours sur la méthode, ch 4.

CHAPTER 26

1. H. S. Wilson, *Origins of West Africa Nationalism* (London, 1969), p. 167.

CHAPTER 27

1. N. Chomsky, *Knowledge of Language* (Wesport, CT: 1986), p. 14.

CHAPTER 28

1. D. A. J. Pernikoff, *Bushido: The Anatomy of Terror* (1943).

CHAPTER 29

1. I. Berlin "My Intellectual Path", *New York Review of Books*, 14 May (1998); *The Power of Ideas*, ed. H. Hardy (Princeton, 2002), p.12.

CREDITS

CHAPTER 1: p. 2 Francisco Goya y Lucientes, Spanish, 1746-1828. Boy Staring at an Apparition (1824-1825) Carbon Black and watercolor on ivory (Black wash heightened with vermilion and brown) 6.03 x 6.03cm (2 3/8 x 2 3/8 in.) Museum of Fine Arts, Boston. Gift of Eleanor; p. 7 © The Natural History Museum, London; p. 8 Howard S. Friedman/Pearson Education/PH College; p. 12 The Jane Goodall Institute, www.janegoodall.org; p. 16 Charles & Josette Lenars © Charles & Josette Lenars/COR-BIS All Rights Reserved; p. 17 Michael & Patricia Fogden/© Michael & Patricia Fogden/CORBIS All Rights Reserved; p. 18 Peter/Georgina Bowater/Creative Eye/MIRA.com; p. 19 Novosti/Photo Researchers, Inc.; p. 22 AKG Images/Jurgen Sorges.

CHAPTER 2: p. 26 © Kevin Flemming/CORBIS All Rights Reserved; p. 28 © Louie Psihoyos/CORBIS All Rights Reserved; p. 30 Theya Molleson, Natural History Museum of London; p. 32 © Joe McDonlad/CORBIS All Rights Reserved; p. 36 © Caroline Penn/CORBIS All Rights Reserved; p. 37 Ashmolean Museum, Oxford, England, U.K.; p. 39 Hittite Museum, Ankara, Turkey/ET Archive, London/SuperStock; p. 43 © Michael Holford; p. 44 Andrew McRobb © Dorling Kindersley.

CHAPTER 3: p. 50 © Copyright The British Museum; p. 54 M. Andrews/Ancient Art & Architecture Collection Ltd.; p. 57 TOP Erich Lessing/Art Resource, NY; p. 57 **BOTTOM** 57 bottom Werner Forman Archive; p. 58 Giraudon/Bridgeman Art Library; p. 62 Borromeo/Dancing girl. Bronze statuette from Mohenjo Daro. Indus Valley Civilization. National Museum, New Delhi, India. Borromeo/Art Resource, NY; p. 65 Michael Holford; p. 66 Royal Museums of Art and History, Brussels, Belgium. Copyright IRPA-KIK, Brussels, Belgium; p. 67 Lowell Georgia/Corbis/Bettmann; p. 71 Courtesy of the Library of Congress.

CHAPTER 4: p. 74 © CM Dixon/ HIP/The Image Works; p. 77 The Art Archive/Dagli Orti; p. 82 The Art Archive/Heraklion Museum/Dagli Orti; p. 84 © Erich Lessing/Art Resource, NY; p. 87 Eric Lessing/Art Resource, N.Y.; p. 88 The Art Archive/Dagli Orti; p. 91 Werner Forman/Art Resource, NY.

CHAPTER 5: p. 96 The Art Archive/Dagli Orti; p. 99 "Human-headed winged bull and winged lion (lamassu). Alabaster (ypsum); Gateway support from the Palace of AshurnasirpallII (ruled 883-859 BCE). Limestone. H: 10' 3/11/2". L: 9' 1". W: 2' 1/2". The Metropolitan Museum of Art, Gift of John D. Rockefeller, J; p. 104 Ronald Sheridan/ © Ronald Sheridan/Ancient Art & Architecture Collection Ltd; p. 105 The Art Archive/Museo Di Villa Giulia Rome/ Dagli Art; p. 107 The Art Archive/Archaeological Museum Sofia/Dagli Orti; p. 108 Lewandowski/Ojeda/Sarcophagus of a married couple on a funeral bed. Etruscan, from Cerveteri, 6th BCE. Terracotta. Lewandowski/Ojeda. Musee Louvre, Paris France. RMN Reunion Des Musees Nationeaux/Art Resource, NY; p. 109 AGE Fotostock America, Inc.; p. 116 116 Michael Holford.

CHAPTER 6: p. 124 Courtesy of the Freer Gallery of Art, Smithsonian Institution, Washington, D.C.; p. 127 © Tim Page/ CORBIS All Rights Reserved; p. 130 Erich Lessing/Relief, Israel, 10th-6th Century: Judean exiles carrying provisions. Detail of the Assyrian conquest of the Jewish fortified town of Lachish (battle 701 BC). Part of a relief from the palace of Sennacherib at Niniveh, Mesopotamia (Iraq). British Museum; p. 132 Courtesy of the Library of Congress; p. 134 "THE GOOD SHEPHERD", marble, Height: as restored cm 99, as preserved cm 55, head cm 15.5. Late 3rd century A. D. Vatican Musuems, Pio-Christian Museum, Inv. 28590. Courtesy of the Vatican Museums; p. 136 www.photos.com/Jupiter Images; p. 139 Christopher and Sally Gable © Dorling Kindersley; p. 141 Mark de Fraeye/Photo Researchers, Inc.; p. 144 Erich Lessing/Art Resource, N.Y.

CHAPTER 7: p. 150 Robert Clark/Robert Clark Photography; p. 157 The Art Archive/Picture Desk, Inc./Kobal Collection; p. 159 Bridgeman Art Library; p. 164 Romisch-Germanisches Museum der Stadt Koln/Rheinisches Bildarchiv; p. 165 © The Detroit Institute of Arts, USA/Bridgeman Art Library; p. 166 Kit Kittle/CORBIS All Rights Reserved; p. 168 © KEREN SU/DanitaDelimont.com; p. 170 p. 172 Werner Forman Archive Ltd; p. 175 Robert Frerck/Getty Images Inc. - Stone Allstock.

CHAPTER 8: p. 180 © Justin Kerr; p. 184 Canali Photobank; p. 188 R. Sheridan/Ancient Art & Architecture Collection Ltd.; p. 189 Werner Forman Archive; p. 192 © Ancient Art & Architecture/DanitaDelimont.com; p. 193 © Gallo Images/CORBIS All Rights Reserved; p. 195 The Art Archive/Dagli Orti; p. 197 Art Archive; p. 202 Dagli Orti/Picture Desk, Inc./Kobal Collection; p. 204 China Tourism Press. Wang, Jian Jun/Getty Images Inc.-Image Bank.

CHAPTER 9: p. 210 Fujita Museum Of Art; p. 215 The Art Archive/British Museum; p. 216 James Stanfield/NGS Image Collection; p. 217 © Michael Holford; p. 219 Natia Chakvetadze; p. 220 Picture Desk, Inc./Kobal Collection; p. 221 © Chris Lisle/CORBIS All Rights Reserved; p. 226 Scala/Art Resource, N.Y.; p. 229 Courtesy of the Library of Congress; p. 232 Reuters America LLC/ © Reuters/CORBIS.

CHAPTER 10: p. 236 © Carmen Redondo/CORBIS All Rights Reserved; p. 242 Sachsische Landesbibliothek p. 243 © Erich Lessing/Art Resource; p. 245 Werner Forman Archive Ltd; p. 248 Christopher Rennie/Robert Harding World Imagery; p. 253 © Luca Tettoni/Robert Harding; p. 254 Library of Congress; p. 256 National Museum of Ireland.

CHAPTER 11: p. 262 Kanai Morio/Tokyo National Museum/DNP Archives; p. 266 © Staffan Widstrand/CORBIS All Rights Reserved; p. 269 Courtesy of the Library of Congress; p. 271 © Kazuyoshi Nomachi/HAGA/ The Image Works; p. 272 Andrew Gunners/Getty Images-Digital Vision; p. 276 Japan Society; p. 278 Leiden University/Institute of Biology; p. 279 Bayerische Staatsbibliothek; p. 282 By permission of The British Library; p. 283 Rheinisches Bildarchiv, Museen Der Stadt Koln.

CHAPTER 12: p. 286 Library of the Topkapi Palace Museum; p. 288 Bibliotheque Nationale, Paris, France/Bridgeman Art Library; p. 289 By permission of The British Library; p. 293 Monasterio de El Escorial, El Escorial, Spain/Index/Bridgeman Art Library; p. 294 H. Lewandowski/Musee du Louvre/RMN Reunion des Musees Nationaux, France. Art Resource, NY; p. 297 Bridgeman Art Library; p. 300 Paul H. Kuiper/CORBIS-NY; p. 302 V & A Picture Library; p. 307 The Art Archive/Freer Gallery of Art; p. 308 The National Palace Museum.

CHAPTER 13: p. 314 © The Trustees of the British Museum; p. 317 The Bridgeman Art Library International/Bibliotheque Nationale, Paris, France/ The Bridgeman Art Library; p. 320 Akg-Images/VISIOARS/AKA-IMAGES; p. 321 Copyright Museum of Imperial Collections, Sonnomaru Shozo Kan; p. 323 The Metropolitan Museum of Art, Purchase, Bequest of Dorothy Graham Bennet, 1993 (1993.256) Photograph © The Metropolitan Museum of Art; p. 324 © Galen Rowell/Corbis All rights reserved; p. 325 The Art Archive/Bibliotheque Nationale, Paris; p. 328 National Palace Museum, Taipei, Taiwan/ The Bridgeman Art Library; p. 329 Library of the Topkapi Palace Museum; p. 330 © George G. Schmid/Corbis All rights reserved; p. 333 Dallas and John Heaton/The Stock Connection; p. 335 © National Maritime Museum Picture Library, London, England; p. 336 Canali Photobank.

CHAPTER 14: p. 342 © Josef Polleross/The Image Works; p. 354 Museum of London; p. 349 © Bildarchiv Preussischer Kulturbesitz/Art Resource, NY; p. 351 Aka-Images/AKA-IMAGES; p. 354 Bibliotheque Nationale, Paris/Bridgeman Art Library; p. 357 p. 360 SEF/Art Resource, NY; p. 362 © 1991 The Metropolitan Museum of Art; p. 365 The Granger Collection; p. 366 Frank Khoury/Museum purchase 86-12-2. Photograph by Frank Khoury. National Museum of African Art, Smithsonian Institution; p. 367 Dallas and John Heaton/The Stock Connection, p. 368 © Charles & Josette Lenars/Corbis All rights reserved.

CHAPTER 15: p. 374 Courtesy of the Harvard Map Collection, Harvard College Library; p. 376 Courtesy of the Library of Congress; p. 378 National Archives of South Africa; p. 379 Photograph © 1984 The Metropolitan Museum of Art; p. 382 Bodleian Library, University of Oxford; p. 390 Library of the Topkapi Palace Museum; p. 391 Courtesy of the Library of Congress; p. 399 Instituto de Arte Hispanico, Barcelona, Spain; p. 402 Courtesy of the Library of Congress; p. 404 © Michael Freeman/CORBIS All Rights Reserved.

CHAPTER 16: p. 410 By permission of The British Library; p. 414 By permission of The British Library; p. 417 Courtesy of the Library of Congress; p. 418 Copyright Rijksmuseum Amsterdam; p. 419 Courtesy of the Library of Congress; p. 421 Bibliotheque Nationale de France; p. 424 V&A Images/Victoria and Albert Museum; p. 428 Courtesy of the Library of Congress; p. 430 The Hispanic Society of America/Hispanic Society of America.

CHAPTER 17: p. 434 © Jonathan Blair/CORBIS All Rights Reserved; p. 437 Koninklijke Bibliotheek, The Hague, The Netherlands; p. 440 Courtesy of the John Carter Brown Library at Brown University; p. 441 Musee des Beaux-Arts et d'Archeologie, Besancon, France/ Lauros/Giraudon/ The Bridgeman Art Library; p. 442 The Granger Collection, New York; p. 445 Courtesy of the Library of Congress; p. 448 Library of the Topkapi Palace Museum; p. 449 Charles Cavaliere; p. 450 The Art Archive/Mus[eacute]e Guimet Paris; p. 454 Courtesy of the Library of Congress; p. 457 Library and Archives of Canada website, www.collectionscanada.ca.

CHAPTER 18: p. 462 © Richard List/CORBIS All Rights Reserved; p. 465 Bildarchiv Preubischer Kulturbesitz; p. 466 Versucung Christi (1547), Gemalde, Bonn, Landschaftsverband Rheinland/Rheinisches Landesmuseum Bonn. Inv. Nr. 58.3; p. 467 Courtesy of the Library of Congress; p. 468 Jeffery Dykes/Photograph courtesy Peabody Essex Museum; p. 469 Courtesy of the Library of Congress; p. 470 Joseph Sohm, Visions of America/Corbis/Bettmann; p. 472 of the Library of Congress; p. 474 Courtesy of the Library of Congress; p. 475 Jerry Hardman-Jones/Art Quarterly; p. 478 The Bridgeman Art Library International; p. 481 © Erich Lessing, Art Resource, NY; p. 482 Courtesy of the Library of Congress; p. 484 Courtesy of the Library of Congress.

CHAPTER 19: p. 488 By permission of The British Library; p. 494 Courtesy of the Library of Congress. Rare Book and Special Collections Divisoin; p. 495 Archiv fur Kunst und Geschichte, Berlin; p. 497 Courtesy of the Library of Congress; p. 498 V&A Images/Victoria and Albert Museum; p. 498 Courtesy of the Library of Congress; p. 502 502 © The Metropolitan Museum of Art; p. 506 Breamore House, Hampshire, England; p. 507 Museo De America.

CHAPTER 20: p. 516 The Art Archive/Museo de Arte Antiga Lisbon/Dagli Orti; p. 519 Courtesy of the Library of Congress; p. 522 Courtesy of the Library of Congress; p. 523 Private Collection/ Agnew's, London, UK/ The Bridgeman Art Library; p. 526 Photograph courtesy Peabody Essex Museum; p. 527 The Bridgeman

C-1

Art Library International; **p. 529** Courtesy of the Library of Congress; **p. 532** © The Bridgeman Art Library; **p. 533** The Master and Fellows of Cambridge University Library; **p. 534** National Library of Australia, Canberra, Australia/ The Bridgeman Art Library.

CHAPTER 21: p. 538 © Wolfgang Kaehler/CORBIS All Rights Reserved; **p. 541** Musee du Louvre/RMN Reunion des Musees Nationaux, France. SCALA/Art Resource, NY; **p. 548** Library of Congress; **p. 549** Dagli Orti (A); **p. 552** Douglas Waugh/Peter Arnold, Inc.; **p. 555** Robertstock/Classicstock.com; **p. 556** Andy Crawford © Dorling Kindersley, Courtesy of the University Museum of Archaeology and Anthropology, Cambridge; **p. 558** John Trumbull (American 1756-1843),"The Surrender of Lord Cornwallis at Yorktown, 19 October 1781", 1787-c. 1828. Oil on canvas, 53.3 x 77.8 x 1.9 cm (21 x 30 5/8 x 3/4 in.) Yale University Art Gallery, Trumbull Collection.

CHAPTER 22: p. 562 Bristol City Museum and Art Gallery, UK/ The Bridgeman Art Library; **p. 564** Musees de Saint-Malo; **p. 566** Musee Lambinet, Versailles/Giraudon/Art Resource, N.Y.; **p. 568** Collection of the National Palace Museum. Taiwan, Republic of China; **p. 570** Ruth and Sherman Lee Institute for Japanese Art at the Clark Center, Hanford. CA; **p. 572** Courtesy of the Library of Congress; **p. 574** Giraudon/Pierre-Antoine Demachy, "Festival of the Supreme Being at the Champ de Mars on June 8, 1794." Obligatory mention: Musee de la Ville de Paris, Musee Carnavalet, Paris, France. Bridgeman-Giraudon/Art. Resource, NY; **p. 577** Royal Geographical Society, London, UK/ The Bridgeman Art Library; **p. 579** Sotheby's Picture Library/London; **p. 581** Gianni Dagli Orti/Corbis/Bettmann; **p. 583** Prado, Madrid, Spain/ The Bridgeman Art Library.

CHAPTER 23: p. 588 Photograph courtesy Peabody Essex Museum; **p. 590** Courtesy of the Library of Congress; **p. 591** The Art Archive/Oriental Art Museum Genoa/Dagli Orti (A); **p. 597** Courtesy of the Library of Congress; **p. 598** Science Museum London/ Bridgeman Art Library; **p. 599** © British Empire and Commonwealth Museum, Bristol, UK/ Bridgeman Art Library; **p. 604** Courtesy of the Library of Congress; **p. 606** Asian Art & Archaeology, Ic./Corbis; **p. 608** © CORBIS All Rights Reserved; **p. 610** image Works/Mary Evans Picture Library Ltd.

CHAPTER 24: p. 614 Toho/The Kobal Collection; **p. 617** Sheffield Galleries & Museum Trust; **p. 619** Dagli Orti (A)/Picture Desk, Inc./Kobal Collection; **p. 621** © Wolfgang Kaehler/CORBIS All Rights Reserved; **p. 622** Courtesy of the Library of Congress; **p. 623** National Archives of South Africa; **p. 626** Image Works/Mary Evans Picture Library Ltd; **p. 629** Courtesy of the Library of Congress; **p. 630** Corbis/Bettmann; **p. 631** Courtesy of the Library of Congress; **p. 634** The Master and Fellows of Cambridge University Library; **p. 635** Photograph courtesy Peabody Essex Museum.

CHAPTER 25: p. 638 The Art Archive/Eileen Tweedy; **p. 641** Courtesy of the Library of Congress; **p. 646** Picture Desk, Inc./Kobal Collection; **p. 647** KIT Koninklijk Instituut voor de Tropen/Royal Tropical Institute, Amsterdam; **p. 649** Mary Evans Picture Library; **p. 651** © The Trustees of the British Museum; **p. 652** Courtesy of the Library of Congress; **p. 655** Courtesy of the Library of Congress; **p. 658** 658 Courtesy of the Library of Congress; **p. 659** Picture Desk, Inc./Kobal Collection;; **p. 661** Library of Congress.

CHAPTER 26: p. 664 Auckland City Art Gallery, New Zealand/Bridgeman Art Library; **p. 668** The Jewish Museum/George Emanuel Opitz (1775-1841), "Dedication of a Synagogue in Alsace," c. 1820. The Jewish Museum/Art Resource, N.Y.; **p. 670** ©

Judith Miller/Dorling Kindersley/Sloan's; **p. 671** Courtesy of the Library of Congress; **p. 673** Courtesy of the Library of Congress; **p. 674** © CORBIS; **p. 676** top Michael Graham-Stewart/Private Collection/The Bridgeman Art Library; **p. 676** bottom W. & D. Downey/Getty Images; **p. 682** Caleb Bingham (American, 1811-1879), "Stump Speaking," 1853-54. Oil on canvas, 42 1/2 x 58 in. Saint Louis Art Museum, Gift of Bank of America; **p. 685** G. Pellizza da Volpedo "The Fourth Estate". Milano, Galleria Civica D'Arte Moderna. © Canali Photobank.

CHAPTER 27: p. 692 Manuscripts and Archives, Yale University Library; **p. 695** Courtesy of the Library of Congress; **p. 699** Courtesy of the Library of Congress; **p. 700** Courtesy of the Library of Congress; **p. 702** ALBERT EINSTEIN and related rights TM/© of The Hebrew University of Jerusalem, used under license. Represented exclusively by Corbis Corporation; **p. 704** © CORBIS; **p. 708** Gisele Freund/Photo Researchers, Inc.; **p. 712** Umberto Boccioni, "Unique Forma of Continuity in Space". 1913 (cast 1931). Bronze, 43 7/8" x 34 7/8" x 15 3/4" (111.4 x 88.6 x 40 cm). Acquired through the Lillie P. Bliss Bequest. The Museum of Modern Art/Licensed by Scala-Art Resource, N.Y.; **p. 713** Robert Holmes/Corbis/Bettmann; **p. 715** J.M. Janzen/The University of Kansas.

CHAPTER 28: p. 718 © Herge'/Moulinsart 2006; **p. 721** French School, (20th century)/Private Collection/The Bridgeman Art Library; **p. 724** Imperial War Museum, Negative Number Q1460; **p. 725** Margaret Bourke-White/Getty Images/Time Life Pictures; **p. 726** Museo Nacional Centro de Arte Reina Sofia; **p. 727** © Topham/The Image Works; **p. 729** Corbis/Bettmann; **p. 731** Courtesy of the Library of Congress; **p. 734** Nick Ut/AP Wide World Photos; **p. 735** © Swim Ink 2, LLC/CORBIS; **p. 736** Private Collection/ The Bridgeman Art Library; **p. 738** Courtesy of the Library of Congress; **p. 741** © Bettmann/CORBIS All Rights Reserved; **p. 742** ©Ali/CORBIS All Rights Reserved; **p. 743** AP Wide World Photos.

CHAPTER 29: p. 748 Courtesy of the Library of Congress; **p. 750** The Art Archive/ Picture Desk, Inc./Kobal Collection; **p. 751** Reprinted by the permission of the American Cancer Society, Inc. All Rights Reserved; **p. 754** AP Wide World Photos; **p. 757** Corbis/Bettmann; **p. 759** © Reuters NewMedia Inc./CORBIS; **p. 760** Dr. Silvia W. de Groot; **p. 761** Luc Gnago/Corbis/Reuters America LLC; **p. 763** © Robert Vos/ANP/epa/Corbis; **p. 765** © Liu Liqun/CORBIS All Rights Reserved; **p. 767** MARK EDWARDS/Peter Arnold, Inc.; **p. 768** Damir Sagolj/ © Reuters/CORBIS; **p. 770** Courtesy of the Library of Congress.

CHAPTER 30: p. 774 David Reed © David Reed/CORBIS All Rights Reserved; **p. 778** Peter/Georgina Bowater/Creative Eye/MIRA.com; **p. 779** Simon Harris/Robert Harding World Imagery; **p. 780** Getty Images Inc. - Hulton Archive Photos; **p. 781** Courtesy of the Library of Congress; **p. 784** Mark Ralston/Corbis/Reuters America LLC/ © Mark Ralston/Reuters/Corbis; **p. 788** National Oceanic and Atmospheric Administration NOAA; **p. 791** World Wide Photos.

PART OPENER p. 3 Image supplied courtesy of Prof. Chris Henshilwood, University of Bergen, Norway; **p. 49** William L. Clements Library, University of Michigan; **p. 123** British Museum, London, UK/Bridgeman Art Library;; **p. 179** By permission of The British Library; **p. 260** By permission of The British Library; **p. 313** Ryukoku University Library; **p. 411** World Museum Liverpool, National Museums Liverpool; **p. 515** Kobe City Museum/DNP Archives; **p. 587** National Library of Australia; **p. 691** Barrett Lyon.

A

DVD-ROM CONTENTS

28. World Order and Disorder: Global Politics in the Twentieth Century

29. The Pursuit of Utopia: Civil Society in the Twentieth Century

London stock exchange, 1920s
Man on the moon, 1969
March on Washington I, 1963
March on Washington II, 1963
May Day celebrations in Tiananmen Square I
May Day celebrations in Tiananmen Square II
Mayan religious ceremony
Movie theater, New York, 1926
Nazi executing Russian civilians
Nikita Krushchev visiting an Albanian factory
Operation Desert Storm
Poverty, southern United States
Rape of Nanjing, 1937
Segregated movie theatre, Mississippi, 1939
Segregation, USA I, 1950s
Segregation, USA II, 1950s
Shanghai, 1920s
Soviet agriculture
Soviet collective agriculture, 1950s
The Holocaust I
The Holocaust II
Tientsin China, 1924
Tokyo and Nuremberg war crimes trials I
Tokyo and Nuremberg war crimes trials II
Warsaw ghetto
Women bathers, 1920s
Yugoslavs at well, 1920s

30. The Embattled Biosphere: The Twentieth-Century Environment

Text Sources

European criticism of American environmental policies, 2007

Nelson Mandela, Closing Address at the 13th International AIDS Conference, July 2000

Rachel Carson, *Silent Spring,* 1962

The Kyoto Protocol to the United Nations Framework Convention on Climate Change, Article Two

Visual Sources

Tin mining, Indonesia
Traffic in Rio de Janiero, 1940
Hoover Dam
Plague hospital, Bombay
Smog in Los Angeles, 1954
Date market, Algeria
Construction of the Aswan dam, Egypt
Cocoa harvesting in Ghana
Central American market
Cairo traffic
UN sprays DDT over Seoul
Polio vaccination
Ozone poster
International space station
Hurricane Katrina
The Earth at night

Note: Every effort was made to contact every copyright holder on this DVD. If there are any corrections or omissions, please contact us and we will make the revision in the next version of the DVD.

YOU SHOULD CAREFULLY READ THE TERMS AND CONDITIONS BEFORE USING THE DVD-ROM PACKAGE. USING THIS DVD-ROM PACKAGE INDICATES YOUR ACCEPTANCE OF THESE TERMS AND CONDITIONS.SINGLE PC OR MAC LICENSE AGREEMENT AND LIMITED WARRANTYREAD THIS LICENSE CAREFULLY BEFORE OPENING THIS PACKAGE. BY OPENING THIS PACKAGE, YOU ARE AGREEING TO THE TERMS AND CONDITIONS OF THIS LICENSE. IF YOU DO NOT AGREE, DO NOT OPEN THE PACKAGE. PROMPTLY RETURN THE UNOPENED PACKAGE AND ALL ACCOMPANYING ITEMS TO THE PLACE YOU OBTAINED THEM.

1 GRANT OF LICENSE and OWNERSHIP: The enclosed computer programs ("Software") are licensed, not sold, to you by Prentice-Hall, Inc. ("We" or the "Company") and in consideration of your purchase or adoption of the accompanying Company textbooks and/or other materials, and your agreement to these terms. We reserve any rights not granted to you. You own only the disk(s) but we and/or our licensors own the Software itself. This license allows you to use and display your copy of the Software at a single location for academic use only, so long as you comply with the terms of this Agreement.

2. RESTRICTIONS: Except for backup, you may not copy the documentation or the Software. You may not reverse engineer, disassemble, decompile, modify, adapt, translate, or create derivative works based on the Software or the Documentation. You may be held legally responsible for any copying or copyright infringement, which is caused by your failure to abide by the terms of these restrictions.

3. TERMINATION: This license is effective until terminated. This license will terminate automatically without notice from the Company if you fail to comply with any provisions or limitations of this license. Upon termination, you shall destroy the Documentation and all copies of the Software. All provisions of this Agreement as to limitation and disclaimer of warranties, limitation of liability, remedies, or damages, and our ownership rights shall survive termination.

4. LIMITED WARRANTY AND DISCLAIMER OF WARRANTY: Company warrants that for a period of 60 days from the date you purchase this SOFTWARE (or purchase or adopt the accompanying textbook), the Software, when properly installed and used in accordance with the Documentation, will operate in substantial conformity with the description of the Software set forth in the Documentation, and that for a period of 30 days the disk(s) on which the Software is delivered shall be free from defects in materials and workmanship under normal use. The Company does not warrant that the Software will meet your requirements or that the operation of the Software will be uninterrupted or error-free. Your only remedy and the Company's only obligation under these limited warranties is, at the Company's option, return of the disk for a refund of any amounts paid for it by you or replacement of the disk. THIS LIMITED WARRANTY IS THE ONLY WARRANTY PROVIDED BY THE COMPANY AND ITS LICENSORS, AND THE COMPANY AND ITS LICENSORS DISCLAIM ALL OTHER WARRANTIES, EXPRESS OR IMPLIED, INCLUDING WITHOUT LIMITATION, THE IMPLIED WARRANTIES OF MERCHANTABILITY AND FITNESS FOR A PARTICULAR PURPOSE. THE COMPANY DOES NOT WARRANT, GUARANTEE, OR MAKE ANY REPRESENTATION REGARDING THE ACCURACY, RELIABILITY, CURRENTNESS, USE, OR RESULTS OF USE, OF THE SOFTWARE.

5. LIMITATION OF REMEDIES AND DAMAGES: IN NO EVENT, SHALL THE COMPANY OR ITS EMPLOYEES, AGENTS, LICENSORS, OR CONTRACTORS BE LIABLE FOR ANY INCIDENTAL, INDIRECT, SPECIAL, OR CONSEQUENTIAL DAMAGES ARISING OUT OF OR IN CONNECTION WITH THIS LICENSE OR THE SOFTWARE, INCLUDING FOR LOSS OF USE, LOSS OF DATA, LOSS OF INCOME OR PROFIT, OR OTHER LOSSES, SUSTAINED AS A RESULT OF INJURY TO ANY PERSON, OR LOSS OF OR DAMAGE TO PROPERTY, OR CLAIMS OF THIRD PARTIES, EVEN IF THE COMPANY OR AN AUTHORIZED REPRESENTATIVE OF THE COMPANY HAS BEEN ADVISED OF THE POSSIBILITY OF SUCH DAMAGES. IN NO EVENT SHALL THE LIABILITY OF THE COMPANY FOR DAMAGES WITH RESPECT TO THE SOFTWARE EXCEED THE AMOUNTS ACTUALLY PAID BY YOU, IF ANY, FOR THE SOFTWARE OR THE ACCOMPANYING TEXTBOOK. BECAUSE SOME JURISDICTIONS DO NOT ALLOW THE LIMITATION OF LIABILITY IN CERTAIN CIRCUMSTANCES, THE ABOVE LIMITATIONS MAY NOT ALWAYS APPLY TO YOU.

6. GENERAL: THIS AGREEMENT SHALL BE CONSTRUED IN ACCORDANCE WITH THE LAWS OF THE UNITED STATES OF AMERICA AND THE STATE OF NEW YORK, APPLICABLE TO CONTRACTS MADE IN NEW YORK, AND SHALL BENEFIT THE COMPANY, ITS AFFILIATES AND ASSIGNEES. THIS AGREEMENT IS THE COMPLETE AND EXCLUSIVE STATEMENT OF THE AGREEMENT BETWEEN YOU AND THE COMPANY AND SUPERSEDES ALL PROPOSALS OR PRIOR AGREEMENTS, ORAL OR WRITTEN, AND ANY OTHER COMMUNICATIONS BETWEEN YOU AND THE COMPANY OR ANY REPRESENTATIVE OF THE COMPANY RELATING TO THE SUBJECT MATTER OF THIS AGREEMENT. If you are a U.S. Government user, this Software is licensed with "restricted rights" as set forth in subparagraphs (a)-(d) of the Commercial Computer-Restricted Rights clause at FAR 52.227-19 or in subparagraphs (c)(1)(ii) of the Rights in Technical Data and Computer Software clause at DFARS 252.227-7013, and similar clauses, as applicable.

Should you have any questions concerning this agreement please contact in writing: Legal Department, Prentice Hall, One Lake Street, Upper Saddle River, NJ 07458. If you need assistance with technical difficulties, call: 1-800-677-6337. If you wish to contact the Company for any reason, please contact in writing: Art Media Editor, Prentice Hall, One Lake Street, Upper Saddle River, NJ 07458.